The Cultures of the West

A History

Volume 2: Since 1350

Clifford R. Backman
Boston University

New York   Oxford
OXFORD UNIVERSITY PRESS

Oxford University Press is a department of the University of Oxford.
It furthers the University's objective of excellence in research,
scholarship, and education by publishing worldwide.

Oxford   New York
Auckland   Cape Town   Dares Salaam   Hong Kong   Karachi
Kuala Lumpur   Madrid   Melbourne   Mexico City   Nairobi
New Delhi   Shanghai   Taipei   Toronto

With offices in
Argentina   Austria   Brazil   Chile   Czech Republic   France   Greece
Guatemala   Hungary   Italy   Japan   Poland   Portugal   Singapore
South   Korea   Switzerland   Thailand   Turkey   Ukraine   Vietnam

For titles covered by Section 112 of the US Higher Education Opportunity Act,
please visit www.oup.com/us/he for the latest information about
pricing and alternate formats.

Published by Oxford University Press
198 Madison Avenue, New York, New York 10016
http://www.oup.com

Oxford is a registered trademark of Oxford University Press

Library of Congress Cataloging-in-Publication Data
Backman, Clifford R.
  The cultures of the West : a history / Clifford R. Backman.
    p. cm.
  ISBN 978-0-19-538889-3 – ISBN 978-0-19-538890-9 – ISBN 978-0-19-538891-6
  1. Civilization, Western.   2. Religion and civilization.   3. Science and civilization.
  4. Philosophy and civilization. I. Title.
  CB245.B324 2013
  909'.09821--dc23
                    2012033151

9 8 7 6 5 4 3

Printed in the United States of America on acid-free paper

This book is for
Graham Charles Backman
Puero praeclaro, Scourge of Nations;

and for my mother
Mary Lou Betker,
with my best love;

and in memory of my brother
Neil Howard Backman, USN (ret.)
(1956–2011)
who found his happiness just in time.

BRIEF CONTENTS

CONTENTS

When Western science revived in the 16th century, it did so once again hand in hand with Christian faith. It is a modern conceit that science advanced only when it divorced itself from religion; that divorce became finalized only in the 19th century. The Scientific Revolution therefore needs to be understood as an offshoot of religious history.

The whole of society became obsessed with rule-making and breaking. Rules of etiquette, standards of spelling and usage, norms for musical composition and visual art, academic curricula, domestic architecture, even the subtle social demands of fashion—all these felt the pressure to conform.

18. The Birth of Modern Politics 666
1815–1848

19. Nationalism and Identity .705
1801–1903

20. The God Problem 745
1799–1907

To analyze human nature scientifically, the new generation felt, was to cheapen it by reducing people to machines. The human heart, in a clinical sense, can be studied as a matter of medical science—but the passions it houses are mysterious, darkly powerful, beyond reason.

However it is defined, nationalism was and remains a potent force. It may in fact be the most vital element in modern political history.

What people took away from the new physics was the broader idea of relativity— no fixed points, no absolute time, no absolute space. And the more we learned about the universe, the more immense, confusing, unexpected, and for some more frightening it seemed to be.

From the introduction of gunpowder weapons and the creation of mass armies, the frequency and scale of massacres in wartime have increased dramatically. The mere pressing of a button or the pulling of a trigger can produce carnage to equal that at Thermopylae or Actium, Hastings or Hattin, Breda or Lepanto.

The West has entered the 21st century in full-throttle disputes over the purpose and limits of government and the responsibilities of individuals in society.

List of Maps

Introduction: Why History?

Through most of my school years I hated history; it seemed a dull exercise in memorization, a slightly sophisticated version of the game of trivial pursuit. Names and dates, followed by more names and dates. *The Battle of Actium was fought in what year? 31 BCE. Name the three ships that sailed to the New World with Christopher Columbus in 1492. The Niña, the Pinta, and the Santa María. Who fought in the Battle of Lepanto? The Holy League (Spain, Venice, the Papal State) and the Ottoman Turks, in 1571. Who delivered the sermon entitled "Sinners in the Hands of an Angry God"? Jonathan Edwards, in 1741. When was the Interstate Commerce Commission established? 1887. Whose assassination in 1914 triggered the start of World War I? Archduke Ferdinand of Austria.* And so on. Important facts all, but deadly boring when treated, as they invariably were, merely as data points to be learned by rote and recited on demand. Occasionally my teachers assigned map quizzes, usually pertaining to battles, which pleased the part of me that enjoyed pretending to be a field commander drawing up my forces to launch brilliant attacks on incompetent enemies. But then all pleasure disappeared when we were subsequently given photos of paintings and sculptures that "illustrated what life was like" in whatever time period was then under discussion. My failure was total. Try as I might, I never could find much to say, or think, or feel, or care about in 17th-century Dutch still lifes ("Oh, look! A loaf of bread!") or 18th-century French rococo landscapes filled, to my jaded eye, with prissy aristocrats in fake settings. No, history bored me, but I was good at it and so kept at it. (Good grades mattered.) My breakthrough moment came in college, when, with the help of my then-girlfriend, I realized that what I hated was not history itself but most of my history teachers—those dry, pinched souls who crushed everything that was vital, interesting, and important out of the great drama of human life. Out of my life, at any rate. History, after all, is the story of people, and anyone who finds people interesting ought therefore to find history interesting. If a person finds history boring, the problem lies either with him, as an unimaginative lout, or with the way in which the history is presented. Rejecting immediately, of course, the former as impossible in my case, I decided firmly on the latter. Blame the messengers, in other words, not the message. Over the years, I have become increasingly convinced of the correctness of this view. In their desire to present all the facts, most of my teachers—and most of the historians they had us read—simply drained all the life out of the subject.

Part of the problem lay in method. Teaching and writing history is difficult, in large part because of the sheer scope of the enterprise. Should one barrage a student or a reader with facts, clearly and objectively stated, and expect her to see the meaningful patterns in them, or should one discuss the patterns, the Big Ideas, and the deeper questions of human life confronted by any particular society in the past, and then allow her to teach herself enough factual details to corroborate and illumine those larger themes? Both approaches have value, and each has its own weaknesses. Most large-scale history books tend to choose the first option and make a fetish of their factual comprehensiveness and strict objectivity of tone. The problem with this approach is that it too often works only for those few who are already true believers in history's importance and leaves most students and readers yawning in their wake. I knew a fellow in college who was one of these true believers; he could recite the names and dates, in order, of every king of England and every archbishop of Canterbury from 1066 to the present. Impressive, in a nerdy way. But he had no idea at all how to explain the causes of England's civil war in the 17th century, or why the British voted their national hero, Sir Winston Churchill, out of office immediately after the end of World War II. Probably for both good and ill, I choose the latter option—to teach and write history by emphasizing ideas and trends, and the values behind them; to engage in the debates of each age rather than to narrate who won them. Once people are genuinely interested in a topic and can see the reasons to care about it, it seems to me, they can pick up the essential facts by themselves. Moreover, experience has taught me that they will do so.

Four years ago, when Oxford University Press invited me to write a general history of the Western world, I warned them that my approach to the topic would be a bit out of the ordinary. I wanted to write a book that would irritate people, inspire them, confuse them, make them question themselves, and sometimes enlighten them, but certainly always engage them. There are enough books already published to make bored readers fall asleep over. My first eccentricity, if that is what it is, is that I wanted to write a book that had opinions and argued with readers. No one falls asleep in an argument, I figured. My second eccentricity, I warned, is that I do not believe in Western civilization as it is usually defined. I believe instead in what I call—and what nearly became the title of this book—the Greater West. It's time to explain.

———————————— + ————————————

There are as many histories of any society as there are historians willing to write them. The shape, themes, and degrees of detail in each result from whatever each author considers of greatest importance—politics, social development, technology and science, economics, gender relations. A focus on any particular theme produces a different understanding of who we have been and therefore who we are. Like the changing patterns in a child's kaleidoscope, the smallest shift of attention or emphasis reveals new configurations of ideas and insights into the way we see ourselves. No single vantage point can claim primacy; as Albert Einstein (1879–1955) theorized and subsequent scientists affirmed, the truths revealed by every perspective in the cosmos are equally true to each observer. But that does not mean one cannot be wrong. "Facts are stubborn things," wrote the American statesman John Adams (1736–1826), in a very different context, "and whatever may be our wishes, our inclinations, or the dictates of our passion, they cannot alter the state of facts and evidence." Historians can disagree, for example, about the specific causes of an event like the Franco-Prussian War (1870–1871), or about its consequences for subsequent generations; but the factual realities of those specific people in those specific places, performing those specific actions, cannot be tampered with. The challenge of writing history, but also its deepest value and most enduring purpose, is in the selection and assemblage of those facts, and the conclusions one draws from them.

To follow a single theme, or a clutch of them, is one way to mediate between comprehensive factuality and meaningful interpretation, and hence the preference by most writers of large-scale histories to select discrete vantage points, to trim the material in such a way that emphasizes, for example, political events. Seen this way, the history of the Greater West emerges as a centuries-long march toward the development of the modern democratic nation-state. A focus on social themes traces the evolution of social classes, the family, interethnic relations, and dominant moral codes. An economic approach emphasizes the everyday common struggle to survive in the world—the production of food, developments in manufacture and commerce, the passing on of property—and culminates not only in modern prosperity but in the belief in a fixed set of economic laws that govern human life. The unspoken corollary of this approach is that it is the recognition of this set of laws to which modern prosperity owes thanks; capitalism thus appears not as a customary practice or an ideology but as a subdiscipline of natural science.

This book too adopts a thematic approach, but a theme seldom utilized in contemporary histories. While paying due attention to other aspects of Western development, it focuses on what might be called the history of values—that is, on the assumptions that lie behind political and economic developments, behind intellectual and artistic ventures, and behind social trends and countertrends. Consider for example, the achievements of the Scientific Revolution (1500–1750). The advances made in fields like astronomy (Nicolaus Copernicus, Johannes Kepler, Galileo Galilei), chemistry (Robert Boyle), and medicine (William

Harvey) did not occur simply because individuals smart enough to figure out new truths happened to come along. Harvey's discovery of the circulatory system was possible only because the culture in which he lived had begun, albeit hesitantly, to allow the dissection of human corpses for scientific research. For many centuries, even millennia, before Harvey's time, cultural and religious taboos had forbidden the desecration of bodies. But the era of the Scientific Revolution was also the era of political absolutism in Europe, a time when prevailing sentiment held that the king was all that stood between mankind and barbarism. Any enemy of the king—for example, anyone convicted of a felony—therefore deserved the ultimate penalty of execution and dissection. No king worship, no discovery of the circulation of the blood. At least not at that time.

Similarly, the search for underlying value assumptions illuminates the effort to explain the gloomy outlook, bordering on nihilism, of the modernist movement of the early 20th century. For the preceding hundred years Europe's traditional Christianity had wavered and withdrawn in the face of industrialism, migration, economic despair, and the intellectual assaults of Darwinian evolution, the so-called higher criticism of the Bible, and the radically new physics of quantum theory and relativity. The trauma of World War I simply was a bloody culmination of the longer trend of the loss of religious belief. A godless universe might still have an underlying order and purpose, but quantum theory and relativity demolished any hope of finding them. For the most stubborn holdouts determined to retain a belief in a meaningfully ordered cosmos, though, World War I crushed any last shreds of hope. If nothing is permanent, true, and purposeful, the modernists thought, then human life is a wasteland of pointless impressions, blind desires, and empty hopes.

> What are the roots that clutch, what branches grow
> Out of this stony rubbish? Son of man,
> You cannot say, or guess, for you only know
> A heap of broken images, where the sun beats,
> And the dead tree gives no shelter, the cricket no relief,
> And the dry stone no sound of water. Only
> There is shadow under this red rock,
> (Come in under the shadow of this red rock),
> And I will show you something different from either
> Your shadow at morning striding behind you
> Or your shadow at evening rising to meet you;
> I will show you fear in a handful of dust.
>
> (T. S. Eliot, The Waste Land, 1922)

On the other hand, the collapse of order was liberating to some. Just as modernist poets like Eliot freed themselves from rhyme and meter, so too did modernist music (Arnold Schoenberg, Paul Hindemith, Igor Stravinsky, Alban Berg) discard traditional compositional structure and tonality. In painting, movements like Dadaism and cubism explored nonrepresentational forms and played with the very idea of visual sense.

A history that emphasizes the development of values inevitably distorts the record to some extent, for obviously not every person living at a given time held those values. Medieval Christians did not uniformly hate Jews and Muslims, believe the world was about to end, support the Inquisition, and blindly follow the dictates of the pope. Not every learned man and woman in the 18th century was "enlightened" or even wanted to be. The young generation of the 1960s was not composed solely of war resisters, hippies, drug aficionados, feminists, and rock-music lovers who celebrated free love in the muddy fields at Woodstock (although many people now of a certain age like to pretend that they were then). With this caveat in mind, however, it remains possible to offer general observations about the ideas and values that predominated in any era. This book privileges those ideas and sensibilities and views the events of each era in relation to them.

And it does so with a certain amount of opinion. To discuss value judgments without ever judging some of those values seems cowardly and is probably impossible anyway. Most large-scale histories mask their subjectivity simply by deciding which topics to discuss and which ones to pass over; I prefer to argue my positions explicitly, in the belief that to have a point of view is not the same thing as to be unfair. Does this risk confusing the reader who might mistake my opinion for accepted fact? Possibly, I admit. But education is as much about teaching students to evaluate arguments as it is about passing on knowledge to them, and students cannot learn to evaluate arguments if they are never presented with any. Or if they are asleep.

In a second departure from tradition (which in this case is really just habit), this book interprets Western history on a broader geographic scale than other historians do. All full-scale histories of Western civilization begin in the Fertile Crescent, the ancient region made up of Mesopotamia (in modern-day Iraq), Palestine (modern-day Syria, Lebanon, and Israel), and Egypt—but after making a quick nod to the origins of Islam in the 7th century they focus almost exclusively on western Europe. Attention moves like the sun ever westward, through ancient Greece to Rome, thence to Britain, France, and Germany (with a bit of Italy and Spain thrown in when unavoidable), and finally embraces America once it emerges from its international isolation in the 20th century. The Muslim world thereafter enters the discussion only when it impinges on European actions. This book overtly rejects that view and insists on including the region of the Middle East in the general narrative, as a permanently constitutive element of the Greater West. For all its current global appeal, Islam is essentially a Western religion, after all, one that has its spiritual roots in the Jewish and Christian traditions and the bulk of whose intellectual foundations are in the classical Greco-Roman canon. To treat the Muslim world as an occasional sideshow on the long march to western European and American world leadership is to falsify the record and to get the history wrong. Most textbooks touch repeatedly on the Islamic world, of course, but do so only in episodic fashion—and those episodes are invariably whenever Europe and the Middle East are in conflict.

A simple analogy shows the poverty of this approach. Consider any long intimate relationship you have had—perhaps a romantic tie, a family connection, a work colleague, or a long friendship. If someone were to write the history of that relationship but in the process examined only the arguments you had, it could not possibly (no matter how detailed and "objective") be an accurate history of the relationship. It could not possibly be even an accurate history of the arguments, since it would view them entirely out of context. That is the situation with the Greater West. The "European world" and the "Middle Eastern world" have been in a continuous relationship for millennia, buying and selling goods, sharing technologies, studying each other's political ideas, influencing each other's religious beliefs, learning from one another's medicine, facing the same challenges from scientific advances and changing economies. We cannot explain who we are if we limit ourselves to the traditional scope of Western history; we need a Greater Western perspective, one that includes and incorporates the whole of the monotheistic world. Nearly every one of the fundamental turning points in European history (the developments of agriculture, literacy, urban life, monotheistic religion, religious heresy; debates over tolerance, over intellectual freedom, over the rights of women; the Black Death; the invention of gunpowder; the discovery of the larger global world; the challenge of secularism, the debate over reason, the Enlightenment (called *al-Nahda* in Arabic); the catastrophic conquests of Napoleon Bonaparte; the changes brought by rapid industrialization; the First and Second World Wars, the Cold War; and the rise of modern feminism, liberalism, and conservatism) have been experienced jointly by the European and Middle Eastern societies. And not only have we confronted the same challenges, we have interacted with each other intimately in our responses to each new development. Only by broadening our focus can we do justice to each other and to the reality of how our histories have played out. This expanded view introduces a rafter of new difficulties, for apart from the unfamiliar nature of much of the new material, it forces the additional compression and selection of more traditionally mainstream matters.

I am very much aware of the risks involved by this approach. In order to discuss, for example, the campaigns to reform and modernize Islamic understandings of women's roles in society in the early 20th century, this book gives less attention to many of the most significant activists for women in Europe and the United States. A woman like Aletta Jacobs (1854–1929), the first university-trained female physician in the Netherlands, a champion of women's health and the right to suffrage, deserves more space than she receives here (although I point out that she is discussed at greater length here than in any other book of this sort). I wanted to make room, however, for women like Huda'i Sha'arawi (1879–1947), the pioneering Egyptian feminist. The payoff seems worth it, if the end result is a broader recognition that the Islamic world's development has closer parallels with the European and American society than has generally been thought or acknowledged.

Since religious belief has traditionally shaped so much of Greater Western culture—whether for good or ill is every reader's responsibility to determine—I have placed it at the center of my narrative. Even for the most unshakeable of modern agnostics and atheists, the values upheld by the three great monotheisms have had, and continue to have, a profound effect on the development of our social mores, intellectual pursuits, and artistic endeavors. The history of religion does not explain all of Greater Western history, but it is as useful a handle as any to grasp the whole, as are politics, economics, society, and intellectual life. It seems to me to be worth trying, especially since religious misunderstanding and friction dominate so much of our current attention.

In another break with convention, the book incorporates an abundance of primary sources into the narrative. I have always disliked the boxed and highlighted source snippets that pockmark so many of today's textbooks. Any teacher who is honest knows that most students do not read them. It seems to me that any passage worth quoting is worth working into the text itself—and I have done so, with some brio. But a word about them is necessary. For the first three chapters I have needed considerable help. I am ignorant of the ancient Middle Eastern languages and have relied on the current version of a respected and well-loved anthology from my own undergraduate days.[1] When discussing the sacred texts of Judaism, Christianity, and Islam I have used their own authorized translations. Simple courtesy, it seems to me, calls for quoting a Jewish translation of the Bible when discussing Judaism; a Catholic, Orthodox, or Protestant Bible whenever discussing those main branches of Christianity; and the English version of the Qur'an prepared by the

---

[1]   Nels M. Bailkey and Richard Lim, *Readings in Ancient History: Thought and Experience from Gilgamesh to St. Augustine*, 7th ed. (Wadsworth, 2011).

royal publishing house in Saudi Arabia when discussing Islam.[2] Last, some of the political records I cite (for example, the Cairo Declaration of Human Rights) are quoted from their official English versions. But apart from these special cases—all duly noted—every translation in this book, from chapter 4 onward, is my own.

SUPPORT MATERIALS FOR *THE CULTURES OF THE WEST*

The Cultures of the West comes with an extensive package of support materials for both instructors and students.

- **Companion Web Site (www.oup.com/us/backman):** For students, the site includes quizzes, flashcards, documents, interactive maps, and links to YouTube videos. Access to the student site is unrestricted. For instructors, the site includes an instructor's resource manual that provides for each chapter, a detailed chapter outline, suggested lecture topics, learning objectives, suggested Web resources and digital media files. It also includes, for each chapter, approximately 30 multiple-choice, short-answer, true-or-false, and fill-in-the-blank questions as well as approximately 10 essay questions.
- **Instructor's Resource DVD:** Includes PowerPoint slides and JPEG and PDF files for all the maps and photos in the text; an additional four hundred map files, in PowerPoint format, from *The Oxford Atlas of World History*; and approximately 250 additional PowerPoint-based slides organized by theme and topic. The DVD also includes the Instructor's Resource Manual, and the test questions can be customized by the instructor.
- **Sourcebook for *The Cultures of the West*, Volume One: To 1750:** Edited by Clifford R. Backman and Christine Axen, it includes approximately two hundred text sources in Western civilization, organized to match the chapter organization of *The Cultures of the West*. Each source is accompanied by a head-note and reading questions. Free when bundled with the text.
- **Sourcebook for *The Cultures of the West*, Volume Two: Since 1350:** Edited by Clifford R. Backman and Christine Axen, it includes approximately two hundred text sources in Western

---

2   *Tanakh: The Holy Scriptures,* by the Jewish Publication Society; *New American Bible,* published by the U.S. Conference of Catholic Bishops; *New Revised Standard Version,* published by Oxford University Press; and *The Orthodox Study Bible.* For the Qur'an I have used *The Holy Qur'an: English Translations of the Meanings, with Commentary,* published by the King Fahd Holy Qur'an Printing Complex (A.H 1410).

civilization, organized to match the chapter organization of *The Cultures of the West*. Each source is accompanied by a head-note and reading questions. Free when bundled with the text.

- **Mapping the Cultures of the West, Volume One: To 1750:** Includes approximately forty full-color maps, each accompanied by a brief headnote. Free when bundled with the text.
- **Mapping the Cultures of the West, Volume Two: Since 1350:** Includes approximately forty full-color maps, each accompanied by a brief headnote. Free when bundled with the text.
- **Now Playing: Studying Western Civilization Through Film:** (available in both student and instructor editions) is a concise print supplement that provides synopses, recommended scenes, and discussion questions for thirty of the most commonly assigned films in Western Civilization classes. Qualified adopters can receive a Netflix subscription with their adoption. *Now Playing* can be bundled with The Cultures of the *West* at no additional cost.
- **E-book for *The Cultures of the West* (both volumes):** An e-book is available for purchase at **http://www.coursesmart.com.**

BUNDLING OPTIONS

The Cultures of the West can be bundled at a significant discount with any of the titles in the popular Very Short Introductions or Oxford World's Classics series, as well as other titles from the Higher Education division world history catalog (**http://www.oup.com/us/catalog/he**). Please contact your OUP representative for details.

ACKNOWLEDGMENTS

Working with Oxford University Press has been a delight. Brian Wheel is the person who talked me into attempting a new history of the Greater West. I am grateful for the confidence he showed in me and for all the encouragement he offered. Charles Cavaliere, Brian's successor, served as point man, guiding me through the entire project with grace and kindness. His cheery enthusiasm kept me going through many a difficult hour. If the prose in this book has any merit, please direct your compliments to John Haber, prince of editors. I shall miss working with him. Lauren Aylward, Theresa Stockton, Lisa Grzan, Eden Kram, Meg Botteon, Kim Howie, and the rest of the staff shepherded me through the marketing and production phase and deserve all the credit for the wonderful physical design of the book—images, captions, layout, and font.

Some two dozen external reviewers, anonymous to me, read various chapters of this book as they emerged from my printer. Those who did not wish to remain anonymous include Robert Brennan, Cape Fear Community College; Gregory S. Brown, University of Nevada–Las Vegas; Scott G. Bruce, University of Colorado–Boulder; William Caraher, University of North Dakota; John Cox, University of North Carolina–Charlotte; Jason Coy, College of Charleston; Lynda Pinney Domino, Simpson College; Steven Fanning, University of Illinois at Chicago; Irina Gigova, College of Charleston; Laura Hutchings, University of Utah; Andrew Jenks, California State University–Long Beach; Erik N. Jensen, Miami University; Andrew Keitt, University of Alabama–Birmingham; Thomas A. Mason, Indiana University–Purdue University Indianapolis; David Matz, St. Bonaventure University; Charles A. Maxfield, DeSales University; Martin Menke, Rivier College; David A. Messenger, University of Wyoming; Peter J. Myers, Palo Alto College; Stephen Norris, Miami University; Devin Pendas, Boston College; Michael Redman, University of Louisville; Pete Rottier, Kent State University; Mark Edward Ruff, Saint Louis University; Wendy Sarti, Oakton Community College; Thomas J. Schaeper, St. Bonaventure University; Linda Bregstein Scherr, Mercer County Community College; Stuart Smyth, University at Albany–SUNY; Laurie Sprankle, the Community College of Allegheny County; Jane Strother, Campbell University; Victoria Thompson, Arizona State University; Hans P. Vought, SUNY–Ulster County Community College; Janet M. C. Walmsley, George Mason University; David White, McHenry County College; and Matthew Donald Zarzeczny, the Ohio State University. Reading their criticisms felt at times like falling face-first into a threshing machine. (You know who you are, reader no. 6!) I am grateful nonetheless for every comment they offered; our profession depends on people offering honest criticism of one another's work. If I have not accepted every one of their suggestions, they should still feel proud of the work they did. This is a better book, and I hope that I am a better teacher, because of their unsung efforts.

My doctoral student at Boston University, Christine Axen, has been a support from the start. She has taught with me, and occasionally for me, through the last three years, and I appreciate the time she took away from her own dissertation research to assist me on this project—pulling books from the library, running down citations, suggesting ideas. Now that Oxford has asked me to prepare a companion volume of primary texts for this book, Christine has proved such an immense help that she will share the title page with me when that volume appears.

To my wife, Nelina, and our sons, Scott and Graham, this book has been an uninvited house guest at times, pulling me away from too many family hours. They have put up with it, and with me, with patience and generosity that I shall always be thankful for. Their love defines them and sustains me.

With so many good people supporting me, I should have finished sooner. I'll do better next time.

About the Author

Clifford R. Backman is Associate Professor of History at Boston University, where he has taught since 1989. He is author of *The Decline and Fall of Medieval Sicily: Politics, Economy, and Religion in the Reign of Frederick III, 1296–1327* (1995) and *The Worlds of Medieval Europe* (Oxford University Press, 2003). His current projects are a biography of King James II of the medieval Crown of Aragon and a study of Arnau de Vilanova, the infamous heretic who was the personal physician to four successive popes.

A Note to the Reader

I follow a few basic conventions. Instead of the old BC (Before Christ) and AD (Anno Domini) designations for centuries, I use the new norms of BCE (Before the Common Era) and CE (Common Era). Dates are given, whenever possible, for every figure mentioned in the book. Political leaders are identified by the years they were in power—hence (r. 0000–0000) means that he or she *ruled* during those years, and, in the modern era, (g. 0000–0000) means that he or she *governed* during them. All other dates, unless otherwise noted, are life- and death-dates.

One of the chief difficulties of the "Greater Western" approach is the sheer number of unfamiliar names. The history of the Islamic Middle East, this book argues, has to take into account national or ethnic differences, as much as the more familiar distinction between Sunni and Shia Muslims. To help with this, I have indicated wherever possible the ethnicity of an individual. [A] denotes an Arab. [K] indicates an ethnic Kurd. [P] identifies a Persian (Iranian). [T] signals that the person is a Turk. The reasons for these designations will be clear as the chapters unfold.

The Cultures of the West

A History

TEMPLA DOMVM EXPOSITIS·VICOS·FORA·MOENIA·PONTES·
VIRGINEAM·TRIVII·QVOD·REPARARIS·AQVAM·
PRISCA·LICET·NAVTIS·STATVAS·DARE·COMMODA·PORTVS·
ET·VATICANVM·CINGERE·SIXTE·IVGVM·
PLVS·TAMEN·VRBS·DEBET:NAM·QVAE·SQVALORE·LATEBAT·

CHAPTER 11

Renaissances and Reformations

1350–1550

The Renaissance, the period in Europe roughly from 1350 to 1550, is one of the few eras in Western history that named itself. The cultural elite of the time believed they were living in an age of self-conscious revival. They were bringing back to life the ideas, moral values, art, and civic mindedness that characterized, they believed, the two high points of Western culture: Periclean Athens and Republican Rome. One of the first to use the term was the Italian writer, painter, and architect Giorgio Vasari (1511–1574), who celebrated a new epoch of civilized life. After a thousand years of medieval brutality and barbarism, Vasari claimed, Italian artists and thinkers

THE GREATER WEST, ca. 1550

◀ **Pope Sixtus IV** Sixtus IV (r. 1471–1484) is remembered for building the Sistine Chapel, establishing the Spanish Inquisition, and developing the Vatican Library. Record collection had long since become professionalized in the papal court; in fact, references to standing administrative offices with bureaucratic support date back to the 6th century, but a formal library was another matter. Sixtus saw the need for a centralized permanent collection of the church's manuscripts. Pope Nicholas V (r. 1447–1455) was the library's actual founder, but Sixtus greatly expanded and reorganized it and also made it available to scholars. Sixtus was a Franciscan, one of the last of his order to hold the papacy, but quickly became enamored of the pomp and splendor of the Renaissance court. He appointed a half dozen of his nephews to the College of Cardinals, including Giuliano della Rovere—the tall figure in the center—who later became Pope Julius II (r. 1503–1513), the target of Erasmus's great satire *Julius Excluded from Heaven*.

had bravely restored the lost perfection of art and philosophy as known to the ancients. An earlier Renaissance writer on education, Pier Paolo Vergerio (1370–1444), insisted that only the study of the classical liberal arts can lift society from the moral and spiritual decay of the medieval era. "Only those liberal arts," he proclaimed, "are worthy of free men; they alone can help us to attain virtue and wisdom . . . [and fill in the gaps in our moral knowledge] which the ignorance of the past centuries has intentionally created."

Una rinascità—a "rebirth" of classical values that gave fresh hope and creative energy to Europe. It also led to the greatest eruption in Greater Western religion since the birth of Islam—the Protestant Reformation.

"I FIXED UPON ANTIQUITY"

Not everyone in the Renaissance shared Vasari's and Vergerio's sense of the near mythic magnificence of antiquity, and it took some time for the English version of the word *rinascità* to catch on. It did not acquire positive connotations in English until John Ruskin (1819–1900) used it in his famous study of architecture *The Stones of Venice* (1851): "This rationalistic art is the art called Renaissance, marked by a return to pagan systems" (1.1.23). Most of Vergerio's and Vasari's contemporaries were simply grateful to have been born after the filthy muddle of the Middle Ages. Francesco Petrarca (1304–1374), usually regarded as the first Renaissance man, expressed this nostalgia for the deep past of Rome and Athens. In an open letter written toward the end of his life, called the *Letter to Posterity*, he recalls his youthful studies:

> I had more of a well-rounded mind than a keen intellect, and was naturally inclined to every type of virtuous and honorable study but especially to moral philosophy and poetry. After a while, it is true, I began to neglect poetry in favor of sacred literature, in which I soon found a buried sweetness that I had previously acknowledged to be there but only in a perfunctory way; now however I found its sweetness so great

CHAPTER TIMELINE

1304–1374
Petrarca

ca. 1440
Gutenberg's
printing press

1466–1536
Erasmus

1492–1556
Pietro Arentino

1434
Cosimo de Medici
assumes power
in Florence

1463–1494
Giovanni Pico
della Mirandola

1469–1527
Niccolò
Machiavelli

that poetry became a mere afterthought for me. Out of all the subjects that intrigued me, I fixed especially upon antiquity—for the truth is that our own age repels me and has always done so. Indeed, were it not for the love of those I hold dear, I would rather have been born in any age but our own. I have spent most of my life thinking about other eras, in fact, as a way of ignoring my own, and that is why I have always loved the study of history.

> The three ideas most characteristically associated with the Renaissance—classicism, humanism, and modern statecraft—represent no essential break with medieval life at all. They may in fact be thought of as the culmination of medieval strivings.

However, the Renaissance—or the early part of it, anyway—shared more with its preceding age than it wanted to admit. The three ideas most characteristically associated with the Renaissance—classicism, humanism, and modern statecraft—represent no essential break with medieval life at all. They may in fact be thought of as the culmination of medieval strivings.

CLASSICISM, HUMANISM, AND STATECRAFT

The cult of classical learning and literature had its origins in early Western monastic life. Novice monks had long been directed to study the Roman poets Virgil and Horace, the historians Suetonius and Sallust, and the playwrights Terence and Seneca. It was their means to learn Latin before being granted access to the Scriptures and the patristic literature. The works of Aristotle, Ptolemy, Galen, and Euclid, moreover, had dominated university education from the start. But the great scholars of the Renaissance broadened this core canon by seeking out long-lost manuscripts; virtually anything by a classical author was of interest. Petrarca himself unearthed Cicero's *Letters to Atticus*, lying unused and unknown on a dusty library shelf in Verona for centuries, and brought out a new edition of it.

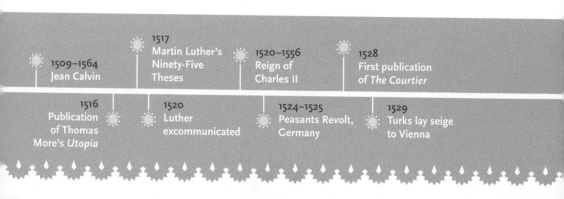

1509–1564
Jean Calvin

1517
Martin Luther's
Ninety-Five
Theses

1520–1556
Reign of
Charles II

1528
First publication
of *The Courtier*

1516
Publication
of Thomas
More's *Utopia*

1520
Luther
excommunicated

1524–1525
Peasants Revolt,
Germany

1529
Turks lay seige
to Vienna

What distinguished the Renaissance approach to the classics was a passionate conviction that they contained all that humans have best thought and best expressed. It was simply impossible not merely to be educated but to be a complete, satisfied, and accomplished human being without knowing the wisdom of the ancients. Pier Paolo Vergerio described the classical canon as "the only literature whose study helps us in the pursuit of virtue and wisdom, and brings forth in us those most sublime gifts of body and mind that ennoble men's spirit and that are properly regarded as second only to virtue itself as our most dignified attainment." This was more than mere affectation. Poseurs seldom engage in such intense archival and philological work. Renaissance scholars traveled through scores of libraries and archives, sifted through piles of manuscripts, corrected the minutest scribal errors, and commented prolifically on the cultural context and multiple meanings of a writer's text. Moreover, these scholars put their learning to use in works of their own, in every genre from poetry to stage drama, epistles to essays, histories to philosophical treatises.

The concern in this period to develop human potential, to value the particular, and to assert the inherent dignity of each person is called **Renaissance humanism**. The idea itself was not new, but the degree of emphasis placed on it was. The catastrophes of the 14th century, after all, had inspired many to doubt the values and assumptions of the high medieval era—the belief in a rationally ordered cosmos, a benevolent deity, the naturalness of a hierarchically structured society, the conviction that good will triumph over evil. The Black Death, after all, had shown no apparent concern to kill only the wicked, and the other calamities of the time had made people grow suspicious of systems of thought or social organization. What does one do, when everything a society takes for granted has been shown to be a sham? The world is a perilous place, a mad, painful jumble of impressions, sensations, thoughts, desires, fears, and inchoate longings. One struggles

The Cult of the Classics Renaissance artists and writers regularly turned to classical Rome, and to a lesser extent to Periclean Athens, for inspiration, finding in these worlds the best models for the conduct of individual life and civil society. There was of course an element of affectation in this, but more generally it derived from a sincere conviction that the most practical guides to good living came from the pre-Christian world. This page from a new translation of Pliny's *Natural History* printed for a Florentine banker—Filippo Strozzi (1428–1491)—is a case in point. More than four years were spent on its production, and the costs involved totaled over 125 gold florins.

in vain to create anything like order or meaning. The best one can do is to find comfort, beauty, or value in the broken shards of the world scattered at one's feet. Humanism celebrated such simple pleasures: the precise arch of an eyebrow or the drape of a garment in a painting, the warm hue of sunlight entering a window, the sense of balance within an enclosure created by the artful placement of objects, the beautiful potential energy in a tensed coil of muscle. A focus on the particular called for a representational art, one attuned to the hard but transitory reality of objects in time. Medieval art had more widely used symbolic and allegorical representations.

Scholars in the Renaissance still wrote in Latin, but most of the creative literature of the age was in the vernacular. This too mimicked medieval practice, but reflected a different reason. In the Middle Ages, scholarship was written in Latin because it was the common tongue of the learned. Physicians in Spain could communicate with physicians in Hungary or Denmark; mathematicians in England could be read in Portugal or Poland. In the Renaissance, however, scholars wrote in Latin (or sometimes in Greek) out of a conviction in the intrinsic superiority of the classical languages. Latin and Greek, in the "pure" forms used in ancient times, were seen as uniquely capable of expressing complex thought. Imagine a demand today to make Shakespearean English the only form of English worthy of public discourse. Anyone who could read a computer manual in that language would be a rare person indeed—and not necessarily a better person because of it.[1]

The most famous of Renaissance descriptions of humanism came from Giovanni Pico della Mirandola (1463–1494), a brilliant polymath. His "Oration on the Dignity of Man" lays out the fundamental elements of the movement in elegant language:

> I read somewhere of a Muslim writer named Abdullah who, when asked to identify the most wondrous and awe-inspiring thing to appear on the world's stage, answered, "There exists nothing more wondrous than Man." Hermes Trismegistus expressed the same view when he wrote, "What a great miracle is Man, Asclepius!"
>
> But when I began to consider the reasons behind these opinions, every particular of their arguments for the magnificence of human nature failed to persuade me.

---

[1] Scholars sought to take the living Latin and Greek they had inherited and purge them of what they considered barbarisms and corrupt usages.

The unconvincing arguments include man's existence as a rational creature or as master of the physical world.

What strikes Pico della Mirandola as the essential and glorious point about humans is rather something else: to us alone has God given the freedom and ability to be whatever we want, to become whatever we desire, and to achieve whatever we wish. A flower has no choice but to bloom, wither, and die; a stone may serve as a building block, a projectile, or a hindrance in the road, but it has no destiny of its own, no yearning to become something. Humans alone, he insists, are free to be whatever we wish to be.

> You alone, being altogether without limits and in possession of your own free will, . . . have it within you to establish the limits of your own nature. . . . Alone at the dark center of his own existence, yet united with God, Who is Himself beyond all created things, Man too exists beyond every created thing—and who can help but stand in awe of this great Fate forger? Even more: How is it possible for anyone to marvel at anything else?

To describe Man as, essentially, his own Creator was to flirt with heresy—and Mirandola did in fact run afoul of the church. To his credit, he admitted that he had overreached on several matters, issued a number of corrections and retractions, and announced his interest in becoming an obedient monk. He died suddenly at age thirty-one, however. Someone had slipped arsenic into his wine. His fate should not distract us, though, from recognizing the fundamentally religious nature of humanism. Humanism was not a secular philosophy. It sought to define the place of humanity in God's divine plan, to parse the relationship between Man and God, and so to glorify both.

The third major element of the Renaissance was statecraft. The concept of a state is a relatively modern one—and a legal fiction. A state as a thing in itself, independent of the people who comprise it and following its own norms and rules, requires a degree of abstraction. Simply to gather a number of people to live in the same space, after all, does not make a city. A city, by definition, is a legal entity, with power—the power to tax, for example, or to administer justice, to legislate, or to police miscreants. It exists on paper and in law, and it makes its powers available to those who dwell within it. Earlier notions of government had regarded the state as a network of personal relationships, but not necessarily as a distinct object. It had the king at the center, with his web of obligations and privileges to his nobles, his commoners, and the church. Exceptions to this model existed, of course, but until the 13th century they were in the minority.

Renaissance theorists and power brokers, taking their cue from late medieval writers like Brunetto Latini (1220–1294) and Marsiglio di Padova (1275–1342), thought of the state in a new way. The political state was a thing, a part of the natural world, and it functioned according to rules. Political leaders who understood this governed most effectively, because they could direct the state by means of its own internal logic. Statecraft therefore involved understanding systems of law, taxation, and economy. It involved the intricacies of diplomacy and negotiation, the mechanisms of crowd control, the manipulation of public opinion, and the knowledge of when to deceive or to exert force. Idealism had no part in it, and politics became a hard science rather than an expression of personal desire. For that very reason, however, it offered the perfect site for educated men of the

The Ambassadors   A powerful but somber piece by Holbein the Younger. Called *The Ambassadors*, it depicts a French nobleman dispatched to London on a diplomatic errand, together with his friend, a French bishop. Together they represent the active and the contemplative modes of life, with objects representing knowledge, power, and art in the background. The diagonally oriented object in the foreground, when looked at obliquely, is a skull representing Death.

Renaissance. Conscious of their abilities, and dedicated to the ancient Roman virtue of civic-mindedness, they could take their proper place within the world by mastering its rules and methods.

THE POLITICAL AND ECONOMIC MATRIX

Europe needed men of ability, Italy especially. Italy was by far the most developed urban society in Europe, followed closely by southern France and eastern Spain. Yet its political scene was a mess. The northern city-states, where the Renaissance began, had long been under the leadership of the German emperor, at least in name. His titular sovereignty dated to the 10th century, when Otto I subdued the region and gained the imperial crown. In the intervening three hundred years, emperors had brought armies over or around the Alps, intermittently but repeatedly, to assert their claims. And most of Italy's city-states opened their gates, bowed deeply, and paid their ritual and financial tribute. But once the armies were safely back in Germany, the Italians instantly returned to their independent republican ways.

The rise of the Hohenstaufen dynasty, however, had altered the rules of the game dramatically. Its joint rule over northern Italy and the Kingdom of Sicily (the result of a marriage alliance) included the southern third of the peninsula. That made urgent the need felt by many northerners to end permanently the imperial claims over their territories. Others, however, saw some utility in the on-again, off-again imperial connection, and so opposed autonomy. This scenario, in which the papacy became deeply involved, led to strife between and within each of the city-states. The Papal State, caught as it was between Hohenstaufen power bases to the north and the south, spent nearly the entire 13th century in diplomatic and military stratagems to break the power of the German/Italian/Sicilian connection. By the time of the 14th century's disasters, northern Italy was a mercenary's dreamscape. Wars large and small, palace coups, assassinations, plots, pillagings, enforced exiles, and institutional corruption had spread everywhere (see Map 11.1).

A unique feature of the Italian scene, however, helped pave the way for the Renaissance. Italian nobles tended to live within the cities, even though their rural estates were distant, and hence they played an active role in urban culture that nobles in Continental Europe did not. That included both ancient lineages and wealthy commoners whose riches had helped them purchase aristocratic titles. Moreover, the elitist bias against trade and commerce that characterized northern aristocratic society was much less virulent in Italy. Hence, by the start of the 15th century, an alliance had developed between the urban aristocrats and the mercantile and banking families of the bourgeoisie. This allowed them

MAP 11.1   Renaissance Italy

to usurp republican government, to institute direct and often tyrannical control over the city-states. Most who did so, mimicking the 1st-century emperor Augustus, maintained the fiction and rituals of republican government while establishing despotic rule.

Most city-states thus had actual, if barely functioning, republican governments between 1350 and 1450 (the first half, roughly, of the Renaissance), but despotic governments from 1450 to 1550 (the second half). In Florence, for example, the Medici family, which had risen through the ranks in banking and textiles, gained a noble title shortly after 1400. Through three generations—under Cosimo de' Medici (r. 1434–1464), Piero de' Medici (r. 1464–1469), and Lorenzo de' Medici (r. 1469–1492)—they governed a pretend republic. In 1531 the family became the hereditary dukes of Florence (later elevated to the status of an archduchy) and placed three family members on the papal throne during the Renaissance—Leo X (r. 1513–1521), Clement VII (r. 1523–1534), and Leo XI (r. 1605). (A fourth pope, Pius IV [r. 1559–1565], had the birth name of Giovanni Angelo Medici but was unrelated.) In Milan, the famous Visconti and Sforza families followed similar trajectories, with the Visconti family taking the ducal title in 1369 and holding it

The Medici as the Magi Wealth has its privileges, among which has been the tradition of artists inserting portraits of their patrons into their religious paintings. Traditionally this was done by placing the patron somewhere within the frame of the original biblical story, but with this painting of the Three Magi coming to worship the child Jesus, the painter has gone one step further by portraying Lorenzo de' Medici and his family members as the Magi themselves. The imposition is apt, since the gifts brought by the Magi (gold, myrrh, and frankincense) were symbolic of the finance and spice trading that brought the Medici their enormous wealth. The painting is by Benozzo Gozzoli (1420–1497).

until the family line died out in 1447. At that point the Sforza family (of peasant origins, with several generations of mercenary soldiers thrown in) took over and governed by fiat until 1535. The d'Este family in Ferrara, who had led local politics since 1264, won a ducal title in 1452 (and another in 1471) and held on to power until 1597. Likewise the Gonzaga family in Mantua, where they ruled without stop from 1328 to 1708.

The concentrations of wealth and power in these city-states, and in others like them, made possible elaborate systems of patronage, which gave a tremendous boost to intellectual and artistic life. Again like Augustus, Renaissance despots put their resources to work in the public sphere. They commissioned scores of palaces, chapels, public fountains and market squares, mausoleums, fortifications, libraries and museums, schools, and hospitals. All were done in the newest styles and were richly decorated with paintings, sculptures, frescos, and tapestries—and they provided hundreds of opportunities for scholars, artists, and architects. Art was not for art's sake alone in the Renaissance. It expressed humanist values and aesthetics while serving to elevate the civic spirit. It also promoted the glory and wisdom of the patron whose support made the art possible.

The depressed economy contributed as well, since labor costs were comparatively low. The building frenzy of the 14th and 15th centuries therefore represented a jobs program: it bolstered support for the regimes by putting people to work. Manufacturing still limped along, since the shrunken population meant a decreased need for most goods; the demographic recovery was slow across Europe. The city of Toulouse, for example, had numbered thirty thousand in the early 14th century, and by the early 15th it had only eight thousand. Within Italy, Genoa had lost more than one-third of its population; Bologna and Milan had each lost half; Florence had lost three-fourths. Many towns did not regain their 13th-century populations until the 20th century. Moreover, the ongoing struggles against the Ottomans, who pressed their frontiers to the gates of Vienna, interrupted trade with Asia. Even with such drastically reduced numbers, the drift of rural poor into the cities ensured a constant labor surplus. Labor costs therefore were cheap, making the vast construction projects of the Renaissance possible.

The rich are with us always. Even in a depressed economy, concentrations of capital exist and often grow, so long as the possessor is lucky or clever (or corrupt) enough to seize the opportunities. In the Renaissance, those opportunities existed, especially in finance and armaments. With so much construction to perform and so much war to wage, those with capital were able to lend it at handsome rates of interest. Meanwhile manufacturers found markets always in search of weaponry and construction equipment. Venice's Arsenal—its shipbuilding factory—employed three thousand laborers at the start of the 15th century. Tax records from that time show that two-thirds of the city's merchants made at least six thousand ducats per year, and one-half of those fortunate merchants actually made well over twelve thousand. Seven merchants actually had annual incomes of over 140,000 ducats.[2] Such severe inequities in the distribution of capital ensured that rents and wages worked in favor of the elite. So did the power of the guild leaders and urban nobles. In Milan and Basel, a mere 5 percent of the population controlled one-half of each city's wealth. No wonder they had the ability to commission palaces, endow museums and libraries, dress in expensive silks and furs, and commission such splendid works of art. The Renaissance, for all its cultural glories, was a miserable time to be a poor farmer or a simple workman— which is precisely what the overwhelming majority of people were.

THE RENAISSANCE ACHIEVEMENT

Art and intellectual life tend to thrive when supported. The cult of patronage— that is, the eager support of painters, sculptors, poets, and scholars as a sign of one's cultivation—and the appreciation of individual talent gave a tremendous impetus to new forms of expression and the pursuit of knowledge. The influx of scholars and artists from the east also contributed, as the Ottomans closed in on the remnants of Byzantium. One Sicilian humanist, Giovanni Aurispa (1376–1459), rushed to Constantinople in the years leading up to the Turkish siege and came back with over two hundred manuscripts that might otherwise have gone up in flames. Copyists were hired by the hundreds in every city to get texts like these reproduced and circulated.[3] The invention of the printing press by Johannes Gutenberg in 1440 allowed books to pour over Europe like a tide. Aldus Manutius (1450–1515) was the most celebrated of humanist publishers; his printing house in Venice produced editions of well over a hundred Latin and Greek texts before his death.

Vernacular literature, or literature in local languages rather than Latin, also began to appear in print. This is important because most of the truly memorable literature produced in the Renaissance was in the common, not the learned, tongues. Petrarca's great sequence of sonnets and love-songs to his beloved Laura (the *Canzoniere*) have proved enduringly popular, while his Latin epic poem about the Roman general Scipio Africanus—called *Africa*—is turgid and lifeless. Much better is Ludovico Ariosto's (1474–1533) immense, and immensely

---

2   A Venetian ducat of that time was minted of roughly 3.5 grams of gold (one-eighth of an ounce). Gold, in 2012 U.S. dollars, has hovered around $1610 per ounce. A very rough estimate of the value of 6000 ducats, therefore, would be perhaps $1,200,000. In Shakespeare's play *The Merchant of Venice*, the amount loaned by Shylock to Antonio, on surety of "a pound of flesh," was half that amount.

3   By the start of the 15th century, Florence had opened the first lending library in Europe: one could actually borrow the books and take them home rather than having to read them on site, as before.

entertaining, mock-epic *Orlando Furioso* ("Crazed Roland"). It tells of the mad adventures of Charlemagne's knight Roland, who loses his mind when his beloved Angelica falls in love with a Muslim prince and moves to China. Then he turns into a one-man juggernaut, rampaging through Europe, Asia, and Africa and destroying everything in sight.

Not many Renaissance stage plays have lasted; only two are still widely read and produced today. Pietro Aretino (1492–1556), known in his lifetime as the "Scourge of Princes" for his scathing wit and willingness to blackmail the prominent when short of funds, wrote several brilliant bawdy comedies—along with a considerable amount of technically clever pornographic poetry.[4] The best, a comedy called *La cortigiana* ("The Woman Courtier"), tells of an upright wealthy citizen from Siena who receives an appointment as a papal cardinal. Traveling to Rome for his installation, he sees a beautiful young woman sitting at a window and decides he must have her as a mistress. The comedy ensues when a scheming con artist tries to teach the elderly man how to flatter and entice the young beauty—all the while pursuing a plan of his own.

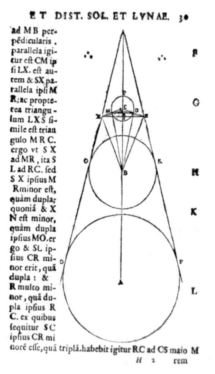

Greek to Me   The Romans, being of a pragmatic bent, became expert innovators in engineering but showed relatively little interest in pure science, and hence the science inherited by the scholars of the Middle Ages was based firmly on, and consisted largely of commentary on, the science of the ancient Greeks. The page shown, from a book printed in Pisa, Italy, in 1572, depicts a passage from *On the Distances and Sizes of the Sun and Moon* by Aristarchus (3rd century BCE). The text and drawing examine the ratios of the diameters of the sun, Earth, and moon and calculate how they affect the light and dark portions visible during a lunar eclipse.

The other great Renaissance comedy is *La mandragola* ("The Mandrake Root"), by Niccolò Machiavelli (1469–1527). The play, which appeared in 1518, tells of another upright elderly man, Nicia, newly married to a stunning but sexually shy beauty named Lucrezia. Unable to convince his bride to sleep with him, the foolish husband confides in a dashing young ne'er-do-well named Callimaco who, desiring Lucrezia for himself, hatches a plot. He tells Nicia that he has

---

4   A 2008 performance of Aretino's *Songs of Lust*, set to modern music, was withdrawn in London after complaints about their obscene content.

learned, through careful study of ancient Greek scientific manuscripts, of a potion made from mandrake root. When given to a woman, it instantly enflames her with a lust that cannot be denied. The drug has an unfortunate side effect, however: the first man to have sex with the woman will die immediately afterward. Nicia declares that he wants Lucrezia, but not enough to die for it. Callimaco then announces, tremblingly, unwillingly, that he himself suffers from an unspecified mortal illness and has only a few days to live. So great is his admiration for Nicia and his desire to perform a useful service before he dies that he volunteers for the suicide mission.

La mandragola surprises most people who read or watch it. They usually come to the play knowing Machiavelli from another work of his, a small political treatise called *The Prince*. In 1499 the people of Florence had overthrown the Medici despot and restored republican government. Machiavelli, a Florentine, loved and served its republic with passionate dedication for thirteen years, from 1499 to 1512—as a diplomat, civil servant, and military overseer. Late in 1512, however, a counter plot restored Lorenzo de' Medici to power. Machiavelli was dismissed, arrested for conspiracy, tortured, and ultimately released. In retirement at his country estate, he then gave himself over to study and writing.

The Prince, although he never published it, was the first thing Machiavelli wrote. (He circulated it among a small circle of friends and dedicated it to Lorenzo de' Medici—probably in hopes of winning a position in the new government.) It is a notorious book, praised by some for its clear-eyed realism about how political power actually works and vilified by others as little more than a how-to manual for thugs. To modern readers, inured by long experience of politicians' lies, manipulations, and occasional crimes, the book no longer shocks. Stable society, Machiavelli argues, results more from stable order than from benevolent instability. Therefore a prince's first responsibility is to secure his own power, even if the exercise of that power is unjust. Ruthlessness should not be pursued for its own sake, but a wise prince will never rule it out altogether. A prince ought always to maintain an upright public appearance, but behind the scenes he should use any means at his disposal—including lying, cheating, stealing, or killing—in order to maintain power. Although *The Prince* never uses the phrase, its essential message is that in politics the end justifies the means.

Clear-Eyed Realist   Niccolò Machiavelli (1469–1527) and a page from his philosophical masterpiece, *The Discourses on Livy*, in praise of republican forms of government.

Once the book was published, five years after Machiavelli's death, people read it with a shudder of horror. Machiavelli's defenders point to the chaotic state of Italian politics at the time, with French, German, Savoyard, and Spanish invaders at every turn. *The Prince*, they suggest, is simply a plea for a no-nonsense messianic figure who would restore Italian liberty. Perhaps. His letters, though, suggest that Machiavelli was a man of republican Florence, first, last, and always. He would have been delighted to see Ferrara, Mantua, Milan, Pisa, or Venice crushed by a foreign army if that were to Florence's gain. Complicating matters, he dashed off *The Prince* in a few weeks. Machiavelli then spent four years (1513–1517) composing his major work, *Discourses on Livy*, which elaborates a complex and passionate argument on the superiority of republican government over any other type of political organization.[5] "Governments of the people are superior to any government by a prince" (1.58).

Less controversial were Marsilio Ficino (1433–1499) and Baldassare Castiglione (1478–1529). Ficino was a celebrated philosopher who spent his career at the Medici court. He had mastered classical Greek as a young man and became a devout exponent of Neoplatonism. His greatest achievement, in fact, was a translation into Latin of the entire corpus of Plato's writings, which he completed in 1470 but did not publish until 1484 (having taken some time, meanwhile, to prepare for the priesthood). Until then, Plato had hardly been known in Latin Europe, and Western intellectual life had been long dominated by Aristotle. Ficino's other major works include a long treatise, *On Platonic Theology*, which explicates Christian doctrine on the immortality of the soul using Platonic ideas. He argues that the unique, characteristic destiny of the human soul is to investigate its own nature, but such investigation inevitably results (at least temporarily) in confusion and misery. Hence the ultimate goal of the soul is to rise above physicality, to become disembodied, and to achieve union with the divine. As a hybrid philosophical and mystical treatise, it is a stunning exercise. Ficino was the tutor of many Neoplatonists, most famously of Giovanni Pico della Mirandola, the author of the "Oration on the Dignity of Man."

Castiglione came from an ancient noble family near Mantua and spent his entire life in the circle of social and political elites. He served as a personal aide and confidante to the marquis of Mantua and then to the duke of Urbino and spent several years in Rome as an ambassador to the papal court, then several more as papal nuncio to the royal court of Spain in Madrid. He is remembered primarily for *The Courtier*, which is a kind of memoir written in the form of a fictional philosophical

---

[5] "No properly run republic should ever find it necessary to overlook the crimes of any given citizen because of his supposed excellence" (Machiavelli, *Discourses* 1.24).

dialogue. In it he laments the passing of the Renaissance's golden era, when humanism was at its height. By the 16th century Italy was overrun by ambitious foreigners, and courtly life as Castiglione had known it (or at least as he chose to remember it) had declined into a tawdry arena of power grabbing, money grubbing, and social climbing. He depicts fictionalized versions of the companions of his youth—elegant, charming, cultivated, effortlessly superior to everyone—who spend four evenings in an extended conversation about the qualities of an ideal courtier.

To Castiglione the courtier is above politics: he graciously advises any figure deemed worthy of attention but does not advocate any particular political philosophy. This marks a shift from the original ideal of humanism, which expected a passionate civic spirit from its adherents. Castiglione's figures expound on the need for courtiers to appreciate music and poetry, to excel at dancing, sports, and refined conversation, to understand the importance of fashion as well as affairs of state. In short, courtiers should exist beautifully, all the while exuding an air of nonchalance and unpracticed elegance. *The Courtier* was extraordinarily popular, going through more than one hundred editions between its appearance in 1528 and 1616. Its significance lay in its elegiac mood: at a time when Europe's nobles were being displaced from political life, Castiglione consecrated for them the qualities that lifted them forever above the common rabble.

THE PROTESTANT RENAISSANCE

As the ideas and values of the Renaissance spread northward, they took on new styles, concerns, and emphases. Ultimately, if indirectly, they led to the shattering of the religious unity that had marked Latin Europe since the advent of Christianity.

It took some time for humanism to catch on in the north. The prolonged agony of the Hundred Years' War in England and France certainly impeded the spread of the new learning. So did the resistance of the universities of Paris and Oxford—both strongholds of Aristotelianism. As for Germany, intellectual life there had long been centered in the royal and aristocratic courts. The royal court at Munich, for example, had been a refuge for scholars like Marsiglio di Padova and William of Ockham in the 14th century, when both had fallen out of favor in Paris and Oxford, respectively. Now Germany had fractured into hundreds of principalities (nominally under the authority of the Habsburg dynasty—the weak successors to the crushed Hohenstaufens—but effectively autonomous), and its relatively few universities did not rush to embrace new ideas.[6] When humanism

---

[6]   Munich did not acquire a university until 1472. Even then, the university was at Ingolstadt, several miles away.

did finally begin to take root, around the year 1500, it did so in an altered form known as **Christian humanism**.

Like humanism in Italy, Christian humanism rejected scholastic system building and looked to the past for new models of thinking and behavior. However, Christian humanists showed a strong preference for texts and traditions that contributed directly to religious faith. Their goal was not to become better all-round individuals but better Christians. Consequently, they focused less on the writings of the ancient philosophers and poets and more on the early writings of the Christians—especially the New Testament itself. In the visual arts, the northern Renaissance likewise showed much less interest in depicting classical pagan themes. Rather, painters and sculptors avidly adopted Renaissance techniques to produce striking new presentations of biblical imagery. The Christian humanists were passionate reformers, dedicated to promote Christian education and practical piety through the preparation of newer and better texts. Their often-stated goal was backward looking: to restore Christian faith to its original purity as practiced in the apostolic community.

The Christian humanists were not yet anti-Catholic, only anticlerical. The shortage of priests had always been direr the further north one traveled in Europe, with exceptions in cities like Paris, London, and Mainz, but the problem had been persistently acute since the Black Death. Clergy at the grassroots level were in painfully short supply, and those who were available were often poorly trained. Hence northerners had developed strong traditions of lay piety. They focused less on the church's sacramental life and more on the simple reading of Scripture, the singing of hymns, and communal prayer. Religious fraternities and sororities abounded, offering many a life of organized piety, education, and moral rigor that deemphasized ecclesiastical dogma and ritual. The best

The Four Holy Men   "A panel on which I have bestowed more care than on any other painting" is how Albrecht Dürer (1471–1528) described this powerful group portrait, completed in 1526. It depicts, from left to right, Saint John the Evangelist, Saint Peter (holding his ever-present key to paradise), Saint Mark, and Saint Paul the Apostle (who carries a copy of the Bible and a sword, the latter being a reference to his martyrdom). Dürer was a passionate supporter of the Lutheran Reformation, and the bottom portion of each panel (since lost) bore passages from Luther's German translation of the Scriptures. The intensity of the men's expressions and the classical simplicity of their dress testify to the spiritual earnestness of the Protestant Reformers—being awed and humbled by the magnificence of what they regarded as the rediscovered beauty and majesty of the Word.

known of these organizations was the Brethren of the Common Life, established in 14th-century Holland and spreading quickly across northern Europe. Its most famous alumni were Desiderius Erasmus (1466–1536) and Martin Luther (1483–1546).

ERASMUS: SATIRIST AND ITINERANT SCHOLAR

Erasmus was arguably the greatest of all humanist scholars, admired for the breadth of his classical learning, his quick wit and generous spirit, and the elegance of his writing. The illegitimate son of a Dutch priest in training and a physician's daughter, he grew up in Rotterdam and received his primary education at home. In 1483, however, both of his parents died in a new outbreak of the plague. Supported by the Brethren of the Common Life, Erasmus entered a series of monastic and lay-fraternal schools, where he was unhappy with the frequently dour discipline but delighted in their extensive libraries. In 1492, brilliant but penniless, he took monastic vows, entered an Augustinian house, and was soon ordained to the priesthood. He hated monastic life, though, and thought most of his fellow monks to be joyless and haughty automatons. Fortunately, a bishop from Cambrai, not far away in northern France, heard of Erasmus's brilliance and took him on as a personal secretary in 1495. The bishop urged Erasmus to pursue more formal study and sent him to the University of Paris.

Once he had finished his degree, Erasmus set out for England, where he had been invited to lecture at the University of Cambridge. Freed from the bishop's service, Erasmus spent the rest of his life as an itinerant scholar, lecturing at various universities and visiting one noble court after another. Chronically short of funds, he was offered many lucrative academic posts throughout his life but declined them all, preferring his freedom. He also rejected several offers to be appointed a Catholic bishop and two nominations to the College of Cardinals. He studied and wrote constantly, even while traveling. In fact, he claimed to have written much of his most famous work, *The Praise of Folly* (1509), while on horseback during a trip to England to visit his friend Thomas More. He died in Basel in 1536.

Despite such an unsettled life Erasmus produced an astonishing amount of writing. His letters alone fill eleven fat volumes in their standard edition. He wrote in three distinct voices. His most popular works were witty satires like *The Praise of Folly* that aimed to entertain people while nevertheless pointing out society's flaws and foibles. Folly here delivers a monologue on the crucial but unappreciated role she has played in human history. Everyone from kings and princes to peasants and peddlers, she claims, owe something to her for the simple reason that humans all prefer foolishness to common sense. Every page of history proves her point. In works like this, or his popular *Colloquies* (1518), Erasmus lampoons pedantic teachers, hypocritical clerics, greedy landlords, shrewish wives, petulant youths, preening nobles, untrustworthy merchants, and others with a wit that is pointed but almost never mean-spirited.

Erasmus's most notorious satire is a prickly piece called *Julius Excluded* (1513), a lengthy sketch depicting a confrontation at the Gates of Heaven between the recently deceased Pope Julius II (r. 1503–1513) and Saint Peter. Julius is drunk when he arrives and tries to unlock the gates with the key to his private money chest. Asked to account for his many sins, ranging from murder to sodomy, Julius replies that his sins were all forgiven "by the pope himself"—meaning, of course, Julius himself. When Saint Peter refuses to admit Julius into heaven on account of his excessive concern for

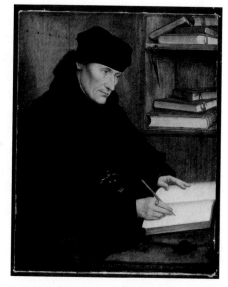

Erasmus of Rotterdam   Given the fact that he was the most traveled, best connected, and highly regarded religious scholar in Europe, there are surprisingly few contemporary portraits of Erasmus, the man who made a heroic last-ditch effort to reform Catholic Christianity before Martin Luther's break with Rome. This portrait, by fellow Dutchman Quentin Metsys (1466–1530), captures the quiet determination of the man. Despite his gift for satire and enjoyment of good (and sometimes bawdy) humor, Erasmus dedicated long years of work to exposing problems within the Catholic Church and promoting a spiritual rejuvenation that would keep all Christians within the arms of the church. His failure marks an important turning point, since most of the great reforms in the church in earlier centuries had been inspired from without. From Erasmus's time to the present, Catholic reform has been largely driven from within the institutional leadership.

worldly power and war making, the pope throws a fit, threatens to excommunicate Peter, and announces that he will raise an army to burst through the gates and take Paradise by force.[7]

Erasmus also composed a long series of moral polemics, earnest in tone yet intended for a general audience. In these books—like *Handbook of the Christian Soldier* (1503), *Education of a Christian Prince* (1516), and *The Complaint of Peace* (1517)—he condemns empty religious formalism and urges people to seek out the vital spirit of Christ as depicted in the Bible. They should live simply,

---

[7]   At one point the pope complains to Saint Peter, "You would not believe how *seriously* some people take little things like bribery, blasphemy, sodomy, and poisoning!"

honorably, peaceably, and with sincere conviction. These satirical and serious works were immensely popular: it has been estimated that, by Erasmus's death in 1536, some 15 percent of all the printed books purchased in Europe had come from his pen. In his third vein, Erasmus toiled at the most detailed and exacting textual scholarship—revised and annotated editions of the writings of the Latin fathers Saint Ambrose (d. 397), Saint Jerome (d. 420), and Saint Augustine (d. 430). He followed these projects with his masterpiece, a new critical edition of the Greek New Testament (1515), whose fifth and final version appeared in 1535. Known as the Received Version (*Textus receptus*), it was used by most early translators of the New Testament into English and other vernaculars. These works had a much smaller readership, understandably, but he regarded them as his chief legacy to the world.

MARTIN LUTHER: THE GIFT OF SALVATION

Among those who used Erasmus's New Testament as the basis for a vernacular translation was Martin Luther, the German monk whose agonized quest for salvation triggered the break with the church known as the **Protestant Reformation**. Like the humanists who sought to restore ancient morals, Luther sought to re-create what he believed to be Christian belief and practice as they had existed in the apostolic Church. He saw himself as a restorer, not a revolutionary, a liberator rather than an insurrectionist. The distinction is important, for it helped to set the stage for the brutal course the conflict ultimately took. Luther, a brilliant biblical scholar, had the gift of presenting his ideas in clear, forceful language that ranged easily in emotional pitch from exquisite descriptions of God's loving kindness to the coarsest verbal abuse of his foes (who consisted of anyone who disagreed with him). His charisma, energy, and passionate feeling were immense; he needed such powerful drive, for his ultimate goals—once he decided that compromise with the church was impossible—were nothing less than the complete overthrow of Catholic tradition and the resetting of the Christian clock, so to speak, fifteen hundred years back.

> Like the humanists who sought to restore ancient morals, Luther sought to re-create what he believed to be Christian belief and practice as they had existed in the apostolic Church. He saw himself as a restorer, not a revolutionary, a liberator rather than an insurrectionist.

Luther was born—proudly—of modest, laboring stock in northern Germany. His hardworking parents instilled piety and order in him from an early age, and when it came time for his education they sent him to a school run by the Brethren of Common

Life, the same group whose austere and rigid discipline had so disillusioned the young Erasmus. Hoping to establish his son in a legal career, Luther's father sent him to the University of Erfurt, but Martin was drawn instead to theology and the classical languages. In 1505, aged twenty-two, he shattered his father's hopes by taking vows as an Augustinian monk. A mere two years later he was ordained a priest.

His vocation brought him no peace, though. Belief in God tormented Luther, for he could see no way to please him. God's majesty was so immense, so vast, and so inconceivably great, that Luther found it impossible to believe that anyone could merit salvation. No one de-

A Restorer, not a Revolutionary   Martin Luther (1483–1546), in a portrait by Lucas Cranach the Elder (1472–1553). Apart from his work as an artist, Cranach was an early enthusiast for the printing press, and in time became one of Martin Luther's publishers. He is revered as a saint in both the Episcopal and Lutheran Churches in the United States.

serves to be saved, he believed, for the simple reason that no one can deserve to spend eternity in God's presence. How can anyone possibly claim to merit that? And yet that was precisely what Christian tradition told him to pursue—a life of prayer, repentance, good works, and devotion that would earn him the salvation Christ had promised to everyone who did so. Luther observed his monastic discipline with fanatical determination, even to the point where his abbot feared for his sanity. And yet the fear that nothing he did could possibly justify his standing before God never left him. So sharp grew his agony, he later wrote, that he began to despise God for having created a game that we cannot win—and then punishing us with eternal torment for losing it:

> Even as a blameless monk I still felt certain that in God's eyes I was a miserable sinner—and one with a very troubled conscience—for I had no reason to believe that God would ever be satisfied by my actions. I could not love a righteous God who punished the unrighteous; rather, I hated Him. I was careful never to blaspheme aloud, but on the inside, in the silence of my heart, I roiled and raged at God, saying, "Is it not enough for You that we, miserable sinners all, are damned for all eternity on account of original sin [the notion that, as a result of Adam and Eve's

misbehavior, all human beings come into the world with a moral stain upon them from birth]? Why do You add to our calamity by imposing the Ten Commandments on us as well? Why add sorrow upon sorrow through the Gospel teachings, and then in that same Gospel threaten us with judgment and wrath?"

But then came the breakthrough. Having been sent by his exhausted abbot to teach theology at the University of Wittenberg, Luther, in 1513, was preparing lecture notes on Saint Paul's Epistle to the Romans, a text he had read countless times before, when suddenly a new insight flashed through his mind:

> I pondered these words night and day until, at last, God had mercy on me and gave me to understand the connection between the phrases "The justice of God is revealed in the Gospel" and "The just will live through faith" [Romans 1.16–17]. I suddenly began to understand that God's justice—that is, the justice by which a just person may live for-ever—is a gift of God won by faith. . . . All at once I felt reborn, as though I had entered Paradise through gates thrown wide open, and immedi-ately the whole of Scripture took on a new meaning for me.

In other words, *of course* God knows that we do not "deserve" salvation. But salvation is God's gift to us, and he simply wants us to have it anyway.

After this flash of insight, the rest of the Scriptures' meaning lay open, as though Luther was seeing it for the first time. To be righteous in the eyes of God, one did not have confess one's sins to a priest, give alms to the poor, or earn indulgences by ritual devotions like pilgrimages or vigils. One did not have to follow disciplines like praying cycles of the rosary or not eating meat on Fridays. One attains righteousness simply by having faith in Christ; one must accept the salvation he offers as an unmerited gift. This idea became canonized in Luther's understanding as **justification by faith alone** (*sola fide* in Latin). It results not from our merit but from God's grace alone (*sola gratia*), as ex-pressed uniquely through Christ's sacrifice on the Cross (*solo Christo*). More-over, everything that God requires of us is expressed not through the teaching authority and tradition of the church but through the words of Scripture alone (*sola Scriptura*). Anything beyond biblical teaching is superfluous to salvation at best, and an impediment to it at worst. Few of these ideas were new. In fact, many of them had been enunciated by Saint Augustine (d. 430), the founder of Luther's own monastic order. But Luther carried them to a degree far beyond Augustine or any other theologian.

REBELLION AGAINST THE CHURCH: "NINETY-FIVE THESES"

Luther's theology offended the church because it made the church irrelevant. From the time of the Gregorian Reform in the 11th century, the church had developed its theology of salvation, with itself as intermediary. The church and the believer worked together to effect salvation, through teaching and ministry, the sacraments and pious action. The relationship was not a crude contract, although many saw it that way and had been making similar complaints since at least the second half of the 14th century.

What prompted Luther's rebellion against the church was not merely his new understanding of Scripture—for it was not, after all, new. Rather, it was his ire over the church's practice of selling **indulgences**, a donation to the church as a means of satisfying the requirements for the forgiveness of sin. From the 12th century on, Catholic doctrine had understood penance for sin to have four elements: contrition, confession, absolution, and satisfaction. One first has to repent honestly for what one has done; second, one must confess the sin fully to a priest; then, third, one receives absolution from that priest if the confession is sincere and genuine; and fourth, one must then make some sort of restitution for what one did. An indulgence—earned by some explicit act of charity or devotion—was a way of meeting the fourth demand. A special donation to the church was one way of earning the indulgence. Hence, while it was not an act of "purchasing forgiveness," it certainly could look like one—especially if the process was abused. And it was, egregiously, in Luther's time.

Many people had criticized the practice, including Erasmus. The Renaissance popes, as involved as ever in Italian politics, had waged wars against various despots, had tried to resist the advancing Ottoman Turks, and had expanded the church's network of universities across Europe. As a result, they were in constant and desperate need of funds, and many turned to the offering of indulgences as a reliable means of raising cash. An enormous campaign spread throughout Germany and Italy to raise funds for the construction of the new Saint Peter's Basilica in Rome (designed in part by Michelangelo and Bernini). In 1517 Martin Luther, just recently released from his spiritual tortures, witnessed the abusive and predatory selling of

Anti-Catholic Propaganda This anonymous woodcut of 1520 by a German satirist depicts the devil (complete with wings and clawed feet) sitting on a letter of indulgence and holding a money collection box. The devil's mouth is filled with sinners who presumably bought letters of indulgence in good faith, thinking they had been absolved from their sins.

indulgences in both places and was outraged. The symbolic starting point of the Protestant Reformation was not his biblical epiphany in 1513 but his Ninety-Five Theses—condemning the theology of indulgences.

The **Ninety-Five Theses** are simply a list of assertions that Luther declares himself prepared to argue—but the arguments themselves are not part of the text. This sort of posting bulletins of ideas was a common practice in universities of the time. Like the modern practice of publishing the prospectus of one's doctoral dissertation, it invited argument and discussion. He got it. Pope Leo X (r. 1513–1521) spent three years examining Luther's position and finally responded with a papal bull on June 15, 1520, called *Exsurge Domine* ("Arise, O Lord"). He condemned forty-one of the theses as heretical, and he gave Luther sixty days to reconsider his position and withdraw the offending statements. Luther answered back by publicly burning his copy of the bull on December 10, exactly sixty days after it was issued. After this, there was only one action Leo could take: On January 3, 1521, the pope excommunicated Luther. From this point on, little effort was made to mend fences. The people of Germany flocked to Luther's message by the thousands, and then by the tens of thousands. Within a few years the religious unity of Christian Europe was permanently sundered.

"The Pope is the Antichrist, and the Catholic Church is the most unruly of all crooks' lairs, the most brazen of all brothels, and the Kingdom itself of Sin, Death, and Hell," Luther wrote in a late book titled *On the Roman Papacy: An Institution of the Devil*. Pope Leo, for his part, dismissed Luther as "a German drunkard who will mend his ways once he sobers up." The language is not edifying. But once the rift between Luther and the church was opened, it developed quickly into an unbridgeable chasm. What began as an in-house theological dispute took on more and more political and social pressures. Two political issues were of special significance: the constitutional arrangement within Germany, and the threat posed by the Turks.

For two centuries the four hundred or so princes of Germany had enjoyed independence from imperial control, while the relatively weak Habsburgs went about adding to their domain in eastern Europe and by marrying available heiresses throughout the Continent. When Charles V (r. 1520–1556) came to the throne, he succeeded, by a genealogical quirk, to several lines of Habsburg-family legacies. These territories, when considered in the aggregate, put him in the unexpected position of having the German princes surrounded (see Map 11.2). His formal title(s), used on all his official records, ran as follows: "Charles, by grace of God the elected Holy Roman Emperor, forever August, King in Germany, King of Italy, Castile, Aragon, León, both Sicilies, Jerusalem, Navarra, Granada, Toledo, Valencia, Galicia, Majorca, Sevilla, Sardinia, Cordova, Corsica, Murcia, Jaen, the Algarves, Algeciras, Gibraltar, the Canary Islands, the Western and

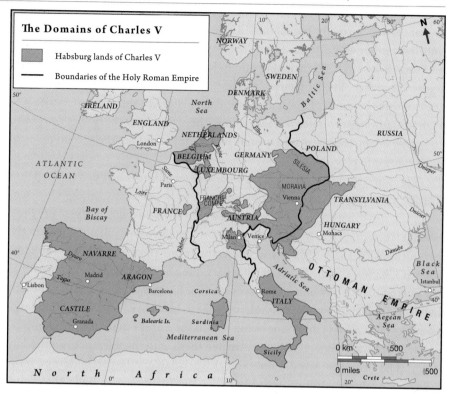

MAP 11.2   The Domains of Charles V

Eastern Indies, the Islands and Mainland of the Ocean Sea, etc. etc., Archduke of Austria, Duke of Burgundy, Brabant, Lorraine, Styria, Carinthia, Carniola, Limburg, Luxembourg, Gelderland, Athens, Neopatria, Württemberg, Landgrave of Alsace, Prince of Swabia, Asturia and Catalonia, Count of Flanders, Habsburg, Tyrol, Gorizia, Barcelona, Artois, Burgundy Palatine, Hainaut, Holland, Seeland, Ferrette, Kyburg, Namur, Roussillon, Cerdagne, Zutphen, Margrave of the Holy Roman Empire, Burgau, Oristano and Gociano, Lord of Frisia, the Wendish March, Pordenone, Biscay, Molin, Salins, Tripoli and Mechelen, etc."

By constitutional tradition, Charles had no cause to take advantage of his position by imposing his rule on the princes. However, since he was, as emperor, the defender of Catholicism, he considered seriously his obligation to combat the Protestant heresy. The princes, for their part, had good reason to support Luther: he had essentially given them control of the new churches.

Luther's *Address to the Christian Nobility of the German Nation* (1520) had laid out his vision for the organization and administration of his reformed church. Since there was no supreme spiritual authority—each believer needing only his Bible and his own conscience—the Protestant Church needed only secular administration and guidance. For that, Luther turned to the princes.

A prince who formally broke with Rome and converted to Lutheranism was entitled, Luther wrote, to confiscate the Catholic ecclesiastical lands, properties, and wealth within his principality and to lead the administration of the new reformed churches. The temptation was great, but most princes feared that seizing the extensive holdings of the churches and monasteries would cause Charles V to rush to Catholicism's defense. Hence, even though most of the nobles converted to Lutheranism, they hesitated to start plundering. But then the second political issue came into play.

The Turkish threat was complicated. Ottoman forces had driven deep into Europe, after taking Constantinople in 1453, in hopes of weakening Christendom. Charles V, naturally, spearheaded the effort to hold them at bay. Many Protestant princes hoped to form an alliance with the Ottoman sultan, Suleiman the Magnificent (r. 1520–1566), who had come to his throne at roughly the same time as Charles V came to his. Such a pact, they hoped, would leave Charles as the surrounded party and thereby neutralize his power. Diplomatic relations between Protestant rulers and Suleiman were extensive. The Turks had large numbers of Jews and Christians living within the European part of their empire, and for the time being, at least, they treated them with the tolerance required by dhimmi law. Dhimmi law did not protect Christian and Jewish buildings, however, and Suleiman advanced steadily. When the Turks overran Buda, the capital of Hungary, they delighted in destroying churches and synagogues throughout the city. Indeed, they set aflame a collection of Renaissance art as rich as anything in Florence or Milan.[8]

Suleiman's advance compelled Charles to mobilize his forces; but since the Turks were not threatening Habsburg lands directly, Charles bided his time. The Lutheran princes kept negotiating with Suleiman, to keep the pressure up. An alliance did not happen, but Suleiman concluded that Charles was too weak to offer any real resistance and so launched a fresh attack in 1526, quickly taking most of Hungary. After a brief pause he advanced his army at far as Vienna, to which he laid siege in 1529. At this point even the Protestants were worried. Luther published in that same year the pamphlet *On the War against the Turks*, in which he called for a united European front against the Ottomans yet rejected as un-Christian the notion of a Crusade. Suleiman's siege failed, however, and the Turkish advance was temporarily stopped.

With so much at stake in terms of geopolitics, it is not surprising that the rhetoric of the religious dispute became feverish. Catholics and Protestants at all levels of society hurled abuse at each other. Erasmus and Luther, for a while, maintained a

---

[8]   Buda—supposedly named after Bleda, Attila the Hun's older brother—much later incorporated with the small nearby town of Pest, to become today's Budapest.

civilized debate in print over theological issues like free will, the workings of divine grace, and the interpretation of Scripture. (The two men never met personally.) Other than that, though, most of the religious battle was in poisonous language. When large numbers of German peasants were persuaded by radicals to rise up in arms against their landlords in 1524 and 1525 in a rebellion known as the **Peasants' Revolt**, Luther responded savagely. While the peasants had been stirred by Luther's insistence on the dignity of all believers, he called on the princes to take bold action.

If his aim was to scare the peasants into submission, *On the Thieving, Murderous Hordes of Peasants* was a brilliant success:

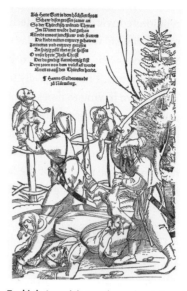

Turkish Atrocities   Throughout the 16th and 17th centuries the Ottomans made repeated efforts to expand their control in southeastern Europe, twice getting as far as the gates of Vienna. This woodcut depicts popular fears of Turkish savagery. "Such amusements are common in all wars," warned Erasmus in 1530, when this image was published. The Turks did commit atrocities like those shown here, but no more so than what European Catholics and Protestants inflicted on one another (and what both sometimes inflicted on the Jews) throughout the Wars of Religion.

> Therefore every one of you who can should act as both judge and executioner.... Strike them down, slay them, and stab them, either in secret or in the light of day ... for you ought always to bear in mind that there is nothing more poisonous, dangerous, or devilish than one of these rebels.... For baptism frees men's souls alone; it does not liberate their bodies and properties, nor does the Gospel call for people to hold all their goods in common.... Fine Christians these peasants are! There can hardly be a single devil left in hell—for I do believe they have all taken possession of these peasants, whose mad ravings are beyond all measure.... What a wonderful time we live in now, when a prince can better merit heaven by bloodshed than by prayer!

Most of the rebels, denied Luther's expected support, laid down their weapons at once. The rest were quickly defeated in a battle at Frankenhausen in May 1525, and the revolt ended. The rebel leader, an apocalyptic firebrand named Thomas Müntzer, was executed. The cost of victory was high, however. As many as one hundred thousand people lost their lives.

After this, the "Protestantization" of Germany gained pace, as the princes rushed to support Luther's program and seized church lands and treasuries. Sincere religious conviction undoubtedly motivated them, but political and economic factors obviously were also at play. By formally adopting the Lutheran cause, princes acquired—with Luther's own blessing—the authority to appoint pastors to the new churches. This effectively placed the nobles in charge of the entire institution. Freed from having to meet their former fiscal obligations to Rome or to recognize the authority of ecclesiastical courts, the princes likewise ensured the obedience of the new Lutheran churches to noble demands. The policies they developed came to be summarized by the phrase *Cuius regio, eius religio* ("The religion of the ruler determines the religion of the land"). And most of the princes promoted the new *religio* in order to strengthen their grip on the *regio*.

THE REFORMATION GOES INTERNATIONAL

Like other reformers before him and since, Martin Luther believed that those who joined him in rebellion would agree with him on what to replace tyranny with. But things seldom turn out that way. People, it seems, unite more easily in opposition to a present evil than they rally around a new vision of future good. With its spread beyond Germany, especially in the legacy of Jean Calvin, Protestantism in fact thrived on divisions.

When Luther began his revolt, many among the pope's advisors recommended immediate and dramatic action. Luther, after all, seemed intent on tearing down the entire Catholic tradition. However, just as many others counseled a quietist approach. Once Luther validated the idea that people can interpret the Scriptures for themselves, they pointed out, they would soon disagree with Luther's interpretations as much as they disagree with Rome's. The rebellion would then splinter into countless factions and soon disappear under its own dead, fractured weight.

Each group of advisers was half right. At the start, Luther saw his actions as a much-needed campaign to correct flaws in Catholic belief and practice, not as a drive to destroy the church. He was a reformer, not a revolutionary. Dramatic counter-action was indeed called for, but not in the urgent sense recommended by the alarmists. As for the second group, they saw correctly the coming splintering of the reformers into rival groups, but their assumption that division meant failure was wrong. They had severely underestimated the extent of anticlerical feeling—and the intense resentment of the church's abuses and failings. By the time they realized their mistake, it was too late. Luther and his followers had flooded Germany with polemical pamphlets, sermons, hymnals, catechisms, and above all the Bible itself in translation.[9]

---

[9]   Luther and his followers understood the power of the new technology of printing.

It took a generation, more or less, for Luther's ideas to catch on outside of Germany. His basic ideas were known. How could they not be, considering the enormity of the scandal he had caused? However, Luther wrote most of his works in German—since vernacular Scripture reading and vernacular worship were so central to his theology. And translators did not rush to bring his works into other tongues. Luther had taken care to produce a number of pamphlets and broadsides in Latin, to encourage the spread of the revolt. His ongoing debate in print with Erasmus—the most revered scholar in the Christian world—also kept his program in the spotlight. Still, when Protestantism did start to spread, it did so on the heels of the spread of Christian humanism. Many saw that intellectual effort as preparation for the spiritual regeneration coming out of Germany.

Not all northern humanists were, or became, Protestant. Many of the most famous, in fact, remained staunchly Catholic. What contributed to the spread of Protestantism was not humanism itself but rather the dialogue between Renaissance and Reformation. It was the spirit of questioning, of returning to ancient sources. Many heard that dialogue and clung ever more fiercely to the Catholic tradition. Many others, though, who might otherwise never have thought it possible, heard in the debate a calling to a wholly new, and newly holy, path.

SCHOLARS AND ACTIVISTS

The best of the Christian humanist scholars were all dedicated Catholics: Guillaume Budé (1467–1540), Jacques Lefèvre d'Étaples (1455–1536), Cardinal Francisco Ximénez de Cisneros (1436–1517), and Joan Lluís Vives i March (1493–1540). Other writers—primarily Protestants like Ulrich Zwingli (1484–1531), Jean Calvin (1509–1564), and John Knox (1514–1572)—remain better known and were more historically significant because of their activities in the world. But pure scholars should have their due, too.

Budé was a classical linguist, one of the finest Greek scholars of his generation. Supported by the French royal court, he produced a Greek lexicon that remained the standard for scholars for nearly two hundred years. He was also the founder of the school that later became the Collège de France and of the library that ultimately grew into the Bibliothèque Nationale, both in Paris. Lefèvre, also a royal favorite, was an industrious writer of biblical commentaries as well as editions and translations of patristic texts. In 1530 he published the first ever translation of the entire Bible into French.

De Cisneros held immense power in Spain: he was the archbishop of Toledo, was twice the regent for the crown, and served as grand inquisitor at the high point of that institution's power in Spain. As a statesman Cisneros was blunt and direct even to the point of cruelty. He was not at all averse to ordering the forced baptism

Polyglot Bible A page from the Complutensian Polyglot Bible (1514–1517) published by Cardinal Francisco Cisneros, one of the great humanistic achievements of the Renaissance. The three main columns present the Biblical text in Hebrew, Latin, and Greek, while underneath are printed passages in Aramaic (Targum), where they survive, and alternative readings. The Complutensian edition was used extensively by the English translators who produced the King James Bible (Authorized Version) in 1611.

of the Moors of southern Spain and the burning of the Arabic manuscripts in the library at Granada. As a scholar, he was patient in the extreme: he spent fifteen years producing the Complutensian Polyglot Bible—an impressive work that reproduced, in parallel columns, the best texts then available of the entire Bible in Aramaic, Greek, Hebrew, and Latin.

Lluís Vives, a much more sympathetic figure, dedicated long years to social reform as well as to reform within the church. He was an earnest champion of education for women and welfare for the poor. The fourth-generation son of a *converso* family—that is, a family that had once been Jewish—he witnessed the Inquisition's execution of his father, grandmother, and great-grandfather.[10] And although he never wavered in his Christian commitment, he left Spain as soon as he could and never returned. After studying in Paris, he became a professor of philosophy at Oxford and spent his time between Oxford and the royal court in London, where he served as private tutor to the Tudor family.

PROTESTANTISM WITHOUT LUTHER

Among the Protestant humanists, the most influential were Ulrich Zwingli and Jean Calvin. Zwingli left behind over twenty volumes of writings—sermons, biblical exegesis, topical essays, some poetry—but little of this is read by anyone other than specialists. His impact was in the world of action rather than thought. He was born to a Swiss farming family and received a good though unremarkable education. In 1498 he enrolled at the University of Vienna, but was expelled for reasons no one has ever discovered. He was ordained a priest and spent several years as a military chaplain. A crisis of conscience, however, led him to withdraw

---

[10] Scholars use *inquisition*, with a lowercase *i*, to refer to the inquisitorial process in the Middle Ages. Uppercase *Inquisition* is reserved for the Renaissance, when what had been a medieval process turned into a formal institution.

from his post and take up duties as a simple parish priest in a small village in Switzerland. This position gave him ample time for self-education, and in a few years he had mastered Greek and acquired a usable knowledge of Hebrew.

By 1516 personal study of the Scriptures had inspired him to doubt the value of much Catholic doctrine and ritual. But he was too timid to admit his opinions in public until Martin Luther began his public work in 1517 with the Ninety-Five Theses. Zwingli then dedicated himself to the twin goals of supporting Luther's Reformation and securing Switzerland's independence from French, Italian, and imperial meddling. He formally broke with Rome, and by 1522 most of the German-speaking cantons of Switzerland had done the same and had placed themselves under Zwingli's leadership. He moved to Zurich, which became second only to Luther's Wittenberg as the unofficial capital of the Protestant movement.

Zwingli's brand of Christianity differed from Luther's in a number of specifics. In fact, Zwingli, who did not meet Luther personally until 1529, is one of the very first examples of a Protestant who broke away from the movement's founder. He died in battle against armies from the Catholic southern portion of Switzerland, and the embryonic church he had created became subsumed by the new church created by Jean Calvin.

A brief but violent interlude, however, preceded Calvin on the scene. Several dozen radical members of Zwingli's church at Zurich quit Switzerland and took up residence in exile at Münster, in northwestern Germany. Disgusted by what they considered the immoral joining of Protestant religion with secular government (Luther and the German princes, Zwingli and the Swiss town councils), they established themselves as an apocalyptic sect known as the **Anabaptists**.[11] Their name means "rebaptizers," for the group rejected infant baptism as meaningless by itself and called for a second baptism in adulthood. They also embraced a literal reading of Scripture, polygamy (although the extent of this is still debated), and the imminent approach of Christ's Second Coming. The sect came under the charismatic leadership of Jan van Leiden, who proclaimed himself the successor to the King David of Biblical times and his Münster church as the reincarnation of the Jerusalem Temple. Zwingli and Luther both denounced the group, as did all the Catholic rulers of the time. Persecutions followed as Münster was stormed by the Catholic prince (and bishop) of the city, the Anabaptists were tortured and executed, and their sympathizers across Europe were arrested.

---

[11]   Crushed by its enemies, the Anabaptist movement disappeared. The Mennonite church, founded by Menno Simons (1496–1561) of Holland, is a late offshoot that still survives.

By the time Jean Calvin established his own Reformed Church in Geneva, the conflict between rival Christianities had moved well beyond a war of words. Most of the Scandinavian territories (Finland was the exception) had declared for Lutheranism by the end of the 1520s. Lutheranism had also sunk deep roots in northern Germany and parts of Poland, Hungary, and the Low Countries. England was, for the time being, still staunchly Catholic, although Henry VIII's (r. 1509–1547) marital woes led him to break with Rome over the course of the 1530s (see Map 11.3).

MAP 11.3   The Protestant Reformation, ca. 1580

CALVIN: PROTESTANTISM AS THEOLOGY

At first glance, Calvin seems an unlikely revolutionary. Quiet, reserved, intensely bookish, he studied (under pressure from his father) for a legal career at the University of Bourges, where he fell under the spell of humanist classicism. At about the same time—somewhere around 1530—he had an evangelical conversion that changed his entire life. He described the event in the introduction to his later *Commentary on the Psalms:*

> All at once, God overpowered my mind, which at that point was far more incorrigible in such matters than one might expect in one so young, and opened it [to the Truth]. Having been given this sampling of, this introduction to, true godliness, I instantly burned with such a passion to have better knowledge of it that, even though I never abandoned my other studies entirely, I pursued them with much less drive than before.

If his account is accurate, his was an intellectual rather than mystical conversion, although it was no less passionate for that. True to his bookish nature, he turned almost immediately to writing the first edition (1535) of his main work, *Institutes of Christian Religion,* which he continued to revise until his death. (Its final and definitive editions appeared in 1559 in Latin and in 1560 in French.)

The *Institutes* was the first work to lay out the emerging theology of Protestant Christianity in a systematic, logical, organized way. Here is a representative passage, on how the Reformed Church uses discipline:

> It is necessary, likewise, to distinguish between different kinds of sins, for some are only minor infractions whereas others are enormous and enormously wicked crimes. In order to correct the latter, mere warnings and reproofs do not suffice, and one must resort to sterner measures—as Paul shows [1 Corinthians 5.1–5] when he does not allow himself to rest content after having condemned the man of Corinth who had committed incest, but immediately excommunicates the man after his conviction for the crime. Now we begin to see how the spiritual authority of the Church, which corrects sins according to God's Word, preserves our health, orders our lives, and establishes bonds of unity among us; for whenever the Church banishes from the community those guilty of adultery, fornication, theft, robbery, sedition, false witness, or any other crimes of that sort, or when it banishes those stubborn people who criticize God's Holy Judgment, even after having been admonished for lesser sins, it [the church] exercises no unauthorized rational power but only the jurisdiction that God Himself has given it. In order that no one may refuse to

recognize this judgmental power of the Church, or think that it represents only the opinion of the community of believers, God Himself bears witness that [the church's judgment] it is nothing less than His judgment of the case, and that what the Church does upon earth is ratified in Heaven. For the Church has by God's Own Word the authority to condemn the wicked and to receive the penitent back into the favor of the Church. Anyone who believes that the Church could even exist without this power to discipline is sorely mistaken—for how could we do without the very thing that God saw fit to give us? The reasons why this is necessary will be made clear in its action.   *(Institutes of Christian Religion 4.12.4)*

Martin Luther, like his model Saint Augustine, had been far too impulsive a writer ever to write anything like this.

Calvin shared Luther's central, defining notion of an infinitely majestic, all-powerful, and all-knowing God whose transcendent might and will is in absolute control of the entire cosmos. But Luther softened this commanding image by emphasizing the infinitely merciful, because unmerited, love that God feels for us. Calvin stressed instead the unfathomable mystery of God's justice. Since he is all-knowing, argued Calvin, God has known since the moment of Creation which human beings were to be saved and which were to be damned—and these fates are sealed absolutely by the sheer force of God's will. There is nothing any human being can do to alter his or her fate. Does this mean that many apparently "good" people will be punished in hell while many apparently "bad" people are rewarded in heaven? Yes, it does; but this, to Calvin, is simply the consequence of our complete inability to understand God's purpose, rather than a sign of God's supposed hypocrisy. We must remain faithful to the belief that God's ways are ultimately and supremely just, even if we cannot comprehend them. In essence, what Calvin called for was an attitude of radical humility before God, an absolute submission of the soul to the Almighty's wisdom, power, and righteousness.

Unlikely Revolutionary   Sketches of Jean Calvin (1509–1564), the founder of the Reformed (Presbyterian) Church, made in a notebook by one of his university students who preferred doodling to taking lecture notes.

But this is not an attitude of passivity. It is precisely because we cannot know whether we are among the **Elect** (his term for those predestined for salvation) that Calvin demands of his followers the strictest possible adherence to moral standards. To the Elect, he writes, good ethical behavior will come naturally and be the sign of their chosen status. To those who are not elected, their moral behavior will not affect their ultimate fate in the slightest—but they therefore have all the more reason to live according to a godly standard. The joy of such a life is in fact the only meaningful pleasure they will have before confronting the eternal torments of hell. Membership in good standing in the Reformed Church—Calvin's name for the branch of Christianity he established—is a likely indicator that one is among the Elect. Membership in the despised Roman Catholic Church or the Orthodox Churches is as likely an indicator as a life of gruesome sinfulness that one is not. But while being a Calvinist immeasurably improved one's odds of salvation, it alone determined nothing. The central concern of life therefore should not be the destiny of our individual souls but the fulfillment of God's purpose on the entire earth.

Calvin's teachings found receptive audiences all around Europe. Apart from its success in Switzerland, Calvinism became the dominant creed in Holland (where it became known as the Dutch Reformed Church), in Scotland (where it was called the Presbyterian Church), in parts of France (where Calvinists were called Huguenots), and in parts of England (where they were ultimately called Puritans). The theocratic state he established in Geneva earned a well-deserved reputation for severity, but Geneva also earned a reputation for modest, honest, and godly behavior. Calvinist communities emphasized simplicity and austerity in worship. Anything that smacked of Catholic ritual or hierarchical structure was eschewed. Instead, churches were communities of equals—joined together in prayer, Scriptural reading, hymn singing, and listening to sermons. How can there be a pecking order among the Elect? Sermons indeed form the centerpiece of Calvinist worship, since they are by nature ruminations on Scripture. Calvin himself was too gifted a scholar to insist on only literal readings of the Bible, although he tended to seek out symbolic or other interpretations only after considering the literal first.

Still other reformers and groups branched off to form new denominations, but these were considerably smaller in size and tinged with elements of ethnic or national rebellion. Lutheranism and Calvinism were the two with the greatest international appeal, and by the middle of the 16th century they had torn the religious fabric of Europe asunder. Only in the late 20th century, in the aftermath of two World Wars and the Holocaust, would there arise serious efforts to reconcile the fissures in Christianity.

THE REBIRTH OF SATIRE

Religious upheavals reflected developments in other aspects of cultural life. The conjunction of increasing literacy rates and the mass availability of printed texts generated a demand for literary entertainment unlike anything the Western world had experienced before. Not that the love of literature was itself new, but oral tradition could now give way to print on paper. Reading became a common pleasure of everyday life, no longer the reserve of scholars and monks. Printing houses across Europe poured out a steady stream of poetry, histories, stage dramas and comedies, travelogues, essays, memoirs, popular science tracts, and collections of letters and speeches.

Not everyone in Europe was reading Erasmus, Luther, and Calvin constantly—which is probably a good thing. In addition to Machiavelli and Aretino, three European writers stand out in the first half of the 16th century: Thomas More (1478–1535), Ulrich von Hutten (1488–1523), and François Rabelais (1493–1553). They could hardly have been more different in their personalities and life stories, but the most famous works of all three were satires.

Satire had been one of the most popular literary genres among the Romans. The English word satire, which appeared for the first time in 1509, in fact derives from Latin *satura* (denoting a witty poem that ridicules vice), not from Greek *satyricos* (which refers to the lewd stage comedies that accompanied tragedic festivals). A few Greek writers had practiced satire—Menippus (3rd century BCE) is the best example—but the Romans excelled at it. "Satire is all ours," once bragged Quintilian (36–96 CE), Rome's greatest literary scholar. But satire had all but disappeared during the Middle Ages. Levity about the world's idiosyncrasies and human foibles did not appeal very much to the monks who established the classical canon in their scriptoria. With the rise of classical humanism, however, satire came back to life. There were, after all, plenty of people to satirize: warmongering popes, fey aristocrats, affected scholars, grasping financiers, humanistic despots, self-absorbed artists.

UTOPIAS AND BOOK BURNINGS

Erasmus helped to revive prose satire with his *Praise of Folly*, and satire in prose, in fact, became the preferred style in the 16th century. His close friend Thomas More penned a popular though curiously dour *Utopia* (1516).[12] It consists of two parts, the first being an imaginary discussion between More and a traveler-adventurer named Raphael Hythlodaeus on the various ills then besetting Europe. High on the list are the enclosure movement, poverty, religious intolerance, the failure of

---

12 More is best known as the royal chancellor who refused to recognize Henry VIII's divorce and paid for it with his head.

systems of justice, and the propensity to war. In the second part, Hythlodaeus describes for More his travels to a "perfect society"—a far-distant island in the Atlantic named Utopia (which is an Anglicized version of the Greek phrase "no place").

Utopia is a crescent-shaped island, two hundred miles across, in which the population lives in scattered communities of about seventy-five thousand each. All goods are held in common; citizens take turns, in two-year shifts, farming the land and working at artisanal crafts; medical care and primary education are free and available to all. There are no lawyers; all wives are subservient to their husbands, to whom they must confess their sins once every month; and the penalty for pre- or extramarital sex is enslavement. There are a lot of slaves, consequently, who do most of the hard labor. Although meant as a satire, there is

Utopia This woodcut by Ambrosius Holbein (1494–1519)—older brother of the famous artist Hans Holbein (1497–1543)—was the frontispiece for a 1518 edition of *Utopia*. Against a backdrop of the fictional island, Raphael Hythlodaeus describes the Utopian way of life to More.

nothing in *Utopia* to make a modern reader laugh, for More was largely humorless. (According to a family memoir he laughed at court jesters when they made pratfalls, but at little else.) He tried and failed on that score. *Utopia* remains a valuable book, though, not least for the insight it provides into its author's mind.

Far more successful as satire is the fictitious *Letters of Obscure Men* (1517) by Ulrich von Hutten, a swashbuckling imperial knight and occasional humanist writer. Born to a noble family in northern Germany, he grew up in a castle near the ancient settlement of Fulda. His parents dispatched him to a monastery when he was eleven, apparently to insure against his elder brother's claim upon the family estate. Six years later, in 1505, Ulrich escaped and wandered from city to city, leading a roguish life as an occasional student (he attended four universities in Germany), a poet, an amateur humanist scholar, and a willing sword for hire. Around 1509 he appeared in northern Italy, working as a mercenary soldier between stints at the universities of Pavia and Bologna. But by 1512 he was back in Germany serving as a Free Imperial Knight.

In 1515 the Duke of Württemberg killed a beloved cousin of his whose wife he had designs on. Ulrich responded by publishing blistering Latin poems that ruined the Duke's reputation and led ultimately to his overthrow. They made Ulrich famous, and in 1517 Maximilian I (r. 1493–1519) appointed him the poet laureate of the German Empire. In that same year, Ulrich became a passionate supporter of

Martin Luther and coauthored, with his humanist friend Johann Jäger (who used the pseudonym Crotus Rubeanus), the *Letters of Obscure Men*.

Filled with clever wit and broad, coarse humor, the *Letters* purport to be addressed to a prominent nobleman by fanatical Catholic monks and friars regarding why it is necessary to burn Jewish books like the Talmud and anti-Christian polemical literature. The diatribe is in reference to a real event: the debate, several years earlier, between the famed humanist scholar Johann Reuchlin and a group of zealous Catholic inquisitors who had argued for the same cause. (The title echoes the *Letters of Notable Men* that had passed between Reuchlin and his adversaries.) The *Letters* were written in intentionally bad Latin, making much of their humor impossible to convey in English. Reading them, it is clear that Ulrich never lost his hatred of Catholic monks, who might well respond to Protestantism and satire with book burnings, and this book is a settling of old debts. He gives his monks outrageous names like Brother Goatmilker and Brother Shitshoveller, attributes all sorts of lechery to them, and describes them nervously defecating under their robes during public debates. Ulrich's aim is less to defend the Jews (even though he was indeed an opponent of the book burnings) than to ridicule the pretensions and hypocrisy of the Catholics. The aristocrat who receives the letters—a real figure in Ulrich's time—also comes in for a lambasting. The monks sordidly declare their passionate relations with his wife.

A summary cannot relate the brilliant wordplay, sharp character depiction, and intellectual cleverness of the *Letters*. The book deserves to be better known and someday may find the translator it deserves. It was published anonymously, though its authorship was never in doubt. Ulrich spent his last years trying unsuccessfully to urge the independence of the German Empire from papal involvement. He contracted syphilis, and when the disease became acute he took refuge in Switzerland, near Lake Zurich, where he died in 1523.

RABELAIS: THE IN-HOUSE CATHOLIC ATTACK

The best-known of the three satirists was François Rabelais. Little is known for certain about his life. Born to a wealthy country lawyer, he received a sound education. A devout Christian, he entered the Franciscan order sometime around 1510 and about a decade later was ordained a priest. He traveled to libraries around France and earned a reputation as a first-rate classical scholar, but in 1524 he suffered the indignity of having his Greek books confiscated by one of his superiors, who thought they might lead to heresy. Rabelais successfully petitioned Pope Clement VII (r. 1523–34) in 1524 for release from his Franciscan order and to be allowed to join the Benedictines. Through his new order he studied medicine in Paris. However, since he disliked Benedictine life too, he broke his

vows and moved to the University of Montpellier to continue his medical training. He finished in record time, quickly sired two children with a local widow, and
then moved on to practice medicine in Narbonne and Lyons.

In 1532 Rabelais published a brief satirical novel, *The Horrible and Terrifying Words and Deeds of the Renowned Pantagruel, King of the Dipsodes.* When
this proved unexpectedly popular, he followed it with three more volumes that
continue Pantagruel's adventures while also providing, in another volume, the
backstory of Pantagruel's father, Gargantua. The five books are now published
together as a single work, *Gargantua and Pantagruel.* (A supposed sixth book,
written by an opportunistic forger, appeared in 1564, eleven years after Rabelais's
death.) Gargantua and Pantagruel are giants—enormous, misshapen, driven by
inexhaustible appetites of body and mind, and delighting in broad scatological
humor—and the same can be said of *Gargantua and Pantagruel* the novel. It is a
picaresque, a vast sequence of discrete episodes. The closest it comes to offering
a coherent story is a lengthy but loose narrative in Books 3 and 4 about their efforts to help a friend. (Another giant, named Panurge, wishes to locate an oracle
known as the Sacred Bottle for help deciding whether to marry a girl whose fidelity is uncertain.) Though lively, the novel is shapeless, repetitive, and long.

What was its purpose? Rabelais certainly wanted to entertain his readers
and make them laugh.[13] *Gargantua and Pantagruel* and the *Letters of Obscure Men*
are the only truly funny books written in that unfunny century. Being satire, the
laughs they raise come at someone's expense; we laugh because someone is being
ridiculed. Both books have numerous targets, but they share one in particular,
the Catholic clergy. If von Hutten attacks them from the Protestant side, Rabelais
offers a Catholic in-house attack.

The wounds he inflicts, however, result not from rapier wit but a heavy two-
handed broadsword. Much of Rabelais's humor is the clowning of a teenager
who thinks he is clever when he is being gross. He mocks dry-as-dust scholastic
theologians and pompous overfed monks by exaggerating their flaws a hundred-
fold. He lambasts puritanical morality by having his heroes indulge in orgies of
food, sex, and drink that would make a Roman emperor blush. Bodily functions
stain every page. In one early passage (1.17), Gargantua caps off a drinking binge
by untying his codpiece and peeing so much he floods the entire city of Paris,
"drowning 260,418 people, plus women and children." Two other entire chapters
(3.26, 3.28) consist of nothing more than a list of improvised nicknames for a
character, all of them employing a variant of the word "scrotum."

---

[13] "Mirth is my theme, and tears are not; / For laughter is man's proper lot" is the famous ending couplet of
Rabelais' verse preface.

Still, the verbal energy is extraordinary. Rejoicing in his freedom from Church Latin, Rabelais pours words onto the page in a kind of vernacular euphoria. The novel is a hymn to the French language and a celebration of human freedom: freedom to think, to scoff, to lust, to indulge in manic excess, to coin words, to imagine outrageous scenes, to offend, to risk boredom, and to delight in whimsy. Ultimately, it is about the freedom to hope for a better world than the one we live in. As a work of art it has failings, but as the expression of an irrepressible spirit it can never cease to fascinate. And that spirit is humanism.

WHO, WHAT, WHERE

Anabaptists

Christian humanism

Elect

indulgences

justification by faith alone

Ninety-Five Theses

picaresque

Peasants' Revolt

Protestant Reformation

Renaissance

Renaissance humanism

Satire

SUGGESTED READINGS

Primary Sources

Calvin, Jean. *Institutes of Christian Religion.*

Erasmus of Rotterdam. *Julius Excluded.*

———. *The Praise of Folly.*

Hutton, Ulrich von. *Letters of Obscure Men.*

Luther, Martin. *Address to the Christian Nobility of the German Nation.*

———. *The Freedom of a Christian.*

———. *Table Talk.*

Machiavelli, Niccolò. *Discourses on Livy.*

———. *The Mandrake Root.*

———. *The Prince.*

Rabelais, François. *Gargantua and Pantagruel.*

Vasari, Giorgio. *Lives of the Artists.*

Anthologies

Black, Robert, ed. *Renaissance Thought: A Reader* (2001).

Janz, Denis R., ed. *A Reformation Reader: Primary Texts with Introductions* (2008).

King, John N., ed. *Voices of the English Reformation: A Sourcebook* (2004).

Wiesner-Hanks, Merry. *The Renaissance and Reformation: A History in Documents* (2011).

Studies

Baylor, Michael G. *The German Reformation and the Peasants' War: A Brief History with Documents* (2012).

Benedict, Philip. *Christ's Churches Purely Reformed: A Social History of Calvinism* (2002).

Bolzoni, Lina. *The Gallery of Memory: Literary and Iconographic Models in the Age of the Printing Press* (2001).

Caffiero, Marina. *Forced Baptisms: Histories of Jews, Christians, and Converts in Papal Rome* (2011).

Diefendorf, Barbara B. *From Penitence to Charity: Pious Women and the Catholic Reformation in Paris* (2006).

Eisenstein, Elizabeth. *The Printing Revolution in Early Modern Europe* (2005).

King, Ross. *Machiavelli: Philosopher of Power* (2009).

Levi, Anthony. *Renaissance and Reformation: The Intellectual Genesis* (2004).

MacCulloch, Diarmaid. *The Reformation: A History* (2005).

Martines, Lauro. *Strong Words: Writing and Social Strain in the Italian Renaissance* (2001).

Mazzotta, Giuseppe. *Cosmopoiesis: The Renaissance Experiment* (2001).

McGrath, Alister E. *Reformation Thought: An Introduction* (2001).

Nauert, Charles G., Jr. *Humanism and the Culture of Renaissance Europe* (2006).

Oberman, Heiko A. *Luther: Man between God and the Devil* (2006).

O'Malley, John W. *Trent and All That: Renaming Catholicism in the Early Modern Era* (2000).

Ozment, Steven. *The Serpent and the Lamb: Cranach, Luther, and the Making of the Reformation* (2012).

Parks, Tim. *Medici Money: Banking, Metaphysics, and Art in Fifteenth-Century Florence* (2006).

Pettegree, Andrew. *The Book in the Renaissance* (2011).

———. *Reformation and the Culture of Persuasion* (2005).

Randall, Michael. *The Gargantuan Polity: On the Individual and the Community in the French Renaissance* (2008).

Stjerna, Kirsi. *Women and the Reformation* (2008).

Taylor, Barry, and Alejandro Coroleu. *Humanism and Christian Letters in Early Modern Iberia, 1480–1630* (2010).

Wiesner-Hanks, Merry E. *Women and Gender in Early Modern Europe* (2008).

For additional resources, including maps, primary sources, visuals, web links, and quizzes, please go to **www.oup.com/us/backman.**

ARMADA DE CAPITAIS QUE

CHAPTER 12

The Last Crusades

1492–1648

THE AMERICAS IN 1600

ATLANTIC OCEAN

PACIFIC OCEAN

■ Spanish
□ Portuguese

All wars are religious wars in one sense. "There are no atheists in foxholes," asserted a phrase popular in World War II. Even if untrue, it expresses a truism: for many people, the hard fact of death elicits something like religious dread.

Soldiers often take refuge in faith to survive war's horror. But are they drawn to fight in defense of their belief? As part of the religious realignment in Europe, wars left millions dead and much of Western society both economically and morally exhausted. The philosopher Thomas Hobbes (1588–1679) described life itself at this time as a tragic "war of all against all," in which existence was "solitary, poor, nasty, brutish, and short."

◀ **Passage to India**   In 1497 the Portuguese explorer Vasco da Gama (1469–1524) rounded the southern tip of Africa and initiated Europe's first direct contact with the peoples of the eastern African coast; with the help of an Indian ship's pilot he met in the port city of Mombasa (in today's Kenya) the following year, he sailed directly across the Arabian Sea and landed in India. The Arab merchants who then dominated the region gave him a cold welcome, and three years later (1501) da Gama returned at the head of a fleet of warships and seized control of the city of Calcutta. This image from ca. 1558 shows the type of trade ship used by the Portuguese at this stage in their rise to global power. This was a carrack, recognizable by its three (sometimes four) masts, rounded stern, raised fore- and aftcastles, and most especially by its absence of heavy guns. Galleons were the premier warships by the middle of the century; carracks (some of which weighed more than a thousand tons, unloaded) were for transporting vast cargoes.

Moreover, Europe's religious realignments took place within the exciting, yet terrifying, context of an immensely broadened world. The first encounters with the New World brought epidemics that killed as much as 99.9 percent of indigenous Americans. At the same time, it brought demographic and moral changes to Europe, including population growth and a new idea of order rooted in the family. The "war of all against all" also became more specifically a war against others, including witches, Jews, and the East—where the tensions between Sunnis and Shi'a intensified as well. It also led to shifts of power between European nations, including England, the Dutch, and Spain.

THE NEW WORLD

For over four thousand years the entire known world had consisted of three continents: Europe, Africa, and Asia. From the start, the peoples of the Greater West had shown more restlessness and curiosity about the world than any other ancient culture. Phoenician travelers, beginning around 1200 BCE, had journeyed a bit beyond the Straits of Gibraltar and into the Atlantic. The Greeks had circumnavigated the British Isles by 300 BCE, and by the end of the 1st century CE the Romans had made contact with merchant-explorers from China. The latter ventured as far as the Euphrates River shortly after the time of Constantine the Great, around 360 CE, although much later the Ming dynasty closed China off from the outside world.[1] The first Christian missionaries had reached China well before the western Roman Empire fell in 476. Viking raiders had spread out through the Baltic, North, and Mediterranean Seas and had reached a corner of North America by the 10th century. The Muslim Arabs, followed by the Persians and Turks, had carved out vast realms on all three continents and developed techniques to map the

---

[1]   Under their great admiral Zheng He (1371–1433), Chinese fleets made it as far as the mouth of the Persian Gulf, to the Horn of Africa, and probably even up the Red Sea to Jiddah, not far from Mecca.

CHAPTER TIMELINE

1497
Vasco da Gama makes
landfall in India

1521
Conquest
of Mexico

1524–1525
Peasants'
Revolt, Germany

1555
Peace of
Augsburg

1492
Columbus discovers
America; expulsion of
Jews from Germany

1516
Ghetto
established
in Venice

1522–1566
Reign of
Suleiman the
Magnificent

1533
Fall of Inca Empire;
England passes
the Buggery Act

new territories. European stirrings in the Atlantic were thus only the latest phase in a centuries-long tradition of restlessness.

The Portuguese led the way. As early as 1415 their ships began to make contact with the coast of western Africa, down the expanse of what is today the country of Morocco. With the enthusiastic support of the royal Prince Henrique the Navigator (1394–1460), Portuguese fleets sailed next to the Azores and the Canary Islands. By 1445 they had reached the westernmost tip of the continent, at today's neighboring states of Senegal and Gambia. In the 1460s they began to curve eastward under the massive overhanging bulk of the Saharan expanse. Their ships crossed the equator in 1474, and in 1488 they reached the Cape of Good Hope at the southern tip of Africa. Only nine years later, in 1497, under the command of Vasco da Gama (1460–1524), the first European fleet made landfall in India (see Map 12.1). These were journeys of exploration and trade, not of conquest. Da Gama told the local ruler in Calcutta that he was

> the ambassador of the king of Portugal—the ruler of many lands and a man of such wealth that no one in this part of the world can compare; and that for sixty years this king's predecessors had dispatched ships to explore the seas in the direction of India, where they had heard that Christian kings like themselves lived. To connect with these Christian monarchs was the sole aim of their explorations, not to seek silver and gold—for the kings of Portugal possessed such tremendous wealth in these metals as to make them uninterested in whatever gold or silver was to be found in India or any other place.

Da Gama meant hardly a word of this, and it is doubtful his Indian host believed any of it. A genuine spirit of exploration for its own sake motivated those who put to sea and those who financed them. So, however, did an expectation of profit.

1571–1636 Mulla Sadra	1588 Defeat of the Spanish Armada	1618–1648 Thirty Years' War	1632–1677 Baruch Spinoza

| 1572 Saint Bartholomew's Day Massacre | 1598 Edict of Nantes | 1626–1676 Sabbatai Zvi | |

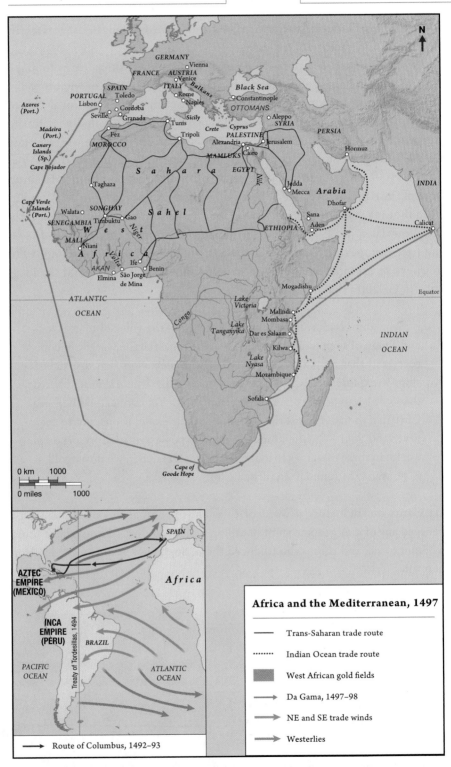

MAP 12.1   Africa and the Mediterranean, 1497

NEW CONTINENTS AND PROFITS

From the early 9th century sub-Saharan gold, spices, slaves, and ivory had been prized commodities in Mediterranean trade. Muslim merchants in Spain and Morocco had first brought these items to Europe, which accounts for the tremendous wealth of cities like Granada and Cordoba. (Tax records show that the Muslim inhabitants of Toledo alone held six thousand black slaves in the 10th century.) These were luxury goods enjoyed by the elites. When Christian forces drove the last Muslim rulers from Iberia in the 15th century, they took over control of this trade and determined to expand it. The commodities exchanged for these luxury items were predominantly textiles, metalwares, glazed pottery, glass, and paper. Not surprisingly, some of the coastal African peoples had embraced Islam in the intervening centuries, but this posed no bar to trade. Money mattered, not faith. When Vasco da Gama reached India in 1497, he mistook Hinduism for a quaint Eastern version of Christianity but identified precisely every precious stone and spice in the markets. Once in Calcutta, the Portuguese quickly established trading posts along the southwestern Malabar Coast of India. Within twenty years they had spread their commercial network to the Malay Peninsula, the Indonesian archipelago, and the Moluccas Islands; within another two decades, by 1542, they had reached Japan. Their first permanent trading post in China, at Macao, was established in 1555 (see Map 12.2).

> Money mattered, not faith. When Vasco da Gama reached India in 1497, he mistook Hinduism for a quaint Eastern version of Christianity but identified precisely every precious stone and spice in the markets.

Cristoforo Colombo's (1451–1506) innovation in 1492 was to propose reaching Asia by sailing directly westward rather than circumnavigating Africa to the south. Colombo was an Italian from Genoa, but he sailed under the Spanish flag of Ferdinand and Isabella. Such international arrangements were common, so no wonder just about every state ever associated with Colombo claims him as a native: to the Spanish he is Cristóbal Colón; streets and squares in Barcelona commemorate Cristòfor Colom; and the Portuguese proudly recall Cristóvão Colombo.[2] A few writers have argued that he was a Jew by ethnicity, but the evidence for this is extremely weak. Still, there is no reason, apart from lazy habit, to call him Christopher Columbus.

Every educated European since the 12th century had known that the world was round. Colombo was unprepared for the size of the globe, and so the length of his historic journey, but not the fact of it. And then he ran into an unexpected speed bump, the New World. Colombo never realized that the Caribbean islands

---

[2]   The English explorer John Cabot, who carried the Tudor flag as far as Newfoundland in 1497, was actually another Italian—Giovanni Caboto (1450–1508), from Venice.

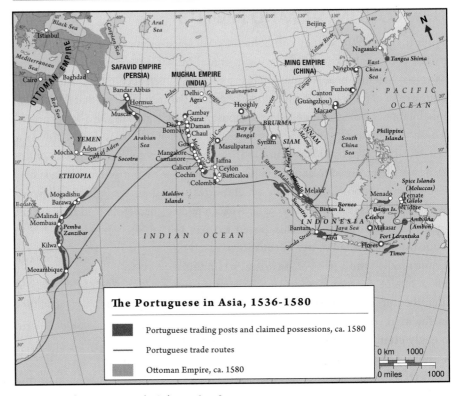

MAP 12.2   The Portuguese in Asia, 1536–1580

he had landed at were in fact the outer islands of two vast new continents. Despite four voyages to the New World, he believed to his dying day that he had sailed to islands just off the coast of Asia (see Figure 12.1). Such misjudgments do not lessen his achievement, however. The Atlantic passage was one of the greatest technical and human-adventure feats in Western history, and it had earth-changing consequences.

In his ship's log, Colombo duly recorded his first encounter with the indigenous people of the islands:

> When it became clear that they welcomed us, I saw that it would be easier to convert them to Our Holy Faith by peaceful means than by force, and so I offered them some simple gifts—red-dyed caps, necklaces of strung beads, and so on—which they received with great pleasure. So enthusiastic were they, in fact, that they began to swim out to our ships, carrying parrots, balls of cotton thread, spears, and other items to trade.... Still, they struck me as an exceptionally poor people, for all of them were naked—even the women, although I saw only one girl among them at the time. Every one of them I perceived to be young (that is, under

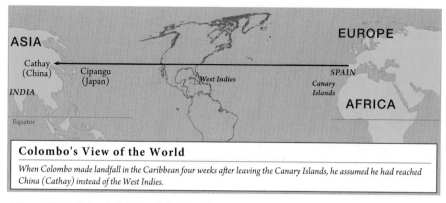

Colombo's View of the World

When Colombo made landfall in the Caribbean four weeks after leaving the Canary Islands, he assumed he had reached China (Cathay) instead of the West Indies.

FIGURE 12.1   Colombo's View of the World

the age of thirty), finely shaped and with handsome faces. . . . They appear to own no weapons and to have no knowledge of such, for when I showed them our swords they reached out and grabbed them by the blades, cutting themselves unexpectedly. . . . When I inquired, by pointing, about the scars visible on some of their bodies, they made me to understand, also by pointing, that people from another island had attacked them and tried to carry them off as slaves, but they resisted. . . . Overall they struck me as being clever, and I believe they would make good servants and could easily become Christian, since they have no religion of their own. They learned quickly to repeat the handful of words we taught them. If it please God, I intend to bring six of them home to Your Majesties, so that they might be taught to speak our language. Apart from the parrots, I saw no animals of any kind on the island.

Colombo's curiously unenthusiastic tone probably reflects his disappointment in the poverty of the people. Expecting the vast riches of China's silk and spice trade, he found instead naked islanders with nothing but ready smiles and a number of parrots. On subsequent journeys he discovered more of the natural wealth available, and his enthusiasm recovered noticeably. Within a few years other adventurers had reached both the North American and South American mainlands, and mapmakers began to appreciate that two entirely new continents had been found.

News of the discovery spread quickly across Europe, and soon wave after wave of explorers and adventurers set sail. In 1513 the Spanish admiral Vasco Núñez de Balboa (1475–1519), standing atop a hill in what is today's nation of Panama, became the first European to see the Pacific Ocean. Only six years later Fernão de Magalhães (Ferdinand Magellan, 1480–1521) set out to circumnavigate the entire globe, an astonishing feat that took three years and claimed the lives of 262 of his

The First Published Image of the New World
Cristoforo Colombo's first report to the Spanish kings of his discovery was published in Basel in early 1494; printed here is one of the illustrations that accompanied the Latin text. It shows Colombo arriving on the shore of "the island of Hispania" in a small landing craft. He offers a goblet as a peace offering to the inhabitants, who appear to be uniformly naked, male, and beardless, gathered at the shore to meet him.

initial crew of 280, including his own. Tales of the wealth available in the New World and in Asia set off a fiercely competitive wave of explorers, soldiers, and government representatives eager to stake out their claims (see Map 12.3).

Geographic location gave an immense advantage to the Atlantic seaboard nations of Europe: Portugal, Spain, France, the Low Countries, and England. The Mediterranean states, which had lived by maritime trade since 3000 BCE, were shut off from the New World bonanza since they could not pass the Straits of Gibraltar—which the Atlantic states had quickly sealed off like a cork in a bottle. Left to trade with Asia only through the Ottoman-controlled land routes, they began a long and slow commercial decline. This resulted in a fundamental change in the structure of the European economy, and by the end of the 16th century economic dominance had shifted away from the Mediterranean. The Atlantic states entered the 17th century as the economic and political powerhouses of Europe.

The Mediterranean states, which had lived by maritime trade since 3000 BCE, were shut off from the New World bonanza since they could not pass the Straits of Gibraltar—which the Atlantic states had quickly sealed off like a cork in a bottle.

The sudden and massive influx of gold from the New World triggered the rise of the Atlantic commercial economies. This gold was seized chiefly from the Aztecs and Mayans of Central America and the Incas of what eventually became Peru and Bolivia. Credit for these seizures belongs above all to the army of **conquistadores** ("conquerors") led by Hernán Cortés (1485–1547), who subdued Mexico in 1521, and Francisco Pizarro (1471–1541), who vanquished the Incas in 1533. The conquerors' forces were astonishingly few in number: Cortés commanded an army of no more than six hundred conquistadores, and Pizarro had only 180. The Europeans' technological advantage is obvious: supplied with firearms, they could mow down the spear-carrying natives with considerable ease. But their victory had been made incalculably easier by an inadvertent biological warfare that preceded them on the scene.

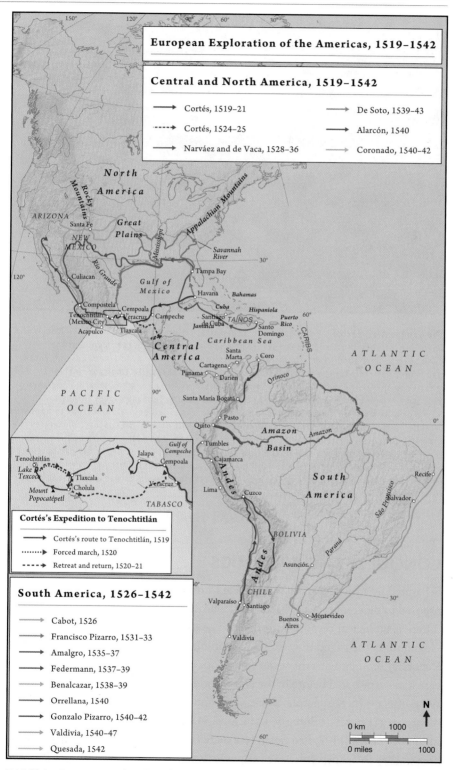

MAP 12.3 European Exploration of the Americas, 1519–1542

The Conquest of Mexico For a quarter century after Colombo's discovery of the New World, Spanish explorers and traders had established settlements only in the islands of the Caribbean; only a handful of expeditions had visited the mainland, to trade. Enough contact was made, however, for the transmission of European diseases like smallpox, influenza, and measles to the indigenous peoples of Central and South America, who, never having been exposed to them before, had no natural resistance to them. In many places throughout the New World as much as 90 percent of the population was killed before any European appeared directly on the scene. This painting, from the second half of the 17th century, illustrates the dramatic conquest of the Aztecs by Hernán Cortés in 1519. The Aztec empire had long been the most powerful (and violent) of the New World kingdoms. Cortés began his campaign with only six hundred soldiers—although he picked up many conscripts on his way to the Aztec capital of Tenochtitlan, shown here in the background—which was a sufficient number to bring down the once-great empire.

CONQUEST AND EPIDEMICS

Separated by a vast ocean, the peoples of Europe and of the New World had been exposed to different types of bacteria and viruses and had consequently developed different biological responses to them. The sailors who landed with Cristoforo Colombo on the island they called Hispaniola (today's Haiti and the Dominican Republic) brought with them the viruses for smallpox and measles. Neither disease had ever existed before in the New World, so they ran unchecked with horrifying effect. On Hispaniola alone, the population, which an early Dominican missionary (Friar Bartolomé de Las Casas, 1484–1566) had estimated to be three million strong in 1492, had fallen to a mere five hundred by 1538. That is a loss greater than 99.99 percent. In the opposite direction, some Europeans contracted a form of syphilis in the New World that seems never to have been present before in Europe. Within a few years, five million Europeans had died of it. Yet the impact on the New World was far greater.[3]

A Franciscan missionary, Friar Toribio de Benavente Motolinia (1484–1568), described how the natives "did not know how to treat the disease ... and consequently died in whole piles, like bedbugs. In many places, in fact, entire households died all at once, and since it proved impossible to bury so great a number of corpses, our

Smallpox Victims The protracted isolation of the peoples of the Americas from the rest of the world made them vulnerable to a battery of diseases European colonists brought with them: the breath of a Spaniard was said to be sufficient enough to kill. These 16th-century illustrations, drawn by a native Mexican artist, depict smallpox victims. In the upper left panel a doctor attempts to treat his patient—undoubtedly he failed.

soldiers simply pulled down the houses over these people, letting their own homes serve as their tombs." Pizarro found similar circumstances favoring him when he stormed through Peru and Bolivia. Even a century later, in far-off Massachusetts Bay, smallpox and measles erased nine-tenths of the Native American population between 1617 and 1619. Such numbers are horrifying to imagine. Motolinia wrote that when Cortés led his men in triumph through the Aztec capital of Tenochtitlan—on the site of today's Mexico City—the soldiers could traverse the entire city stepping only on the corpses of smallpox victims, without ever once setting foot on the ground.

Such unintended suffering does not excuse the outright brutishness of the Europeans. In sailing to Africa, India, and China, the Europeans had shown no interest in conquest and colonization since they were able to acquire what they wanted—nonperishable luxury goods—by simple trade. Their technological advantage, in military hardware, over the sub-Saharan Africans was as great as it was over the indigenous New World peoples, but it did not prompt them to slaughter millions and seize their lands. The smallpox epidemic changed everything, and as a consequence the Europeans instantly developed a different attitude toward the land: here lay two vast and supremely wealthy continents that were, in effect, uninhabited—or near enough to uninhabited to persuade the conquistadores to finish the job. Moreover, the Protestant Reformation accelerated European interest in the New World. They saw not only an opportunity for evangelization,

---

[3] Cortés was able to conquer Mexico in 1521 with only six hundred men-at-arms because 90 percent of the Aztecs had already been obliterated by smallpox by 1520.

but also a means to finance their struggles back home. The coincidence of the discovery of the New World's gold and silver deposits, and the bubbling over of the Catholic-Protestant rift into outright war in the 1540s, was too great to be entirely coincidental.

Once they had seized control of the gold and silver mines, the Europeans set to the large-scale production of cash crops like cotton, sugar cane, and tobacco. These commodities fetched high prices, retained consistent demand, and traveled well across the long distance from New World to Old. The annihilation of the local populace presented a problem, though, since all three crops were exceptionally labor intensive in their production. Without a large infusion of people to work the land, producing them was out of the question. There were only two ways to put people on the land in the numbers needed: settlement and slavery.

NEW CROPS AND THE ENCLOSURE MOVEMENT

It is one thing to explore and trade and another to settle. Europe's expansion could not have become the permanent development it did without demographic changes, including growing populations with reduced access to land ownership. These fundamental changes made it possible, and desirable, to export people—which is another way of describing overseas expansion.

After severe contraction in the late Middle Ages, Europe's population began to grow around 1500 and did so steadily for the next three hundred years (see Figure 12.2). A gradual decline in outbreaks of plague accounts for much of this, but so does improvement in the food supply. Famine has always been nature's principal method of population control. For the premodern world, steady growth in demographic numbers is a sure indicator of steady growth in the availability of food. Europe saw just such a steady growth from the 16th to 18th centuries, for two reasons. First, food exports to the Ottoman-controlled east declined. And second, Europe was introduced to new crops from North and South America—the most important being corn (maize), beans, tomatoes, and potatoes. It is unlikely that these were brought back with the intention of introducing new foodstuffs. Rather, they were probably loaded on ships as victuals for those making the journey back to Europe (see Map 12.4). Most Europeans disdained corn (maize), which they thought inedible for humans; they prized it instead as animal fodder. Tomatoes made exotic sauces and side dishes. Beans and potatoes, though, were radical innovations. By long-standing feudal customs, Europe's

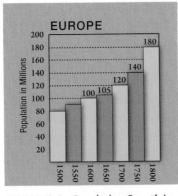

FIGURE 12.2 **Population Growth in Europe, 1500–1800**

manors remained dedicated to grain production, but beans and potatoes quickly dominated the peasants' individual garden plots. Gradually, fields normally left fallow were also given over to the new crops, which helped replenish the soil. Their high yields made them popular, not as market crops but as staples of the peasants' own diets. By the 17th century farmers on the Continent were eating as many as one to two dozen potatoes a day. Not the most satisfying of diets, but infinitely preferable to famine. Potatoes could also be distilled to produce vodka. Other grains that formerly went to peasant diets became available for distilling too.[4]

Increasing food supplies, however, meant declining agricultural prices. Small landholders who could not keep up with their rents therefore risked sliding back in debt bondage, and the manorial lords who lived off those rents faced severe potential drops in their own incomes as well. For many aristocrats, an answer to their trouble lay in the **enclosure movement**: By enclosing farmland—that is, by constructing a border of fences or thick hedgerows around it—landlords could evict their tenants, convert crop fields to meadows, and raise sheep or other herd animals instead. Their labor costs thus declined sharply, and the wool

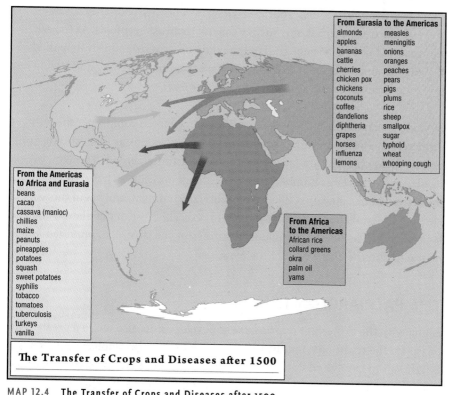

From Eurasia to the Americas

almonds	measles
apples	meningitis
bananas	onions
cattle	oranges
cherries	peaches
chicken pox	pears
chickens	pigs
coconuts	plums
coffee	rice
dandelions	sheep
diphtheria	smallpox
grapes	sugar
horses	typhoid
influenza	wheat
lemons	whooping cough

From the Americas to Africa and Eurasia
beans
cacao
cassava (manioc)
chillies
maize
peanuts
pineapples
potatoes
squash
sweet potatoes
syphilis
tobacco
tomatoes
tuberculosis
turkeys
vanilla

From Africa to the Americas
African rice
collard greens
okra
palm oil
yams

The Transfer of Crops and Diseases after 1500

MAP 12.4   **The Transfer of Crops and Diseases after 1500**

---

[4]   The large-scale production of gin and whisky began—and so did greater alcoholism among the common people, with the usual social ills that accompany it.

generated by their sheep was self-renewing. Moreover, the steady rise in human population meant a steadily growing demand for textiles. In this way landed nobles improved their incomes significantly, but at the expense of the evicted farmers. Lacking the funds to purchase new lands of their own, rural workers had difficulty supporting themselves.

Thomas More had described the problem as early as 1516 in his *Utopia*, in which his narrator explains the rise of crime:

> It's because of sheep. These animals, so naturally mild and so easy to tend, can now be said to have become uncontrollable devourers, consuming even the people themselves; they empty homes, devastate crop fields, and turn whole villages into ghost towns. Anyplace where sheep can be raised to produce fine and rich wool, the nobles, gentry, and even the abbots (those supposed "holy men"!), not content with their rents and yearly fees, and feeling that it is not enough to live in luxurious laziness and do no actual good in the world, but choosing instead to bring actual harm into it, enclose all the land for pasture and put an end to farming. They demolish homes and level villages. The churches they allow to remain, of course, but only so they can use them as sheepfolds. As though they did not waste enough [land] already on coverts and private parks, these fine people are now destroying every human dwelling and letting every scrap of usable farmland run wild. *(Book 1)*

Evicted farm families had few options. The younger men could enter the military or merchant marine, and the females could seek positions as domestic servants, but for many the solution lay in seeking new fortunes abroad. The New World needed settlers in large numbers. It was a difficult decision, to travel thousands of miles from home, take up residence on a foreign continent, and begin the work of clearing the land afresh. But many chose to do so, because of population rise and land hunger. The feverish religious hostilities of the time, too, provided ample reason to quit the Old World for the New.

THE PATRIARCHAL FAMILY

Along with the Protestant reforms, these developments also led to a greater emphasis on the traditional family, with the husband firmly established at its head. But threats to family and state abounded, or were believed to abound, throughout the 16th and 17th centuries. And these threats, popularly believed to come primarily from witches and Jews, were considered so dire that society justified the most extraordinary measures to root them out.

Luther, Calvin, and the other Protestant leaders did not think of themselves as social reformers. When radicals like Thomas Müntzer (1488–1525) interpreted Luther's theology as a call to social rebellion, resulting in the Peasants' Revolt, Luther responded with characteristic vigor and called for the rebels' extermination. The Reformers, in fact, relied on existing social and political structures for their vision of a new Christendom: from feudal princes in Germany to urban elites in Switzerland, the existing social models provided the backbone of the Protestant campaigns.

And a strong backbone was needed, according to Luther, Calvin, and others. Human nature was too depraved, too ensnared in its own sinfulness, to be trusted. Figures of authority were needed to provide discipline. Protestant theology championed the notion of the "priesthood of all believers"—meaning that each individual could discern the teachings of the Bible for him- or herself. But only strong and demanding leaders could make sure that people lived according to the truths they read in Scripture. Hence Luther granted power to the German princes to enforce the teaching of the new Lutheran churches within their domains. Calvin established the town councils of the Elect to supervise, judge, and punish the Reformed citizens of Geneva and elsewhere.

Both men wrote extensive commentaries on the following passage from the New Testament:

> Let every person be subject to the governing authorities, for there is no authority except from God, and those authorities that exist have been instituted by God. Therefore whoever resists authority resists what God has appointed, and those who resist will incur judgment. For rulers are not a terror to good conduct, but to bad. Do you wish to have no fear of the authority? Then do what is good, and you will receive its approval; for it is God's servant for your good. But if you do what is wrong, you should be afraid, for the authority does not bear the sword in vain! It is the servant of God to execute wrath on the wrongdoer. Therefore one must be subject, not only because of wrath but also because of conscience. (*Romans 13.1–5*)

Since sinfulness is present in us from birth, disciplined authority needed to be as much a cornerstone of parenting as was love itself. Hence Protestant social ideology called for the patriarchal family as the fundamental unit of godly society. In that family, the man stood as the undoubted leader, charged with the protection and care of the whole household. The mother was subject to her husband's authority and given the special task of beginning the moral and spiritual education of their children. Luther and Calvin here drew on Saint Paul's Epistles: "Wives, be subject to your husbands as you are to the Lord. For the husband is the head of the wife just as Christ is the head of the church, the body of which He is the Savior. Just as the church is subject to Christ, so also wives ought to be, in everything, to their husbands" (Ephesians 5.22–24).

The Scottish Reformer and founder of the Presbyterian tradition, John Knox (1510–1572), wrote an infamous treatise called *First Blast of the Trumpet against the Monstrous Regiment of Women* (1558).

> To promote a woman to bear rule, superiority, dominion, or empire above any realm, nation, or city, is repugnant to nature; contumely [an insult] to God, a thing most contrary to His revealed will and approved ordinance; and finally, it is the subversion of good order, of all equity and justice. In the probation of this proposition, I will not be so curious as to gather whatsoever may amplify, set forth, or decor the same; but I am purposed, even as I have spoken my conscience in most plain and few words,

The Patriarchal Family   Cornelius Johnson (1593–1661) was a popular portraitist among the English aristocracy of the 17th century. This 1640 painting shows Arthur, 1st Baron Capell (1604–1649), together with his family. Capell was a staunch Royalist in England's Civil War, who personally escorted Queen Henrietta Maria to safety in France in 1646. Captured by Cromwell's forces in 1648, Capell was briefly imprisoned in the Tower of London before being executed. His eldest son, Arthur, shown at the far left here, joined what was left of the Royalist army even though he was only twelve years old at the time. This portrait shows the family posing before their formal garden. Note that of the three females in the picture, one (his wife, Lady Elizabeth Capell) is looking respectfully at her husband, the second daughter (Mary) is gazing at her baby brother, and the eldest daughter (Elizabeth) is looking slyly away to the right; only the males in the picture look directly at the viewer. Is it a coincidence that in this image, completed just before the outbreak of the Civil War, the Capell's garden is empty and storm clouds appear to be gathering over it?

so to stand content with a simple proof of every member, bringing in for my witness God's ordinance in nature, His plain will revealed in His word, and by the minds of such as be most ancient amongst godly writers. And first, where I affirm the empire of a woman to be a thing repugnant to nature, I mean not only that God, by the order of His creation, has spoiled [deprived] woman of authority and dominion, but also that man has seen, proved, and pronounced just causes why it should be. Man, I say, in many other cases, does in this behalf see very clearly. For the causes are so manifest, that they cannot be hid. For who can deny but it is repugnant to nature, that the blind shall be appointed to lead and conduct such as do see? That the weak, the sick, and impotent persons shall nourish and keep the whole and strong? And finally, that the foolish, mad, and frenetic shall govern the discreet, and give counsel to such as be sober of mind? And such be all women, compared unto man in bearing of authority. For their sight in civil regiment is but blindness; their strength, weakness; their counsel, foolishness; and judgment, frenzy, if it be rightly considered.

Husbands and fathers exercised their authority in a variety of ways. Physical discipline was permitted within certain limits, but men were expected above all to lead by setting examples of rigorous and godly behavior. To help them, most Protestant denominations offered some form of personal and family counseling. They also emphasized Bible reading within all family devotions. But since the godly family was the basic unit of godly society, the society itself had an intrinsic right to step in and exert authority when a parent failed. Public shaming, social ostracism, banishment from church life, and imprisonment were widely practiced.

SEXUAL MORALITY

At least in their first two or three generations, Protestant Christians placed a significantly sharper and more constant focus on sexual morality than their Catholic peers. Chastity before marriage and fidelity within it remained the moral ideal for all Christians, but Catholic Europe had long allowed a certain liberality in sexual matters, especially for men. Prostitution, while regulated, had been legal throughout Europe for centuries, for example, and no social stigma fell on the men who frequented prostitutes.[5] One way that Protestants sought to curb prostitution—apart from simply closing down the brothels—was through early marriage. With access to legitimate sexual release, they believed, men would not

---

[5] Men had tended to put marriage off until they were established in a trade, which could take until their thirties.

be tempted to resort to illegitimate means. These earlier marriages helped account for the population increase that marked the century.

The era also witnessed new efforts to combat homosexuality. Same-sex eroticism had been regarded as a sign of weakness since Roman times. Christianity added the notion that the activity was immoral since it denied the procreative function that was sexuality's whole intent and purpose. Until the 13th century, however, homosexuality was not a criminal offense. By 1260 in France, homosexual acts became punishable by death. Comparable measures were instituted across Europe, at both the national and local levels, although it remains unclear how often such laws were enforced. Hostility to homosexuality increased with the need to rebuild the population after the Black Death as well. While Renaissance classicism brought more liberal attitudes, in Florence alone over 15,000 people were arrested for sodomy between 1432 and 1502 (though not all were convicted). The Spanish Inquisition arrested over 1,500 people on charges on homosexual acts between 1540 and 1700.

Protestantism's emphasis on Biblical truth (*sola Scriptura*) sharpened antihomosexual sentiments significantly, although formal condemnations came mostly at the local levels of government.[6] One notable exception was the Buggery Act passed by England's King Henry VIII (r. 1509–1547) in 1533, which remained in force until 1861, when the death penalty it called for was replaced by a sentence of life imprisonment.

Forasmuch as there is not yet sufficient and condign punishment appointed and limited by the due course of the Laws of this Realm for the detestable and abominable Vice of Buggery, [whether] committed with mankind or beast: May it therefore please the King's Highness, with the assent of the Lords Spiritual and the Commons of this present parliament assembled, that it may be enacted by the authority of the same, that the same offence be from henceforth adjudged a felony, and that such an order and form of process therein to be used against the offenders as in cases of felony at the Common Law; and that the offenders being hereof convicted—by verdict, confession, or outlawry—shall suffer such pains of death, and losses and penalties of their goods, chattels, debts, lands, tenements, and [inherited properties], as felons do according to the Common Laws of this Realm; and that no person offending in any such offence shall be admitted to [the king's] clergy; and that Justices

---

6   Just six passages from the Bible explicitly condemn homosexuality, and two are simply New Testament restatements of Old Testament proscriptions. The Scriptures record no direct teaching from Jesus.

of the Peace shall have power and authority within the limits of their commissions and jurisdictions to hear and determine the said offence, as they do in the cases of other felonies.

What makes any type of sexual activity a crime against the state instead of a matter of personal morality? In Protestant Europe, where the state had become the administrative head of the religious community, a sin against public morals was also a crime against civil society. Hence homosexuality—along with adultery, masturbation, foul language, gambling, and drunkenness—required a civil response. Protestants read the Bible as mandating the two-parent, heterosexual,

"A Jan Steen Household" Jan Havickszoon Steen (1626–1679) was a prolific and popular genre painter of the Dutch Golden Age, who made a handsome living from his scenes of everyday life among common town and country dwellers. Sometimes comic, sometimes tragic, and sometimes a mixture of the two, his paintings were known for their attention to the crowdedness and chaos of domestic living—to such a point that even today a common Dutch colloquialism describes a messy, squalid space as "a Jan Steen household" (*een huishouden van Jan Steen*)—a phrase roughly comparable to the American expression "a pigsty." This painting is one of his moralistic images, showing the dangers of drunkenness. (Steen grew up in a family of tavern keepers, and knew what he was talking about—or rather painting.) Apart from the unbecoming postures of the two figures in the foreground and the uninviting physical scene, a woman and two companions (musicians?) are stealing the drunken pair's cloaks in the background.

married nuclear family. Any sexual activity outside that norm was in essence a threat to the godly state.

ENEMIES WITHIN: WITCHES AND JEWS

Popular belief in witchcraft had roots in pre-Christian classical, Germanic, and Celtic culture. Ancient and medieval beliefs differed from those of the early modern era, however. Earlier Europeans had held that some individuals (thankfully, not many) are simply born with an intrinsic ability to summon supernatural forces at will, which they used for good or ill. In contrast, people of the 16th and 17th centuries developed the belief that magical powers resulted from an explicit and conscious contract made between the witch (who could be male or female) and Satan. Witchcraft was now believed to be intentional—a power that an individual chose to acquire—rather than an innate, though freakish, ability possessed from birth. And that made popular fear of it all the stronger, especially given the era's particular emphasis on human weakness and sinfulness. If people could be so easily coaxed into a pact with Satan, then witchcraft could conceivably take over our world and bring about its ruin. A witch was not merely someone "possessed of powers" but someone actively engaged in evil, and the danger he or she represented required immediate action.

That action consisted of mania, arrest, trial, torture, and execution on a scale that is difficult to comprehend. Campaigns against witches began to increase markedly toward the end of the 15th century but became frenzied after 1560, once Europe's religious disputes turned violent. From 1560 to 1670, nearly two hundred thousand people across Europe were accused of witchcraft and subjected to judicial persecution or mob violence (see Figure 12.3). Roughly one quarter of them were executed. Those who confessed and repented—which required identifying other witches and agreeing to testify against them—were briefly imprisoned, frequently marked by a tattoo, fined, and released. Yet they were socially shunned for the rest of their lives. Germany, Switzerland, and eastern France had the most witchcraft trials per capita. And while there seems to be no substantial difference between the frequency of Protestant and Catholic prosecutions of witchcraft, it does appear that the Protestant-Catholic divide played a role: witchcraft mania struck most ferociously where Protestants and Catholics were most even in number. The witches who appeared in stage dramas like William Shakespeare's *Macbeth* were realistic characters to audiences, in addition to whatever symbolic role they played in the text. In the end, however, no country was immune to witchcraft.

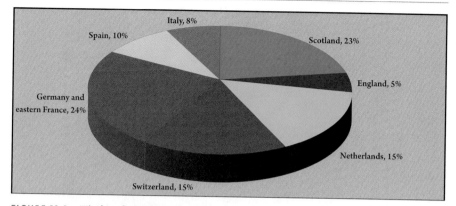

FIGURE 12.3   **Witchcraft Trials, 1450–1750**

Neither was any sex. Both men and women were believed capable of sell-ing their souls to Satan, although at least three-quarters of those arrested for witchcraft, and nearly 90 percent of those executed for it, were women. (Ire-land was the sole exception: roughly 90 percent of its prosecuted witches were male.) Popular assumptions about women's nature—as emotional, impulsive, passionate, demanding creatures—fueled the phenomenon. Women were re-garded as generally weaker than men, but especially in regard to sex. Ideas about sexuality, derived from ancient Greek medicine, held that female lust, once aroused, was insatiable.[7] Only a demonic lover like Satan, it was assumed, could satisfy a woman's sexual longing—and that was precisely the appeal used by the devil to ensnare his victims. Men who became witches were gener-ally assumed to have been enticed into it by women who had already given themselves over to satanic lust.

In this way, the witchcraft craze accords with the period's concern with sexuality in general. Ironi-cally, the era's emphasis on early marriage was directly related to its fear of unchecked sexuality. It demanded being the "godly wife and mother" responsible for her children's moral education, the subjection of wives to their husbands, and the sacralization of domestic life. A force as powerful and unpre-dictable as a woman's body needed to be firmly controlled—or else all hell, literally, could break loose.

> A force as powerful and unpredictable as a woman's body needed to be firmly controlled—or else all hell, literally, could break loose.

---

[7]   Many of the constraints placed on women—such as limiting their appearance in public or regulating their dress—were justified as protecting them from their own inability to control their passions.

Burning the Enemy Within A convicted witch being executed in Amsterdam in 1571.

THE JEWS OF THE EAST AND WEST

The era was cruel to Jews as well. Late medieval hostility to Jews had resulted in a series of expulsion orders, first from England (1290), then from France (1306) and Germany (numerous times), and finally from Spain (1492) and Portugal (1497). Forced from one territory to the next, the Jews gradually concentrated in the Low Countries, Italy, North Africa, and the Ottoman Empire, where the **Ashkenazic** and **Sephardic** traditions of Judaism once again confronted one another (see Map 12.5).

For the host countries, the sudden increase in the Jewish populations aggravated social tensions and led many to segregate the Jews into **ghettos**. Regulations like these had been common since the 12th century. The surge in Jewish numbers within those districts, however, frequently led to new legislation limiting the Jews' freedom to move and act within the larger community. Venice established the first modern ghetto in 1516, but other cities were quick to follow.[8] Life in these communities was often difficult, since Jews from many backgrounds were thrust shoulder to shoulder, within a larger social context of economic decline and Christian hostility. The economic decline occurred largely because of the shift of economic power from the Mediterranean—where the Jews had taken refuge—to the Atlantic seaboard, which happened at the same time. Only those Jews who had migrated to the Low Countries moved into a society of economic growth.

---

8 The word *ghetto* likely derives from the Italian *borghetto*, meaning a "small borough" or "precinct."

MAP 12.5   Expulsions and Migrations of Jews 1492–1650

Not surprisingly, as most Jews' social and economic lives grew shaky in the 16th and 17th centuries, many found solace in new messianic movements, especially in the Ottoman state, which, after 1515, included the Holy Land. Jewish refugees from Europe generally received a cordial welcome from the Ottoman rulers Bayezid II [T] (r. 1484–1512) and Selim I [T] (r. 1512–1520), who encouraged Jews to settle in the Holy Land.[9] Many Jews, upon arriving in the Holy Land, expressed surprise at the squalor into which the cities had fallen. An Italian refugee, R. Obadiah of Bertinoro, sent a letter back to friend in which he estimates there being "only about seventy [Jewish] households in all of Gaza," while in Hebron he found "only twenty households, ... half of them coming from Spain and just recently arrived." In Jerusalem itself he found "only seventy households left, all of them poverty-stricken and with no means of support. ... Anyone who has food to last a year, or the means to procure it, is considered wealthy here."

In Italy, led by charismatic adventurers like Solomon Molcho (1500–1532) and David Reubeni (1490–1541), and in the Ottoman Empire, inspired by R. Isaac Luria (1534–1572) and R. Hayyim Vital (1543–1620), thousands of Jews believed in the

---

[9]   Spanish Jews set up the first printing press in the Ottoman state. Two Sephardic Jews, Joseph Hamon and his son Moses Hamon, served for a total of thirty years as personal physicians to the sultans.

imminent arrival of the long-promised messiah. These four figures, and others like them, preached a message of intense spiritual and social reform to prepare for the restoration of the Davidic Kingdom. These movements involved a minority of the Jews, but they were popular enough to make the rulers of their host countries concerned about the potential for social unrest.

Reubeni was an especially enigmatic figure, known today primarily through his diary. A curly haired and heavily bearded dwarf, he had a striking appearance. He probably came from the large Jewish community at Cranganore in India, but at some point he traveled to Khaybar, in today's Afghanistan. In 1522 he appeared in Sudan, speaking to crowds about a large Jewish kingdom in the east, supposedly ruled by his brother Joseph. For some reason, Reubeni also claimed to be a direct descendant of the Prophet Muhammad. His life's aim was to create a military alliance between European royalty and his supposed royal brother to open a two-front war upon the Ottoman Empire. In 1524 he went to Rome, entering the city while riding a white horse, and was received by Pope Clement VII (r. 1523–1534). With Clement's recommendation in hand, he approached the Portuguese king João III (r. 1521–1557), the rulers of Milan and of Venice, and finally the Habsburg emperor Charles V, each of whom promised some form of aid. (In Italy he made friends with Solomon Molcho, the son of Jewish parents who had converted to Christianity. Solomon reconverted to Judaism and, at Reubeni's encouragement, circumcised himself.) Reubeni's habit of complaining to these rulers about their treatment of native Jews, however, turned them against him. Sometime around 1531 he was arrested in Italy and sent to Spain, where he was tried by the Inquisition. No official record of his trial or execution survives, but a later chronicle records that in 1541 "a Jew from India who had come to Portugal" was put to death by the Inquisition at Llerana in southern Spain. His diary survives in the Bodleian Library in Oxford and was published in 1895.

When Sabbatai Zvi (1626–1676) came along and preached his own version of messianic deliverance, he found an enormously receptive audience. He was from Smyrna (modern Izmir, Turkey). **Kabbala**, a mystical interpretation of scripture developed by rabbis, had originated centuries before. In 1648, however, in fulfillment of a kabbalistic prophecy, Zvi declared himself the Messiah and ultimately moved to Istanbul, where he converted a Jewish scribe who promptly forged an ancient-looking revelation document from the patriarch Abraham.

> I, Abraham, confined for forty years to life in a cave, spent a long time in pondering when the miraculous time of deliverance might come, when suddenly, a heavenly voice cried out: "A son named Sabbatai will be born to Mordechai Zvi in the year 5386 [1626]. He, the great Messiah, will humble the Serpent and take his seat upon my throne."

Armed with this, Zvi preached to Jews throughout the Ottoman lands—Istanbul, Athens, Alexandria, Cairo, Gaza, Jerusalem, Aleppo—and gained followers everywhere. Jews as far away as Italy, France, Germany, and the Netherlands joined the movement. At least one entire community, at Avignon, made preparations to quit the city and move with all their belongings to Jerusalem, to join the anticipated new kingdom.

Zvi went so far as to issue a universal proclamation to all Jews:

> Sabbatai Zvi, the first-born son of YHWH, and the Messiah and Redeemer of all the people of Israel, to all the sons of Israel, sends Peace. Since you have been thought worthy to behold the great Day of Fulfillment promised by YHWH through His prophets, all your sorrows and lamentations must end and be turned to celebrations, your fasts be turned into feasts, and your tears must cease. Rejoice, instead, with psalms and hymns! Let your days of sadness and despair become days of jubilation! For I have appeared!

A Messiah on His Throne
Sabbatai Zvi (1626–1676) was a Sephardic Jew who grew up in Smyrna (modern Izmir) in western Anatolia. A sensitive lad, troubled by violent mood swings, he began to experience mystical revelations in 1648 that intimated he was the long-expected messiah of the Jewish people. It is unclear how much he believed these revelations at first, and how many followers he acquired, but in 1665, after receiving a number of confirming signs that dispelled all doubt, he and his followers publicly proclaimed his messianic mission. This page from a prayer book, published in Amsterdam in 1666, shows him enthroned, with angels bringing him a heavenly crown. Note the lower image, which has him presiding over a table at which are gathered the representatives, presumably, of the Twelve Tribes of Israel. The Hebrew word *tikkun* in large print in the center of the image means the "restored harmony" expected to be provided by the messiah.

As unlikely as it sounds, the proclamation generated enormous excitement throughout the international Jewish world. Zvi's portrait began to be printed in Jewish prayer books (frequently appearing next to images of King David). His initials were carved on synagogue walls and embroidered onto flags, and prayers for him were inserted into Jewish liturgies.

The speed of the Sabbatean cult's rise reflects the misery and difficulty of Jewish lives. Persecutions of the Jews grew in number and ferocity throughout the era, leading many to find hope only in a miraculous deliverance. Even a number of Christian groups enthused over the supposed Messiah's arrival, although they were probably more excited by the idea of the Jews leaving Europe than they were about their liberation. But the Ottoman ruler Mehmed IV (r. 1648–1687) grew concerned about

Zvi's popularity. Afraid that large numbers of Jews migrating to Israel would push for its independence, he began to pressure Zvi to stop his activity. Zvi responded, on September 16, 1666, by suddenly announcing his conversion to Islam—for which Mehmed rewarded him with great wealth, a prominent position at court, and several new wives. To Jews everywhere, the blow was devastating, and the Sabbatean movement fell apart instantaneously.

Most of the founders of Protestantism were surprised by the refusal of the Jews to convert to Christianity. For centuries, figures like Martin Luther believed, the Jews had bravely and correctly held out against the false teachings of the Catholics. "If I had been born a Jew," he wrote in *On Jesus Christ Having Been Born a Jew* (1523), "and if I had witnessed such idiots and buffoons [as the Catholics] trying to teach and administer Christian truth, I would as soon have turned myself into a pig as into a Christian." But surely, most Reformers confidently felt, once the beautiful Gospel truth was restored by the Protestants, the Jews would rush to accept it. Conversion would be their reward for enduring centuries of Catholic idiocy and persecution. "We will receive them with open arms, permit them to trade with us, to work with us, live among us, hear our Christian preaching, and witness our Christian way of life." When that failed to happen, the reaction was severe.

Luther himself penned many private letters to friends in which he railed against Jewish perfidy. He also released his wrath publicly in several viciously anti-Semitic tracts, the most notorious being *On the Jews and Their Lies* (1543):

> What ever shall Christians do with the damned, rejected Jews? We can hardly tolerate having them live among us as they do—for if we do, now that we know of their lies, hatred, and blasphemy, we will be complicit in their evil. We are powerless to convert them, but powerless too to put out the unquenchable fire of God's wrath, of which the prophets wrote.... Here is what I recommend. First, we ought to burn down their synagogues and schools, and bury underground whatever is immune to fire, so that no one ever again needs to see a single stone or cinder of them.... Their homes too should be set ablaze and destroyed.... Let all their prayer books and copies of the Talmud be taken from them, for it is by means of these that they propagate their idolatry, their lies, their foul cursing, and their blasphemies.

The tract goes on like this for two hundred pages. Luther was arguably no more anti-Semitic than many of his peers, but he was among the most influential and outspoken. His works may not have persuaded tolerant Christians to become otherwise—and it deserves pointing out that many individuals disagreed with Luther, in print. Yet his uniquely authoritative position among Protestants probably encouraged and confirmed many anti-Semites in the bigotry they already had.

The early modern era, in sum, was marked by harsh religious tensions compounded by severe economic dislocations. Small wonder, then, that so many dispossessed Christians fled to the New World. Small wonder, too, that so many dispossessed Jews fled to the Old.

WARS OF RELIGION

When societies employ force, they often justify their action by recourse to the divine. The ancient Hebrews, for example, considered some wars ethically justifiable as self-defense (*milhemet hovah*). Other wars, however, such as their conquest of the Promised Land from the Canaanites, they deemed to be a religious obligation (*milhemet mitzvah*), a manifestation of YHWH's victory over the false gods of the peoples of the Palestinian plain. The Greeks never entered battle, when they could help it, without first making offerings to the gods and looking for signs of heavenly favor or disfavor. They found divine revelation in everything from cloud patterns in the sky to the spray of blood in the sacrifice of an animal. In ancient Rome the constitutional authority to declare war laid not with the emperor, the consul, or the Senate but with the *fetiales*—the college of priests.

> Still, the church struggled for centuries to determine a Christian ethic for war. How can one justify even a war of self-defense when the greatest heroes of the church were martyrs? Can one be a soldier and a Christian at the same time?

Christianity posed a problem to medieval warriors (if they bothered to think about it), since Jesus's message had focused so intently on peace. He offered no resistance to those who sought to do him harm and forgave those who had already done it. Fortunately for the warlords, though, Dark Age–era Christianity emphasized Jesus as the stern Lord of Heaven, the All-Powerful Judge of Last Days, rather than the Prince of Peace. Still, the church struggled for centuries to determine a Christian ethic for war. How can one justify even a war of self-defense when the greatest heroes of the church were martyrs? Can one be a soldier and a Christian at the same time?

Medieval Muslims had less trouble with the matter: the Prophet himself had been an avid soldier, and the Holy Qur'an enjoined all believers, under certain circumstances, to take up arms for the faith. The Islamic empire had been achieved by the sword first and proselytizing later. The pious names (*laqab*) adopted by the early caliphs illustrate this attitude: al-Saffah ("the Slaughterer"), al-Mansur ("the Conqueror"), al-Muntasir ("the Victorious").

For Protestant Christians the moral sovereignty of the Bible posed no absolute bar to violence. They could point to Old Testament precedents, and the New Testament, too, opened the door to force. "Do not think that I have come to bring peace to the earth," warned Jesus. "I have not come to bring peace, but a sword.

For I have come to set a man against his father, and a daughter against her mother, and a daughter-in-law against her mother-in-law; and one's foes will be members of one's own household" *(Matthew 10.34–36)*.

Most Christians do not read this passage as inciting conflict. It simply recognizes that commitment to the new faith can introduce dissension even within a family. But others noted that Jesus himself used violence on at least one occasion, described in all four gospels, when he encountered the money changers in the Temple: "Making a whip of cords, he drove all of them out of the temple . . . [and] poured out the coins of the money changers and overturned their tables" (John 2.13–15). Moreover, the Gospel writers passed up the perfect opportunity to condemn all military activity—when crowds came to John the Baptist, asking what they needed to do in order to be saved. John replied not that soldiers needed to renounce the army but only that they should "not extort money from anyone by threats or false accusation, and be satisfied with [their] wages" (Luke 3.14).

Stories like this may not have been on everyone's mind in the 16th and early 17th centuries. Yet wars raged widely (see Map 12.6). The brief but bloody Peasants' Revolt in Germany in 1525 served as a kind of prologue to the other conflicts of the age, since it involved the four chief elements—religious conflict, economic conflict, social conflict, political conflict—characteristic of the era. The blows to Christian unity quickly reached France, but in England the adoption of Protestantism in fact signaled the end of a long civil war and the start of a new golden age. It took the Thirty Years' War in Germany, however, to embroil all of Europe.

THE PEACE OF AUGSBURG AND THE EDICT OF NANTES

The Protestant movement was only eight years old when the Peasants' Revolt erupted, but it had already progressed far enough to shred permanently any sense of Christian unity. Encouraged by Luther's open approval, the Protestant nobles responded in force and crushed the rebellion. The experience sharpened more antagonisms than it resolved, however, and set the stage for the coming battle with the emperor Charles V. The Catholic nobles in southern Germany—none of whom had stood up to support the peasants—feared the aroused might of their Protestant peers and looked to Charles to restore order.

But while they hoped for Protestantism's defeat, the Catholic princes were chary of Charles's ending up with more power in Germany as a result. When Charles finally began military action in the 1540s, support from the Catholic princes was at best occasional and at worst verged on treason. For this reason, the war quickly degraded into an inconclusive series of advances and defeats. Finally, when it appeared certain that neither side could gain a clear victory, Charles and

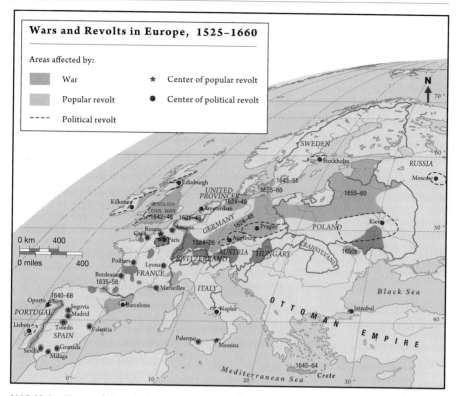

MAP 12.6   Wars and Revolts in Europe, 1525–1660

the Lutheran princes agreed to a compromise settlement. Known as the **Peace of Augsburg** (1555), it granted Lutheranism legal recognition and established *cuius regio, eius religio*, already encountered in chapter 11. With this policy, the religion of the local ruler determined the state religion of the principality, with certain guarantees offered to the rights of the religious minority.

Any hopes that the Augsburg compromise might serve as a model for other countries failed the first test, and in 1562 France became embroiled in a religiously charged civil war that raged for over three decades. The problem was that the Augsburg treaty had recognized the legal validity of Lutheranism but had not done so for Calvinism (since Calvin's version of Christianity had a negligible presence in Germany). And Calvin, who now lived across the Swiss border, in Geneva, longed to secure legitimacy for his followers back home.[10]

His chance came in 1562, when control of the French monarchy came up for grabs. The young King Francis II had died in 1560 after only one year on the throne, leaving his even younger brother, Charles IX (r. 1560–1574), to succeed

---

[10]   By 1562 nearly one-fifth of the French population was Calvinist—primarily in the southern and eastern parts of the realm.

him. The question of the regency—that is, of someone appointed to run the government on Charles's behalf until he came of age—exposed political rivalries and religious antagonism as well. Each of the two leading noble families had ties to royalty, but one was Catholic and the other Calvinist. The Catholic faction was led by the duke of Guise, while the prince of Condé and Henri de Navarre led the Calvinists—who were called **Huguenots** in France. The queen mother, Catherine de' Medici, formed yet another faction of her own. Although essentially a court conflict between aristocratic rivals, the war quickly engulfed the whole population. The leaders of each faction appealed to the masses and turned a dispute over the *roi et loi* ("king and law") into a fight over *foi* ("faith"). Mob violence determined the course of the war almost as much as the actual armies did, for Catholics and Calvinists everywhere attacked each other. They ransacked each other's churches and plundered each other's shops and households. Clergy on both sides urged the fight onward.

The war's grimmest episode was the **Saint Bartholomew's Day Massacre**, a week-long orgy of violence that began as an assassination plot and turned into a mass riot (August 23–29, 1572). The Huguenot leaders had come to Paris to celebrate the wedding of Henri de Navarre, the Huguenot leader, to Marguerite de Valois, the sister of French king, Charles IX (r. 1560–1574). The marriage was intended to ease relations between Catholics and Protestants by uniting their causes in the royal family, but Catherine de' Medici hoped to put a decisive end to the fighting by plotting their murder. The murders spurred mobs to action, and soon crowds in other cities had joined in. When the killing finally ended, thousands of Protestants lay dead, the victims of shooting, strangling, knifing, and drowning. In addition to Paris, massacres took place in Angers, Bordeaux, Bourges, Gaillac, La Charité, Lyons, Meaux, Orléans, Rouen, Saumur, Toulouse, and Troyes—all cities that had reverted to Catholic rule. The riots sparked Protestant fury, predictably, and the Huguenots redoubled their efforts to bring down the royal house, aided now by sympathetic Protestants from Germany and the Netherlands. Catholic Spain responded in turn by sending its troops into southern France. France's civil war threatened to engulf all of Latin Europe.

The whole miserable struggle ended when the next French king, Henri III (r. 1574–1589), was murdered at more or less the same time as the Huguenot leader, the Duke of Guise. Henri de Navarre, married to Princess Marguerite, acceded to the throne. Although the Protestant champion, he made the cool calculation that France, being 80 percent Catholic, had to have a Catholic king. "Paris is worth a Mass," he reportedly declared, then announced his conversion to Catholicism. It took several years to convince the Catholics of his earnestness and to mollify the disappointment of the Protestants. In the end,

No "Restored Harmony" Here   On August 23, 1572, a plot to assassinate leaders of the Huguenot faction in Paris—probably but not certainly instigated by Catherine de' Medici—inspired a terrifying wave of mob violence by thousands of the city's Catholics against their Protestant neighbors. Some estimates put the number of Protestants killed in the riot as high as thirty thousand. The original target of the assassination plot, Gaspard de Coligny, the military leader of the Huguenots, can be seen hanging out of a window to the right. (He was only wounded, but was subsequently executed.) Catherine de' Medici is at the far back, toward the left, emerging from the Louvre and examining a pile of Protestant corpses.

though, he won the support of both and began a long reign that is widely regarded as one of the high points of French history—as Henri IV (r. 1589–1610). In 1598 he promulgated the **Edict of Nantes**, which guaranteed religious freedom, under certain restrictions, throughout the realm. This edict, together with the Peace of Augsburg, established a legal right to believe as one wishes—but in both cases freedom of religion was technically imposed on the people by the king, rather than arising from a demand bubbling up from the populace. In other words, it was a power of the monarch to impose, not a right claimed by the people. For a brief spell the Continent had achieved peace, but it had not attained tolerance.

THE CHURCH OF ENGLAND

Meanwhile, a different sort of religious settlement had evolved in England. There a civil war known as the **War of the Roses** (1455–1485) had erupted soon after England's humiliating defeat in the Hundred Years' War (1337–1453), as various factions fought to shift the blame for England's loss and to win the throne.[11] The War of the Roses never involved large numbers of commoners, but it decimated the English nobility. When the war ended in 1485, a relatively minor aristocrat named Henry Tudor became king, largely by attrition. Ruling as Henry VII (r. 1485–1509), he understood that he could make no elaborate claims of distinguished lineage or heavenly favor—and he did not attempt to do so. He governed modestly and frugally, making sure not to upset the delicate truce. Henry was quick to recognize the potential of the New World discoveries, though, and he invested heavily in developing England's meager maritime capability.

When his son Henry VIII (r. 1509–1547) came to the throne, the kingdom had begun its climb to wealth and power on the international stage. Portraits of Henry VIII convey an aura of manly vitality and newfound wealth altogether absent from portraits of his cautious father. They differed not only in personality but royal self-regard. Henry VIII's portraits exude confidence, swagger, and more than a touch of the gaudiness of the nouveaux riches—for that is precisely what the Tudor monarch was becoming. His marriage in 1509 to Catherine of Aragon, the daughter of the king of Spain, was a corporate merger of the two leading Atlantic seaboard powers. It promised to secure England's new dominant position in Europe for generations to come.

But then came the matter of divorce. Catherine, a pious, loving woman but without a robust physique, had produced several sickly children, and only one—a daughter, Mary—had survived infancy. By 1525, after sixteen years of marriage, it seemed likely that Catherine would not produce the male heir Henry so desperately needed. He decided to divorce her. This move offended Rome (since the marriage had happened only by means of a special papal grant in the first place), the royal house of Spain (since their princess was being publicly humiliated), and the German emperor (since he was Catherine's nephew, and was already smarting from his losses to the Lutherans in his realm). After much dramatic though failed diplomacy, Henry decided in early 1533 to break with the Catholic Church and establish the **Church of England**, or Anglican Church. It was a Protestant church with the monarchy as its supreme head.

Henry famously had six wives before he died. The first had given him Mary, the second produced his only son, Edward, and the third gave birth to another daughter, Elizabeth. Wives four and five gave him nothing but misery, and number six brought genuine affection and comfort to his last years. In creating the Anglican Church, however, Henry did more than establish yet another form

---

[11]   The War of the Roses took its name from the white and red roses on the respective heraldic badges of the noble houses of York and Lancaster.

of Protestantism; he brought England directly into the turmoil raging across Europe. Another version of Christianity was arguably the last thing Western culture needed at the time. Worse, it set the two countries leading the exploration of the New World and the new international economy at odds with one another. England and Spain, briefly united in Henry's marriage to Catherine and on the brink of becoming a joint superpower, instead remained bitter rivals through the rest of the century. Henry's action did result in an enormous increase in royal income, though. He ordered the suppression of every Catholic monastery in the realm and seized all their holdings—which may have amounted to one-fifth of the real estate in England and Wales. The Tudors used this wealth, along with their New World riches, to buy support in both houses of Parliament.

At Henry's death in 1547, the throne passed to his son Edward VI (r. 1547–1553). Only ten at his accession, he never emerged from the shadow of the regency council established for him. The steps made to eradicate Catholicism were undone when Edward fell ill and died, and the throne passed, after some intrigue, to his elder half sister, Mary (r. 1553–1558). Mary, as the daughter of the scorned Catherine of Aragon, was resolutely Catholic and determined to restore Catholicism. Her reign has entered popular memory as a nightmare of religious violence, earning her the nickname of "Bloody Mary." In reality, she was quite popular at first, especially with the many Catholics who still remained in the kingdom. Even many Protestants sympathized with her after her father's break with Rome. But her decision to marry Felipe of Spain in 1554 changed matters and dispelled any hopes that a peaceful religious settlement might be reached. (In Germany, the Peace of Augsburg was still a year away.)

A wave of political purges and religious persecutions marred her last three years on the throne, with roughly three hundred Protestant leaders hunted down as enemies of the crown and killed. Their stories were told—with more love for melodramatic detail than for historical accuracy—by John Foxe in his *Book of Martyrs*, first published in 1563. (Its actual title was *Actes and Monuments of these Latter and Perillous Days, Touching Matters of the Church*). The work is enormous, longer even than the Bible. And for a while it had nearly as much authority over English Protestants; a decree in 1570 ordered that a copy of it be placed in every cathedral church in England.[12]

Mary died childless, and the crown passed to her half sister, Elizabeth I (r. 1558–1603), in whose reign England reached the apogee of international power and prestige. Commonly regarded as England's golden age, this was the era of

---

[12]   Until the start of the 19th century, the three most widely disseminated books in England and America were the Bible (Authorized Version), John Bunyan's *A Pilgrim's Progress*, and Foxe's *Book of Martyrs*.

the poet-playwrights Christopher Marlowe (1564–1593), William Shakespeare (1564–1616), the pirate-adventurers Sir Francis Drake (1540–1596) and Sir Walter Raleigh (1552–1618), and the composers William Byrd (1543–1623) and Thomas Campion (1567–1620). Elizabeth secured a religious settlement that established the Anglican Church as the official faith, with the monarch as its supreme leader. This compromise was a hybrid of Catholic ritual and Protestant theology, and it proved amenable to a majority of her subjects. She placed legal restrictions on Catholic holdouts, but she was even sterner with the more radical wings of the Protestant movement, such as the Puritans, who began to see the New World as more inviting.

"The Only Defense of the Christian Faith"
Engraving dated 1596 of England's Queen Elizabeth I (r. 1558–1603), showing her as erect and unyielding as the marble pillars on either side of her. She holds the usual signs of royal power (orb, scepter) but stands between two unusual other symbols: the falcon atop the left-hand pillar, feeding her young, and the falcon to the right, who rises as a phoenix. The inscription at the bottom (supplemented by a boilerplate poem beneath) lauds her as "the only defense of the Christian faith." The defeat of the Spanish Armada in 1588 had marked the highpoint of her popularity. Owing to economic troubles and a protracted war in Ireland, though, by the late 1590s she was losing control over her privy council and some of her popular regard with the masses, a slow slide that continued until her death. This image seems part of an effort to boost her public image.

Elizabeth increased England's involvement in the new Atlantic economy, which brought her into direct conflict with Spain. She promoted the piracy campaigns of Sir Francis Drake against the Spanish fleets returning from the New World, laden with gold and silver. She also underwrote further exploration of North America. Given the already tense relations between England and Spain, Elizabeth's actions were sure to cause further trouble— which came in 1588 when Felipe II (r. 1554–1598) sent his famous armada to invade England. After the smaller, lighter English fleet defeated these massive warships, England's involvement in the hornets' nest of Continental politics only became more intense.

Spain was also fighting at the time against the Netherlands, which had formed part of the Habsburg Empire. Smarting under Catholic rule, the staunchly Calvinist Dutch revolted against Felipe in 1566. They fought over religion, of course, but even more important was the money to be made in the New World. The Dutch resented having to send a portion of their earnings to Madrid, and they therefore sued for independence. England was happy to see Spain lose to the

Netherlands, and so gave the Dutch whatever overt and covert assistance they could afford.[13] The benefits proved obvious. With Spanish naval might curtailed, England established its East India Company in 1600. The Dutch founded their own East India Company in 1602, leaving them and England as the two most prominent European trading nations in the subcontinent. In North America, England built its first settlement in Virginia in 1607, and the Dutch colonized the southern portion of the island of Manhattan in 1612. Spain thus entered the 17th century in a state of severe economic decline.

THE THIRTY YEARS' WAR

These economic rivalries, political aspirations, and religious conflicts culminated in the last and bloodiest of the Wars of Religion: the **Thirty Years' War** (1618–1648), between Protestants and Catholics in Germany, drew in all of Europe. Like the other wars of the era, this conflict sprang from other motives than religious faith. Nor was the war inevitable, even though, with hindsight, it is easy to see it coming. Most of the European countries became involved in it, in one way or another. The war dragged on for so long in part because the Atlantic states profited from it: so long as the Germans remained mired in civil strife, they could not interfere with or compete against the English, Dutch, French, and Spanish who were busy plundering North and South America. All of the fighting took place in German territories, which makes sense given that the war was as much about Germany's constitutional problem as it was about religion (see Map 12.6).

Its effects were devastating: roughly one-fifth of the entire German population died. France and England both sent assistance to both sides of the conflict. When the Protestants were winning, they aided the Catholics; and when the Catholics were winning, they sent aid to the Protestants. The Dutch helped whichever side promised to help them keep their independence from Spain. Denmark entered the conflict with the aim of seizing northern German territory for itself. The king of Poland joined the fighting in order to defend the Catholic faith. He also claimed the throne of Sweden and hoped for papal and imperial recognition of his claim. The Swedes, for their part, fought to defend Protestantism—and to gain a military alliance with Orthodox Russia against Catholic Poland.

As with the Hundred Years' War between England and France, the significance of the Thirty Years' War lay in how it was fought rather than in the dreary narrative of which side won which battle in any given year. This was the first European-wide war. It was also the first war in which most of the fighting used modern

---

[13]   The playwright Christopher Marlowe served briefly as a spy for Elizabeth in Holland.

weapons based on gunpowder. Armed commoners now formed the overwhelming bulk of the armies, marching in formation, with lines of muskets flanked by cumbersome but mobile artillery. Under the command of cavalry officers still drawn from the upper classes, the armies were larger than any that had taken the field before. At the first battle of Nördlingen in 1643, for example, close to 50,000 soldiers took part, and 10,000 lay dead on the field by battle's end. Only two years later a second battle was fought on the same site, with 30,000 soldiers entering the fray and only 20,000 coming out alive. Similar slaughter took place at Breitenfeld in 1631, at Lützen in 1632, at Breda in 1634, at Thionville in 1639, at Jankau in 1635, and at Lens in 1648. Corpses lay rotting by the thousands in fields all across central Europe.

Among the most vivid testimonies to the war's savagery is a remarkable novel by Hans Jakob Christoffel von Grimmelshausen (1621–1676). Kidnapped by Hessian soldiers when he was only ten, he was captured in battle and redrafted into military service by several armies until the war's end in 1648. His novel, *The Adventurous Simpleton*, appeared in 1668 and tells of a young simpleton who, like

Armies before Professionalization   The small northern French town of Aire-sur-la-Lys had the misfortune of being near Calais, England's vital port entrance into France, and hence always fought over. Between the Hundred Years' War (1337–1453) and the Thirty Years' War (1618–1648) it was besieged nearly a dozen times. This painting from the latter conflict shows the crude makeup of mass armies: no longer the aristocratic-led cavalry, and not yet the professionalized infantry of the Age of Absolutism.

von Grimmelshausen, witnesses horrors and is pressed into service. An early scene sets the tone:

> At first I did not intend to force you, gentle reader, to accompany these soldiers to my father's homestead, for I know what evil things are about to happen there; but the nature of my story requires me to leave some record of the brutal acts performed, time and again, by those involved in the war here in our Germany.... After stabling their horses, the soldiers all set about their appointed tasks, the sum of which was the utter ruin and desolation of our farm. Some began to slaughter all of our animals and set them stewing or roasting, so that it appeared as though they were preparing a jolly feast; but others ransacked our house from top to bottom.... Whatever they did not want to cart away they tore to pieces. A few started to thrust their swords into the haystacks and bales of straw, to find any hidden sheep or swine they could add to the slaughter.... Our maid Ursula, shame to tell, was dragged into the stable and so roughed up that afterwards she refused to come out. Then they took one of our hired workmen and stretched him out flat upon the ground, and, prying his mouth open with a bit of old wood, they dumped a slop bucket full of shit and piss down his throat. They called this a "Swedish cocktail."

After rounding up other farmers in the neighborhood, the soldiers began interrogating them.

> First they took the flints out of their pistols, jammed the farmers' thumbs into the opened space, and used the pistols as thumbscrews to torture them as they would witches. One poor fellow, even though he had confessed to no crime at all, they thrust into the oven, and lit it. They wrapped a rope around another fellow's head and twisted it with a piece of wood until blood gushed from his mouth, nose, and ears.... I cannot report much about what happened to the women, young girls, and maidservants of the district, for the soldiers prevented me from seeing it; but I remember hearing pitiful screams coming from each corner of our house. *(1.4)*

Much of the novel's horror comes from Grimmelshausen's identifying the soldiers simply as *soldiers*. He often does not differentiate between Bavarians, Saxons, Austrians, Thuringians, Swedes, Dutch, French, Spaniards, Danes, Poles, Lutherans, Calvinists, or Catholics. They are all simply soldiers, there are no meaningful

Title Page of *The Adventurous Simpleton* (1668) The first great German-language novel. Its author, Hans Jakob Christoff von Grimmelshausen (1621–1676), like the novel's main character, was abducted as a child and pressed into service in several armies throughout the Thirty Years' War. Unlike the novel's hero, Grimmelshausen never flew to the moon or visited the center of the Earth.

sides to the conflict, and the war is its own repellent cause and justification. But the novel offers more than scenes of savagery. Simpleton runs away from the army and finds his way through a dizzying series of unpredictable adventures. He turns himself into a populist highwayman à la Robin Hood; he impersonates a woman; he takes the place in high society of an aristocrat; he becomes a con artist and a religious pilgrim; he explores a utopian society of mermaids and mermen who live at the bottom of a lake in the Black Forest. At turns hilarious and horrifying, the novel depicts a treacherous world without order. It is a chaotic quest not for a Holy Grail but for simple human decency and the tiniest bit of stability in life.

Grimmelshausen wrote several other novels, each a sequel to his first, usually narrated by a minor character from *Simpleton*. The series recalls Geoffrey Chaucer's *Canterbury Tales* in its shifting kaleidoscope of experiences and views. Though little read today, Simpleton is the greatest German novel before Goethe, and it has never been surpassed as a depiction of war as collective insanity.

WARS OF RELIGION: THE EASTERN FRONT

Christian Europe was not the only theater of conflict. Events in the Middle East, too, turned violent in the 16th and 17th centuries, thanks to a similarly toxic mixture of religious, economic, and ethnic enmity. Three large, multiethnic states dominated the Islamic world around 1500: the Ottoman Empire, the Mamluk Sultanate in Egypt and Syria, and Safavid Persia. Twenty years later only two remained, and they challenged each other for leadership of the Muslim world for the next two hundred years.

Turks and Persians, heading up the Sunnis and Shi'a, respectively, were the standard-bearers of Islam. Ethnic Arabs held decidedly second-class status in both societies, and efforts to alter their position failed before the military might of the dominant regimes. Bayezid II [T] (r. 1481–1512) and his son Selim I [T] (r. 1512–1520) were anxious to continue the policy of aggressive Ottoman expansion and drove the Turkish army northward into the Black Sea, westward into the Balkans, southward toward Egypt, and eastward toward Persia. Bayezid even constructed a large naval fleet that defeated the Venetians in 1503 and left the Turks in command of the eastern Mediterranean sea-lanes. Bayezid had a more peaceful side to his personality, though, and took particular delight in managing the palace schools (sometimes even volunteering to examine students personally) and in fostering trade.

Selim—whose nickname Yavuz ("the Inflexible") describes his personality—began his reign with a near paranoid fear of Persian designs on his realm and spent his first two years in power executing forty thousand suspected Safavid sympathizers in Anatolia. Non-Muslims fared better under these two than did non-Sunni Muslims. Nearly a quarter million Jews emigrated to the Ottoman realm after the European expulsions and settled in Anatolia and Palestine. Like many of their predecessors and courtiers, however, Bayezid and Selim practiced an eclectic form of Islam. It was formally Sunni but tinged with a passionate admiration for **Sufism**.

The Turkish affinity for Sufism may have had its roots in the shamanistic cults of pre-Islamic times. But whatever its origins, it frequently set the Turks at odds with the more staid Sunni and Arabic majority they governed. Urged on by heavyweight scholars like Ibn Taymiyya [K] (1263–1328) after the fall of the Persianized Abbasids, Arab leaders in the 14th century had again placed the **'ulama** ("brotherhood," or "community") at the center of Sunni life. In this conservative view, the traditions of the Qur'an, **hadith**, and **sunnah** were paramount, and all forms of speculative theology and metaphysical innovation were denounced.

Ibn Taymiyya's career, together with those of his acolytes, can in fact be thought of as a small-scale Islamic analog to the Protestant Reformation:

- It demanded a strict return to the authority of early texts.
- It called for stripping away every aspect of religious life not specifically called for in those texts.
- It condemned as heretics all who disagreed with them or who used their ideas for other purposes.
- It was openly hostile to all forms of monastic life and to the cults of popular saints.
- It considered the earliest religious community (the Twelve Apostles for Luther, the Companions of the Prophet for Ibn Taymiyya) the most perfect in its observance of confessional life.

All of these traits were shared by the Sunni and Protestant reformers.[14] Ibn Taymiyya's party attacked Sufism as fundamentally un-Islamic, since it emphasized ecstatic union with God over strict observance of his laws. His immediate

---

[14] In modern times Taymiyya inspired Muhammad ibn Abd al-Wahhab [A] (1703–1792), the founder of Wahhabism, the official doctrine of Saudi Arabia.

acolytes included Ibn Kathir [A] (1301–1372) and Ibn al-Qayyim al-Jawziyya [A] (1292–1350). Little had changed by the 15th century, except for the even deeper entrenchment of the conservative position.

THE WANING OF THE SULTANATE

The Ottoman economy peaked under Selim I's son and heir Suleiman I [T] (r. 1520–1566). Suleiman, the contemporary of Charles V in Europe, is known in Europe as "Suleiman the Magnificent." In the Muslim world, he is called "Suleiman the Lawgiver" in recognition of his work in codifying the great mass of legislation he inherited from his predecessors. He also made the imperial administration more efficient. He was a successful warrior as well, extending Ottoman power to Hungary.[15]

With the opening of the Atlantic trade, however, the Ottoman economy gradually slowed and stagnated. Population increase both fueled the initial growth and brought about the stagnation. When the economy was still expanding, immigration increased significantly. The arrival of the Jews formed only a part of this; a much greater factor was the influx of Muslims from Egypt and Syria and parts of Persia. Cities like Edirne, Trabzon, and Iznik grew by as much as 80 percent, while scores of others grew by 40 to 50 percent. Rural villages increased by 30 to 40 percent over the 16th century. Ultimately, overpopulation set in and was felt first in the countryside. Available farmland grew scarce, and local authorities responded by permitting the clearing of forests. Woodland, never abundant in much of the region, became even scarcer and contributed to a loss of commercial diversity. Adding to the trouble was the influx of gold and silver from the New World, which led to inflation. In 1580, for example, it took sixty silver Turkish coins to equal one gold ducat (then the international standard currency of account), but only ten years later it required 120. By 1640 it took 250. The price of basic commodities like wheat increased by a factor of twenty between 1500 and 1600.

As in Christian Europe, economic misery made religious and ethnic tensions worse. Popular resentment of ethnic and religious foreigners, especially of the relatively newcomer Sufis and Shi'a, increased. Street violence between factions forced local officials to take more direct and heavy-handed actions to keep the peace. But this required money. Over the 16th and 17th centuries, therefore, the power of the Ottoman sultanate waned. Provincial governors and urban or district commanders

---

[15] Suleiman ultimately led his armies all the way to the gates of Vienna (which they failed to take).

Now It's Istanbul, Not Constantinople   A painting from 1537 showing a bird's-eye view of the now-Turkish capital of Istanbul. The picture still follows the medieval tradition of orienting maps with east at the top; a modern viewer needs to turn his or her head sideways to the left. The Hippodrome and the former Church of Hagia Sophia (now renamed the Ayasofya Mosque and renovated to include two minarets) are the two largest structures visible. Though subject to brutal pillage after its 1453 fall to the Ottomans, the city recovered quickly and became a welcoming refuge for Jews who fled the rising religious antagonisms of the 16th and 17th centuries.

first demanded the right to collect their own taxes and then used the revenue to finance their new political muscle.

The sultan's loss of fiscal and political power catalyzed the conservative trend in religion. **Madrasas** across the Ottoman state declared their opposition to any sort of speculative thought. Preachers condemned public morals for straying from the early 'ulama.[16] Even the natural sciences, which had been one of the glories of Islam in the medieval period, came under attack. When Murad III [T] (r. 1574–1595) had an astronomical observatory built in 1579, local preachers—mostly

---

[16]   Especially popular targets for preachers were the new enthusiasms for coffee and tobacco, brought over from the New World.

Arabs—condemned it as an offense against Allah to attempt to unravel the secrets of the act of creation and hired mobs to tear it down.

NEW CENTERS OF INTELLECTUAL LIFE

The creative centers of intellectual life thus moved from the Ottoman center to Egypt and Persia. Cairo emerged as the vital site for scientific work. It was also the home of Ibn Khaldun [A] (1132–1406), whose great *Muqaddimah* ("Introduction to History") posited a new philosophy of history, based on materialism—or the pursuit of worldly goods rather than spiritual ends. Safavid Persia, by contrast, became the center for metaphysics. Its great achievement was a philosophical program known as **illuminationism** (*al-hikmat al-ishraq*), starting with a learned Sufi named Shahab al-Din Suhrawardi [P] (1155–1191). Its central figures were al-Amili [P] (1546–1622), Mir Damad [P] (d. 1631), and especially Sadr ad-Din al-Shirazi [P] (1571–1636)—better known in the Islamic world by the name **Mulla Sadra**. The author of *Transcendental Wisdom*, he remains the most influential thinker in the Persian philosophical tradition down to the present. A key feature of illuminationist, or ishraqi, thought is its effort to harmonize Sufism, Shi'ism, and rational philosophy.

Illuminationism was in fact a common feature of Greater Western philosophical thinking of the age, although European and the Middle Eastern thinkers arrived at it by different trajectories. In western Europe it is expressed in the philosophies of Baruch Spinoza (1632–1677) and Gottlieb Leibniz (1646–1716). Spinoza, a heretical Jew excommunicated by his Amsterdam synagogue, was also a heretical illuminationist. He argued for a highly original form of pantheism that asserted that God was Nature Itself (*natura naturans*, in his posthumously published masterpiece—the *Ethics*) and that every facet of and occurrence in nature (*natura naturata*) is a necessary consequence of God's existence. But the identification of God and Nature should not elicit an attitude of wonderment and awe from human beings. To Spinoza, human life has no divinely ordained purpose and the occurrences of nature possess no supernatural meaning; they simply *are*. The rational study of nature leads to no spiritual revelation, only to a rational understanding of God's manifestation within nature—which, Spinoza insists, is illumination enough for anyone.

> To Spinoza, human life has no divinely ordained purpose and the occurrences of nature possess no supernatural meaning; they simply *are*.

Leibniz, by contrast, sees divine emanation everywhere. He rejects pantheism in favor of an idea to which he gave the awkward name of monadology; all forms of natural life are composed of fundamental units he calls monads, which contain within themselves all the qualities of the life-form they make up.

Spinoza   Baruch de Spinoza (1632–1677) was the greatest Jewish philosopher since Maimonides, although his ideas led to his receiving a writ of *herem*—a form of excommunication in Jewish law. The wording of the writ is striking. Its central portion reads as follows: "The leaders of this holy community, long familiar with the evil ideas and actions of Baruch de Spinoza, have tried repeatedly and by numerous stratagems to turn him from his evil ways; but we have failed to make him mend his wicked ways—in fact, we hear fresh reports every day about the abominable heresies he practices and teaches, and the monstrous deeds he continues to perform. . . . And [therefore] we have decided that the said Baruch de Spinoza should be excommunicated and expelled from the people of Israel. . . . [Wherefore], in accordance with the will of the Holy One (may He be ever blessed) and of this Holy Congregation, and in the presence of the holy scrolls of the Torah, with their 613 commandments, we hereby excommunicate, cast out, curse and damn Baruch de Spinoza with the same form of excommunication with which Joshua condemned Jericho, with the curse with which Elisha cursed the boys, and with all the curses which are written in the Book of the Law. Cursed be Baruch de Spinoza by day and cursed be he by night; cursed when he lies down and cursed when he rises up; cursed when he goes out and cursed when he comes in. The Lord will not spare him; His righteous anger and wrath will rage against this man, and bring upon him all the curses written in the Law. May the Lord blot out his name from under heaven, and condemn him to separation separate from all the tribes of Israel with all the curses of the covenant as they are contained the Law."

The concept is difficult to grasp—and Leibniz himself had difficulty in expressing it—but may be thought of, for organic matter at least, as something akin to a particular life-form's unique genetic code. God himself, says Leibniz, is not present in nature, as Spinoza would uneasily have it, but his intent is present in the system of monads. The study of nature does not bring us, therefore, into God's presence, but it does illuminate for us the workings of his mind.

In Persia, illuminationism derived from the attempt to harmonize Islamic doctrine with classical Greek thought and the mystical elements of Zoroastrianism, and hence to give Sufism a measure of intellectual respectability within the larger Muslim world. Elements of illuminationism date to the 12th century but the theory was given its fullest and most brilliant expression in the work of Mulla Sadra, the greatest Muslim philosopher of the modern era. Mulla Sadra's most important book, *The Four Journeys of the Intellect* (1638), maps out four stages in the route to spiritual and philosophical enlightenment. He dissects the cognitive processes that lead from the understanding of the physical world to a consideration of the essence of God and the nature of the relationship of humans to the Creator. Illumination is both a divine blessing and a technique of enlightenment, an aspect of spiritual discipline.

Sadra does not see God in creation like Spinoza; neither does he behold a divine intelligence in it like Leibniz. Rather, he sees a mystical unity in creation that parallels the unity of God himself and draws the enlightened believer into a stronger desire for spiritual ascent, a return to the Oneness at the heart of all things. Sadra thus pulls together and harmonizes Sufi mysticism, Aristotelian rationalism, and Neoplatonic emanationism.

> Philosophy is the process of perfecting the human soul by coming to a true understanding of things-as-they-are, which is achieved—when it is achieved at all—through rational demonstration rather than intuition or appeal to prior authority. By means of philosophy, we come to resemble our Creator, and this allows us to perceive and ascribe a rational order to His creation.

Most of Arab Islam adhered to a staid and increasingly conservative form of Sunni Islam, eschewing scientific and metaphysical innovation in favor of rigid tradition. As early as the late 14th century Ibn Khaldun had observed that most of the creative intellectual energy in the Islamic world came from non-Arabs. From the *Muqaddimah*:

> All the great grammarians have been Persian, . . . all the great legal scholars. . . . Only the Persians still write great books and dedicate themselves to preserving what is known. Thus, a saying attributed to the

Prophet himself rings true: "If Knowledge was suspended from the highest ceiling in heaven, the Persians alone would get it." . . . All the intellectual arts, in fact, have long since been abandoned by the Arabs and become the sole preserve of the Persians.

The encouragement given to non-Arab Islamic and pre-Islamic traditions by the Ottomans thus stemmed from a sincere interest in promoting innovation and enquiry, but it also served a political purpose by providing a counterweight to the Arab-centric views holding sway from the Arab Peninsula through Palestine and Syria. It also provides another example of the interconnected nature of the cultural life of the Greater West.

THE OTTOMANS: FROM STRIFE TO WARFARE

Tensions between the Ottomans, their Sunni Arab base, and the Shi'i Safavids grew increasingly bitter. The Ottomans' economic stagnation worsened, while Safavid Persia not only carved out its own Islamic identity, but challenged the very notion that the center of Muslim civilization lay with the Arabs and Turks. The pulse of vital Islamic life, Persians insisted, had moved permanently eastward to Iran. The Persian **shah** (emperor) Ismail (r. 1501–1524), who believed himself divine, ordered the immediate conversion of all Sunnis in Iran to Shi'ism on penalty of death. And he made good on the threat by executing tens of thousands, confiscating their homes and goods, closing their mosques, and absconding with the funds for their schools. He also urged the Turkish people to overthrow the Ottomans. As a colorful warning to the Ottoman ruler (Bayezid II), Ismail had another political rival killed, had the skin removed from his corpse and ordered it stitched around a life-size straw figure of the man, and sent it to Istanbul.[17]

Predictably, wars broke out between the two states (see Map 12.7) and continued through the reign of Ismail's son Tahmasp I [P] (r. 1524–1576). Religious hatred intensified with each new reign. Ismail II (r. 1576–1578) played a role in Persia analogous to that of England's Mary Tudor. He tried to force the realm to reconvert to Sunni Islam, but the purges and persecutions he ordered became so bloody that his closest supporters poisoned him after only two years on the throne. Occasional persecutions of Iran's Jewish and Christian communities broke out in the 16th century, but in the 17th religious relations improved significantly. In general, as the Shi'a became more firmly established and were less involved in strife with Sunni holdouts, they eased up on oppression of Jews and Christians. Moreover, many Jewish immigrants from further west earned the shah's gratitude by

---

[17] Ismail kept his rival's skull—gold-plated and encrusted with jewels—and used it as a drinking cup.

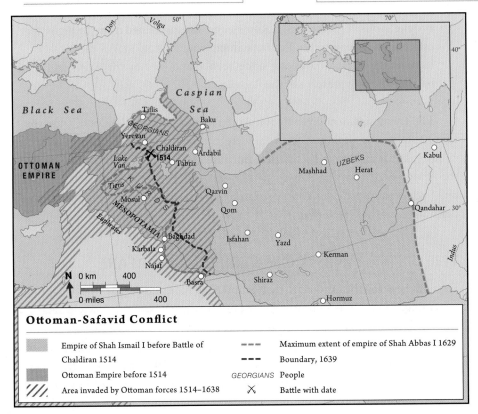

Ottoman-Safavid Conflict

▨ Empire of Shah Ismail I before Battle of Chaldiran 1514	– – – Maximum extent of empire of Shah Abbas I 1629
▨ Ottoman Empire before 1514	– – – Boundary, 1639
▨ Area invaded by Ottoman forces 1514–1638	*GEORGIANS* People
	✗ Battle with date

MAP 12.7   **Ottoman-Safavid Conflict**

introducing him to gunpowder and the casting of heavy artillery. The desire by rulers like Abbas the Great [P] (r. 1588–1629) to increase Iran's export of silk textiles and Persian rugs also opened the way for Armenian Christians, long expert in the crafts, to thrive under Safavid rule.

Ottoman relations with the west remained uneasy, especially with Habsburg Austria and Venice, their neighboring rivals for control of trade routes. The absence of a natural boundary between the Turkish and the Austrian realms kept mutual concerns for safety at a high level. And with the relative decline of Mediterranean trade relative to the Atlantic, control of the sea-lanes in and out of the Levant became all the more important. At the Battle of Lepanto in 1571 an alliance of naval forces led by Venice and King Felipe II of Spain defeated the Turkish fleet and decimated its corps of experienced officers. The so-called Long War (1593–1606) against Austria highlighted the need to modernize the Ottoman army with gunpowder weaponry, but resistance to Western technology among the Arab populace made this an unpopular development.

TABLE 12.1 **Sultanate of Women**

NAME	YEARS IN POWER	MOTHER OF	WIFE OF	ETHNICITY
Ayşe Hafsa	1520–1534	Selim I	Suleiman I	Tatar
Nur-Banu	1574–1483	Selim II	Murad III	Venetian
Safiye	1594–1603	Murad III	Mehmed III	Venetian
Hatice	1617–1621	Ahmed I	Osman II	Serb
Kösem	1623–1648	Ahmed I	Murad IV and Ibrahim I	Greek
Turhan Hatice	1648–1683	Ibrahim I	Mehmed IV	Ukrainian

Just as unpopular and destabilizing was the repeated phenomenon of women running the imperial government. The era of the 16th and 17th centuries in general—but especially the period of the 1640s and 1650s—is referred to as the **Sultanate of Women** (*kadınlar saltanatı* in Turkish; see Table 12.1). During the reigns of several weak-minded rulers, such as Ibrahim I (r. 1640–1648), and several minorities, such as that under Mehmed IV (r. 1648–1687), the leading members of the imperial harem effectively controlled the government. Taking the title of "queen mother" (*valide sultan* in Turkish), these women ran the state, directed foreign policy, and oversaw the fiscal system. What made matters worse, from the point of view of their disgruntled, mainly Arab, subjects, was the fact that most of these women were non-Muslim by birth and their embrace of Islam was therefore suspect. (The Ottomans made a point of marrying as many Christian-born wives as possible, as a nod to their Christian subjects.) In the 16th century the most prominent sultanas were Nur-Banu and Safiya, who either ran or helped to run the Ottoman state in the years 1574–1583 and 1595–1603, respectively. Both of Venetian descent, they restored relations with Venice after the battle of Lepanto and strengthened commercial ties between their empires. Two figures who especially stood out in the 17th century were Kösem, the Greek-born mother of Ibrahim, and her Turkish daughter-in-law Turhan Hatice, whose rivalry was as much personal as political and ended with Kösem's assassination in 1651.

The 16th and 17th centuries, in sum, were not necessarily more religious or more filled with religious hatred than earlier periods in Christian or Islamic history. However, religion became enmeshed in economic and ethnic rivalries of an unusually large scale. Money and the ties of blood intensified religious antagonisms until they reached a degree of fanaticism unlike anything that had existed before, with the possible exception of the medieval crusades. Such antagonisms would not reach this fever pitch again until the 20th century.

WHO, WHAT, WHERE

Ashkenazic

Church of England

conquistadores

Edict of Nantes

enclosure movement

ghettos

hadith

Huguenots

illuminationism

Kabbala

Madrasa

Mulla Sadra

Peace of Augsburg

Saint Bartholomew's Day Massacre

Sephardic

shah

Sufism

Sultanate of Women

sunnah

Thirty Years' War

'ulama

War of the Roses

SUGGESTED READINGS

Primary Sources

Diaz, Bernal. *The Conquest of New Spain.*

Grimmelshausen, Hans Jakob Christoffel von. *The Adventurous Simpleton.*

Las Casas, Bartolomé de. *A Short Account of the Destruction of the Indies.*

Montaigne, Michel de. *Essays.*

Mulla Sadra. *The Four Journeys of the Intellect.*

Anthologies

Diefendorf, Barbara B. *The Saint Bartholomew's Day Massacre: A Brief History with Documents* (2008).

Kors, Alan Charles, and Edward Peters, eds. *Witchcraft in Europe, 400–1700: A Documentary History* (2000).

Pryor, Felix, comp. *Elizabeth I: Her Life in Letters* (2003).

Symcox, Geoffrey, and Blair Sullivan. *Christopher Columbus and the Enterprise of the Indies: A Brief History with Documents* (2005).

Studies

Buisseret, David. *The Mapmaker's Quest: Depicting New Worlds in Renaissance Europe* (2003).

Bonney, Richard. *The Thirty Years' War, 1618–1648* (2002).

Briggs, Robin. *Witches and Neighbors: The Social and Cultural Context of European Witchcraft* (1996).

Clark, Stuart. *Thinking with Demons: The Idea of Witchcraft in Early Modern Europe* (1999).

Dale, Stephen F. *The Muslim Empires of the Ottomans, Safavids, and Mughals* (2010).

Diefendorf, Barbara B. *Beneath the Cross: Catholics and Huguenots in Sixteenth-Century Paris* (1991).

Dursteler, Eric R. *Renegade Women: Gender, Identity, and Boundaries in the Early Modern Mediterranean* (2011).

Fairchilds, Cissie. *Women in Early Modern Europe, 1500–1700* (2007).

Fritze, Ronald. *New Worlds: The Great Voyages of Discovery, 1400–1600* (2005).

Greyerz, Kaspar von. *Religion and Culture in Early Modern Europe, 1500–1800* (2007).

Hartz, Glenn. *Leibniz's Final System: Monads, Matter, and Animals* (2006).

Holt, Mack P. *The French Wars of Religion, 1562–1629* (2005).

Israel, Jonathan I. *European Jewry in the Age of Mercantilism, 1550–1750* (1989).

Kamen, Henry. *Spain, 1469–1714: A Society of Conflict* (2005).

Kaplan, Benjamin J. *Divided by Faith: Religious Conflict and the Practice of Toleration in Early Modern Europe* (2007).

Kleinschmidt, Harald. *Charles V: The World Emperor* (2004).

MacHardy, Karin. *War, Religion, and Court Patronage in Habsburg Austria: The Social and Cultural Dimensions of Political Interaction, 1521–1622* (2003).

Moris, Zailan. *Revelation, Intellectual Intuition, and Reason in the Philosophy of Mulla Sadra: An Analysis of the Al-Hikmah Al-'Arshiyyah* (2003).

Nadler, Steven. *Spinoza's "Ethics": An Introduction* (2006).

———. *Spinoza's Heresy: Immortality and the Jewish Mind* (2002).

Newman, Andrew J. *Safavid Iran: Rebirth of a Persian Empire* (2008).

O'Malley, John W. *Trent and All That: Renaming Catholicism in the Early Modern Era* (2000).

Parrott, David. *Richelieu's Army: War, Government, and Society in France, 1624–1642* (2001).

Peirce, Leslie. *Morality Tales: Law and Gender in the Ottoman Court of Aintab* (2003).

Pursell, Brennan C. *The Winter King: Frederick V of the Palatinate and the Coming of the Thirty Years' War* (2003).

Thomas, Hugh. *Rivers of Gold: The Rise of the Spanish Empire* (2004).

Wiesner-Hanks, Merry E. *Early Modern Europe, 1450–1789* (2006).

Wilson, Peter H. *The Thirty Years War: Europe's Tragedy* (2009).

For additional resources, including maps, primary sources, visuals, web links, and quizzes, please go to **www.oup.com/us/backman.**

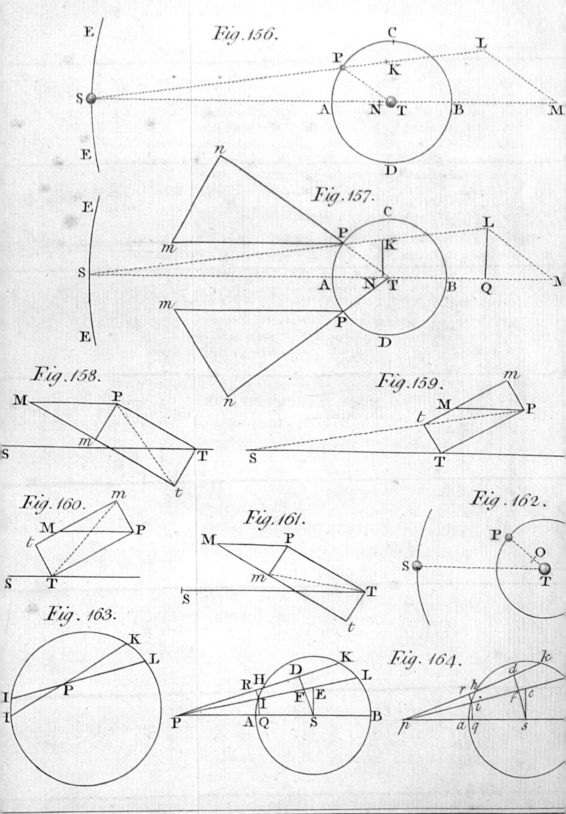

Fig. 156.

Fig. 157.

Fig. 158.

Fig. 159.

Fig. 160.

Fig. 161.

Fig. 162.

Fig. 163.

Fig. 164.

CHAPTER 13

Science Breaks Out and Breaks Through

1500–1700

In the 13th century a Franciscan scholar from England named Roger Bacon (1214–1294) gleefully tore into everyone around him who thought of themselves as scientists. He could, and did, find fault in anyone. Phrases like "damned fools," "ignorant asses," "inept buffoons," and "miserable idiots" pepper his writings in his own colorful Latin. Science, he argued, had been for too long a prisoner to philosophers who never thought to test their abstractions against the evidence of their senses.

THE GREATER WEST, ca. 1700

◀ **The Geometry of Gravity** Sir Isaac Newton's *Principia* (1687) was the closest thing the world had yet seen to a scientific Theory of Everything and dominated the field of physics until the start of the 20th century. This plate from the original edition illustrates some of Newton's theorems visually. The top image (Figure 156), for example, illustrates his thoughts on the gravitational interaction of three bodies: a central and fixed star, represented by the letter T, and two planets in orbit around it, P and S.

When a renowned figure like Albertus Magnus (1206–1280) came to lecture at the University of Paris and was received "like a second Aristotle," Bacon reacted bitterly: "Never before in the history of the world has there been committed a[n intellectual] crime as perverse as this."

Ironically, Bacon's assault on scientists marked the beginning of what we call today the Scientific Revolution. Bacon did not oppose grand theories in themselves. Rather, he believed that the only valid way to reach them was through observation. "Experimental science is the Queen of All Sciences, the goal of all our speculation," he wrote in his *Opus Maius* ("Large Study"). But even that was not sufficient. One had to master all the sciences—including mathematics, optics, astronomy, botany, and physics—before one could even begin to theorize about any one of them. Bacon spent many years achieving just that mastery, as well as learning Greek and Hebrew (and possibly a smattering of Arabic), in order to reach the grand synthesis that he believed only he could achieve. In the end, however, struggles within the Franciscan order forced Bacon into house arrest and silence; he never had the chance to elaborate his grand Theory of Everything.

In the 17th century Sir Francis Bacon (1561–1626) earned fame for his brilliance in law and philosophy, and he cultivated friendships among England's most wealthy and privileged people. Bacon (of no known relation to his medieval namesake) could, and did, flatter anyone. Bacon spent his last five years on the philosophical work that had always fascinated him. He planned a massive, comprehensive work to be called the *Great Instauration*—meaning the great refounding of the entire Western intellectual tradition—but completed only a handful of discrete books that were to form parts of the whole. His *Novum Organum* ("New Instrument") in 1620 reworked Aristotelian logic, while *The New Atlantis* in 1627 was a utopian fantasy. He envisioned, like Roger Bacon had several centuries earlier, a grand masterwork, a complete synthesis of human intellectual understanding. His focus, however, was on the process of analysis rather than on the gathering of data or the testing of hypotheses. Given facts A and B, what conclusions or assumptions can we validly draw from them—and how can we distinguish the valid from the invalid?

Both Bacons addressed the same problem, although from different angles: what are the intrinsic flaws in human thinking? What errors stand between us and Truth, and how can we overcome them? The world overwhelms us with data, impressions, facts, and observations, and our history overwhelms us with ideas, theories, opinions, and conjectures. We need a clear guide to dealing with all this input. How can we know that we are thinking properly?

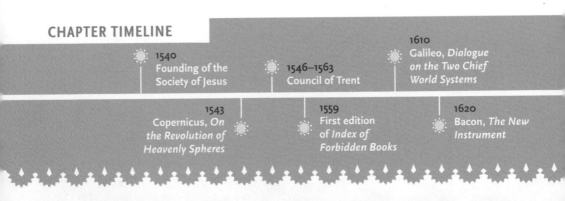

CHAPTER TIMELINE

1540
Founding of the
Society of Jesus

1546–1563
Council of Trent

1610
Galileo, *Dialogue
on the Two Chief
World Systems*

1543
Copernicus, *On
the Revolution of
Heavenly Spheres*

1559
First edition
of *Index of
Forbidden Books*

1620
Bacon, *The New
Instrument*

The **Scientific Revolution** of the 16th and 17th centuries was not a rejection of tradition, unlike Renaissance humanism, but a new phase in its development. The astonishing discoveries of the age placed science at the center of intellectual life in a way that was unique to the West. Fields like mathematics, medicine, and astronomy had always played important roles in intellectual culture. Plato's Academy, remember, expected everyone to master geometry before beginning philosophical study. However, in the 16th and 17th centuries they did more than place the sun at the center of the solar system, discover the universal law of gravitation, and defy the Inquisition and the Islamic retreat from science. They also came to define intellectual life and establish the standards by which it developed and was judged. The story from Bacon to Bacon helps to explain why.

THE COPERNICAN DRAMA

Science interested few people during the Renaissance; at best it formed a minor hobby for some. Like the classical Romans they emulated, Renaissance thinkers showed a keen interest in applied technology but spent little time on pure science. One partial exception was the great artist Leonardo da Vinci (1452–1519), whose curiosity about the natural world and eye for observation inspired him to make intricate drawings of human anatomy, various forms of plant and animal life, and types of machines. He even performed a few human dissections, on the sly. But while such work reflected a strong intuitive grasp of how things in the material world function, they are still not science—which may be one reason why Leonardo left these studies to private journals and notebooks. The only other Renaissance figure who may qualify as a scientist was the Swiss physician Philip von Hohenheim, better known by his nickname of Paracelsus (1493–1541). His understanding and practice of medicine was thoroughly medieval, although he did some pioneering experimentation with various chemicals and minerals in the treatment

1637
Decartes, *Discourse on Method*

1687
Newton, *Principia Mathematica*

1660
Royal Society Founded (London)

1752
Murder Act of 1752 allows bodies of executed murderers to be dissected (England)

Drawing of a Fetus in a Womb Leonardo da Vinci (1452–1519) performed as many as three dozen human dissections in his lifetime (he also dissected several cows and monkeys), which gave him unparalleled knowledge of the body. He prepared over two hundred detailed drawings for publication as a book on anatomy. As shown in this drawing of a fetus, he also wrote extensive notes. The book, *A Treatise on Painting*, was never published in his lifetime. This image also shows da Vinci's use of "mirror writing," which he used not for any secret purpose but simply because he was left-handed and found it easier to write this way without smudging the page.

of disease. His most significant discovery was the development of laudanum—a tincture of opium dissolved in alcohol that was used to treat a host of maladies until the early 20th century. Paracelsus is otherwise remembered primarily for the popular legends that arose around his involvement in alchemy.

The revival of pure science began with developments in astronomy. The revival sprang from a new model by Nicolaus Copernicus (1473–1543) of the motion of the planets, confirmed by careful calculations by Tycho Brahe (1546–1601) and Johannes Kepler (1571–1630). And it led Galileo to a direct confrontation between science and the church. Cosmology had formed a key component of Western science and philosophy from the beginning, going back to the ancient Greeks. The geocentric model handed down for two thousand years posited a static earth at the center of the universe, with the sun and other "moveable stars" (the planets) swirling about it in perfect circular orbits. The unmoving "fixed stars" comprised bright points on the ceiling of Creation. The universe was thus a single, finite, enclosed entity with mankind—Nature's masterpiece—at its center. Christians, to the extent they thought about such things at all, saw no reason to challenge the geocentric model, and indeed felt that it contributed to the Christian view of Man as God's supreme creation. Science was religion's handmaiden. God created the universe, in fact, in order to provide humans with a home. To study the workings of the natural world, therefore, was to most Christians a way of praising God and strengthening faith by deepening our appreciation of God's Creation. Throughout the Middle Ages in fact the church was the primary institution, and often the only one, promoting the study of science. When Western science revived in the 16th century, it did so once again hand in hand with Christian faith. It is a modern conceit that science advanced only when it divorced itself from religion; that divorce became finalized only in the 19th century. The Scientific Revolution therefore needs to be understood as an offshoot of religious history.

Flaws in the geocentric model were evident from the start. Even to the naked eye, the movement of the planets across the night sky was irregular: the transit of Venus (a mini-eclipse caused when Venus passes between Earth and the sun) was just one such irregularity. If the planets all move in ever-widening perfect concentric circles around a stationary Earth, how could the orbits of Venus and the sun intersect in this way? Over the centuries astronomers had come up with scores of intricate arguments to explain away the inconsistencies of the geocentric model, but with each new refinement the system seemed less and less viable.

Sometime around 1510 the German-Polish astronomer Nicolaus Copernicus (Mikołaj Kopernik in Polish) began to develop a different model that resolved many of the irregularities. This **heliocentric** model posited that the sun was the fixed center, and Earth was one of the planets in orbit around it. By 1514 he had begun to circulate his findings among a handful of friends. They spent years gathering more precise observational data, and Copernicus continued to refine his hypothesis. His book, *On the Movements of the Heavenly Bodies*, was not published until 1543, the year of his death.

When Western science revived in the 16th century, it did so once again hand-in-hand with Christian faith. It is a modern conceit that science advanced only when it divorced itself from religion; that divorce became finalized only in the 19th century. The Scientific Revolution therefore needs to be understood as an offshoot of religious history.

Copernicus had feared the book would set off a firestorm within the Catholic Church, but it did not. As early as 1536 a scientifically inclined cardinal, Nikolaus von Schönberg, had already written to him, encouraging his work:

> It was several years ago that I first heard of your skills, about which so many people were constantly speaking, and first developed such high regard for you. . . . What I learned was that you had not only mastered the knowledge of the ancient astronomers but had in fact created an entirely new cosmology according to which the Earth moves [in orbit] while the sun actually holds the most fundamental or central place in the universe. . . . At the risk of intruding upon your activities I want to urge you, with the utmost seriousness, to make these discoveries of yours known to scholars, and please to send me (as soon as is feasible) your writings on the workings of the universe, together with your data tables and anything else you may have that pertains to this important matter.

More criticism came from Protestant leaders, for whom the explicit teachings of Scripture carried more weight. Luther himself is often said to have condemned "that damned fool Copernicus" for challenging the authority of Scripture. (In reality, there is little evidence that Luther was fully aware of Copernicus's work.) Church condemnation did come, but not until some six decades later when the debate had shifted to Galileo's elaborations of the heliocentric theory and his claims for the scientific process that propounded it.

Copernicus had prepared for some resistance. In the preface to his book, he directly addressed the reigning pope, Paul III (r. 1534–1549). His book, he said, offered a simple hypothesis, an explanation of planetary movements that accommodated the available data far better than any permutation of the geocentric model. He closed with a dignified appeal to the church's concern for scholarly truth:

> I have no doubt that our most skilled and talented mathematicians will concur with my findings, so long as they are willing to investigate, with all the honest seriousness that scholarship requires, the arguments I have set forth in this book in support of my theories. But still, in order that everyone, both the learned and the nonlearned, may see that I hide from no man's judgment, I have decided to dedicate these findings of mine to Your Holiness, rather than to another, for even in this remote part of the world where I reside Your Holiness is regarded as preeminent in dignity for the position you hold, for your love of learning, and even for your interest in mathematics. . . . And if there should be any amateurs who (not letting their ignorance of mathematics stand in the way of a chance to pass judgment on such matters) presume to attack my theory because it contradicts some passage of Scripture that they misinterpret for their own purposes, I simply do not care; in fact, I dismiss their opinions as mere foolishness. . . . Mathematics is written for mathematicians. . . . I leave it to Your Holiness and all learned mathematicians to judge what I have written.

He defends his method more than his conclusions. What follows, in other words, is a set of mathematical proofs subject only to the critical review of mathematicians. He makes no theological or even astronomical claims, but argues only that his model conforms to the available data more precisely than earlier models.

Word of Copernicus's work spread quickly around Europe, and a number of scholars elaborated on the heliocentric theory. The Danish astronomer Tycho Brahe, for example, devoted his career to making ever more precise chartings of planetary movements and stellar positions. This improved data made possible the next major leap in astronomy, when Brahe's German pupil Johannes Kepler formulated three famous axioms of planetary motion. These axioms hold that the planets move in ellipses around the sun, that they move at nonuniform speeds, and that the

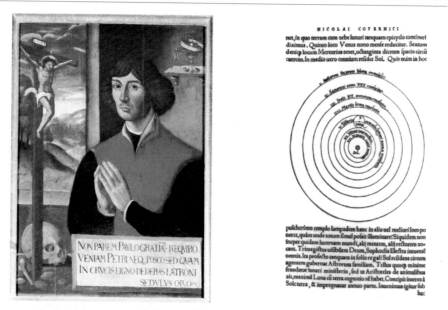

Nicolaus Copernicus A portrait of Mikołaj Kopernik (Nicolaus Copernicus; 1473–1543) emphasizing his Catholic piety, and a page from his book *On the Revolution of the Heavenly Spheres*, which he published just before his death.

velocity of each planet throughout its orbit is in direct proportion to its distance from the sun at any given moment. Kepler had fought a childhood battle with smallpox that had left him very nearsighted. Unable to gather his own observational data, he used the mountain of astronomical tables and star charts left behind by his teacher. With these, he validated his model with a mathematical precision that few of his contemporaries could equal or even understand. Even Galileo initially ignored it.

GALILEO AND THE TRUTH OF NUMBERS

Galileo Galilei (1564–1642) was a genius in astronomy, mathematics, and physics, as famous in his day as Albert Einstein was in the 20th century. His achievements in any one of those fields alone would warrant his being remembered.[1] Trained in mathematics, which he later taught at the University of Padua, he learned astronomy largely on his own and with the use of his telescope. In *The Starry Messenger*, the first report of his astronomical discoveries in March 1610, he describes the most significant of his discoveries: the moons of Venus. The force of this discovery is often difficult for modern readers to appreciate. The geocentric model made no allowance for smaller bodies in orbit around the planets. Everything, in the classical view, orbited the Earth. Yet here was direct evidence against it.

---

[1] Galileo was a skilled tinkerer too, renowned for his redesign of the telescope (invented by Hans Lippershey, of the Netherlands) and of the geometric compass (used by surveyors and artillerymen).

Galileo's Drawing of the Surface of the Moon   Galileo Galilei (1564–1642) developed but did not invent the telescope. He was not even the first to write about its uses for astronomy. By the time he published *The Starry Messenger* (1610), in which this sketch of the lunar surface appears, a Jesuit missionary in Beijing had already published a book about the telescope—in Chinese—for Wanli (r. 1572–1620), one of the last of the Ming Dynasty emperors. But Galileo did build the best of the early telescopes, and with it he made the then-astonishing discovery that the moon's surface was rough and pockmarked, as shown above.

The elaborate mathematical arguments of Copernicus and Kepler were easily ignored. By the astronomers' own admission, they were nothing more than conjectures, a way to make the numbers fall into neater computational alignment. Few people then alive even understood them. But Galileo's discovery was as solid and incontrovertible as the New World continents that Cristoforo Colombo had run into in 1492. Anyone with a telescope (and Galileo himself sold them, as a business venture, on the side) could look up in the sky and see Venus's moons for themselves. Galileo's findings were confirmed by none other than Christoph Clavius, the most prominent expert in mathematics and astronomy in the church, and the city of Rome gave Galileo a triumphant welcome in 1611.

Yet years later he was arrested and forced to recant. What had changed? Two factors principally, and Galileo shares in the blame for the first. In 1623 he published a treatise on comets in which he made a crucial mistake: he argued that comets were not physical objects but only optical illusions—tricks of refracted sunlight. Moreover, in putting forth this (wrong) hypothesis, he went out of his way (not unlike Roger Bacon) to insult astronomers who had asserted (correctly) that comets were in fact fiery solid bodies passing through the solar system far beyond the orbit of our moon. Several of those astronomers, however, were highly regarded clerics who taught at the church's college in Rome, and the papal court was in no mood to countenance such outright rudeness. Several years earlier, in 1616, the church had condemned the heliocentric model as contrary to Scripture, and Galileo was given a friendly warning to refrain from promoting or teaching Copernicanism. He complied, for the most part; but the offensive passages in his treatise on comets called for some sort of response.

If Galileo's first problem was scientific and political, his second concerned Scripture. What happens when scientific conclusions and Biblical statements are in conflict? In his letter to the Grand Duchess Christina, published in 1615, he argues that the Bible should be interpreted in a way that makes it compatible with the scientific finding. Here he invited a debate that Copernicus and Kepler had studiously avoided. They had presented heliocentrism as a mathematical theory only. Although aware that it contradicted Scripture, they offered no opinion about which form of truth was preferable. Galileo, however, brought the Copernican claims into direct open conflict with Scripture—and he made it clear that in his mind the Bible had to accommodate science, not vice versa.

That opinion, combined with his offensive mockery of the church's leading astronomers, turned the tide against him. Several clerics denounced him from the pulpit, and the scandal grew until Galileo was finally called before the Inquisition at Rome in 1632. Galileo's crime was not that he accepted the heliocentric theory; it was that he asserted it as incontrovertible truth. Science, Galileo held, was self-confirming. The Bible was not merely wrong, it was irrelevant. "The purpose of the Holy Spirit is to tell us how to get to Heaven," he wrote, "not to tell us how the heavens operate." And that is what brought on his condemnation.

> Galileo, however, brought the Copernican claims into direct open conflict with Scripture—and he made it clear that in his mind the Bible had to accommodate science, not vice versa.

Science and religion in the Greater West had always known tension, but the strain was proof of their close relationship. Apart from Jewish and Muslim scholars, every Western scientist of any note since the fall of the Roman Empire had been a sincere Christian, often at odds with the church but always identifying with it. And every Jewish and Muslim scientist had been a devout, if sometimes unorthodox, believer.[2] The first identifiable atheist—that is, one who expressly denies the existence of any deity whatsoever—in Greater Western history was not a scientist at all but a German seminary dropout. Matthias Knutzen (1646–1675) published three pamphlets in 1674 denying "God, any Authority from On High, and all sects and their ministers." All that is needed to live a moral life, he wrote, is "to harm no one, live honestly, and give each person his due."

Scripture, Galileo implied, allows room to maneuver; science, though, does not. The Church's position—and, to include the Protestants, the churches' position—was that two thousand years of tradition should not be overthrown because of some opaque mathematical formulas that relatively few people understood properly. The problem, essentially, was epistemological rather than theological: What exactly does it mean, "to *know* something"? At what point can mere humans justifiably declare that a given statement is universally true?

---

[2]   Copernicus and Galileo were both devout Catholics, and Brahe and Kepler were pious Protestants.

THE OTHER SCIENTIFIC REVOLUTION: THE COUNCIL OF TRENT, 1546–1563

Epistemology, or the study of nature of knowledge itself, implies teaching, which brings us to how Christian society responded to the challenges of the era. The Protestant Reformation is only the most obvious of the problems it confronted. Just as significant were the growth of modern monarchies, the early stages of capitalism, the missionary challenge of the New World, and the development of the new science. But the period's difficulties can be, and often have been, overstated. Seen in terms of the actual changes it prompted, the early modern crisis paled in comparison with the Middle Ages, when the church reinvented itself from top to bottom in order to help Europe emerge from the post-Carolingian ruin. The Roman Catholic Church of 1100, say, was a radically different institution from what it had been in 900, whereas the church in 1700 remained essentially what it had been in 1500; if anything, it was even more conservatively so. The reputed dying words of Pope Paul IV (r. 1555–1559) provide an apt epilogue to the Renaissance-era papacy: "Of all the pontificates since the time of Saint Peter, mine has been the most lamentable. Oh, how I regret everything that has happened. Pray for me!"

And yet they overstate the case. The church in fact responded vigorously, and, perhaps surprisingly, that response did not exclude the growth of science. One might even call it the other scientific revolution.

Reform was certainly needed, and figures like Erasmus and More had spent their lives calling for it. Even the most worldly of Renaissance popes recognized that many of the faithful were put off by the church and its cumbersome institutions. The problem was how to find reforms that would please everybody. Through much of the 14th and 15th centuries, when the Holy See was a political football of the Italian nobility, a movement arose to strengthen the role of general councils in ecclesiastical governance. The popes, many of them more concerned with their personal fates than with the office they held, opposed this "conciliarism" vehemently, but the resulting deadlock only aggravated the problems that both sides were supposedly trying to confront. The success of Protestantism produced urgent calls for a general council; papal dithering only made the calls more insistent.[3] But then, surprisingly, the Protestant juggernaut stalled. By 1540 every state in Europe that would become Protestant had done so; no new national-scale conversions were won by any of the major Protestant branches.

---

3   Pope Leo X (r. 1513–1521) famously dismissed Martin Luther at first as "some drunken German who will repent once he sobers up."

Beginning with Pope Paul III (r. 1534–1549), the court in Rome finally took the lead in bringing on reform. He appointed a commission of high-ranking clerics to investigate church abuses, whose final report, published in 1536, laid bare scores of problems in the administration of the church, the actions of the episcopacies, and shortcomings in parish life. In 1537 he issued a bull condemning the enslavement of the indigenous peoples of the New World; in 1540 he confirmed the formation of the Jesuits, a teaching and missionary order; and in 1542 he authorized the creation of the Holy Office—the Roman Inquisition. Last, after securing guarantees that its proceedings would be subject to papal approval, he called for a full ecumenical council to study and propose solutions to the general reform of Catholic life (which has come to be known as the **Counter-Reformation**). This **Council of Trent**, which convened (with a few intermissions) from 1546 to 1563, was the most important assembly of its kind until the Second Vatican Council of 1963–1965.

Although the religious revolt in northern Europe was obviously its trigger, the Council of Trent was more than a response to Protestantism; efforts at reform had begun long before Luther appeared on the scene. Nevertheless, the council's initial actions offered no hint of compromise but rather highlighted the differences between what it regarded as Catholic truth and Protestant lies. If anything, they asserted the Catholic position with even more force than before. The problem confronting the church, they believed, was not with doctrine itself but with the ways in which doctrine was taught to the people. The changes most needed were therefore in leadership and organization.

After Paul III, Pope Julius III (r. 1550–1555) devoted himself to personal pleasure—in particular, his infatuation with an illiterate, fourteen-year-old street beggar named Innocenzo. Julius moved Innocenzo into the Vatican palace (and the papal bedroom), awarded him several wealthy benefices, appointed him the abbot of the monastery of Mont Saint-Michel, and made him a cardinal. But the popes

Catholic Reform　Pope Paul III (r. 1534–1549), in an oil portrait by Titian (Tiziano Vecellio; 1490–1576) and the high pomp of the Council of Trent (1545–1563), which laid out the plan for the Catholic Counter-Reformation.

who succeeded him pressed the council to reach even farther in its ambition: Paul IV (r. 1555–1559) and Pius IV (1559–1565).[4] The Council ordered a streamlining of the church bureaucracy, outlawed ecclesiastical pluralism (the practice of a single individual holding appointments to serve in multiple parishes of dioceses), and heightened the responsibility of bishops to oversee the life of their provinces. Most important of all, it charged them with improving the education of their clergy and of the flocks they served. To assist them, the church helped to build hundreds of new parish schools to train teachers for them. At the higher levels, the church increased the funding for universities and reorganized curricula.

THE SOCIETY OF JESUS

Several new ecclesiastical orders joined the campaign and dedicated themselves specifically to education: the Ursulines ("Company of Saint Ursula"), founded in 1535 and papally approved in 1544, created a network of schools for girls across Europe and soon in the New World. More famous still was the Society of Jesus, commonly called the **Jesuits**, found by Saint Ignacio de Loyola (1491–1556) in 1540. "A Society founded for a single, central purpose—namely, to strive for the defense and propagation of the Faith, and for the progress of souls in Christian life and doctrine," the Jesuits dedicated themselves to preaching and teaching at all educational levels, although historically they have tended toward higher education. Founded as they were by a former soldier—Loyola, a Spanish noble and career military man, experienced a conversion while recuperating from severe battle wounds received in 1521—the Jesuits formed a compact and highly centralized organization. They took vows of poverty, chastity, and absolute obedience to their superiors, especially to the pope, and became the church's most successful tool in bringing Christianity to the outside world.

Within ten years of their founding, the Jesuits had established mission schools in India and Japan, and by 1600 they had extended their reach into South and North America and into sub-Saharan Africa. And since the Council of Trent particularly emphasized the doctrinal point that for Catholics, unlike Protestants, doing "good works" was an essential requirement of Christian living, the reformed church stepped up its involvement in charitable work among the world's poorest peoples. The combined efforts of these new orders, especially in their conflation of schoolroom teaching and service, helped gain many converts in the New World. They even returned many Protestant believers in southern Germany, parts of Bohemia, and throughout Poland-Lithuania to Catholicism.

---

[4]   Julius is the last pope known to have been sexually active and the last pope to have been explicitly homosexual.

Education requires books, how-ever, and education in the Catholic faith faced a further obstacle: non-Catholic books were easily available too. The post-Trent church confronted the problem—or thought they had done so—by producing an **Index of Forbidden Books**. The first version of the *Index*, promulgated in 1559, was regarded as too severe in its strictures, and a revised and slightly moderated version appeared in 1564. The *Index* was continually updated over the centuries, with over forty editions published between 1564 and its suppression in 1966, making it the longest institution-alized censorship in Western history. It was also, arguably, the least effective, since few of the condemned books ever went out of print. In fact, the *Index* rep-resented a perfect shopping list for in-dividuals who wanted to read materials

Jesuit Missionaries The Jesuits were pivotal in revitalizing the Catholic Church's evangelical and educational missions. In this 18th-century painting from Lima, Peru, the order's founder, St. Ignatius Loyola, appears in the center, flanked by two loyal followers, St. Francis Borja and St. Francis Xavier. At the bottom, figures representing Africa, Asia, North America, and South America bear witness to the extent of Jesuit missionary activity.

officially denied them. True, 90 percent of the books ever placed on the list were dense theological treatises that non-Catholics or lay Catholics were unlikely ever to read in the first place. Even so, the 1564 *Index* singles out quite an impressive list of writers. It condemned the works of Pietro Aretino, Sir Francis Bacon, Jean Calvin, Nicolaus Copernicus, Desiderius Erasmus, Henry VIII of England, Martin Luther, Niccolò Machiavelli, François Rabelais, and William Tyndale (an early translator of the Bible into English). Also forbidden were the Qur'an and the Talmud. Later editions added the *Essays* of Michel de Montaigne and the scientific writings of Johannes Kepler and Galileo Galilei.

Jesuit training emphasized all-round education, so that society members would be prepared for any educational or missionary challenge the papacy might throw their way. Even today, the training of a Jesuit takes up to thirteen years. Though grounded in classical humanism, Jesuit education branched off into mathematics and astronomy. Several of the leading scholars of the age were Jesu-its. Fr. Christoph Scheiner (1573–1650) was a German astronomer who discov-ered sunspots independently of Galileo; he also wrote one of the first treatises on the physiology of the human eye. Fr. Alexius Sylvius Polonus (1593–1653) was a Polish astronomer like Copernicus and specialized in the design of ever more refined telescopes. Although primarily an engineer, he nevertheless used his instruments, mastery of mathematics, and Copernican theory to compose a new work on the design of the solar calendar.

Another influential Jesuit, Fr. Carlo Borromeo (1538–1584), was no scholar but dedicated his career to promoting a better-educated clergy. Coming from a wealthy aristocratic family (his mother was a Medici), he used his personal fortune and the large income from his position as archbishop of Milan to found numerous colleges and seminaries. He also established the Academy of the Vatican Nights, an informal symposium to keep church leaders informed of the newest learning.

Most Jesuit astronomers accepted Galileo's work up through *The Starry Messenger*. Fr. Roberto Bellarmine (1542–1621) did, even after he was made a cardinal and placed in charge of the Inquisition. A theologian by training, Bellarmine first attracted attention as a professor at the Roman College, where, in addition to teaching priests-in-training, he wrote the four-volume *Disputation Regarding the Controversies in the Christian Faith* (1593), in which he systematically confronted the theological positions of the leading strains of Protestantism. The English and German governments in fact endowed several university professorships whose specific mission was to devise counterarguments against Bellarmine's book.

When Galileo's work was investigated by the tribunal in 1610, Bellarmine understood the science well enough to accept his discoveries—and arranged for the dropping of charges against him. He added a private warning not to proclaim Copernicanism publicly. Galileo followed the advice and pursued other research until 1623, when a cardinal who was friendly to him and supported his research—Maffeo Barberini, another Jesuit—was elected as Pope Urban VIII (r. 1623–1644). Galileo took this as a sign that the heliocentric theory was finally going to win public acceptance, and so he turned again from his work in physics to astronomy. By 1632 he had written his treatise *The Two Chief World Systems*, but he blundered. The new treatise was written in the form of a dialogue between geocentric and heliocentric astronomers, and even though Galileo was careful to make the heliocentrists capitulate at the end, he nevertheless made the old-style astronomers look foolish. Even worse, he named the spokesman for the traditionalists Simplicio ("Simpleton"). He should have known better. When Inquisitors petitioned to place Galileo on trial, an irritated Urban allowed them to proceed.

As Galileo learned, tone matters. The church had promoted scientific work for centuries and had a tradition of accepting ideas and discoveries not immediately reconcilable with doctrine. It understood that knowledge proceeds by probing, doubting, and testing. What matters is patience and humility. Galileo had sufficient patience but lacked modesty when it came to his work. Other Catholic scientists of the era presented new findings every bit as jarring to traditional sensibilities as

Galileo Galilei, by an Unknown Painter   To the right is a depiction of his trial by the Inquisition.

Galileo's, but presented them as discoveries in progress rather than indisputable truths. A German named Athanasius Kircher (1601–1680) was a pioneer of microbiology and linguistics.[5] An Italian physicist named Francesco Maria Grimaldi (1618–1663) made the first observations that led to the wave theory of light; he also compiled the first map of the lunar surface that described its geological features in detail. These men understood scientific research as a never-ending process, a slow groping toward truth, but one that can never declare final success. The infinite complexity of the universe precludes such hubris. But Galileo effectively altered the rules, or at least claimed that the rules were alterable and that pure truth—final and complete—was attainable. His revolutionary breakthrough was not heliocentrism in itself but the argument that the scientific method justifies itself, ratifies itself. Biblical authority and intellectual tradition mean nothing in the face of empirical data and rigorous mathematical logic. The separation of science from religion, in other words, was not a divorce. It was an annulment.

> Biblical authority and intellectual tradition mean nothing in the face of empirical data and rigorous mathematical logic. The separation of science from religion, in other words, was not a divorce. It was an annulment.

INQUISITION AND INQUIRY

Inquisition is a historical term, a word denoting a specific phenomenon of the past. One could even call it a technical term since it describes a precisely defined and regulated judicial process established by the Catholic Church in 1184. That process

---

[5] Kircher was the first to describe microbes, and he correctly identified ancient Egyptian hieroglyphics with the Coptic language. He also wrote an entire encyclopedia of the Chinese language.

evolved over time, naturally, but even into the 19th century the word referred to a special type of investigation, conducted by ecclesiastical or secular authority, for the sake of public safety. To this extent, it is like the word "fascism"—a multifaceted but technically precise historical referent. But Inquisition, like fascism, is also a popular term, loosely used to describe almost any investigative process or institution that one deems profoundly unfair.

The Inquisition of the early modern era differed significantly from its medieval forebear. Pope Lucius III (r. 1181–1185) had established the Inquisition as a way of stopping the unjust execution of people for dissident religious beliefs. False beliefs within Christianity—heresy—was a sin against the church but was also a crime against the secular medieval state, and in the 12th and 13th centuries the aristocratic courts of Europe were quick to act against heretics—convicting them, killing them, and confiscating their property. The church took a dim view of heresy but championed the idea of intellectual free inquiry. Lucius's decree of 1184 helped to codify a strict, narrow definition of actionable heresy and brought state exercise of authority over heretics under the church's jurisdiction. As brutal and backward as the medieval Inquisition is to modern sensibilities, it is important to note that the number of people killed for dissident Christian beliefs across Europe declined sharply after the Inquisition's establishment.

Even so, ugly is ugly; and even without the use of physical torture (and most inquisitions never resorted to it) the threatening nature of the inquiry, its potential for unspeakable cruelty, was obvious and coercive. That ugliness grew, and the cruelty became a standard operating procedure, in the early modern era when the Inquisition was officially taken over as an institution of the governments. In the 16th and 17th centuries the monarchical states in France, Portugal, and Spain assumed control of it—as did the lesser princes in Germany, Italy, and the Low Countries—and used it to terrorize dissidents and control political opponents. Churchmen actively colluded in the process, certainly, but the notorious Inquisition of the time was as much an indicator of the loss of church power as it was an index of religious and intellectual intolerance.

Although some supported the idea, the Inquisition was not the weapon of choice for dealing with the Protestant Reformation. The Protestants, after all, declared their own separation from Rome and hence no longer came under the church's jurisdiction; later, the policy of *cuius regio, eius religio* granted a certain degree of toleration across the Catholic-Protestant divide. The Inquisition instead focused on three principal targets: witches, false converts from Judaism and Islam, and scientists. The witchcraft craze has been discussed. The issue of false converts was a complex one, arising from financial envy, racial prejudice, and unease about aristocratic stature. The conversion of nonbelievers to Christianity was a desire central to Christian aspirations since the dawn of the religion, but fanatical worries arose from the 15th century onward that many of Europe's converts were converts in name only—people who publicly proclaimed their Christianity but privately retained their Jewish or Muslim practice. Such suspects were referred to as crypto-Jews and crypto-Muslims.

The concern was not merely that they were religious frauds but that there was something intrinsic to their makeup. Some element in their collective blood-lines, it was feared, permanently tainted their Christianity and kept them from a genuine and full commitment. That would have been bad enough, for most of the bigots of the time; but what made matters even worse was the upward social mobility of the professional classes of the Renaissance and after. Noble families in economic decline often married wealthy, ambitious urbanites from the rising merchant economy. For them, the danger of exposing their pure noble blood to the inferior and possibly diseased elements in Jewish or Muslim blood set off a clamor of concern. Crypto-Jews and crypto-Muslims, in other words, were perceived as a threat to noble security and privilege as much as a threat to faith.

The last class of Inquisitorial victims, the proponents of the new science, are the most difficult to generalize about. Their names have become causes célèbres over the centuries. Giordano Bruno (1548–1600), a Dominican friar, mathematician, and cosmologist, provides the most dramatic example. Bruno had little training in science but much amateur enthusiasm for it. Seizing eagerly upon Copernican

Expulsion of the Moriscos from Spain   This painting by Pere Oromig depicts the expulsion of the Moriscos (suspected pseudo-converts from Islam) from the coastal town of Vinaròs, in eastern Spain, in 1609. Moriscos comprised nearly one-third of the population of this part of Spain at the time.

heliocentrism, he soon went further—without any good scientific reason for doing so. He argued that the universe is infinitely large, that the fixed stars were suns like ours that have planets of their own in orbit around them, and that the existence of life on these planets is a likelihood. He consequently denied the special nature of human beings as part of God's Creation, which was tantamount to denying the special role of Christ as the savior of humankind. His admirers over time have given him too much credit: he spun out so many ideas about science that the chance of at least some of them turning out to be true was high. He was an intelligent man, but it is a mistake to consider him a scientist in the sense that Galileo was. Nevertheless, he fell victim to the Inquisition. The court followed its usual tactic of delay, negotiation, and appeal; if Bruno would have only agreed to keep a low profile for a few years, he might well have been given his freedom. But he refused and was executed in a public square in Rome, with his ashes dumped into the Tiber River.

The most famous case of all is that of Galileo. Two inquiries into his science occurred, one in 1616 and another in 1633. The 1616 tribunal, led by Cardinal Bellarmine, reiterated the church's partial condemnation of heliocentrism and let Galileo go with a warning. Copernican theory could continue to be discussed and investigated, so long as it was presented only as a mathematical hypothesis instead of incontrovertible truth. Sixteen years later, having won further fame with his discoveries in optics, physics, and the study of tides, as well as his mathematical theory of infinite sets, Galileo breached his 1616 agreement. In his *Dialogue on the Two Chief World Systems*, he argued openly for the heliocentric model as the indisputable truth. Hence the Inquisition's action against him arose from the complaint that he had broken a contract with the church as much as from his scientific views. The formal judgment rendered by the tribunal reads as follows.

> Seeing that you, Galileo, ... were denounced by this Holy Office in 1615 for asserting the truth of the false doctrine, maintained by some, that the sun is the unmoving center of the universe and that the Earth moves in orbit around it ...
>
> And seeing that ... it was agreed that if you refused to stop [proclaiming this theory as decided truth] this Holy Office could order you to abandon the teaching altogether ... and that you could therefore be subject to imprisonment ...
>
> And seeing that ... your *Dialogue on the Two Chief World Systems* has recently been published ... in which you try to give the impression that the matter is still undecided, calling it only "probable" ... and that you confess that numerous passages of the book are written in such a way that a reader could in fact draw the conclusion that the arguments for [heliocentrism] are irrefutable ...

We conclude, proclaim, sentence, and pronounce that . . . you have made yourself strongly suspected of heresy.

His punishment was house arrest and penance, and the Inquisition ordered his *Dialogue* to be burned. Galileo agreed and spent his last years in quiet work.[6] In 1638 he published his last major work, the *Discourses on Two New Sciences*, which treats problems of motion, acceleration, and mathematical theory. His trouble with the Inquisition was clearly related to, but not solely composed of, his belief in heliocentrism itself; rather, the immediate issue was his breaking of a sacred vow.

The more general and important issue, though, was in the debate about truth itself. Discussing Copernican theory was something the church's own astronomers did with enthusiasm. But to leap from enthusiasm to dogmatic certainty was

Measuring Acceleration   This model reproduces Galileo's experiment for measuring the acceleration of falling bodies. By placing bells at various places along the inclined plane and measuring time via the small pendulum at the plane's top, Galileo was able to show that the distance traveled by a ball rolled down the plane was always proportional to the square of the time elapsed. (A medieval scholar, Nicholas Oresme (1320–1382), had already determined that, but his discovery had been forgotten by Galileo's time.) More truly original was Galileo's determination, contrary to Aristotelian physics, that the speed with which objects fall is a vacuum—hence neutralizing the effects of air resistance—is independent of their mass.

---

[6]   The legend that Galileo at his verdict muttered under his breath "Even so, it moves" is most likely false. The first instance of it appears in a fanciful Spanish painting after his death.

something few were prepared to do, and the church believed it had a responsibility to warn people not to rush into making that leap. The case of Galileo and the Inquisition marks an important turning point in intellectual history—the rise of a belief in *quantification*. If the numbers in Theory A work more precisely and consistently than the numbers in Theory B, this belief goes, then Theory A is for that reason alone accepted as true. But is that really the case? By every imaginable quantitative index, the United States won the Vietnam War—but did it? Conversely, all of the numerical data published by Bernard Madoff for twenty years showed that his investment schemes were fraudulent—and yet knowledgeable investors still poured billions of dollars into his criminal business. Anyone who has ever argued that their scores on standardized exams do not reflect the reality of their knowledge and skills is holding to a position consonant with that of the Inquisition. Right or wrong, the Inquisition trusted God's Word more than it trusted mathematical formulas.

> Anyone who has ever argued that their scores on standardized exams do not reflect the reality of their knowledge and skills is holding to a position consonant with that of the Inquisition. Right or wrong, the Inquisition trusted God's Word more than it trusted mathematical formulas.

THE REVOLUTION BROADENS

It is unclear how much all of these discoveries and debates mattered outside the walls of academia and of the church. History books always present intellectual infighting as high drama, but outside the ivory tower academic squabbles often appear squalid or even silly. (Is it a coincidence that novels about life in academia are always comedies?) To a 17th-century peasant shoveling manure out of a cow stall, it probably did not matter whether that manure was at the fixed center of the universe or if it was in orbit around the sun. All he cared about was getting it out of the barn before the landlord came and beat him for not keeping up with his duties. But discoveries in other fields mattered a great deal at the time, because of their immediate practical value. Increasingly, too, they mattered because of ethical tensions as older taboos declined, especially in regard to Islam.

In medicine, William Harvey (1578–1657) identified the circulation of blood in the human body via the intricate system of heart, veins, and arteries. The existence of internal organs and tissues came as no surprise, but physicians had never understood their individual functions or their working together as a system. Harvey's work opened the door to comprehending the human body as an integrated organism. In chemistry, Robert Boyle (1627–1691), extrapolating from the atomic theory inherited from ancient Greece, described the molecular structure of compounds. In physics he both determined the role of air in the propagation of sound and derived **Boyle's law**, which states that the volume and pressure of a gas at constant temperature vary inversely. These discoveries helped in deriving new chemicals and stabilizing air pumps. In biology Robert Hooke (1635–1703) employed a compound microscope to discover the cellular structure of plants, which, when studied over time, gave hints of the actual process of growth. Organic life, Hooke was the first to assert, is an ongoing process of growth and decay according to natural principles. By analyzing fossils he came close to developing a full-blown theory of evolution almost two hundred years before Darwin.

All this points to an important development. If Galileo had effectively removed God from the workings of the physical cosmos, later scientists began to discover the structures that took the place of Providence. However useful these discoveries might have proved, could they compensate for the loss of a divine purpose in life? When one takes away the idea that the universe functions, however mysteriously, according to a heavenly plan, then one risks the fear of a random, meaningless existence. The poet John Donne (1572–1631) described this feeling

TABLE 13.1 Major Works of the Scientific Revolution, 1500–1700

1543	*On the Revolutions of the Heavenly Spheres*	Nicolaus Copernicus (1473–1543)
1543	*On the Makeup of the Human Body*	Andreas Vesalius (1514–1564)
1600	*On the Magnet and Magnetic Bodies*	William Gilbert (1544–1603)
1609	*The New Astronomy or Celestial Physics*	Johannes Kepler (1571–1630)
1610	*The Starry Messenger*	Galileo Galilei (1564–1642)
1614	*The Wonderful Law of Logarithms*	John Napier (1550–1617)
1619	*The Harmonies of the World*	Johannes Kepler
1620	*The New Instrument*	Sir Francis Bacon (1561–1626)
1628	*On the Motion of the Heart and the Blood*	William Harvey (1578–1657)
1632	*Dialogue on the Two Chief World Systems*	Galileo Galileo
1635	Academie française founded	
1637	*Discourse on Method*	René Descartes (1596–1650)
1653	*On the Arithmetical Triangle*	Blaise Pascal (1623–1662)
1658	*The Spirit of Geometry*	
1660	Royal Society of London founded	
1660	*New Experiments Physico-Mechanical*	Robert Boyle (1627–1691)
1661	*The Skeptical Chymist*	
1687	*Principia Mathematica*	Sir Isaac Newton (1643–1727)

of loss and confusion in "An Anatomie of the World" (1611), written for an aristocratic patron on the anniversary of the death of his wife:

> Then, as mankind, so is the world's whole frame
> Quite out of joint, almost created lame,
> For, before God had made up all the rest,
> Corruption ent'red, and deprav'd the best;
> It seiz'd the angels, and then first of all
> The world did in her cradle take a fall,
> And turn'd her brains, and took a general maim,
> Wronging each joint of th'universal frame.
> The noblest part, man, felt it first; and then
> Both beasts and plants, curs'd in the curse of man.
> So did the world from the first hour decay,
> That evening was beginning of the day,
> And now the springs and summers which we see,
> Like sons of women after fifty be.
> And new philosophy calls all in doubt,
> The element of fire is quite put out,
> The sun is lost, and th'earth, and no man's wit
> Can well direct him where to look for it.
> And freely men confess that this world's spent,
> When in the planets and the firmament
> They seek so many new; they see that this
> Is crumbled out again to his atomies.
> 'Tis all in pieces, all coherence gone,
> All just supply, and all relation;
> Prince, subject, father, son, are things forgot,
> For every man alone thinks he hath got
> To be a phoenix, and that then can be
> None of that kind, of which he is, but he.
> This is the world's condition now.

The poem expresses above all the pain that follows a great personal loss. Yet it
succeeds because the dread of a shapeless and unintelligible universe was felt so
widely at the time. "The world's condition now" seemed one of decay and doubt;
ordered existence is so jumbled and out of joint that one does not even know
"where to look for it." Even God himself, the poem laments, could do nothing
to set matters aright, since "corruption ent'red, and deprav'd the best" before a
divine order could be introduced.

Sic Transit Gloria Mundi   Done in Spain in 1655, this painting serves as a sly cautionary comment. A sleeping nobleman dreams of wealth, power, knowledge, art, beauty, and military prowess, only to have an angel enter the dream, holding a banner that reminds him that death is the end of all things.

It is a powerful poem that should be read whole; the passage here comprises perhaps one-sixth of it. Not all scientific discoveries, it asserts, are advances, for they come at a cost. Take the discovery of the circulation of blood. This breakthrough occurred not simply because William Harvey happened to come along and figure it out. It became possible only with the dissection of human bodies—corpses, mostly, but some still alive.

THE ETHICAL COSTS OF SCIENCE

Deep cultural taboos against the desecration of the body had forbidden dissections for millennia. These taboos predate Christianity and even Judaism. The elaborate funeral rites of the Egyptians and Mesopotamians, with their careful cleansing and wrapping of the body, the incantation of prayers and hymns, the presentation of offerings, the ceremonial burial or burning of the remains under the guidance of priests—all these document a powerful need to treat the dead with decorum. At the end of Homer's *Iliad*, Achilles drags Hector's dead body behind his chariot as he circles Troy. For Achilles it is a moment of triumph; for the reader or listener, it is a moment of moral horror: How can the great Greek hero behave so monstrously? Does Achilles even deserve our interest? To an ancient audience, the scene cast doubt on all that had gone before. In Sophocles' great tragedy *Antigone*, the drama turns on the treatment of the dead. Before the story begins, Antigone's brother Polyneices had led a rebellion against King Creon, who defeated the rebels on the battlefield and ordered that their corpses be left to rot in the field, "prey to the wild dogs and vultures." Antigone's tragedy is to be caught between the king's command and the laws of her religion, which demand proper burial rites for the dead. At the play's conclusion she chooses to bury her brother and accepts her own inevitable execution for disobeying the king.

William Harvey was able to make his great discovery because, by the 17th century, many Western states had come to believe that certain individuals *deserved* to have their bodies desecrated; it was a final supreme punishment for the worthlessness of their lives. After Harvey's breakthrough, detailed knowledge of the operation of the internal organs followed quickly, but these advances required a new horror: the careful cutting open of victims while they were still alive. Harvey himself participated in some of this. The wretches to whom this was done spent weeks, and sometimes months, in constant agony.[7]

Who were these miserable people? It varied from state to state, but in general the possibility of dissection after death awaited anyone convicted of murder, treason, or counterfeiting. Theft too opened the door to the cutting table, if the person one stole from was well-connected. (Heretics and witches did not need to fear the dissector's knife; they were burned at the stake. Besides, it was assumed that they were unnatural and so would not contribute to the understanding of normal human physiology.) A hardness of heart toward certain sectors of society had to exist before Harvey could make his discovery. Many people felt a concern that scientific knowledge can come at too high a price, ethically speaking, for the benefits it brings. Even today, people today seldom stop to wonder where the thousands of cadavers used each year in our medical schools come from. Individuals who donate their bodies to science make up only a fraction of the bodies used. The rest are the unclaimed remains of America's homeless population, donated by our county morgues. Practices vary from state to state in the United States. Illinois, for example, requires county medical examiners to keep unclaimed bodies for sixty days before releasing them to medical schools; Maryland requires a wait of only fourteen days. Medical examiners in New York, however, are allowed to release unclaimed cadavers within twenty-four hours.

---

7   Physicians would make strategically placed incisions, then peel away layers of skin and muscle, in order to observe, for example, the full process of digestion from stomach to bowel.

Two Views of Human Dissection   On the left, Rembrandt van Rijn (1606–1669) shows a dignified exhibition of the start of a lesson on human anatomy; at this time, religious and civil law permitted a handful of dissections to be performed, under strictly regulated conditions. On the right, William Hogarth (1697–1764) shows a considerably more careless and cavalier approach, after Absolutist law permitted the dissection of those convicted of felonies.

But the picture becomes cloudier the more we look at it. Dissections actually were fairly common in the Middle Ages in the Mediterranean regions of Europe and in the Middle East. In Muslim Spain a physician named Ibn Zuhr [A] (1091–1161) performed dissections for research and several autopsies. He was in fact the first physician to deny that the human body was composed of four humors— though he found few people who believed him—and he invented the medical procedure now known as tracheotomy. A physician to Saladin himself, al-Baghdadi [P] (1162–1231), anatomized the corpses of a famine that struck Egypt in 1200, where al-Baghdadi had traveled in order to meet the great Maimonides.

In Christian Europe decrees forbidding the dissection of human remains for the purpose of transporting them to a distant burial site appeared as early as the 1160s, but these were not prohibitions of dissection generally. When in the Third Crusade (1189–1193) the German emperor Frederick Barbarossa (r. 1152–1190) drowned in a river in Asia Minor, his troops, wanting to bury him whole in Jerusalem, tried to preserve his body in vinegar. The human body, it turns out, does not pickle very well, and as Frederick decomposed, the crusaders buried his flesh, organs, and bones in three separate sites. By the late 13th century, in fact, dissections for the teaching of anatomy were standard in the leading medical schools such as the University of Montpellier. At the University of Bologna, another center for medical research and teaching, dissections were performed annually from 1315 on and were made available to the public. It was only in northern Europe that human dissections were both taboo and illegal, and those countries had a less developed scientific tradition. England forbade human dissections until the 16th century, and even after authorizing them on criminals, the law permitted a total of only ten per year throughout the kingdom.[8] Thus the acceptance of dissection came specifically in Protestant Europe, where it was reserved for social malefactors.

THE ISLAMIC RETREAT FROM SCIENCE

The ethical cost of science detached from religious faith may not have troubled the Muslim world in the same way as it did in parts, at least, of the Christian West. At least it seems that way, but science had largely disappeared from Muslim intellectual culture, displaced by legal and theological studies, historical writing, and poetry. From the 7th to the 11th centuries the Islamic world had excelled in every science—medicine, physics, astronomy, mathematics—on both the theoretical and practical levels, leaving Latin Europe far behind. By the 13th century, however, the Latin West had taken the lead. Throughout the Renaissance, much of the Islamic world was too engulfed in warfare and internal strife to continue supporting scientific academies and observatories. The arrival of the Ottomans and Mongols, the rise to power of the Safavids in Persia, and the political recalibrations all three caused drove intellectual effort into philosophical and historical pursuits in the effort to redefine the very nature of Islamic identity. The new conservative element in Islam, exemplified by Ibn Taymiyya in Damascus, dominated the

Law in the Ottoman Empire A page from a legal handbook, *The Confluence of the Currents* (*Multaka al-abhur*) by Ibrahim al-Halabi (1459–1549). Al-Halabi was from Aleppo and spent the first half of his long life in Syria and Egypt, studying and then teaching Hanafi law—one of the four main schools of legal thought in Islam. Around 1500 he moved to Istanbul and became the imam at the great mosque built by the sultan Mehmed II (r. 1451–1481). The *Multaka*, published in 1517 and shown here with some of its many annotations by later writers, remained the authoritative Hanafi text for the next three hundred years.

curricula in the madrasas from the 14th century onward and kept the schools' focus intently on the Qur'an, hadith, and sunnah. Their goal was to produce pious and obedient Muslims, not to advance learning. Memorization of the traditional canon was the goal, not the pursuit of new knowledge. Except for Mamluk Egypt, science in the Islamic world stagnated in the early modern era.

This decline did not go unnoticed. The great scholar Mustafa Katip Çelebi [T] (1609–1657) famously bemoaned the shortcomings of his age:

> There are so many ignorant people . . . their minds as dead as rocks, paralyzed in thoughtless imitation of the ancients. Rejecting and belittling all

---

8 The Murder Act of 1752 finally allowed the body of executed murderers to be available for dissection. France, Germany, and the Low Countries allowed the anatomization of anyone convicted of gross felonies.

new knowledge without even a pause to give it any consideration, they pass themselves off as learned men but really are just ignoramuses who know nothing about the world or the heavens.... The [Qur'anic] admonition— "Have they not contemplated the kingdom of Heaven and Earth?" [7.184]— means nothing at all to them, and they seem to think that to "contemplate the Earth and sky" means to stare at them like a cow.

He was not alone in his complaint. Even one of the Mughal emperors of Muslim India, Muhi ad-Din Muhammad Aurangzeb [P] (r. 1658–1707), lamented the fall in intellectual stature of Islam. In a diatribe against one of his early tutors, he harshly condemned what passed for education in the Muslim world:

> And what were some of the things you taught me? You taught me that France was a small island whose greatest king had previously been the king of Portugal, then of Holland, and then of England! You taught me that the kings of France and of Spain are just like our own petty provincial princes!... God be praised! What impressive knowledge of geography and history you had! Wasn't it your duty to teach me about the ways of the world's nations—their exports, their military might, their methods of warfare, their customs and religions, their styles of government, their diplomatic aims?... Instead, all you thought I needed to know was Arabic grammar and law, as though I was a judge or jurist.... By the time my education was finished I knew nothing at all of any science or art, except how to toss off some obscure technical terms that no one really understands!

Throughout much of the Ottoman Empire, frustration at the increasingly arid curriculum of the madrasas drove the more creative minds on to new schools known as *khanqas*, where the emphasis was on Sufi mysticism. Poetry, music, and metaphysical writing formed the core of this schooling, much of it powerfully imaginative and emotive. (Graduates from the khanqas frequently celebrated the completion of their studies by hurling the textbooks from their madrasa years into wells.) But science was still ignored. Memorization and transmission trumped exploration at every turn, leaving the European world unchallenged in its pursuit of scientific truth.

THINKING ABOUT TRUTH

Having severed its connection with the religious intellectual tradition, European science needed new standards. That includes standards of practice, criteria for determining the quality of evidence and argument, and principles for defining scientific truth. Without such agreement, scientific progress would be fitful at best, permanently hobbled at worst. Suppose one conducts an experiment several times and always achieves the same result. At what point may one legitimately conclude that this result is *always* the result—the natural and inevitable result of that experiment? Five times? Five hundred times? Five thousand times? When does it cease to be a mere result and become a conclusion? When does a general conclusion become an accepted scientific theory, and when does it finally become—the Holy Grail of research—a law of nature? Starting with Galileo and those who supported him, science had sloughed off its ancient standards and criteria but had yet to agree upon new ones to replace them. Even science, it turned out, needs a philosophy.

The 17th century was replete with efforts to establish this new philosophy, as new findings emerged from laboratories and lecture halls across Europe. Two of the most significant figures in this effort were Sir Francis Bacon (1561–1626) and René Descartes (1596–1650), and Isaac Newton (1642–1727) then made their ideas the foundations for mathematically precise scientific laws.

Francis Bacon we have already introduced. As the son of a career courtier, he grew up in high society, learned its manners, and became accustomed to its privileges. (His father, Sir Nicholas Bacon, had been the lord keeper of the Great Seal to Elizabeth I.) He worked as a lawyer and held a seat in Parliament. In 1589 he finally gained his first position in the royal administration and worked his way up, until, in the reign of James I (r. 1603–1625), he made it to the top of the pile, serving as lord chancellor and—a last plum—his father's old position as keeper of the Great Seal. But Bacon had expensive tastes. Even with all his income, he built up enormous debts, which may or may not have led to his taking bribes. Scandal swirled around him for several years as his enemies and creditors colluded to bring him down. In 1621 he finally fell from power in disgrace. Though he was allowed to keep his properties and aristocratic titles, he was barred from all political life and from most of privileged society.

A profoundly cautious man, except when it came to his spending habits, he advocated an uncompromising empirical approach to all knowledge, the gradual acquisition of discrete fact after fact, observation after observation, all of them subjected to repeated testing to insure their accuracy, until one has finally assembled enough data to hazard a general hypothesis. Mankind is prone to drawing hasty assumptions, he argued in *The New Atlantis*, and the only antidote is the patient accumulation of tested and retested facts.

Francis Bacon   Sir Francis Bacon (1561–1626) in all his finery, before his fall.

Roger Bacon, the medieval Franciscan, had already identified four barriers to intellectual progress, errors so common as to be nearly universal:

> There are, in fact, four distinct impediments along the pathway to Truth—stumbling blocks, if you will, that get in the way of every man, no matter how learned he may be, and frustrate anyone who strives to reach the Truth. These impediments are: first, the precedents established by ill-equipped earlier authorities; second, long-established customs; third, the passionate sentiments of the ignorant masses; and fourth, our own habits of hiding our ignorance by the ostentatious display of what we think we do know.

Francis Bacon likewise identified four problems, which he called "illusions" (*idola* in Latin). Here he located the source of error in human nature, our own habits of thinking, the words we use, and tradition. While the correlation is not exact, he clearly had the earlier Bacon in mind:

> There are four types of illusions that bedevil the human mind— illusions to which, in order to keep them distinct, I have attached particular names. These are the illusions of the tribe, illusions of the den, illusions of the marketplace, [and] finally illusions of the theater. . . .
>
> The *illusions of the tribe* are the fallacies inherent in human nature, . . . [above all] the human tendency to consider all things in relation to itself, whereas everything that we perceive via our senses and reason is actually just a reflection of ourselves, not of the universe. The human mind resembles nothing so much as a flawed mirror, and like such a mirror it imposes its own characteristics upon whatever it reflects, and distorts and disfigures it accordingly.
>
> The *illusions of the den* are the fallacies inherent in each individual. Every mind possesses—in addition to the fallacies common to all men everywhere—its own individual den or cavern whose qualities intercept and corrupt the light of Nature as it receives it. This may result from each person's individual and unique disposition, from his education, his interaction with others, or his reading. . . .
>
> There are also what I call the *illusions of the marketplace*, the illusions created by the daily interactions and conversations we have with each other—for we speak through language but words have been formed arbitrarily . . . and they throw everything into confusion. . . .
>
> Finally, the fallacies I call the *illusions of the theater*. By this term I mean those mistakes that creep into men's minds from the teachings of different

philosophies and from erroneous arguments. We must regard every philosophical system yet designed or imagined as nothing more than a play that has been staged and performed—a charade, in other words.

He saw scientific thinking as the careful piling up of individual bricks of knowledge to create a solid edifice. But Bacon himself never did any actual science; a wealthy aristocrat and career administrator, he was accustomed to telling other people how to do their jobs. Descartes, on the other hand, practiced what he preached.

DESCARTES AND THE QUEST FOR TRUTH

René Descartes received a good Jesuit education as a youth, but when he left school he was, he wrote, "filled with so much doubt and false knowledge that I came to think that all my efforts to learn had done nothing but increase my ignorance." In 1618 he met a gifted Dutch mathematician named Isaac Beeckman (1588–1637), and for entertainment they invented mathematical problems for each other. From this sort of play Descartes came to realize that geometric forms likes lines and curves, when marked on a graph, could be described by algebraic formulas. Thus was born **analytical geometry**, a discovery that set the trajectory for Descartes's intellectual life. As he began to elaborate on his original finding in 1619, he all but disappeared for nine years—moving from city to city, from France to Italy and the Netherlands, never telling anyone his addresses (which he changed regularly anyway), and gradually selling off the properties he had inherited from his parents. "To live well, live in secret" became a favorite personal motto. He emerged from self-exile in 1628 in the Netherlands, where he remained for twenty years, though still moving frequently. He moved to Sweden in 1649 at the request of its queen, who appointed him her tutor, but caught pneumonia and died in February 1650.

Descartes's greatest achievements were in mathematics and philosophy.[9] The invention of analytical geometry, apart from its inherent value, made possible the later discovery of calculus and mathematical analysis (differential equations and the like). His best-known work, however, remains the *Discourse on Method* (1637), which he wrote as an introduction to a volume of several scientific papers. In it he presents not only his own working method as a scientist but a creed, a set of principles that guide one to true knowledge, a hybrid of science and philosophy.

---

[9]   Descartes also made numerous advances in optics, meteorology, physics, and even physiology. As a young man, he dissected cows.

He vows "never to accept something as true which I did not distinctly know for myself to be true." Rather than encouraging skepticism and doubt, however, Descartes advocates passionately for certainty. Doubt is not a philosophy, but merely a tool—and Descartes detested thinkers like Montaigne who seemed to him to regard skepticism as the end point of human endeavor. For Descartes, it is the point at which one needs to start thinking the hardest. But what does "knowing" consist of? And what, precisely, is truth?

Descartes   René Descartes (1580–1666), the French mathematician and philosopher.

Descartes begins with a distrust of the senses. The data we gather about the world through our senses cannot be fully trusted for the simple reason that our sense perceptions are imperfect. That includes things we observe with our eyes, or the sensations that derive from touch or smell. Optical illusions are common; people often hear sounds or voices that are not actually present, or fail to hear those that are. Individuals who have lost a limb frequently report feeling an itch on a part of their body that is no longer there. Knowledge based on sense data, therefore, can never be entirely trusted, since it depends on a flawed system of observation—a fact that undermines the very foundation of experimental science. One can try to validate one's data by performing an experiment numerous times and gathering the data with scrupulous repetitive care. Nonetheless, logically speaking there is no absolute certainty that an experiment that repeatedly renders one result after five million consecutive attempts may not suddenly give a different result on the five-million-and-first.

True and absolute knowledge, if possible at all, must therefore derive from a different source than empirical observation. For Descartes that source is logic. Logical thought is itself an absolute reality, or, as he famously put it, "I think, therefore I am" (*Cogito ergo sum* in Latin). I can doubt everything I see, everything I hear, everything I touch, smell, or taste. I can even doubt whether I am alive. But even in the absence of all sense data, my thinking mind—all by itself—knows that I am doubting, knows that I am thinking about thinking, and therefore I know absolutely that I exist.

"Congratulations," one might say. "You exist. So what?" But Descartes's insight contains the germ of a revolution in scientific and philosophical thought. Absolute truth, he argues, is theoretical instead of physical, and the theoretical expression of physical reality is ultimately more real than any physical manifestation of it. Consider, for example, a circle. One can express the idea of "circleness" by drawing one on a piece of paper, but also by describing it in words. "A figure in two dimensions made up of all the points equidistant from a single central point." The description in words is one level of abstraction above the physical drawing on paper. But one can move to an even higher level of abstraction by describing a circle in algebraic notation, as a mathematical formula. This, to Descartes, is an absolute truth, because this formula will describe all circles, in every place and throughout all time. If scientific investigation seeks to understand the truth about circles, it must work at this abstract level. Only here can absolute truth exist and be understood.

> Descartes described an entire universe guided by an immense, internally consistent, and utterly logical set of laws and formulas that the human mind can grasp—and this way of thinking has dominated Western scientific life ever since.

Descartes described an entire universe guided by an immense, internally consistent, and utterly logical set of laws and formulas that the human mind can grasp—and this way of thinking has dominated Western scientific life ever since. Scientific research of all types—whether in physics, chemistry, microbiology, astronomy, medicine, or any other field—begins with an assumption that everything operates according to a set of natural laws. The goal of research is to peel back the covering of the universe and see the logical structure underneath. It may be a coherent structure of unimaginable complexity, but we do not doubt that it is there and that it makes rational sense.

Modern physics, for example, includes the laws of quantum mechanics and of general relativity. Both are universally accepted, and yet they seem to contradict one another fundamentally. Do physicists therefore give up their research grants with a shrug? "Physics . . . it was worth a try, but I guess it just doesn't work." Obviously not. They continue their work on the assumption that still another paradigm exists, one that we have yet to discover but which is absolutely out there, that reconciles our two apparently irreconcilable current systems.

John Donne had complained that the universe is "all in pieces, all coherence gone." Descartes was the first to argue convincingly that another type of system, based on fixed and unalterable natural laws, can take the place of Biblical and classical authorities—and that humans can figure them out. Just as the human mind exists within, but also beyond, the body, the abstract laws of nature exist within and beyond the physical universe. They guide it, shape it, drive it, and ennoble it with purpose.

NEWTON'S MATHEMATICAL PRINCIPLES

The first person to deliver on Descartes's promise was Sir Isaac Newton (1643–1727), the greatest scientist in Western history before Albert Einstein (1879–1955). He came from an undistinguished family and received a fairly standard education at a boarding school. As a boy he enjoyed tinkering with machines, a hobby he continued throughout his life.[10] He earned a bachelor's degree in 1664 from Cambridge University in classical studies, but by that time he had already started to teach himself mathematics and physics by reading the works of Descartes. When the plague swept through England, he withdrew to his family's rural home, where he began his work in optics and in the calculation of infinite series. The first resulted in his discovery that light can be broken into the spectrum of colors and has the properties of a wave, and the second resulted in his discoveries of integral and differential calculus. Within two years he had become the leading mathematician of his age and earned a prestigious professorship at Cambridge, where he remained for thirty years. He spent his last thirty years in London serving as master of the Royal Mint and president of the Royal Society.

Newton's greatest achievement was his *Philosophiae Naturalis Principia Mathematica* ("Mathematical Principles of Natural Philosophy"), published originally in 1687. It is not light reading. Newton was a cranky, obsessive loner who loathed being disturbed in his work, especially by people who could not understand the complexity of his thinking—which was just about everyone. Only three hundred copies of the first edition of the *Principia* were printed, which was probably well more than the number of people capable of making sense of it. Newton insisted on having empirical data as the basis for his high-flying mathematical formulations, and hence the *Principia* skips from topic to topic, wherever there is sufficient data to begin computing. Nevertheless, the variety and number of topics Newton addresses add up to a comprehensive theory about the physical world.

Its fundamental and astonishing idea is the theory of universal gravitation. The idea that things such as apples fall to the ground was hardly startling news. What prompted Newton's thinking was the question of why the planets do not fall to the Earth's surface. Plainly there is evidently nothing holding them in orbit in the sky. Physical theory had been based for centuries on the belief that motion was an intrinsic quality of all matter. Water flows because that is what water does; the atoms that propel our bodies forward are in constant movement because movement is life itself. Death, in this view, is a cessation of natural movement. Newton argued instead that motion results from the interaction of objects, and he showed that the interaction can be calculated precisely by taking into account their mass, velocity, and direction of motion. In this way he developed the physical concept of force. But he then complicated matters by introducing another idea—what he called the "weight" (*gravitas* in Latin) or attraction that all

---

[10]   Newton invented the reflecting telescope—one that uses a curved mirror rather than a second lens to focus captured beams of light.

physical objects feel toward one another whether they are in a static or dynamic state. Thus was born the idea of gravity.

In his descriptions of gravity, which he further showed to be determined in permanent ratios according to mass, distance, and force, he produced a comprehensive explanation for physical actions as simple as an apple's fall from a tree and as complex as the elliptical orbits of the planets in the solar system. Descartes had shown the logical necessity of a universal set of natural laws governing all matter. Now Newton provided the mathematical formulas that those laws consisted of. The universe was not only internally coherent according to a single, though undeniably massive, set of laws, but those laws were knowable, calculable, and provable. When Newton died in 1727, he was given a hero's funeral and buried in Westminster Abbey.

THE CHOICES FOR WESTERN SOCIETY

The immediate impact of the Scientific Revolution was moderate, but it changed Western culture profoundly. The universe became in the popular mind less of a divine and glorious mystery and more of a fascinating mechanism, with all that is good and bad in that transition. The new tenets included the belief in a rational explanation for everything we experience, the considered reliability of an idea that is based on quantifiable evidence, and the habit of privileging the demonstrably logical over the intuitive. All came increasingly to characterize much of Western thought. Western society, being the most open to the rational exploration of the world and the exploitation of its potentialities, became poised to do just that (see Map 13.1).

> The immediate impact of the Scientific Revolution was moderate, but it changed Western culture profoundly. The universe became in the popular mind less of a divine and glorious mystery and more of a fascinating mechanism, with all that is good and bad in that transition.

Not that there were not sounds of alarm raised. When the Royal Society, England's premier institution for the promotion of science, was established in London in 1660, some warned that it was nothing short of the beginning of a Satanic apocalypse. One prominent Anglican clergyman, Robert South (1634–1716), denounced the members of the society in a sermon in 1667 as

> the profane, atheistical, epicurean rabble ... who have lived so much in the defiance of God ... a company of lewd, shallow-brained huffs [blowhards] making atheism and contempt of religion the sole badge of wit, gallantry, and true discretion. ... The truth is, the persons here reflected upon are of such a peculiar stamp of impiety, that they seem to be

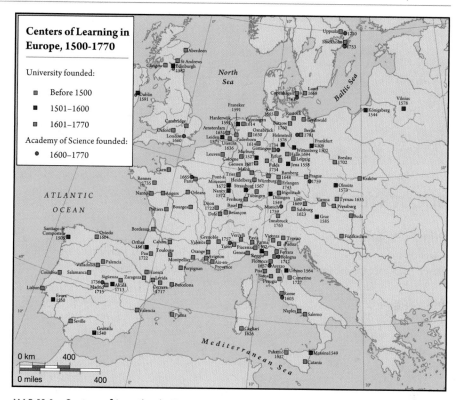

MAP 13.1   Centers of Learning in Europe, 1500–1770

a set of fellows got together, and formed into a diabolical society, for the finding out new experiments in vice.

Developments in the Christian West and the Islamic West now sharply diverged. Europeans came increasingly to view the world as knowable, explorable, and understandable. In fact, it became something that the West could dominate. At the same time, the Islamic world took a pronounced inward turn, eschewing science and exploration in favor of a reexamination of tradition. Neither path was intrinsically right or wrong, but both resulted from conscious cultural choices and as the expressions of value. The consequences of those choices would be felt for centuries to come.

WHO, WHAT, WHERE

analytical geometry	heliocentric
Boyle's law	*Index of Forbidden Books*
Council of Trent	Inquisition
Counter-Reformation	Jesuits
Epistemology	Scientific Revolution

SUGGESTED READINGS

Primary Sources

Bacon, Francis. *Novum Organum.*

Descartes, René. *Discourse on Method.*

Galilei, Galileo. *The Starry Messenger.*

Hobbes, Thomas. *Leviathan.*

Anthologies

Donnelly, John Patrick, ed. and trans. *Jesuit Writings of the Early Modern Period, 1540–1640* (2006).

Finocchiaro, Maurice A., ed. and trans. *The Essential Galileo Galilei* (2008).

Hellyer, Michael. *The Scientific Revolution: The Essential Readings* (2008).

Jacob, Margaret. *The Scientific Revolution: A Brief History with Documents* (2009).

Studies

Biagioli, Mario. *Galileo's Instruments of Credit: Telescopes, Images, Secrecy* (2007).

Bireley, Robert. *Religion and Politics in the Age of the Counterreformation: Emperor Ferdinand II, William Lamormaini, S. J., and the Formation of the Imperial Policy* (2011).

Blackwell, Richard J. *Behind the Scenes at Galileo's Trial* (2006).

Brooke, John, and Ian Maclean, eds. *Heterodoxy in Early Modern Science and Religion* (2006).

Dear, Peter. *Revolutionizing the Sciences: European Knowledge and Its Ambitions, 1500–1700* (2009).

Evans, Robert J. W., and Alexander Marr. *Curiosity and Wonder from the Renaissance to the Enlightenment* (2006).

Feingold, Mordechai. *The Newtonian Moment: Isaac Newton and the Making of Modern Culture* (2004).

Gaukroger, Stephen. *The Collapse of Mechanism and the Rise of Sensibility: Science and the Shaping of Modernity, 1680–1760* (2011).

———. *The Emergence of a Scientific Culture: Science and the Shaping of Modernity, 1210–1685* (2006).

———. *Francis Bacon and the Transformation of Early-Modern Philosophy* (2001).

Godman, Peter. *The Saint as Censor: Robert Bellarmine between Inquisition and Index* (2000).

Henry, John. *Knowledge Is Power: How Magic, the Government, and an Apocalyptic Vision Inspired Francis Bacon to Create Modern Science* (2004).

Jardine, Lisa. *Ingenious Pursuits: Building the Scientific Revolution* (2000).

Lindemann, Mary. *Medicine and Society in Early Modern Europe* (2010).

Park, Katharine. *Secrets of Women: Gender, Generation, and the Origins of Human Dissection* (2010).

Park, Katharine, and Lorraine Daston. *Early Modern Science* (2006).

Shea, William R,. and Mariano Artigas. *Galileo in Rome: The Rise and Fall of a Troublesome Genius* (2003).

Spiller, Elizabeth. *Science, Reading, and Renaissance Literature: The Art of Making Knowledge, 1580–1670* (2004).

Tutino, Stefania. *Empire of Souls: Robert Bellarmine and the Christian Commonwealth* (2010).

For additional resources, including maps, primary sources, visuals, web links, and quizzes, please go to **www.oup.com/us/backman.**

CHAPTER 14

From Westphalia to Paris: Regimes Old and New

1648–1750

"Those who did not live in the 18th century before the [French] Revolution do not know life at its sweetest," declared the French career diplomat Charles de Tallyrand-Périgord (1754–1838). An egoist right to the tips of his fingers, Tallyrand knew what he was talking about. The period of the Ancien Régime ("Old Regime"), from 1648 to 1789, was a time of unparalleled privilege and delight for the European upper aristocracy. Its belief in absolute order spread throughout society as well, inspiring a demand for norms in the arts and even everyday life. While England's civil wars led to a constitutional monarchy, the Islamic world in fact grew more conservative. As international trade grew and a new economic system came into being, however, Europe faced a new round of crises and war. Urban manufacturing and commerce had long since become the main engines of economic life, but the landed

THE GREATER WEST IN THE AGE OF ABSOLUTISM

Peterhof
Potsdam
Schönbrunn
Versailles

○ Palaces built by Absolutist monarchs

◀ **Teaching Manners**
Enlightenment Europe placed profound importance on proper manners, one example being the publication of the first etiquette manuals for "proper" urban families. In this painting by Jean-Baptiste Chardin (1699–1779), a governess upbraids her charge for having dirtied his hat—presumably having dropped it on the ground during a tennis match.

elite still enjoyed various rental incomes, judicial fees, annuities, ecclesiastical and governmental sinecures, and military revenues. That was more than enough for them to live in lavish comfort, especially given their most closely held privilege— exemption from paying taxes. While agreement between states brought peace, it too further concentrated wealth and power, and philosophy rose to the occasion with an argument for tyranny.

This was the **Baroque Age**, when fabulously ornate palaces, churches, summer residences, concert halls, libraries, museums, theaters, pleasure gardens, and private academies sprang up by the hundreds across Europe. Most were filled to bursting with paintings and sculptures and rang with the music written by liveried court composers and played by servant musicians—all for the enjoyment of the wealthy, powdered, perfumed, and brilliantly attired nobles. Their images, coats of arms, and marble-inscribed names bedecked everything in sight. The display sought not merely to impress but to overwhelm the viewer with its expressive power. And that meant the power not of the architect, artist, or composer, but of the nobleman whose authority and station made such glories possible. Europe's elites had always enjoyed their privileges, but seldom on this scale.

The all-encompassing grandeur was designed to stun the people into a state of paralyzed awe. But such a display was possible only by means of a brutal hoarding of wealth. Few periods in Western history ever saw a more intense concentration of power and wealth among the elites—or such widespread penury and suffering by the common people. The German poet Johann Wilhelm von Goethe (1749–1832) described Europe's peasant farmers as "caught between the land and the aristocracy as between an anvil and a hammer." Not a comforting image— especially when one realizes that Goethe did not make the observation out of sympathy for the commoners' plight, but merely as a recognition of what was and needed to be.

CHAPTER TIMELINE

1643–1715
Reign of Louis XIV
(France)

1649
Charles I
of England
beheaded

1670
Molière, *The Middle
Class Gentleman*

1648
Treaty of
Westphalia

1651
Hobbes, *Leviathan*

1675
Founding of Bedlam
Asylum (England)

THE PEACE OF WESTPHALIA: 1648

By 1648 most of Continental Europe was exhausted by over one hundred years of brutal warfare. Unable or unwilling to continue the carnage, all sides sued for peace. The **Peace of Westphalia** (1648) is an umbrella term for a collection of individual treaties that ended the hostilities. It rearranged political borders, created a framework of mutually agreed upon principles, and established a network of recognized sovereign governments. Over one hundred delegations had participated in the negotiations, which had taken seven years: sixteen nations, sixty-six German imperial principalities, and twenty-seven nongovernmental interest groups (such as churches, corporations, and guilds). This was the first general diplomatic congress in Western history, and it provided a model for subsequent international assemblies.

The peace dramatically revised the political map of Europe by splitting some states, joining others, carving out new independent entities, and moving many traditional boundaries (see Map 14.1). In so doing, it paid little attention to preserving ethnic domains. The goal instead was to produce a balance of power between the states created by the peace. If each new state was roughly equal in power to its neighbor, the thinking went, then wars would be less likely to break out between them. But to create such a balance, sheer acreage was not enough to consider; population density, economic and technological development, access to ports and rivers, and the availability of natural resources all had to be factored in. The resulting map shows several new states (an independent Denmark, Holland, Portugal, and Switzerland, for example) scattered amongst the larger territorial powers (Austria-Hungary, Bavaria, Brandenburg-Prussia, France, Poland-Lithuania, Spain, and Sweden). Moreover, countries now had a mechanism for creating alliances in order to check an ambitious neighbor. This eased tensions by allowing each state to control its own foreign policy in a meaningful way. Even small states like Denmark or Holland had strategic strengths that made them valuable allies. Threatening to withdraw their

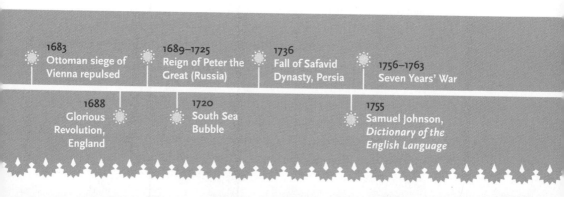

1683
Ottoman siege of
Vienna repulsed

1689–1725
Reign of Peter the
Great (Russia)

1736
Fall of Safavid
Dynasty, Persia

1756–1763
Seven Years' War

1688
Glorious
Revolution,
England

1720
South Sea
Bubble

1755
Samuel Johnson,
*Dictionary of the
English Language*

MAP 14.1   Europe in 1648

support from an alliance could make even a large state like France or Spain reconsider their policies.

The Westphalia treaties also reaffirmed the principle of religious establishment—the idea that the ruler of each state could determine its official religion (*cuius regio, eius religio*)—while guaranteeing the freedom of other faiths and denominations within certain prescribed limits. Strictly speaking, religious establishment meant more than a preference for any particular faith or denomination and was distinct from theocracy. Rather, it created a formal relationship between the state and the specific church. Religious establishment in the modern sense, in which the established church serves as an organ of the state, was a product of the Protestant Reformation: England established the (Anglican) Church of England

The Landed Gentry   Thomas Gainesborough (1727–1788) was the premier portraitist of 18th-century England, which was ironic since he had a profound dislike for the upper classes. His speed was admired as much as his skill, which kept a constant stream of commissions coming his way. In this dual portrait (1750) of Robert and Frances Andrews, a wealthy gentry couple, Gainesborough slyly lets some of his disdain for his subjects show. The couple looks distinctly out of place in the tranquil setting, like foreign objects imposed on the countryside. Mrs. Andrews, then only eighteen, sits stiffly on an elaborate wooden bench. The area of her lap was left deliberately unfinished, perhaps to allow for the inclusion of a baby in the future. Mr. Andrews, aged twenty-four, has a look of forced nonchalance. Gainesborough has pushed the couple to the side in order to spend more time painting the landscape (his real artistic love). No workers, implements, or farm animals are on the scene, except for a small herd of sheep far in the distance, which gives the land an eerily lifeless look.

in 1533, and the (Lutheran) Church of Sweden came into formal existence in 1536. Most of the states carved out by the Peace of Westphalia had in practice established churches, although few had the formal legal structures uniting church and state as did England and Sweden.

This sprawl of new or heavily revised territorial states left most monarchs without serious rivals for power. Where councils and parliaments had provided a limited check on royal ambitions, few of these customs survived intact. The aristocracy remained wealthy, privileged, and secure in their control of the agrarian countryside, but also unable to unite in opposition to royal aims. The new states were professional bureaucracies—uninviting to most nobles, who found it more to their liking to remain in their baroque palaces and chateaux than to crowd into expensive cramped quarters in the busy capital cities. Moreover, individual rulers could now consolidate extensive, centralized authority over their common subjects, so long as they avoided using that power to threaten their neighbors. In other words, the alliances and guarantees that aimed to prevent a king from intimidating his neighbors actually helped him to tighten his grip on his own subjects. In this way the peace helped to trigger the rise of royal **absolutism**, or a king's absolute power—not as a consciously deliberated policy, but rather as the unintended consequence of the quest for a balance of power.

THE ARGUMENT FOR TYRANNY

The argument for tyranny is a simple one, to its enthusiasts: it provides freedom. That may seem contrary to common sense, but the argument is sound. We define freedom by what we are free *from*. Many people, quite understandably, think of freedom as independence, or not being subject to control. To others, however, true freedom consists of freedom from chaos. The restoration of order after a long period of anarchy can thrill people with a sense of regained liberty—the liberty of a reliable, well-regulated tranquility.

The argument is an old one. The Archaic- and Classical Age Greeks celebrated their tyrants (*tyrannoi*, like Solon and Psistratus) and wrote them into their constitutions, as necessary correctives to democracy's occasional tendency to drive the cart into a ditch. The Roman Republic too allowed for constitutional dictatorship, a temporary though renewable grant of unlimited authority to revise the laws, reform government, and command the military. Julius Caesar had been a dictator—and a popular one at that until he appointed himself dictator for life, which made him effectively a king and all but assured his own assassination. In times of crisis, as when an airplane is spinning out of control or a ship is foundering in a storm, the rights to individual self-expression and self-determination do not further the cause of rescue. There is no time to hold elections, seek consensus, and let everyone on board freely express views about what to do. Instead, the argument goes, salvation requires a single firm hand on the controls and a single strong voice barking orders to an obedient crowd. Tyrants can make mistakes, of course, but they at least have the potential of saving the ship. Noisy, messy democracy and respect for independence of thought and action in such a plight only guarantees a crash.

The catastrophic wars of religion and civil wars before them, many now argued, were the result of liberalizing, mass-driven politics. In retreating from traditional authority since the 12th century, Europe had nearly committed suicide and had all but lost its collective mind in the crazed pursuit of witches.

The aristocracy needed to parade its power, boast of it, and glorify it in everything it did. And the higher the aristocrat, the greater the need for spectacle.

Only a restoration of patriarchal society, headed by noble male authority, could save the West from ruin. But this could not be done quietly or subtly. The aristocracy needed to parade its power, boast of it, and glorify it in everything it did. And the higher the aristocrat, the greater the need for spectacle. Kings, of course, needed to parade their glorious position more than anyone else.[1] Jean Domat (1625–1696), a prominent jurist and royal favorite, justified the ostentation:

> Law grants the sovereign many rights, one of which must be the right to public display of anything that gives evidence of the grandeur and majesty needed to express the authority and dignity of his high and wide-ranging office.... God Himself [after all] wants monarchs to augment the authority He has shared with them, in ways that promote the awed respect of the people, and this can be achieved only by the grandeur conveyed by the brilliance of their palaces.

The Peace of Westphalia did not institute absolute monarchy in any formal sense, but it did establish the conditions that made its rise likely. Some early indicators of royal dictatorship had emerged even before the peace. In France the rapid concentration of power by the monarchy had begun under King Louis XIII (r. 1610–1643), whose chief minister—(Armand-Jean du Plessis) Cardinal de Richelieu (1585–1642)—summed up the problems confronting the throne when he first came to power in 1624:

> The Protestants acted as though they shared the state with you, the nobles, as if they were your equals rather than your subjects, and the governors of the provinces as though they were monarchs of their own offices. These scenarios set a bad example, one so harmful to the kingdom that even Your most loyal courts were influenced

Richelieu Armand-Jean du Plessis, Cardinal-Duc de Richelieu (1585–1642), was the sickly younger son of a low-ranking noble family, who grew to become the most powerful figure in the kingdom of France after the king himself. Richelieu believed firmly in the necessity of an absolutist monarchy; only a strong central monarch, ably guided and determined to exert his authority energetically, could maintain civil order. His rapid rise in the church and the French government went hand in hand. Consecrated a bishop in 1608, he became France's secretary of state in 1616; in 1622 he was made cardinal, and two years later he was Louis XIII's chief minister—a post he held until his death.

---

[1] Privilege, in the Age of Absolutism, was not a consequence of power but the very essence of it.

by it and were driven—unreasonably—to build up their authority to the detriment of Your Own. Might I add that every individual seemed to measure his worth by the boldness of his presumption, . . . each one deeming the privileges he held from You valuable only to the extent that they satisfied his greedy fantasies. . . .

Sure in the knowledge of how much good a king can accomplish when he puts his power to proper use, I, in my confidence, dared to promise Your Majesty that You would soon regain control of Your state and that before much time elapsed Your wisdom and courage, together with God's blessing, would put the realm on a new path. I swore to Your Majesty that I would spare no effort and would use whatever power it pleased You to grant me to ruin the Protestants, to break the stiff-necked pride of the aristocracy, to return all Your subjects to Your dutiful service, and to restore Your name to the high position it deserves in foreign lands. *(Political Testament, ch. 1)*

Richelieu accomplished all this and more with a mix of careful negotiation and heavy-handed intimidation. He neutralized most of Louis XIII's foes thanks to his network of domestic and international spies, his ability to charm, and his willingness to bribe, and above all his ruthless conviction that only an all-powerful throne could keep France safe and strong. Richelieu's passion for order and security is as evident in his personal life as in his public policies, and in this he represents many of the qualities of the Age of Absolutism.

THE SOCIAL CONTRACT

Richelieu's dedication to a supremely powerful monarchy was instinctive, but more than one philosopher of the time reached a similar position. None of these thinkers directly created absolutism as a political force, but they help explain the sentiments that gave rise to it. The philosopher most closely associated with the theory of absolutism is Thomas Hobbes (1588–1679). Hobbes was not England's first philosopher, nor even her first political philosopher; he was, however, the first to write philosophy in English. A contemporary of René Descartes, with whom he corresponded, and Sir Francis Bacon, Hobbes spent most of his adult life as a tutor and secretary to William Cavendish, the second Earl of Devonshire, which left him ample time to take advantage of the earl's magnificent library. He had broad interests that included history, law, mathematics, and physics, as well as philosophy. Forced to spend time in exile in Paris after the arrest and subsequent execution of King Charles I in 1649 because of his strong royalist views, Hobbes returned in 1651 with the completed manuscript of his best-known work, *Leviathan*.

Although his own life was comfortable, Hobbes's philosophy owed much to the violence and misery of his age. He emphasizes the instincts for self-preservation and self-regard that are natural to all people. Our polite, civilized behavior toward one another is an acquired attribute, one that masks and hopefully controls our baser passions for food, wealth, power, pleasure, and status. The problem, he argues, lies in the finite nature of the things we desire. Seeking always to satisfy ourselves, we unavoidably live in a state of constant competition with one another. "The war of all against all," as he memorably put, corrodes our civilized veneer and leads us into periodic anarchies like the one Europe suffered after 1500. Moreover, people are unequal in abilities—some being stronger, others faster, still others more cunning, or more agile. The war of all against all therefore becomes a permanent state, with

> no place for industry, because the fruit thereof is uncertain; and con-
> sequently no culture of the earth; no navigation or use of the commodities
> that may be imported by sea; no commodious building; no instruments of
> moving and removing such things as require much force; no knowledge of
> the face of the Earth; no account of time; no arts; no letters; and which is
> worst of all, continual fear and danger of violent death; and the life of man
> solitary, poor, nasty, brutish, and short.

It is a pessimistic view of life. (A long-ago student of mine once submitted an essay on the horrors of the early modern era "in which life was, in Hobbes's view, 'solitary, poor, nasty, British, and short.'") But it is not altogether surprising, given the agonies Europe had experienced since the discovery of the New World, the Protestant Reformation, the Wars of Religion, civil wars, Inquisitions, and witchcraft mania.

Hobbes sees only one way out of the misery of the state of nature: limitless sovereign authority. Only by transferring our innate rights of self-determination to a governing authority entrusted with absolute power over the people can we hope to free ourselves from chaos. Interestingly, Hobbes does not much care whether the absolutist government is a monarchy, an oligarchy, or a democracy. All that matters is that the government, whatever its form, has unquestioned power to compel obedience. Unlimited and indivisible power to legislate, adjudicate, execute, and enforce, in a single sovereign entity, is the only way to live an ordered, peaceful, and prosperous life. Of course it also fails to prevent the abuse of that power; but Hobbes counters this charge with two assertions. First, no absolute tyranny can ever be worse than absolute chaos. And second, when people recognize their complete obedience to the Sovereign Authority, a stable and peaceful enjoyment of life really does result. Their total submission

The Social Contract   Title page of the first edition (1651) of *Leviathan* by Thomas Hobbes (1588–1679), the first work of political science in English.

> Government, which bears responsibility for preserving social stability, may therefore legitimately assert its will on the community whenever it deems it necessary to do so. Renunciation of personal liberty, in other words, is the price of peace; but the truest form of freedom, Hobbes insists, lies in that very renunciation.

to the Sovereign Authority will temper any possible inclination that authority might have to abuse its power.

Leviathan is a difficult book to read. Its archaic English—all four hundred pages of it—defeats all but the most determined readers. (I have modernized its spelling and punctuation.) But it deserves attention. A darker yet more substantial work than Machiavelli's *Prince*, *Leviathan* elaborates what later became known as **social contract** theory. This theory holds that when people decide to live in community they enter a covenant with each other, compromising their individual free wills in return for the benefits of society. Government, which bears responsibility for preserving social stability, may therefore legitimately assert its will on the community whenever it deems it necessary to do so. Renunciation of personal liberty, in other words, is the price of peace; but the truest form of freedom, Hobbes insists, lies in that very renunciation.

Richelieu and Hobbes were not the only 17th-century figures to argue for absolutism, but they are the most interesting. Both men were brilliant, moody, and pessimistic about human nature, and each worked diligently to bring their ideas to fruition—Richelieu in deed, Hobbes on the page. Had they met, they might have recognized one another as kindred spirits despite their religious differences. For all his worldliness, Richelieu was a devout Catholic, and scholars still debate whether Hobbes was an atheist.[2] Each also had humane pursuits. Richelieu collected classical manuscripts (later donated to the Sorbonne, of which he was the

---

[2]   Can one be committed to Christianity while endorsing secular absolutism? Hobbes says yes, but was he just trying to avoid inflaming the still-smoldering religious antagonisms of his age?

chief executive), founded the Academie française (the premiere literary society in France), patronized painters and sculptors, and ardently promoted theatre. Hobbes dabbled in mathematics and physics, published his own translations of Thucydides and Homer, and wrote a vivid history of the English Civil War. Still, both men shared unsettling and ominous views about human nature and the hard realities of life. Their influence was profound, and the fears they articulated were shared by many—fears that allowed absolutism to take root and flourish. For a while on the Continent, it could enjoy even popular support.

ABSOLUTE POLITICS

The dominant dynasties, and the most representative, of the Old Regime were the Bourbons in France, the Habsburgs in Austria and (a separate branch of the family) in Spain, the Hohenzollerns in Brandenburg-Prussia, and the Romanovs in Russia. A web of intermarriages that in some cases went back generations or even centuries connected the royal families to one another. Even so, ties of affection were minimal and always gave way to politics. Standing armies became arms of the state, as royal families undertook vast building projects to display their rule. Mercantilism, the economic system to support their disastrous self-indulgence, also devastated much of the population.

Despite the supposed "balance of power" established at Westphalia, France was the dominant Continental state in every way. With somewhere between 15 and 18 million people, France around 1648 had twice the population of Spain and three times that of England. With its superior resources concentrated among the upper orders, all of whom lavished funds on the arts, French culture flowered. This was the age of the playwright Molière (1622–1673), the painter Nicolas Poussin (1594–1665), and the composer Jean-Baptiste de Lully (1632–1687). Young King Louis XIV set immediately to increasing the size of his army, in the hope of matching France's cultural clout with its military muscle.

Brandenburg-Prussia, by contrast, was a surviving remnant of the old Holy Roman Empire, steeped in tradition and pride but for the moment a poor, defenseless, war-shocked ruin. Much of the worst fighting of the Thirty Years' War had taken place here, leaving large stretches of the countryside desolate and many towns depopulated. Economic development came slowly, and most commercial, technological, and institutional innovations appeared here one or two generations after they had taken root in England, France, or Holland.

Habsburg Austria had a long genealogy going back to the Middle Ages, but the traumas of the 17th century had left much of its land depleted and demoralized. The Ottoman Turks advanced upon Austria almost as soon as the

Another Siege of Vienna   In 1683 the Ottomans again marched against the Habsburg Empire (their first effort having been in 1529). The Turks had an army of nearly one hundred thousand soldiers. The Habsburgs called on their Polish and Lithuanian allies to join in the defense and carried the day. In this painting by the Flemish artist Frans Geffels (1624–1694), the Turks have launched their assault on the city. The Poles and Lithuanians have not yet appeared on the scene. According to legend, as part of the celebration over their defeat of the Turks the Viennese bakers' guild created a new pastry: the croissant, which was designed to mimic the Islamic crescent, visible on the Turks' flag above the tent on the left. The idea is that every time one tears open a croissant, one is in effect calling the Turks a rabble of puff pastries.

Westphalia agreements were signed; by 1683 they had reached Vienna, which they besieged for two months before giving up.[3] (Forces from Poland, Russia, Venice, and the papacy joined the subsequent Austrian counteroffensive.) The Turkish defeat reenergized Austrian pride, an emotional swell that led to a sharp improvement in economic and social stability. This was the era of Austria's climb as a cultural capital, especially the cities of Salzburg and Vienna; the first Austrian composer of note, Heinrich Ignaz Franz Biber (1644–1704), almost single-handedly turned Salzburg into a pilgrimage site for music lovers. The background to the Romanov dynasty lay in a decade-plus of famines, civil wars, and foreign invasions known as the Time of Troubles (1601–1613).

Mikhail I Romanov (r.1613–1645) came to power just before the Thirty Years' War engulfed Europe and died before it ended, but he took advantage of Europe's deadly self-absorption to drive out the (Polish-Lithuanian) invaders besetting his country and solidified his control over all of Russia. When Piotr I (Peter the Great) came to power in 1689, he brought with him the style and techniques of autocratic rule that he had learned earlier when traveling in the west. Together they laid the foundation for a czarist state that would last until 1917.

---

[3]   The Turks used the ancient temple of the Parthenon in Athens as their main munitions storehouse. When Venetian artillery units took aim on it, the temple was blasted into the ruin it is today.

TABLE 14.1   **The Age of Absolutism**

AUSTRIA (HABSBURG)	BRANDENBURG-PRUSSIA (HOHENZOLLERN)	FRANCE (BOURBON)	RUSSIA (ROMANOV)	SPAIN (BOURBON)
Leopold I 1658–1705	Friedrich Wilhelm 1640–1688	Louis XIII 1610–1643	Mikhail I 1613–1645	Felipe I* 1621–1665
Josef I 1705–1711	Friedrich III 1688–1713	Louis XIV 1643–1715	Alexei 1645–1676	Carlos II* 1665–1700
Karl VI 1711–1740	Friedrich Wilhelm I 1713–1740	Louis XV 1715–1774	Theodore II 1676–1682	Felipe V 1700–1746
Maria Theresa 1740–1780	Friedrich II the Great 1740–1786	Louis XVI 1774–1792	Ivan V 1682–1689	Ferdinando VI 1746–1759
Josef II 1780–1790	Friedrich Wilhelm II 1786–1797		Peter I the Great 1689–1725	Carlos III 1759–1788
Leopold II 1790–1792	Friedrich Wilhelm III 1797–1840		Katerina I 1725–1727	Carlos IV 1788–1808
Franz II 1792–1835			Peter II 1727–1730	
			Anna 1730–1740	
			Ivan VI 1740–1741	
			Lizaveta 1741–1762	
			Peter III 1762	
			Katerina II the Great 1762–1796	
			Pavel 1796–1801	
			Aleksandr I 1801–1825	

* The last two Habsburg kings of Spain

POLICE STATES

Autocracy is not conceptually difficult to grasp, since dictatorships follow a few set patterns of development. The regimes of the 17th and 18th centuries were above all police states. Raw military muscle and the willingness to use it both secured and expressed their power. The king's army in France mustered merely 20,000 soldiers in 1661; by 1700 it numbered 400,000. The Prussian army in the Thirty Years' War had consisted mostly of unreliable mercenaries, with the result that Swedish forces had ravaged the countryside almost at will. After 1648 the Prussian monarch began to assemble a professional standing army of his own. It began small: between five and six thousand men. But by 1750 it had ballooned to 180,000. Control of the Austrian army was given to a professional military officer from France, Prince François-Eugène of Savoy (1663–1736), who oversaw its transformation from a ragtag mixture of old feudal forces and mercenaries into a national institution with modern methods of supply, training, and command. After only a few years' work, he had increased the size and quality of the Austrian forces to such an extent that they drove one hundred thousand Ottoman Turks eastward from Austrian lands by 1687, after which he turned the army around and expelled a French force from the west. Austria thus entered the 18th century with a professionalized army of nearly one hundred thousand men.

The transformation of the Russian military was even more dramatic. Long consisting of an informal conglomeration of semifeudalized noble cavalrymen known as **streltsi**, the army was disbanded and brutally purged of political rivals by Tsar Piotr I in 1698. Piotr was determined to bring Russia in line with Europe, in terms of economic and political development, and resolved not only to catch up with Europe but to do so by emulating it. He modeled his new army along French and Prussian lines, put his soldiers in Western-style uniforms, gave them Western weapons (muskets and artillery), and hired Western officers to train them.

These massive new armies drew from the lower orders of their respective societies for the rank and file; men from the urban and professional classes or the lower nobility dominated midlevel officer ranks. The highest ranks were still primarily the purview of the high nobility, but tended to include only those for whom the military was a lifelong career. Only Prussia used a military draft; in every other country, volunteers served. And there was no shortage of volunteers. The king's army offered commoners three meals a day, a salary, solid training, and the possibility of a pension after a certain number of years in service—things they had little or no chance of attaining on their own. These were "drum and bugle" armies, divided into companies that fought in formation using long, unbroken lines. Discipline was harsh and frequently brutal: beatings, fines, half rations, and imprisonment were common. The penalty for breaking ranks was flogging. Executions were common too. In Austria, Prince François-Eugène liked to perform them personally on soldiers who failed to obey orders on the battlefield. Piotr I once personally executed five soldiers accused of rebellion, after allowing others to prepare the way by torturing the men first.

The Peace of Westphalia, however, was largely successful in maintaining a relatively peaceful Europe. Conflicts remained, a couple of them even large-scale matters, but Europe between 1648 and the start of the French Revolution in 1789 was a much more peaceful place than it had been in the 140 preceding years. Most of the wars of the era arose from Louis XIV's grandiose plans to create a greater France, or more accurately to secure a number of extranational regions that might buffer France from external attack: the War of Devolution (1667–1668), the

Franco-Dutch War (1672–1678), the War of the League of Augsburg (1688–1697), and the War of the Spanish Succession (1701–1714). Louis came to regret his overreaching, although not until the very end of his life. On his deathbed, Louis is reported to have advised his heir (his great-grandson Louis XV): "Don't follow the bad example I've set."[4]

Why then were such enormous armies created? With fewer foreign and civil wars to fight, the soldiers were put to use policing their own populations. Soldiers marched the streets and plazas, stood in university lecture halls, observed church services, watched crowds entering and leaving theaters, policed the countryside, guarded government buildings, and monitored harbors. They guarded city gates, performed maneuvers in town squares, staffed prisons (one of the new inventions of the age), and inspected printing houses. Without such vast reserves of manpower, royal absolutism was unthinkable. Maintaining the

Prussian Military Discipline   By the middle of the eighteenth century, the Prussian line infantry made full use of flintlock muskets and bayonets, as well as drilling, which involved the rotation of the front and rear lines after each salvo. "If my soldiers were to think, not one of them would remain in the army," Frederick II of Prussia is reputed to have said. The painting above shows Frederick's forces charging directly into the fire of the Austrians at the Battle of Hohenfriedberg in 1745, which the Prussians won.

---

[4]   Louis on his deathbed: "I was too quick to start wars, and I kept them going out of vanity. . . . Be a peaceful ruler, and devote yourself above all to easing the suffering of your subjects."

military—paying salaries, providing weapons and uniforms, serving meals, offering housing, supporting pensioners—remained a central concern of every monarch of the 17th and 18th centuries. The costs even in peacetime were enormous; the occasional conflicts of the age drove the expenditures exponentially higher.

Old Regime monarchs also relied heavily on separate companies of royal commissioners and civil servants—called *intendants* in France, and known collectively as the **Directory** in Prussia—who traveled through the provinces and inspected the handling of royal and administrative affairs. These commissioners held jurisdiction over all matters relating to public finance (whether collecting it or paying it out), public safety, and justice. They also formed part of the kings' extensive networks of intelligence gatherers. Drawn chiefly from the urban professional classes, commissioners served the king personally and did not hold public office, and hence they received their own salaries directly from the royal purse. They were expensive supervisors to maintain, since the kings not only paid their salaries but also equipped them with trappings appropriate to a representative of the king. In Prussia, in fact, all government positions of high and middling rank were reserved for military personnel, which effectively excluded much of the traditional aristocracy from power. It also made the king's position all the more secure, since literally everyone who worked in his government received a salary directly from him. In return for their exclusion from government, the nobles received royal permission to reinstate serfdom on their estates.

SELF-INDULGENCE WITH A PURPOSE

Expensive too were the sometimes grand, sometimes grotesque, building projects of the age. Palaces and churches decorated with baroque profusion arose by the score, year after year, as did lecture and concert halls, libraries and museums, scientific laboratories, and academies. Louis XIV, stung by rebellions and resistance in Paris, moved outside the capital and began construction of the immense palace complex at Versailles, which became the permanent seat of power from 1682 on. And other rulers built their own imposing piles too.[5]

Versailles itself had been a small rural village of only a thousand inhabitants fifty years earlier. Louis's palace—known properly as the Château de Versailles—transformed the simple hunting lodge that had previously existed on the spot into a spectacularly vast edifice that housed the entire royal court. The Château possessed well over a half million square feet of floor

---

[5]   Friedrich II of Prussia built the palace at Potsdam, just outside Berlin; Piotr I of Russia built Peterhof; the Habsburgs in Austria established the palace of Schönbrunn, just outside Vienna.

The Château De Versailles With 2,300 rooms, a roughly equal number of ornate windows, and over 600,000 square feet (55,000 square meters) of floor space, the Château de Versailles is by far the grandest public structure built in the Age of Absolutism. Intended to showcase royal splendor and the French culture that the king personified, every bit of material used to build, furnish, and decorate Versailles was produced in France. In this painting (1668) one can see the extensive park and gardens as well as the château itself.

space (55,000 square meters) divided among seven hundred rooms, most of them magnificent. Thousands of paintings, drawings, sculptures, tapestries, and precious objects lined the walls and adorned every room. The effect on a first-time visitor is overwhelming—not so much for its beauty (although it is indeed beautiful) as for the audacity of its grandeur.

Louis's decision to build a new home for his court was self-indulgent but with a purpose. By creating a single space for the royal government and by demanding the constant attendance of France's aristocrats, Louis was able to keep an eye on the nobles and keep them under his sway. Louis never forgot that his reign began with an aristocratic rebellion against him. Called the **Fronde**, this rebellion (1648–1653) had not targeted Louis personally; the king was only ten years old when the trouble began.[6] Instead, the Fronde was a reaction against the royal finance minister Cardinal Jules Mazarin (1602–1661), the successor to Cardinal Richelieu, who had imposed a tax on judicial officials and sought to curtail

---

[6] *Fronde* is the French word for slingshot—a favorite weapon of the Paris rebels, who used them to shatter the upper windows of the royal buildings.

a number of aristocratic privileges. It took five years to quell the rebellion, and Louis resolved to keep a permanent eye on the nobles by requiring their presence under his own ornate new roof. To make his job easier, he had the palace lined with secret passages, one-way mirrors, and peepholes; and he maintained a large private staff to spy on the goings-on in every room. The Duc de Saint-Simon (1675–1755), whose keen-eyed *Memoirs* provides an irreplaceable view of life at court, summarized the key role of Versailles as a means of controlling the nobles:

> [Louis] loved splendor, grandeur, and opulence in everything and inspired similar tastes in everyone in his court, even to the point where the surest way to earn a royal favor—perhaps the honor of receiving a word from him—was to spend extravagantly on something like a horse and carriage. . . . There was a sly political purpose in this, for by making conspicuously expensive habits the fashion at court (even making them a sort of requirement for people of a certain rank) he forced the members of his court to live beyond their means, which inevitably brought them to depend on royal favors in order to maintain themselves. But this [habit of indebtedness] turned out to be a plague that gradually infected the entire country, for in no time at all it spread to Paris, then to the army, and finally to the provinces, and now a man of any social standing at all is judged solely by the costliness of his daily habits and the extravagance of his luxuries. Such foolhardiness—the result of vanity and ostentation— has brought vast worry in its wake and threatens to result in nothing short of a national disaster and utter collapse.

This was prescient: the story of the French economy in the 18th century is one of constant and compounded indebtedness, a fiscal rot of staggering proportions that ultimately brought down the entire regime. For the present, however, the spending continued at an astonishing pace.

It is doubtful that Saint-Simon ever spoke so boldly to the king himself about the danger. A far braver man was François Fénelon (1651–1715), a Catholic priest appointed in 1689 as tutor to Louis XIV's grandson. As part of his teaching Fénelon composed a novel in 1694, *The Adventures of Telemachus*, which describes the travels and education of the son of the famed Greek king Odysseus. The novel mounts a stinging attack on the ideas of divine-right monarchy and absolutism. "Good kings are quite rare," it says at one point; "in fact, the majority of them are rather poor." It also denounces as evil the pursuit of glory through war and the sickening love of luxury. Fénelon's book became hugely popular across Europe and was translated into a half dozen languages. (It also provided the plot for Mozart's 1781 opera *Idomeneo*.)

Louis XIV hated it but recognized the good effect Fénelon's tutoring had on his grandson, a famously spoiled brat. He was brave enough to speak out in a 1694 letter to the king:

> Sire, for thirty years now Your ministers have broken every ancient law of this state, in order to increase Your power. They have infinitely increased both Your income and Your expenses, but in the process have impoverished all of France and have made Your name hated—all for the sake of the luxury of Your court. For the last twenty years these same ministers have turned France into an intolerable burden to her neighbors through bloody war. Wanting nothing but slaves, we now have no allies. And in the meantime, Your people are starving and rebellion is growing. You are thus left with only two choices: either to let the rebellion spread, or to resort to massacring the very people whom You have driven into desperation.

In 1696 Fénelon was appointed archbishop of Cambrai, but the following year was relieved of his position as tutor.

MERCANTILISM AND ABSOLUTISM

Supporting the absolutist regimes was a varied set of economic policies known collectively as **mercantilism**. For about 250 years, from roughly 1500 to 1750, this was the prevailing model for understanding and managing the economic life of northern Europe: England, France, and the Netherlands were the chief centers of mercantilist thinking, with Austria, Germany, Spain, and Sweden comprising a second tier. The Mediterranean economy also contained mercantilist elements but was less dominated by them overall. Mercantilism, in general, defined economic wealth as tangible assets: the money in circulation, land and mineral resources, the available precious metals, the aggregate of physical goods that can be produced from nature's resources. Global wealth therefore is static. Since the Earth is not increasing in size, the amount of economically valuable material is therefore fixed, and the aim of commerce is thus to maximize the amount of valuable stuff—actual specie and goods—in one's possession. The two most efficient means of doing so are to increase the amount of bullion in one's possession, either through mining precious metals or by appropriating the bullion of others, and to export more commercial goods than one imports.[7] But either way,

---

[7] In a closed system, one becomes richer than one's rivals by gathering more of the available "pieces" of wealth; the number of "pieces" in the system, however, remains constant.

Mercantilist Center The town of Bristol was founded shortly before the Norman Conquest of 1066 and for a while was important chiefly at the launching place for English armies on their way to Ireland. The discovery of the New World raised its significance enormously, and by the 17th century Bristol was the second-largest and busiest port in the kingdom. Between 1600 and 1750 Bristol was the principal site from which English slave-traders shipped African slaves to the New World. This painting, ca. 1760, shows the busy quay, where goods were loaded and unloaded.

the world economy is a "zero-sum game"—meaning that growth is reduced to mere hoarding. Wealth is thus a matter of distribution rather than creation.

Mercantilism thus champions **protectionism**—the blocking of imports by tariff barriers, usually, and, if necessary, by law. The system, since it was based on the idea of artificially manipulating the distribution of wealth, also welcomed the awarding of monopolies by government (in return for sizeable bribes and licensing fees), the fixing of prices and wages, the blocking of competition, and the imposition of high domestic taxes. In a world of finite wealth, the reasoning went, assets must be concentrated in a small number of hands. Only this could enable the grand expenditures such as those needed to defend the realm, administer the government,

> Mercantilism, in other words, did not aim at the prosperity of an entire people, nor did it think that possible to achieve. Rather, its purpose was to concentrate wealth among as few individuals as possible.

and maintain social order. Mercantilism, in other words, did not aim at the prosperity of an entire people, nor did it think that possible to achieve. Rather, its purpose was to concentrate wealth among as few individuals as possible. The absolutist regimes perfected their policies over the 17th and 18th centuries—and in the process drove their own subjects into the direst poverty. (It is worth pointing out, by way of illustration, that the economic policies of China in the late 20th and early 21st centuries include many mercantilist elements.)

The classic statement in defense of mercantilism came from Thomas Mun (1571–1641), an English merchant and member of the board of directors of the English East India Company. He wrote *England's Treasure by Foreign Trade* in 1630, although it was not published until 1664. In it he argues, among other things, for the forced lowering of domestic wages. If the people of England cannot afford to purchase food, clothing, and other consumer goods, he points out, then the government will have larger amounts of those commodities available for export, which brings more money into the royal purse.

Modern thinking commonly regards mercantilism as nonsense, which raises the question of whether people in the early modern era were economic idiots. In reality they were far from it. Given the social bias against commerce as a "common" activity, Europe's nobility and most of its intelligentsia gave little thought to how economies function. The very idea of an economy as an existing, organic system remained a foreign concept. Money, goods, land, and raw resources were things one could put in one's hand, feel the heft of, and know to be real. An economy, on the other hand, is an abstraction, an invisible system of interactions that obeys supposedly fixed laws. Producing, selling, and consuming goods are aspects of human agency, but the notion of "an economy" or "a market" as an autonomous thing that determines human action requires a conceptual leap. And few people in early modern Europe were capable of or interested in making such a leap. Merchants understood that a scarcity of goods—as when, for example, a drought results in decreased crop yields—meant that they could charge a higher price. However, they interpreted this not as a scientific "law of the market" but simply as a scenario they could exploit. When 16th-century Spain imported tons of gold bullion taken from the New World, the country expected to acquire enormous wealth. What it got instead was an inflationary spiral unlike anything Europe had ever seen, the collapse of the currency, and the ruin of vast stretches of the peninsula. Compounding the problem, the Spanish rulers spent this money on a colossal scale—on palaces, museums, churches, artwork, and the army—rather than investing it in wealth-generating industry.[8] But no one at the time, in Spain or elsewhere, would have agreed that there was any connection. *That*, they would

---

[8]   Spain did not fully recover as an economic power until the late 20th century.

have insisted, makes as little sense as asserting that eating of massive amounts of food could result in a dramatic loss of weight.

MERCANTILISM AND POVERTY

Mercantilism served two specific purposes. First, it generated impressive amounts of revenue for the leading merchants and financiers of the age, who benefited from monopolies, protectionist policies that banned foreign competition, and the relative decline of domestic markets—thanks to the poverty of the bulk of the population. With captive markets in overseas colonies, too, high prices could be demanded with impunity. Second, mercantilism produced enormous returns for the governments, which made money from bribes and monopoly licenses, high tariffs on imported goods, onerous taxation of the common people, and investment in the commercial activities of the leading mercantile firms. If mercantilism did not create prosperity for the nation, that was never its aim. All that mattered was the preservation of the state and the institutions it controlled.

Mercantilism had been at work in France and Spain since the 1530s, in England since the reign of Elizabeth I, and in most of the rest of Europe after 1648. Its effects were stark. In contrast to the baroque splendor of aristocratic palaces and ornate churches was the grinding, humiliating poverty of the peasantry, village laborers, and local artisans and craftsmen. A French official's report on conditions among the rural populace of Normandy in 1651 paints a brutal picture:

> The most consistent food source here are the rats that the people hunt, so desperately hungry are they. They also eat plant roots that the farm animals will not touch. One can scarcely find words adequate to describing the horrors one sees everywhere. . . . This report, in fact, actually understates those horrors, rather than, as one might think, exaggerates them, for it describes only the tiniest fraction of the suffering in this district, suffering so dire that only those who have actually seen it can understand its scope. Hardly a single day passes in which at least two hundred people do not die. . . . I attest to having personally seen whole herds of people—men and women, that is, not cattle—wandering the fields between Rheims and Rethel, rooting in the dirt like pigs, and finding nothing edible, but only rotting fibers (and even these are only plentiful enough to feed half the herd), they collapse in exhaustion and have no strength left to continue searching for food. . . . The rest survive on a

Peasant Life   A small Dutch farm family prays before sharing
a single bowl of gruel. Note the absence of a table, but the
presence of an open fireplace—a common site of accidents,
especially involving infants. Two ladders serve as a staircase
leading up to the sleeping quarters. Though small, the home
is perfectly clean and well-ordered. The emphasis in this
engraving (1653) is not on the harshness of peasant life but the
spirit of simplicity and piety among the hardworking poor.

substitute for bread that does not deserve the name, made as it is from a
mixture of chopped straw and dirt.

As dire as these conditions were, they were an improvement from the last years
of the Religious Wars, for the simple reason that the people no longer had to
avoid marauding bands of desperate soldiers from nearly every nation in Europe.
Goethe's description of people "trapped between the land and the aristocracy as
between an anvil and a hammer" takes on new vividness.

The question must be asked: Given such unspeakable suffering, why did
people accept absolutist government—or at least not actively oppose it? The only
answer is that things were even worse during the Religious Wars. One can hardly
exaggerate the bloody, murderous horror that plagued Europe before 1648.

DOMESTICATING DYNAMISM: REGULATING CULTURE

European culture, too, was subject to a form of absolutism, but not simply as an extension of royal power. The whole of society became obsessed with rule making and breaking. Rules of etiquette, standards of spelling and usage, norms for musical composition and visual art, academic curricula, domestic architecture, even the subtle social demands of fashion—all these multiplied under the pressure to conform. All came to express explicit standards of value, certainty, decorum, and taste. Such standards have existed in every age, but they have seldom dominated life as they did in Old Regime Europe.

> The whole of society became obsessed with rule making and breaking. Rules of etiquette, standards of spelling and usage, norms for musical composition and visual art, academic curricula, domestic architecture, even the subtle social demands of fashion—all these multiplied under the pressure to conform.

The baroque style, which had emerged with the Catholic Counter-Reformation, had emphasized dynamic energy and raw emotional power. Roughly half the paintings by Peter Paul Rubens (1577–1640) glorify Catholic themes; most of the rest portray the magnificence of Europe's royals and high aristocrats. In music, the Baroque zenith was reached by the father-son team of Alessandro (1660–1725) and Domenico Scarlatti (1685–1757) and Antonio Vivaldi (1678–1741). Most music lovers today rank Johann Sebastian Bach (1686–1750) as the greatest baroque composer.[9]

Bach insisted that "all music should be for God" (*"Alle Musik soll für Gott sein"*). But as the style spread from Italy and Spain to the rest of Europe, its focus shifted to glorifying the monarchies. What else stood between the people and Hobbesian chaos? The courts slowly replaced the dynamism of the baroque with the controlled formal tone of **classicism**. In the visual arts this was the age of Nicolas Poussin (1594–1665) and Charles Le Brun (1619–1691); in theatre, of Pedro Calderón de la Barca (1600–1681), Pierre Corneille (1606–1684), and Jean Racine (1639–1699); in literature, of John Milton (1608–1674) and John Dryden (1631–1700). The strictures of formal classicism eased in the 18th century, but the insistence on proper composition, content, and form continued.

The Absolutist Age also saw the first comprehensive dictionaries of the European languages. Bilingual dictionaries, the sort to help English speakers learn French, or vice versa, had existed since the invention of the printing press. But dictionaries as normative reference works for native speakers and writers were another matter altogether. Nearly two dozen hastily produced English

---

[9]   In his own time, however, Bach was considered just a good provincial musician (especially as an organist). A figure of *real* stature would have composed operas, which Bach refused to do.

dictionaries had been published between 1550 and 1750, in a rush to capitalize on the dramatic spread of literacy made possible by print. Only with Samuel Johnson (1709–1784), however, was the extensive, critical, and prescriptive *Dictionary of the English Language* (1755) finally published.

Johnson's nine-year labor was a watershed event. A dictionary, after all, is a rulebook, one that asserts, for example, that the word *chair* is spelled C-H-A-I-R and in no other way—not chaar, chaire, chayr, chare, chaere, char, or any other phonetic estimation. (To date, for example, seven authentic signatures of William Shakespeare's have been found, and he spells his name differently each time.) It sets meanings and defines usage; it standardizes and regulates syntax.[10] Johnson's *Dictionary* succeeded where earlier efforts had failed, and it remained authoritative until the publication of the complete *Oxford English Dictionary* in 1928. In France, a team of scholars produced the *Dictionnaire de l'Académie française* in 1698. The *Vocabolario degli Accademici della Crusca* had appeared in Italy even earlier, in 1612, and the *Diccionario de la lengua española* arrived in 1780. The German language, by contrast, did not acquire a comparable dictionary until the Grimm brothers (of fairy-tale fame) began to compile their *Deutsches Wörterbuch* in 1838.

Ecstatic Divine Love   Gian Lorenzo Bernini (1598–1680) carved this famous statue of Saint Theresa of Avila in 1645. Theresa was a Carmelite nun whose mystical revelations formed the backbone of her books of confessional and theological writings. Her best-known books are *The Way to Perfection, The Inner Castle,* and her absorbing autobiography. In this last book (actually the first one she wrote) she describes one of her visions, this one of a heavenly angel: "In his hand I saw a long spear of gold, from the point of which a small flame showed. It was as though he thrust it repeatedly into my heart, piercing my innermost parts; and whenever he pulled the spear out it was as though he drew my heart out as well, leaving me all on fire with love for God. The pain was so great it made me moan—and yet this great pain was so sweet that I wanted it never to end."

---

[10]   Prior to Johnson, the spelling of English words was left to each writer's personal preference. So long as the reader could tell what word the writer meant, it meant little how the word used was spelled.

DECENCY AND MODESTY

If language needed standardization and control, so much more did daily behavior. Norms of social behavior had long been determined by local custom. Books of etiquette date back to the Middle Ages, when treatises on "courtesie" were required reading for the higher nobility of the late 12th and 13th centuries. Generalized works of etiquette for the urban classes, however, became increasingly common in post-Westphalia Europe. Richard Strathwaite (1588–1673) published a trilogy of guides—*The English Gentleman, The English Gentlewoman,* and *Description of a Good Wife*—that established norms of behavior that lasted a hundred years; Eleazar Moody's *School of Good Manners* (1715) was an enormously popular guide for parents who wanted to raise well-behaved children. In Italy, Baldassare Castiglione's *Il libro del cortegiano* (1528; in English as *The Book of the Courtier* in 1561) had established the norms for proper comportment in the Renaissance, but was overtaken in the 17th and 18th centuries by texts aimed at bourgeois society.

Table Knife and Fork   Most Europeans had traditionally used only knives and spoons at table. Forks, though known since Roman times, were used only as kitchen tools, if at all. Renaissance Italy reintroduced the use of table forks, although it is unclear whether this resulted from the desire to emulate the Romans or to limit one's exposure to disease—since people commonly carried their own knives and forks with them in a box. As a rule, the farther north and west from Italy, the slower the adoption of the fork. In Germany and England especially, forks were long considered effeminate affectations; and the people of the American colonies did not embrace them until the late 18th century. The knife and fork shown here were made in Germany in the 17th century.

This is the society lampooned in the great comedy *The Middle-Class Gentleman* (*Le bourgeois gentilhomme,* 1670) by Molière (the pen name of Jean-Baptiste Poquelin [1622–1673]), whose very title is a part of the joke. A bourgeois commoner is attempting to behave with noble manners, as if one can become civilized by mimicking polite behavior. But a laughing matter in 1670 became serious business a generation later, as books on table etiquette, polite conversation, proper dress and comportment, and the rearing of well-behaved children grew in popularity. A French guide from 1729 helped explain the proper use of a new invention—the napkin:[11]

---

11   Until the early 18th century, polite diners used the edges of the tablecloth to cover their laps and wipe their hands.

When at table one ought always to use a napkin, plate, knife, spoon, and fork; in fact it is now considered to be utterly improper to be without any one of these.

The proper thing is to wait until the highest-ranking dinner guest unfolds his napkin before unfolding one's own, but if everyone at table is a social equal, they should all unfold their napkins at the same time and without ceremony.

It is poor manners to use the napkin to wipe one's face, and even poorer manners to wipe one's teeth; but the grossest behavior of all is to use the napkin to blow one's nose.

This text from 1729 signals change in its very title: *La Salle: Les règles de la bienséance et de la civilité chrétienne* ("The Room: The Rules of Propriety and of Christian Civility"). And as for bodily comportment:

Decency and modesty demand that one keeps covered all the parts of the body, except the head and hands, when in society. Moreover, one should take every care never to touch with one's bare hand any part of the body that must remain properly covered; if one absolutely must do so, it must be done with the greatest discretion. A polite person simply must become accustomed to suffering small discomforts without twisting, rubbing, or scratching. . . .

When one needs to urinate, one should always withdraw to a private place—for it is permissible to perform natural functions (and this is true even for children) so long as one does it where one is not seen. It is nevertheless altogether impolite to emit wind from one's body—either from below or above—even if it is done without any sound.

Contrast an English guide from 1619, written in verse:

Let not your privy members be
laid open to be viewed;
it is most shameful and abhorr'd,
detestable and rude.

Retain not urine, nor the wind
which do thy body vex;
so [long as] it be done in secrecy,
let that not thee perplex.

The Teatro San Carlo in Naples   Built in 1737, then rebuilt after a fire in 1816, this is the oldest continuously used opera house in Europe. The original upholstery was blue; the red was used after a fire. Seen at the center here is the royal box, where members of the Bourbon dynasty sat. It was designed specifically for the staging of operas, with the auditorium built in a U-shape and tiered; an orchestra pit, so as not to overwhelm the singers; and all the backstage areas and equipment as needed for any theatrical production. Opera houses were expensive, and most of those built in the 17th and 18th centuries resulted from the patronage of royals and high aristocrats. By maintaining the system of tiered balconies as the reserve of the upper classes, the seats of the main floor could be opened to non-nobles. Thus opera, by its very popularity, helped to maintain the social system by embodying the privileged hierarchy while allowing the commoners to share in the delight made possible by aristocratic largesse.

Guidebooks laid out rules for conversation, letter writing, dress, the issuing of invitations, and behavior at occasions such as weddings, funerals, balls, and theaters.

Regulation reigned in other areas of life too. In music, most of the major compositional forms moved toward formal definition: fugues and sonatas initially, and eventually concertos and symphonies. Every opera had to have its text (libretto) approved by state censors before it could be staged, to make sure the plot carried no subversive messages. Just as significantly, popular pressure gradually demanded further norms in opera—such as the strict separation of comedy (opera buffa) and tragic opera (opera seria), the use of plots from classical drama or from French neoclassical theater, and the Italian language.[12]

---

12   Women were forbidden to take the stage in regular theater productions. Opera, however, offered them the chance to perform alongside men.

The period from 1680 to 1740 also saw the peak in popularity of castrati in the leading male roles. Castration before puberty prevented the natural deepening of the male voice, enabling the singer to sustain a high and flexible musical register. Moreover, the loss of testosterone production resulted in the weakening of the joints—which caused castrati to develop exceptionally long limbs and ribs. Their increased chest capacity allowed them extraordinary lung power, which aided their projection. So great was the demand for castrati and so lucrative were the potential rewards they could win that as many as three thousand young singers across Europe submitted to the operation annually during this peak period.

THE BIRTH OF PRIVATE LIFE

Aspects of domestic, even private, life became subject to innovative strictures, too. Societies were brought up on the idea of maintaining order at all costs. For most urban dwellers, living quarters by long tradition had been single open-space rooms above the workshop, tavern, or storefront in which they worked. The details of private life were conducted communally. Over the 17th and 18th centuries, however, domestic architecture took on interior walls, even among those with modest incomes. The activities of daily life—sleeping, cooking and eating, tending to hygiene, and socializing—were to be performed in discrete rooms. It is no accident that the word *privacy* was coined in the 17th century; before then, neither the word nor the concept existed. Even the human body became subject to a kind of control. Common people throughout the Middle Ages and Renaissance had worn simple garments that sheathed the body, whereas the 17th and 18th centuries saw the general introduction of underwear of various types. Henceforth, everyday dress for both men and women involved undergarments—not just to provide warmth but to support and control the body's movement. Cultural regulation like this was not imposed by government but arose naturally.

> Henceforth, everyday dress for both men and women involved undergarments—not just to provide warmth but to support and control the body's movement. Cultural regulation like this was not imposed by government but arose naturally.

As standards of expected behavior rose, manners improved, and aesthetic values became defined and codified. In turn, attitudes toward those who failed to observe the new niceties grew harsher. Aristocratic culture had always prided itself on the chasm that separated it from the dirty masses, but a sense of cultural elitism began to emerge among bourgeois Europeans at this time as well. As a result, efforts spread to instill better behavior among the lower orders, some of them altruistic, others not. Centuries-old peasant entertainments like carnivals (rural festivals that usually preceded Lent) were discouraged from the pulpit and judicial bench alike.

A Clean, Well-lit Place   The interior of a well-to-do burgher's house in 17th-century Holland. The Dutch prided themselves on their sense of order and balance. The family that lived here was obviously wealthy but not ostentatious. The woman in the front room plays a harpsichord; to the left of the door is a four-posted bed. Each room opens onto the other, and each is filled with light.

English Puritan ministers railed against the evils of taverns, dances, country fairs, and popular folk songs. Protestant ministers in Germany struggled to stamp out rural irregularities in communal worship.

In the cities, the urban poor were no longer objects of pity and almsgiving but were denounced in sermons, speeches, broadsides, and newspapers (another invention of the age) as lazy, deceitful, uncouth, and potentially dangerous. New institutions arose to deal with them: poor houses, hospitals (hospices, that is), and reformatories. These institutions performed the valuable services of removing the unsightly destitute from polite society, and then either rehabilitating them (if possible) by teaching them a craft or effectively imprisoning them. In 1676 Louis XIV went so far as to order every city in France to build and maintain a hospital for warehousing the worst off of the urban poor.

In England, people whose behavior violated basic norms but who had not broken the law frequently ended up in Bedlam. Although the hospital dates back to the 13th century, in 1675 it became the first asylum for the mentally ill.[13] The

---

[13]   In 1725 Bedlam was divided into separate wings for those considered curable ("patients") and incurable ("lunatics").

idea caught on, and asylums soon dotted the European landscape. So too did prisons. Prior to the 18th century, jails or dungeons were simply holding areas for those waiting until judicial punishment (execution, lashing, maiming, or a simple fine) was carried out. But after 1700 state after state preferred to remove criminals (in noncapital cases, at least) from society altogether, and lengthy incarceration became the punishment of choice. Those whose presence offended polite society became isolated, institutionalized, and removed from the scene.

THE ENGLISH EXCEPTION

England rose to the top tier of European nations in the second half of the 16th century. When Elizabeth I died in 1603, however, a constitutional crisis threatened to undo the internal stability of the realm and endangered England's position in the international economy. In response, the new Stuart dynasty asserted greater absolutism, but it ended in civil war.

Elizabeth, of course, had never married, and so the Tudor dynasty ended. After some intrigue, the throne passed to James Stuart, the great-grandson of Henry VIII's sister. This marked the beginning of the trouble-plagued Stuart dynasty, which lasted, with interruptions, until 1714. Being Scottish, James I (r. 1603–1625) faced rude resistance from the start despite the legitimacy of his succession.[14] More than ethnic prejudice was at work in this, however, for James was a passionate advocate of royal absolutism. Before coming to power in England he had published a tendentious book called *The True Law of Free Monarchies* (1598), in which he argues that since kingship existed "before any estates or ranks of men . . . [and] before any parliaments were held or laws made," it is therefore unnatural for a king's power to be checked in any way. The argument is as weak as James's stubbornness was strong, and the struggle to balance royal ambitions and Parliamentary rights ultimately characterized the history of the entire Stuart dynasty.

James restated his position in a speech to the English Parliament in 1610:

> The state of monarchy is the supremest thing upon earth, for kings are not only God's lieutenants upon earth and sit upon God's throne, but even by God himself they are called gods. There be three principal [comparisons] that illustrate the state of monarchy: one taken out of the word of God, and the two other out of the grounds of policy and philosophy. In the Scriptures kings are called gods, and so their power after a certain relation compared to the Divine power. Kings are also compared to fathers of families; for a

---

[14]   James, who ruled as James VI in Scotland (r. 1567–1603), was the first to style himself the king of "Great Britain."

king is truly *parens patriae*, the politic father of his people. And lastly, kings are compared to the head of this microcosm of the body of man. . . . I conclude then this point touching the power of kings with this axiom of divinity, that as to dispute what God may do is blasphemy . . . so is it sedition in subjects to dispute what a king may do in the height of his power.

Colossally and ideologically vain, James I also had a near-pathological fear of assassination.[15] His childhood in Scotland had been filled with political deceits, palace intrigues, kidnappings, and numerous murder plots. The horror of his early years made him distrustful of those around him, and once in power in Edinburgh and London he resolved that institutions like parliaments, courts, and churches were mere service organizations of the monarchy rather than sharers of power. Although he had been brought up as a Catholic, James found that Anglicanism suited his self-regard, for it identified the king as undisputed head of the church. He embraced the faith and endorsed the Act of Supremacy, which asserted that only an avowed Anglican could ever sit on the throne in England. His greatest achievement was his support for a new English translation of the Scriptures intended specifically for his newly adopted church—the so-called **King James Bible**, known officially as the Authorized Version.

The seldom-read dedication to the King James Bible provides a good example of absolutist ideology. It begins:

Great and manifold were the blessings, most dread Sovereign, which Almighty God, the Father of all mercies, bestowed upon us the people of England, when first he sent Your Majesty's Royal Person to rule and reign over us. For whereas it was the expectation of many who wished not well unto our Sion, that, upon the setting of that bright Occidental Star, Queen Elizabeth, of most happy memory some thick and palpable clouds of darkness would so have overshadowed this land, that men should have been in doubt which way they were to walk, and that it should hardly be known who was to direct the unsettled State; the appearance of Your Majesty, as of the Sun in his strength, instantly dispelled those supposed and surmised mists, and gave unto all that were well affected exceeding cause of comfort; especially when we beheld the Government established in Your Highness and Your hopeful Seed, by an undoubted Title; and this also accompanied with peace and tranquility at home and abroad.

---

[15] In childhood, James had seen more than one family member cut down. He regularly wore a heavy dagger-proof tunic under his royal garments.

But among all our joys, there was no one that more filled our hearts than the blessed continuance of the preaching of God's sacred Word among us, which is that inestimable treasure which excelleth all the riches of earth; because the fruit thereof extendeth itself, not only to the time spent in this transitory world, but directeth and disposeth men unto that eternal happiness which is above in heaven.

Then not to suffer this to fall to the ground, but rather to take it up, and to continue it in that state wherein the famous Predecessor of Your Highness did leave it; nay, to go forward with the confidence and resolution of a man, in maintaining the truth of Christ, and propagating it far and near, is that which hath so

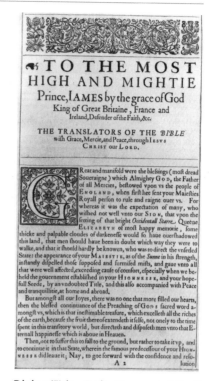

Divine Writ Dedication page of the first edition of the Authorized (King James) Version of the Bible (1611).

bound and firmly knit the hearts of all Your Majesty's loyal and religious people unto You, that Your very name is precious among them: their eye doth behold You with comfort, and they bless You in their hearts, as that sanctified Person, who, under God, is the immediate author of their true happiness. And this their contentment doth not diminish or decay, but every day increaseth and taketh strength, when they observe that the zeal of Your Majesty toward the house of God doth not slack or go backward, but is more and more kindled, manifesting itself abroad in the farthest parts of Christendom, by writing in defence of the truth, (which hath given such a blow unto that Man of Sin as will not be healed,) and every day at home, by religious and learned discourse, by frequenting the house of God, by hearing the Word preached, by cherishing the teachers thereof, by caring for the Church, as a most tender and loving nursing father.

James fervently believed in mercantilism and followed its tenets in order to escape financial dependency on the Parliament. Wanting to increase English power in North America, he established the colonies at Jamestown (1607) and

Plymouth (1620), in what would eventually become the states of Virginia and Massachusetts. He also tried, though unsuccessfully, to arrange a marriage between his son Charles and a Spanish princess. He awarded many monopolies and collected enormous licensing fees, which raised opposition from the gentry; but he compensated them by creating (and selling to the highest bidders—most of whom came from the gentry) an unprecedented number of new noble titles. The "baronetcy" was his signature invention, and he happily bestowed this honor on anyone who would pay his asking price of 10,000 pounds. Many purchasers came forward. When James first came to the English throne in 1603 the House of Lords had fifty-nine members; when he died in 1625 the House had more than twice that number. He also granted more than two thousand knighthoods.

CIVIL WAR AND RESTORATION

When Charles I (r. 1625–1649) became king, opposition to the Stuarts had grown to the point where Parliament openly demanded constitutional reforms. Charles had inherited his father's vanity and stubbornness, however, in addition to his titles, and had no intention of compromising royal prerogatives. Unfortunately for him, he also inherited England's involvement in the Thirty Years' War. Meeting commitments to numerous parties in that struggle placed ever-greater pressure on royal finances, but Parliament passed a Petition for Right (1628) that denied the crown additional taxes and restricted the king's judicial authority. The following year Charles summoned a new Parliament, immediately arrested nine of its leaders, and dissolved the assembly; no new Parliament met for eleven years, during which time Charles bullied new fees and levies from the provinces. By 1640 king and country were wholly estranged. When Parliament did convene again in that year, the legislators prepared a "Grand Remonstrance"—a lengthy list of formal complaints about royal abuses of authority. Charles's troops again stormed the Parliament, but were resisted. Civil war had begun.

The Parliamentary forces were disorganized at first but soon came under the leadership of Oliver Cromwell (1599–1658), a Puritan in religion and a member of the gentry by social status. Without much military experience, he nevertheless rose quickly through the officer ranks of the Parliamentary forces. He was one of the three or four most powerful figures on the scene when the army defeated Charles in battle and took him prisoner in 1645. Few people wanted to abolish the monarchy altogether, and most hoped to force the king to some sort of compromise. When news came that Charles was in secret negotiations with Royalist sympathizers to launch a Scottish invasion of England, however, patience was at an end. Parliament placed Charles on trial for treason in 1648, and when the tribunal returned a guilty verdict Cromwell was one of the signatories to the king's death warrant. Charles was beheaded on January 30, 1649.

But the people who had opposed the monarchy soon found that, having removed the king, they could not agree on what to replace him with. Dissension broke out almost immediately; after several tense weeks, Cromwell took over the government by general acclamation. For the next eleven years he governed the Commonwealth of England, Europe's most radical experiment to date in representative government. Despite his best efforts, Cromwell failed to put together an administration that could outlast him. When he died in 1658, the Commonwealth quickly fell apart, and Parliament summoned Charles I's exiled son, who had taken refuge in Holland, to return to England and restore the monarchy. Charles II (r. 1660–1685), a carefree hedonist by nature, agreed to certain limits on royal power and took the throne amid a general sense of celebration. After twenty years of government by dour Puritans, the people welcomed Charles's love of pleasure and laughter and his reopening of the theater houses.

The party was short-lived, however, since an outbreak of bubonic plague in 1665 and the Great Fire of London in 1666 destroyed much of the city and took tens of thousands of lives. Charles now adopted a more serious approach, although he never managed to keep his living expenses within the budget the Parliament had set for him. In 1672 he attempted to force through a royal declaration that removed all legal penalties from the practice of Roman Catholicism, but backed down when Parliament resisted. Doubts about Charles's own religious loyalty filled the rest of his years on the throne.

Charles had no legitimate heir, since his wife's pregnancies had all ended in miscarriages and stillbirths. (He had married a Portuguese princess, Catarina de Bragança, who was unpopular with the English on account of her Catholicism and her lasting inability to learn English.) And so the crown passed in 1685 to Charles's brother James II (r. 1685–1688), who was openly Roman Catholic and determined to introduce absolutism.[16] James's short reign was filled with dissension, since the Parliament refused to remove the legal strictures that limited Catholic rights. Even more worrisome was the new king's desire for a much larger standing royal army. England had traditionally never kept soldiers in uniform and on the public payroll during peacetime. James's proposal, moreover, appeared too much in line with the actions of the post-Westphalian monarchs across Europe and stirred the Parliament into dramatic action.

In 1688 a group of leading members of Parliament invited the Protestant ruler of Holland, Prince William of Orange, to invade their realm and depose

---

[16]   Charles II was received in the Roman Catholic Church on his deathbed. James II had formally converted to Catholicism while growing up on the Continent during the Commonwealth.

James. (William was married to James II's daughter Mary.) William agreed. James initially thought he could defeat the invaders but soon realized otherwise, and so he fled the scene. He was soon captured by William's men, who, with William's consent, allowed him to escape to France—where he lived out his days in the court of Louis XIV. Since the coup proceeded without significant violence (James's soldiers deserted him en masse), it is known as the **Glorious Revolution**. Without shedding a drop of blood, England had staged a successful revolution, brought down an unpopular monarch, and brought to power a popular royal couple dedicated to Protestantism and constitutional rule.

OTTOMAN MIGHT AND ISLAMIC ABSOLUTISM

The Islamic world in the 17th and 18th centuries consisted of three empires that were also de facto absolutist states, although their regimes lacked the philosophical underpinnings found in Europe: the Ottoman Empire, Safavid Iran, and Mughal India (see Map 14.2). Language and culture distinguished them as much as political regimes. The Ottomans controlled the Arabic-speaking nations, the

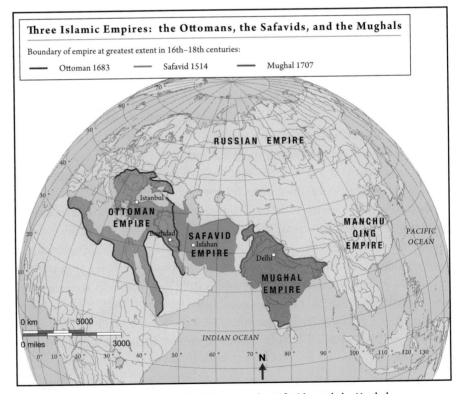

MAP 14.2   Three Islamic Empires: the Ottomans, the Safavids, and the Mughals

Safavids governed the Persian speakers, and the Mughal dynasty ruled over the numerous language groups of the vast Indian subcontinent. Important religious distinctions existed as well, with Sunni Islam dominating among the Arab peoples and Shi'ite Islam practiced by the bulk of Persian speakers. Though overwhelmingly Muslim, none of these states was religiously monolithic, for large Christian and Jewish populations continued to reside in them.

Ottoman military encroachments on Europe had continued well into the 17th century, and at least three times (1529, 1532, and 1683) their armies had advanced as far as Vienna. According to one tradition, the battle of 1683 was followed by a citywide celebration, for which the Viennese bakers' guild developed a new pastry—the croissant. This supposedly mocked the Islamic crescent that appeared on the Turkish army's banners. The powerful Ottoman forces were symbolically reduced to puff pastries.

After 1683 the Turks were put on the defensive for the first time in their history, a position exacerbated by the ascendancy of European merchant fleets in the Indian Ocean. Since they had previously lost control of the eastern Mediterranean at the battle of Lepanto in 1571, the new setbacks occasioned two new developments for the Turks. First, they gradually relinquished control over the furthest provinces of their empire—Morocco and Algeria, along the North African coast, which henceforth became independent states. To resist Spanish dominance in the western Mediterranean, these new states encouraged the "Barbary pirates" to attack ships on either side of the Gibraltarian Strait. Second, they delegated more power to provincial governors, with a system of tax farming that assigned local fiscal control to leading families. These steps were not, however, a complete capitulation of authority. Turkish autocracy had always differed from European absolutism in a fundamental way. Since the 15th century the monopoly of power was held by the dynastic house of Osman rather than by any specific individual. The sultan in Istanbul, as leader of the royal family, held primacy of place over his relatives, but power was rightfully held by every representative of Osman's line. The empire's system of government was therefore an oligarchical absolutism, but was no less absolutist for that.

Like that of its Western contemporaries, Ottoman absolutism was based on military might. The most important component of the army was the large corps of **Janissaries**, standing infantry units that resembled the military-religious orders of the Christian Middle Ages in their rigorous discipline, austerity, and spiritual vows. These "new soldiers" (the literal meaning of the Turkish word *yeniçeri*) were formed of Christian children from the Balkans and the Caucasus who were forced into military service and converted to Islam—just as had been the practice centuries before with the Mamluk slave-soldiers. They were sworn to celibacy during their years in the army, granted pensions and the right to marry upon retirement, and accorded exceptionally high social status. By the 17th century civil government was largely dominated by former Janissaries. At that time too the traditional practice of drafting Christian children into the corps (called *devşirme*) was abolished, as ethnically Turkish families sought to place their own children in the corps, in hopes of social advancement. Given the relative decrease in their military activity after 1683, the Janissaries were increasingly used (again like their European counterparts) as domestic police forces. In this role they maintained order, quelled revolts, and represented the ever-watchful eye of the sultan and his family.

SAFAVID PLEASURES

The Safavid dynasty in Iran had been established in 1501. It had established Shi'ism as the state religion and reasserted the Persian identity of the nation, after the Abbasid, Mongol, and Tatar interludes. The Safavids had emerged from a heterodox Sufi order and regarded themselves as either the earthly representatives of the Shi'i Hidden **Imam** or as the Hidden Imam himself. Given their religious origins, they were not likely to recognize any checks on their power. To be prudent, they complemented the religious basis of their claims to absolute authority by relying on the unwavering support of a large and potent army. Most of their army was composed of regular infantry units that served only as needed. More significant for maintaining the regime was a unique network of militant units known collectively as the **Qizilbash**. These companies—identifiable by the distinctive red-topped headpieces they wore (and from which they take their name)—regarded the Safavid ruler as divine. So great was their zeal that the Qizilbash customarily went into battle without any type of defensive armor. They were convinced that Allah and their Safavid lord's blessing would protect them from harm.[17]

Under the greatest Safavid **shah**, Abbas I [P] (r. 1587–1629), the Persians recaptured Baghdad and established commercial ties with both the British and Dutch East India Companies. Baghdad had never fully recovered from the devastation wreaked on it by the Mongols and may have held as few as fifty thousand people. An elaborate irrigation network had made the river valleys fertile since Sumerian times. Now that too lay in ruins, and most of Iraq had become a patchwork of scrubby pastoral zones loosely but violently controlled

---

[17] The Qizilbash still exist as a distinct religious community in Afghanistan, Azerbaijan, Iran, and Pakistan. The third president of modern-day Pakistan, Agha Yahya Khan (1969–1971), was Qizilbash.

by rival tribes. But Baghdad itself still mattered as a forward defensive position against a renewed Ottoman offensive. Friendly ties with the East India Companies were vital, since conflicts over control of the sea-lanes had shifted commercial routes away from the Persian Gulf and toward the Red Sea, on the other side of the Arabian Peninsula. The shift threatened to cost the Iranians considerable revenue.

Like the European monarchs, the shahs centralized their nation's wealth as much as they did its political power, and they spent as lavishly on themselves as did Louis XIV. Magnificent palaces, pleasure gardens, libraries, astronomical observatories, and public adornments filled the cities. They built mosques and madrasas by the dozen and restored older centers of worship that had been damaged during the Mongol and Tatar years. In Iraq the holy shrines in the cities of Karbala and Najaf—dear to the Shi'a—were rebuilt and again became important sites of pilgrimage. Abbas II [P] (r. 1642–1666) extended his realm northward into Afghanistan, taking the strategic city of Kandahar from the Mughals, and ruled over a thriving and peaceable realm.

But the later Safavids gave in to the pleasures of their lavish lifestyle and spent more time enjoying themselves than in governing, which led to the dynasty's downfall in 1736. Several decades of turmoil ensued until, in 1796, a new dynasty took over—the **Qajar**—which held absolute power over Iran until 1925. The founder of the new dynasty, Muhammad Khan Qajar [P] (r. 1794–1797), had been castrated as a young boy by a rival for leadership of the Qajar tribe, and the experience contributed to his predilection for cruelty and violence.[18] While Muhammad was assassinated in 1797, the Qajar shahs still focused resolutely on maintaining their political power and the wealth that made it possible. Yet they also distanced themselves from the theocratic ideology of the Safavids. Religious and legal authority thus devolved from the court-appointed officials (qadis) of earlier times to the caste of scholars in shariah law produced by the madrasas. In the case of Shi'ite Islam, these were predominately clerics who held the title of **mullah** ("guardian"). Leadership of the mullahs fell to a higher office still, the **ayatollah** ("sign from God," literally). By the end of the 18th century, Iran had evolved into a dual absolutist state: political and military might was monopolized by the secular state under the autocratic control of the shah, while religious authority remained the preserve of an elite corps of mullahs led by their clerical superiors, the ayatollahs.

---

[18]   Muhammad once ordered the blinding of twenty thousand men in a city that resisted his authority. He also had the Georgian city of Tbilisi burned to the ground and its entire Christian population put to death in 1795.

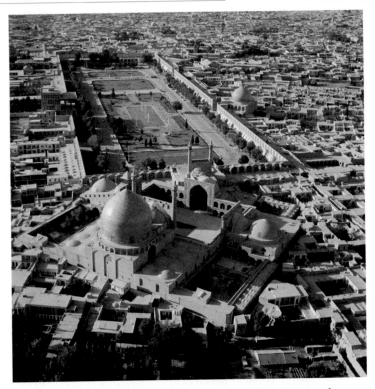

Isfahan Isfahan, in central Iran, was the capital of Safavid Persia from 1598 to 1795. Located on a high plain just east of the Zagros Mountains, its high elevation—comparable to that of Denver, in the United States—makes for chilly winters. It snows usually once a year. Summers, though, are hot. Shown in this image is the Shah Mosque, built in 1611 and considered one of the great masterpieces of Persian architecture. The large square behind it (the Naqsh-e Jahan Square) was built to serve a purpose analogous to that of the Château de Versailles—that is, it housed all the Safavid rulers' leading nobles and ministers of state, keeping them all in his direct sight. The mosque itself comes off the square at a unique angle, so that the towering entrance arch (called an *iwan*) and the central dome of the mosque can both be seen from everywhere in the square. Visible to the right of the great dome is a smaller, lower dome that marks the "winter mosque"—a smaller, warmer site for use during the cold winters.

THE END OF ORDER

Absolutist Europe and constitutional England formed the center of a vast network of international trade (see Map 14.3). It proved a hybrid of commercial, colonial, mercantilist, and capitalist practices. It also turned on new markets, sustained by slavery and domestic labor, and it added enough uncertainty on top of sheer human misery to bring an end to order.

World Trade Networks, ca. 1750

——— Trade networks

MAP 14.3   World Trade Networks, ca. 1750

Starting with Sweden in 1664, Europe's leading countries created royal or national banks that quickly developed systems of credit to finance manufacturing, commerce, and development. Strict mercantilism demanded the use of precious-metal coins, and aristocratic Europe's demand for Asian luxury goods never abated. Hence there was drainage of gold and silver from the West, which led to the introduction of paper money. Released from dependence on actual bullion, the new national banks dramatically increased loans, bonds, and other opportunities to invest. Credit now became available "on account," as promises to repay. National stock exchanges soon followed. Joint-stock companies like the British East India Company, the Dutch United East India Company, and the South Sea Company benefitted from the influx of investments. Their charters granted them monopolies on certain manufactures and trades, which allowed many to build impressive long-term returns. But involvement in this wealth creation was limited to those with excess capital, or wealth to invest, which was still a small percentage of the population. Mercantilist practices kept most laborers' wages at rock-bottom levels, and price controls and domestic taxes kept most skilled draftsmen from setting aside investment capital. As a result, most of the benefits of the international economy went to a small number of investors.

Investment was a new concept. The idea behind it—that capital itself, not people, can *do work*—is an abstraction that few fully understood. In purchasing stock, one is not buying a good or service, but rather the right to share in the profit generated by the future production and sale of those goods or services. Moreover, it takes money to produce goods and services, which usually means borrowing. In purchasing stock, one is also purchasing a share of a company's debt. Elaborate legal and financial arrangements can equally beguile and confuse those entering the market. The combination led frequently to speculative "bubbles" that ruined thousands of investors.

The most famous crash was the **South Sea Bubble** of 1720. The South Sea Company had been formed in London in 1711 in order to trade with the Spanish colonies in North America. To finance its activities, the company purchased England's national debt (then some 50 million pounds) in return for the right to exchange government bonds for shares in the company. Bondholders who despaired of the government's ability to redeem its bonds were thrilled by the possibility of New World riches and rushed to invest in the company. Soon a wave of speculation drove share prices to unprecedented heights, and the company encouraged the buying frenzy. It announced ever more spectacular ventures that it intended to undertake, like the manufacture of a (nonexistent) machine that could desalinate seawater—not to mention an ultrasecret "undertaking of great profit in due time to be revealed." Shares rose from 150 pounds each to over 1,000 pounds before the inevitable crash came and investors were wiped out.

THE SLAVE TRADE AND DOMESTIC SUBJUGATION

Among the most reliable investments were New World agriculture and the slave trade that enabled it. Until the 19th century, when settlers moved westward across the Great Plains, the New World did not produce food for export. Crops like potatoes, tomatoes, and corn (maize) were introduced into European farming and consequently were not shipped across the Atlantic. But sugar cane, cotton, and tobacco did not grow well in Europe. Being non-perishable, they could also be transported over-seas to generate enormous profits, but they were labor-intensive crops. The need for slaves thus grew, as did the demand for the crops. Throughout the 18th century be-tween seventy-five thousand and one hundred thousand African slaves were shipped across the Atlantic annually, until the slave trade was finally abolished (by France in 1793, England in 1807). Exact accounting is impossible, but somewhere around twelve million sub-Saharan Africans were brought to the New World in chains. The greatest number of them went to the Caribbean Islands, where they perished in hor-rifying numbers while working the sugarcane fields. Roughly a half million were sent to what eventually became the American South (see Map 14.4).

The profits generated by slave-produced New World agriculture were enor-mous. England's colonial profits rose from 10 million pounds to 40 million pounds between 1700 and 1776. France saw its revenues increase from 15 to 250 million livres in the same period. But the profits of the era were not distributed throughout society; they went to the highest social strata. Domestically, the rural economy was a ruin. As much as 20 percent of the European population lived in abject poverty.

The introduction of maize and potatoes alleviated famine in Europe, but also raised a new danger—alcoholism. Crops no longer needed for food could be con-verted into distilled spirits, which provided the poor with an escape from the drear-iness and hardship of their lives. Before, liquor distil-lation had primarily been a secret of monasteries, which used it to support themselves. By now, how-ever, the Protestant Reformation had advanced the knowledge of distillation across Europe. Gin became the hard liquor of choice among the poor, since it was so plentiful and cheap. By 1740, in England, gin production was nearly six times the nation's beer production—and all of it was drunk locally. The city of London alone had over six thousand gin shops, which sold cheap gin in bottles with rounded bot-toms. This meant that the bottles could not be set down without risking a spill, which in turn urged the buyer to drink the entire bottle. When the government in 1736 tried to reduce consumption by imposing a heavy tax on gin, crowds took to the street by the thousands until they won a repeal of the tax.[19]

Those poor not killed off by drink often succumbed to disease, since the physical conditions in which the poor lived were appalling. In the district of

---

[19]   As liquor became a favorite item for governments to tax, people operated their private stills at night, so that the smoke produced would not be seen. That is why homemade liquor is known as moonshine.

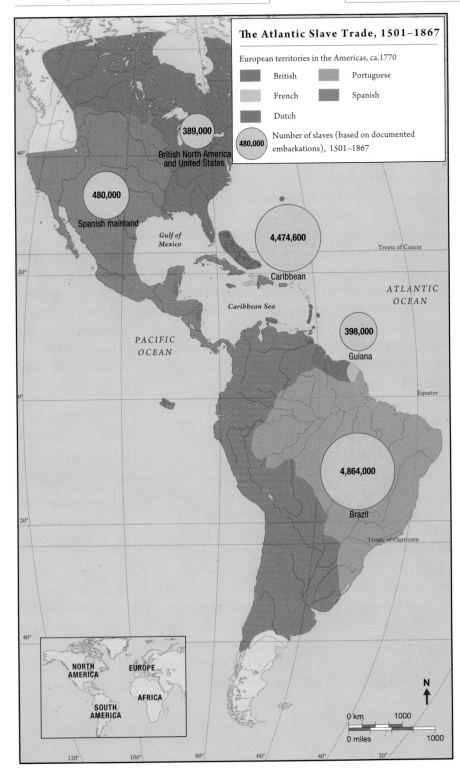

The Atlantic Slave Trade, 1501–1867

European territories in the Americas, ca.1770

- British
- French
- Dutch
- Portuguese
- Spanish

480,000 Number of slaves (based on documented embarkations), 1501–1867

389,000 — British North America and United States

480,000 — Spanish mainland

4,474,600 — Caribbean

398,000 — Guiana

4,864,000 — Brazil

MAP 14.4   The Atlantic Slave Trade, 1501–1867

Brittany, in northwestern France, dysentery killed one hundred thousand in a single year (1779). Until the middle of the 18th century, only one-half of all children born lived to the age of ten, and only one-half of the females who made it to their tenth birthday survived until their fortieth. Pregnancy and childbirth were a death sentence for most of them.

Rural women became wage earners through the **putting-out system** of textile manufacture, which became increasingly widespread in the 18th century. Also known as **cottage industry**, this system transferred cloth production from towns to the countryside. Women had woven cloth for their families for centuries, but in the Middle Ages textile production had shifted to cities, where it came under the control of guilds that regulated production and set prices. The putting-out system returned the center of cloth making to the rural economy, as new merchants sought to avoid the urban guilds and improve profits. These entrepreneurs typically purchased bulk quantities of raw wool and cotton, which they distributed throughout rural districts, often following routes claimed by competing entrepreneurs. Then they retraced their steps, collecting the finished cloth from women and taking it to urban markets. Rural families needed this work desperately. Wages remained low, but by assigning tasks like carding or spinning to their children, countrywomen

The Working Poor   An example of cottage industry. In an attic room, an Irish family beats flax in order to expose the fibers contained within; once cracked open, the flax fibers are then soaked in water, removed, and spun by hand into linen thread.

were able to produce more finished cloth. Once redeemed, it often made the difference between life and death.[20]

THE RETURN OF UNCERTAINTY

Given the miseries of the age, the passivity of the people in the face of the excesses of absolutist society is striking. Even the most dramatic political action, like England's civil war and revolution, was undertaken by bourgeois and aristocratic factions. The underclass had seldom known prosperity and independence—and so had grown not to expect them. Disruptions could still spark them into action, as the rebellions of the 11th and 14th centuries showed. Yet as long as absolutism kept the peace, as it generally did between 1648 and 1700, peasants complained of their lot but seldom rose up against it.

The reappearance of warfare after 1700 added just the uncertainty, insecurity, and violence needed to trigger mass unrest. First came the War of the Spanish Succession (1702–1713). When King Carlos II died without an heir in 1700, France's Louis XIV and Austria's Leopold I—each of whom was married to a sister of Carlos's—greedily eyed the Spanish crown and its enormous overseas empire. Carlos's will had named an heir to the throne: the grandson of his sister, the closest male relative available. But Louis hoped to win the crown for himself before the young man, Felipe V, took power. Louis consequently invaded Spain; he also invaded the Spanish Netherlands, which brought him into a parallel war with England. The English army at this time was led by a career soldier named John Churchill, who defeated Louis's forces and brought the islands of Gibraltar and Menorca, plus France's New World territories of Newfoundland and Hudson's Bay, into England's possession.[21]

A subsequent conflict was the War of the Austrian Succession (1740–1748), which arose when ambitious outsiders challenged Maria Theresa's succession to the throne. Several countries joined into this fray, less to advance claims of their own than to do anything they could to weaken the Habsburg family in general. But the largest and most devastating conflict of the age was the **Seven Years' War** (1756–1763), which pitted Great Britain, Brandenburg-Prussia, and some smaller German principalities against an alliance of Austria, France, Russia, Saxony, and Sweden. This last war arose, in general, in response to the changes made to the Westphalian "balance of power" by the earlier two conflicts.

---

[20] Cloth was the leading commodity in this system, but not the only one. Leatherwork, soap and candle making, and even metalwork formed part of the economy too.

[21] His achievement resulted in his being created the First Duke of Marlborough, which raised the Churchills to the status of one of England's greatest noble families.

The War of the Spanish Succession had its North America parallel in Queen Anne's War. The War of the Austrian Succession correlated with King George's War. The Seven Years' War in Europe was matched with the French and Indian War. Together, these wars produced horrendous casualties. The Seven Years' War alone resulted in over a million deaths. Roused by the vast ruin of the countryside, the disruption of trade, the wasted expenditure, and the callous abuse of the peasantry, popular voices began to rise up and to demand change. Bread riots, calls for peace, and complaints over endless governmental deficits arose across Europe. Demonstrations against the treatment of the many by the very, very few sprouted from Ireland to Austria and from Sicily to Sweden. Surely something could be done to restore order. As the century progressed, new voices arose in response, voices dedicated to the idea that change was possible, necessary, and within reach. The world was a dark place that needed new light and hope.

WHO, WHAT, WHERE

absolutism	mercantilism
Ancien Régime	mullah
ayatollah	Peace of Westphalia
Baroque Age	protectionism
classicism	putting-out system
cottage industry	Qajar
Directory	Qizilbash
Fronde	Seven Years' War
Glorious Revolution	shah
Imam	social contract
Janissaries	South Sea Bubble
King James Bible	streltsi

SUGGESTED READINGS

Primary Sources

Fénelon, François. *The Adventures of Telemachus.*

Hobbes, Thomas. *Leviathan.*

Molière. *The Middle Class Gentleman.*

Tocqueville, Alexis de. *The Ancien Régime and the French Revolution.*

Saint-Simon. *Memoirs.*

Richelieu. *Political Testament.*

Anthologies

Beik, William. *Louis XIV and Absolutism: A Brief Study with Documents* (2000).

Gregg, Stephen H., ed. *Empire and Identity: An Eighteenth-Century Sourcebook* (2005).

Helfferich, Tryntje, ed. and trans. *The Thirty Years War: A Documentary History* (2009).

Wilson, Peter H., comp. *The Thirty Years War: A Sourcebook* (2010).

Studies

Bennett, Martyn. *Oliver Cromwell* (2006).

Bergin, Joseph. *Church, Society, and Religious Change in France, 1580–1730* (2009).

Casale, Giancarlo. *The Ottoman Age of Exploration* (2010).

Clark, Christopher. *Iron Kingdom: The Rise and Downfall of Prussia, 1600–1947* (2006).

Cracraft, James. *The Revolution of Peter the Great* (2006).

Dale, Stephen F. *The Muslim Empires of the Ottomans, Safavids, and Mughals* (2010).

Fowler, William M., Jr. *Empires at War: The Seven Years' War and the Struggle for North America, 1754–1763* (2005).

Harris, Tim. *Revolution: The Great Crisis of the British Monarchy, 1685–1720* (2006).

Hufton, Olwen. *Europe: Privilege and Protest, 1730–1788* (2001).

Hughes, Lindsey. *Russia in the Age of Peter the Great* (2000).

Ingrao, Charles. *The Habsburg Monarchy, 1618–1815* (2000).

Jones, Colin. *The Great Nation: France from Louis XV to Napoleon, 1715–99* (2003).

Levi, Anthony. *Louis XIV* (2004).

Linebaugh, Peter. *The London Hanged: Crime and Civil Society in the Eighteenth Century* (2006).

Martinich, A. P. *Hobbes* (2005).

Matthee, Rudolph P. *The Politics of Trade in Safavid Iran: Silk for Silver, 1600–1730* (2006).

Newman, Andrew J. *Safavid Iran: Rebirth of a Persian Empire* (2008).

Ormrod, David. *The Rise of Commercial Empires: England and the Netherlands in the Age of Mercantilism, 1650–1770* (2003).

Prak, Maarten. *The Dutch Republic in the Seventeenth Century: The Golden Age* (2005).

Quataert, Donald. *The Ottoman Empire, 1700–1822* (2000).

Rowlands, Guy. *The Dynastic State and the Army under Louis XIV: Royal Service and Private Interest, 1661–1701* (2002).

Smith, Jay M. *Nobility Reimagined: The Patriotic Nation in Eighteenth-Century France* (2005).

Streusand, Douglas E. *Islamic Gunpowder Empires: Ottomans, Safavids, and Mughals* (2010).

Szabo, Franz A. J. *The Seven Years' War in Europe, 1756–1763* (2007).

Wheatcroft, Andrew. *The Enemy at the Gate: Habsburgs, Ottomans, and the Battle for Europe* (2009).

Whisenhunt, William B., and Peter Stearns. *Catherine the Great: Enlightened Empress of Russia* (2006).

Zagorin, Perez. *Hobbes and the Law of Nature* (2009).

For additional resources, including maps, primary sources, visuals, web links, and quizzes, please go to **www.oup.com/us/backman.**

CHAPTER 15

The Enlightened

1690–1789

The **Enlightenment** is a term coined in the second half of the 18th century to describe an array of intellectual and cultural activities of the 1700s. Most of these new ideas, though not all of them, aimed to improve European life by setting its economic, political, religious, and social developments along paths dictated by reason and critical inquiry, rather than by tradition and blind faith. The **philosophes**—as the Enlightenment writers came to call themselves[1]—both continued and broadened the Scientific Revolution by carrying over the scientific method of inquiry from the functioning of the natural world to the human one. Their subject might be the mechanics of Absolutist government, the growth of legal traditions, the development of moral codes, the workings of a national economy, or the functioning of the mind or heart. Any field of human endeavor, when examined rationally, could be understood; and anything that could be understood could be improved.

THE GREATER WEST IN THE ENLIGHTENMENT

At least it seemed that way for the first great figures of the Enlightenment, including John Locke, Pierre Bayle, Adam Smith, and Denis Diderot. For very different reasons, Voltaire and Jean-Jacques Rousseau found grounds for harsh

◀ **A Meeting of a Masonic Lodge in Vienna, 1790** Mozart was said to be a member.

CHAPTER OUTLINE

skepticism—often directed at one another. Many Jews saw the Enlightenment as an opportunity to reassert their place in western Europe. In the face of widespread poverty and its consequences, however, the Enlightenment had uncertain answers, and assessing its impact is by no means simple. The Enlightened writers and publicists had widely varying interests but also widely varying aims. Historians have traditionally emphasized the role of the reformist wing of the movement, those figures who wanted to address abuses and excesses within existing society and government but without fundamentally replacing either. Another wing of the movement though was significantly more radical and sought either the destruction or wholesale replacement of the mores and institutions of the time. Whether moderate or radical, the men and women of the Enlightenment carried out the first major reform effort in centuries that aimed not to reestablish a supposedly better society of the past but to envision and create a wholly new world based on original ideas, practices, and values. Not since the 12th century had so many people devoted themselves so completely and excitedly to the thrill of the new.

THE ORIGINS OF THE ENLIGHTENMENT

The philosophes did not pursue ideas for their own sake; a pragmatic impulse drove the whole enterprise. The men and women of this movement were overwhelmingly public figures rather than dry university academics. (Many in the European professoriate agreed with the Enlightenment program, but few of them wrote well enough to play much of a part in it.) Like the "public intellectuals"

---

[1]   The term philosophes came into general use during the 1740s. Before that, the writers preferred to call themselves les Lumières ("the Enlightened Ones").

CHAPTER TIMELINE

1685
Louis XIV revokes
Edict of Nantes

1690
Locke, *Two Treatises on Government* and *An Essay on Human Understanding*

1696
Boyle, *A Historical and Critical Dictionary*

1688
Glorious Revolution
(England)

1694–1778
Voltaire

1712–1778
Rousseau

of today, they wanted to effect the immediate improvement of human life and to realize the all but certain promise of progress—if only the world would heed their message.

They found that message in response to a return of religious intolerance in France and a detested king of England. With John Locke, the Glorious Revolution and a limited form of democracy had a philosophical justification. With Pierre Bayle, religious freedom had its first great champion.

They were, as a group, the most self-confident thinkers since the scholastic writers of the 13th century. How could they be otherwise? Newton had proven that the universe is massively complex but rationally constructed; it functions according to a coherent system of natural laws. Mankind, as part of that universe, also obeys fixed laws—at least as a physical organism. If the rational mind can decipher the workings of the universe, how hard could it be to figure out the supposed mysteries of human activity and behavior? Why not develop new modes of action that are more in accord with rational principles? And how could such a scheme fail to bring about a better and more progressive world, one stripped of contradiction, idiocy, superstition, and intolerance? The work of the philosophes, in the words of one of them, Immanuel Kant (1724–1804), would help mankind to grow "out of its self-inflicted immaturity." Its immaturity results from man's failure "to use his own rational intelligence instead of being led along by someone else. . . . Dare to learn something! Anyone who persists in this immaturity, whether out of laziness or cowardice, makes it easy for others to think and act for him." The first stirrings of the movement arose in the 1690s, but its heyday was from 1740 to the outbreak of the French Revolution in 1789.

Like the leaders of most intellectual movements until the 20th century, the philosophes brimmed over with self-confidence and optimism. Their writings show the extraordinary breadth of their knowledge as well as the sharpness of

1713–1784
Denis Diderot

1764
Beccaria, *Of Crime and Punishment*

1779
Lessing, *Nathan the Wise*

1729–1786
Moses Mendelssohn

1776
Smith, *The Wealth of Nations*

their gifts for sarcasm and for tossing off witticisms that sound clever but say little. Consider just a sampler:

Diderot: "From fanaticism to barbarism is but a single step."
"What a delightful comedy this world would be, if only we played no part in it."

Hume: "Generally speaking, errors in religion are dangerous; those in philosophy only ridiculous."

Lichtenberg: "We call some actions vices simply because they are performed by ugly people."
"A book is a mirror: if an ass peers into it, don't expect an Apostle to peer back out."

Montesquieu: "[An author is] a fool who, not content with boring everyone around him during his lifetime, insists on boring generations yet to come."

Rousseau: "As long as he is not actually insane, a man can be cured of every folly except vanity."
"Those who are slowest to make promises are those who keep them most faithfully."

Voltaire: "Theology amuses me so. In it we see human insanity at its fullest."
"[Optimism] is an obsession with saying 'All is well' even when one is in Hell."

> The philosophes may have been the most influential group of talented amateurs in European history, not only because of their influence on their own age but because of the way they and their assumptions about human nature still affect us today.

With a few exceptions—David Hume (1711–1776) and Immanuel Kant, most notably—their knowledge was broad rather than deep, and at their worst they were infuriatingly flippant. Yet they brought to most of their work remarkable talents for clarity and shrewdness, and a dedication to practical reform. They wrote in many genres—essays, treatises, novels and stories, encyclopedia articles, letters, histories, poems, and stage dramas—to reach the broadest possible audience. The philosophes may have been the most influential group of talented amateurs in European history, not only because of their influence on their own age but because of the way they and their assumptions about human nature still affect us today.[2]

---

2   We are all, in the words of one of the philosophes' most earnest modern critics, still "Voltaire's bastards."

LEARNING FROM OUR WORST MISTAKES

Whatever else historians mean by the term Enlightenment, they do not mean a coherent set of ideas. Like the medieval scholastics they resemble, the philosophes represent a method of thinking rather than a body of thought. Their efforts all originated in the conviction that the bulk of human misery results from the irrationality of our actions, traditions, beliefs, institutions, and values. Simply remove the uncritical and witless assumptions that guide what we do with our lives; replace them with finely reasoned alternatives that can be logically supported, measured, and calibrated; and then watch mankind progress into a clearer, better, happier, and more productive life. The philosophes were not necessarily utopians. Hume, for example, for all his geniality of tone, should never be read by depressives. Yet they remained firm believers in man's ability always to make life better. One of the best-known pieces of literature produced by the Enlightenment—Voltaire's fable *Candide*—satirized the utopianism that had spread among some of the movement's truest believers.

Several factors triggered the Enlightenment, not the least of which were Louis XIV's reckless decision in 1685 to revoke the Edict of Nantes and the Glorious Revolution in England in 1688. The Edict of Nantes, promulgated in 1598 by France's king Henri IV, had established the official policy of religious toleration, and for nearly one hundred years this policy had preserved the peace between Catholics and Huguenots. Louis XIV knew little about religion (and was said by his sister-in-law never to have opened a Bible in his life). But he knew that he preferred a hierarchical Catholicism under royal control to a Protestant theology that privileged individual conscience over obedience to authority. At a stroke, Louis's action to revoke the edict stripped French Protestants of their legal rights. He seized the nearly one hundred cities placed under Huguenot control by the edict, drove their civic officials into exile, shut down their schools and churches, and banned all Protestant public activities. Forced to choose between conversion and banishment, approximately two hundred thousand French Protestants went into exile in Holland, England, and Brandenburg-Prussia. This renewal of persecution, coupled with fears about Louis's expansionist territorial aims, prompted the Holy Roman emperor Leopold I (r. 1658–1705) to cobble together a defensive alliance with England and the Low Countries (along with Sweden and several German principalities) called the **League of Augsburg**.

Meanwhile, in England, Parliament forced the detested Catholic king James II from the throne in 1688. Early in 1689 the Parliament drafted the Declaration of Rights that stipulated that henceforth all English monarchs were required to be Anglican, that freedom of speech was guaranteed, and that Parliament controlled the levying of taxes. The leaders of Parliament then offered the English throne to

James II's Protestant daughter Mary, who had married the Dutch stadtholder, or chief magistrate, William III of Orange. William was Louis XIV's nemesis and was determined to lead the forces of the league against France. Fighting began in 1689 and lasted for eight years. The Treaty of Rijswijk (1697) established a shaky peace, but the damage had been done: the horrors of the 16th and 17th centuries threatened to rise from the dead.

But the specter of the return of religious intolerance, of vain saber rattling, and of the economic misery created by flat-out war also sparked new efforts to rethink the attitudes of the age; hence the Enlightenment. Aristocratic and upper-middle-class readers had long enjoyed keeping up with new developments in science, but more and more thinkers were drawn to the critical investigation of human behavior. What is it that leads human beings, whether individually or communally, to act as they do? Is it possible to develop a science

Persecution and Exile   The city of La Rochelle had long been a center of Huguenot life. After the Edict of Toleration was issued in 1598, direct persecution against French Protestants ceased but tensions remained. In 1622 the leaders of La Rochelle rebelled against King Louis XIII and were quickly put down; five years later, though, spurred on by English sympathizers, they rebelled again. This time Cardinal Richelieu came in person to oversee the siege of the city, which lasted fourteen months. Continued strife finally resulted in this scene from 1661, when three hundred Huguenot families were sent into exile. Louis XIV had risen to the throne in that year, and his intention to revoke the Edict of Toleration was well known.

of humanity? And if we can understand ourselves better, can we learn to avoid our worst mistakes?

LOCKE AND THE ADMINISTRATION OF THE COMMONWEALTH

The inquiry began with the publication in 1690 of John Locke's *Two Treatises on Government* and *An Essay Concerning Human Understanding*. Pierre Bayle's *Historical and Critical Dictionary* quickly followed in 1697. Locke (1632–1704) is commonly regarded as the first philosophe. Drawn initially to science, he studied medicine at Oxford University while reading philosophers like Descartes and Leibniz in his spare hours. In 1666 he met Lord Ashley, later the Earl of Shaftesbury, and joined his household as a general counselor. Locke provided medical care for the family, advised the earl on commercial and financial matters, arranged the marriage of the earl's heir, and oversaw the education of the Shaftesbury children. At one point Locke even performed a lifesaving operation on the nobleman. In 1672, when Shaftesbury became the lord chancellor of England, Locke was appointed to a secretarial position with the Board of Trade, an experience that seems to have sparked his interest in politics. When Shaftesbury fell from power in 1676 Locke moved to the Continent and spent the next decade living primarily in France and Holland, enjoying the support of various noble patrons, and working on the book that would become the *Essay on Human Understanding*.

But politics interrupted his studies once again when a number of the figures busily planning the Glorious Revolution made contact with him in Holland. At their urging, Locke quickly produced *Two Treatises on Government*, which provided a philosophical justification for Parliament's dismissal of James II and its transfer of the crown to William and Mary. In the treatises he attacks the notion of absolutist monarchy. In its place, his model sees all government as the expression of a social contract between the members of a community. This contract consists of recognizing that in choosing to live together, people tacitly agree to compromise their individual autonomy and to delegate to the government the power to adjudicate conflicts and administer the law.

But Locke, who spent his adult life among the propertied classes and enjoying their patronage, defined the central function of government as the administration of the commonwealth—which meant its property. He argued that all political rights begin with the "individual property interest"—that is, the ownership of property. Government is therefore legitimate only when it is composed of or chosen by individuals whose property comes under the state's jurisdiction. It is a moderate, limited form of democracy: only those people who own property, whether defined as land or commercial interest, have a rightful voice in determining the government's shape and activity. When a ruler such as James II violates the social contract, the propertied classes may justifiably resist him and even, as proved necessary in this case, remove him from office.

Locke's dictum that civil rights consist primarily of the rights to "life, liberty, and property" was cribbed by Thomas Jefferson when he wrote the American Declaration of Independence (1776). Jefferson, of course, altered Locke's position significantly, turning it into the better-known phrase "life, liberty, and the pursuit of happiness." Less well known is that Locke would probably have been horrified by the American revolutionaries, viewing them as rebels against the legitimate claims of the propertied men in England whom the colonists served. Some writers have asserted that Jefferson's change of phrase is itself an Enlightenment achievement: the invention of happiness. Such a concept could never have existed, the argument runs, until the philosophes placed the means of actually acquiring it within all men's and women's reach. "Happiness is a new idea here in Europe," wrote Louis Antoine Saint-Just (1767–1794), and some modern writers take him at his word. They shouldn't. Earlier writers like Aristotle, Saint Augustine, Geoffrey Chaucer, Giovanni Pico della Mirandola, or François Rabelais would have scoffed at the notion that no true concept of happiness existed in their times.[3]

Locke's understanding of government stands in sharp contrast to Thomas Hobbes's argument in *Leviathan*—the text to which Locke was implicitly responding. To Hobbes, the function of the state is to govern the people. Since we are all essentially equal in nature, our competing desires for self-fulfillment condemn us to constant competition, rivalry, and struggle, and government is therefore necessary to keep our hostile tendencies in check. Locke turns Hobbes's argument on its head: the essential role of the state is not to govern the people but to manage and administer its material wealth, or "property," as Locke put it. The state does not decide who gets which property; that would go against Locke's conviction that the private ownership of property is an intrinsic human right. The state does, however, set the terms by which those who already possess property may keep it, transfer it, and manage it—all of which it does by establishing laws regarding the rights of ownership, by setting taxes on property, and by setting inheritance norms. And Locke goes a step further. Since the state's fundamental function is to administer the collective property of the nation, only those who possess that property have the right to participate in government. Government

---

3   Saint-Just was a pornographer turned revolutionary who championed the despotism of Robespierre. He was known as the "Archangel of the Terror." Happiness, to him, was a well-oiled guillotine.

thus resembles a medieval guild, in which only those who engage in a particular craft or trade may set the rules for that craft or trade's activities.

BAYLE AND RELIGIOUS TOLERATION

Pierre Bayle (1647–1706) is the most enigmatic and beguiling of the philosophes. Born just before the Treaty of Westphalia, he came to public attention in 1686 with an attack on Louis XIV's decision to revoke the Edict of Nantes, called *An All-Catholic France*, which he followed with *A Philosophical Commentary* in the next year. This latter work is a touchstone—the first major treatise in Europe's history to champion the idea of religious toleration. The argument he makes for tolerance is, however, flawed. The question, as Bayle frames it, comes to this: Is it ever right to compel a person to change his belief even if the belief he holds can be proven false? He insists that the answer is no, since the choice of belief must be regarded as an intrinsic individual human right. Although he presents an array of real and imaginary case studies to buttress his position, he never confronts head-on the obvious counterargument: If a belief can be proven to be not only wrong but actually harmful, surely the morally correct thing is to stop unnecessary harm from being done. Adolf Hitler sincerely believed in the moral rectitude and historical necessity of annihilating the Jews of Europe. Was it therefore morally wrong to oppose him by force? Ought his beliefs to have been tolerated? Obviously not. Still, Bayle's work deserves note as a historical first.

Bayle continued his scholarly efforts with his most accomplished work—*A Historical and Critical Dictionary*, a sprawling, eccentric encyclopedia that began to appear in 1696. Despite its massive size, the *Dictionary* was by far the biggest "best seller" of all the philosophical works of Europe in the 18th century. Published in four fat folio volumes—more than three thousand pages—it is a wild collection of articles on topics ranging from ancient Greek philosophies to the erotica of Bayle's own time. It made, and still makes, delightful browsing, since Bayle allows himself to veer off on any tangent that holds his interest. Indeed, there are more tangents than text: over 90 percent of the *Dictionary* consists of lengthy footnotes, addenda, marginalia, spin-off mini-essays, and sometimes even footnotes to the footnotes. But the fun has a serious purpose. Time and again theodicy—the question of why evil exists—emerges as a central theme making the whole structure cohere.

Bayle examines the question philosophically, historically, theologically, linguistically, in art and literature, as a practical matter of law, even in a way that prefigures anthropology. "Mankind is evil and miserable," he writes; "everywhere one looks there are prisons, hospitals, gallows, and beggars. History, one might say, is nothing but the narrative of man's crimes and sufferings." But why is this so, if the world was created for us by an omnipotent and loving God? Bayle returns to the question over and over, but in bits and pieces, as though the question is too horrifying to contemplate for too long. If God is all-loving, he argues, he would destroy evil if he could—and yet evil obviously exists, so one must conclude that God cannot stop it. Bayle will have none of this, since it concludes in essence that God is not God. On the other hand, assuming that God could destroy evil if he wanted to, then he must not want to—in which case he is not all-loving. This too Bayle rejects. In the end, he suggests (though he never says so explicitly) that the question of evil has no rational explanation. The coexistence of an all-loving, all-powerful God and rampant, unremitting evil is simply a mystery that we must accept and acknowledge our inability to comprehend.

> In the end, Bayle suggests (though he never says so explicitly) that the question of evil has no rational explanation. The coexistence of an all-loving, all-powerful God and rampant, unremitting evil is simply a mystery that we must accept and acknowledge our inability to comprehend.

Yet this is not a failed exercise. Bayle's whole point is present here, though somewhat veiled. By his exuberant, continuous reexamination of the question, his implicit message is the fundamental and best argument for tolerance: the only proper human response to religious mystery is to recognize the inability of human beings to comprehend heavenly mysteries. No one can or should ever be so certain of his convictions that he deems it right to persecute those who disagree with him. We must tolerate, in other words, because we can never be sure.

Bayle is seldom read anymore, which is a shame. In his own time he was lauded as perhaps the greatest nonscientific mind in centuries. The German philosopher Gottfried Leibniz (1646–1716) described him as "one of the most brilliant men of our time, a man whose eloquence is as great as his intellect." Voltaire, in a generous mood, praised him as "the greatest master of logic who ever wrote." His influence on the later philosophes can hardly be overstated; and if he came to few positive conclusions in his work, that surely was part of his point.

FREE MARKETS AND RATIONAL PUNISHMENT

The Enlightenment drew writers from across Europe, but the movement's geographic centers were Amsterdam, Edinburgh, Geneva, The Hague, Leiden, London, and Milan. Paris was not an important center of this activity until Voltaire brought the new thinking there in the 1740s, when the political atmosphere proved more amenable to reform. From these centers the writers of the

Enlightenment poured forth a dazzling stream of ideas on every aspect of human life.

John Locke was interested in epistemology—the study of how we acquire knowledge and of what it means "to know" anything. However, as we have seen, he also provided a philosophical underpinning for forms of governance that draw their justification from the consent of the governed. His concern for rational foundations quickly spread from government to economics, with Adam Smith; to crime and punishment, with Cesare Beccaria; and to education, with Denis Diderot.

Adam Smith (1723–1790) published *The Wealth of Nations* in 1776 in order to prove the inevitable failure of mercantilism and the inevitable success of free-market capitalism. Mercantilism is wrong, he argues, for the simple reason that it is irrational: it assumes that people will passively accept their own poverty and oppression—all in order to support a regime that absorbs all available capital for its own ends. Capitalism, on the other hand, is based on a far more rational view of human motivation. It allows people the freedom to make their own economic choices and to reap the rewards of their own success. But in order for this to happen, markets must have open competition and freedom from price fixing. He therefore warns against cartels—powerful monopolies or agreements between firms—quite as much as against interference by the state.[4]

Smith thus redefined the notion of a **market**. The word no longer meant merely a physical site where commerce occurs, but rather a pattern of human behavior. Commerce was now seen as following set laws, since all individuals, in any free economic exchange, will act rationally in their own best interest. And these laws are based on the economic choices people make from among a limited supply of goods, along with the competition between firms for buyers—in other words, supply and demand:

> The natural effort of every individual to better his own condition, when suffered to exert itself with freedom and security, is so powerful a principle, that it is alone, and without any assistance, not only capable of carrying the society to wealth and prosperity, but of surmounting a hundred impertinent obstructions with which the folly of human laws too often encumbers its operations.

---

[4] "People of the same trade seldom meet together even for merriment or diversion, but that the conversation ends in some conspiracy against the public, or in some contrivance to raise prices."

Rational self-interest also guided the investigations of Cesare Beccaria (1739–1794) into economics and into law. His *Elements of Public Economy* (published posthumously, in 1804) anticipated some of Adam Smith's ideas on the need for economic policies that produced wealth for the entire populace by opening up markets to natural forces of competition, supply, and demand. His greatest work, however, was his study *Of Crimes and Punishments* (1764). A system of criminal justice, he argued, should aim to promote social security and order rather than to seek revenge upon malefactors. It thus ought to consider the causes of crime as much as punishment. After all, it is preferable for society to prevent crimes from happening than to punish their perpetrators after they have occurred. Hence any just society will actively seek to eradicate poverty, which Beccaria sees as the principle cause of crimes against property. For crimes against humanity, the aim of a judicial system should be to rehabilitate criminals who are emotionally unbalanced and to teach them to understand themselves, the consequences of their actions, and the paths to personal improvement.

Punishment of crimes is necessary, he insists, but is more effective when it is imposed in a rational way. Toward that end, punishments should be only as severe as necessary in order to promote social order. Anything more severe, he argues, is tyrannical and merely provokes attitudes of resentment and hostility that make the criminal all the more likely to commit another offense. Punishments must also be consistently applied. The certainty of punishment, not the severity of it, deters crime more effectively.

An 18th-Century Scene from an Italian Prison   The prisoner in the center of the image is being drawn up in the *strappado* torture.

Freeing individuals from corrupt and irrational practices, whether in politics, the marketplace, or civic life, will lead to the improvement of society for the simple reason that most of the Enlightened regarded human nature as essentially good. Though ineluctably based in self-interest, human behavior is also naturally social. We are equipped, in other words, with an ability to recognize in rationally chosen compromises an indirect means of satisfying self-interest. We are intrinsically good and when given freedom to act will consistently choose the good.

DIDEROT AND THE CIRCULATION OF THE ENLIGHTENMENT

Perhaps the most heroically energetic and resilient philosophe was Denis Diderot (1713–1784). While he was far from the best thinker or writer in the movement, he was perhaps the most important in getting Enlightened ideas into print and into circulation outside the closed society of the salons.[5] He was the central force behind the great *Encyclopédie*, the vast compendium of all the new learning in science, philosophy, economics, law, technology, art, and religion. Diderot was among the most utilitarian of the philosophes, a true believer in the cause of saving the world from tyranny, superstition, and ignorance. Here is how he himself put it, in the *Encyclopédie*'s entry "Encyclopedias":

> The aim of an encyclopedia is to gather in one place the knowledge scattered all over the world; to display the general content and organization of that knowledge to one's contemporaries; and to pass this knowledge on to later generations—so that the achievements of the past may be useful to the future; so that our children, by so improving their own minds, may become more virtuous and more happy; and so that we may not perish without having proved a benefit to all mankind.... For we have long had need of a rational age [such as ours], in which men would no longer look to classical authorities for the truth, but to the study of nature itself.

Despite its size—thirty-five volumes of print and images—or perhaps because of it, the *Encyclopédie* sold extremely well. Four thousand subscribers ordered copies before it was even in print. Thomas Jefferson purchased a set, and Empress Catherine of Russia, hearing of Diderot's financial woes,

---

[5]   Diderot, like Ezra Pound later for modernism, had a wonderful ability to spot talent in others. He was tireless in encouraging, prodding, supporting, and publishing new authors.

purchased his entire library and hired Diderot, at a generous stipend, to be her "librarian" and guardian for the books. The books were shipped to Saint Petersburg after Diderot's death in 1784 and are now a special collection within the Russian National Library. But the *Encyclopédie* was not the only such effort; the 18th century, in fact, was a golden age for such enterprises. Just as 13th-century scholastics filled European libraries with *summas* on every topic, the Enlightened of the 18th gave birth to a glut of encyclopedias: Pierre Bayle's *Dictionnaire historique et critique* (1697), Ephraim Chambers's *Cyclopaedia* (1728), Gianfrancesco Pivati's *Nuovo dizionario scientifico e curioso, sacroprofano* (1744), Johann Heinrich Zedler's *Universal-Lexicon* (1754), and the first edition of the *Encyclopædia Britannica* (1768) are merely the best-known examples of this remarkable genre.[6]

Pages from the *Encyclopédie*   The *Encyclopédie* reflects the personal interest of Denis Diderot in technology for its own sake and as a tool for social reform. The illustrations above depict scenes of sheet-glass manufacture and locksmithing.

---

6   Thomas Dobson's *Encyclopaedia* (1789–1798) was the first American encyclopedia. It copied much from the *Encyclopædia Britannica* and was soon replaced by the *Encyclopedia Americana*.

VOLTAIRE AND THE LIMITS OF OPTIMISM

As it happened, the two most influential of all the Enlightened were considerably less optimistic about human goodness and its ability to overcome the demands of society: François-Marie Arouet (1694–1778), who published under the pen name of Voltaire, and Jean-Jacques Rousseau (1712–1778). Both were prima donnas, but they differed profoundly in their origins, temperaments, aims, and styles.

Voltaire doubted the essential goodness of mankind, or at least of the lower orders of it. He believed in the possibility of human progress, but a progress firmly directed by a political and intellectual elite—of which he regarded himself and others like him as the indispensable leaders. The commoners, however, whether farmers in the countryside or laborers in the towns, he loathed as degenerate brutes incapable of rising above ignorance. Rousseau, on the other hand, came from those lower orders and held tightly to the conviction that goodness is the essential characteristic of all human beings. It is society itself that corrupts the individual—especially the privileged classes with whom Voltaire was so comfortable. The power of the privileged, to Rousseau, derives from its enslavement and brutalization of the common man. Given these differences, it is no surprise to learn that the two men despised each other.[7]

Voltaire was born in Paris to a wealthy, bourgeois family. He was educated at the Jesuit Collège Louis-le-Grand, where he excelled in languages and law, and after graduation took a job as secretary to the French ambassador to Holland. This might have been the start of a successful government career, but his impulsive romantic entanglements and his habit of poking sarcastic barbs at his social superiors kept getting him in trouble. He was imprisoned twice—once in the Bastille after publishing satirical verses about the prince regent—and released the second time only when he promised to flee the country. After an offhand witticism, a nobleman had Voltaire beaten by hired thugs—to which Voltaire responded by challenging him to a duel. But since Voltaire came from a lower social rank, his challenge enraged aristocratic society even more than the original insult. He remained in England for three years. His early writings, mostly poetry and stage dramas,

Voltaire (1694–1778)   The leading figure of the Enlightenment in France and tireless champion of free speech and religious toleration.

---

[7]   Rousseau, who died on July 2, 1778, is said to have died happy since he had lived long enough to learn of Voltaire's death on May 30.

however, were popular enough to keep him writing, although they make very poor reading today.

The years he spent in England marked the turning point in his life. Quickly learning English, he moved easily through educated society and met many of the most prominent figures in England's political and intellectual life. He observed English law and government, studied Newtonian physics, and avidly read the works of John Locke. The culmination of his experience was the grand state funeral given to Isaac Newton. Returning to Paris, Voltaire published his *Philosophical Letters on the English* (1733), which instantly propelled him to the front ranks of the intellectuals of his time. The *Letters* extol the rationalism of English life over the irrational, superstitious, and corrupt Continental world; he contrasts the modesty and gentleness of the Quakers with the rigid intolerance of the Calvinists, yet praises a constitution that permits both to practice their faiths freely despite the existence of an established Church of England. He marvels at the Quakers' absence of priests ("'We have none, my friend,' he replied, 'to our great happiness.'") and denounces the Presbyterians (who "wear the most severe expressions, . . . preach through their noses, and call [all other Christian denominations] 'whores of Babylon'"). He also praises the English for their judicial system, their open trade, their dedication to promoting science.

The *Letters* were a sensation with the reading public, which is why the government ordered the book to be banned and copies to be burnt. Voltaire went once again into exile, this time to a remote village, where he lived in the chateau of his mistress, the Marquise de Chatelêt. For the next twelve years he poured out a stream of pamphlets, plays, histories, poems, scientific papers, essays, and letters that made him the most prominent philosophe of the age. (The standard edition of his complete works today fills more than one hundred volumes.) His two principal concerns were religious toleration and freedom of speech. Political freedom meant little to him, since the unwashed masses neither needed nor deserved it. Besides, their educated superiors would profit less from democracy than from Enlightened ideas put into efficient practice by an absolutist regime guided by philosophes such as himself.

The death of the Marquise in 1749 left Voltaire deeply mournful, and he sought a new chapter in his life in Berlin. He accepted an invitation to reside with, debate with, and act as counselor to Frederick the Great of Prussia, the most rigidly absolutist ruler then in Europe. Yet his air of self-satisfaction, his sarcastic gaiety, and his inability to resist challenging all forms of authority (even those he was in agreement with) lead to a speedy falling out with the deeply serious-minded Frederick. After yet another brief imprisonment—this time in Frankfurt—Voltaire then went to Geneva and lived there just long enough to make himself unwanted. He moved at last to a brilliant estate at Ferney, near the French-Swiss

The Lisbon Earthquake   On November 1, 1755, a massive earthquake struck the city of Lisbon, followed by widespread fires and a tsunami. As many as sixty thousand of the city's two hundred thousand people died, and roughly 85 percent of the city's buildings were destroyed. This painting depicts the catastrophe in religious terms, with avenging angels swooping through the dark sky to cut down sinners amid popular calls to penance and renewed devotion.

border, where he remained for the last twenty years of his life. It was at Ferney that he wrote his best-known work, the novella *Candide* (1759).

The inspiration for the tale was a catastrophic earthquake that flattened Lisbon in 1755, killing perhaps as many as sixty thousand people and demolishing almost 90 percent of the city's buildings.[8] The tragedy shocked Europe, and the suffering of the survivors challenged many people's confidence in the rational ordering of the world and the conviction that man can understand it. *Candide*, for all its usual Voltairean humor, provides a first glimpse of the bitterness and pessimism that increasingly marked Voltaire's latter years. It also mercilessly satirizes the optimism of his rival philosophes—especially Rousseau, whom Voltaire regarded as vulgar, gullible, and naïve.

The novella tells of the title character and his thick-headed tutor Dr. Pangloss, whose fundamental teaching is that "everything is for the best in this, the best of all possible worlds." They stagger from one disastrous misadventure to another, in the search for Candide's lost love, the beautiful but vacuous Lady Cunegonde,

---

8   Experts today reckon the severity of the Lisbon quake as 9.0 on the Richter scale. (The strongest earthquake ever recorded was 9.5, in Valdivia, Chile in 1960.)

and for the mythical kingdom of El Dorado. Candide and Pangloss suffer through wars, famines, plagues, imprisonments and tortures, earthquakes, shipwrecks, and slavery with stoic resolve. Experiencing nothing but evil, they cling to their belief that everything happens for a reason and toward some positive end. By the end, Candide concludes that the most anyone can do is to tend to what is within one's reach. In the face of the world's evils, one must "cultivate one's own garden." Pangloss, however, remains unenlightened and optimistic.

ROUSSEAU: "MANKIND IS BORN FREE"

Jean-Jacques Rousseau, Voltaire probably would have said, was never enlightened to begin with. Rousseau shared Voltaire's enormous egoism but in every other way was his polar opposite. Born in 1712 to a working-class family in Protestant Geneva, Rousseau was orphaned at an early age and had a hardscrabble youth, working at odd jobs and sleeping wherever he could. In constant poverty and ill health, he developed a bitter and nervous temperament. Even after he had achieved renown and a modicum of wealth, he remained convinced that people were persecuting him. Almost entirely self-educated, Rousseau turned himself into a polymath by sheer will: he composed music, wrote novels, studied politics and philosophy, promoted new techniques of education, and acquired an amateur's knowledge of science. Brilliant but maladjusted, possibly paranoid, he spoke endlessly of his own virtue while complaining that no one understood him. He scolded everyone for their immorality, yet he had five children with his illiterate servant girl and placed each one in an orphanage. In his letters and his *Confessions*, one of the most fascinating autobiographies ever written, he at once exaggerates his own sins and exonerates himself anyway. Bad as he was, others were worse.

Jean-Jacques Rousseau (1712–1778) Author of the *Discourse on the Origins of Inequality* (1754) and *The Social Contract* (1762), and a tireless enemy of Voltaire.

Yet this unstable misanthrope had a more profound influence on Western culture than any other figure of his time. At the heart of Rousseau's thinking was an unshakable belief in the fundamental goodness, decency, and equality of people. All the corruption and evil of this world, he insisted, was the fault of society—and not just the particular society of France in the *Ancien Régime*. It is the sheer fact of socializing, of living in community, that introduces injustice, pain, and unhappiness in human life. "Mankind is born free, but we see him everywhere in chains." That is the memorable opening of the *Discourse on the Origins of Inequality*, one of his best-known works. To live in community means to relinquish one's freedom, to accept compromises of one's desires and will. We may gain a degree of civility in the process, but civilization itself plants the seed of corruption in our souls. And we see this corruption in the unfair hierarchies of wealth, privilege, and power that exist.

Thus far, most of the Enlightened would have agreed. But Rousseau goes farther. Simply redistributing wealth and influence, he says, will not solve anything. The real problem is the concern for wealth and power that civilized life creates. Rejecting economists like Smith, Rousseau insists that the point of Enlightenment is to make people good, not rich. He similarly resists efforts like Diderot's to educate the masses in practical matters. To Rousseau, any philosophy that aims to help people enjoy material comfort and self-determination is wrongheaded, if not delusional. Human happiness, he insists, derives from a persistent pursuit of life's meaning. What is the good life, and what is happiness? Only by asking questions like these can hope to achieve either. Even if we never discover the answers, the very search for answers will make us better and happier. In the end, it is the effort to retain our humanity in the face of the world's brutality that gives life meaning and makes it endurable.

Rousseau does take some concrete positions. He rejects Locke's argument that ownership of property establishes a political right, since everyone, rich and poor alike, has surrendered freedom in entering the social contract. The only legitimate form of government will embrace the mandate of the majority—what he calls the General Will. As a believer in human goodness, Rousseau affirms that the General

> To Rousseau, any philosophy that aims to help people enjoy material comfort and self-determination is wrongheaded, if not delusional. Human happiness, he insists, derives from a persistent pursuit of life's meaning.

The Noble Savage Jean-Jacques Rousseau did the most to popularize the idea of the **noble savage**—that is, the non-Europeans who are untainted by civilization's corrupting forces—but the notion was widespread before him. This handsome 1783 painting by Sir Joshua Reynolds (1723–1792) offers a romanticized portrait of a Tahitian native brought back to England by Captain James Cook.

Will must always be correct. It may not secure the highest economic yield (as Smith would ask), promote the best technical skills (with Diderot), or crush religious superstition (with Voltaire). It simply expresses the truest desire of the people, which will always promote the well-being of all. Our natural altruism, our concern for others, can guide social life once we overcome our shortsighted individual desire. Provided that the law governing society derives from and expresses the General Will, the freedom of each individual consists of obedience to it. Rousseau thus championed a radical democracy that offended the aristocracy while rejecting rational progress, which offended most of the Enlightened.[9]

Most of the Enlightened rejected religion absolutely. Some, however, took recourse to **deism**. Deists grudgingly believed in a single and possibly benevolent God who created the cosmos—but who plays no active role in it. Like a clockmaker, he builds his machine, winds it up, then sets it ticking. Deists like Hume, Voltaire, and Diderot insisted that the universe, from the moment of its creation, has operated solely according to rational principles. Since God plays no role in our lives, we owe him nothing more than a vague gratitude. More significantly, since God is unknowable, all dogmatic assertions are meaningless—which means that the teachings of all organized religions are without value. Churches—whether Catholic, Protestant, or Orthodox—have no right to command our obedience. A dual policy of religious freedom and of freedom from religious intolerance is essential to human progress. As Voltaire memorably put it:

> It is quite understandable that the fanatics of one sect want to wipe out the fanatics belonging to another, . . . but to have forced [someone like] Descartes to flee to Holland in order to avoid the wrath of the stupid . . . is an eternal shame upon our nation.

Later, in his popular *Philosophical Dictionary* (1764), he defends deists as people

> who do not claim to know how God punishes the wrong, or how He promotes the good, or how He forgives—for [the deist] is not presumptuous enough to boast that he knows God's nature; instead, the deist simply takes comfort in the knowledge that God is good and just.

The calm reasonableness of his tone, however, cannot make up for deism's obvious flaw: it is intellectually lazy. That helps explain why it failed to catch on with the general public. It accepts a divine Creator as a convenient cover, since science has failed to explain the universe's existence, only to cast the Creator aside and bolt for

---

9   In subordinating individual desires to the General Will, Rousseau has sometimes been seen as the creator, in theory, of fascist totalitarianism.

the nearest exit. Why would he go to the trouble of creating a universe only to show no interest in what happens in it? Deism does not even attempt an answer. Voltaire was even known to order servants to leave the room before letting conversation on religion begin. The lower orders, he felt, could never hope to understand his Enlightened ideas, so best not to irritate their ignorance by letting them overhear.

The deists deserve respect for their dedication to religious tolerance and their willingness to risk exile and imprisonment for its sake. But deism was the only major Enlightenment idea to disappear from European life after the 18th century.

JEWISH ENLIGHTENMENT

The promotion of reason and tolerance certainly appealed to Europe's Jewish populations. Many Jews supported the Enlightened goal of fighting superstition and ignorance, which were sources of anti-Jewish hatred. To secular Jews, an Enlightened world without religion would be a world without religious violence. And of violence they had had their fill.

By 1500 hardly any Jews still resided in western Europe, thanks to late-medieval and later expulsions in England (1290), France (1292), Spain (1492), and Portugal (1496). Most Continental Jews migrated east into Germany and then to Poland. The confederation then known as the Polish-Lithuanian Union dates back to 1385. By the 17th century it included what are today the nations of Poland, Ukraine, Belarus, Latvia, and Lithuania—and there they enjoyed a welcome and a degree of tolerance that they had seldom known in the west (see Map 15.1). Most of the exiled Sephardim migrated to Holland and the Ottoman Empire, although substantial numbers settled in southern Italy and North Africa as well. But matters changed when Poland became ensnared in political and social convulsions in the mid-17th century, including the so-called Polish-Swedish War (1600–1629) and the Northern War (1655–1660).[10] Fleeing once more from oppression, several hundred thousand Jews returned to western Europe, whose nations gradually—and grudgingly—revoked their bans on Jewish presence.

England was the last western country to revoke its ban, in 1655. Not everyone was pleased. The poet John Dryden (1631–1700), for one, complained in his best-known poem, *Absalom and Achitophel* (1681):

> The Jews, a headstrong, moody, murmuring race,
> God's pampered people, whom, debauched with ease,
> No king could govern, nor no God could please.

---

[10] In the Khmelnytsky Rebellion of 1648 alone, well over a hundred thousand Jews were slaughtered by rampaging Cossack troops.

MAP 15.1   Jewish Communities in Poland-Lithuania

It is important to note, however, that the "Jews" here in fact represent the people of England. Dryden is using the Biblical tale of Absalom and Achitophel's rebellion against King David (2 Samuel) to describe the political struggle in England. David represents Charles II, whose followers were known as the Tories. Absalom and Achitophel stand for the Earl of Shaftesbury and the Duke of Monmouth, whose supporters were the Whigs. The poem's anti-Semitic overtone went down smoothly with Dryden's readers. Nonetheless, Jews had returned to an Enlightened Europe apparently dedicated to reform and reason.

Traditionally, most Jews had sought to secure a peaceful, though parallel, existence with Christian society. From their segregated communities, under the leadership of their rabbis, they had ventured out into the gentile world to conduct business. They could even engage, within limits, in the broader intellectual and social life—but returned at day's end to the community and its ritual life under the Law. Jews had retained their distinctive identity for centuries, wearing traditional clothing, observing dietary restrictions, performing their mitzvahs, keeping their languages alive, and perpetuating the traditions of Jewish intellectual life. Now many Jews were determined to reestablish Judaism in the west, not as a separate, segregated society but as an integral part of the new progressive world.

Amsterdam Synagogue   Emanuel de Witte (1617–1692) painted this interior view of the Portuguese Synagogue in the Dutch capital in 1680. This was the synagogue whose leaders excommunicated Baruch de Spinoza "with the excommunication with which Joshua banned Jericho, with the curse with which Elisha cursed the boys, and with all the curses which are written in the Book of the Law."

HASKALAH AND HASIDISM

The Hebrew term for enlightenment is **haskalah**, the name of one of the two main developments in European Jewish history in the 18th century. The Haskalah movement accepted the idea of assimilation, or seeking to integrate Jews into the main European populace and culture. Moses Mendelssohn (1729–1786), a Prussian autodidact who became Judaism's greatest philosopher since Maimonides, encouraged, if not complete assimilation, at least a dignified integration with gentile society. Israel Jacobson (1768–1828), the founder of Reform Judaism, deemphasized Jewish teachings that he regarded as merely ritual instead of moral or ethical and therefore essential. They recommended the decline of Jewish vernaculars like Yiddish and Ladino, which only kept Jews segregated from the European world, in favor of traditional Hebrew and the gentile vernaculars. Mendelssohn translated the entire Bible into German.

The **Hasidim** occupied the other end of the spectrum and the other end of Europe. Founded by the Polish rabbi Israel ben Eleazar (1696–1760), also known as the Ba'al Shem Tov ("Master of the Good Name"), Hasidic Judaism represented a revivalist spirit rather than a new set of ideas regarding observant life. The Hasidim (literally, "the Pious Ones") decried Ashkenazic rabbinic Jewish life as too rule-bound, soul-deadening, and formulaic. At the same time, they found the mystical-philosophical Kabbalistic elements of Sephardic Judaism too foreign. What R. Eleazar emphasized instead was a more vividly emotional and uplifting style of worship. Centered in the home instead of the synagogues, the Hasidim adhered strictly to Jewish Law but did so under the leadership of charismatic zaddikim ("holy men"), who led their congregations in joyous singing and dancing. The Hasidim maintained that sincerity of prayer, charity performed with warmth and eagerness, and sensitivity to God's ever-present reality are more pleasing in heaven than uninspired rituals. Eastern European Jews became known for the vitality of their worship and their communal lives. From these two developments—Haskalah and Hasidism—arose the Reform, Conservative, and Orthodox traditions of modern-day Judaism.

THE JEWS AND EUROPE'S AMBIVALENCE

Europeans were, as ever, ambivalent about the Jews. Most favored integration—that is, incorporating the Jews into society at least in terms of law and governance—but were opposed to outright assimilation, an idea that raised the uncomfortable notions of intermarriage and socializing on equal terms. The problem was described by Charles-Henri de Clermont-Tonnerre, in a debate in the National Assembly in 1789:

> We must deny everything to the Jews as a nation, but grant them everything as individuals. We must not recognize the authority of their judges—rather, they need to recognize the authority of ours. They should not be allowed to exist as a distinct political entity or power within our state; and accordingly we must not grant legitimacy to the discrete laws by which they have lived as a separate community. Each Jew, as an individual, must be a citizen [of France]. To any who say, "That is not what they want!" I can only reply: "If they do not want to be citizens, then they should say so openly, and be banished. It is insupportable to retain a polity of noncitizens within our state—a nation, as it were, within our nation."

Although many Jews did assimilate, they were not necessarily welcomed into the broader streams of society. Among the more paranoid of anti-Semites, the Jews' willingness to assimilate was proof of their supposed desire to attack Christian society from within. Friedrich II of Prussia issued an edict in 1744 that expelled all Jews from the city of Breslau, except for ten merchant and financial families. A similar enactment for the city of Berlin added that the few Jews who were allowed to remain in the capital could do so only on the condition that they refrain from marrying and bearing children. That was in 1750, the same year as when Maria Theresa of Austria evicted the Jews from the whole of Bohemia, only to invite them back, later, with the inspired idea of requiring them to pay a fee every ten years for the right to remain.[11] Nevertheless, numerous **Acts of Toleration** that offered full or partial constitutional rights to Jews were promulgated in country after country: Holland (1657), the British colonies (1665, 1740), Britain itself (1753), France (1781), Austria (1782), Spain (1789), and Hungary (1791).

But changes in law occur in advance of changes in popular opinion as often as they occur in response to them, and popular prejudices against Jews remained common across the Continent. The best hope for the future therefore lay not in the conversion or assimilation of the Jews but in the promotion of tolerance as a secular, civil virtue applicable to all regardless of faith. This was Spinoza's point when he wrote in his *Theological-Political Treatise* (1670) that all nations, even the Jews themselves, must surrender their self-appointed roles as the unique possessors of heavenly blessing, since "every man's happiness and true blessedness consists in enjoying the Good, not in indulging in the belief that he alone, to the exclusion of all others, is enjoying it. Anyone who thinks himself to be somehow more blessed and fortunate than his neighbors is therefore actually ignorant of both happiness and good fortune." Other Enlightened writers, notably Voltaire and Kant, ridiculed Judaism as a faith yet championed Jewish rights of full citizenship and had several Jews among their close friends.

The German playwright and philosopher Gotthold Lessing (1729–1781) wrote two plays that dramatized the plight of European Jewry—*The Jews* (1754) and *Nathan the Wise* (1779)—and presented (scandalously, for the time) Jewish characters who were more virtuous and kindhearted than their Christian neighbors.[12] In the latter play, which takes place during the Third Crusade, there is a scene in which the title character tells the Muslim warlord Saladin a parable. A wealthy, powerful, and noble-spirited man possessed a beautiful ring that enabled

---

[11] In 1752, Maria Theresa promulgated a decree limiting all Jewish families to having a single son—or else face eviction.

[12] Few Enlightenment plays appeal to modern tastes. Has anyone ever seen a production of Voltaire's *Oedipus* (1718), often cited as the greatest tragedy of the 18th century?

its wearer to enjoy God's special love and favor, and decreed that the ring shall be passed down the generations with each owner giving it to the son he loved the most. After several generations, one owner decided that he loved all three of his sons equally and so had two exact replicas of the ring made. None of the three heirs therefore knew for certain which ring was the original. In that situation, Lessing writes, the choices are stark: either the sons and their successors fight one another eternally, each certain that his own ring is the true one, or they decide to live together in peace in the hope that his ring is authentic and that its authenticity is proven by the excellence of its wearer's moral behavior. The parable is apt as a description of Lessing's hope for religious toleration and as a general expression of the spirit of the reformers. The only solution to religious strife, they maintained, is secular virtue.

THE UNENLIGHTENED

Competing ideas and tensions existed among the Enlightened about the lower orders of society as well, who still comprised the overwhelming bulk of the population. Some writers—Locke, Hume, Voltaire, and Kant especially among them—regarded the idea of radical democracy as sheer lunacy. But as poverty and its consequences spread, what was to be done? For Locke and Voltaire, to give common farmers and laborers a political voice equal to that of the educated and propertied was an offense to intelligence and good taste. To Hume, distinction by birth was as fixed as distinction by race. Just as "there never was a civilized nation of any other complexion than white," so too the notion of the civilized mass of common people was unimaginable. As for Kant, the only political or civic freedom he could envision was one of freedom of the Enlightened from the tyranny of the brutish common folk:

> In truth, only a ruler with a large and disciplined army at his disposal can say, "Debate as much you wish, but obey me!" An ironical fact thus emerges—that the greater the degree of civic freedom, the more limited the freedom of the spirit; but a lesser degree of civic freedom allows the [Enlightened] mind to grow to the utmost it is capable of doing.

As for Voltaire, he wrote movingly in his great *Treatise on Toleration*:

> It takes no great art, no specially trained eloquence, to show that all Christians should have tolerance for one another—but I am going one step further and asserting that all men should be regarded as brothers to one another. What? A Turk, my brother? A Chinaman, my brother?

A Jew? A Siamese? To which I respond: Yes! Absolutely! After all, are we not all children of the same Father, all created by the same God?

And yet Voltaire's personal letters and diaries, which fill 102 volumes in their standard edition, make plain that he despised Jews. Racial vituperation and caricature pour off their pages with numbing regularity. His anti-Semitism, like Martin Luther's in the 16th century, was certainly no worse than that of his contemporaries, yet his stature lent prejudice a shameful degree of legitimation. His views of the lower orders were no less odious. He finds them ignorant, brutish, foul-smelling, lazy, simplistic, incapable of understanding or appreciating the noble work of the philosophes.

The Simple Pleasures of Life   Louis Le Nain (1593–1648) was one of three French artist brothers, all of whom signed their works with only their family name, thus making it difficult to tell which brother painted which painting. The confusion is fitting, in its way, for the closeness and good cheer of the brothers is a common element in their paintings. Whether portraying a panel of city aldermen, a group of friends around a gaming table, or, as here, a peasant family listening to their grandfather play a song on his pipe, the Le Nain brothers show commoners' lives with dignity and grace.

Few of the philosophes or those who read them felt any shame about disregarding the lowest levels of society. Millions of peasants lived on the edge of poverty and famine. Those who could not pay their rent were driven from the land. In France alone nearly a quarter million peasants, on average, lost their farms per year over the 18th century and, having no place to go, migrated into the cities. Across Europe, from Ireland to Poland, between 10 and 20 percent of all city dwellers were indigent laborers who depended entirely on charity for survival. The possibilities this raised for crime led local governments to build ever more workhouses, where the indigent presumably could earn their keep by doing low-grade manufacturing labor. In reality, nearly a quarter of them died within six months of entering the poorhouse.

The number of these institutions across Europe more than doubled from 1700 to 1789, with the bulk of that increase occurring after 1740. (The population of Europe increased by only 30 percent over the same period.) With these demographic shifts came new social problems. By 1789 nearly one-fifth of all childbirths in Europe occurred out of marriage, a key factor in which was the number of poor women who entered domestic service to the better-off. In the German principalities, the rate of out-of-wedlock births quadrupled from 1700 to 1800. Many novels of the era, such as the immensely popular *Pamela, or Virtue Rewarded* (1740) by Samuel Richardson, narrate the drama of young girls in service at the mercy of their employers.[13]

Poverty grew more visible as it worsened, since the cities became choked with unemployed, starving crowds. The problem was exacerbated by disputes over whose responsibility they were. Traditionally, Europe's poor had depended on churches, religious confraternities, guild-supported hospices, and almsgiving by those lucky enough to have money to spare. Caring for the indigent was generally not regarded as a responsibility of the state. But the numbers of the wretched, and the social ills associated with their condition, became so acute that radical new approaches were needed.

Jonathan Swift (1667–1745) offered an ironic one with his famous essay "A Modest Proposal" of 1729, to deal with the teeming swarms of orphan children in Ireland:

> I am assured by our merchants, that a boy or a girl before twelve years old is no salable commodity; and even when they come to this age they will not yield above three pounds, or three pounds and half-a-crown at most on the exchange; which cannot turn to account either to the

---

13   Nor were servant girls the only victims of lecherous rakes. Richardson's richest novel, *Clarissa*, tells of the repeated attempts to seduce the virtuous maiden (of good birth) of the title.

parents or kingdom, the charge of nutriment and rags having been at least four times that value.

I shall now therefore humbly propose my own thoughts, which I hope will not be liable to the least objection. I have been assured by a very knowing American of my acquaintance in London, that a young healthy child well nursed is at a year old a most delicious, nourishing, and wholesome food, whether stewed, roasted, baked, or boiled; and I make no doubt that it will equally serve in a fricassee or a ragout.

His point was satirical, but the essay raises few laughs. A far more charitable and admirable man, Samuel Johnson, wrote that "a decent provision for the poor is a true test of civilization" and opened his own home to a parade of the needy. Yet even he reserved his charity for the "deserving poor"—those who could not care for themselves because of physical or mental debility. Like most of his contemporaries, Johnson expected the unhandicapped poor either to fend for themselves or to accept misery as man's natural condition.

The philosophes, for the most part, failed to do much better. Rousseau, as we saw, argues that man's natural compassion is corroded by the competition for material goods. Economic and social privilege therefore legitimate and perpetuate one another. When Voltaire received a copy of the *Discourse*, he thanked Rousseau for his "newest attack on the human race." His characteristic sarcasm might be dismissed as lighthearted, but a note Voltaire wrote in the margin gives his real opinion away: "Here it is—the philosophy of a wretch who wants nothing more than for the rich to be robbed by the poor."

> To most of the Enlightened, the uneducated laboring masses were simply a fact of nature, and no rational reform of society and civil life could change it.

The philosophes were not utterly heartless. They spoke fervently against the injustices that made the lives of common peasants and laborers worse. Gabriel Bonnot de Mably (1709–1785), for one, asserted the equality of all persons before the law, as well as the equality of their material needs—an early form of communism. But they did not see elevating the lowest strata of society as important, or even desirable. To most of the Enlightened, the uneducated laboring masses were simply a fact of nature, and no rational reform of society and civil life could change it. Even de Mably maintained that peasants were stupid and ignorant. They deserve sympathy, he argues, only because their poverty, which previously had been voluntary, had become institutionalized by absolutism. The philosophes, in sum, aimed at the rational reform of polite society. The great toiling bulk of mankind did not need liberty, wealth, and rights. They only needed better masters.

ASSESSING THE ENLIGHTENMENT

In the context of Europe's intellectual history, the significance of the Enlightenment can hardly be exaggerated. The philosophes generated new ideas, contributed enormously to culture, and inspired later generations to follow in their steps. They promoted political, social, and economic change, and their intellectual, and often personal, courage was extraordinary. But their failures, too, were many. Voltaire's *Candide* and Rousseau's *Emile*—both phenomenal successes in their time—are hard to read today as art. Diderot's plays are rarely performed. The 18th-century poets who are most read today were not part of the Enlightened program and often viewed it skeptically: in England, Alexander Pope (1688–1744) and Samuel Johnson (1709–1784); in Germany, Johann Wolfgang von Goethe (1749–1832) and Novalis (Friedrich von Hardenberg, 1772–1801); in Spain, Juan Meléndez Valdés (1754–1817). Only Edward Gibbon (1737–1794), among the philosophes, produced anything regarded today as literary art of the first rank. His great *History of the Decline and Fall of the Roman Empire* is still viewed as a masterpiece of English prose.

Readers of the Enlightened were numerous and avid. The *Encyclopédie* appeared in thousands of private and public libraries all over France, as did its English, German, and Italian counterparts in those countries (see Map 15.2).

MAP 15.2   Subscriptions to the *Encyclopédie*.

Rousseau's *Emile*, like Voltaire's *Letters on the English* and *Philosophical Dictionary*, was known to tens of thousands. Lectures and public readings by Locke, Smith, Diderot, Beccaria, and others were enjoyed by untold numbers; and their ideas circulated through innumerable salon meetings. They fought against censorship by cleverly disguising their messages, by circulating to an extent under the governments' radar, by book smuggling across borders, and by the black market. But who exactly read these works and embraced their ideas, and what does that say about the sympathies of the Enlightened for others?

Some of the Enlightened's most fervent readers and supporters came from the aristocracy itself. Indeed, a number of the leading philosophes were themselves noble born, such as the Baron de Montesquieu. But it is a mistake to give them too much credit here. The relative size of the European aristocracy, as a demographic percentage, had declined significantly in the preceding two hundred years, owing to baronial war making and the absorption of smaller estates and baronies into larger ones. By the middle of the 18th century hereditary aristocrats made up a small portion of the European population, overall. Generally, the figure was 1–2 percent in England and France and increased as one moved eastward and southward through the Continent from there: 4–5 percent in Germany, 5–6 percent in Italy and in Austria-Hungary, 7–8 percent in Spain, and as much as 9–10 percent in Poland-Lithuania. Russia then provided a firm backstop with a return to a restricted 1–2 percent—although the bulk of these lived in western Russia's regions around Moscow and St. Petersburg, regardless of where their landholdings actually were.

Allowing for differences between countries, approximately 3–4 percent of the European population consisted of the hereditary aristocracy. The nobles found many of the philosophes' ideas worth investigating, but usually only those dealing with technical matters. It was one thing to improve agricultural yields, make mining more efficient, or develop better means to transport rural goods to urban markets. Beyond that, though, few dared or cared to venture. They expected legal privileges and monopolies, not open markets. Mercantilism and feudal privilege guaranteed their income, and Enlightened ideas attracted them only if they could increase their profit margins. Faced with runaway inflation, the nobles insisted with ever greater force on their rights and the seigniorial dues owed them by the peasants. These dues dated back to the 13th century and included payments to use the lord's utilities—namely his mill, oven, and winepress. (Needless to say, the peasants were forbidden to use anyone else's, for good measure.) Peasants commonly owed special taxes on commodities like salt. They had to build and maintain the roads—and then cart the nobles' goods to market.

All this revenue supported the maintenance of chateaux and country houses, fine carriages, the patronage of art and music, clothing of fine silks and ornament, plumed hats, powdered wigs, and (for the women) astonishing hairdressings and gowns. Opportunities for wealth were growing in the capitalist trade

A Feather in Your Cap?   This engraving from Denis Diderot's great *Encyclopedia* shows a group of women haberdashers making feather ornaments to adorn various wigs and gowns.

centered in the cities; but social prejudices made it difficult for aristocrats to sully themselves by doing business with common merchants. Making matters worse, a number of absolutist regimes (France and Spain, most notoriously) made it illegal for them to do so. Burdened by high costs, and with few alternate means of drawing income, many nobles fell into debt and relied on loans to maintain their standards of living.

Some nobles were drawn to Enlightened ideas about society, law, government, and religion—but they were very few. In general, countries with a higher proportion of nobility (Italy, Austria-Hungary, Spain, Poland-Lithuania) also had more impoverished nobles—who, in turn, felt more threatened by change. Noble readers of the philosophes in those countries were very few indeed. In England, France, and Germany, the nobles proved more willing to investigate Enlightened activity.[14] John Locke and David Hume owed much of their living to the patronage of society's greats. Immanuel Kant was revered by countless more Prussians than who actually read and understood him. Diderot had a few noble patrons who could be relied upon to help him out of his legal troubles; and the Baron de Montesquieu and the Marquis de Condorcet actively participated in

---

14   No fewer than thirty of the 160 author-contributors to Diderot's *Encyclopédie* were noble.

the Enlightened movement. But the overwhelming bulk of the aristocracy deeply distrusted more radical philosophes like Diderot and Rousseau and tried hard to marginalize or imprison them.

The main audience for the Enlightened, then, was the middle class—especially the upper strata of it, the professional classes. This comprised well-heeled financiers and merchants, industrialists, medical and legal professionals, and local civil servants. Many of these individuals were as wealthy as many aristocrats and lived lives of extraordinary material comfort. The Enlightened allowed them important roles in intellectual and artistic life that might enhance their reputations. **Salons**, learned societies, patronage of artists and composers, support for theatrical companies were more than just means to promote the new learning. They also controlled its funding and shaped its development. John Locke's wealthy patrons, for example, influenced the development of his political thought, with its stress on property rights; it is impossible to imagine those patrons supporting Rousseau in the same way.

By the 18th century this well-to-do middle class, the **bourgeoisie**, was large enough to support an ambitious campaign. The total population of France, for example, increased from roughly 22 million in 1700 to approximately 30 million in 1800—a gain of about 33 percent. But within that population the number of wealthy bourgeoisie increased 300 percent. Europe now had a highly developed urban culture. The greatest city of all was London, with just over a million people;

Example of an Enlightenment Salon   Here a group of philosophes gathers to hear a reading of Voltaire's play *The Orphan of China* (1755). It cannot have been painted by an eyewitness, since no one is asleep.

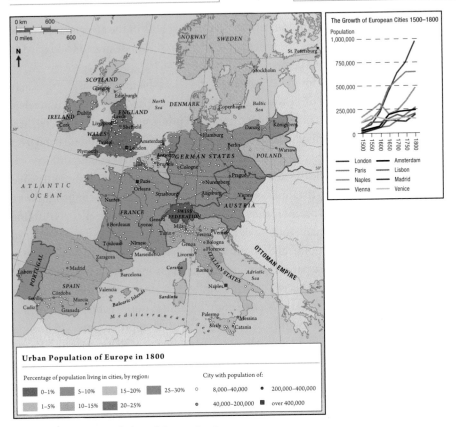

MAP 15.3   Urban Population of Europe in 1800

Paris came next, with 600,000; the next tier was occupied by Berlin, Vienna, and Saint Petersburg, with about 200,000 each. Rome and Milan had slightly fewer, perhaps 150,000 each. Scores of smaller cities, too, could maintain universities, support scientific academies, offer lectures in public halls—and host salons and establish Masonic lodges (see Map 15.3).

> Freemasonry was thus an 18th-century version of keeping a private Facebook account. Here a controlled and closed circle of friends could stay in touch, trade ideas, and promote new projects.

Masonic lodges date to the 17th century, perhaps starting in Scotland. They were essentially private clubs, whose members were sworn to secrecy about their activities.[15] For a nobleman, mingling in public with commoners was social suicide. As Freemasons, however, nobles could socialize with well-to-do commoners, either to arrange business dealings or to support programs such as the Enlightenment. Freemasonry was thus an 18th-century version

---

15   Symbols like pyramids and illuminated eyes made Masonic lodges appear to descend from medieval guilds or secret societies like the Knights Templar. Some of this imagery appears today on U.S. currency.

of keeping a private Facebook account. Here a controlled and closed circle of friends could stay in touch, trade ideas, and promote new projects. In *War and Peace*, Leo Tolstoy sends his main character, Pierre Bezuhov, into the lodges in search of his own brand of enlightenment.

The Catholic Church condemned **freemasonry** as evil. The church saw it as a conspiracy to destroy the divinely ordained institutions that kept the world in order. (This response explains the nonsense in novels like *The Da Vinci Code*.) However, by 1750 Masonry had spread as far east as Poland and Russia, and as far west as the American colonies, where figures like George Washington and Benjamin Franklin were members. In Paris alone, in the 1770s, there were well over ten thousand Masons. Through such stratagems as these, Enlightened ideas spread much further than they could simply through book sales.

Most urban professionals clearly supported the scientific and aesthetic programs of the Enlightened. They favored breaking away from mercantilism and unleashing the free market—which is hardly surprising, since they were the ones most likely to benefit. They advocated Enlightened reforms in education as well, to promote science and technological development. None, however, spoke out in favor of public education for the masses. They desired instead vocational training for urban workers, with the elites in control of the curriculum, leaving higher matters like philosophy and political theory to leaders of the new society.

On political matters, the elites were divided. Enlightened despotism still seemed the best of all possible political worlds to many. This group advocated a thorough reform and improvement of the current systems of governance, but not a revolution. But by the 1770s the pendulum was swinging in favor of a clean break with the past, a destruction of the Old Regime, and the creation of a new form of republic. This is also the decade in which Voltaire's reign as the supreme philosophe began to give way to Rousseau's. But the radical philosophes disagreed with their moderate colleagues mostly in degree. Both political programs were based on the rationality of the human world. Humans might be essentially good (to the radicals) or at least potentially good (to the moderates). Either way, they had it within their power to create happiness here on earth, if only they adapted their behavior to the laws of nature.

> To critics of the Enlightenment, both then and now, the world hardly works according to universal laws. The very belief is itself unreasonable and a new form of oppression; it merely substitutes one system of human bondage for another.

To critics of the Enlightenment, both then and now, the world hardly works according to universal laws. The very belief is itself unreasonable and a new form of oppression; it merely substitutes one system of human bondage for another. In economics, they say, it encourages docile acceptance of what the masters of **laissez-faire** capitalism desire. Moreover, it gives those masters a morally odious excuse. They can claim to be unable to change the system that keeps them enriched and in power. This is just what Karl Marx argued in the 19th century, and Diderot and Rousseau may have hinted at it as well.

Were the Enlightened truly the champions of the common man? Most of them did not pretend to be. They wanted a world based on merit and reasoned argument rather than inherited privilege. If they saw themselves as the unique possessors of that merit, they were simply being human. Rousseau, above all, radicalized the Enlightenment by speaking passionately to the lower orders. He came from them, and he urged them to disregard the fancy theories of the powdered and pampered salons. He especially despised Voltaire as a hypocrite. Voltaire died rich, yet a bitter man, for he was never granted the peerage he so desperately desired. Lauded by all as a champion of freedom, he had been shunted aside by a vulgar upstart from Geneva. When Rousseau cast the light of his reason on the Enlightened, he found them wanting, and he called on the masses to take their fates into their own hands. He was fortunate to have died in 1778, for he never saw the results of that call.

WHO, WHAT, WHERE

Acts of Toleration	laissez-faire
bourgeoisie	League of Augsburg
deism	market
Enlightenment	noble savage
freemasonry	philosophes
Hasidim	salons
Haskalah	

SUGGESTED READINGS

Primary Sources

Bayle, Pierre. *Historical and Critical Dictionary.*

Beccaria, Cesare. *On Crimes and Punishments.*

Diderot, Denis. *Encyclopedia.*

Hume, David. *An Enquiry Regarding Human Understanding.*

Locke, John. *An Essay on Human Understanding.*

———. *Two Treatises on Civil Government.*

Montesquieu, Baron Charles de. *The Spirit of the Laws.*

Rousseau, Jean-Jacques. *Confessions.*

———. *Discourse on the Origins of Inequality.*

———. *The Social Contract.*

Smith, Adam. *The Wealth of Nations.*

Voltaire. *Candide.*

———. *A Philosophical Dictionary.*

Source Anthologies

Hyland, Paul, ed. *The Enlightenment: A Sourcebook and Reader* (2001).

Jacob, Margaret C. *The Enlightenment: A Brief History with Documents* (2000).

Studies

Anderson, Fred. *Crucible of War: The Seven Years' War and the Fate of Empire in British North America, 1754–1766* (2000).

Berg, Maxine. *Luxury and Pleasure in Eighteenth-Century Britain* (2005).

Blanning, T. C. W. *The Culture of Power and the Power of Culture: Old Regime Europe, 1660–1789* (2002).

Blom, Philipp. *Enlightening the World: "Encyclopédie," the Book that Changed the World* (2005).

Buchan, James. *The Authentic Adam Smith: His Life and Ideas* (2006).

Dale, Richard. *The First Crash: Lessons from the South Sea Bubble* (2004).

Damrosch, Leo. *Jean-Jacques Rousseau: Restless Genius* (2007).

Doyle, William. *Aristocracy and Its Enemies in the Age of Revolution* (2009).

Feiner, Shmuel. *Haskalah and History: The Emergence of a Modern Jewish Historical Consciousness* (2004).

———. *The Jewish Enlightenment* (2003).

Groenewegen, Peter D. *Eighteenth-Century Economics: Turgot, Beccaria, and Smith and Their Contemporaries* (2002).

Hess, Jonathan M. *Germans, Jews, and the Claims of Modernity* (2002).

Israel, Jonathan. *Democratic Enlightenment: Philosophy, Revolution, and Human Rights, 1750–1790* (2011).

———. *Enlightenment Contested: Philosophy, Modernity, and the Emancipation of Man, 1670–1752* (2006).

———. *Radical Enlightenment: Philosophy and the Making of Modernity, 1650–1750* (2001).

McMahon, Darrin M. *Enemies of the Enlightenment: The French Counter-Enlightenment and the Making of Modernity* (2001).

Munck, Thomas. *The Enlightenment: A Comparative Social History, 1724–1794* (2000).

Pearson, Roger. *Voltaire Almighty: A Life in Pursuit of Freedom* (2005).

Porter, Roy. *The Creation of the Modern World: The Untold Story of the British Enlightenment* (2000).

Saul, John Ralston. *Voltaire's Bastards: The Dictatorship of Reason in the West* (1992).

Straub, Kristina. *Domestic Affairs: Intimacy, Eroticism, and Violence between Servants and Masters in Eighteenth-Century Britain* (2005).

Sutcliffe, Adam. *Judaism and Enlightenment* (2003).

Zaretsky, Robert, and John T. Scott. *The Philosophers' Quarrel: Rousseau, Hume, and the Limits of Human Understanding* (2009).

For additional resources, including maps, primary sources, visuals, web links, and quizzes, please go to **www.oup.com/us/backman.**

DÉCLARATION DES DROITS DE L'HOMME ET DU CITOYEN,

Décrétés par l'Assemblée Nationale dans les séances des 20, 21, 23, 24 et 26 août 1789, acceptés par le Roi

PRÉAMBULE

LES représentans du peuple François, constitués en assemblée nationale, considérant que l'ignorance, l'oubli ou le mépris des droits de l'homme sont les seules causes des malheurs publics et de la corruption des gouvernemens ont résolu d'exposer dans une déclaration solemnelle, les droits naturels, inaliénables et sacrés de l'homme: afin que cette déclaration constamment présente à tous les membres du corps social, leur rappelle sans cesse leurs droits et leurs devoirs, afin que les actes du pouvoir legislatif et ceux du pouvoir exécutif, pouvant être à chaque instant comparés avec le but de toute institution politique, en soient plus respectés; afin que les reclamations des citoyens, fondées désormais sur des principes simples et incontestables, tournent toujours au maintien de la constitution et du bonheur de tous.

EN conséquence, l'assemblée nationale reconnoit et déclare, en présence et sous les auspices de l'Etre suprême les droits suivans de l'homme et du citoyen.

ARTICLE PREMIER

LES hommes naissent et demeurent libres et égaux en droits: les distinctions sociales ne peuvent être fondées que sur l'utilité commune.

II.

LE but de toute association politique est la conservation des droits naturels et imprescriptibles de l'homme: ces droits sont la liberté, la propriété, la sureté, et la résistance à l'oppression.

III.

LE principe de toute souveraineté réside essentiellement dans la nation, nul corps, nul individu ne peut exercer d'autorité qui n'en emane expressement.

IV.

LA liberté consiste à pouvoir faire tout ce qui ne nuit pas à autrui: Ainsi, l'exercice des droits naturels de chaque homme, n'a de bornes que celles qui assurent aux autres membres de la société la jouissance de ces mêmes droits; ces bornes ne peuvent être déterminées que par la loi.

V.

LA loi n'a le droit de défendre que les actions nuisibles à la société. Tout ce qui n'est pas défendu par la loi ne peut être empêché, et nul ne peut être contraint à faire ce qu'elle n'ordonne pas.

VI.

LA loi est l'expression de la volonté générale; tous les citoyens ont droit de concourir personnellement, ou par leurs représentans, à sa formation: elle doit être la même pour tous, soit qu'elle protege, soit qu'elle punisse. Tous les citoyens étant égaux a ses yeux, sont également admissibles a toutes dignités, places et emplois publics, selon leur capacité, et sans autres distinction que celles de leurs vertus et de leurs talens

VII.

NUL homme ne peut être accusé, arrêté ni détenu que dans les cas déterminés par la loi, et selon les formes qu'elle a prescrites; ceux qui sollitent, expédient, exécutent ou font exécuter des ordres arbitraires, doivent être punis; mais tout citoyen appelé ou saisi en vertu de la loi, doit obéir à l'instant, il se rend coupable par la résistance.

VIII.

LA loi ne doit établir que des peines strictement et évidemment nécessaire, et nul ne peut être puni qu'en vertu d'une loi établie, et promulguée antérieurement au délit, et légalement appliquée.

IX.

TOUT homme étant présumé innocent jusqu'à ce qu'il ait été déclaré coupable, s'il est jugé indispensable de l'arrêter, toute rigueur qui ne serait pas nécessaire pour s'assurer de sa personne doit être sévèrement réprimée par la loi.

X.

NUL ne doit être inquieté pour ses opinions, mêmes religieuses pourvu que leur manifestation ne trouble pas l'ordre public etabli par la loi.

XI.

LA libre communication des pensées et des opinions est un des droits les plus precieux de l'homme: tout citoyen peut donc parler écrire, imprimer librement: sauf à répondre de l'abus de cette liberté dans les cas déterminés par la loi.

XII.

LA garantie des droits de l'homme et du citoyen nécessite une force publique; cette force est donc instituée pour l'avantage de tous, et non pour l'utilité particuliere de ceux a qui elle est confiée.

XIII.

POUR l'entretien de la force publique, et pour les dépenses d'administration, une contribution commune est indispensable; elle doit être également répartie entre les citoyens en raison de leurs facultés

XIV.

LES citoyens ont le droit de constater par eux même ou par leurs représentans, la nécessité de la contribution publique, de la consentir librement, d'en suivre l'emploi, et d'en déterminer la quotité, l'assiette, le recouvrement et la durée.

XV.

LA société a le droit de demander compte a tout agent public de son administration.

XVI.

TOUTE société, dans laquelle la garantie des droits n'est pas assurée, ni la séparation des pouvoirs déterminée, n'a point de constitution.

XVII.

LES propriétés étant un droit inviolable et sacré, nul ne peut en être privé, si ce n'est lorsque la nécessité publique, légalement constatée, l'exige evidemment, et sous la condition d'une juste et préalable indemnité.

AUX REPRESENTANS DU PEUPLE FRANCOIS

CHAPTER 16

The War against Absolutism

1789–1815

In the minds of many, the French not least among them, the Revolution of 1789 is the prime divider of European history, the watershed moment that announced the dramatic and bloody beginning of the modern age. Of the drama and blood there is no doubt. The Revolution overthrew monarchy, abolished aristocracy and the decayed remnants of feudalism, instituted representative government, and asserted the innate human rights of liberty, freedom of expression, and equality before the law. It proclaimed the beginning of a new era of enlightened independence. Along the way it also slaughtered tens of thousands of victims, triggered a continental war, terrorized into silent obedience the very people it purported to free, ruined fortunes, and crushed forms of religious and cultural life that had buoyed human spirits through centuries of deprivation and struggle.

THE GREATER WEST, ca. 1800

It also led to an equally tumultuous and bloody aftermath that transformed the whole of Europe—and not just in the direction of liberty and modernity. The rise of Napoleon in France brought reform elsewhere, as he sought to expand his empire. Meanwhile an opening between Europe and the Turks invited parallel changes in Islam.

A REVOLUTION IN WESTERN HISTORY?

◄ **The Declaration of the Rights of Man and the Citizen** The central document of the French Revolution, enacted by the National Assembly on August 26, 1789.

Much of the vocabulary of modern political life derives from the Revolution. Factions are described as "left," "right," "centrist," or "radical";

institutions promote their aims through "declarations" and "agendas"—which their opponents dismiss as "propaganda." The "will of the people," not the privileges of the mighty, is the touchstone for political rectitude. Even the ideology of a faction, including those dedicated to "terrorism," derives from the Revolution. So large does the Revolution loom in most Western minds that it is the first single political event given an entire chapter in most general histories of Europe. (In this respect it joins the two World Wars to form a triad of Most Important Events in Western History.)

> So large does the Revolution loom in most Western minds that it is the first single political event given an entire chapter in most general histories of Europe.

But other people disagree. For all its physical and philosophical carnage, after all, the Revolution changed nothing, they say. France began the year 1789 with a financially and morally corrupt political system. It persecuted millions in order to serve the interests of a self-regarding and indulgent minority, while wrapping itself in an aura of irreplaceability. And when the Revolution ended ten years later, with Napoleon in dictatorial charge, France had simply replaced one brutal regime with another. Much of France's subsequent political history, they argue, has consisted merely of a perpetual swing of the pendulum from one extreme to another: the French Republic (1792–1804), then Empire (1804–1814), then Second Republic (1848–1852), then Second Empire (1852–1870), then Third Republic (1870–1940), then Vichy and Nazi-occupied France (1940–1945), then Fourth Republic (1946–1958)—which was followed, in the aftermath of the definitive collapse of empire with the loss of Algeria, by a Fifth Republic (1958–present).

In 1989, on the eve of the bicentennial of the French Revolution, Britain's then–prime minister Margaret Thatcher was invited by the leading Parisian newspaper *Le Monde* to comment on the significance of the Revolution for advancing the cause of human rights in the world. She replied, with her customary directness, that she thought the Revolution had contributed nothing at all:

CHAPTER TIMELINE

| 1729–1797 | 1758–1794 | 1789–1807 |
| Edmund Burke | Maximillian Robespierre | Selim III, Ottoman sultan |

| 1737–1809 | 1789 | 1792 |
| Thomas Paine | Beginning of the French Revolution | Founding of the French Republic; Wollstonecraft, *A Vindication of the Rights of Man* |

Human rights did not begin with the French Revolution. . . . [but] really stem from a mixture of Judaism and Christianity. . . . [Here in England we] had 1688, our quiet revolution, where Parliament exerted its will over the king. . . . It was not the sort of Revolution that France's was. . . . "Liberty, Equality, Fraternity"—[France's revolutionaries] forgot *Obligations* and *Duties*, I think. And then of course the "Fraternity" went missing for a long time.   (*The Downing Street Years*)

Le Monde's angry headline the next day complained: "Thatcher Says Human Rights Did Not Begin in France."

So was the French Revolution one of the three most important events in Western history, or was it an inconsequential spasm of violence? Or is the truth somewhere in between? But if the latter, then why does the Revolution still elicit such powerful sentiments? Even in the eyes of its contemporaries, the Revolution appeared in widely varying guises. To Edmund Burke (1729–1797), one of the founders of modern political conservatism and a passionate champion of America's break from England, the Revolution showed only that the French people had proven themselves to be

the ablest architects of ruin that had hitherto existed in the world. In that very short space of time they ha[ve] completely pulled down to the ground, their monarchy; their church; their nobility; their law; their revenue; their army; their navy; their commerce; their arts; and their manufactures. . . . [There is a danger of] an imitation of the excesses of an irrational, unprincipled, proscribing, confiscating, plundering, ferocious, bloody and tyrannical democracy. . . . [In religion] the danger of their example is no longer from intolerance, but from Atheism; a foul, unnatural vice, foe to all the dignity and consolation of mankind; which seems in France, for a long time, to have been embodied into a faction, accredited, and almost avowed.

1799
Napoleon
becomes consul

1805
Battle of Trafalgar

1815
Battle of Waterloo

1804
Napoleon crowned
emperor

1812
Napoleon invades
France

1821
Death of Napoleon

TABLE 16.1   **Timeline of the French Revolution**

	NATIONAL ASSEMBLY, 1789–1791
June 20, 1789	Tennis Court Oath.
July 14, 1789	Storming of the Bastille.
Aug. 26, 1789	Assembly adopts The Declaration of the Rights of Man.
Oct. 5, 1789	Women's March on Versailles.
Nov. 2, 1789	All church property in France is nationalized.
Feb. 13, 1790	Suppression of monasteries and religious orders.
May 19, 1790	Feudalism abolished by National Assembly.
Feb. 28, 1791	400 nobles arrested at Tuileries Palace.
June 25, 1791	The royal family is caught trying to flee the country.
Sept. 14, 1791	Louis XVI formally accept new Constitution.
	LEGISLATIVE ASSEMBLY, 1791–1792
Oct. 1, 1791	National Assembly is dissolved; Legislative Assembly assumes power.
January, 1792	Food riots begin in Paris, last until March.
Feb. 7, 1792	Austria and Prussia form alliance to crush Revolution.
Mar. 20, 1792	Assembly adopt guillotine as official means of execution.
Apr. 20, 1792	France declares war on Austria and Prussia.
July 30, 1792	Austria and Prussia invade France.
Aug. 13, 1792	Louis XVI and family arrested after the storming of the Tuileries Palace.
	NATIONAL CONVENTION, 1792–1795
Sept. 20, 1792	Legislative Assembly dissolved. National Convention takes power.
Sept. 21, 1792	Monarchy abolished. French Republic declared.
Dec. 3, 1792	Louis XVI brought to trial.
Jan. 21, 1793	Execution of Louis XVI.
Apr. 6, 1793	Committee for Public Safety created.
June 10, 1793	Jacobins take control of Committee for Public Safety.
Sept. 5, 1793	The Reign of Terror begins.
Oct. 16, 1793	Marie Antoinette executed.
March 28, 1794	Death of Marquis de Condorcet in prison.
March 30, 1794	Danton executed.
May 8, 1794	Antoine Lavoisier executed.
July 28, 1794	Robespierre executed.
July 14, 1795	*Marseillaise* selected as the French national anthem.
Aug. 22, 1795	Constitution ratified.
Oct. 26, 1795	National Convention dissolved.
	THE DIRECTORY, 1795–1799
Nov. 2, 1795	The Executive Directory takes power.
May 10, 1796	Battle of Lodi.
June 4, 1796	Siege of Mantua.
Oct. 17, 1797	Treaty of Campo Formio.
July 21, 1798	Napoleon wins Battle of the Pyramids
Aug. 24, 1799	Napoleon leaves Egypt.
Oct. 9, 1799	Napoleon returns to France.
Nov. 9, 1799	Napoleon dissolves the Directory (18th Brumaire).
Dec. 24, 1799	Napoleon assumes power under title of Consul.

And yet the overthrow of the French monarchy led other Englishmen, like the young poets William Wordsworth (1770–1850) and Samuel Coleridge (1772–1834), to race to the Continent to witness firsthand the creation of a utopian new world. As Wordsworth wrote:

> Bliss was it in that dawn to be alive,
> But to be young was very heaven!—Oh! Times,
> In which the meager, stale, forbidding ways
> Of custom, law, and statute, took at once
> The attraction of a country in romance!
> When Reason seemed the most to assert her rights,
> When most intent on making of herself
> A prime Enchantress—to assist the work,
> Which then was going forward in her name!

Whether for the nobility of its aims or the vulgarity of its methods, the Revolution still fascinates and impassions.

REVOLUTIONARY ROAD

The great German poet Johan Wolfgang von Goethe (1749–1832) may not have had France in mind when he stated that "revolutions are never the fault of the people, but of the government," but the judgment fits the French case—at least as an immediate cause. The Old Regime was in fiscal free fall from 1750 on—long before the revolution turned radical.

Wars with Spain, Holland, Austria, and Prussia had drained money from the treasury at an astonishing rate, but the losses simply made war even more necessary: the crown, having already sucked every possible sou out of the domestic economy, needed more lands and people to plunder in order to maintain their place. Then, too, France had lent considerable support to the American Revolution, not from a desire to see democracy supplant monarchy everywhere but from a conviction that anything that undermined England's power indirectly favored France's. Crop failures plagued the kingdom at midcentury too, driving rent payers into arrears and their landlords into still-deeper debt themselves. When royal and aristocratic expenditures continued unabated, the result was a vast web of indebtedness. France had no national bank to regulate the fiscal rot, which forced the throne to live off short-term, high-interest loans from private sources. By the late 1770s fully 50 percent of the annual national budget went simply to paying the interest on the debt. Finance ministers came and went with steady regularity, some advocating fiscal restraint (a repulsive idea, to the court) and others supporting exuberant spending as a means of stimulating the economy. Heavier taxes were levied on the commoners to the point where massive protest loomed. No one seemed to know how to stop the downslide.

Louis XV (r. 1715–1774) had succeeded to the throne as a young child, and during the regency established for him (under the Duke of Orléans), much of the French aristocracy had worked tirelessly to secure and extend their privileges—especially exemption from having to pay most taxes. The ancient aristocratic-led system of legal courts (**parlements**) was reintroduced, and aristocratic councils replaced royal bureaucrats at every level of government. Louis tried to overturn these changes when he reached majority age. In 1771 he deployed the army to dissolve the parlements and oust the aristocratic governing councils; the next decade witnessed a continued back-and-forth between king and aristocracy that would have been unthinkable in the days of Louis XIV, but the gaping maw of national debt emboldened people to attempt the inconceivable. Meanwhile, Enlightened ideas about economic and social reform gained support at court as a means of forestalling disaster. Amid cries of alarm over royal tyranny trampling the traditional liberties of the nobles, Louis ordered a lifting of mercantilist policies restricting the grain trade, abolished the guild structure, and promoted religious toleration for France's eight million Protestants. All of this was bad enough, as far as the aristocracy was concerned—but then Louis announced his support, in 1775, for a comprehensive land tax. The announcement sparked a firestorm of complaint.

Calls for such a tax were nevertheless repeated throughout the 1770s and 1780s as the only possible way to address the crisis. Further royal steps included abolishing serfdom, condemning the use of judicial torture, and reforming the prisons, but these measures—though generally popular—required new debt financing, which only added urgency to the call for the nobles to relinquish their tax exemptions. By 1787, amid bread riots by the peasantry and loud denunciations of royal abuses of power, an aristocratic council demanded the reestablishment of the historical French legislative body known as the **Estates General**. This body, which had not met since 1614, had previously held jurisdiction over tax issues; the nobles calling for it to convene rested their hopes in a simple statistical fact: the legislature, being made up of three bodies (or estates)—one for the nobility, one for the clergy, and one for the commoners—was sure to ratify the aristocracy's position supporting tax exemption because every single one of the eight thousand–plus ecclesiastical offices represented in the clerical estate was held by a member of the nobility. No matter how loudly the **Third Estate**, the commoners, bellowed for reform, the abolition of the nobles' tax emption would lose by a two-to-one vote.

In the spring of 1789 elections were held around France to select the estates' delegates. Representatives of the commoners compiled detailed records of local

The Three Estates   French cartoon from 1789 depicting three fattened members of the privileged classes riding atop a naked, chained, and blindfolded commoner (who is also being spurred in a most unfortunate place). The riders are an aristocrat, a bishop, and a judge. The cartoon's message is clear.

grievances to be brought to Paris; these grievance notebooks (*cahiers des doléances*) offer fascinating views of the attitudes and concerns of the common populace. An example comes from a small commune on the river Orge, not far from Paris:

> The order of the Third Estate of... Dourdan, filled with gratitude for the fatherly kindness of Our King Who deems it fitting to restore our rights and customs of old, and setting aside for the moment our present sufferings and debilities... begs Him to accept this statement of our grievances, complaints, and remonstrances.... This estate formally petitions:
>
> That no citizen should ever lose his freedom except according to the dictates of the law; ... that no letters nor other writings sent through the public mail be the cause of the detention of any citizen, except in the case of treason or conspiracy against the state; ... that the property of all citizens be respected as inviolable; ... that every poll tax be abolished... and

replaced by a tax on land and real property. . . and that the burden of this
new tax be imposed equally on every class of citizen without distinction; . . . that the venality of civil offices be abolished; . . . that statutes
limiting admission to officer status in the military to members of the
nobility be rescinded; . . . that today's militia, which devastates the countryside, pulls workers away from their field labor, forces people into pre-
mature and ill-advised marriages [commoners could avoid being pressed
into the militias by marrying], and subjects individuals to secret and arbitrary taxes, be abolished and replaced by a public, volunteer army.
(*Archives parlementaires de 1787 à 1860*, ed. Jérôme Mavidal and Èmile
Laurent [Paris, 1862], ser. 1, vol. 3, pp. 250–254.)

But as the representatives gathered in Paris in June, the clerical and aristocratic
estates decided to bar the Third Estate representatives from admission to the assembly—at which those representatives proclaimed themselves, together with the
king, the sole legitimate government of France and began to write a new constitution. The Revolution, which had begun as a revolt of the nobles against the demands
of the king and people for a land tax, had now become a popular movement to establish a constitutional monarchy that abolished aristocratic privilege.

The Oath of the Tennis Court, June 20, 1789   Representatives of the Third Estate gathered angrily on
the largest available open space, a tennis court—for what came to be known as the Tennis Court Oath.

THE REVOLUTION TURNS RADICAL

To this point the Revolution had called merely for the reform of the state, not its destruction. By the end of 1789 the National Assembly, as the new government was called, had stormed the Bastille and freed the (surprisingly few) political prisoners held captive there, had abolished feudalism (although providing compensation for the nobles' losses), had issued a Declaration of the Rights of Man and Citizen, and had confiscated and sold all the ecclesiastical lands in the nation in order to pay off the royal debt. Nevertheless, the new government failed to win active national support. Across France most peasant farmers and laborers, presumably fearing an aristocratic backlash, did little more than seize the opportunity to destroy the local records that documented their particular obligations to their landlords, then quietly returned to their work while waiting for the political fracas in Paris to settle down. Rumors spread quickly of noble-backed gangs of thugs roaming the countryside seeking rebellion-sympathizing peasants to attack. A corps of six thousand Parisian women marched to Versailles and brought the royal family back into the city, both to prevent them from leaving the country and to enlist them in joining the new regime.

But it became clear throughout 1790 and 1791 that the Revolution in Paris was not winning the hearts and minds of the nation as a whole. And as it did, the leaders of the new government began to split into factions, each offering a more thoroughgoing platform of change in hopes of winning support. The two dominant parties were the Girondists and the Jacobins, the former favoring a reformed constitutional monarchy and the latter being dedicated to a more radical democracy—although it is difficult to identify specific political programs to any given faction, since policies, proposals, and personalities changed so rapidly among them.

In 1792, after three years of steadily decaying order, France was invaded by Austria and Prussia, who were determined to come to the aid not of Louis XVI but the ideal of absolutism. The military situation was dire, for although France's army was large, over two-thirds of its aristocratic officer corps had long since fled the country, leaving most of the military units leaderless. Even worse, most of those officers had joined the counter-Revolutionary forces. Sensing disaster, Louis and his family tried to flee the country but were caught at the border and brought back to Paris in chains. The Jacobins, by this time led by Maximilien Robespierre (1758–1794), a passionate ideologue who believed that anything standing in the way of the Revolution had to be eradicated, eventually seized control of the government through its leadership of the innocent-sounding Committee for Public Safety. But Robespierre and his committee believed fervently that the enemies of the Revolution would stop at nothing to undermine it, and so began to purge the new government's ranks of individuals and parties whose loyalty to the radical cause was suspect.

The Guillotine   An 18th-century model of a guillotine. Intended as a humane means of execution, the guillotine inadvertently became the central symbol of the Revolution. Its first use was in 1792; the Reign of Terror ended with the beheading of Robespierre himself in mid-1794. Since estimates of the number of people guillotined during the Terror range from fifteen thousand to forty thousand, and since most executions took place in Paris itself, a dedicated spectator could have seen an average of twenty-five to sixty beheadings a day. And in fact great crowds of observers did show up regularly—so many that entrepreneurial vendors printed and sold programs of the daily schedule of beheadings.

The outbreak of pro-royalist rebellion in the far west of France convinced Robespierre that all the achievements of the Revolution to date were threatened. In a shockingly brutal wave of violence in the name of the supposed purification of society—known as the **Reign of Terror** (1792)—Robespierre's clique engineered the arrest of over three hundred thousand French men and women in only nine months, some forty thousand of whom were executed. Defending the harshness of his methods, Robespierre later wrote:

If virtue is the wellspring of popular government in times of peace, then virtue combined with terror is the wellspring of such a government in time of revolution: virtue (without which all terror is fatal) *and* terror (without which all virtue is impotent). For terror is nothing more than swift, sure, and inflexible justice—indeed, it emanates from virtue and is not so much an independent principle as it is a natural consequence of the general idea of democracy when applied to our country's most urgent needs.... Subdue the enemies of liberty by terror [if you must]! You are right to do so, as founders of our Republic. Government, in a Revolution, is a despotism of liberty against tyranny. (*Report on the Principles of Public Morality, 1794*)

Machiavelli would have been proud of the sentiment, and perhaps envious of the superior style, had he lived to read Robespierre. But Robespierre was speaking in a context of catastrophic national emergency, since the Revolution was endangered by foreign invasion, aristocratic plots, and internal dissension. France's internal strife had to be quelled as quickly as possible in order to avoid annihilation.

Robespierre, who fell from power in 1794 and was himself guillotined, remains a divisive figure. Immediately after his death, his political enemies destroyed most of his papers and vilified him as a fanatical dictator—the portrait that long fixed his historical image. In the 19th century, however, groups representing the working-class French, then undergoing the horrors of the industrial revolution, revived his memory as a persecuted champion of the people. While his methods were harsh, they argued, his goals of eradicating the inequitable distribution of wealth in society and of ensuring the availability of education and work for all were admirable.[1]

The pace of revolution increased through the next two years. The government (renamed the National Convention) executed Louis XVI and criminalized the practice of Christianity, replacing it with the pallid cult of the Goddess of Reason. They adopted a new calendar that renamed all of the months of the year, forcibly introduced the metric system, confiscated the property of all "enemies of the Revolution," and instituted a national military draft. The draft was necessary since Britain, Holland, and Spain had joined Austria and Prussia in the invasion of the country. Spain wanted to defend absolutism; England, which had executed its own King Charles I in 1649 and lived to regret it, hoped mostly to keep France preoccupied with a land war so that it could not challenge England's primacy in the international sea-lanes. Holland's involvement was defensive, since France had launched a surprise attack on it in 1795, in order to provide a counterweight to England and to round up many of the French nobles who had fled to that country.

NAPOLEON AND THE WAR AGAINST ABSOLUTISM

As internal decay and external threat increased, and the Revolution's very existence seemed threatened, the Directory (yet another renaming and retooling of the central administration) summoned its most successful general to Paris to take control of the government, institute martial law, and restore order. His name was Napoleon Bonaparte (1769–1821).

Actually, his name was Napoleone di Buonaparte. Descended from a minor Italian baronial family, he was born and raised on the French-controlled island of Corsica. At the age of ten he moved to Autun in east-central France and enrolled in an elementary military academy, which he followed five years later with a course of study at the elite École militaire in Paris, where he trained to be an artillery officer; in 1785 he received his commission as a second lieutenant in the French army. When the Revolution broke out in 1789, he was back in Corsica and soon was involved in the civil struggle there between factions loyal to the monarchy, to the Jacobins, and to Corsican independence. He supported the Jacobin cause from the start and soon earned the rank of lieutenant colonel. By 1793 he

---

[1]   The British novelist Hilary Mantel indeed presents a sympathetic portrait of Robespierre in A *Place of Greater Safety* (2006).

was back on the Continent and leading campaigns against France's foreign invaders. His early successes on the field and his publication of a pro-Jacobin pamphlet brought him to the admiring attention of the Committee on Public Safety, which promoted him to brigadier general.

Robespierre's fall in 1794 resulted in Napoleon's brief fall from favor, but when he fought off a royalist challenge to the Directory the following year, his restoration was complete. Awarded the position of commander of the interior, Napoleon led the war against the Austrians, who were invading France via Italy. His successes led to another ambitious campaign into Egypt (where he had been sent by Directory leaders who, fearing Napoleon's growing prestige, wanted him out of Europe for a while), in an effort to weaken England's maritime commercial ties with India.[2]

His abilities as military commander made him a natural choice to take over the government once it reached its worst state of decay and strife; not that he was invited to do so. At some point during his Egyptian campaign he learned of the imminent collapse of the Directory and raced back to Paris with his troops in October 1799. A few weeks later, on November 10, 1799, he staged a coup d'état and became the dictator of France—although he had the sense to take the less ominous-sounding title of consul.[3] He initially shared power in a triumvirate that included the Abbé de Sieyès and Pierre-Roger Ducos, two holdovers from the Directory, although he dominated the government from the start. By 1802 all pretense of shared power was done away with, and Napoleon was the sole master of France.

The record of his accomplishments is lengthy and well known. After quelling France's internal conflicts and driving off her foreign invaders, Napoleon set himself to overhauling nearly every aspect of French civil life, problems he attacked with extraordinary energy and intelligence. His contemporaries, whether they admired him or hated him, marveled at his charisma and drive. "A man like me does not care if a million people die" in pursuit of a goal, he once declared. (At the time he said it, he meant it rhetorically; he later put the statement to the test on the battlefields, though.) He rewrote the national constitution and enshrined the notion of egalitarianism before the law and universal suffrage. He created the most fair and comprehensive taxation system France had ever had, abolished all feudal and local customs, and enacted a systematic law code for the entire country. This **Napoleonic Code** emphasized individuals' rights to property,

---

[2]   In legend Napoleon used the Sphinx as a practice target for artillery. Its nose and beard were in fact broken off in the 14th century on orders of a Muslim cleric—outraged that local farmers, to improve their harvest, had made ritual offerings to it.

[3]   According to the Revolutionary calendar, Napoleon become consul on the 18th of Brumaire—the title of a famous essay by Karl Marx.

standardizing the legal structures for contracts, leases, and establishing stock corporations. He also prohibited the creation of merchant guilds, industrial cartels, and trade unions. He then went on and constructed France's first system of national education, with primary and secondary schools (*lycées*) in every major town, established a teachers' training college in Paris, organized a network of military and vocational schools for those drawn to specific professions, and crowned the whole system with a national university.

Yet Napoleon could show pragmatism as well. He invited the exiled nobles willing to swear loyalty to the new constitution to return to France, a shrewd maneuver that brought vast amounts of stolen treasure back into the realm, along with the talent pool of many experienced military and civil officials. Another practical compromise was Napoleon's decision to restore the legal recognition and practice of Catholic and Protestant Christianity; although personally an Enlightened deist, he saw the value of religion as an instrument of social cohesion. While he guaranteed freedom of religious expression, he also arranged that all clergy received their pay directly from the central government, a move that kept Napoleon firmly in control of the churches.

All Men Are Created Equal   This allegorical drawing depicts reason and nature, represented by the two robed female figures on the left, celebrating the equality of whites and blacks in the new revolutionary order.   The black man holds the Rights of Man; on the picture's left demons of injustice flee to wreak havoc elsewhere.

Although he proclaimed himself a Republican, Napoleon did not permit all freedoms. He retained strict limits on freedom of speech and of the press, for example, which made it difficult for any individuals or parties to oppose his will or question his policies. (His defenders argue that the restrictions that Napoleon imposed were simply the standards of communications control to which he was accustomed from the army.) He also denied political rights to women: they were not allowed to vote, to enter contracts, or to hold bank accounts, and they remained the legal dependents of their fathers and husbands. Although he could be personally gallant toward the women in his private life (of whom there were many), he did not hesitate to state his opinion about the different positions of men and women in society. "A husband must possess absolute authority over his wife," he once declared, "and must have the right to say to her, 'Madam, you shall not go out of the house; you shall not go to the theater; you shall not pay a visit to such-and-such a person. And as for the children you bear—they are mine.'"

Napoleon relished his popular image as the savior of the Republic but he also believed in his unique personal authority. He had read much history in his school days and revered the Roman leader Octavian/Augustus, who had saved the Roman Republic by keeping its institutions and customs even while running them with an iron fist. His vision for France was along those lines. To the tips of his fingers and the end of his days, Napoleon believed in France's destiny to lead all of Europe and in his own destiny to lead France in the effort. But that meant addressing the problem of absolutism—for although it had been successfully stamped out in France, it still held sway in nearly every country in Europe, and each one of those regimes was determined to see France's Revolu-

Napoleon Enthroned   The oil portrait by Jean-Auguste Ingres (1780-1867) was first exhibited at the Paris Salon of 1806, where it had a chilly reception. Stiff and imposing, the figure of Napoleon holds the scepter of Charlemagne in his right hand. A stylized version of the German imperial eagle appears on the carpet at his feet. In the background over his left shoulder is a shield representing the states of Italy. Nothing about the painting is subtle – which helps explain its unpopularity.

tion fail. By 1804 he was ready to act. He arranged for an imperial coronation to be performed in Paris by the pope himself, and at the last moment he snatched the crown from the startled pontiff's hands and placed it on his own head.

There would be no question of his subordination to Rome. He was his own man, the ruler of his own state. But an emperor by definition needs an empire. And so he conquered Europe.

THE RUSH TO EMPIRE

As sheer narrative Napoleon's conquests make a long but straightforward tale, full of dramatic, impressive, frequently startling and moving episodes; but they are not conceptually difficult to grasp. In quick succession, between 1805 and 1812, he conquered the Netherlands, Bavaria, the Austrian Empire, northern Italy, the Rhineland Confederation, Saxony, Prussia, Poland, Spain, the Kingdom of Westphalia, and the Kingdom of Naples—nearly the whole of the Continent (see Map 16.1). A series of coalitions among various European powers against Napoleon had determined, more or less, the sequencing of these campaigns, but the general aim behind them was present in Napoleon's mind from the start. Megalomania and a desire for glory certainly played their part in this rush to empire. Napoleon's ego was as large as the continent he conquered, and many of the people of France shared his dream of domination. The French army was a truly national institution, being filled by conscription, and like the republic it fought for, it was organized as a meritocracy. Each victory on the battlefield therefore did more than score a military success; it validated the Revolution itself.

> The French army was a truly national institution, being filled by conscription, and like the republic it fought for, it was organized as a meritocracy. Each victory on the battlefield therefore did more than score a military success; it validated the Revolution itself.

The French in fact followed each victory with another revolution, toppling each opponent's government, abolishing its centuries-old feudal privileges, rewriting its constitution and civil laws, dismantling its mercantilist practices and dated tax codes, retooling its justice and educational systems, and establishing (often for the first time) freedoms of speech and worship. The justification for their work was simple: the nefarious and corrupt network of absolutist regimes in Europe, by the sacred ties established between them in 1648, would never allow the French Revolution to succeed, and therefore had to be destroyed. Since it had been established as a *system* for controlling Europe, absolutism anywhere on the Continent would always conspire to undermine republicanism anywhere else, even if only to discourage its growth within its own domestic borders.

MAP 16.1 Napoleonic Europe, 1799–1815

The proof of this reality, to the French, lay in the unilateral invasions of their country as soon as the republic had been established. The conquest of Europe after 1805 therefore was not aggressive imperialism but defensive (though preemptive) anti-Absolutism.

Of course, it was easy to concoct such an excuse. Did the French truly believe it? Did Napoleon himself? Or was this mere after-the-fact rationalizing? This is the crucial issue for those who, from Napoleon's time to our own, try to form a judgment about the emperor. Admirers of Napoleon saw (and see) him as the bold man of action. To them, he brought down a near-universal tyranny; in sweeping away its dead traditions, he made possible the creation of a modern Europe based on individual rights and the championing of merit over inherited privilege. His detractors saw (and see) a power-mad glory hound who simply replaced one form of tyranny with another. At most they did (and do) grant him his military genius and his better-than-average gift for self-justification.

Across Europe, in country after country, Napoleon did dismantle the old order and attempted to install the new—although he was also careful to install a loyal member of his own family as the new king. We see a glimpse of his aims, for example, in a letter he sent in 1807 to his brother Jerome, whom he had installed as the king of Westphalia—the very site of the formal birth of absolutism:

> My chief concern is for the well-being of your [new] subjects, not only as it affects your standing and my own, but also because of the impact it has on the whole condition of Europe. Do not listen to anyone who says that your subjects, being so long accustomed to servitude, will fail to feel gratitude for the freedoms you bring to them—for the common people of Westphalia are more aware than such individuals would have you believe, and your rule will never have a secure basis without the people's complete trust and affection. Quite simply, what the German people desire and pressingly demand is that men without rank but of genuine ability will have an equal claim upon your favor and advancement, and that every trace of serfdom and feudal privilege... be done away with. Let the blessings of the Napoleonic Code and of public trials that use juries be the centerpiece of your administration.... I want all your subjects to enjoy liberty, equality, and prosperity alike and to such a degree as no German people has yet known.... Everywhere in Europe—in Germany, France, Italy, Spain—people are longing for equality and liberal government.... So govern according to your new constitution. Even if Reason and the Enlightened ideas of our age did not suffice to justify this call, it still would be a smart policy for anyone in your position—for you will find that the genuine support of the people is a source of strength to you that none of the absolutist monarchs neighboring you will ever have.

If genuinely felt, the sentiments Napoleon expresses here suggest an idealism behind his conquests that might mitigate the harsher conclusions made about his character. Even so, it is difficult to overlook the fact that his conquests came at the high cost of approximately three million battlefield deaths.

THE CONTINENTAL SYSTEM

He replaced mercantilism everywhere with a new set of economic policies that he termed the **Continental System**. This system had two aims. First, it sought to create an integrated Continental economy by establishing permeable borders for the transfer of goods, services, and labor across Europe; by encouraging freedom of movement and assuring individual rights to property, the plan hoped to awaken a dormant entrepreneurial spirit. People no longer held in place by outdated customs would be free to seek opportunities wherever they might occur and thus create the truly meritocratic society Napoleon claimed to desire. But the second aim of the Continental System was both its real purpose and the cause of its own failure: to bring about the collapse of Britain by imposing a strict trade embargo on it. Soon after proclaiming himself emperor, Napoleon had made several attempts at a naval attack on Britain, but these attempts had all ended in failure—most notably at the Battle of Trafalgar (1805). The Continental System essentially closed all European ports to British shipping and redirected all Continental trade to markets within the continent itself. The overseas colonies of all Continental powers were likewise sealed off from British commercial contact. The hope was that Britain, unable to acquire sufficient raw materials for its industries and denied access to its most significant markets, would weaken to the point of collapse, at which point Napoleon's administration could sweep into London and take over.

The system succeeded at neither goal. The embargo against Britain actually helped to turn the island into an economic superpower, because it effectively removed all competition from England's aggressive expansion into global markets. Without any rivals on the scene, the British were able to extend their domination across southern and eastern Asia. France could hardly encourage Europeans

Unfettered Trade   Cartoon depicting a happy British merchant conducting trade with Nanjing and Beijing without competitors, as a result of the Continental System imposed on Europe by Bonaparte.

to trade solely with other Europeans while their armies were tearing apart the countryside. Moreover, he needed capital to keep funding the war effort; this need for cash is what led to the sale of the vast French-held territories in the central part of what became the United States—the Louisiana Purchase (1803). England's dominance at sea, well established in the Atlantic Ocean by 1805, became world-wide with Napoleon's ultimate fall in 1815. England proved able, in fact, to block most Continental shipping even along the European coastline, which forced the system's trade to proceed strictly over land, which was much more costly. Neither did the system work to generate an economically united Europe. The vast and complicated work of de-absolutizing the Continent—reallocating property, writing constitutions, instituting new civil law codes—while pressing the military campaigns ever further to the east, made it impossible to direct sufficient funds toward creating the new manufactures, supply lines, markets, currency exchanges, and tariff structures needed to make the system succeed.

The system did result in one significant change, however. By dismantling feudal ties and encouraging the freer movement of labor across Europe, Napoleon's policies accelerated the most important demographic shift of the era, namely the rise of **urbanism**. In 1800 only 2 percent of the Continental population lived in a city; by Napoleon's downfall in 1815 this percentage had doubled. (Some countries, such as Italy, had considerably higher degrees of urbanization. Others, such as Poland, were almost entirely agrarian.) This leap was made up not only of rural migration into cities but of peoples migrating from one country into another. Polish former peasants appeared in German cities; Hungarian farm laborers took up residence in Austria and Italy; Spanish workers appeared in France. Many of these individuals, barred by language or ethnic prejudice from obtaining jobs in skilled trades, ended up as domestic laborers—cooks, maids, footmen, servants, gardeners. Those lucky enough to belong to the middle class thus became able for the first time to employ large corps of domestic staff, as the swelling of urban population drove down the cost of such labor. By 1810 in Paris, for example, roughly one-fifth of the entire urban population worked in domestic service, and most of these were in service to middle-class, bourgeois families rather than upper-class high society.

Immigration like this, on this scale, produced profound social changes. For the bourgeoisie, the standard of daily living rose remarkably. Freed from doing their own cooking, cleaning, house tending, and child rearing, they were able to indulge themselves in a more comfortable existence of leisure. For the immigrants, their own family relations tended to break off, since it was predominantly individuals, not entire families, who moved into the towns to find employment. The cities thus swelled with isolated job seekers rather than cohesive family units. Young women unable to find work in domestic service or in other trades

Urban Workers   "Street scenes" is the title of this illustration from an early 19th century German periodical published in Stuttgart, a city whose population more than tripled over the course of the century. Shown here, clockwise from upper left, are a milkmaid, fishmonger, coachman, fruit seller, organ grinder, and figurine-seller.

were therefore reduced to prostitution as a means of survival. By 1815 Paris alone had over thirty thousand active prostitutes, and London had twice as many. The social ills that frequently attend prostitution—violence, alcohol or drug addiction, disease, abandoned children—soon followed. Young men unable to find work frequently drifted into crime too, and the dramatic rise in urban crime led to the formation of modern police forces. Awareness of the rising troubles in the cities also inspired the governments of the early 19th century to begin compiling official statistics on population growth, degrees and patterns of poverty, the need for housing and urban infrastructure, the lack of education, and access to clean water and sewers.

Napoleon's wars, in the end, altered Europe's history every bit as much as the Revolution altered France's. The positive achievements or gains of the era may or may not be directly credited to the Revolution, but the absolute and irreversible clearing away of the Old Regime by Napoleon made those achievements possible. (And that holds whether or not it was truly his personal goal, and not merely an excuse for a love of dictatorship.) Europe after 1815 was an altogether different place from what it had been in 1789.

> Napoleon's wars, in the end, altered Europe's history every bit as much as the Revolution altered France's. The positive achievements or gains of the era may or may not be directly credited to the Revolution, but the absolute and irreversible clearing-away of the Old Regime by Napoleon made those achievements possible.

HOW TO JUDGE A REVOLUTION

Within weeks of the Storming of the Bastille in 1789, the British statesman Edmund Burke (1729–1797) began writing *Reflections on the Revolution in France*. Published in 1790, the book takes the form of a letter written to a friend and sets out Burke's reasons for believing that the Revolution would end in abject failure and misery. He may have predicted correctly, but had he truly known how to judge a Revolution? For the pamphleteer Thomas Paine (1737–1809), justice, not stability, is the true index of political legitimacy.

Mankind, Burke argues, is inherently conservative—meaning that our natural instinct is to hold securely what we value and to desire to pass those things on to our heirs. These values include but are not limited to property and wealth: morals, religious beliefs, emotional connections, and notions of identity also constitute the human legacy and are worth keeping. But an impulse to conserve does not preclude change, he asserts. A stable society will always allow a degree of freedom and experimentation, and even encourage them, and will leave a path open for individuals to achieve on their own merits. Burke insists, however, that the fairest and strongest society will be one that evolves from, rather than breaks with, its past. "A spirit of innovation is generally the result of a selfish temper and confined views. People will not look forward to posterity, who never look backward to their ancestors."

Even more important, Burke argues that inequality among people is not intrinsically evil. Indeed, it cannot be so, since it is natural. Some people are simply smarter than others; some run faster; some are more skilled with their hands; some are given to contemplation rather than action. He is not speaking of any individual's metaphysical worthiness, only of their unique, specific characteristics. To insist that everyone is equal is to lie in order to appear kindhearted. Social and economic distinction, therefore, are natural. A well-regulated society will not allow social inequality to be oppressive, he contends, and yet any society that does away with social inequality is itself oppressive:

> Even more important, Burke argues that inequality among people is not intrinsically evil. Indeed, it cannot be so, since it is natural.

> Believe me, Sir, those who attempt to level, never equalize. In all societies, consisting of various levels of citizens, some description must be uppermost. The levelers, therefore, only change and pervert the natural order of things.... The Chancellor of France, at the opening of the Estates, said, in a tone of oratorical flourish, that all occupations were honorable. If he meant by that only that no honest employment was disgraceful, he would not have gone beyond the truth. But in asserting that anything is honorable, we imply some distinction in its favor.... Do not imagine that I wish to confine power, authority, and distinction to blood and names and titles. No, Sir. There is no qualification for government but virtue and wisdom, actual or presumptive. Wherever they are found, they have, in whatever state, condition, professions or trade, the passport of Heaven to human place and honor.... Everything ought to be open, but not indifferently, to every man.

Burke suggests that we need to think in terms of degrees of freedom and model our government after the social structure that is natural to any given community. Gradual but constant evolution is the best guarantor of stability—and Burke shares (although he would have denied it) Hobbes's notion that government's primary function is to provide stability, not justice. He does not oppose justice as a principle, but he sees it as the consequence of a stable society rather than as a vague ideal to be pursued at any cost. In pursuing such heady though foggy-minded ideals as liberty, equality, and fraternity, Burke belives, the Revolution was doomed at its birth. Moreover, he concludes his *Reflections* with a prediction:

> When the leaders choose to make themselves bidders at an auction of popularity, their talents, in the construction of the state, will be of no service. They will become flatterers instead of legislators—the instruments, not the guides, of the people. If any of them should happen to propose a scheme of liberty, soberly limited and defined with proper qualifications, he will be immediately outbid by his competitors who will produce something more splendidly popular. Suspicions will be raised of his fidelity to the cause. Moderation will be stigmatized as the virtue of cowards, and compromise as the prudence of traitors, until, in hopes of preserving the credit which may enable him to temper and moderate, on some occasions, the popular leader is obliged to become active in propagating doctrines and establishing powers that will afterward defeat any sober purpose at which he ultimately might have aimed.

A revolution, in other words, *any* revolution, will always fail because those who lead it are united only in their opposition to what they have overthrown. Once the work of creating a new government begins, unity will end. Former partners in revolution will become rivals in politics. To win out over each other, the rivals will keep offering the public increasingly generous, popular, and radical promises. Soon, angry accusations of being an "enemy of the revolution" will fly through the air, arrests and executions for treason will multiply, and riots will ensue. The revolution will spin out of control until finally someone comes along who, in order to save the gains made by the revolution, restores order by force. That means "propagating doctrines and establishing powers" that will undermine the entire enterprise by creating a new version of the very order that the revolution overthrew. In other words, the revolution spins from Louis XVI to the Estates General, to the Girondists, to the Jacobins, to Robespierre and the Terror, to civil war, to Napoleon—from autocracy to autocracy. Burke published his book in 1790 before any of this happened, and he died in

1797 before seeing the end of the process, but he seems to have predicted each stage perfectly.

Others saw the Revolution differently. In England, Thomas Paine wrote *The Rights of Man* (published in two parts, 1791–1792), in which he rebutted Burke's analysis. Paine asserted that human rights are innate, granted by Nature rather than bestowed by government; therefore any state that restricts or subverts the rights of its citizens may be opposed and brought down.[4] Government can retain its legitimacy only by supporting the intrinsic rights of its citizens. It was in this spirit that Paine grew distrustful of Napoleon and ultimately abandoned France, calling the emperor "the completest charlatan that ever lived."

Paine had immigrated to America in 1774 as an enthusiast for the colonies' push for independence and stayed there until 1787, when he returned to London. In 1792 Paine went to Paris to witness the Revolution firsthand and was elected to serve in the National Assembly even though he could speak no French. Robespierre

France as a Storm-Tossed Ship   This 1796 British map fancifully depicts Revolutionary France as a ship in distress. Note the broken prow-mast and the cut-away anchor in the Bay of Biscay; two aft-sails have become unmoored; and a storm brews ahead even while the ship founders on rocks at the bottom.

---

4   *The Rights of Man* was so popular and caused such scandal in London that Paine was tried in absentia for sedition against the crown.

hated him and arranged for his arrest in 1793. Released the following year, Paine remained in France until he returned to America in 1802.

Another initial supporter of the Revolution was Mary Wollstonecraft (1759–1797), a reformer for women's rights, who responded to Burke with two passionate tracts. *A Vindication of the Rights of Man* (1791) and *A Vindication of the Rights of Woman* (1792) dismissed Burke's notion of liberty as a smokescreen to protect the interests of the propertied classes, when it is the rights of the lower orders that must be respected. She argued that traditional society has brutalized women and degraded them to a subhuman level, leaving the only rational choice for reform to be the destruction of all existing social mores and the political regimes that support them. Wollstonecraft too rushed to Paris to witness the Revolution, in 1793. Within two years, though, she grew disillusioned with the violent turn of events, and, after a disastrous romantic liaison added personal misery to her political disappointment, she returned to England.

Reactions to the Revolution across the Continent likewise ranged widely. The Absolutist regimes responded by sending their armies into France, but among the general population of Germans, Italians, Dutch, Piedmontese, Spaniards, and even Russians there were many who cheered the French on. Ludwig van Beethoven famously admired Napoleon and intended to dedicate his Third Symphony to him, until the imperial coronation in 1804 led him to tear the dedicatory epistle to shreds. The poet Johann Wolfgang von Goethe (1749–1832) was too conservative and elitist to support revolutionary egalitarianism; in fact, he served as an advisor to German forces fighting French troops in 1792 and 1793. Yet when he met Napoleon in 1806, he declared *"Voilà, un homme!"* ("Behold, a Man!") and accepted with pleasure the emperor's award

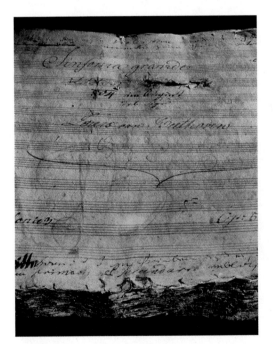

Beethoven's Third Symphony   First page of the manuscript of Ludwig von Beethoven's Third Symphony. According to legend, Beethoven had been an early admirer of Bonaparte and had intended to dedicate the symphony to him, but was enraged when Napoleon crowned himself emperor. He reportedly crossed out Napoleon's name so angrily that he tore a hole in the manuscript, as shown.

of the Cross of the French Legion of Honor, which he continued to wear for the rest of his life. While Napoleon clearly fascinated his non-French contemporaries, and while many of them welcomed liberation from the absolutist regimes he toppled, most of them chafed against rule by Napoleon's Revolutionary agents. The French conquests, in fact, helped trigger a rise in nationalistic fervor across Europe. Peoples humiliated by Napoleon's quick victories reacted by expressing a desire to unify and establish ethnically and culturally based states to forge their own destinies, rather than follow the path laid out for them by Napoleon.

DOWNFALL

Napoleon's brilliance as a charismatic leader, military commander, administrator, and legal and social reformer were extraordinary, but so were his deficiencies. He had little understanding of naval warfare and no understanding at all of economics. He trusted his own judgment over that of his advisers. He underestimated the extent to which ethnically based national identity mattered to the peoples of Europe. Worst of all, he had no interest in the things he did not understand, and so gave them insufficient attention. All of these weaknesses played a role in his ultimate military defeat and fall from power.

The Continental System never worked. Europe's coastline, all 3,100 miles (5,000 kilometers) of it, proved impossible to police, and merchant-smugglers were resourceful when it came to avoiding the harbor police. Moreover, by ceding control of the sea-lanes to the British, the Continental System simply allowed the British to secure international markets in the Americas and Asia that proved so lucrative as to turn Britain into an economic superpower. Britain also used its capital to invest in domestic infrastructure, such as networks of roads and canals, to facilitate further development. The Continent, subsumed as it was in war and reconstruction, could not match such investment. Until 1810 British goods slipped through the trade barriers and were readily available across Europe. Even the wasteful War of 1812 between Britain and America—fought over the issue of British searches of American vessels to make sure they were not trading with France—did not weaken the British position with respect to the Continent.

Napoleon also miscalculated when he overthrew the Spanish king Ferdinand VII in 1808 and replaced him with his own older brother, Joseph Bonaparte. The dismantling of absolutism in Spain failed when Napoleon ordered the suppression of roughly two-thirds of the monasteries and convents in the realm and confiscated their property. The displaced Spanish nobility allied with the disenfranchised clergy to lead resistance against the invaders. Unable to defeat the Bonapartist forces in open battle, the Spanish fighters waged instead a guerrilla war that kept a large number of French troops (over three hundred thousand of them) mired in an unwinnable conflict when they were sorely needed elsewhere in Europe. Small wonder that Napoleon complained of his "Spanish ulcer."

Meanwhile, family troubles added to his indigestion. Although an energetic womanizer, Napoleon dearly loved his wife Josephine; but like England's Henry VIII in the 16th century, Napoleon agonized over his wife's supposed failure to give him a son. Convinced that he needed an heir to continue his life's work, he reluctantly arranged for a Parisian bishop to annul his marriage to Josephine in 1810, so he could remarry. Pope Pius VII (r. 1800–1823) refused to perform the annulment, which is why Napoleon turned instead to a local bishop (who, like all the French clergy, was on Napoleon's payroll). He set his sights initially on the younger sister of Tsar Aleksandr I of Russia (r. 1801–1825), whose two daughters had recently died, leaving the succession to the throne in doubt; rather than invade Russia—then the last substantial absolutist state in Europe—Napoleon hoped simply to acquire it as a dowry. Aleksandr, however, refused the match even though he was, at the time, Napoleon's ally in a grand (and delusional) plan: they hoped to drive the Ottoman Turks from Europe and carry the conquests of a unified Catholic and Orthodox Christendom as far as India.[5]

Aleksandr was a complicated character himself—emotional, idealistic, contradictory, and given to dramatic shifts of mood. His relations with Napoleon went from initial revulsion to implacable opposition of "the oppressor of Europe and the disturber of the world's peace." Yet he was dazzled by Napoleon's brilliance when they met, and he became unswervingly loyal in return for his help in bringing Finland and Poland under tsarist rule. The pact against the Turks soon followed. Aleksandr even insisted on his love for Napoleon after French forces had invaded Russia in 1812; only the French sacking of Moscow turned that love back to hatred.

Napoleon married instead Marie-Louise, the daughter of the Austrian emperor Franz II (r. 1804–1835), who soon gave him the son he so desperately wanted. The birth of this son (also named Napoleon) signified an important change in people's perceptions of the emperor—even among the French. The destroyer of inherited privilege had himself produced an heir to whom he intended to pass on the government of all of Europe. Anti-Napoleon pamphlets began to circulate, and some government advisors began to urge the emperor to restrain his ambition. One of those advisors, his former foreign minister Charles-Maurice de Talleyrand, even started to negotiate secretly with Franz II over how France might be governed if Napoleon should fall.

---

5   Leo Tolstoy provides extraordinarily sensitive portrayals of Napoleon and Aleksandr in *War and Peace.*

In June 1812 Napoleon invaded Russia with an army of roughly six hundred thousand men—perhaps the largest single force ever mustered in European history to that time. Russia responded by avoiding direct clashes while maintaining a rearguard action, drawing the French further and further into the enormous landmass. In September Napoleon entered Moscow, after pounding through Russia's last defensive stand at the battle of Borodino. He found the capital virtually deserted and two-thirds of it aflame. Hopelessly exposed and left unsupplied, the French marched back to Paris, hoping to make it back before the brutal Russian winter set in. Aleksandr's forces harassed the French enough to slow them down miserably, and the onset of winter did the rest of the damage.[6]

Napoleon was able to hold on to power for two more years, but his position in Europe, and even in France, was never the same. Overthrown by the Republic and imprisoned initially on the Mediterranean island of Elba, he escaped but was defeated by the British at the battle of Waterloo in 1815. He was then imprisoned on the island of Saint Helena in the middle of the South Atlantic, more than a thousand miles from any mainland. He died, fittingly, of a cancerous ulcer on May 5, 1821. (Rumors of Napoleon's murder by arsenic poisoning have been thoroughly disproven.)

Napoleon's legacy continues to divide people. No one doubts his exceptional talents and charismatic energy, but few people accept uncritically his own judgment of himself—in the memoirs he dictated during his seven years on Saint Helena:

> [My] imperial government was a kind of Republic... [because I was] summoned to take control of the government by the voice of the nation itself.... There has never been, in fact, a king who was more truly a "people's sovereign" than I was.... If I were to return [to power] I would establish my empire once again upon the ideals of the Jacobins, for Jacobinism is a volcano that threatens all orders of privileged-based society. I could reproduce it easily even in Prussia... and with the power of Prussia at my disposal I could use [Jacobinism] as a club to smash Austria and Russia.

As for his miserable end:

> My body is in the hands of wicked men but my soul is free. I am prouder here on Saint Helena than if I were sitting again on my throne, appointing kings and handing out crowns.... If I had succeeded [by

---

6   Only forty thousand of the original six hundred thousand made it back from Russia to France by December; most of the dead fell victim to starvation, exposure, and exhaustion.

Charting a Disaster A striking image (called a cartogram), created by Charles Joseph Mainard in 1869. It grafts a chart onto a map, showing the depletion of Napoleon's army as it marched from Poland to Moscow and back. The constantly narrowing line represents the decline in French forces heading east (brown) and then returning west (black). The line below the main figure tracks the temperature of the brutal Russian winter. Edward Tufte (1942-), a pioneer in the field of data visualization, describes Mainard's cartogram as the "best statistical graph ever drawn."

adding a reformed Russia to my empire] I would have been remembered as the greatest man ever to have lived.... [But my] martyrdom will strip away my reputation as a tyrant.... In time [I will acquire] a crown of thorns.

He made permanent some of the most important achievements of the Revolution—the equality of all people (or men, at least) before the law; the rights of personal freedom of thought, belief, and expression; the individual right to property; the abolition of serfdom. He created Europe's first national system of public education. He established a fair and rational system of taxation. And then he brought those reforms to the nations he conquered. But in the process he created an imperial tyranny. His wars cost millions of lives. Among the French alone, perhaps 20 percent of all deaths that occurred between 1799 and 1815 resulted from his military actions.

In the end, he showed little remorse. He believed above all in France's destiny to lead Europe and in his own destiny to lead France. To have achieved anything less would have been tragic, and to have failed to answer the cause of glory would have been worse than death. "Death, after all, is nothing," he declared; "but to spend one's life defeated and without glory is to die anew every day."

LEAVING THE EAST BEHIND

The Ottoman Empire underwent profound decentralization during the 17th century. It also confronted a new threat from Romanov Russia, which expanded aggressively southward to the Black and Caspian Seas. By 1774 Russia's Catherine the Great (r. 1762–1796) had extended her control to a narrow strip along the northern rim of the Black Sea, where she founded the port city of Odessa. Only nine years later she annexed the whole of the Crimean peninsula and even briefly held a portion of Romania (see Map 16.2). For the Ottomans, having already lost much of eastern Europe and the Balkans area to the Austrian Habsburgs, these setbacks seriously undermined the strength of their empire and triggered a number of internal reforms—not all of them welcome. For the moment, the most pressing need was to reform the military.

The Janissaries had dominated the Turkish army since the 13th century but had long since been surpassed in organization, training, and overall might by the Western national armies. The Janissaries, in fact, had become an elitist and conservative force in the empire, interested primarily in securing their privileges and maintaining the status quo. The ruler Selim III [r. 1789–1807] brought in military

MAP 16.2 Ottoman Losses in the Balkans and Crimea, 1699–1774

advisers from the French Republic, who helped him to abolish the semifeudal structure of the army, established foundries for the building of modern artillery weapons, retrained the infantry, and provided new instruction in naval warfare. Selim also established a separate printing press solely for the publication of technical manuals, engineering texts, and up-to-date geographical atlases. Angered by these new developments, the Janissaries rose in revolt in 1807, assassinated Selim, and installed a cousin, Mustafa IV [T] (r. 1807–1808), who ruled briefly until he was murdered by his own brother, Mahmud II [T] (r. 1808–1839).

Mahmud tried to continue the reforms begun by Selim III, but with mixed success. Aspects of public finance were modernized, along with provincial legal practices. For example, local governors had long enjoyed their administration of provincial Courts of Confiscation. These courts gave local officials the right to personally confiscate the property of convicted criminals—and the practice triggered the amount of abuse one might expect from such an arrangement. Mahmud closed these courts entirely. He tried to develop a modern navy as well. The Turks had become maritime nonentities ever since losing the battle of Lepanto in 1571, and since then the empire had seen its control of the shipping routes in the Persian Gulf and the Indian Ocean lost to the British.

The French Revolution had inspired these attempts at reform, and the Turkish opening to Western ideas and technologies contributed to a fashionable vogue for Turkish culture in the West—as in the Turkish setting of Mozart's opera *Die Entführung aus dem Serail* (*The Abduction from the Seraglio*, 1782). The Revolution also invited elements of Western culture to take new root in the Islamic world. Ottoman mosques began to incorporate baroque styles of decoration; summer palaces adopted rococo designs. Perhaps most striking, Turkish wall paintings began to copy the European fashion for depicting dramatic battle scenes—complete with dashing generals astride rearing warhorses, crowds of infantry dead on the field, air thick with artillery smoke. The paintings did not merely introduce representational figures, to the exclusion of more traditional geometric and Arabesque patterns; they also vividly depicted human triumphs, sufferings, joys, pleasures, and despairs. Developments in French poetry, French theater, and French dress were eagerly reported by Turkish writers. Even the 18th-century craze for breeding tulips and creating elaborate gardens to house them caught on with the Ottomans.

Napoleon's campaigns through Egypt and Syria brought the cultural romance to a quick end, and after most of the Habsburg state had fallen to his forces, the Ottomans began to fear they were next. They were saved by the on-again, off-again alliance between Napoleon and Aleksandr of Russia, which ultimately drew French attentions away. But the lesson had been learned, and the push to modernize dominated the rest of the 19th century. The government gave a name

The Tulip Period   This late 18th century Turkish manuscript painting shows a crowd, mostly female, relaxing in a park. It appears in a work called "The Book of Women" and represents—although it does not come from—the so-called Tulip Period in Turkish history (1718-1730), when Ottoman society consciously oriented itself in favor of Enlightened Europe. Notable here are the social mixing of men and women, the Western-style building in the background, the absence of veils (and the visibility of the women's hair), the woman in the foreground smoking a pipe, and the beardless man accompanying her.

to the movement: **Tanzimat** ("reorganization"). Its central planks would be economic development and the integration of the empire's non-Muslims and non-Turks into civil society, by granting them civil liberties and promoting a new type of egalitarianism in Islamic society. These efforts, however, faced determined resistance by Arab groups interested instead in establishing their own ethnically based nationalism.

In its own way, the history of the Ottoman world curiously paralleled that of the Europeans in the 18th century: attempts to dismantle outdated systems of privilege were followed by reform efforts based on notions of equality and the increased social and economic interaction of ethnic groups. And these in turn were resisted by nationalistic forces determined to develop on their own. Napoleon's downfall in 1815 brought a reprieve; but dramatic action would be needed.

WHO, WHAT, WHERE

Continental System	Reign of Terror
Estates General	Tanzimat
Napoleonic Code	Third Estate
parlements	Urbanism

SUGGESTED READINGS

Primary Sources

Bonaparte, Napoleon. *Memoirs.*
Burke, Edmund. *Reflections on the Revolution in France.*

De Las Cases, Emmanuel-Auguste. *The Life, Exile, and Conversations of the Emperor Napoleon.*

Robespierre, Maximilien. *Virtue and Terror.*

Sieyès, Abbé de. *What Is the Third Estate?*

Walter, Jakob. *The Diary of a Napoleonic Foot Soldier.*

Anthologies

Blaufarb, Rafe. *Napoleon: Symbol for an Age; A Brief History with Documents* (2007).

Dwyer, Philip, and Peter McPhee, eds. *The French Revolution and Napoleon: A Sourcebook* (2002).

Larsen, Anne R., and Colette H. Winn, eds. *Writings by Pre-Revolutionary French Women* (2000).

Studies

Bell, David A. *The First Total War: Napoleon's Europe and the Birth of Warfare as We Know It* (2008).

Birn, Raymond. *Royal Censorship of Books in Eighteenth-Century France* (2012).

Brown, Howard G. *Ending the French Revolution: Violence, Justice, and Repression from the Terror to Napoleon* (2007).

Censer, Jack, and Lynn Hunt. *Liberty, Equality, Fraternity: Exploring the French Revolution* (2001).

Cole, Juan. *Napoleon Napoleon's Egypt: Invading the Middle East* (2007).

Doyle, William. *The Oxford History of the French Revolution* (2002).

Dwyer, Philip G., ed. *Napoleon and Europe* (2003).

———. *Napoleon: The Path to Power* (2008).

Edelstein, Dan. *The Terror of Natural Right: Republicanism, the Cult of Nature, and the French Revolution* (2010).

Englund, Steven. *Napoleon: A Political Life* (2004).

Faroqhi, Suraiya. *The Ottoman Empire and the World around It* (2006).

———. *Subjects of the Sultan: Culture and Daily Life in the Ottoman Empire* (2005).

Hanson, Paul. *Contesting the French Revolution* (2009).

Hathaway, Jane. *The Arab Lands under Ottoman Rule, 1516–1800* (2008).

Israel, Jonathan. *A Revolution of the Mind: Radical Enlightenment and the Intellectual Origins of Modern Democracy* (2009).

Kates, Gary. *The French Revolution: Recent Debates and New Controversies* (2005).

Lawday, David. *The Giant of the French Revolution: Danton; A Life* (2011).

Masters, Bruce. *Christians and Jews in the Ottoman Arab World: The Roots of Sectarianism.* (2004).

———. *The Origins of Western Economic Dominance in the Middle East: Mercantilism and the Islamic Economy in Aleppo, 1600–1750* (2008).

McPhee, Peter. *The French Revolution, 1789–1799* (2002).

———. *Living the French Revolution: 1789–99* (2009).

———. *Robespierre: A Revolutionary Life* (2012).

Mousset, Sophie. *Women's Rights and the French Revolution: A Biography of Olympe de Gouge* (2007).

Murphey, Rhoads. *Ottoman Warfare, 1500–1700* (1999).

Scurr, Ruth. *Fatal Purity: Robespierre and the French Revolution* (2007).

Simonetta, Marcello, and Noga Arikha. *Napoleon and the Rebel: A Story of Brotherhood, Passion, and Power* (2011).

Tackett, Timothy. *When the King Took Flight* (2004).

Woloch, Isser. *Napoleon and His Collaborators: The Making of a Dictatorship* (2001).

For additional resources, including maps, primary sources, visuals, web links, and quizzes, please go to **www.oup.com/us/backman.**

CHAPTER 17

Industrialization and Its Discontents

1750–1850

Man has been a tool user since the Neolithic Age. From the time of the first stone implements, the brute labor needed for subsistence was performed by men and women, and sometimes children, holding tools in their hands. The Bronze and Iron Ages were in fact defined by tools.

INDUSTRIALIZATION IN THE GREATER WEST, ca. 1850

Level of industrial output per capita (100=UK in 1900)
- 0–15
- 16–30
- 60–75

Increase in level of industrial output per capita 1830–1850
- ○ 50–100%
- ● over 100%

The next major leap came with harnessing animals to larger tools like plows and wagons. By the Middle Ages both the water-wheel and windmill captured the energy of the natural world, putting it to use in everything from milling grain to producing paper. The Renaissance created tools of increasing sophistication—telescopes and microscopes come quickly to mind—but as late as 1750 most goods were overwhelmingly the result of tools held in human hands. This was especially true of food and textiles—the two commodities that humans consume the most over their life spans. Through the centuries, labor had become more efficient, and the West had learned new ways to use natural resources. But human labor, with all its limitations, still defined economic activity. Well into the 18th century, it required the labor of eight people to feed and clothe ten people. That is an improvement on the roughly 9.5:10 ratio of Sumerian times, but still backbreaking physical labor, twelve hours a day.

The industrial revolution changed that forever. It also led to crushing conditions and the cultural movement known as Romanticism.

◀ **Interior of a Typical Coal Miner's Home, 1880s** Coal fueled the Industrial Revolution, and mining it was one of the most brutal and dangerous jobs of the 19th century. This photo depicts a typical one-room tenement of a coal miner's family, ca. 1889.

ENGLAND'S HEAD START

Starting in Britain in the second half of the 18th century, power-driven machines altered Western life profoundly, permanently, and absolutely. Industrialization created new economies, new cities, and new social relations, and it brought all of these changes on with startling speed. And the people of the time were quick to recognize the implications of mechanization.

The early English Romantic poets William Blake (1757–1827) and William Wordsworth (1770–1850) described the effects on industry on the human soul and the natural world as dire and ruinous. In a brief poem that serves as a prologue to his long epic *Milton*, Blake refers to an ancient legend that Jesus, in his youth, had visited England. Blake asks:

> And did those feet in ancient time
> Walk upon England's mountains green?
> And was the holy Lamb of God
> On England's pleasant pastures seen?
> And did the Countenance Divine
> Shine forth upon our clouded hills?
> And was Jerusalem builded here
> Among those dark Satanic mills?
>
> Bring me my bow of burning gold:
> Bring me my arrows of desire:
> Bring me my spear: O clouds, unfold!
> Bring me my chariot of fire!
> I will not cease from mental fight,
> Nor shall my sword sleep in my hand
> Till we have built Jerusalem
> In England's green and pleasant land.

CHAPTER TIMELINE

1765
Development of the spinning jenny

1769
First water-powered spinning machine

1799
First documented use of the phrase "industrial revolution"

1806
Fichte, "Address to the German Nation"

1818
One-third of the G(
states join Custom

The "dark Satanic mills" possibly refer to the massive grain mills that lay only a few miles from Blake's home in London, but in a larger sense they describe the smoke-billowing factories then spreading across all of England.

The first documented use of the phrase **industrial revolution** to describe a new economy driven by factories and a growing workforce appears in a letter written in 1799 by a French diplomat visiting England, who saw industrialization as a positive development. (He also claimed that the English had stolen the idea from the French.) Nevertheless, awareness of the changes brought by machine power was everywhere. As Friedrich Engels wrote in *The Condition of the Working Class*

Dark Satanic Mills   *Coalbrookdale by Night* (1801) by Philip James de Loutherbourg. The Madeley Wood furnaces shown here were owned by the Coalbrookdale Company, which was the first industrial firm successfully to use coke as a fuel. Coke is the residue from a controlled burning of coal with a restricted supply of oxygen; it burns at a significantly higher temperature and produces higher-grade metals in the smelting and refining processes.

1819
Peterloo Massacre, England

1824
Glasgow Young Men's Society for Religious Improvement founded

1826
Janissaries abolished in Ottoman Empire.

1832
Cholera epidemic kills hundreds of thousands in Europe

1850
Britain crisscrossed by six thousand miles of rail; population of London reaches 2.5 million

in England in 1844, "An industrial revolution was a revolution which at the same time changed the whole of civil society."

Like so much of the West's economic history, the basis of the industrial revolution lay in demographic change, or a growing population. Improvements in food production and advances in medicine had combined to spur a consistent increase in the European population ever since the 16th century; in the late 18th and early 19th centuries, though, the rate of increase grew dramatically. Larger domestic populations meant larger potential markets for manufactured goods. At the same time, Europe's international contacts meant increased opportunities to acquire raw materials and new targets for selling goods. The expansion of literacy, too, meant a more highly skilled labor force.

To take advantage of these conditions, one needed money—or access to it. It took financing to start private commercial ventures on a large scale. The mercantilist systems on the Continent had made that all but impossible. But when Napoleon demolished that system, national banks and stock exchanges came into existence, and financial markets could provide the capital, or funds for investment, needed. By 1815 most of Europe was ready to industrialize. England, though, had a fifty-year head start. Having avoided the burden of absolutism, left unaffected by the turmoil of the French Revolution, and intentionally ignored during the Napoleonic era, it had become an economic superpower.

> By 1815 most of Europe was ready to industrialize. England, though, had a fifty-year head-start. Having avoided the burden of absolutism, left unaffected by the turmoil of the French Revolution, and intentionally ignored during the Napoleonic era, it had become an economic superpower.

England's population in 1780 had stood at roughly eight million people; by 1850 it had grown to eighteen million. By 1880 it had reached twenty-six million.[1] This created a large demand for goods like food, clothing, furniture, and housewares; it also provided cheap labor. According to the "Iron Law of Wages" made popular by the English economist David Ricardo (1772–1823), population growth always outpaces industrial productivity, and that fact drives labor wages down to subsistence levels—what he termed "natural wages." Cheap labor was the primary fuel propelling the industrial economy forward, and it remained so into the 20th century.

New technologies from the Scientific Revolution and the Enlightenment had dramatically improved crop yields. A single acre of farmland in 1750 produced around fifteen bushels of wheat, but by 1850 it produced twenty-seven bushels. Careful breeding of animals had resulted in sheep that in 1850 produced twice as much wool annually as they had done in 1750, and cows produced more milk as

---

[1]   The engine of growth was the countryside, where improved medical care had lowered the mortality rate of children and mothers. The smallpox vaccine was available after 1790.

Agricultural Management   Thomas Weaver (1774-1843) painted this scene of Thomas Coke, 1st Earl of Leicester (1754-1842), inspecting a flock of sheep on his thirty thousand acre estate at Norfolk. Coke had enclosed most of his lands and encouraged the "scientific agriculture" of the time by experimenting with new types of feed and fertilizer and new techniques of animal breeding.

well. Higher productivity caused a decline in prices, which meant, theoretically, more disposable income for the purchase of manufactured goods. England, in simple terms, had an active market economy in the 18th century, as the Continent would not until well into the 19th. In Spain, France, the German states, eastern Europe, and Russia, agricultural economies were still at the subsistence level. The overwhelming majority of the people (as many as 90 percent in some territories) ate what they produced and made their own clothes. In the absence of any "disposable income," or spending money, economic demand was nonexistent.

England had achieved its unique status by eliminating its small-scale farmers. Big landowners had driven most of their farmers off the land through a combination of increased rents, buyouts, and evictions; they then consolidated this land into large-scale holdings that they could farm more efficiently. Or they could "enclose" the land and give up crop farming altogether, in favor of raising sheep and cattle for wool and dairy products. Acres of land that might have needed two hundred people to farm now needed only twenty to tend the herds and flocks. This decreased the landowners' labor costs while increasing their incomes. Instead of a countryside dotted with small farmers, England became divided among a small class of large landholders and a more numerous class of agricultural laborers who worked for wages.

Wage workers now used their incomes to purchase commodities that peasants had once made for themselves. Money had taken root as the foundation of the national economy. That new industrial economy, based on money, is capitalism. It is a system based on markets—on the supply of and demand for money, goods, and services.

Clothing was, after food, the most important purchase most people made. Even today, textiles make up the second-largest commodity consumed worldwide. The growth of the population naturally meant a need for more textile production. For England, which had been a mass wool producer since the Middle Ages, the new demand was especially for cotton—which was available from the southern United States. If enough American raw cotton could be brought to England, and if England could arrange its industrial capacity correctly, it could not just meet all domestic needs; it could also produce finished cloth for export. And political turmoil on the Continent left the English without any competitors on the international market. England had outlawed slavery in the 18th century, but that did not stop them from doing business with the slave-owning American South. American cotton and British wool formed the basis of industrial expansion.

> England had outlawed slavery in the 18th century, but that did not stop them from doing business with the slave-owning American South. American cotton and British wool formed the basis of industrial expansion.

INNOVATION AND INFRASTRUCTURE

Social and cultural factors played a role too. First, by the 18th century Britain was largely free from powerful guilds. Guilds had been central to the development of the medieval economy, but they were ill suited to a capitalist system, since their control of prices and production levels undermined the free play of supply and demand. In Habsburg Austria, for example, if demand rose for a given commodity, then the guilds that controlled the commodity would not necessarily increase production. After all, a guild derived much of its profits from government subsidies and membership fees rather than from commerce itself. Without an incentive to increase production, there was little reason to experiment with new technologies that might produce more goods more efficiently. England's remaining guilds were too weak and marginal to check market forces.

Second, an entrepreneurial culture had taken root in England in the 17th century (as it had done in Holland too) that encouraged economic growth. On the Continent, the nobility often believed that manufacture and commerce were "common" pursuits, beneath the dignity of an aristocrat. That class-based prejudice existed among the British, but to a far lesser degree. So long as he conducted his business in a dignified and gentlemanly way, an English lord's reputation did not necessarily suffer—which made access to capital for industry easier. Moreover, the English constitution had developed in such a way as to center real power in the House of Commons, whose members largely were drawn from the bourgeoisie, which was most interested in promoting trade. Third, the British legal system encouraged business by establishing the rights of property and allowing tradesmen to take out patents on the technologies they developed. Secure in the right to the rewards of one's own innovation, manufacturers, financiers, and shippers were more willing, and eager, to innovate.

While the manufacturing sector in England was spurred to new life, it quickly realized the limits of its means of production. Consider the textile industry. The putting-out system, which hired people to work in their own homes, had sufficed for a while, but the new demand for cloth far outpaced its ability to produce. Adding more carders, spinners, and weavers to the system helped, yet by the middle of the 18th century a drive to find more efficient machines had begun. England by this time controlled a vast colonial empire whose many millions of subjects needed everything from clothes to furniture, beer to kitchen utensils, housewares to agricultural tools. Entrepreneurs had ample incentives to increase their output; demand for goods like textiles, after all, was *elastic*: lower prices produced greater demand. Investment in new technology, such as the flying-shuttle loom, alone doubled a single weaver's ability to produce cloth. But now that weaving capacity had increased, there was incentive to increase the capacity of spinners to produce thread for the weavers. This led in 1765 to the development of the spinning jenny, a machine that could spin more than one spool of yarn at a time.

The most dramatic innovation, however, came in 1769 with the first water-powered spinning machine, which was quickly replaced by spinning machines and looms operated by steam engines. The application of steam power to textile production truly revolutionized the industry and began a social and economic revolution. Such machines, running continuously, day after day, could produce quantities of finished cloth previously unimaginable—and given the economies of scale, such production was highly profitable. They remained highly profitable, too, even though their productivity led to a decline in the price of the cloth. Early industrial factories driven by steam were immense, noisy, dangerous, and hot places that were miserable to work in; but the machines, if properly tended, never tired. By 1810 amounts of finished cloth that in 1750 had required over two hundred skilled workers to produce needed only a dozen semiskilled machine operators. With factory cities fast filling with displaced farm populations looking for work, the downward pressure on wages made it possible for entrepreneurs to invest large sums in machinery while still reaping huge profits. These and other innovations

Spinning Machines   Quarry Bank Mill, in Cheshire, England, was the largest textile mill in Britain by 1830. Originally water-powered, the spinning machine (called the "mule") was driven by steam engine after 1810. Until the practice was outlawed in 1847, the Quarry Bank Mill relied heavily on unpaid child labor.

changed completely the way large numbers of people worked and lived, and they shaped much of the rest of the 19th century.

The final necessary ingredient, in order to launch Britain's industrial revolution, was its development of the national infrastructure—the roads and waterways that brought the nation together. Without the ability to move bulk quantities of raw materials into the new factories and to efficiently ship large inventories of finished goods out to market, the producers' innovations were all for naught. Here geography favored the British. While large enough to support a population of tens of millions, Britain was yet a small enough island that the idea of uniting it with a comprehensive transport system seemed feasible. Investments in coastal barges, and in expanding harbors to accommodate them, enabled the movement of coal—the chief fuel of industry—around the island. Smaller river barges allowed shipments to move up and down the rivers, while a new network of interior canals connected rivers to one another. By 1815 the British had constructed some four thousand miles of canals, linking up their counties to such a degree that goods could be moved easily from any place in the realm to another. New networks of roads, and ultimately of railroads, completed the task, making Britain's physical infrastructure the most extensive and efficient in the world.

It had to be, given the enormous weight of the raw materials needed in the factories. Coal was available in enormous quantities, as was iron ore. Only the lack of means to move these resources efficiently had impeded their full use. Coal burns at a higher temperature than wood (the most common fuel in use before the 19th century), which made it more effective in steam production. Moreover, a by-product of coal called coke burns at an even higher temperature still, making it the fuel of choice for refining iron ore into usable iron, and ultimately for producing steel. Britain's coastal and river barges moved coal and coke by the hundreds and thousands of tons. The development of wrought iron made it possible, in the 1820s, to move heavy freight overland by railcars driven by steam engines.

An English engineer developed the first steam engine capable of pulling a train. Trains themselves had been in use for well over a century by that time, but they had been pulled along the tracks by teams of horses and had been used principally for transporting loads of coal from the mines. With the new steam-powered engine, freight could be moved anywhere affordably—so long as the tracks were in place. England thus began constructing an elaborate system of railroad tracks from mines and quarries to factories and markets all across the country. By 1830 a mere one hundred miles of track existed, but within twenty years a network of more than six thousand miles of track crisscrossed the country (see Map 17.1).

The unique combination of Britain's natural and cultural geography, its ability to inspire and capitalize on new technologies, and its legal and economic adaptability set the nation decades ahead of Continental Europe. Through the rest of the 19th century, it struggled to respond to the social problems created by industrialization, even while continuing to innovate and develop new technologies. Its challenge was to maintain its now dominant position in the world.

TRYING TO CATCH UP TO ENGLAND

The diplomats who redrew the political map of Europe at the **Congress of Vienna** in 1815 showed little enthusiasm for developing an industrial economy. More than anything, the statesmen, who represented more than two hundred separate states and princely houses, wanted to turn back the clock—if possible, all the way back to 1648 and the Treaty of Westphalia. Most of the parties favored the restoration of monarchical governments across Europe, along with the economic and social programs that had traditionally supported them. Too much had changed, however, to allow that. Whatever its faults, the Continental System had freed people from serfdom and encouraged their migration to manufacturing and commercial centers—enough that the majority of the people wanted to move ahead into the new economic world opened up by Britain.

Industrializing Britain by 1850

Industries:

🔲	Textiles
🔲	Pottery
◼	Copper mining and smelting
◻	Tin mining and smelting
🔲	Iron extraction and smelting
◆	Lead mining
✳	Metalware and cutlery
⚑	Salt, soap, chemicals, and glass manufacture
⛁	Shipbuilding
▨	Coalfield
▪	Major port
—	Navigable river
⊔⊔⊔	Major canal
▬▬	Major railway

MAP 17.1   Industrializing Britain by 1850

European industrialization differed from the British version in profound ways. First, Britain's commanding lead in international markets meant that Continental industry aimed instead to serve domestic markets. The European population, after all, was large enough to merit such attention, and by carefully assigning tariffs and import quotas, the Continental states could protect their newer industries from British competition. Second, the post-1815 states played even more central roles in industrialization than the government had done in England. The Continental governments not only built infrastructure but invested directly in the fledging industries—especially heavily capitalized industries like railroads—and in the building of factories. Third, important general differences emerged in the way each Continental country industrialized. France, for example, tended to favor the production of luxury items like glassware, china, and fine housewares; in Germany specialty domestic commodities predominated, like linens, timepieces, tools, and kitchenwares, as well as state-used commodities like ships and weaponry.

Once again, demography and geography played important roles in the ways industrialization progressed. In France, for example, the population grew at a healthy rate, but considerably slower than its neighbors (see Figure 17.1). In 1700 the French population was somewhere near twenty million, and by 1850 it had grown to approximately thirty-five million, a steady but otherwise unremarkable growth rate of not quite 2 percent annually. Over the same period, Britain's population had leaped from five million to twenty million (a growth of nearly 5 percent per year), while Germany's had increased from fifteen million to thirty-four million (about 3.5 percent per year). This meant that the need to increase food production that had driven the British rush to industrial production was lacking in France. Their traditional means of feeding themselves sufficed, which enabled the French to focus on luxury goods, niche markets that had smaller gross sales but higher profit margins.

This served France well, for the maintenance of a traditional peasantry on the land had kept the urban labor pools from growing excessively large,

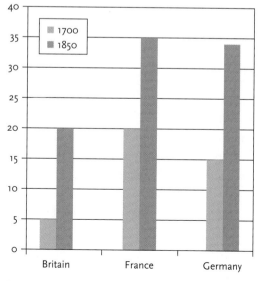

FIGURE 17.1   Population of France, Britain, and Germany, 1700–1850

as had happened in England. But it came at the price of France—once Europe's largest and most prosperous economy (even though the wealth was hoarded at the highest levels)—becoming a second-tier commercial power.[2] Indeed, France's more measured industrial development resulted in generally less dire social disruptions, compared to those suffered by the British and Germans, and the basic structures of much of French life in the countryside survived until the end of the 19th century.

The Congress of Vienna had consolidated Germany's three-hundred-plus independent territories to a mere three dozen larger entities. This augured well for German industrial growth, especially given the rapidly expanding population, but the reigning conservative impulse after 1815 inclined each new state to adhere strictly to its own laws and customs. Merchants wanting to move goods across territorial borders had to contend with multiple sets of tolls and tariffs, multiple laws and jurisdictional systems, and multiple currencies; few were willing to make the effort. Germany therefore began to industrialize, although on a regional rather than a national level. The consequently lower levels of investment capital available meant that few entrepreneurs could afford expensive coal-fired machinery and had to rely on water-powered factories. This in turn meant that Germany's first factories were limited to areas in mountainous regions with access to fast-flowing streams, like Saxony and Silesia. Led by Prussia, one of the three dozen German principalities, a Customs Union (*Zollverein*) was created in 1818 and had enrolled one-third of the German states within twenty years, creating not a full-fledged free-trade zone but a set of streamlined partnerships. Members agreed to observe Prussian customs and regulations, in order to promote industry. In this way, Prussian leadership in the move toward eventual German reunification can be seen decades before the political movement itself took root. The Customs Union hired British equipment and engineers to develop the German coal industry and train them to build and maintain a railroad system. By 1850 nearly four thousand miles of rail track had been laid in Germany, and industrial development had progressed to such a degree that one could say that industrialization brought about the unification of Germany.

Many European states failed to industrialize at all after 1815: Austria, Italy, the Netherlands (though not Belgium), Poland, Portugal, Russia, Scandinavia, and Spain. The reasons for this failure were unique to each territory, but most involved some combination of a lack of natural resources, a shortage of capital, and a disinclination of labor to adopt new skills and technologies. In Austria and Spain, for example, geography worked against them. Fully two-thirds of the area of the

---

2   French cities like Bordeaux, Lyons, Montpellier, and Vienna, formerly busy centers of trade, became sleepy provincial towns.

Austrian-Hungarian Empire consisted of major mountain ranges that impeded infrastructural development. In Spain, the majority of the peninsula consisted of a hot upland plain, called the *meseta*, that was poor agricultural land, with few metal or mineral resources and little water. In Italy—which after 1815 was still divided into over a dozen petty kingdoms and principalities—intense regional pride and a cultural disinclination to change frustrated efforts to unify and industrialize. Though agriculturally rich, and with long-established traditions of artisanal crafts and professional (that is, financial, legal, and medical) expertise, few Italians valued the ideas of industrialized labor and mechanized production. What industrial production did exist, such as power-driven silk weaving in Lombardy, was performed on a part-time basis; seasonal female laborers simply filled in their days between the planting and harvesting of their crops. Even as late as 1861, in unified Italy's first national census, there were three times as many Italian farmers as there were industrial workers, and the majority of those workers were women working part-time.

Europe lagged behind Britain in railroad development, as in everything else, but did its best to catch up. In 1830, when England had established its first hundred

Italian Farm Workers   Italy was among the last of the western European countries to industrialize. These Italian farm workers, photographed sometime in the early 1900s, were still using oxen to pull their mower, long after other countries had introduced more modern techniques.

miles of track, France had a mere twenty miles of track to compare—and there was none anywhere else on the Continent. Belgium, however, began to construct a system immediately and by 1835 had established a network that covered the entire (although admittedly small) country. By 1850, though, things had changed. Germany, which by 1840 was funneling one-third of all its industrial investment capital into the railroads, had developed a grid of over 3,600 miles of track, and France's rail line had grown to roughly 1,800 miles. Underdeveloped Austria, by contrast, had a mere 850 miles of track, and Italy had not even half of that amount (see Map 17.2). The general picture that emerges suggests that railways proved most successful when connecting areas already starting to industrialize, but they

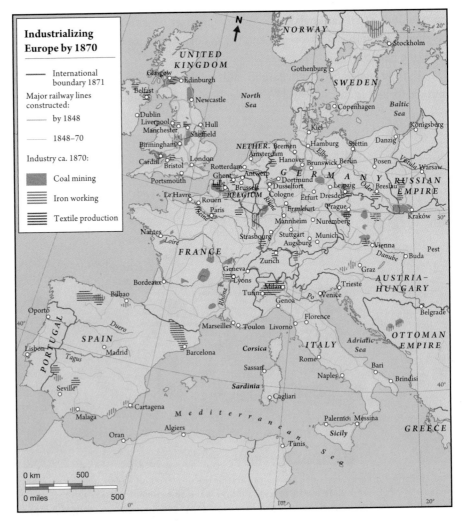

MAP 17.2   Industrializing Europe by 1870

themselves were seldom enough to initiate industrialization. And furthermore, whereas industrialization greatly expanded national economies, the wealth it generated exacerbated rather than relieved social inequities.

TRYING TO CATCH UP TO EUROPE

The Muslim world after 1800, for the most part, had only one of the many elements that had been essential to trigger industrialization in Europe: a growing population. The other elements—investment capital, an openness to technical innovations, secure access to raw materials, a reliable transport infrastructure, flexible market economies, and a system of government amenable to entrepreneurialism—were in short or irregular supply.

Census records for the Ottoman state are spotty, although the general pattern seems clear: after a dramatic downturn in population during the 18th century, the 19th saw strong population growth, from roughly seven million at the start of the century to about twenty million by its end. The growth was not evenly spread, however, with the lion's share of it happening in the empire's European provinces. (Generally speaking, the further east and south one traveled in the Ottoman Empire, the lower the population density.) This increase took place within a shrinking imperial geography, since Morocco, Algeria, and Tunisia had all broken away from Ottoman control by 1835 (see Map 17.3). As a result, the population density effectively doubled. Moreover, the political and social scene grew unsteady as the Ottoman Empire's hold over the western half of the Islamic world weakened.

Historians, especially European historians, tend to portray the Ottoman state as in a gradual but nonstop decline after 1700. Certainly the defeat of their last great campaign to take Vienna in 1683 was a watershed, and territorial retreat against the Austrian-Hungarians and the Russians was disheartening. Yet as late as 1750 the Ottomans were still the rulers, in terms of area, of the largest state in the Western world. The empire showed great resilience and was open to many reforms. Indeed, the 18th and 19th centuries were marked, if anything, by continuous waves of reform as the rulers labored to address the myriad ethnic, religious, economic, and social problems confronting it. This was not blind flailing. Taking their cue from the great Spanish Arab scholar Ibn Khaldun (1332–1406), whose ideas inspired many of the enacted or merely proposed reforms (and whose famous book *The Introduction to History* [*Muqaddimah*] was translated into Turkish at this time), the Turks crafted a variety of reforms that would hold together the fabric of Islamic society. These considered the interplay between the attractive forces of religious allegiance, economic interdependence, and political tradition on

> Yet as late as 1750 the Ottomans were still the rulers, in terms of area, of the largest state in the Western world.

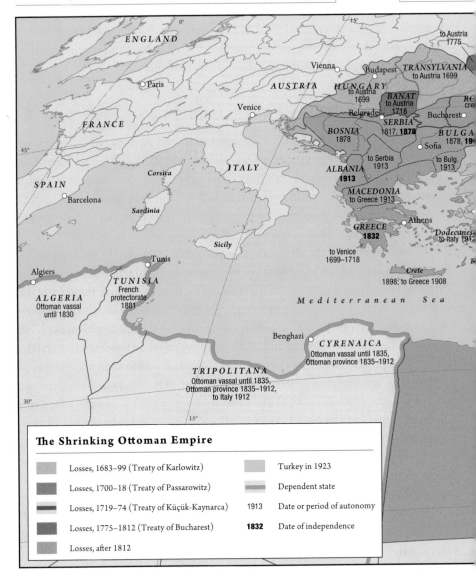

MAP 17.3   **The Shrinking Ottoman Empire**

the one hand and the divisive, centrifugal forces of ethnic or tribal localism, social division, and technological underdevelopment on the other.

Numerous Turkish writers of the time, echoing the efforts of their Enlightenment contemporaries in Europe, commented on the reform efforts emanating from the Istanbul court. One was Sari Mehmed Pasha (d. 1717), the son of a grocer who rose ultimately to the position of imperial treasurer, who saw the fundamental problem in the empire as the blurring of distinctions between the Muslim ruling class and their tax-paying non-Muslim subjects:

The admission of non-Muslims to the military ranks must be stopped, for nothing but trouble can result when those who are not descendants of cavalry officers are turned suddenly into cavalry officers.... Provincial town dwellers and farmers deserve to be protected, and their welfare increased by doing away with all [governmental] abuses; at the same time we should bend every effort to helping the people become prosperous—but it would be wrong to indulge the non-Muslims too much. (*The Book of Advice for Viziers and Governors*)

This did not bode well for the Christians and Jews in the empire. And while Mehmed Pasha's opinions were not official policy, the unease in the empire frequently resulted in popular hostility against religious minorities.

Another watershed was Napoleon's 1798 invasion of Egypt. This had been a short-lived conquest, but the event showed clearly how Muslim military might was falling behind that of Europe. Thereafter, periodic separatist movements arose throughout the Ottoman Empire, which were usually encouraged by Russia and Austria-Hungary. These setbacks forced the Turks to invest time and money in rebuilding the military that they would otherwise have committed to developing their industrial capacity. They settled on a strategy of replacing their traditional patchwork system of administration—one that had insured as much of each province's local customs as possible—and instead mandated a single system of law, granted citizen status to all, and abolished tax exemptions for privileged groups. In the early 19th century the ruler Selim III (r. 1789–1807), having witnessed the might of the French forces, tried to modernize the Turkish army along European lines but was stopped by a revolt of the Janissaries. His successor, Mahmud II (r. 1808–1839), took the drastic step of abolishing the Janissaries altogether in 1826. In their way, these reforms were progressive and echoed the egalitarian sentiments then current in European thinking, but they were anathema to much of the Muslim populace, most of whom angrily rejected the notion of equal status before the law for their non-Muslim neighbors.

"THE SICK MAN OF EUROPE"

Ottoman trade with Europe took place under the aegis of a group of trade agreements known somewhat ominously as **capitulations**. These agreements had previously been occasional arrangements that guaranteed Turkish and European merchants access to one another's markets for a mutually agreed-on period of years. By 1815, however, most capitulations overwhelmingly favored the Europeans. In fact, they did little more than grant European traders the right to enter Ottoman markets at will—in return for vague European promises to aid the Ottomans diplomatically in their territorial disputes with Austria-Hungary and Russia. Moreover, most capitulations ceded jurisdiction over all foreign traders and visitors to the foreigners' resident diplomats, and granted jurisdiction over foreigners whose home countries had no ambassador in Istanbul to whatever countries did have diplomatic representation there. They even allowed selected foreign governments to extend their own trading privileges to Christian and Jewish subjects of the Ottoman state.

The net effect of these capitulations was twofold. First, the empire's Mediterranean trade fell almost entirely into the hands of the Europeans precisely at the time when Europe began to industrialize. (Commerce in the Black Sea, Red Sea, Persian Gulf, and Indian Ocean remained in Muslim hands and usually exceeded, in annual revenue, the amount lost in the Mediterranean to the Europeans.) Second, popular resentment of Christians and Jews, whether Ottoman subjects or not, flared up significantly along with popular displeasure at what the empire's Muslim subjects regarded as the ruling dynasty's weakness and corruption.

A French traveler through the Middle East at the end of the 18th century summarized his impressions of relations between the Turks' Muslim and non-Muslim subjects this way:

> [Christian and Jewish merchants in Egypt] are confined to separate quarters where they live among themselves and have hardly any communication with the outside world; they dread such contact, in fact, and emerge from their neighborhoods as seldom as possible in order to avoid the insults thrown at them by the common people . . . and the bullying of the Mamluks. . . . Living as they do in a kind of perpetual imprisonment, they are constantly fearful—that perhaps an outbreak of plague will force them to blockade themselves in their houses, or perhaps a revolt somewhere will cause their neighborhood to be plundered, or perhaps the leader of some Islamic faction will extort money from them.

His view of relations in Damascus was no better:

> Turks, in fact, never speak of the [Muslim] people of Damascus without mentioning that they are the biggest troublemakers in the whole empire. . . . But they are quick to add too that the Christians there are more vile and troublesome than anywhere else. . . . The Damascene Arabs, for their part, hate the Christians too, and this hatred is fomented by their continual contact with Mecca . . . for Damascus is the general meeting point for all Islamic pilgrims coming from the north of Asia, just as Cairo is for the Muslims coming out of Africa. . . . Most European travelers and merchants agree . . . that the empire's Greek Christian subjects are a wicked, deceitful, abject, and insolent lot, whether they prosper or not. . . . For since the Turks treat the Greeks with the haughtiness and contempt they usually reserve for slaves, the Greeks cannot help becoming what they are regarded as. Forced constantly to lie, or to avoid violence by sly behavior, they indulge in obsequious flattery, deceit, and cheating of every kind.
> (C. F. Volney, *Travels in Egypt and Syria* [1785])

Even allowing for the traveler's ready stereotyping, the strain between communities is palpable.

Numerous efforts to revive the economy emanated from the court at Istanbul, but all failed. The Ottomans invested heavily in steamships, which increased the productivity of maritime trade, but were slow to develop railroads. Whatever rail lines they had in the 1800s were almost entirely limited to their European provinces; Anatolia, Palestine, and Egypt remained undeveloped in this regard. Farming methods did not undergo the transformative change they did in Europe, largely because most of the arable land remained in individual family farms; they were never consolidated into the larger holdings necessary to make the expense of new technology bearable. Without a corresponding increase in production, rural society did not develop the market economy characteristic of Europe. In terms of manufacture, the empire never successfully freed itself of the guild structure, and hence incentives to increase production failed to materialize despite the continuing interest in Ottoman goods like silks, carpets, and textiles. The most noticeable change in the manufacturing sector of the 19th century was the

Industrialization Comes to the Ottomans A silkweaving mill in Bursa, Turkey, in the late 19th century. Note the younger girls who tended the boiling basins where the older and more-skilled women extracted and cleaned the silk. Silk manufacture had been a specialty in Bursa since the 16th century. Since Islamic tradition forbade, and generally still forbids, Muslim men to wear silk—they regard it as effeminate—silk cloth was primarily an export commodity, and a highly profitable one.

increase in the percentage of women in the workplace, but their labor was by hand. Mechanization was insignificant.

Without local market economies, access to investment capital, incentives to increase production, and a reliable infrastructure for transport, the empire could not industrialize and hence had no chance to catch up with the fast-growing European economy. As the "sick man of Europe"—as Westerners began to call the Ottoman state in the 19th century—Istanbul's hold over even its reduced empire continued to slip, prompting more efforts by the provinces to secede. The most famous and significant of these secessions was Greece's successful revolt in 1832.

LIFE IN THE INDUSTRIAL AGE

Until the industrial revolution the word "unemployment" did not exist in English. In earlier centuries the word "unemployed" had been widely used, but almost always in relation to an object instead of a person: tools might lie unemployed on a workman's shelf; a workman himself, however, never "was unemployed." He was simply poor. Daniel Defoe, in his great *Journal of the Plague Year* (1756), described the ghostly emptiness of the London city streets with a reference to "coaches... left unemploy'd for five or six days"; yet people themselves, even the poorest among them, were seldom without work to do. Industrial society, however, was rife with unemployment. It indeed depended on it, for surplus labor kept wages down to a level that justified the capital risk of entrepreneurship.

But unemployment was only one of the dire new developments created by industrialization. Hardly a single aspect of Western society remained unaffected. Everything from the role of the state to the structure of the family, from women's roles in society to the material standards of living, from the urban landscape to school curricula, and more, were altered in one way or another. Much of 19th-century history, in fact, can be read as a long effort to adapt to the changes brought on by the industrial revolution.

The easiest change to quantify is the increase in urban development— although the word "development" may be misused here. What occurred was largely the unchecked, uncontrolled, riotous, and blighted increase in the number and size of cities wherever the mechanization of labor took root. In 1800 Europe had a mere twenty-two cities with populations of 100,000. By 1850 that number had grown to forty-seven. The populations of cities both old and new likewise skyrocketed. By 1850 London's population stood at an astounding 2.5 million people, making it easily the largest city in Europe. Paris had roughly 1.5 million; Berlin and Naples each had a half million; Vienna held approximately 400,000; and Brussels held 250,000 (see Map 17.4). These leading cities had ballooned not only with industry

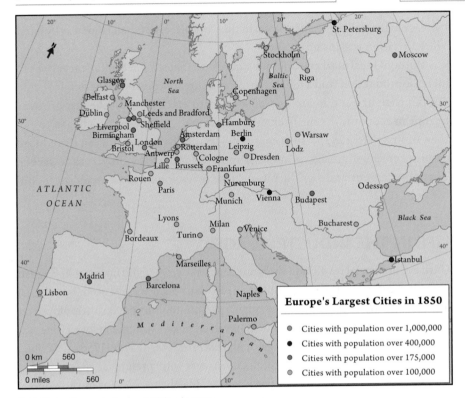

MAP 17.4   Europe's Largest Cities in 1850

but also with the financial and government administrations needed to manage it. There were lesser, though still large, centers—like Barcelona, Budapest, Hamburg, Lyons, Palermo, Rouen, and Stockholm. But even with these, the capacity to cope with such unprecedented increases in numbers failed miserably. For everyone except the reasonably prosperous—perhaps the top 15 percent of the urban population—living conditions ranged from the bad to the almost unspeakably awful.

Workers, the unemployed, migrants, and their families were squeezed into filthy hovels with poor sanitation, little warmth, and inadequate supplies of fresh water to drink. Lacking any kind of sewage system, people relieved themselves in chamber pots and simply flung the refuse into the street.[3] Chemical smog and coal smoke filled the air; prostitution and violent crime were rampant. In the worker slums of Lille (population in 1872: 158,000) fully one-third of the population lived in cellars. In Stockholm several thousand poor families, who lived primar-

---

3   By the mid-19th century, the ratio of urban inhabitants to flush toilets was still an alarming 200:1 in most industrial cities.

Shantytown   The word *shantytown* originated in North America and came into general use in the middle of the nineteenth century to denote the ramshackle dwellings of poor Irish immigrants. It quickly was taken over, however, to describe the slum areas that sprang up outside industrialized cities. This scene presents a dewy-eyed vision of one such shantytown in Germany. The poor are clearly poor, but almost picturesquely so. Notice the well-dressed genteel couple in the center, who are handing out money to the children.

ily in the hilly areas surrounding the archipelago that makes up the center of the city, actually lived in holes they had dug in the ground. Census records from 1847 show that in one Irish working-class neighborhood in London, St. Giles, no fewer than 461 people lived jammed together in only twelve houses. Cholera and tuberculosis (then called consumption) were endemic and according to some estimates accounted for over 50 percent of all deaths in factory cities in the 19th century. A single wave of cholera in 1832 killed 32,000 people in Paris alone and another 7,000 in London; worse still, the same epidemic carried off 250,000 in Russia. The effects of tuberculosis were even more dire.

Local and national governments responded with housing codes, the expansion of sewage systems, and efforts to control crime, but were seldom able to keep pace with the misery. Factory workers, vulnerable to reduced wages created by the great abundance of labor, generally earned too little to support their families, and consequently women and children had to work too. In textile manufacturing, in fact, fully one-half of the pre-1850 labor force was made up of women and children as young as seven. Conditions for the workers were often dismal. Work days were frequently twelve or even fourteen hours in length, and discipline could be brutal.

An English woman who worked hauling carts of coal out of a mine shaft described her work to a government-inquiry panel in this way:

> I was married at 23, and went into a colliery when I was married. I used to weave when about 12 years old; can neither read nor write. I . . . make sometimes 7 [shillings] a week, sometimes not so much. I am a drawer [cart puller], and work from 6 in the morning to 6 at night. Stop about an hour at noon to eat my dinner; have bread and butter for dinner; I get no drink. I have two children, but they are too young to work. I worked at drawing when I was in the family way. I know a woman who has gone home and washed herself, taken to her bed, delivered of a child, and gone to work again under the week. . . .
>
> [When hauling coal] I have a belt round my waist, and a chain passing between my legs, and I go on my hands and feet. The road is very steep, and we have to hold by a rope; and when there is no rope, by anything we can catch hold of. There are six women and about six boys and girls in the pit I work in; it is very hard work for a woman. The pit is very wet where I work, and the water comes over our clog-tops always, and I have seen it up to my thighs; it rains in at the roof terribly. My clothes are wet through almost all day long. . . .
>
> My cousin looks after my children in the day-time. I am very tired when I get home at night; I fall asleep sometimes before I get washed. I am not so strong as I was, and cannot stand my work so well as I used to. I have drawn till I have [worn the] skin off me; the belt and chain is worse when we are in the family way. [My husband] has beaten me many a times for not being ready [to have sex]. I [was] not used to it at first, and he had little patience. . . .
>
> I have known many a man beat his drawer. I have known men take liberties with the drawers, and some of the women have bastards.
>
> (*Parliamentary Papers, 1842, vol. 15*)

In France, factory workers were long required to carry a document called a *livret* ("booklet"), which was a kind of worker's passport. Foremen and superiors in a factory regularly wrote comments in an employee's livret, citing his or her mistakes, tardiness, poor attitude, breakages, or ill discipline. Applicants for factory jobs were required to produce their booklets for their prospective employers to review.

Apart from the demeaning nature of these conditions, industrial work also fostered economic and social dependency, since workers lived more or less at the mercy of their employers. Textile factories often provided housing for their unmarried female workers—the cost of boarding being deducted from their

a

b

**Engraving from *A Treatise on the Winning and Working of Collieries* by Matthias Dunn
(1848)** It shows a boy pulling a loaded cart through a shaft in a Welsh coal mine
(a). Children sometimes started to work in the mines as young as age seven. Below, a
woman drags a heavy load of coal up an incline, assisted by two children (a boy and a girl,
apparently) at the rear (b). From the coal region of Midlothian, in Scotland, ca. 1848.

wages—which meant that many women literally spent their whole working lives
on the job site. Children sent to work in their youth ended up crippled and deformed, unable to care for themselves in their adult years. One observer of the
child workers in the cotton mills left this vivid description:

> When I visited Bradford, in Yorkshire, in 1838, being desirous to see
> the condition of the children—for I knew that they were employed at
> very early ages in the worsted business ... I asked for a collection of
> cripples and deformities. In a short time more than 80 were gathered in
> a large courtyard. They were mere samples of the entire mass. I assert

without exaggeration that no power of language could describe the varieties, and I may say, the cruelties, in all these degradations of the human form. They stood or squatted before me in all the shapes of the letters of the alphabet. This was the effect of prolonged toil on the tender frames of children at early ages.   *(Parliamentary Debates, 3rd ser., vol. 245)*

All that was left for one thus ruined was to join the public welfare rolls. Given such wretched conditions, it is not surprising to learn that alcoholism became rampant—although it is a shock to discover that the problem was so extensive that in many cities the businesses staggered their scheduled paydays in order to minimize the number of drunks on city streets at any given time. Neither is it surprising that workers and indigents alike began to riot. Labor strikes and demonstrations shook northern England as early as 1811. In France the silk-weaving center of Lyons erupted in worker rebellions in 1831 and again in 1834—the latter revolt resulting in several hundred deaths and the arrest, conviction, and deportation of approximately ten thousand city dwellers.

RIOTS AND REFORM

A riot over starvation wages by linen weavers in Silesia (then part of Prussia, today located in Poland) in 1844 gained such renown that the Romantic poet Heinrich Heine (1797–1856) commemorated their struggle in verse. "The Silesian Weavers" appeared in 1844, in the immediate aftermath of the revolt. Many of his poems were set to music by Franz Schubert and Robert Schumann. Karl Marx was also a fan and was the first to publish Heine's "Germany—A Winter's Tale" (also 1844). It is easy to see how lines like these, from "The Silesian Weavers," would appeal to Marx:

> Doomed is our king, the rich man's king,
> who remained unmoved by our suffering
> and snatched the last penny out of our hands
> before giving us over to his thuggish bands.

In Manchester, the "Peterloo Massacre" occurred in 1819 when private militias hired by the local factory owners showed up at a popular demonstration of workers. Speakers there were calling for universal suffrage and secret ballots as the only means of getting the government to address urban problems effectively. When the most popular of the speakers, a firebrand named Henry Hunt, began his speech, the militias swung into action:

> The commanding officer then approaching Mr. Hunt, and brandishing his sword, told him that he was his prisoner. Mr. Hunt, after enjoining

the people to tranquility, said, that he would readily surrender to any civil officer on showing his warrant, and Mr. Nadin, the principal police officer, received him in charge. Another person, named Johnson, was likewise apprehended, and a few of the mob; some others against whom there were warrants, escaped in the crowd.

A cry now arose among the military of "Have at their flags!" and they dashed down not only those in the cart, but the others dispersed in the field; cutting to right and left to get at them. The people began running in all directions; and from this moment the yeomanry lost all command of temper: numbers were trampled under the feet of men and horses; many, both men and women, were cut down by sabers; several, and a peace officer and a female in the number, slain on the spot. The whole number of persons injured amounted to between three and four hundred. The populace threw a few stones and brick bats in their retreat; but in less than ten minutes the ground was entirely cleared of its former occupants, and filled by various bodies of military, both horse and foot. Mr. Hunt was led to prison, not without incurring considerable danger, and some injury on his way from the swords of the yeomanry and the bludgeons of police officers; the broken staves of two of his banners were carried in mock procession before him. The magistrates directed him to

Cutting the Workers Down to Size Cartoon showing police putting down the labor strikers at the Peterloo Massacre in 1819, in Manchester.

be locked up in a solitary cell, and the other prisoners were confined with the same precaution. The town was brought into a tolerably quiet state before night, military patrols being stationed at the end of almost every street. *(Annual Register)*

Unrest continued to grow throughout the century, giving rise to passionate debate over what to do about the myriad negative consequences of industrialization.

Not all was doom and gloom, however. Private charities and organized efforts to relieve urban suffering proliferated by the thousands across Europe.[4] A private enterprise called the Society for the Diffusion of Useful Knowledge appeared in 1824, dedicated to teaching the masses everything from new job skills to personal hygiene. In Paris the church-run Society of Saint Vincent de Paul formed in 1835 to provide clothing, food, and rudimentary education to workers and transients. Meanwhile the French government-funded network of night schools, called Polytechnic Associations, made vocational training available to over one hundred thousand people by 1850.

WOMEN AND CHILDREN LAST

Women were affected by industrialization in ways that men were not. Initially, women made up more of the workforce, at least in some industries: England's textiles factories, in fact, notoriously hired women and children to a disproportionate degree. Women and children made up as much as 75 percent of the labor force in some areas. A woman received less than half the wages a man did in factory work. Working women in the 19th century also differed from their forebears in a significant way: they lived apart from their families. In rural areas, women had put in as many hours of daily labor as men did, but since workplace and domestic space were the same, no fundamental division between work and family existed. In many factories, the female laborers were single girls or women who had left the family farm in search of work. Cut off from their traditional social units, they had to forge new connections in a strange and dangerous new urban setting. Married women with one or two children were often able to rely on new friends or neighbors to help with childcare while they put in long hours at the factory. But as her family increased in number, it grew increasingly difficult for a woman to keep working, no matter how badly the family needed her wages, and so she dropped out of the workplace. Factory owners were quick to seize on the

---

[4]   London was the site of nearly five hundred relief organizations by midcentury.

Women at Work in a French Textile Mill   Everyone looks healthy, happy, and, well, industrious.

children themselves as replacement workers; children earned less than half of even the discounted wages of women, after all. It took the Factory Act in 1833 to restrict and regulate (though not ban) child labor.[5]

Unmarried women were vulnerable to sexual exploitation, either from demanding factory bosses, seducing boyfriends, or criminal attackers. Public health workers recorded that approximately one-third of all the babies born in an industrial city in England or France in the 1820s and 1830s were born out of wedlock. Throughout France, an average of thirty thousand newborns were abandoned at foundling hospitals and orphanages annually. Thousands more each year—although no one can know the precise number—were victims of infanticide. Prostitution formed another aspect of exploitation. Industrial cities swarmed with it. After all, factory work and employment in domestic service to the wealthier families could absorb only a fraction of the working-class women packed into urban slums.[6] Many of those with no other means to support themselves turned to sex work. Paris had roughly thirty thousand streetwalking prostitutes in the

---

[5]   The Factory Act outlawed child labor for those under the age of nine. It set a maximum limit of nine hours of labor a day for children aged nine to thirteen.

[6]   The word *slum*, according to a popular though dubious folk etymology, emerged in the Industrial Revolution as a slang variant of the word *slime*, to describe the filthiness of the hovels into which workers were packed.

Workhouse   The St. Marylebone Parish Workhouse was established in 1730. By 1834 it had acquired several new and enlarged buildings. Refugees from the Irish Potato Famine drove its occupancy to over 2200. This photo dates to 1901, after a new wave of construction added two five-story blockhouses to the site. During World War I it also housed Belgian war refugees.

1830s; London had over twice that number. Concerns about the spread of disease rose accordingly.

In order to deal effectively with the social consequences of industrialization, Western governments began to create special bureaus for the collection of data: commissions on public health, on housing, on working conditions, on urban crime, on municipal codes and infrastructure, all appeared for the first time in the early 19th century, and the data they gathered form the basis of our understanding of the problems Europe faced as its economy mechanized. But the states were not the only institutions involved. Private charities, trusts, and societies formed by the hundreds, each usually dedicated to a particular urban problem. Catholic religious orders established scores of hospitals, old-age homes, soup kitchens, and orphanages. Protestant groups instituted Bible-reading societies, evangelical gatherings, temperance societies (to fight the alcoholism rampant among the industrial poor), and workhouses. In Scotland, the "Glasgow Young Men's Society for Religious Improvement"—a forerunner of today's YMCA—was formed in 1824 to provide healthy alternatives to urban crime, alcohol, and sexual license.

Private religious groups inaugurated the idea of Sunday schools as places where young people could gather to study the Scriptures and sing hymns. Half of all British working-class children received reading instruction at Sunday schools. Among the many problems facing the slums was a dire shortage of places of worship. In Berlin, for example, the churches in the city, combined, could seat about twenty-five thousand people on any given Sunday, but there were well over eight hundred thousand people living in Berlin. Without churches, the faithful had to extemporize. Some whole denominations emerged, either as completely new phenomena or as revitalized versions of older denominations, and most of them depended on a heightened emotionalism that responded to the desperate needs of the people. Among these new denominations were the Methodist, Quaker, and Baptist branches of Protestant Christianity. In the United States, itself beginning to industrialize in the North, some of the new denominations included the Latter-day Saints (the Mormons) and the Seventh-day Adventists; the second half of the century saw the establishment of the Jehovah's Witnesses and the Salvation Army.

THE ROMANTIC GENERATION

Romanticism was the most pervasive and influential cultural phenomenon in the first half of the 19th century. Everyone agrees on that. What few historians can easily do, however, is state exactly what Romanticism was. Between 1899 and 1932 a brilliant historian named Henri Pirenne (1862–1935) published the massive seven-volume *History of Belgium*, and when he reached the 19th century and came to the topic of Romanticism he briefly halted. A careful scholar, given to detail and precision, he indulged himself and came up with 152 separate definitions of it. Rather than compete with Pirenne, it may be better to back away from precision and describe Romanticism—vaguely, perhaps, but not inaccurately—as a generational mood that tended to prefer emotion and instinct over structural order and rational thought. Just as reference to the '60s generation calls up images of attitude, aesthetic style, political concerns, and social rebellion, so too does the term "Romanticism" denote sentiments about human life, nature, and the workings of the world.

Of course, not every young person in the United States in the 1960s wore long hair, experimented with drugs and "free love," listened to an electrified Bob Dylan, marched on Washington to protest the war in Vietnam or in support of civil rights, or sought to create a new social order by establishing communes. Neither did every young adult in the first decade or two of the 19th century wear long hair, experiment with opium and Byronic free love, listen to Beethoven, set out to join Greece's nationalist rebellion against the Ottoman Empire, or seek a new social order by overthrowing bourgeois values in favor of an anarchic utopia of like-minded souls in communion with one another. But individuals in each era did so—enough to give each age its identity.

We can see the Romantic temperament expressed most clearly in the arts, especially in literature. Compare a few lines of Samuel Johnson (1709–1784) and William Wordsworth (1770–1850). The differences between the poems are stark:

> Where then shall Hope and Fear their objects find?
> Must dull Suspense corrupt the stagnant mind?
> Must helpless man, in ignorance sedate,
> Roll darkling down the torrent of his fate?
> Must no dislike alarm, no wishes rise,
> No cries attempt the mercies of the skies?
> Enquirer, cease, petitions yet remain,
> Which Heaven may hear, nor deem religion vain.
> Still raise for good the supplicating voice,
> But leave to heaven the measure and the choice,
> Safe in His power, whose eyes discern afar
> The secret ambush of a specious prayer.
> Implore His aid, in His decisions rest,
> Secure, whate'er He gives, He gives the best.
> Yet when the sense of sacred presence fires,
> And strong devotion to the skies aspires,
> Pour forth thy fervours for a healthful mind,
> Obedient passions, and a will resigned;
> For love, which scarce collective man can fill;
> For patience sovereign o'er transmuted ill;
> For faith, that panting for a happier seat,
> Counts death kind Nature's signal of retreat:
> These goods for man the laws of Heaven ordain,
> These goods He grants, who grants the power to gain;
> With these celestial Wisdom calms the mind,
> And makes the happiness she does not find. *(Johnson, "The Vanity*
> *of Human Wishes," ll. 343–368)*

Johnson's carefully measured, stately rhythms and strong rhymes bespeak order and stoic calm, even while the poem asserts the supreme need to reconcile the infinite longings of the heart with the world's harsh and finite realities. Happiness does not exist outside of ourselves, like an as-yet undiscovered continent; but we can attain something like it, the poem hints, by the calm acceptance of our limits, hopeful under the eye of a mysterious but loving God.

Wordsworth's poem, in contrast, follows a regular but less rigid metrical scheme, avoids rhyme altogether, and emphasizes throughout the world's sensuous delight:

> O there is blessing in this gentle breeze,
> A visitant that, while he fans my cheek,
> Doth seem half-conscious of the joy he brings
> From the green fields, and from yon azure sky.
> Whate'er his mission, the soft breeze can come
> To none more grateful than to me; escaped
> From the vast City, where I long have pined
> A discontented Sojourner—Now free,
> Free as a bird to settle where I will.
> What dwelling shall receive me? in what vale
> Shall be my harbour? underneath what grove
> Shall I take up my home? and what clear stream
> Shall with its murmur lull me into rest?
> The earth is all before me: with a heart
> Joyous, nor scared at its own liberty,
> I look about; and should the chosen guide
> Be nothing better than a wandering cloud,
> I cannot miss my way. I breathe again;
> Trances of thought and mountings of the heart
> Come fast upon me; it is shaken off
> That burthen of my own unnatural self,
> The heavy weight of many a weary day
> Not mine, and such as were not made for me. *(Wordsworth,*
> *The Prelude, 1.1–23)*

The poet feels more than he thinks, exults rather than analyzes. He sets out from the hated City into the world of wild nature where he can breathe again, confident that he cannot fail to find his way.

Both poems are magnificent, but they work on the reader in different ways—and that difference is the result of Romanticism. Another pairing—this time in the field of music—might start with the floating melodic piano line that introduces the well-known chorale by Johann Sebastian Bach, "Jesu, Joy of Man's Desiring." Its lovely, long, regular run of eighth notes contrasts with the four-note blast that begins Ludwig von Beethoven's Fifth Symphony. This is not to say that Bach's music lacks passion or that Beethoven's lacks structure (although many early critics and musicians complained of exactly that, when attempting to play Beethoven). Rather, these two passages of music affect the ear and stir the soul in different ways—intentionally. Bach's music is sublimely beautiful and moving—and yet one is always aware of its cool, intricate structure. Beethoven's music can astonish us with its power—and yet part of its effect arises from the uneasy sense it inspires that Beethoven himself is at times barely in control of the surging passionate wave he is unleashing. Romanticism exalted, and exulted in, that sense of passionate abandon.

Romanticism, or forms of it, appeared broadly throughout Western culture, in philosophy, popular attitudes, painting, and politics, as well as poetry and music. Indeed, it is this very all-pervasiveness that makes Romanticism difficult to pin down. How can one summarize coherently a culture shared by personalities as vastly different as Charles Baudelaire (1821–1867), the decadent French poet, and Otto von Bismarck (1815–1898), the "Iron Chancellor" of the German Empire?[7] In its most general sense, Romanticism was an intellectual reaction against the 18th-century Enlightenment ideals of order, discipline, and reason. To analyze human nature scientifically, the new generation felt, was to cheapen it by reducing people to machines. The human heart, in a clinical sense, can be studied as a matter of medical science—but the passions it houses are mysterious, darkly powerful, beyond reason.

> To analyze human nature scientifically, the new generation felt, was to cheapen it by reducing people to machines. The human heart, in a clinical sense, can be studied as a matter of medical science—but the passions it houses are mysterious, darkly powerful, beyond reason.

Moreover, the Enlightened view of the world had resulted in a bloody revolution and millions of dead from Paris to Moscow. It was thus hard to justify maintaining its core tenets about the rational reform of society and the inevitability of progress. At the same time, Romanticism rejected the mechanized horrors of industrialism and the bourgeois values that championed it. Industrial capitalism, after all, gave every appearance of valuing commodities more than people, of regarding human beings merely as workers, consumers, and nothing more. For Thomas Carlyle (1795–1881), as he expresses in his essay "Signs of the Times" (1829), it cheapened existence itself by cynically squashing every humane value and attribute:

> Were we required to characterise this age of ours by any single epithet, we should be tempted to call it, not an Heroical, Devotional,

---

[7]   Baudelaire: "To say 'Romanticism' is, in essence, to say 'Modern Art.' It is to speak of intimacy, spirituality, color, the aspiration to the infinite—as expressed by every tool available to the arts." ("The Salon of 1846")

Philosophical, or Moral Age, but, above all others, the Mechanical Age. It is the Age of Machinery, in every outward and inward sense of that word; the age which, with its whole undivided might, forwards, teaches and practises the great art of adapting means to ends. Nothing is now done directly, or by hand; all is by rule and calculated contrivance. For the simplest operation, some helps and accompaniments, some cunning abbreviating process is in readiness. Our old modes of exertion are all discredited, and thrown aside. On every hand, the living artisan is driven from his workshop, to make room for a speedier, inanimate one. The shuttle drops from the fingers of the weaver, and falls into iron fingers that ply it faster. . . . There is no end to machinery. Even the horse is stripped of his harness, and finds a fleet firehorse yoked in his stead. Nay, we have an artist that hatches chickens by steam; the very brood-hen is to be superseded! For all earthly, and for some unearthly purposes, we have machines and mechanic furtherances; for mincing our cabbages; for casting us into magnetic sleep. We remove mountains, and make seas our smooth highway; nothing can resist us. We war with rude Nature; and, by our resistless engines, come off always victorious, and loaded with spoils.

The poem by Heinrich Heine quoted earlier, "The Silesian Weavers," imagines a group of women tending an industrial loom as they weave a death shroud for the German nation; witch-like, they weave a trio of curses into the cloth— denouncing God, the king, and the hellish industrialized country they have all become victim to.[8] To rebel against mechanization, utilitarianism, middle-class values, and bourgeois respectability was, in the early 19th century, a declaration of the freedom of the soul. To a lesser extent, Romanticism was also a nationalistic response against French predominance in the political and cultural spheres, and hence was a rebellion against the Napoleonic era.

Because of its rebellious nature, Romanticism was very much a young person's movement. Most of the writers commonly associated with Romanticism— Friedrich Schelling (1775–1854), Stendahl (Marie-Henri Beyle; 1783–1842), Lord Byron (1788–1824), Percy Bysshe Shelley (1792–1822), John Keats (1795–1821), Thomas Carlyle (1795–1881), Mary Shelley (1797–1851), Aleksandr Pushkin (1799–1837), Victor Hugo (1802–1885), Mikhail Lermontov (1814–1841)— were all under the age of forty (and many under the age of thirty) in 1815. The older Romantics were Johann Wilhelm von Goethe (1749–1832), William Blake

---

[8] Heine: "O Germany, we're spinning out your pall, / Weaving our triple curse through it all."

(1757–1827), William Wordsworth (1770–1850), Samuel Taylor Coleridge (1772–1834), and Novalis (Georg Philipp Freiherr von Hardenburg; 1772–1801). Generalization about so broad a range of writers is difficult, but they did share a tendency to privilege the instinctive, impulsive, creative spirit in humans over the rational and analytical.

The Romantic generation believed in "genius"—meaning by this word an individual's imaginative capacity, the passionate and spiritual instinct that allows us to feel connected to nature and to one another. The only true happiness people can attain in life, it follows, is to live in intimate harmony with our sensations and passions. This is not necessarily to promote hedonism; the desire to please and serve others can be as sincerely felt a passion as sexual lust or any other selfish impulse. Indeed, most of the Romantics believed that ethnic and cultural groups possessed a kind of collective genius—a shared spiritual intimacy that allows members of a race to understand one another intuitively.

This sense of cultural cohesion strongly influenced a development later in the century, nationalism, when native groups broken apart artificially by the Treaty of Vienna struggled to reunite. They sought a world of organic states brought to spiritual perfection by their unique identities. The German Romantic philosopher Johann Gottlieb Fichte (1762–1814) put it thus, in his "Address to the German Nation" in 1806:

Encountering Wild Nature   A work by Theodore Chasseriau (1855) depicting Macbeth and Banquo as they encounter the three witches, in Shakespeare's *Macbeth*.

Men who speak the same language are joined to each other by Nature herself, through countless invisible bonds, long before any human art begins; such men understand one another and can always make themselves understood with perfect clarity; they belong together, and they possess a single, indivisible nature. . . . Only when a [united] people is left to itself, so that it can create and develop in harmony with its own unique genius, and only when every individual within each group develops himself in accord with that shared genius—while also in harmony with his own individual genius—then, and only then, does the divine creative spirit manifest itself as it ought.

To remain in contact with the intuitive, passionate self—whether the individual or the collective self—was the only guarantee of a satisfying life to the Romantics. Life should be mysterious, at least to some extent. Reason is a tool to be deployed whenever needed, they felt, but it does not define humanity; to those who allow Reason to dictate their entire view of life and regard every activity and observation as an opportunity for analysis, the Romantics respond with an urgent alarm to wake up from their methodical dullness before they effectively turn into machines themselves.

The dangers were many, and they threatened all of society. "Only the material, the immediately practical, not the divine and spiritual, is important to us," wrote Carlyle. "The infinite, absolute character of Virtue has passed into a finite, conditional one; it is no longer a worship of the Beautiful and Good, but a calculation of the Profitable. . . . Our true Deity is Mechanism." Industrialization not only brought penury and suffering to millions at the bottom of the economic scale, it also cheapened everyone's lives by reducing them to a mechanical, bureaucratic, institutionalized monotony. When the machines take over, the Romantics urged, our souls die.

WHO, WHAT, WHERE

capitulations	industrial revolution
Congress of Vienna	Romanticism

SUGGESTED READINGS

Primary Sources

Babbage, Charles. *On the Economy of Machinery and Manufactures.*

Carlyle, Thomas. "Signs of the Times."

Engels, Friedrich. *The Condition of the Working Class in England in 1844.*

Ricardo, David. *On the Principles of Political Economy and Taxation.*

Anthologies

Breckman, Warren. *European Romanticism: A Brief History with Documents* (2007).

Frader, Laura Levine. *The Industrial Revolution: A History in Documents* (2006).

Wu, Duncan, ed. *Romanticism: An Anthology* (2005).

Studies

Allen, Robert. *The British Industrial Revolution in Global Perspective* (2008).

Berend, Iván. *History Derailed: Central and Eastern Europe in the Long Nineteenth Century* (2003).

Bilenky, Serhiy. *Romantic Nationalism in Eastern Europe: Russian, Polish, and Ukrainian Political Imaginations* (2012).

Burnette, Joyce. *Gender, Work, and Wages in Industrial Revolution Britain* (2008).

Clark, Gregory. *A Farewell to Alms: A Brief Economic History of the World* (2008).

Cohen, Deborah. *Household Gods: The British and Their Possessions* (2006).

Crump, Thomas. *A Brief History of the Age of Steam: The Power That Drove the Industrial Revolution* (2007).

Flanders, Judith. *Inside the Victorian Home: A Portrait of Domestic Life in Victorian England* (2005).

Holmes, Richard. *The Age of Wonder: How the Romantic Generation Discovered the Beauty and Terror of Science* (2009).

Hudson, Pat. *The Industrial Revolution* (2007).

Landes, David S. *The Unbound Prometheus: Technological Change and Industrial Development in Western Europe from 1750 to the Present* (2003).

McLane, Maureen N. *Romanticism and the Human Sciences: Poetry, Population, and the Discourse of the Species* (2006).

Mokyr, Joel. *The Gifts of Athena: Historical Origins of the Knowledge Economy* (2004).

Pollard, Lisa. *Nurturing the Nation: The Family Politics of Modernizing, Colonizing, and Liberating Egypt, 1805–1923* (2005).

Pomeranz, Kenneth. *The Great Divergence: China, Europe, and the Making of the Modern World Economy* (2001).

Richardson, Alan. *British Romanticism and the Science of the Mind* (2005).

Sunderland, David. *Social Capital, Trust, and the Industrial Revolution, 1780–1880* (2007).

Swade, Doron. *The Difference Engine: Charles Babbage and the Quest to Build the First Computer* (2002).

Weightman, Gavin. *Industrial Revolutionaries: The Making of the Modern World, 1776–1914* (2009).

Wrigley, E. A. *Energy and the English Industrial Revolution* (2010).

For additional resources, including maps, primary sources, visuals, web links, and quizzes, please go to **www.oup.com/us/backman.**

CHAPTER 18

The Birth of Modern Politics

1815–1848

The diplomats who convened at the Congress of Vienna (1814–1815) did more than redraw the map of Europe. They also tried to turn back time by returning European politics to the familiar rule of kings. The high idealism of the French Revolution, they felt, had resulted in nothing to recommend it. What was needed was to reestablish an older tradition that, while perhaps not perfect, did at least have the benefit of stability in its favor. They feared the revolutionary virus and a country's capacity to wreak havoc on its neighbors—two dangers associated with France. Hoping to contain and eradicate both, they crafted a long series of decrees, treaties, and protocols. These agreements created a new balance of power between the nations by reconfiguring international borders and by introducing a measure of constitutional government under royal leadership.

CIVIL UNREST IN THE GREATER WEST, 1819-1831

They also brought about a philosophical division between conservatism and liberalism, the two sets of beliefs that would dominate most of European political development for the next two centuries. By midcentury, however, both views were challenged by social upheavals and by Marxism, a new philosophy of history and revolution. And none of these fully encompassed changes in family life and the budding rights of women.

◀ **Revolutionary Fervor** A sacred call to "Brotherhood" inspires the people from all Europe in their march against monarchy, privilege, and social hierarchy. To Karl Marx, the rebellions of 1848 offered the promise of worker solidarity; to his dismay, nationalist passions got in the way.

CONSERVATISM IN POWER

The restoration of monarchies was the fundamental strategy of the diplomats. This is hardly surprising, since the royal families driven from power by Napoleon had spent the intervening years plotting their return. Complicating matters, though, was the fact that many of the dynasties created by Bonaparte—such as the new Duchy of Warsaw and the Kingdom of Piedmont-Sardinia—had acquired a certain amount of popular support. Representatives of five major powers dominated the **Congress of Vienna**: Austria, Britain, France, Prussia, and Russia. Further complicating matters was the new political division between liberalism and conservatism.

The main figure of the Congress, though, was Klemens von Metternich (1773–1859), an Austrian aristocrat and the chief diplomat for the Habsburg emperor. Metternich had been born in the age and social milieu of absolutism and aristocratic privilege, and throughout his long and active life he never wavered in his conviction that the people of Continental Europe were not ready for democracy. He did not disagree with democracy in principle, but believed that it worked only in certain highly limited circumstances. Above all, Metternich insisted, a politically stable democratic society arose only from gradual, evolutionary change in political structures. The radical surgery represented by political revolution was guaranteed to fail and to bring misery to any society that attempts it. (Metternich met Edmund Burke briefly in 1794, during a visit to England; the men took an immediate, instinctive liking to one another.)

The issue for Metternich was not the desire of the powerful to maintain their status but the impatience of revolutionaries who believed they could pass over periods of organic growth that were in fact essential before democracy could begin. Metternich wrote in his *Memoirs*:

> The nature of Man is unchanging. The principal needs of any society are always and ever shall be the same; any differences that appear to exist between human societies are simply the result of the varying influences (different climates, different fertility of soil, existence as an island as

CHAPTER TIMELINE

1753–1821
Joseph-Marie
de Maistre

1806–1873
John Stuart Mill

1818–1883
Karl Marx

1773–1859
Klemens von
Metternich

1814–1815
Congress of
Vienna

1825
Decembrists revolt,
Russia

opposed to a continental territory, etc.) that Nature has effected upon them. Such influences undoubtedly have consequences far beyond the fundamental material realities of life: they can establish and shape unique needs of the most advanced kind, and can even determine the laws of a society and influence the development of its religion.... It is true of institutions as well; their origins are frequently obscure, but they then progress through stages of evolution until they reach a developmental peak, only at last to decay. Like Man himself, and following the same natural laws, they have a period of infancy, then of youth, then of full adult vigor and intelligence, then of decline. But throughout this natural process they retain at all times two key elements that never relinquish or see a diminution of their everlasting power—namely, the dictates of religious and social morality, and the limits established by geography.

Conservatism thus values tradition and stability above the individual. As Metternich saw it, it was realism, pure and simple, a common-sense recognition that human life takes place within a physical and cultural geography to which it must adapt. Not all things are possible, and therefore to desire all things is impractical. Change is of course possible, but only when it comes about gradually.

Although the conservatives carried the day at Vienna and remained in power throughout Europe for most of the next thirty years, not everyone shared their dream of return to a stable past. In the first place, these others argued, the stable old order revered by conservatives had been neither stable nor ordered. The most wretched misery, confusion, and resentment had always roiled just beneath the surface. It was merely that the aristocrats had paid no attention to any of it until the revolutionaries took their privileges away. Besides, a monopoly of privileges by social elites does not constitute a cultural tradition, or at least not a tradition that is worth preserving. What the opponents of the Treaty of Vienna wanted, therefore, was a new alternative, a society built upon a different notion. Liberalism—as this opposing political view came to be called—assumed the intrinsic goodness of all

1830
Conservatives lose power in Britain; uprisings throughout Europe.

1838
Beginning of Chartist movement

1857
Matrimonial Causes Act (Britain)

1834
New Poor Law

1848
Rebellions throughout Europe; publication of *The Communist Manifesto*

1861
Mrs. Beeton's Book of Household Management

Diplomats at the Congress of Vienna in 1815   To a man, they were all members of their countries' aristocracies, and the Treaty they produced reflected that fact.

people and argued that people, if left to manage their own lives, would choose what is good, honorable, and fair. Liberals called therefore for civil liberties, equality under the law, the right to vote, and a free market economy.

Conservatism and liberalism alike were newly coined words. The word conservatism appeared in English for the first time in 1835. The adjective "conservative" dates back to Chaucer, but it was used in a political sense beginning only in 1830 when it appeared in an article by John W. Croker (1780–1857) in the *Quarterly Review*: "attached to the Tory, and which might with more propriety be called the Conservative, party." The word "liberalism" was coined in 1819 by Lady Morgan (Sydney Owenson), when she wrote admiringly of a friend that "he is worthy of a conversion to Liberalism."[1]

Croker, an Irish statesman and member of the British Parliament, is best remembered for a blisteringly hostile review he wrote of the poem "Endymion," by John Keats. So ferociously did Croker attack the poem that Keats's fellow poet Lord Byron quipped that it may have accounted for Keats's early death. This from Byron's *Don Juan*, canto XI:

> John Keats, who was killed off by one critique,
> Just as he really promised something great,

---

[1]   John Henry Newman on religion, in his *Apologia Pro Vita Sua*: "The more serious thinkers among us are used . . . to regard the spirit of Liberalism as the characteristic of the destined Antichrist."

If not unintelligible,—without Greek,—
Contrived to talk about the gods of late,
Much as they might have been supposed to speak.
Poor fellow! His was an untoward fate.
'Tis strange the mind, that fiery particle,
Should let itself be snuff'd out by an article.

Of course, not just the vocabulary of politics was changing. The 19th century crackled with intellectual energy as people from Dublin to Istanbul, from Lisbon to Moscow, struggled to find new ways to order civic life. The profoundest and most intriguing drama of the age came not from the political struggles between monarchists, conservatives, liberals, socialists, and anarchists (to choose just five of the leading factions across the continent). It was the intellectual wrestling between the emerging new political traditions and developments in economics, science, philosophy, art, and religion. Like a child's kaleidoscope that changes shape with every turn of the wrist, the cultural landscape of Western civilization shifted, and was forced to shift, with every new development in the understanding of the world, the human heart, and the human mind. Like other creatively chaotic periods in history—the era of Second Temple Judaism, for instance, or post–Dark Age Greece, or the Europe of the 14th and 15th centuries—the 19th century demanded the thinking through of everything afresh. To a surprising degree, we are still engaged in their struggles.

> Like a child's kaleidoscope that changes shape with every turn of the wrist, the cultural landscape of Western civilization shifted, and was forced to shift, with every new development in the understanding of the world, the human heart, and the human mind.

ROYALISM AND NATIONALISM

The English educator Thomas Arnold (1795–1842) wrote in a letter to a friend in 1840 that "the principle of Conservatism has always appeared to me to be not only foolish, but to be actually *felo de se* [an attack upon itself]: it destroys what it loves, because it will not mend it." None of those who attended the Vienna congress would have agreed—or would have dared to say so, even if they did. One conviction dominated the assembly: only strong centralized governments, guided by noble traditions, served by professionalized bureaucracies, and backed by large national armies, could pull Europe back from the brink of disaster. But an entirely new and urgent issue presented itself, and it worked against the neo-royalist platform of the congress: the need to industrialize, and to do so quickly. Industrialization required investment and entrepreneurship, and the people most interested in entering the new economy demanded more—recognition of the rights of personal property, a role in shaping government policies, and a relatively free market. Capitalism in the new era existed to serve itself first. The government benefited only secondarily from taxation, which provided it with reliable revenue but without impeding innovation and economic growth.

The congress kept the two aims of strong monarchical government and an industry-friendly economy in sight, but did so to the exclusion of other considerations. When the diplomats put their pens to the map of Europe, they took into account royal desires, military capabilities, industrial resources, access to markets and harbors, and agricultural potential. The so-called Holy Alliance of the five major powers represented at Vienna swore to support one another:

> Any state which undergoes a change of government due to revolution by that fact alone ceases to be a member of the European Alliance. . . . And if on account of that change other states are threatened, the European Powers bind themselves, by peaceful means or if necessary by arms, to force the guilty state back into the bosom of the Great Alliance.

All this produced a sprawl of states that were roughly equal to one another in military and economic potential (see Map 18.1). States thus existed in a balance of power that would discourage any one state from provoking its neighbor. To an extent the congress succeeded, since Europe avoided international war until 1860.

However, the congress failed, or refused, to consider a critical desire of the mass populations, the desire for nationalism. Most wanted to unite along ethnic lines and thereby create nations that expressed ethnic and national *genius*—the collective consciousness of a distinct culture. The lines drawn in Vienna dismembered such desires. The Polish people, for example, were forced into an unnatural division, with their people dispersed between Prussia, Russia, and Austria-Hungary. The Italians, politically riven since the end of the Roman Empire, remained divided into a dozen principalities. For nearly fifty years, Europe's reformers looked back at the Congress of Vienna as a gathering of callous reactionary elites parceling out the family silver to one another, while the legitimate desires of the people were crushed.

The policies of the new regimes were indeed conservative. They restored the royal families to power in Austria-Hungary, France, Prussia, Russia, and Spain; they also restored a dozen lesser princes to small buffer-zone states between the major powers. The returned monarchs quickly brought back all the facets of absolutism that they could get away with. Austria's Franz I (r. 1804–1835), for example, censored every medium of public communication and set up elaborate networks

MAP 18.1   **Europe in 1815**

of spies and informants in order to stamp out any hint of radicalism.[2] France's
Louis XVIII (r. 1814–1824) abolished the Estates General and established in its
place a two-chambered legislature made up of a Chamber of Peers (the aristocracy) and the Chamber of Deputies. Membership in the latter was restricted to
the wealthiest bourgeois, those most likely to inaugurate France's industrial development. Prussia's Friedrich Wilhelm III (r. 1797–1840) gained territories in
the 1815 settlement, especially the early industrial centers of the Ruhr valley in

---

[2]   A somber, brooding personality, he was Franz I of Austria but Franz II of the Holy Roman Empire. That
    old empire, however, was dissolved and carved up in the 1815 accords.

the Rhineland and Westphalia, making Prussia for a while the leading German state in Europe. But he also cracked down sharply on any form of rebellion or demand for reform. In Spain, Ferdinando VII (r. 1814–1833) nullified the liberal constitution drawn up in 1812 by the Napoleonic regime, reinstated the Inquisition, imprisoned the leaders of the Spanish Parliament, and declared a return to divine-right absolutism. Even dismembered Italy made several attempts to overthrow the restored regimes, the largest occurring in 1821.

Popular opposition to conservatism resulted in numerous crackdowns. In 1817, for example, amid celebrations to mark the three hundredth anniversary of Martin Luther's rebellion against the Catholic Church, university students in Wartburg demanded a loosening of government controls over education. They ended up being chased and clubbed by police, and the governments of the German Confederation imposed strict new censorship regulations over student publications. They installed overt and covert surveillance networks on campuses everywhere, with commissioners whose job was to preserve the ideological stability of the universities.

Lord Byron   The great Romantic poet Lord Byron (1788-1824), portrayed in fanciful Turkish garb by Thomas Phillips in 1813 after his return to England from a two years' trip to the continent and as far east as Constantinople. After publishing the first volume of Childe Harold's *Pilgrimage*, as he put it, "I awoke one morning and found myself famous." For the rest of his short life Byron was a famous for his scandalous love-life as he was for his poetry. In his last two years, however, he dedicated himself to as great a cause: the liberation of Greece from Ottoman rule. He died at Missolonghi, while leading a rebel band on a campaign to attack Lepanto.

In 1821, Greek patriots rose up against the Ottoman Turks, whose control over Greece had been reconfirmed at Vienna. When the Russian tsar Aleksandr I (r. 1801–1825) sent troops to aid the rebels—Turkey's loss being Russia's gain—the conservative alliance pressed Russia to stop. All official aid to the Greeks was indeed halted, but by this point, under the influence of Romanticism, popular sentiment across Europe had swung strongly in favor of the Greek cause. When the poet Lord Byron popularized the Greek drive for independence with his own personal heroics, public pressure on the Ottomans and their conservative supporters increased; Greece subsequently won its independence in 1828. The ruins of the Parthenon became a symbol of that struggle. Between 1801 and 1812 the former British ambassador to Greece, Thomas Bruce, the Earl of Elgin, under an agreement with the Ottoman government, removed a large number of statues and marble friezes from the Parthenon in Athens, shipped them to London, and sold them to the British government. These "Elgin Marbles," once cleaned and secured in the British Museum, were enormously popular but controversial. The Greek government, formally established and internationally recognized as of 1830, denied that Lord Elgin's supposed authorization to take the sculptures was genuine, insisted that the Ottoman government had had no right to allow such a thing anyway, and demanded the Elgin Marbles' immediate return to Greece. Nearly two hundred years later, they are still pressing their case.

In Spain, the continued presence of antiroyalists inspired a new wave of repressive measures. These culminated, in 1823, with over two hundred thousand French troops being sent into the country in defense of the Bourbon dynasty. In Russia, the death of Aleksandr I in 1825 triggered an attempt to create a liberal government by a group of rebels known as the Decembrists. The new tsar, Nicholas I, put them down with great severity and inaugurated the most conservative government in all of the West. The new century seemed off to a poor start.

THE MORAL COMPONENT OF CONSERVATISM

Liberal-minded people, including historians, tend to portray conservatism as a reactionary movement. They see it as an effort by elites to retain their privileges at the expense of common people, common sense, and natural progress. There is something to be said for that view of the post-Vienna crowd, but in the end it is neither accurate nor just. A core of strong ideas lay at the heart of conservatism—ideas that deserve to be taken seriously. Many of those ideas can be traced back to Edmund Burke's *Reflections on the Revolution in France*, which is commonly regarded as one of the foundational texts of political conservatism. Another important source for conservatism was the *Essay on the Generative Principle of Political Institutions* by the French-Savoyard diplomat Joseph-Marie de Maistre (1753–1821).

> More so than liberalism, conservatism has a philosophical basis, one that emerges from a central ethical question: How should people live? In particular, how should people live when living together?

More so than liberalism, conservatism has a philosophical basis, one that emerges from a central ethical question: How should people live? In particular, how should people live when living together? Conservatism recognizes the rights of individuals, but also the responsibilities that individuals have toward one another. It emphasizes the mutual duties that bind us together and create a cohesive society; in a conflict between individual desires and social requirements, the claims of society reign supreme. Those social claims have any number of origins—cultural tradition, religious conviction, economic requirement, and political or social security, among them; and any successful and legitimate government must work within the parameters established by them. These forces are perhaps not as immutable as a mountain range, but they can hardly be ignored.

Conservatism thus values traditions—including religion, established norms of morality, and social continuity. Its ethical goal is the preservation of the group rather than the gratification of the individual. As its name suggests, conservatism *conserves* something, preserves it, and desires its continued existence: and the "it" is, in a word, tradition. Burke makes the point:

> If civil society be the offspring of convention, that convention must be its law. That convention must limit and modify all the descriptions of constitution which are formed under it. Every sort of legislative, judicial, or executory power are its creatures. They can have no being in any other state of things. . . . Government is not made in virtue of natural rights, which may and do exist in total independence of it. Government is a contrivance of human wisdom to provide for human wants. Men have a right that these wants should be provided for by this wisdom. Among these wants is to be reckoned the want, out of civil society, of a sufficient restraint upon their passions. Society requires not only that the passions of individuals should be subjected, but that even in the mass and body, as well as in the individuals, the inclinations of men should frequently be thwarted, their will controlled, and their passions brought into subjection. This can only be done by a power out of themselves. . . . But as the liberties and the restrictions vary with times and circumstances, and admit of infinite modifications, they cannot be settled upon any abstract rule; and nothing is so foolish as to discuss them upon that principle.
>
> To avoid therefore the evils of inconstancy and versatility . . . we have consecrated the state, that no man should approach to look into its defects or corruptions but with due caution; that he should never dream of beginning its reformation by its subversion; that he should approach to the faults of the state as to the wounds of a father, with pious awe and trembling solicitude. . . . Society is indeed a contract. Subordinate contracts for objects of mere occasional interest may be dissolved at pleasure—but the state ought not to be considered as nothing better than a partnership agreement in a trade of pepper and coffee, calico or tobacco, or some other such low concern, to be taken up for a little temporary interest, and to be dissolved by the fancy of the parties. It is to be looked on with other reverence; because it is not a partnership in things subservient only to the gross animal existence of a temporary and perishable nature. It is a partnership in all science; a partnership in all art; a partnership in every virtue, and

in all perfection. As the ends of such a partnership cannot be obtained in many generations, it becomes a partnership not only between those who are living, but between those who are to be born. *(Reflections on the Revolution in France)*

Similarly, Joseph-Marie de Maistre emphasized the organic nature of authentic political constitutions, which he saw as the by-product of social development, rather than the creation of human minds:

> The more we study the role of human agency in the development of political constitutions, the more convinced we become that it plays the smallest of roles and is in fact a mere tool [of the larger social development]. To my mind there remains no reason to doubt the absolute truth of these four propositions: first, that the basic principles underlying all political constitutions exist prior to the laws themselves; second, that any [legitimate and enduring] constitutional law is, and must be, the natural development or sanction of a pre-existing, though unwritten, right; third, that the most essential, intrinsically constitutional, and fundamental rights are those which remain unwritten—and indeed cannot be put in written form without endangering the state; and fourth, that the inherent weakness and vulnerability of any constitution is directly proportional to the extent that it exists in written form. *(Essay on the Conservative Principle of Political Institutions)*

Conservatism does not, on the whole, deny the need for change, but it is deeply skeptical of humans' ability to create entire new systems of religious belief, economic policy, political action, and social order. Such things, conservatives maintain, require time-tested, gradual development. As Burke had emphasized, revolutionary passions are ultimately self-defeating and leave misery in their wake. Napoleon's career was not one of tragic failure but of stupidly predictable failure, since what he had tried to accomplish was not natural. His downfall therefore did not result from his having been corrupted by power but from his having been a revolutionary in the first place. Conservatism appealed, and still appeals, to minds inclined to accept that the world has its own ways and that our abilities to reshape it to our liking are limited. The world as it actually exists is not egalitarian. Attributes like talent, intelligence, skill, beauty, wealth, and social position are simply not dealt out in equal measures to all people; hierarchies exist everywhere in nature and are, therefore, natural. Egregious abuses of privilege ought of course to be opposed. But opposition to hierarchy itself, and not just to its occasional abuses, is unnatural, historically uninformed, and philosophically indefensible.

The conservative governments of the early 19th century hardly wished to halt the course of history. Rather, they wanted to insure that the shock of industrialization did not obliterate all that was good and necessary in the European tradition. For there was no doubt about the need to industrialize. The process had begun before the signatures were dry on the Treaty of Vienna. But industrial capitalism seemed to conflict with the traditional society championed by the conservatives, since it valued individual enterprise and innovation. Capitalism depends on the freedom of capital and labor to move, the breaking of old customs and institutions, and the cool, calculating mentality of business—ledgers, inventories, market forces, interest rates, supply routes, tax incentives. The challenge was to achieve the economic benefits of industrial development without jettisoning the values—king, country, church, tradition—of the old order.

Consider, for example, the vast numbers of urban poor. Since the industrial economy profited from the enormous surplus of available labor, factory owners had no incentive to alleviate suffering—at least not until the social unrest created by their misery affected the workplace. The conservative governments recognized the need for public support for the poor, but tried to tailor these welfare programs in ways that would return the indigent to village societies. According to the Poor Law, originally enacted in England in the 16th century, a welfare

A New Institution but an Old Order   John Croker is credited with coining the term 'Conservatism.' He also established a British institution that came to be closely associated with it—the Athenaeum Club. Originally intended as a quasi-academic club—a club for men "of eminence in science, literature, the arts, and public service," according to house rules—it soon attracted British peers, Anglican bishops, and Cabinet members. It admitted its first female member in 2002.

recipient received a monthly payment in the parish where he was born. The idea behind this plan was that the traditional networks of family, friends, church, and local squire would assume the responsibility of tending to his or her needs; the government's role was in essence to complement, but not to replace, traditional and natural methods of caring for the poor.

The moral component of conservatism had a powerful appeal. The role of government, as conservatives saw it, was to maintain and support a moral life, and they opposed efforts to insert the state into roles best left to individuals and the organic communities to which they belong. The obligation to aid the poor is immediate and personal, conservatives maintained: if I am aware of a family in my neighborhood that is in dire need of help, then I have a personal duty to come to its aid if I can. To hold that the government ought to provide aid for all the indigent is foolhardy, for it is the most indirect, inefficient, and impersonal way of bringing assistance where it is needed. It is also morally wrong, since it means my passing along the problem to someone else. In its insistence on local solutions to local problems, and on personal responsibility instead of government initiative, conservatism appeals to the desire for moral behavior and social connection.

THE CHALLENGE OF LIBERALISM

As strong as conservatism's appeal was, it lost ground to the steady opposing pull of liberalism. The second of the three main political traditions of the modern West (socialism being the third), **liberalism** regards the primary function of government to be the promotion of freedom instead of order. By 1830, as industrialization rushed ahead, the conservatives' hold on government weakened across Europe, and they even lost control in several nations. Rapid urbanization on the Continent made it difficult to contain and suppress the demands for social reform and political participation. These demands from the laboring population coalesced into the liberal alternative.

True to its name, liberalism has proven more changeable over the last two centuries, freely discarding some values while taking on new convictions, as conditions warranted. However, it has retained its dedication to freeing individuals from undue control. If conservatism rests on the foundation of preserving the best of society's past, liberalism, in general, seeks to liberate individuals from the strictures of inequality, injustice, and intolerance. As John Stuart Mill (1806–1873), liberalism's answer to Edmund Burke, wrote in a letter to a newspaper, "A Liberal is he who looks forward

> If conservatism rests on the foundation of preserving the best of society's past, liberalism, in general, seeks to liberate individuals from the strictures of inequality, injustice, and intolerance.

for his principles of government; a [conservative] looks backward" (*Morning Star,* July 6, 1865). Compare a cutting comment from a prominent conservative periodical: "What lurking conspirator against the quiet of his native government . . . has failed to ask and receive the protection of our Liberals?" (*Blackwood's Magazine,* February 1828). Or this retort from a Canadian newspaper of 1832: "We shall first notice the slanderous imputations cast upon the Liberals, that they are a discontented set of men, ever on the watch to find occasion of complaint and clamour" (*The Liberal,* September 20, 1832).

At least from the time of John Locke in the late 17th century, liberals have asserted the fundamental equality and goodness of human beings:

> To understand political power right, and derive it from its original, we must consider, what state all men are naturally in, and that is, a state of perfect freedom to order their actions, and dispose of their possessions and persons, as they think fit, within the bounds of the law of nature, without asking leave, or depending upon the will of any other man.
>
> A state also of equality, wherein all the power and jurisdiction is reciprocal, no one having more than another; there being nothing more evident, than that creatures of the same species and rank, promiscuously born to all the same advantages of nature, and the use of the same faculties, should also be equal one amongst another without subordination or subjection, unless the lord and master of them all should, by any manifest declaration of his will, set one above another, and confer on him, by an evident and clear appointment, an undoubted right to dominion and sovereignty. (*Second Treatise of Civil Government, ch. 2*)

If people are individually good and equal, then the good society is achieved by leaving them alone as much as possible, to act freely. Any action by government that would curtail individual freedom, then, must be justified by extraordinary argument, since it upsets the natural good ordering of the world. To take the example of the conservative Poor Law, liberalism finds it unacceptable. In tying the welfare recipient to his home parish, the law restricts his freedom of movement, his freedom to seek employment or education, and his freedom to determine his own fate. After the liberals came to power in 1830, they enacted the new Poor Law of 1834, so that welfare payments followed the recipient if he chose to move from one location to another, in search of work or for any other reason. It was a costlier and less efficient system of administration, to be sure—but it maximized the citizen's freedom to act.

Part of the difficulty for liberalism has been the very nature of freedom: it requires identifying what it is we are free from. The debate has beset political thinking ever since Thomas Hobbes made his arguments in favor of absolutism in the early 17th century. As formulated in the 19th century, liberalism meant above all freedom from control by government. This is hardly surprising, given Europe's experience of hierarchy, privilege, and monarchical tyranny, and considering that the strongest support for liberalism came from the new middle class, the **bourgeoisie**. Their newfound economic muscle depended precisely on individual freedom and the rights of property. Their position is easily expressed: so long as one does not coerce others, one ought to be left alone to do what one pleases with one's own property. Society has no right to force an entrepreneur to manage his property in a certain way, just as the entrepreneur has no right to force his workers to accept low pay or miserable working conditions. Freedom of choice is all. A worker who does not like the pay or demands of any given workplace is free to walk away from it and pursue a better situation elsewhere. Better yet, he can cultivate his own entrepreneurial goals. Moreover, any worker who *is* willing to accept a job at low pay, harsh hours, and miserable conditions should be free to do so.

For this reason, 19th-century liberalism championed **laissez-faire** capitalism, or capitalism without government intervention: a deregulated economy was the only way to insure the freedom of every individual to do as he saw fit. Hence liberals opposed wage- and working-condition regulations, fought against high taxes, and resisted the idea of labor unions, even while they encouraged the free movement of the poor who received government assistance. That free movement, of course, is part of what guaranteed the surplus of labor that kept costs at rock-bottom levels.

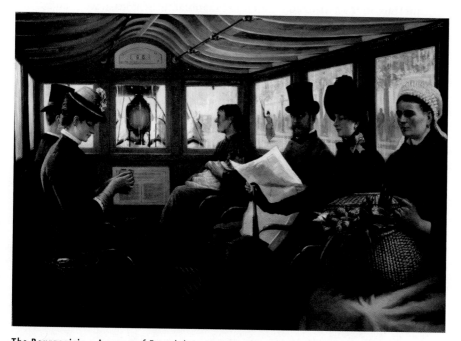

The Bourgeoisie   A group of French bourgeoisie riding in a horse-drawn tram, 1880.

In 1840, legislation was proposed that would reduce factory workdays from twelve hours to ten. In response, a public-relations campaign insisted that government regulation of the marketplace was ill-considered and harmful:

> There are few subjects upon which more erroneous sentiments prevail, than as to the proper objects and limits of legislation. Thus, in our attempts to improve, by legislation, the condition of the poor, we have not only multiplied the number, but reduced them to a state of degradation before unknown. By our poor laws and our charities, we have pauperised, and almost ruined the country. . . . In our commerce and manufactures also, the effects of legislation have been equally mischievous. By our well meant, but injudicious attempt to foster and protect, we have constantly been driving capital from productive into unproductive channels, encouraging the smuggler, checking our commerce, and stunting our manufactures; and our efforts to procure to the operatives a fair remuneration for their labor, has always ended in a reduction of their wages, or in depriving them altogether of employment. Thus, after repeated failures, we have been, in some degree, schooled into knowledge, and have purchased our experience at the usual price. Modern legislation is indeed improving, though the improvement is rather of a negative nature, and consists not so much in passing better laws, as in repealing bad ones. It may be confidently predicted that all further improvement will be of the same kind, and thus, in matters of commerce and manufactures at least, we shall approach continually to a condition of complete and unrestricted freedom. *(London, "Battle of the 10-Hour Day Continues")*

Liberalism has tended to see the world as in constant flux, in contrast to the emphasis on time-honored customs and institutional structures found in conservatism. Since the world is continually changing, the only sensible way of ordering it is to privilege meritocracy, opportunity, and innovation. Let creative minds create, without censorship; let individuals determine their own political fates, through free elections; let people with ideas and drive be free to exercise them and reap the benefits of their success, in free markets.

INDUSTRIAL CAPITALISM AND ITS CRITICS

It was not the plight of the urban poor under industrial capitalism, therefore, that led to the political defeat of the conservatives in 1830. Instead, it was the plight of the entrepreneurs, who wanted to free the new economy from what they regarded as the archaic paternalism of the aristocratic order. The solid middle class of the 19th century joined forces politically with another emerging group, skilled laborers—those whose technical expertise with new machinery allowed them to rise to higher wage levels. Together, they demanded greater clout through the extension of **suffrage**—the right to vote.

In England, the process occurred peacefully, with the conservatives voted out in 1830. In France, by contrast, it took yet another popular rebellion to pull the nobles from power. The reigning Bourbon king, Charles X (r. 1824–1830), had made himself hated by dissolving the liberal-leaning parliament, ordering new elections, and rigging them so that only candidates he had preapproved could win. His timing was rotten, since France had just suffered through a miserable winter and shortages had doubled the cost of most foodstuffs. Spontaneous, angry food riots took places in most of the larger cities. Fearing revolutionary violence, Charles abdicated and passed the crown to his cousin Louis-Philippe (r. 1830–1848)—the last king France would ever have. He granted a new charter that doubled the number of Frenchmen who had the right to vote, but even this number still represented a mere 1 percent of the population (compared to about 8 percent

The New Voters   When the British House of Lords vetoed, in 1831, yet another draft of the Reform Bill that extended the vote to working-class men and re-drew the lines of the country's electoral districts, crowds of demonstrators took to the streets across the nation. The London protestors shown here are carefully presented as proud workers who are loyal to the monarchy.

in England). The outlook for liberal reforms in France looked bleak, except for one thing. Louis-Philippe became not just more conservative as the years went by but also more unpopular, until finally in 1848 he abdicated.[3]

Liberal-led rebellions broke out in 1830 in other parts of Europe too, although the protests failed to effect much real change. Factory workers in the German territories, for example, smashed industrial equipment and demonstrated in factory yards to protest their low pay and long hours. Disaffected Belgians (actually French-speaking Walloons) in the heavily industrialized Netherlands took to the streets and demanded better working conditions, a recognition of their ethnic and linguistic identity, and a new constitution. Disaffected university students and junior military officers campaigned for reform in Poland, seeking a reunification of all Polish people (divided by the Treaty of Vienna among Prussia, Austria, and Russia) and a national constitution—to which Russia responded with an armed attack.

Spain's clash between conservatives and liberals was also violent. The restored Bourbon king, Ferdinand VII (r. 1813–1833), was a diehard absolutist who made only the mildest of compromises with constitutionalism. When he died without a male heir, his throne passed to his daughter Isabella II (r. 1833–1868), who in her early years seemed amenable to a modest reform program. Her claim to the throne was challenged, however, by her ultraconservative pro-absolutist uncle, named Carlos—whose followers were therefore known as "Carlists." The Carlists fought bitterly to restore divine-right monarchy, the authority of the Catholic Church, and traditional society, even at the expense of economic development. Wars with the Carlists hardened Isabella's attitudes, until in her later years she herself had become a royal absolutist. Finally, in 1868, she abdicated the throne after some of her more reform-minded generals voiced their unhappiness against her drift into autocracy. Isabella had twelve children, although doubts remain to this day about their biological father. Her husband, Francisco, was widely reported to be homosexual, and Isabella publicly complained about his supposed effeminacy. She spent her last years in comfortable exile in Paris, but the struggle between Spain's conservative traditionalists and liberal constitutionalists continued into the 20th century with the bloody civil war of the 1930s.

———————————— + ————————————

What the reformers demanded throughout the 1830s and 1840s can be easily summarized: expanded suffrage, decreased taxes, confirmed property rights, deregulated trade and workplaces, and curtailed labor unionization. These issues served the bourgeoisie's interests. As the industrial economy developed, however, becoming more diversified and specialized, so too did the bourgeois class that

---

[3] Louis-Philippe fled to England in disguise and carrying a passport identifying him as one "Mr. Smith."

promoted it. Usually only the great merchants, leading industrialists, and most prominent financiers had access to political power. The rest of the middle classes, from lesser merchants to lawyers and physicians and down to office clerks and school teachers, toiled away without any direct political influence.

Beneath the bourgeoisie was the great mass of the laborers, skilled and unskilled, working long, rigorously enforced shifts in the factories. These came to be known as the **proletariat**—a pejorative term that derived from the Latin, and whose colloquial meaning was "those who smell." They were regarded as the lowest and most vulgar sort of humans, who contributed nothing to the betterment of society except the next generation of workers. (The word *proletarius* in ancient Rome colloquially designated a "stunt cock," a slave whose sexual service gratified his male and female owners.) As reported in a news magazine of the time:

> The proletariat, which has not morally and physically any thing to lose, has allied itself to this revolutionary tendency. . . . This word, which has lately become familiar to all readers of German and French literature, signifies the lowest and poorest classes, those in fact who are totally destitute of property. (*The Daguerreotype, October 16, 1847*)

The bourgeois reformers aimed less at alleviating the proletariat's misery than at improving the efficiency of the economy. Limiting the work week to a maximum of sixty-nine hours for workers aged fourteen to nineteen, for example, reduced the number of jobless poor who received public assistance. Funds for welfare payments and housing subsidies were also redirected to workhouses, where the poor received room and board in return for long hours of unskilled drudgery.[4]

The bourgeois were not necessarily heartless or grasping, and many of them donated generously to the poor. However, much like the early conservatives, they believed that charity was a personal moral duty, not the rightful function of civil government. Many hundreds of private charitable institutions were founded in the first half of the century: orphanages, hospitals, organizations like the YMCA and the Society for the Prevention of Cruelty to Animals, medical clinics, vocational schools (called polytechnics), athletic and hygienic programs, Sunday schools, musical societies, and lending libraries. The problems created by industrialism, however, far outstripped the ability of private, volunteer kindness to address.

Angered by the slow pace and self-serving nature of liberal reform, the urban poor began to organize to demand swifter and more far-reaching reforms. In 1838 the London Working Men's Association drafted a "People's Charter," a petition that they circulated among laborers in city after city, ultimately collecting over six million signatures. This became known as the **Chartist movement,** and it

---

4   Charles Dickens dramatized the starvation level accommodations of the workhouses in *Oliver Twist.*

Gymnastics Class   A sketch (1872) illustrating the popular craze for athletics and fitness at the end of the 19th century in Europe. The scene shown here depicts a gymnastics festival in Bonn, Germany.

provided a model for labor protests across Europe. The Chartists made six essential demands:

1.   universal suffrage (though for men only)
2.   annual elections
3.   secret ballots
4.   elimination of the requirement to own property in order to qualify for public office
5.   fair redistricting of electoral maps; and
6.   guaranteed salaries for those serving in government.

> What society needed, the Chartists insisted, was not only personal freedom from undue governmental control but freedom as well from the unjust control of people's lives by unfettered capitalism.

Without the last, only the rich could afford to enter public service.

Chartism thereby helped to redefine liberalism. What society needed, the Chartists insisted, was not only personal freedom from undue governmental control but freedom as well from the unjust control of people's lives by unfettered capitalism. Just as the power of government needs to be checked by constitutional restraints, lest it devolve into tyranny, so too does the industrial economy require regulation. Otherwise, it will become a system of economic slavery. It took several decades for the new ideas to flourish—starting with yet another round of protests, strikes, street riots, and violent clashes with states and industries.

THE REAL REVOLUTION OF 1848

After at least a decade of discontent, urban workers and the homeless poor across the Continent rose up in violent protest in 1848. With only a handful of exceptions—Britain, the Netherlands, Russia, Scandinavia, and the Ottoman Empire—every Western government confronted mass rebellion of some sort. To some critics, the wave of uprisings looked suspiciously organized, but most regarded them as spontaneous bursts of rage, with each explosion giving encouragement to the next. Demonstrators filled the streets and squares, blockaded roads, smashed factory windows and equipment, and looted and burned stores. Speeches and broadsheets proclaimed the end of political and economic elitism and called for the transfer of power to new governments chosen by full and open democratic processes.

Coming as they did in the aftermath of several consecutive crop failures and growing concern of European-wide famine, these revolts frightened everyone.[5] The French king, Louis-Philippe, had forbidden public assemblies as early as 1835, in an effort to forestall political agitation. But in 1847 the leaders among the radical reformers organized a broad network of large-scale "private banquets," at which reformers plotted their moves and incited their audiences to increase their activity. The decision in January 1848 by the French premier François Guizot (1787–1874) to suppress these banquets triggered an uprising in Paris, which in turn triggered uprisings across Europe (see Map 18.2). Guizot declared himself "an unflinching enemy of universal suffrage—I regard it as the certain ruin of democracy and liberty."

Within a matter of days the protestors had forced Louis-Philippe to abdicate, and a new constitutional republic was established (the Second Republic, in France's back-and-forth political narrative). For the president of the new government, the Republican leaders chose Louis-Napoleon, the nephew of the great emperor. He began modestly. In accepting the new post, he assured the assembly:

> I am guided by no ambition. . . . Having grown up in free countries and learned from the school of hard knocks, I will remain forever faithful to the duties [entrusted to me]. . . . I vow to devote myself entirely, unreservedly, to strengthening this Republic by guiding it to develop wise laws, honest goals, and great and noble deeds, and my greatest honor will be to hand over to whomever succeeds me, after four years in

---

[5] Alexis de Tocqueville described France as "a society cut in half—those who possessed no property were united in envy, and those who did possess anything were united in terror."

MAP 18.2   **Centers of Revolution, 1848**

office, a stable government, with its liberties intact and its genuine progress assured.

Only four years later, however, Louis-Napoleon declared the Second Republic dead, restored autocracy, and took the imperial title of Napoleon III (r. 1852–1870). Thus was born France's Second Empire.

In Italy, the uprisings took many forms. The northern city of Milan, rebelling against Austrian rule, began the year with a popular effort to give up smoking tobacco since the taxes on it were so onerous. The no-smoking demonstration worked too well, however: Austrian soldiers went on a retributive rampage and killed over sixty people. Outrage over the imperial response triggered unrest throughout the peninsula. In Rome, rebels assassinated the prime minister of the Papal State, causing Pope Pius IX (r. 1846–1878) to flee south, where he went into hiding with the temporarily exiled Duke of Piedmont and King Ferdinando II of Naples. Revolutionaries in Palermo succeeded briefly in forming a new government and issuing a constitution. Uprisings throughout the German-speaking territories, including Habsburg Austria, were notable for their insistence on the unification of Germany into a single state. They did not achieve it, but the crowds in Vienna did manage to force Klaus von Metternich, the chancellor, from office. Riots in Berlin resulted in the deaths of hundreds at the hands of Prussian soldiers. Despite promises from the king to introduce a liberal constitution, a conservative new legislature was put into place instead, one that proved the starting point for the career of a new military figure and diplomat, Otto von Bismarck.

The narrative of 1848 is so confusing, in part, because there were as many motives as rebels. Aristocrats feared the unbridled absolutism desired by Louis XVIII of France and Franz I of Austria; industrial capitalists opposed the undermining of property interests through taxation and regulation; urban workers rebelled against horrid work conditions and wretched pay; and the poor took to the streets to demand rescue from famine, crime, and disease. Europe's transition into a modern, developed industrial economy left everyone, it seemed, vulnerable and aggrieved. What brought on such a state of affairs? And how could a stable future be created from so much misery, distrust, and sheer rage? For the time being, most European states retreated in another brief era of law-and-order conservatism.

KARL MARX AND REVOLUTION

The first major figure to suggest an interpretation of this staggering era was a scholar-turned-journalist named Karl Marx (1818–1883). A German Jew, Marx had earned a PhD in philosophy from the University of Jena in 1841, but failed to win an academic position in Germany and turned to journalism. After he was accused of treason in 1844 for supposedly seditious criticisms of the government, Marx, who was then living in Paris with his young family, renounced his Prussian citizenship and made his way to London. Early in 1848 Marx published **The Communist Manifesto**, coauthored with his close friend Friedrich

Das Kapital.

Kritik der politischen Oekonomie.

Von

Karl Marx.

Erster Band.

Buch I: Der Produktionsprocess des Kapitals.

Das Recht der Uebersetzung wird vorbehalten.

Hamburg
Verlag von Otto Meissner.
1867.
New-York: L. W. Schmidt. 24 Barclay-Street.

Title Page of the First Edition of Karl Marx's Masterpiece, *Capital: A Critique of Political Economy* (1867) "I assume from the start that the reader is willing to learn something new and to start thinking for himself." (Preface)

Engels (1820–1895), and shortly thereafter he returned to Germany to participate in the uprisings of that summer.

Marx returned to England in 1849, disappointed in the failure of the rebellions but confident in the eventual victory of reform. He had already laid out a general theory of history in a book called *The German Ideology* (1846), and he spent his remaining years refining his ideas and working to promote economic and social reform. He had relatively little success in his own lifetime, either as a scholar or as a political activist, but he became arguably the single most influential political thinker of the 20th century. Only then were his ideas adopted—in severely reshaped form—by communist parties around the world.

Marxism is essentially a theory about history, and like its creator it is profoundly optimistic. Like Rousseau before him and the Romantics of his own time, Marx believes in the essential goodness of human nature; it is the world that plants the seed of corruption in the heart. All human conflict is at root a conflict over things—gold, lands, animal herds, estates, inheritances, cities, tax revenues, harbors, mines, and trade routes. Clashing ideas and values are real, but secondary, and in fact are usually little more than rationalizations for the conflict over wealth.

> Like Rousseau before him and the Romantics who followed him, Marx believes in the essential goodness of human nature; it is the world that plants the seed of corruption in the heart.

Marx calls this process **historical materialism**. Economic matters, in simplest terms, are the fuel that drives history forward. In all ages, he argues, change has come about through the conflict between those who produce the bulk of society's wealth with one technology and those who produce it under alternative technologies. In a nomadic, pastoral society, for example, ownership of the animal herds decides social status and hence political power. But when that society transitions into agrarian life, a new technology of wealth production is created, namely crop farming; control of land now determines economic value and therefore social status. The conflict between these modes of existence drives the change from a tribal society governed by unwritten customs to a bureaucratic state governed by written laws and contracts (such as land deeds). The rise of manufacturing and commerce propels the development of urban life and yet another stage of historical growth, especially as the urban economy eclipses the rural economy as the main producer of aggregate wealth. Hence the development of parliaments, with power in the hands of representatives from the urban economic elite. In each case, material life shapes social existence. Liberalism's emphasis on limiting society's claims on individual wealth and property therefore creates a society of free individuals.

But liberalism, in Marx's view, makes a fundamental and grievous error: it privileges the very things that we need to do away with—individual happiness and private property. Liberal notions of justice aim to protect us from one

Historical Materialism on Vivid Display Steelworkers, idealized.
William Scott Bell (1811-1890) painted this mural at Wallington Hall,
Northumberland. A viewer can almost hear the men singing a Disneye-
sque tune as they swing their hammers in unison. No smoke, no dirt,
no misery. A little girl even sits contently by while her father nobly
toils. The coke-fueled heat coming out the furnace by which she sits
could reach 2000 degrees Fahrenheit (1200 degrees Celsius).

another, to restrict one person's ability to take or interfere with another person's
property. And this means, Marx insists, that liberalism is essentially a philosophy
of separation, whereas true human happiness consists of community, fellowship,
and shared prosperity. Once we see liberalism as it really is, we will seek to move
past it and to create a harmonious future without selfishness.

Simply put, we must show the world what it is actually fighting
over—for this, in the end, is what people need to recognize, whether
they want to or not. In order to reform society's way of thinking, we must
first help it to realize the way it is actually thinking already; we must
awaken the world from its dreamy image of itself and show its actions for
what they truly are.... Once we have accomplished this, the world will
see that it can actually possess what it has hitherto only dreamed of
[namely, a truly happy and stable society].

So he wrote in a letter to a friend in September 1843.

Marx saw that the motivating forces in history are economic and technological. That insight surprises few readers today, but in its time it was strikingly original. What remains controversial is Marx's conclusion: the production and distribution of wealth determines culture. Marx argues that the struggle to control the means of production determines everything about a society from its political values to its laws, religious life, morals, and intellectual outlook. The process is not even conscious—it does not need to be. Since the class that controls the dominant means of production also controls the state, it can perpetuate its position, just as it promotes its religious and moral values. The leading role in the economy played by industrial capitalists, for example, finds its political expression in the House of Commons, which represents its interest. It also finds its ideological expression in the cultural values of hard work, entrepreneurial drive, and free markets. As for religion, Marx holds that Christianity seems almost tailor-made to create a mass of docile workers: "Blessed are the poor"; suffering ennobles the soul; the affairs of this world do not really matter; reward comes in the next life; "turn the other cheek" to one's oppressors; and love one's enemies. He calls these teachings "slave morality."

> Marx argues that the struggle to control the means of production determines everything about a society from its political values to its laws, religious life, morals, and intellectual outlook. The process is not even conscious—it does not need to be.

But Marx insists that the painful cycle can be broken. Interrupting the march of capitalism will allow human altruism to emerge from its suppressed state. Indeed, the cycle is destined to be broken. The key is the transfer of economic and political power to the great mass of the proletariat.[6] That transfer culminates and concludes the historical process begun ages ago when the first nomad cut furrows in the earth and planted seeds. Marx does not, as some suggest, argue that its outcome is inevitable, but it is predictable. The interplay of economic, technological, and social forces produces the opportunities for social change; but human will and action are required to inaugurate each new development. To Marx, European capitalism in the middle of the 19th century had reached another decisive historical moment.

Since industrial capitalism, he argues, is incapable of self-reform, its death is imminent, but that death will not occur on its own. The struggle to wrest power and pass it to the workers may take a long, concerted effort—and may require force. As he wrote in *The German Ideology*:

> A revolution is required because the ruling class cannot be overthrown in any other way, but also because the working class that

---

6   It was Marx who popularized the word *proletariat*.

dislodges it needs a revolution itself—a revolution that will purge the proletariat of the accumulated [cultural] trash of its past. Only thus can the workers rebuild society.

The act of revolution, in other words, creates the revolutionaries it needs to complete its own process. Marx abhors violence and never advocates it; he calls only for labor strikes, mass demonstrations, relentless political pressure, and the like. His rhetoric is always dramatic, but a call to confrontation is not the same thing as a call to arms.

THE COLLAPSE OF THE "CONCERT OF EUROPE"

Did the uprisings of 1848 significantly alter the political or economic trajectories of Europe? After all, no governments fell from power as a result. Some writers insist that the year nevertheless marks a turning point: the severe economic and social problems catalyzed by industrialization had become impossible to ignore. One could no longer assume that the free market, left to itself, would set society along the path to a natural balance of prosperity, opportunity, and order. Henceforth, both conservatives and liberals would have to compromise their convictions with a practical commitment to economic regulation and government-sponsored social welfare. In this view, the second half of the 19th century represents a series of efforts to strike the right form of compromise.

Such writers also point to 1848 as the point of collapse of the "concert of Europe" created by the Congress of Vienna in 1815. When King Friedrich Wilhelm IV of Prussia (r. 1840–1861) was confronted with armed insurrection in Berlin, he agreed to create a national assembly for Prussia and dissolve his absolute authorities. He thus catalyzed similar settlements for all of the German territories. Moreover, debates over whether to include the ethnic Germans residing in the Austrian-Hungarian Empire brought Austria and Prussia to the brink of war. The possibility of the Habsburg Empire's ethnic Germans seceding from the megastate encouraged the nationalist hopes of the Magyars (ethnic Hungarians), Croats,

> To Marxists, the vast movement of history, like the current of a broad and powerful river, was toward the revolution of the proletariat, the destruction of capitalism, and the evolution of a new, classless society of freedom.

Slovenians, and Czechs, which the Habsburgs quelled only with extreme force. Russia quickly became involved in the dispute, which in turn ignited Turkish concerns. A regional conflict threatened to expand into an international war. The failure of the 1815 settlement was all but officially recognized by the resignation of Klemens von Metternich as the Habsburg's minister of foreign affairs in April 1848—even before most of the year's dramas had occurred.

Other writers regard 1848 not as a pivot point for European history but simply as a road sign confirming the path that Europe was already on. The rebellions and violent responses may have accelerated developments, but they did not fundamentally change the direction of history. To Marxists, the vast movement of history, like the current of a broad and powerful river, was toward the revolution of the proletariat, the destruction of capitalism, and the evolution of a new, classless society of freedom. Events like 1848 encouraged them to believe in the inevitability of **communism**. As *The Communist Manifesto* proclaims (in the English edition prepared by Engels himself):

> Hitherto, every form of society has been based, as we have already seen, on the antagonism of oppressing and oppressed classes. But in order to oppress a class, certain conditions must be assured to it under which it can, at least, continue its slavish existence. The serf, in the period of serfdom, raised himself to membership in the commune, just as the petty bourgeois, under the yoke of feudal absolutism, managed to develop into a bourgeois. The modern laborer, on the contrary, instead of rising with the progress of industry, sinks deeper and deeper below the conditions of existence of his own class. He becomes a pauper, and pauperism develops more rapidly than population and wealth. And here it becomes evident, that the bourgeoisie is unfit any longer to be the ruling class in society, and to impose its conditions of existence upon society as an over-riding law. It is unfit to rule because it is incompetent to assure an existence to its slave within his slavery, because it cannot help letting him sink into such a state, that it has to feed him, instead of being fed by him. Society can no longer live under this bourgeoisie, in other words, its existence is no longer compatible with society.
>
> The essential condition for the existence, and for the sway of the bourgeois class, is the formulation and augmentation of capital; the condition for capital is wage-labor. Wage-labor rests exclusively on competition between laborers. The advance of industry, whose involuntary promoter is the bourgeoisie, replaces the isolation of the laborers, due to competition, by their revolutionary combination, due to association. The development of Modern Industry, therefore, cuts from under its feet the very foundation on which the bourgeoisie produces and appropriates products. What the bourgeoisie, therefore, produces, above all, is its own grave-diggers. Its fall and the victory of the proletariat are equally inevitable.

The revolution of 1848 therefore accelerated historical change. Constitutions may have been jettisoned and franchises rescinded; nationalist aims were thwarted,

The Dream of Universal Brotherhood   A fanciful painting from 1848 showing the nations of Europe all marching, under a heavenly blessing, toward a statue symbolizing human rights. Note the sprawl of broken, discarded crowns and aristocratic shields in the foreground.

workers brought to heel, and the poor forced to submit. But the very success of the powerful and propertied ensured the ultimate success of the revolution. Common workers could now believe in the inevitability of victory, whether or not that victory appeared in a Marxist form, and that belief was the real revolution of 1848. The movement was only in embryonic form by midcentury, with Marx and Engels busily analyzing the workings of politics and economy in print, while organizing and rallying workers into labor unions and political factions in meeting halls. But the communist model they created eventually became the third dominating political and social vision of the modern era, after conservatism and liberalism.

WOMEN AND THE CULT OF DOMESTICITY

It was not only Marxist writers who felt that the dramas of 1848 had changed nothing or little. Millions of women across Europe smarted under new industrial cruelties and old social biases alike. They experienced a feverish jolt of optimism at the turn of the 19th century at the prospect of a reformed and enlightened society that would value them, if not as equals, at least as deserving members of society with legitimate claims, concerns, and demands. Not all were miserable, and it would be foolish to assume that social prejudice defined all of their lives.

The Enlightenment of the 18th century, nevertheless, entailed a critical reexamination of women's roles in Western life.

As it happened, few of the influential figures of the Enlightenment gave the subject of women any sustained thought. Locke, Kant, Herder, Montesquieu, Beccaria, Smith, Hume, Gibbon, and Condorcet say almost nothing about women in their published works, and most of them had little space for women in their private lives too. Diderot, who married for love, created several sympathetic female characters in his plays and novels—the best being a fictionalized portrait of his own sister in the novel *The Nun* (*La religieuse*; 1760)—but never dealt in earnest with the idea of reforming society's treatment of women. The only philosophe to discuss women in society at any length at all was Rousseau. And his views hardly gave hope to those seeking a better position for women in the Enlightened future.

By the second half of the 18th century, most women's lives had not altered significantly from what they had been a hundred years previously. Most women were legally controlled by their fathers until they married, at which point they came under the legal control of their husbands. Customs varied from country to country in regard to dowries, inheritance rights, and property ownership. Little formal education was available, except for those capable of hiring private tutors. Marriage and childbirth were the central events in most women's lives. Peasant and working-class girls usually married in their early twenties, but were considered marriageable by age sixteen; they were usually given to husbands anywhere from five to fifteen years older. By her mid-thirties an unmarried woman was considered a spinster, according to English law. By the end of the 19th century, the British government sent annual shipments of spinsters to its overseas colonies, especially to India, where they might find work as governesses or teachers.

Most women lived in or near poverty. On the Continent, perhaps one-fifth of all people, male and female, faced flat-out starvation-level poverty. Most of these were drawn to cities in search of employment, and their numbers increased under industrialism. Perhaps another 30–40 percent of the population were barely able to support themselves. They had food to survive on and a roof over their heads, but little else. Women brought in extra money by spinning, needlework, laundering, or other simple services, while remaining at home with their children—and that often meant the difference between survival and destitution for their families. One reason for their poverty was the increased cost of living. Taking account of only the basic necessities—housing, food, clothing, and fuel for cooking—the average cost of living for most Europeans increased roughly three to four times faster than wages over the entire 18th century. In Spain alone, the ratio was five to one. These dire conditions helped sustain the practice of female infanticide, despite laws forbidding it; male infants were usually killed only in cases of serious sickness or disability. When poor families could not bring themselves to euthanize infants they could not support, they handed them over instead to orphanages and workhouses.

Women formed a large segment of the workforce and indeed came to dominate certain manufactures. On average, however, they earned only about 40 percent of what male wage earners received, and efforts to unionize labor hardly helped. In fact, these efforts were driven in part by attempts to drive women from the workplace altogether, so that more men could find employment. Industrialism brought another change to family life as well—the physical separation of work space and domestic space. Throughout most of human history, the home was also where one worked—either a farm or a small shop above which the shopkeepers lived. But the factory economy now meant that one went away to the job, while home was a refuge after a long day's labor. The effort to push women out of the job market and "back into the home" thus defined the home as a woman's terrain. It

Domesticity Critiqued   A typically bleak view of family relationships by Edgar Degas (1834-1917). The Bellelli Family, shown here, depicts Degas' aunt with her husband and two daughters. The mother's formal, stiff posture and grim expression, etched sharply against a relatively blank background, contrasts with the distracted, unfocused image of the father, whose busy desk and cluttered background suggests self-involvement. The contrast between the postures of the daughters indicates their divided loyalties in a desolate scene of family alienation. Degas painted this large canvas—it measures roughly six feet by eight feet—while studying in Italy as a young man. His views on marriage never changed.

was also part of a new **cult of domesticity.** For working-class women, programs taught personal hygiene, basic literacy, and simple craftwork like sewing, basket weaving, and shoemaking.

Sex and illegitimacy ran rampant. In Europe, it has been estimated that one of every six deaths across the industrialized world resulted from sexually transmitted disease. The majority of unwed mothers were of the working class, but the fathers of their children came from every social level. Many of the problems of urban society were regarded as moral failings, as opposed to flaws in the economic or political systems. They were also widely blamed on women for making the supposedly unnatural choice of working outside the home, rather than nurturing their families.

> Sex and illegitimacy ran rampant. In urban Europe, it has been estimated that one of every six deaths across the industrialized world resulted from sexually transmitted disease.

Among middle-class women, the cult of domesticity took on even greater sentimentality. Proper society emphasized the importance of the home as a place of refuge, comfort, and nurture for hard-working husbands and fathers. Novels became the most popular genre of popular literature, overtaking poetry, and the overwhelming majority of them dealt with domestic themes: the discovery of love and its culmination in happy marriage and a cozily elegant domestic life.

POPULAR MAGAZINES AND THE NOVEL

Among the most popular new publications of the age were magazines for middle-class women like *La Belle Assemblée, Bell's Court and Fashionable Magazine Addressed Particularly to the Ladies,* and *Wives' and Widows' Gazette of Fashions,* which began to appear in large numbers in every country. These offered advice on fashions, décor, family relationships, home economics, sheet music, and dress patterns, along with serialized fiction and sentimental poetry. Also popular were guidebooks to maintaining happy, efficient, economical, and comfortable homes. The leading example, *Mrs Beeton's Book of Household Management* (1861), became one of the best-selling books of the century.[7] Isabella Beeton was only twenty-five when she published the first edition of this massive book of over 1,100 pages. (She died only four years later of a uterine infection after the birth of her fourth child; her first two had already died.) She made her purpose plain at the start:

> What moved me . . . to attempt a work like this, was the discomfort and suffering which I had seen brought upon men and women by

---

[7]   Over two million copies of *Mrs Beeton's Book of Household Management* sold in the United Kingdom in ten years—more than all the novels of Charles Dickens in his lifetime, combined.

household mismanagement. I have always thought that there is no more fruitful source of family discontent than a housewife's badly-cooked dinners and untidy ways. Men are now so well served out of doors—at their clubs, well-ordered taverns, and dining houses—that in order to compete with the attractions of these places, a mistress must be thoroughly acquainted with the theory and practice of cookery, as well as be perfectly conversant with all the other arts of making and keeping a comfortable home.

Even more blunt is the first page of the opening chapter:

> As with the Commander of an Army . . . so it is with the mistress of a house. Her spirit will be seen through the whole establishment; and just in proportion as she performs her duties intelligently and thoroughly, so will her domestics follow in her path. Of all those acquirements, which more particularly belong to the feminine character, there are none which take a higher rank, in our estimation, than such as enter into a knowledge of household duties; for on these are perpetually dependent the happiness, comfort, and well-being of a family.

While the bulk of its pages consist of cooking recipes, Mrs. Beeton also offers detailed advice on cleaning, first aid, and the oversight of domestic servants; what surprises many modern readers is the attention she gives to legal matters, as in chapter 44:

> In civil cases, a wife may now give evidence on behalf of her husband; in criminal cases she can neither be a witness for or against her husband. The case of assault by him upon her forms an exception to this rule. The law does not at this day admit the ancient principle of allowing moderate correction by a husband upon the person of his wife. Although this is said to have been anciently limited to the use of "a stick not bigger than a thumb," this barbarity is now altogether exploded. He may, notwithstanding, . . . keep her under restraint, to prevent her leaving him, provided this be effected without cruelty.

The millions of middle-class women who read Mrs. Beeton, and other authors like her, prided themselves on their domestic efficiency and propriety.

So too did the popular literature of the age. Not only did novels become the most popular literary genre of the 19th century; the majority of both their readers and authors were women. This marked a sharp shift of opinion from the 18th century, when the new genre was blamed for spreading lax morals. Novels

Guidebook to Happiness   *Mrs. Beeton's Book of Household Management,* published in 1861 when the author was only twenty-five years old, offers an antidote to Degas' gloomy outlook on the family (see page 695). Over 1,100 pages, it guides readers through everything necessary to create a happy, orderly, comfortable bourgeois home. Isabella Beeton died in 1865, from complications in the birth of her fourth child.

dangerously misled young women, it was said, filling their hearts and minds with fantasies of idle romance. As late as 1801, the father-daughter team of Robert and Maria Edgeworth wrote in their popular guide *Practical Education*:

> With respect to sentimental stories, and books of mere entertainment, we must remark, that they should be sparingly used, especially in the education of girls. This species of reading cultivates what is called "the heart" prematurely, lowers the tone of the mind, and induces indifference for those common pleasures and occupations which, however trivial in themselves, constitute by the far the greatest portion of our daily happiness.

Compare this with Thomas Broadhurst's *Advice to Young Ladies on the Improvement of the Mind and Conduct of Life* only a few years later, in 1810:

> She who is faithfully employed in discharging the various duties of a wife and daughter, a mother and a friend, is far more usefully occupied than one who, to the culpable neglect of the most important obligations,

is daily absorbed by philosophic and literary speculations, or soaring aloft amidst the enchanted regions of fiction and romance.

Popular novelists like Jane Austen (1775–1817) or the Brontë sisters (Charlotte [1816–1855], Emily [1818–1848], and Anne [1820–1849]) published their books under male pseudonyms. Jane Austen even took to hiding her manuscripts under piles of knitting and sewing, lest any household visitors discover her life as an author. In 1856 the great writer George Eliot (another woman: Mary Anne Evans [1819–1880]) published a delightfully vindictive article, "Silly Novels by Lady Novelists," in the *Westminster Review*. Eliot castigates writers who

> have evidently never talked to a tradesman except from a carriage window; they have no notion of the working-classes except as "dependents;" they think five hundred a-year a miserable pittance; Belgravia and "baronial halls" are their primary truths; and they have no idea of feeling interest in any man who is not at least a great landed proprietor, if not a prime minister. It is clear that they write in elegant boudoirs, with violet-coloured ink and a ruby pen; that they must be entirely indifferent to publishers' accounts, and inexperienced in every form of poverty except poverty of brains.

But not all the novels were silly. George Eliot's own novels—especially her masterpiece, *Middlemarch*—depict England's rural and village settings with uncommon delicacy and intelligence. In France, the novels of George Sand (Amantine Dupin, Baroness Dudivant [1804–1876]) provide sympathetic portraits of agrarian and working-class men and women who struggle against poverty and social prejudice. Italy's Matilde Serao (1856–1927) published a series of novels in the 1880s whose melodramatic plots were laced with a powerful social conscience driven by her work as a journalist and newspaper editor. Rosalía de Castro (1837–1885), from north-western Spain, was primarily a poet, but her novels detail with dignity and precision the lives of the rural poor. Austrian novelist Bertha von Suttner was the first woman ever to win the Nobel Peace Prize, for her passionate antiwar novel *A Farewell to Arms* (*Die Waffen nieder*; 1889).[8] Annette von Droste-Hulshoff (1797–1848), from an old aristocratic family from the region of Westphalia, is best known in Germany for her religious poetry, but also wrote a disturbing novel called *The Jew's Beech Tree* (*Die Judenbuche*; 1842), which may be the first murder mystery in modern fiction.

---

[8]   The first woman ever to win the Nobel Prize in Literature was Sweden's Selma Lagerlöf (1909).

If women found acceptance, however grudging, on the shelves of booksellers, they still faced determined opposition when it came to legal rights. Even privileged women faced great obstacles. An Englishwoman named Caroline Norton (1808–1877) came from a respectable family with military and colonial connections; her two sisters each married into the nobility, and she wed a prominent barrister and member of Parliament. Her husband, however, turned out to be a violent drunkard whose jealousy prompted him to suspect the lovely Caroline, unfairly, of constant infidelity. His verbal and physical abuse were unrelenting—especially during his many bouts of alcoholic stupor. To make extra money, Caroline began to publish poetry and novels, which were well received and led to friendships with many prominent writers and statesmen. In 1836, unable to take any more violence, she left her husband. Her husband in turn abducted their three children (all sons), refused to let her see them, and sued to gain possession of all her book royalties—arguing successfully in court that everything belonging to a wife is the rightful possession of the husband. For six years she was forbidden to see her boys and received none of her book earnings. In 1842 their eldest son died in a horse-riding accident, after which her husband relented and allowed her occasional visits to the remaining two boys. She had no legal grounds for divorcing her husband—wife beating not being against the law then—and did not become free until his death in 1875.

Caroline Norton devoted many years to the struggle for changes in the laws regarding marriage and divorce. The culmination of her efforts came with the Matrimonial Causes Act of 1857, which gave women the legal ability to initiate divorce; they could also retain possession of a share of the couple's wealth. The act reaffirmed their right—originally granted in 1839, also thanks in part to Caroline Norton—to shared custody of their minor children. Norton wrote a pamphlet-length letter, addressed to Queen Victoria herself—

> the one woman in England who *cannot* suffer wrong; and whose royal assent will be formally necessary to any Marriage Reform Bill which the Lord Chancellor, assembled Peers, and assembled Commons, may think fit to pass, in the Parliament of this free nation; where, with a Queen on the throne, all other married women are legally *NON-EXISTENT.*

She concluded:

> Nevertheless, so long as human nature is what it is, some marriages must be unhappy marriages, instead of following that theory of intimate and sacred union which they ought to fulfill: and the question is,

therefore, what is to be the relation of persons living in a state of alienation, instead of a state of union,—all the existing rules for their social position being based on the first alternative,—namely, that they are in a state of union,—and on the supposition that marriage is indissoluble, though Parliament has now decided that it is a civil contract? Divorced or undivorced, it is absolutely necessary that the law should step in, to arrange that which is disarranged by this most unnatural condition. It becomes perfectly absurd that the law which appoints the husband legal protector of the woman, should not (failing him who has ceased to be a protector, and has become a very powerful foe) itself undertake her protection. She stands towards the law, by an illustration which I have repeatedly made use of,—in the light of an ill-used inferior; and she is the *only* inferior in England who cannot claim to be so protected. *("A Letter to the Queen on Lord Chancellor Cranworth's Marriage and Divorce Bill" [1855])*

Britain stood ahead of the curve, compared with the Continent, in recognizing the legal rights of women.

By the end of 1848 Europe was tiring of revolutions, and with good reason. The overthrow of absolutism and the forced march of industrialism had been wrenching experiences. The people had demanded the restructuring of the state and the reconsideration of longstanding social traditions. Conservatism and liberalism offered new paths out of the chaos; but while significantly distinct from earlier notions of political order, they were not revolutionary. Indeed, conservatism presented itself as the upholder of traditionalism, while liberalism offered itself as the intelligent way to control and channel the forces of change.

The real revolutionary developments of the midcentury were the challenges of Marxism and the campaign for the rights of women. Both were changes of the mind and heart as much as calls to transform the state or workplace. It would take another two or three generations for these changes to take root, but their effects on daily life were dramatic, permanent, and inescapable. These changes, when they came, permanently altered family structures, moral values, notions of state power and obligation, and religious life—as good a definition as any of what *revolution* really means.

WHO, WHAT, WHERE

bourgeoisie	cult of domesticity
Chartist movement	historical materialism
communism	laissez-faire
The Communist Manifesto	liberalism
Congress of Vienna	proletariat
conservatism	suffrage

SUGGESTED READINGS

Primary Sources

Beeton, Isabella. *Mrs. Beeton's Book of Household Management.*

Burke, Edmund. *Reflections on the Revolution in France.*

Maistre, Joseph-Marie de. *Considerations on France.*

———. *Essay on the Generative Principle of Political Constitutions.*

Marx, Karl. *Capital.*

———. *The Communist Manifesto.*

———. *The 18th Brumaire of Louis Napoleon-Napoleon.*

———. *The German Ideology.*

Metternich, Klemens von. *Memoirs.*

Mill, John Stuart. *On Liberty.*

———. *The Principles of Political Economy.*

Norton, Caroline. *English Laws for Women in the 19th Century.*

Tocqueville, Alexis de. *Recollections.*

Anthologies

Leroux, Robert, and David Hart, eds. *French Liberalism in the 19th Century: An Anthology* (2012).

Marx, Karl. *Selected Writings* (2000). Edited by David McLellan.

Tucker, Robert C., ed. *The Marx-Engels Reader.*

Studies

Alexander, Robert. *Re-writing the French Revolutionary Tradition: Liberal Opposition and the Fall of the Bourbon Monarchy* (2007).

Berend, Ivan T. *History Derailed: Central and Eastern Europe in the Long Nineteenth Century* (2005).

Boime, Albert. *Art in an Age of Counterrevolution, 1815–1848* (2004).

———. *Art in an Age of Civil Struggle, 1848–1871* (2008).

Cohen, G. A. *Karl Marx's Theory of History: A Defence* (2001).

Dénes, Iván Zoltán. *Conservative Ideology in the Making* (2010).

Devigne, Robert. *Reforming Liberalism: J. S. Mill's Use of Ancient, Religious, Liberal, and Romantic Moralities* (2006).

Fortescue, William. *France and 1848: The End of Monarchy* (2005).

Gross, Michael B. *The War against Catholicism: Liberalism and the Anti-Catholic Imagination in Nineteenth-Century Germany* (2005).

Kahan, Alan S. *Liberalism in Nineteenth-Century Europe: The Political Culture of Limited Suffrage* (2003).

Kertzer, David I., and Marzio Barbagli, eds. *Family Life in the Long Nineteenth Century, 1789–1913* (2002).

Langewiesche, Dieter. *Liberalism in Germany* (2000).

Leopold, David. *The Young Karl Marx: German Philosophy, Modern Politics, and Human Flourishing* (2007).

Liang, Hsi-Huey. *The Rise of Modern Police and the European State System from Metternich to the Second World War* (2002).

Pitts, Jennifer. *A Turn to Empire: The Rise of Imperial Liberalism in Britain and France* (2006).

Popkin, Jeremy D. *Press, Revolution, and Social Identities in France, 1830–1835* (2001).

Rapport, Michael. *1848: Year of Revolution* (2009).

Sack, James J. *From Jacobite to Conservative: Reaction and Orthodoxy in Britain, c. 1760–1832* (2004).

Sked, Alan. *Metternich and Austria: An Evaluation* (2008).

Sperber, Jonathan. *The European Revolutions, 1848–1851* (2005).

———. *Revolutionary Europe, 1780–1850* (2000).

Vick, Brian E. *Defining Germany: The 1848 Frankfurt Parliamentarians and National Identity* (2002).

Wolff, Jonathan. *Why Read Marx Today?* (2002).

Zamoyski, Adam. *Rites of Peace: The Fall of Napoleon and the Congress of Vienna* (2008).

For additional resources, including maps, primary sources, visuals, web links, and quizzes, please go to **www.oup.com/us/backman.**

CHAPTER 19

Nationalism and Identity

1801–1903

THE GREATER WEST, 1871

O ne of the most dramatic and ubiquitous cultural developments of the 19th century was the phenomenon of passionate, urgent concern for national identity. What does it mean to be
a member of a particular ethnic or cultural group? What makes
one English, German, Hungarian, Polish, or Serbian? Can a foreign immigrant ever be truly assimilated into a new culture? Into
a political state, yes—but that is another matter entirely, a question of mere citizenship. Can an ethnic Russian truly become
Irish, however? Is it possible, or even desirable, for a Dutch man or woman to
become French—and if so, is not some element of his or her "Dutchness" lost in
the process? Attempts to answer questions like these altered the map of Europe.
In turn, those changes led to renewed questions and divisions within European
Jews and a crumbling Ottoman Empire.

It seems odd that questions of identity still haunted peoples who had
lived together for over a thousand years; the explanation lay in the innumerable configurations of their joint existences. Political borders designating
states and countries in past centuries had been drawn variously along dynastic lines, religious lines, geographic lines, lines of military conquest, lines
demarcating zones of economic interest, linguistic lines, negotiated lines of
convenience, and lines based on nothing in
particular. The willful drawing and redraw-
ing of political boundaries at international
congresses like Westphalia and Vienna, or at
scores of local meetings over the centuries
to settle regional disputes, had the effect for
many of making states seem artificial at best

◀ **Fighting for the Nation**
A Greek rebel against Turkish
rule, shown carrying banner
and sword. The image
illustrates the linkage
between Romantic passion
and political nationalism.

- Nationalism in Theory
- Nationalism in Practice: Germany
  and Italy
- Frustrated Nationalism: Hungary
  and Ireland
- Assimilation and Zionism
- Islamic Nationalisms
- Reforming Islam

CHAPTER
OUTLINE

and irrelevant at worst. If the "country" to which one owes political obedience and personal loyalty can be altered by something as small as a signature on a treaty, then how can one honestly feel any sense of deep identification with it? Given such persistent arbitrariness, the absence of any sure sense of communal identity becomes less of a surprise (see Map 19.1).

The upheavals of the late 18th and early 19th centuries only added to the confusion. As late as 1815 just under 10 percent of Europe's population lived in cities with populations above fifty thousand; only fifty years earlier than that, however, the figure had been closer to 2–3 percent. The threefold increase in urban population meant more than a quantitative growth in absolute numbers, for urban populations tend to greater ethnic complexity than rural ones. Farming societies, in other words, are more typically homogenous in their ethnic makeup than urban societies, and so the rise in the number and size of cities meant a concomitant increase in ethnic heterogeneity. Napoleon's Continental System had erased, for a while, at least, the legal barriers to peoples' free movement from one territory to another, as they sought opportunities to learn new skills and access new markets. The result was the presence of sizable communities of resident foreigners in cities across Europe: ethnic Poles living in Berlin or Paris, ethnic Sicilians residing in Milan or Hamburg, ethnic Greeks taking up new lives in Madrid or Genoa, ethnic Portuguese residing in Rotterdam or Lille. When the Continent began to industrialize at speed, post-1815, the pluri-ethnic character of urban life became even more pronounced. Under these conditions, when a city like Munich became home to a confusing sprawl of cultural groups, what did "being German" or "being Bavarian" mean?

NATIONALISM IN THEORY

Edward Augustus Freeman (1823–1892), one of England's great historians in the 19th century, confronted the question in an essay entitled "Race and Language" (1879):

CHAPTER TIMELINE

1801
Act of Union between
England and Ireland

1829
Catholic
Emancipation
Act (Ireland)

1831
Rifa'a al-
Tahtawai, *The
Essence of Paris*

1845–1852
Irish Potato
Famine

1805–1848
Rule of
Mehmet Ali
Pasha in Egypt

1830
Greece wins independence;
Bulgaria secures autonomy
from Ottomans

1839–1876
Tanzimat in
Ottoman Empire

[What of] those parts of the world where people who are confessedly of different races and languages inhabit a continuous territory and live under the same government? How do we define nationality in such cases as these? The answer will be very different in different cases. . . . They may form what I have already called an *artificial nation*, united by an act of its own free will. Or it may be simply a case where distinct nations, distinct in everything which can be looked on as forming a nation, except the possession of an independent government, are brought together, by whatever causes, under a common ruler. The former case is very distinctly an exception which proves the rule, [such a] nation is something different from those nations which are defined by a universal or at least a predominant language. We mark it as an exception, as something different from other cases. And when we see how nearly this artificial nation comes, in every point but that of language, to the likeness of those nations which are defined by language, we see that it is a nation defined by language which sets the standard, and after the model of which the artificial nation forms itself.

Freeman mentions Switzerland as an example of an artificial nation—one composed of several groups, each of which maintains its own language. He sees other examples in the Ottoman and Austrian-Hungarian empires of his time:

While in each Western country some one of the various races which have settled in it has, speaking roughly, assimilated the others, in the lands which are left under the rule of the Turk, or which have been lately delivered from his rule, all the races that have ever settled in the country still abide side by side. So when we pass into the lands which form the Austr[ian]-Hungar[ian] national government, another fragment is ruled by civilized strangers, a third is trampled down by barbarians. The existing states of Greece, Romania, and Serbia are far from taking in the

1848
Europe rocked by revolutions

1858
Romania secures autonomy from Ottomans

1870
Franco-Prussia War

1881
First appearance of the term "anti-Semitic" in English

1903
Publication of *The Protocols of the Elders of Zion*

1853–1856
Crimean War begins

1861
Abolition of serfdom in Russia; unification of Italy

1871
Unification of Germany

1896
Theodore Herzl, *The Jewish State*

MAP 19.1 The Peoples of Europe, ca. 1850

whole of the Greek, Romanian, and Serbian nations. In all these lands ...
there is no difficulty in marking off the several nations; only in no case
do the[se] nations [correspond] to any existing political power.

To Freeman, language defines national identity. But other possibilities exist.
To some writers, one's nationality comprised race, loyalty to a unique political
vision, religious practice, or even native cuisine. Rudyard Kipling (1865–1936),
tireless champion of British imperialism and at one point the most popular writer
in the English-speaking world, identified nationality and sentimentality; one's
nation is simply the place to which one remains loyal in one's heart.

> Our hearts where they rocked our cradle
> Our love where we spent our toil,
> And our faith, and our hope, and our honor,
> We pledge to our native soil.
>
> God gave all men all earth to love
> But since our hearts are small
> Ordained for each one spot should prove
> Beloved over all.

The search for national identity was intrinsically Romantic—self-fascinated, intuitive, multifaceted (and, inevitably, contradictory), and awe-inspiring—and
informed numerous aspects of Romantic thought and expression, from historical
writing like E. A. Freeman's to the political essays of Ernst Renan (1823–1892)
and the poetical-philosophical works (not to mention the music) of Richard
Wagner (1813–1883). Like Romanticism, the influence of nationalism spread
throughout the 19th century. Unlike Romanticism,
the fascination with national identity continued to
be felt throughout the 20th century as well, all too
often in odious and destructive ways.[1]

However it is defined, **nationalism** was and remains a potent force. It may in fact be the most vital
element in modern political history. The word im-
plies more than mere patriotism, although it includes that notion. Nationality in
the 19th-century sense suggests a collective consciousness, a growing awareness
that the members of an individual nation-group share a depth of feelings, values,
and attitudes toward the world. Together, these sentiments give meaning to their

> However it is defined, nationalism
> was and remains a potent force. It
> may in fact be the most vital element
> in modern political history.

---

[1]   George Orwell: "Nationalism is power-hunger tempered by self-deception."

Scots   This lithograph of Queen Victoria's "Four Highlanders" was printed in 1869. Victoria lost her mother and her husband in 1861 and went into deep and prolonged mourning, during which time she lived primarily in Scotland.

aggregate existence and may in fact be the only way to realize a fully meaningful life. In the United States this conviction took the form of a belief in America's manifest destiny to move westward across the Great Plains and extend the national borders to the Pacific coast. In Europe it took the form of popular desire to eradicate the artificial political lines drawn in 1815 and replace them with organic states composed of the political and geographical union of all members of specific national groups: a Germany made up of the aggregate of all ethnic Germans; an Italy that unites all ethnic Italians into a single state; an independent Hungary that gathers all Magyars under an autonomous government of their own.

But the word "nation" did not always have this populist meaning. In the 16th and 17th centuries it was widely used to designate the aristocracy in most countries—that is, the people born into privilege, the people who mattered. That is why the declaration made in 1789 by the revolutionaries locked out of the meeting of the Estates General in Paris—that "we are the nation"—was so radically decisive. Rousseau had argued that a nation composed of all of its people in equal membership would create not only a more just society but a decidedly more powerful, dynamic, and harmonious one. Here the *volonté générale* ("general will") of its constituents would find the freest and most perfect expression. This idea carried through into the Industrial Age, though differing political camps put it to different uses. To most conservatives, nation meant culture, language, and tradition—the political and social norms that bound people together under the paternal care of ancient hierarchies. To liberals, the word described the egalitarian gathering of people under a constitution that recognized rights, guaranteed the claims of property, and promoted individual freedom. To Marxists, a nation was a fiction, an imagined grouping used by capitalists to control industrial production and promote the interests of the bourgeoisie. It is part of the complexity of nationalism that all of these views were, and are, to some extent correct.

The political narrative of 19th-century nationalism is episodic: it took decades either for discrete territories to unite into a single nation or for a subjugated land to break away from foreign domination and establish its independence. The most prominent political successes were the unifications of Germany and of Italy, while the most significant political failures were those of Hungary and of Ireland.

NATIONALISM IN PRACTICE: GERMANY AND ITALY

Germany as a unified political state had not existed since the 13th century, and Italy had ceased to exist as a single nation as many as eight centuries before that. The Congress of Vienna had reshuffled the German territories into a confederation of thirty-eight states and the Italian peninsula into roughly a dozen autonomous petty principalities. The desire for unification was present from the start, although it was hardly universal. The middle classes in both places were the prime movers for unification, for they stood to benefit the most: only by pooling the peoples' resources, they recognized, could the Germans or Italians catch up to industrialized England. National banks were needed to provide financing for start-up manufacturers, for example, and extensive systems of transport and communication had to be established. Moreover, they needed to be established quickly. To those of the working class, a unified state seemed the only feasible way to rein in the abuses and inequities of industrial capitalism. Both groups thus saw national union as the most promising path to both economic growth and social reform. Conservatives in both places balked at both developments and fought to protect their provincialism. The strong Romantic pulse of the young generation, however, inclined them to explore and exalt the collective genius of their cultures at large. It thus complemented the ledger-book mentality of the entrepreneurial class in its press for national union.

The Prussians had taken the early lead in the German Confederation by reforming their military along meritocratic lines. Reorganizing the officer corps signaled the end of the dominance of the old aristocracy (called **Junkers**) in Prussian society and paved the way for other reforms: cities won the right to control their own finances, and German universities were opened to competitive admission. By 1848, tired of conservative foot-dragging and impatient of initial liberal efforts at reform, workers and bourgeois alike proposed schemes for German nationhood at a meeting of the Frankfurt Assembly.

Most of the delegates came from professional circles and confronted a pressing question: Did unification mean the union of all ethnic Germans everywhere or simply of those Germans residing in German-governed principalities? German populations living in Czech-dominated Bohemia, for example, or in Habsburg-controlled Austria, wanted to be included in a "Greater Germany" but could not do so without risking active resistance from their rulers. The Prussian king Friedrich Wilhelm IV (r. 1840–1861) was offered, but declined, the crown of a "Lesser Germany" that omitted those extraterritorial nationals. Not that his refusal had anything to do with the extraterritorial nationals; he refused the crown simply because it had been offered by the people. A true conservative, he declared that the only crown he could ever wear was one that he placed upon his own head, lest he appear to condone liberal attitudes:

> This crown [that you offer] is no real crown. . . . [It] humiliates whoever wears it. . . . It smells of the gunpowder of the revolution of 1848—the most ridiculous, stupid, and vile (although not, thank God, the most evil) uprising of this century. . . . Let me state it outright: If the [true] crown of the united German nation, a crown with a one-thousand-year-old heritage . . . should ever be bestowed again, it will be I and my peers—alone—who bestow it. Woe to those who assume authorities to which they have no right. *("Proclamation of 1849")*

Instead of an early union of the Lesser Germany, what came out of the Frankfurt Assembly was an even weaker version of the former German Confederation.

One thing remained clear: the debate over German unification boiled down to a political rivalry between Prussia and Austria, since either one of these seemed likely to take the lead in a single Greater Germany. As one of the Frankfurt delegates put it:

> There is no avoiding the fact that the whole issue of a united Germany comes down to a simple choice between Prussia and Austria. German life in these two states certainly has its positive and negative characteristics—in the first, the focus is on national union and reform, while in the second the focus is upon mere, and ultimately destructive, dynastic power. In this way, the whole issue of "Germany" is not about a constitution but about power, pure and simple. The monarchy in Prussia thinks about the whole of the German people, while that in Austria never will. *("Speech to the Frankfurt Assembly" [1848] by Johann Gustav Droysen)*

Historians still debate the consequences of the failure at Frankfurt. At the very least, unification, with the support of a broad cross-section of the people, happened only later. Yet it was also caused by a new political alliance between the Prussian monarchy and the military. This direct military element, some argue, forced German nationalism onto a unique path that led unavoidably to Nazism and Hitler. (Historians call this debate the Sonderweg controversy, after the German for "unique path.")

Unavoidably or not, the Prussian military did in fact take over the cause of unification. Under the leadership of Prime Minister Otto von Bismarck (1815–1898), a deeply conservative, complex, and brilliant figure, Prussian arms bullied and beat its neighbors into submission.[2] Bismarck started a war with Denmark (1866) in order to seize the disputed principalities of Schleswig and Holstein, then provoked a "Seven Weeks' War" against Austria (also 1866), which gained another half-dozen territories, while securing Venice (previously under Habsburg control) as his Italian ally. He then engineered the Franco-Prussian War (1870–1871), which returned, among other areas, the Alsace-Lorraine region to German control (see Map 19.2). Bismarck, who regularly wore a military uniform but never served in the army himself, is most frequently remembered for his statement that "the great issues of our time will not be resolved by speeches and parliamentary votes (that was the mistake of the revolutionaries of 1848 and 1849) but by blood and iron." Yet he also declared that "anyone who has ever looked straight into the glazed eyes of a soldier dying on a battlefield will think twice before starting a war."

Bismarck himself had little nationalistic feeling for a "Greater Germany"; his loyalty was first and foremost to Prussia. But since German unification seemed inevitable, he chose to bring it about in his own way, with Prussia very much the dominant element. Bismarck gambled that the German people would support his militarism in return for his championing of liberal social programs that he personally found odious: health insurance, unemployment insurance, and retirement pensions—anything that avoided actual regulation of the marketplace. He was right. Germany became not only a single nation—the

Otto von Bismarck in 1864.

Otto von Bismarck Prussian diplomat and Prime Minister who engineered the unification of Germany.

---

[2] Bismarck neither enjoyed nor glorified war; he was simply willing to resort to it when there seemed no other way to achieve what he desired.

MAP 19.2   **The Unification of Germany**

Second Reich (the first being the medieval empire established in the 10th century)—under Bismarck, but also became both an unfettered industrial-capitalist economy and a social-welfare state. On January 18, 1871, at the end of the Franco-Prussian War, which destroyed the power of the French emperor Napoleon III, the Prussian king Wilhelm II became the emperor of Germany with the following proclamation:

> I, Wilhelm . . . do hereby declare that I have concluded that it is my solemn duty to our common Fatherland to answer the call of the united German princes and free cities and to assume the German imperial

title ... while fully conscious of my responsibility to protect the rights not only of the empire of its loyal German subjects, to maintain peace, and to assure the independence of the German nation (which depends, in its turn, on the united strength of its people). I assume this title in the hope that the German people will be freely able to reap in lasting peace the rewards of its strenuous and selfless wars, within national boundaries that will grant the Fatherland safety from renewed French aggression—a safety that has been lacking for centuries. May God grant that I and my successors on this imperial throne will ever add to the wealth of our empire not by military conquest but through the blessings and gifts of peace, in the realm of national prosperity, freedom, and morality.

It is as concise a summary of nationalist sentiments as one could hope to find.

Once united, Germany accelerated its industrial development and efforts to "Germanize" the population. The first development is self-explanatory: the construction of new factories (especially in steel manufacture, railroads, and arms)

Nationalism and Power   The Krupp Steel Works factory in Essen, Germany. Founded in 1810 as a foundry for producing railway equipment, the Krupp factory turned to manufacturing cannons and other armaments in midcentury. Weaponry quickly became its primary manufacture after 1870. By 1900 Krupp was the largest company in Europe, with over seventy-five thousand employees across the Germany, roughly one-third of whom worked in the original plant at Essen.

and the building of both commercial and military fleets that could challenge England's dominance on the high seas. "Germanization" of the countryside involved the forced assimilation of ethnic minorities and the resettlement of ethnic Germans on farmland confiscated from groups such as the Danes, French, Lithuanians, and Poles. The languages spoken by these groups were forbidden in schools, books, newspapers, theaters, concert halls, museums, courtrooms, the military, and most other public sites.

Bismarck, a devout Pietist Lutheran, also targeted Catholicism as an intrinsically non-German religion. This anti-Catholic campaign was known as the **Kulturkampf** ("culture battle") and lasted from 1871 to 1878. Among the measures the government took were the banning of the Jesuit Order and the breaking of diplomatic relations with the Vatican. Internally, the Reich forbade Catholic priests from mentioning any political issue in the pulpit; clergy found guilty of "political preaching" faced two years' imprisonment.[3] The government also closed roughly one-third of all monasteries. It is difficult to know the extent to which the Kulturkampf targeted Catholics and how much it aimed to undermine the Polish communities now living under the authority of the Reich; Bismarck certainly had little sympathy for either group. In either case, however, it backfired: Catholic representation in the Reichstag doubled over the seven years of government oppression.

Italy's unification equaled Germany's in drama, but it was a drama of a different sort. Political decentralization had not particularly bothered most Italians through the centuries; fragmentation and localism had so long been the norms of Italian life that they were seldom questioned. This sort of particularism, in fact, had preserved much of what was best loved in Italian life—local customs, local cuisines, local dialects, and a strong sense of local identities. Until well into the 19th century, few people on the peninsula thought of themselves as Italians. Instead, they were Beneventans, Florentines, Lucchesans, Neapolitans, Perugians, or Venetians—or, for those with a more regional sense of identity, Ligurians, Sicilians, or Tuscans. The strongest impulse toward national identity came from resentment of foreign domination. At least since the 13th century, the Italian peninsula had been dominated by a shifting matrix of European powers: Angevins, Austrians, Catalans, French, Germans, Savoyards, and Spaniards. In the 16th century Machiavelli had penned *The Prince* as a desperate plea for a native uprising against the foreigners (at that point primarily the French) tearing apart the countryside. The chief villains in the 19th century were the Habsburg

---

[3] By 1878 nearly two thousand Catholic clergy had been either jailed or exiled, including fully one-half of all the bishops in Prussia.

Austrians in the north and the Bourbon French in the south, both of whom had been either placed or ratified in power by the despised Treaty of Vienna. In 1827 the Romantic poet Alessandro Manzoni (1785–1873) published his only novel, often considered Italy's greatest, *The Betrothed* (*I promessi sposi*), which dramatized, among other things, the suffering inflicted on northern Italy by foreign usurpers. (The same author's *Adelchi* (1822) dramatizes the overthrow of a Lombard prince by Charlemagne, the great but meddlesome 9th-century emperor.) The novel is set in the 17th century, when the region around Manzoni's birthplace of Milan was controlled by Spanish forces, but it alludes directly to the dominance of the Austrians in the 19th—a theme of his stage dramas as well.

Popular rebellion broke out in hundreds of small riots and demonstrations.

I MANGIA-MACCARONI

Neapolitans   Two Neapolitan youths in an archetypal pose, eating maccheroni. Naples is the Italian peninsula's largest port city. Commonly thought of as a place of squalor and crime, it was (and still is) the fourth largest urban economy in Italy, and the first Italian city to have a railway line. When Naples joined the Kingdom of Italy in 1861, national unification was complete.

"Italian patriotism is like the patriotism of the ancient Greeks," wrote a prominent Neapolitan official in 1850; "it consists of love for a single town, not for a whole country. Conquest by foreigners is the only thing that ever unites Italians. Left to themselves, they will always split into smaller groups." Another proponent of unification, Giuseppe La Farina (1815–1863), wrote that

Italy's independence should be the aim of every spirited and intelligent man, for neither our schools, commerce, nor industry will ever flourish or develop so long as Austria's boot remains on our necks. . . . To gain freedom politically we must drive out the Austrians who dominate us. To gain freedom intellectually we must drive out the Austrians who keep us the slaves of the Holy See. And to create a national literature, too, we must drive out the Austrians who keep most of our people illiterate. . . . Everything tends toward political unification. Our science, industry, commerce, and arts require it. No great advancements are possible unless we first bring together the skills, minds, capital, and labor of our great nation. . . . Woe to anyone who dares to get in our way!

The only open question, in most Italians' minds, was whether the unified country would be a monarchy (favored by many in the north) or a democracy (the general preference of those in the south). Diplomatic leadership came from the north in the persons of Vittorio Emmanuele II, the king of Piedmont-Sardinia (r. 1849–1861)—which was one of the misshapen countries created in 1815—and his chief minister, Camillo Benso, the count of Cavour (1810–1861). Military and populist leadership, however, came from the south in the person of Giuseppe Garibaldi (1807–1882), a charismatic adventurer who pursued the cause of liberating enslaved peoples everywhere from Tunisia and Brazil to Italy, the United States, and France.[4]

Garibaldi had defeated the Bourbon-controlled south by the end of 1860, while Cavour (with some help from the French) had neutralized Habsburg power in the north by roughly the same time. By 1871 the last remnants of foreign resistance had been overcome, and Vittorio Emmanuele journeyed to Rome and assumed the title of king of Italy (see Map 19.3). The only remaining problem was the Holy See. The pope was not only spiritual leader of the Catholic Church but also the political ruler of part of central Italy since the Middle Ages. His domain had long since been reduced, geographically, but Pope Pius IX (r. 1846–1878) refused to relinquish any aspect of his secular authority and so became "the prisoner of the Vatican." The dispute continued until 1929, when a concordat signed by the Holy See and the Italian government finally ended the matter. But Italy was united only in name. The north remained the center of economic might, with its banks, industry, and commercial links; the south, by contrast, was overwhelmingly rural and poorly educated. Since Italy's political leadership invariably came from the north, the economic disparity between north and south, and the unequal leverage of political power between them, would hamper Italian development for decades.

Wittingly or unwittingly, France played a significant role in the unifications of Germany and of Italy. Napoleon III (r. 1852–1870), who as Louis-Napoleon Bonaparte had served as president of the Second Republic, dreaded another uprising of the common peasants and laborers. Now emperor, he pushed hard for France's industrial and commercial development, even while doing all he could to centralize political authority into something as close to absolutism as he could manage.[5] The goal was to encourage a carefully controlled type of nationalism, one in which popular loyalty was not only to the country but to the state itself. By mobilizing the government behind industrial expansion, he hoped, people would

---

[4] Garibaldi offered his services in the American Civil War—on two conditions: President Lincoln would abolish slavery immediately and make him commander-in-chief of the Union army. Lincoln politely declined.

[5] Napoleon III created the infamous penal colony at Devil's Island off the coast of French Guiana—immediately sending 240 of the Republican leaders who had opposed his coup d'état.

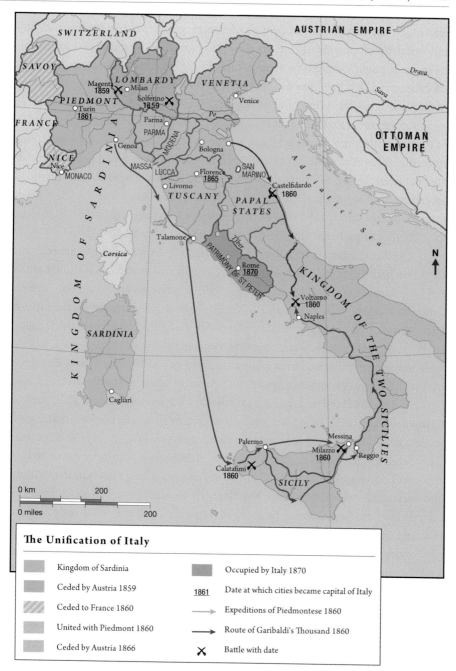

MAP 19.3   **The Unification of Italy**

associate prosperity not with individual entrepreneurship outside of state regulation but with the government—and especially with the ruler at its head.

The emperor controlled state finances, commanded the military, determined foreign policy, and dictated domestic affairs to an impotent national assembly whose existence preserved the fiction of popular democracy. Two policies dear to his heart—industrial development and urban renewal—advanced because of innovations he made in public finance, the most notable being his establishment of the Crédit Mobilier, a publicly held investment bank whose capital financed the construction of the Suez Canal, the quintupling of France's miles of rail lines, and the wholesale re-design of the city of Paris. The redevelopment of the city center involved demolition of well over thirty thousand buildings, wiping out entire neighborhoods, and laying more than 120 miles (200 kilometers) of new roads. A dozen broad boulevards radi-ated out from the Arc de Triomphe, in the heart of the city. These not only provided an esthetic and sentimental focal point to the city; their breadth also made it easier for the emperor's troops and police units to fan out into the neighborhoods, if neces-sary, in order to quell uprisings like those of 1848 (see Map 19.4).

Eager for military glory, Napoleon III rushed inadvisedly into several con-flicts that had pervasive consequences for German and Italian unification. Late in 1853 the Russian tsar Nikolai I (r. 1825–1855) ordered his army into the Turkish-controlled regions of Moldavia and Wallachia—roughly the territory of the eastern and southern part of today's nation of Romania, along the plain where the Danube River meets the Black Sea—arguing that the need to liberate the regions' Catholic and Orthodox populations from Islamic oppression justified the action. But since the quick Russian victory threatened the balance of power in southeastern Europe, France joined England in declaring a retaliatory war against Russia. This was the **Crimean War** (1854–1856), a wasteful and ineptly managed conflict that ended in a truce that left international borders unchanged. Only two years later Napoleon III ordered French military action into then little-known Southeast Asian territo-ries later known as Vietnam and Cambodia. France's strong efforts in the Crimea and success in Asia emboldened Napoleon III to attempt to influence political matters closer to home, and so he plunged into Italy's unification struggle in 1859. His interests were divided: as a devout Catholic he wanted to preserve the auton-omy of the Vatican, but as a nationalist he sincerely wanted to see a unified Italy. And the hard-nosed politician in him sought to wrest some territorial concessions from Cavour in return for military assistance against Austria. In the end, the hard-nosed politician won. French troops helped drive the Austrians from the region around Venice, and for their trouble Cavour and Vittorio Emmanuele II granted France, in 1860, the city of Nice and the area of the French Riviera.

Had Napoleon III ceased his adventures at that point, his reign would have been remembered much more positively than it now is. Instead, he first undertook a bizarre campaign to conquer Mexico. His forces were defeated by a Mexican nationalist force in a battle at Puebla, which took place on May 5, 1862. Worse, he then stumbled into a direct conflict with Otto von Bismarck.[6] The Franco-Prussian War (1870–1871)

---

6 Although French troops remained in Mexico until 1867, Cinco de Mayo lives on as a national holiday.

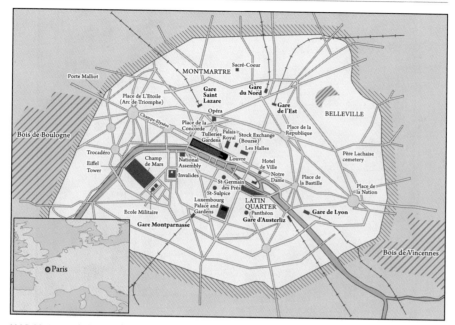

MAP 19.4   Paris in 1890

proved a disaster for France. The Prussian military outmatched France's army, and Bismarck outwitted Napoleon III diplomatically and militarily at every turn. The southern German states of Baden, Bavaria, Hesse, the Palatinate, and Würtemberg all rushed to join Prussia in defending the Fatherland, and after only three months of fighting the French army fell and the emperor himself was captured. Germany declared victory and its imperial unification, and Napoleon III was deposed. France then declared the start of its Third Republic (1870–1940), while the disgraced former emperor fled into exile in London, where he died in early 1873.

FRUSTRATED NATIONALISM: HUNGARY AND IRELAND

Nationalist passions may have been ubiquitous, but victories were not. Two of the most notable failed efforts of the 19th century—although they succeeded in the 20th—occurred in Hungary and Ireland.

Hungary had not been independent since 1526, when the Ottomans crushed the Magyar army and killed the Magyar king at the battle of Mohács. The remaining independent Hungarian nobles had split over what to do next. Some elected a new Hungarian monarch and formed a rump mini-kingdom that lasted only a brief time before being absorbed into the Ottoman Empire, while the others threw their support to Ferdinand I (r. 1526–1564) of Habsburg Austria. Hungary remained divided between Habsburgs and Ottomans until 1687, when a vast military alliance organized by Pope Innocent XI (r. 1676–1689) and

Hungarian Patriot   Lajos Kossuth (1802-1894), the great national champion of Hungarian independence, called for his country's freedom from Austria in a stirring speech to the Hungarian Diet in 1848. "Gentlemen!" he cried, "The fate of our nation is now in our hands...God has placed each one of you in the position of arbiter of the life or death of Hungary!" This drawing shows Lossuth, after his speech, in one of his many appearances around Hungary calling for recruits to the nation's militia.

known as the Holy League (Austria, the Holy Roman Empire, the Venetian Republic, Poland-Lithuania, and Russia, plus others) routed the Turkish army at a second battle of Mohács. Soon virtually all of the Hungarian homeland lay under Habsburg control. The century and a half of Austrian-Ottoman fighting had left much of Hungary in ruins, with many of its cities depleted or flattened and much of its urban population lost to emigration.

Austrian rule, autocratic and frequently brutal, weighed heavily on the Hungarians. Hardly a decade passed without a nativist rebellion somewhere in the Magyar lands. The Habsburgs responded in true absolutist style by destroying strongholds, choking off supplies to cities, forbidding the publication in the Magyar language, and keeping the peasantry (fully 90 percent of the population) dirt-poor.[7] The temporary dismantling of absolutism under Bonaparte gave fresh hope to the people not only by ridding them of a detested monarchy but also by presenting an opportunity

---

7   Hungary refused to use German in government councils or for public records. It thus has the honor of being the European country with the longest tradition of spoken Latin anywhere.

for economic development. Hungary's traditionally diversified subsistence farms gave way to large-scale monoculture that could provide food and materiel to Napoleon's eastward-heading army; the French also developed local roads, bridges, and transport vehicles. The enthusiasm created by the resulting economic boom, combined with the subsequent crushing of political hopes at the retrograde Congress of Vienna in 1815, catalyzed Magyar pride and resentment and sparked new demands for the creation of an autonomous Hungarian state. Led by charismatic leaders like István Széchenyi (1791–1860) and Lajos Kossuth (1802–1894), the Hungarians pushed continually to overthrow the Habsburgs. While they succeeded briefly during the raucous uprisings of 1848–1849 (during which Kossuth dramatically issued the Hungarian Declaration of Independence), Habsburg power was restored by force, with the assistance of tsarist Russia. Kossuth was driven into exile and died abroad. Magyar nationalist hopes lived on, but would not fully revive until the ultimate collapse of the Habsburg Empire in World War I.

By contrast, many of the Irish actually wanted to remain under foreign control. After centuries of British rule and misrule, enough Anglo-Irish Protestants had lived in Ireland long enough to regard the island as their native country. Although a minority of the total population, they were yet sufficiently numerous that the legitimacy of their claims could not be altogether dismissed. But the development of parliamentary government meant that, if Ireland were to gain political autonomy, the Protestants would always remain a minority—and thus, they feared, never receive fair representation in government or full equality before the law. To many loyalists the solution was to deny representation and equality to the Catholic majority by rejecting Irish home rule and prohibiting Catholics from participation in government. Irish nationalism, as it entered the 19th century, thus progressed in two stages—first the struggle for Catholic emancipation, then the fight for home rule. Protestants in Ireland opposed both campaigns.

Since the 16th century, royal writ had effectively restricted political rights in Britain to those willing to take the **Oath of Supremacy**—that is, to recognize the monarch as the supreme head of the church within the realm. This law barred Catholics from holding public office; moreover, anyone who refused to take the oath could be arrested for treason. With very few exceptions, the law had effectively forbidden Irish Catholics to play any part in their own government. Rebellions against England had broken out regularly in the 17th century but were crushed by England's superior armed forces. Legal assaults usually followed on the heels of the military ones. By 1700, for example, Irish Catholics were forbidden to purchase new land or to inherit it from a Protestant, and the law required Catholic landholdings to be subdivided among all surviving sons upon a landholder's death. Over generations these maneuvers undermined Catholic land tenure, turning the Irish majority from free owners to tenants-at-will who could be turned out by their Protestant landlords on a whim. Catholics could not vote, sit on juries, serve in the military, or work as schoolteachers or police. The Anglo-Irish Protestant minority therefore had a monopoly on economic and political power over the entire island.

A brief relaxation of the legal persecution in 1778 produced such a powerful anti-Catholic backlash within England that riots engulfed London, leaving more than four hundred people dead and hundreds more injured. These are known as the "Gordon Riots" (1780), named after Lord George Gordon (1751–1793), who in his position as head of the Protestant Association had led the effort to overturn the easing of legal oppression of the Catholics. Leading a mob of fifty thousand, Gordon tried to present a petition against the legal reforms to Parliament. Blocked from entry into Parliament, the mob then went out of control, destroying Catholic chapels, pillaging the homes of London Catholics, and setting fire to Newgate Prison. It took several days for the English army to quell the riots. Gordon escaped briefly to Holland but afterwards took up residence in Birmingham, where he converted to Orthodox Judaism. In 1788 he was arrested and sent to Newgate Prison, where he died five years later.[8] Hatred and mistrust across religious lines remained deeply engrained as Ireland entered the 19th century.

England recognized that Catholic emancipation would have to be granted eventually, or else the island would never cease to rebel. As a means of retaining control, however, the English now proposed an **Act of Union**, whereby the nominally independent Irish Parliament (composed solely of Protestant Anglo-Irish since the 17th century) was subsumed into the British Parliament. The Irish were slow to warm to the idea, but eventually they agreed, and in 1801 the union took place. Catholic emancipation followed a generation later. By 1829, therefore, Irish Catholics had secured the right to vote and to serve in government. Their smaller numbers, in both the House of Lords and the House of Commons, however, meant that they were unable to form a sufficiently large bloc to affect policy.

Disputes about the nature of Irish nationalism continued to rage. To the majority Catholics, more than half of whom still spoke Gaelic rather than English, the Protestant Anglo-Irish were not Irish at all. By blood, language, law, religion, and custom they were English and therefore foreigners on Ireland's soil. To the Protestants, national identity meant more than biological ethnicity or religious commitment. A nation could be as legitimately defined by dedication to a set of ideals and values—as the example of the United States showed. In the 1790s, in fact, a Protestant lawyer named Theobald Wolfe Tone (1763–1798), inspired by

---

8   The Gordon Riots provide the backdrop to Charles Dickens's novel *Barnaby Rudge* (1841).

the French Revolution, had mounted a campaign for Ireland to solve its political troubles by creating a nonsectarian democratic republic. Enlightenment idealism, he hoped, would dissolve the hatreds that had filled and ruined Irish life. Wolfe Tone went so far as to negotiate a French invasion of the island that would overthrow the parliament in Dublin and establish the new Enlightened Ireland. (The French forces were repulsed quickly, and Wolfe Tone was arrested and convicted of treason. He killed himself while in prison awaiting execution.) The failure of his vision meant that Ireland's competing national identities continued their bloody rivalry throughout the 19th century.

Industrialization only worsened matters. Because of its ties to England, Ireland experienced a wave of industrialization earlier than the European continent, though it never advanced far enough to challenge English manufacturing might. (The English saw to that.) Textile factories predominated, for the production of fine Irish linens, along with breweries and distilleries. These factories were scattered across the country but were found most frequently in counties where the Anglo-Irish Protestants predominated.[9] Most Irish still worked the land and never shared in the prosperity of the factory-owning class. Moreover, farm prices fell dramatically after 1815, when the barriers to trade with the Continent fell, so most farmers fell into ever worse poverty, widening the economic gap between the Catholic majority and the Protestant minority. Manufacturing wealth and agrarian poverty were a volatile mix; the rural poor grew angrier and more violent and even began to organize themselves into networks of underground movements. For the Anglo-Irish, their industrial prosperity meant that they had even more to lose in the event of a successful nationalist rebellion.

The 1820s and 1830s saw repeated attempts at reform. Some of these efforts, like the Catholic Emancipation Act of 1829, which gave Catholic Irishmen (and only men) the right to vote for their own representatives in government, had salutary effects. Others, like the temperance movement, seemed a mixed blessing. By 1842 five million people in Ireland had publicly sworn themselves to total abstinence from alcohol, a figure large enough to worry the owners of the heavily capitalized breweries and distilleries. By 1844 distillery revenues across Ireland had fallen by 50 percent from what they had been only twenty years earlier. Ireland's population in 1844 was roughly 8.5 million, so the number of pledge takers represented

---

9   One landlord described his Catholic tenants and factory workers as "ignorant, prejudiced, vulgar, brutal [people] unacquainted with . . . an efficient police, kind or indulgent landlords, or a respectable clergy."

Conspirators   An Irish cartoon featuring a group of rebels swearing-in (and toasting) a new recruit to the cause of "Captain Rock"—a euphemism for the cause of Irish nationalism.

more than half the country. Landlords began to fear sober tenants, who might thereby organize into a movement, more than drunken rowdies.

Given the slow emergence of something like an organized Irish majority and the willingness of the British to institute at least some reforms, a successful campaign for Irish independence might have come about by midcentury, but then catastrophe struck—the Great Famine (1845–1852). The fungus-like potato blight (*Phytophthora infestans*) is believed to have come to Ireland in 1844 from South America aboard ships transporting guano, a natural fertilizer widely used in western Europe at the time. The blight in fact infected much of western Europe, not just Ireland. Conditions in Ireland, however, allowed the disease to reach its maximum and most deadly effect. By 1845 fully one-third of the entire Irish population lived on potatoes, combined at best with bacon, buttermilk, and cabbage, since potatoes grew so abundantly as to allow even the poorest farmers with the tiniest landholdings a subsistence diet.[10] The blight—for which no cure is known even today—not only wiped out entire crops but infected the soil itself and guaranteed the loss of subsequent plantings as well even if one brought in fresh seed potatoes. Perhaps half of the 1845 harvest was lost, and the blight destroyed three-quarters of the 1846 harvest. Only in 1852 did the blight run its course, leaving Ireland permanently changed and Irish-English relations permanently scarred. In general, the blight was deadlier the farther to the south and the west one traveled (see Map 19.5).

---

[10]   Farm families, especially in the west, ate as many as twenty potatoes per person daily.

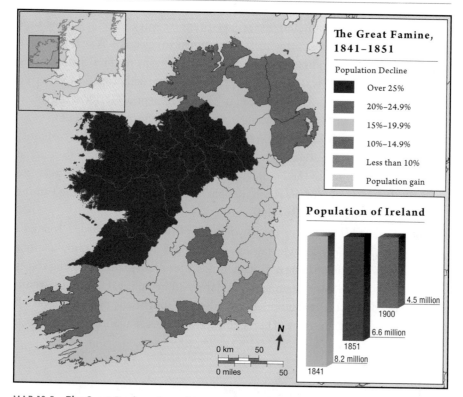

MAP 19.5   The Great Famine, 1841–1851

Somewhere between 1 and 1.5 million Irish died of starvation during the famine, and a slightly larger number, perhaps as many as two million, were forced to emigrate—mostly to America and Canada, in addition to from Britain itself. Nearly one-third of the westward-sailing emigrants died before reaching their new homes, however, making the total mortality figures all the more horrific.

The blight itself was a natural disaster, but one made considerably worse by British mismanagement of the crisis. The British blocked international relief efforts and refused to commit to long-term public works projects that would have enabled Irish workers to purchase foodstuffs from abroad. To Irish eyes, though, the two most odious of Britain's actions throughout the crisis were to

As John Mitchel (1815–1875), a young Irish nationalist, bitterly wrote: "The Almighty, indeed, sent the potato blight, but the English created the Famine."

continue shipping into England large quantities of the unblighted potatoes to make up for England's own native losses and to refuse to redirect Irish grain crops (which provided the raw material for the distilleries and breweries owned by the Anglo-Irish) so that they could feed the people instead. As John Mitchel (1815–1875), a young Irish nationalist, bitterly wrote: "The Almighty, indeed, sent the potato blight, but the English created the Famine."

Sir Charles Trevelyan (1807–1886), assistant treasury secretary at the time, was responsible for orchestrating Britain's response to the crisis. A dedicated civil servant who went on to hold several important positions in the British Empire, Trevelyan nonetheless was a poor choice for dealing with Ireland's suffering, simply because he seemed to approve of it. "The judgment of God sent the calamity to teach the Irish a lesson," he wrote in a pamphlet, *The Irish Crisis* (1848), that was intended to justify his inaction; indeed, he wrote openly that "th[e] calamity must not be too much mitigated. . . . The real evil with which we have to contend is not the physical evil of the Famine, but the moral evil of the selfish, perverse and turbulent character of the [Irish] people." For his service during the Famine, Trevelyan was knighted by Queen Victoria.

In the midst of this horror, the Revolutions of 1848 rocked Europe. Ireland's version of it lasted only a single day before being put down, but the implications of possible revolt loomed large in British minds afterward. Like the leading voices at Westphalia in 1648 or at Vienna in 1815, the leading political figures in Britain resolved to contain the revolutionary impulse and sought any means to forestall Irish independence. The issue of home rule did not emerge again as a live political issue until the 1880s.

The Face of Horror The suffering of the Potato Famine in Ireland is starkly portrayed in this painting from 1850 by George Frederick Watts (1817–1904).

Within Ireland, two essential demographic facts shaped matters. First, many of the most desperate, angry, and radical of the Irish had either died or emigrated. This may explain the political quiescence of Ireland after midcentury, since the presumed leaders of any populist movement were absent. Second, the enormity of the disaster, coupled with some easing of British restrictions on land tenure for Catholics, meant that those Irish who did remain on the land were able to increase their holdings: individual farms grew from as few as five acres to fifteen, or a hundred, or even more, which meant that something beyond mere survival was possible. Industrialization declined overall throughout the island but focused more intensely on the northern counties, such as Ulster, where a large shipbuilding industry took root. In other words, postfamine Ireland was less populous overall, more secure in its resources, and more ethnically and religiously demarcated. For the time being, peaceful order and relative calm and prosperity trumped the urgent demands of the frustrated Irish version of nationalism.

ASSIMILATION AND ZIONISM

The Psalmist's oath in exile has been a mainstay of Jewish prayers and aspirations for centuries: "If I forget you, O Jerusalem, let my right hand wither; let my tongue stick to my palette if I cease to think of you, if I do not keep Jerusalem in memory even at my happiest hour" (Psalms 137.5–6).

Driven into Diaspora by the Romans, the Jews' dream of returning to Palestine remained constant, even if it seldom expressed itself in a mass movement. Some individual and small-group emigration trickled into the region, and on occasion it swelled—at it did, for example, after the establishment of the Crusader states in the 12th century and with the consolidation of the Ottoman Empire in the 16th and 17th centuries. For the most part, though, the bulk of Europe's Jews since the Diaspora chose either to coexist with mainstream Western society or to assimilate, while awaiting the messiah.

While there is no absolutely necessary link between the return to Zion and the appearance of messiah, most Talmudic and **midrashic** writers over the centuries assumed a connection between the phenomena. By the start of the 19th century most Jews expected the two events to happen concurrently. In 1845, however, a European conference of Reform rabbis proclaimed that the appearance of the messiah and the return to Zion could happen separately. The exploits of several would-be messiahs over the years, such as Sabbatai Zvi (see chapter 12) and Jacob Frank (1726–1791), had made many Jews skeptical of messianic claims but still dedicated to the notion of return to the Holy Land.

During the Enlightenment many Jews, especially the more well-to-do, embraced the rationalism of the age, in the hope that in a Europe without religion there would be no religious hatred. Some of these Jews abandoned Orthodoxy, accepted Western gentile forms of dress, diet, and thought, and joined the world of the salons. The great philosopher Moses Mendelssohn (1729–1786) is perhaps the best example of an assimilated, Enlightened Jew. Still others went so far as to accept baptism as a means of gaining entry to mainstream society—like the parents of Karl Marx and of the British statesman Benjamin Disraeli (1804–1881).

Most Western countries had given Jews—officially, at least—something like full civic and political equality by 1871: they struck down guild restrictions that had prohibited Jewish involvement in certain industries and crafts; they opened Europe's universities to Jews; and they permitted Jews to participate in newly emerging professions like journalism. Under the Ancien Régime Jews had not been permitted to reside in Paris; by 1880 more than forty thousand Jews lived there—nearly two-thirds of all the Jews in France. Throughout Germany, Jewish populations in cities of at least twenty thousand inhabitants quadrupled between 1815 and 1871. In Berlin alone the Jewish population increased from three thousand to thirty-six thousnad over that period.

Most Jews in western Europe prospered in these years. Tax rolls tell the tale. England, for example, had admitted roughly ten thousand Jewish immigrants between 1750 and 1815, most of them simple peddlers; yet by 1850 virtually all of their families had achieved middle-class status. In Germany, 80 percent of all Jews reported incomes that made them solidly middle-class.

Assimilation: An Evolutionary Perspective   An anti-assimilationist cartoon. Jews cannot become assimilated into the German nation without losing their Jewish identity.

Given their urbanization, Jews figured large as business leaders, journalists, physicians, and lawyers.[11] Many Jews launched political careers as well. Adolphe Crémieux (1796–1880) served in France's Chamber of Deputies and twice held the position of minister of justice; Gabriel Riesser (1806–1863) became Germany's first Jewish judge. Benjamin Disraeli, mentioned before, was England's first (and still the only) Jewish prime minister.

Romantic nationalism, however, quickly ended the Enlightened dream of a single, unified, rationalized human community, and Jews were once again seen as alien. Resistance to Jewish advancement occurred at the popular level, and it rose as rapidly as the Jews themselves did within society. But racial discrimination, not religious opposition, defined the new anti-Semitism. Marx may have been one of the first Westerners to write publicly about "the Jewish Question," but he was hardly the first to raise it. In 1844 a Frenchman named Alphonse Toussenel (1803–1885) published a vile attack titled *The Jews—Kings of Our Time: A History of Financial Feudalism*, which was quickly followed by Arthur de Gobineau's (1816–1882) *Essay on the Inequality of the Human Races* (1855), one of the first books to argue for the inherent superiority of the "Aryan race."

These books represent the start of a century-long parade of anti-Semitic literature in Europe that culminated in an infamous forgery, *The Protocols of the Elders of Zion* (1903). This Russian work, soon translated into every major European language, purports to represent the blueprint for an international Jewish conspiracy to take over the world. In English the terms anti-Semitic and **anti-Semitism** were coined in 1881, appearing first in the London journal *The Athenaeum* with the laconic observation that "anti-Semitic literature is very prosperous in Germany."[12] Being disproportionately visible in industrial, urban Europe, the Jews were disproportionately blamed for its miseries. That meant everything from low wages and miserable housing for workers to self-satisfied, bourgeois elitism.

> Being disproportionately visible in industrial, urban Europe, the Jews were disproportionately blamed for its miseries.

The Jews' very success was seen as proof of their insidious intent. Surely it cannot be a coincidence that Jews own businesses, publish newspapers, fill the ranks of the medical and legal professions, manage theaters, and help write the laws? Either the Jews are engaged in an international conspiracy or they are simply mean and grasping. In either case, the bigots concluded, we tolerate the Jews at our peril. But not all criticism of assimilation came from outside. Many Orthodox

---

[11]   Jews made up 10 percent of all lawyers in the city of Würtemberg. In Vienna in 1870 fully 40 percent of all medical students were Jewish.

[12]   A German journalist named Wilhelm Marr appears to have invented the word anti-Semitism in 1879.

Jews viewed warily the rise of secularism. Jewish schools now taught secular subjects—geography, mathematics, and European languages—that pushed aside the traditional focus on the study of scripture and the Talmud. The Jewish High Rabbinical Court in Paris in 1808 had asserted the authority of civil law over religious law; in effect, Jews should be French citizens first and observant Jews second. In 1818 authorities in Hamburg issued a new prayer book written in German, not Hebrew, and printed from left to right, unlike Hebrew. It also introduced practices like choirs, organ playing, sermons in the local language, and integration of the sexes, and it dropped from the weekly prayers all references to a Jewish return to Zion.

These tensions resulted in new efforts to establish at long last a Jewish state. Two fundamental convictions form the basis of those efforts, known as **Zionism**. One is the belief in the Jews' unique claim to possession of the Holy Land—a claim as old as the Abrahamic Covenant. The other is recognition of the historical fact that the Jews, despite two thousand years of effort, will never be wholly accepted into Western society. The Viennese journalist Theodor Herzl (1860–1904), who organized the First International Zionist Congress, summed up this view in a powerful pamphlet titled *The Jewish State* (1896):

> The anti-Semitism of today should not be confused with the persecutions that Jews have faced in the past, for while it does have a religious tinge to it in some countries, the principle focus of this new aggression is different. In most places where anti-Semitism thrives, in other words, it does so because of the [civil] emancipation of the Jews. . . . Maybe, if we would be left in peace for a generation or two, we could possibly assimilate completely into the peoples who surround us, but the simple fact is that they will not leave us in peace. Instead, they manage to tolerate us for a short time, but then their hostility returns—again and again. For some reason our prosperity irritates the world, probably because for so many centuries it had grown accustomed to regard us as the most contemptible of the poor. Society's stupidity and mean-heartedness have made it blind to the fact that prosperity has actually weakened our Jewish identity by eradicating those customs that used to distinguish us. . . . We are a single people—our enemies have united us even without our consent. This has happened before. Suffering has brought us together, and in that union we recognize our strength. Surely we are strong enough to found a state of our own, one that will be a model for all states.

The Zionist movement found most of its support among the Jews of eastern Europe. These Jews, in the 19th century, made up roughly two-thirds of the

MAP 19.6   The Pale of Settlement, 1835–1917

The map contents:

SWEDEN

St. Petersburg
(21,000)

Lake
Pskov

Novgorod
(4,700)

Lake
Ilmen

Baltic Sea

BALTIC PROVINCES
(80,000)

KOVNO

VITEBSK

■ Moscow
(9,000)

GERMANY

SUWALKI

VILNA

■ Smolensk
(10,500)

■ Tula
(2,700)

PLOCK

LOMZA

MINSK   MOGILEV

KALISZ   WARSAW   GRODNO   Pripet
Marshes

R U S S I A

PIOTRKOW   SIEDLCE

RADOM

CHERNIGOV

■ Kursk
(4,000)

■ Voroneth
(2,700)

KIELCE   LUBLIN

VOLHYNIA

■ Kharkov
(14,000)

AUSTRIA—
HUNGARY

Kiev

POLTAVA

KIEV

N

PODOLIA

EKATERINOSLAV

0 km   200

0 miles   200

RUMANIA   BESSARABIA

KHERSON

Nikolaev

TAURIDA

Sea of
Azov

The Pale of Settlement, 1835–1917

—— The Pale of Settlement. Russian Jews were confined to this
area by laws of 1795 and 1835.

○ Towns within the Pale which were themselves barred to
Jews without special residence permits.

■ Towns outside the Pale with Jewish inhabitants (figures for 1897).

Sebastopol

Yalta

Black Sea

Kuban
(5,000)

entire world's Jewish population, so success here was essential to the ultimate
spread of Zionism (see Map 19.6).

Anti-Semitism in eastern Europe—including the area known as the **Pale
of Settlement**—was particularly vicious. The Russian tsar and king of Poland
Aleksandr II (r. 1855–1881), despite his liberalizing tendencies, was widely unpopular and the subject of numerous assassination attempts. In fact, in 1881
members of the revolutionary Narodnaya Volya ("Will of the People") Party did
kill him. Although no Jewish individuals or groups had been involved, popular

sentiment blamed the murder on the supposed international Jewish conspiracy. Wave after wave of **pogroms** now rolled through the region, cutting down Jews, destroying synagogues, and setting Jewish books aflame. As a result, more than three million Jews migrated farther westward into eastern and central Europe, desperate and hungry, carrying only the possessions they had on their backs. To these exiles and the eastern European Jews who welcomed them, Zionism was the only solution to the hatred and bigotry that had permeated Jewish history.

Slowly, groups of Jewish settlers also began to return to the Holy Land. Between 1881 and 1914 nearly one hundred thousand Jews had taken up residence there, either living with distant relations and friends or purchasing land from Turkish landlords or Palestinian freeholders. Zionist organizations in Europe created their own financial networks that made capital available to would-be settlers. Many of the Turks who sold their lands were absentee landlords, and some were public officials determined to withdraw from a decaying Ottoman state with their purses full. These were fully legal purchases of property, but that fact did not appease many of the roughly seven hundred thousand Palestinians who lived in the area and dreamed of a free homeland of their own.

The Aftermath of a Pogrom   The aftermath of an anti-Jewish pogrom in Russia, 1881. Survivors pick through the remnants of a Torah scroll, prayer books, and other items in a pillaged synagogue.

ISLAMIC NATIONALISMS

Nationalism roiled throughout the Islamic world just as in Europe. The Ottoman state had expanded far into Europe, with a diverse religious and ethnic makeup, and through the centuries it had likewise struggled to guarantee a degree of religious toleration while preserving Islamic religious law, guarding the holy cities, and maintaining the pilgrimage routes that led to them. Moreover, the flexible structure of Ottoman administration had allowed non-Turks to serve in government and even to rise to positions of political and social prominence. But in the 18th century the empire went on the defensive against expansionist powers in Russia, Austria, and revolutionary France. And with the rise of industrial Europe, the empire as a unifying force for Muslims weakened dramatically, to be replaced by ethnically based nationalist sentiments. The Ottoman gift for accommodation proved no match for the newfound commercial and military might of European states, and the tardy reform efforts of figures like Selim III (r. 1780–1807) crumbled in the face of the increasingly urgent demands for local control over local fates.

Greece wrested her independence from the Ottomans in the 1820s. In the following decade France, which had already humiliated the Muslims during Napoleon's Egyptian and Syrian adventures, invaded Algeria and carved it away from Ottoman rule. At the same time, Tunisia and Egypt instituted political and economic reforms in an effort to secure their independence. The region of Bulgaria had gained autonomy by 1830, with Romania not far behind. Off to the east, the Caucasus territories of Abkhazia, Georgia, Batumi, and Kars were wrenched away by Russia. By 1878 the Ottomans remained in control of only Anatolia, Iraq, Palestine, and the Hijaz—the coastal strip of Arabia that lay alongside the Red Sea, including the holy cities of Mecca and Medina. Persia had long since established itself as an independent—indeed a rival—state under the Safavids and then the Qajars. What had once been a universal Islamic empire stretching from the Atlantic Ocean to India was thereby reduced to a single Middle East state, kept alive by a shaky alliance between its Turkish and Arab leaders.

Nationalistic passions were both fed and challenged by several new strains in Islamic thought. In the 19th century Russian intellectual life was divided between liberals and Slavophiles—that is, between those who promoted Western-style reforms on the one hand and those who urged a return to Russian cultural and religious tradition on the other; 19th-century Islamic thought was divided as well. While many believed that new Muslim countries could be aligned with Europe without abandoning their Islamic character, others advocated instead a thorough turning away from the Greater West and delving deeper into Islamic tradition. An example of the first was the pro-Western reform promoted in Egypt under the dynasty established by **Mehmet Ali Pasha** (r. 1805–1848), more commonly known in the West by the Arabized version of his name, Muhammad Ali Pasha. An example of the second was the intensely conservative reform championed by the dynasty of Muhammad ibn Saud (r. 1744–1765), a tribal prince from a small oasis town in central Arabia.

Mehmet Ali, an ethnic Albanian, arrived in Egypt from Ottoman-controlled Greece at the head of an army as part of the Ottomans' campaign to regain control of Egypt after Napoleon's forces had withdrawn. He assassinated most of his Mamluk rivals for power, which made him popular with the Egyptian masses, and subsequently drove the remaining Mamluk soldiers into the desert. By 1805 he had taken the title of *wali* ("governor") of the country and ruled independently, even though he publicly claimed obedience to the ruler in Istanbul. His most important innovation was a popular army. Mehmet understood the growing weakness of the regime in Istanbul and believed that Egypt was the site for a renewal of Islamic power: its economic might, coupled with its proximity to the holy cities of the Arabian Peninsula, made it the natural successor as leader of the Islamic world. But in order for Egypt to assume that leadership, he believed, the Egyptians themselves had to form the basis of the state, and hence he remodeled the army.

> Mehmet understood the growing weakness of the regime in Istanbul and believed that Egypt was the site for a renewal of Islamic power: its economic might, coupled with its proximity to the holy cities of the Arabian Peninsula, made it the natural successor as leader of the Islamic world.

By 1820 he had conscripted thirty thousand Egyptians and turned them into a disciplined force, and by the end of his life in 1848 the army numbered 150,000 or more. This was the first truly Egyptian military force—with ethnic Egyptians making up the rank and file and gradually staffing the officers' ranks as well—since the days of the pharaohs. Mehmet wanted a modern army too, with modern weaponry, and so he established close ties with industrialized England, from whom he acquired not only modern rifles and artillery but also military trainers to instruct his soldiers. He also put together a new navy with ships purchased from England, France, Italy, and Greece. By 1830 he had constructed his own new shipyard at Alexandria, which began to produce a steady stream of frigates and men-of-war. Once his navy was fully developed, Mehmet launched a combined land and sea attack against the Ottomans, taking Jerusalem, Acre, Damascus, Beirut, and Aleppo in quick succession until, by peace treaty in 1833, he ruled all of Palestine and Syria in addition to Egypt. He also sent a force into Arabia itself, and briefly controlled both Mecca and Medina.

Mehmet Ali ruled as an autocrat but reorganized and professionalized the government along Western lines, with a central cabinet composed of ministries

Negotiating with the Europeans   David Roberts (1796-1864) produced this lithograph of the great social reformer Muhammad Ali Pasha (r. 1805-1848) receiving European dignitaries in his palace at Alexandria, Egypt. Roberts spent several years in Egypt and the Middle East drawing sketches from which he later produced color prints, which he published in nine hugely popular volumes.

of war, finance, foreign relations, education, and commerce. In trade, he directed Egypt's exports away from the Ottomans and toward Europe. He supported the introduction of cotton cultivation along the Nile, and soon Egyptian cotton began to be shipped to the factories of England. As soon as the engineering skill was available, Mehmet Ali also constructed his own textile plants and sugar refineries, too. He appointed European administrators and civil engineers to improve the sanitation of cities, and he hired Europeans to head new military academies and polytechnic (vocational) schools.[13] Newspapers were introduced, appearing in both Arabic and French. New centers for translating European technical manuals into Arabic were set up, along with publishing houses to produce the works.

REFORMING ISLAM

The opening up to Europe helped to inspire an intellectual and cultural revival in Egypt known as **al-Nahda** ("awakening" or "renaissance"), which some writers describe as an Islamic Enlightenment. Most of the thinkers associated with

---

[13] In the 19th century, roughly one-tenth of the urban populations in Egypt died each year from infectious disease.

al-Nahda believed that Muslim society faced being surpassed by Europe's economic, military, and technological might and thus needed to open its arms and minds to ideas from the outside world. As in their great medieval empire, Muslims could actually strengthen and deepen their culture, they believed, for customs from abroad could be harmonized with Islamic values.

The first great figure in the movement was Rifa'a al-Tahtawi (1801–1873). He had been sent to Paris, along with a corps of younger students, by Mehmet Ali Pasha in 1826 in order to learn French, study Western ideas, and develop closer understanding between Europe and the Islamic world. After a stay of five years, Tahtawi wrote a celebrated memoir (*The Essence of Paris*) in which he recounts his group's excitement at learning Western law, philosophy, mathematics, and science. He read Voltaire, Rousseau, and Montesquieu. He wrote volumes on social theory, citizenship and political rights, and moral philosophy. After returning to Cairo, he established the School of Languages (1835), which not only instructed students in languages but also served as a central clearinghouse for ideas about secular government, national identity, and cultural pluralism. Tahtawi believed passionately in the integration of Islam and European culture. This was possible, he argues, because Europe had separated its religion from its political and civic traditions. Key to this integration, he contends, is the notion of **citizenship**—a form of group identity that is not determined by race, creed, or ethnicity. Rather, one chooses to join a community and acts as a member in good standing of it. A nation, in the modern sense, Tahtawi urges, consists of people who share not just an allegiance to a vision of the past but a vision for the future.

> A nation, in the modern sense, Tahtawi urges, consists of people who share not just an allegiance to a vision of the past but a vision for the future.

The other major school of Islamic thought, however, thoroughly rejected, condemned, and demonized modernization. The clerics and writers known ultimately as **Wahhabis** were conservatives and traditionalists, but nationalists too in their way. Named for a mirthless cleric from central Arabia, Muhammad ibn Abd al-Wahhab (1703–1792), the Wahhabi movement declared that the overwhelming majority of Muslims throughout the entire world—Sunni, Shi'a, and Sufi—had fallen into a state of spiritual ignorance and moral barbarism. What had caused this religious desolation? Ignorance of the meaning of the Qur'anic concept of *tawhid*—the "unity" of God. Interpreting this concept in the strictest possible fashion, Wahhabis emphasized that God is the One, the Only, the Creator, the Divine. Any act of religious observance that diverted attention from him was an abomination. Acts such as charity to the poor or the veneration of shrines bestowed on human beings or physical spaces the devotion owed solely to God. As al-Wahhab once wrote:

It is well-known that the Messenger of God (Peace be upon him!) obliged the faithful to observe *tawhid* many years before obliging them to the Pillars of Islam.... *Tawhid* is supreme among religious duties, more important than prayer, alms, fasting, and pilgrimage.

Anything and everything that distracts the soul from recognizing the Supreme One is an abomination. Wahhabism accepts as historical facts the miracles performed by Islamic saints, but it forbids veneration of the saints who performed them or the shrines where they are entombed. That would be idolatry. To give alms to the poor is a religious requirement, but it is idolatrous to do so out of love for the poor rather than love of God. Only by returning to a pure and martial faith—ideally to practices in existence during the lifetime of the Prophet himself—could the moral horror of the modern world be erased and an authentic Muslim society established.

Abd al-Wahhab never articulated a full body of teachings on government. Drawing his inspiration from the 14th-century conservative jurist Ibn Taymiyya, he stressed the moral responsibility of the ruler to destroy all forms of idolatry—if necessary, by force. Any ruler who adhered to Wahhabi ideals and enforced its strict moral code would be acceptable. Al-Wahhab taught that every true Muslim (meaning his followers) must refuse to obey political and clerical authorities who do not maintain the proper attitude toward tawhid. It was not until well after his death in 1792 that his clerical successors began to formulate a coherent set of ideas regarding governance; most drew their main ideas directly from Ibn Taymiyya. Ibn Taymiyya had identified "innovation in religion" as a second abomination, equal to that of idolatry, and called for relentless state action to stamp it out in all its forms. His Wahhabi acolytes did the same in the 19th century.

The Arab prince Muhammad ibn Saud enthusiastically embraced the teachings of the Taymiyya-Wahhabi sect in the middle of the 18th century. Ibn Saud was an ambitious figure, determined to free Arabia from foreign control and create a new Arab-led society that would restore Islam's greatness and purge it of the vile "innovations" that had crept into its practice through the centuries. Two enemies, as he saw it, stood out among many—the Ottomans and the Sufis. By 1765, when Ibn Saud died, he had conquered much of central Arabia and parts of the east. His succeeding son, grandson, and great-grandson extended the conquests, until by 1818 nearly the entire peninsula, including the holy cities, was under their control (see Map 19.7). At this point, the Egyptian reformer Mehmet Ali, acting with the blessing of the Ottoman ruler in Istanbul, launched his own attack on Arabia, to wrest the holy sites from Saudi control and liberate them from Wahhabi doctrine and practice. He succeeded for a time, but Saudi determination and the fast-growing sense of Arab nationalism won control back for them in 1824. This Second Saudi State lasted from 1824 to 1891.

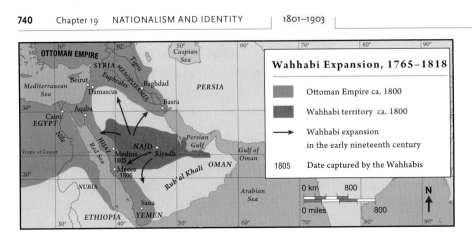

MAP 19.7   Wahhabi Expansion, 1765–1818

A key element of Wahhabism, based on the Taymiyyism of the 14th century, is the notion that only Arabs can reform and save Islam. The religious revelation vouchsafed to the Prophet Muhammad called first for the unification of the Arab tribes and only afterward for bringing the Prophet's message to all mankind. Islamic reform movements throughout history have had an ethnic or nationalist element, beginning with the Shi'a tradition, which asserted the primacy of religious authority among those directly descended from the Prophet. In medieval times, the Abbasids urged the Persianization of Islamic life in order to unify groups embracing the faith. The Almoravid and Almohad movements of the 11th and 12th centuries called for a restoration of rigorous jihad under leadership by the Berbers of North Africa. The arrival of the Seljuk Turks triggered the start of a conservative Sunni crackdown on the Shi'a (though under Turkish leadership), but also broadened the appeal of the Sufi movement. The Mongols and Tatars had no doubts about who was meant to control and reform the Islamic world. And the arrival of the Ottoman Turks encouraged a new openness to non-Islamic culture—although under the Ottomans' own strict control. In the 14th century Ibn Taymiyya was the first figure of note to call for the restoration of Islamic leadership to those to whom Allah himself had granted it, the Arabs. In its 19th-century Wahhabi version, Saudi-based Arab nationalism simply completed a historical cycle that restored leadership to the people who had been privileged to wield it first.

> In its 19th-century Wahhabi version, Saudi-based Arab nationalism simply completed a historical cycle that restored leadership to the people who had been privileged to wield it first.

The fast-crumbling Ottoman Empire, for its part, tried to counter the pro-Western nationalism exemplified by Egypt and the Wahhabi nationalism of the Saudis. The empire's Tanzimat (Turkish for "reform"), which flourished from

1839 to 1876, represented a last-ditch effort to hold onto power.[14] Its essence was to promote civic secularism while protecting religious pluralism. Especially within its shrunken political borders, the Ottoman realm was too diverse, both ethnically and religiously, to conflate religion and civic life. So the Ottomans proposed, if anything, a different kind of nationalism—one based not on race or creed but on secular government and religious freedom. They built more schools, reorganized curricula, and encouraged newspapers and magazines. They enacted

ARMÉE OTTOMANE

SADIK-BEY
Colonel d'infanterie, aide de camp de
S. M. I. le Sultan.

RIZA-BEY
Commandant de cavalerie, aide de camp
de S. M. I. le Sultan.

CHEFKET-BEY
Lieutenant-colonel d'artillerie.

Uniformed Secularism   Portrait of three leaders of the increasingly secular and professional Turkish army. The religiously trained and motivated Janissaries had been disbanded in 1826, after they had attempted a coup. The great reform era known as Tanzimat ("Re-organization") lasted from 1839 to 1876, during which the empire attempted to integrate its non-Muslim subjects more fully into society, while modernizing its institutions and legal processes. In the end, the empire fell victim to the intense nationalist passions of the nineteenth century.

---

[14]   Tanzimat failed to sustain the empire, but it helped to lay the foundations for the modern nation of Turkey after World War I.

laws promising equality for all subjects regardless of faith. They even appointed Christians and Jews to reform councils to advise the government, as well as to the Supreme Judicial Council, which acted as an appellate court. The fact that the Arab world violently rejected these reforms and called for an end to Ottoman power shows the depths of nationalist passions.

WHO, WHAT, WHERE

Act of Union	midrashic
al-Nahda	nationalism
anti-Semitism	Oath of Supremacy
citizenship	Pale of Settlement
Crimean War	pogroms
Junkers	Wahhabis
Kulturkampf	Zionism
Mehmet Ali Pasha	

SUGGESTED READINGS

Primary Sources

Bismarck, Otto von. *Memoirs.*

Fichte, Johann Gottlieb. *Address to the German Nation.*

Herzl, Theodor. *The Jewish State.*

———. *Old New Land.*

Mazzini, Giuseppe. *The Duties of Man.*

Renan, Ernest. *What Is a Nation?*

Seacole, Mary. *Wonderful Adventures of Mrs. Seacole in Many Lands.*

al-Tahtawi, Rifa'a. *The Emancipation of Muslim Women.*

———. *The Essence of Paris.*

Anthologies

Kurzman, Charles, ed. *Modernist Islam, 1840–1940: A Sourcebook* (2002).

Spencer, Philip, and Howard Wollman, eds. *Nations and Nationalism: A Reader* (2005).

Studies

Aksan, Virginia H. *Ottoman Wars, 1700–1870: An Empire Besieged* (2007).

Akşin, Sina. *Turkey from Empire to Revolutionary Republic: The Emergence of the Turkish Nation from 1789 to the Present* (2007).

Anderson, Benedict. *Imagined Communities: Reflections on the Origin and Spread of Nationalism* (2006).

Baron, Beth. *Egypt as a Woman: Nationalism, Gender, and Politics* (2007).

Bayly, C. A. *The Birth of the Modern World, 1780–1914* (2003).

Ceylan, Ebubekir. *The Ottoman Origins of Modern Iraq: Political Reform, Modernization, and Development in the Nineteenth-Century Middle East* (2011).

Çiçek, Nazan. *The Young Ottomans: Turkish Critics of the Eastern Question in the Late Nineteenth Century* (2010).

Clark, Christopher. *Iron Kingdom: The Rise and Downfall of Prussia, 1600–1947* (2009).

Eichner, Carolyn J. *Surmounting the Barricades: Women in the Paris Commune* (2004).

Eley, Geoff. *Forging Democracy: The History of the Left in Europe, 1850–2000* (2002).

Elon, Amos. *The Pity of It All: A Portrait of the German-Jewish Epoch, 1743–1933* (2003).

Fahmy, Khaled. *All the Pasha's Men: Mehmed Ali, His Army, and the Making of Modern Egypt* (2002).

Frankel, Richard E. *Bismarck's Shadow: The Cult of Leadership and the Transformation of the German Right, 1898–1945* (2005).

Gellner, Ernest. *Nations and Nationalism* (2009).

Gerwarth, Robert. *The Bismarck Myth: Weimar Germany and the Legacy of the Iron Chancellor* (2005).

Gross, Michael B. *The War against Catholicism: Liberalism and the Anti-Catholic Imagination in Nineteenth-Century Germany* (2005).

Hall, Catherine, Keith McClelland, and Jane Rendall. *Defining the Victorian Nation: Class, Race, Gender, and the British Reform Act of 1867* (2000).

Harvey, David. *Paris: Capital of Modernity* (2005).

Hewitson, Mark. *Nationalism in Germany, 1848–1866: Revolutionary Nation* (2010).

Khuri-Makdisi, Ilham. *The Eastern Mediterranean and the Making of Global Radicalism, 1860–1914* (2010).

Langewiesche, Dieter. *Liberalism in Germany* (2000).

Lerman, Katharine Anne. *Bismarck* (2004).

Offen, Karen. *European Feminisms, 1700–1950: A Political History* (2000).

Pollard, Lisa. *Nurturing the Nation: The Family Politics of Modernizing, Colonizing, and Liberating Egypt, 1805–1923* (2005).

Porter, Brian. *When Nationalism Began to Hate: Imagining Modern Politics in Nineteenth-Century Poland* (2002).

Smith, Anthony D. *The Ethnic Origins of Nations* (2009).

———. *Nationalism: Theory, Ideology, History* (2002).

Wawro, Geoffrey. *The Franco-Prussian War: The German Conquest of France in 1870–1871* (2005).

Wetzel, David. *A Duel of Giants: Bismarck, Napoleon III, and the Origins of the Franco-Prussian War* (2003).

For additional resources, including maps, primary sources, visuals, web links, and quizzes, please go to **www.oup.com/us/backman**.

CHAPTER 20

The God Problem

1799–1907

"God is dead." Many people know this quotation from the German philosopher Friedrich Nietzsche (1844–1900), if only from having seen it scrawled on bathroom walls, where it often comes with a rejoinder: "Nietzsche is dead—God." However, Nietzsche's statement was not, as many readers assume, a bold declaration of intellectual freedom after centuries of superstition and thought control. For him, the death of God was tragic, perhaps the worst calamity ever to befall mankind. His insight highlights the dilemmas of one of the 19th century's most striking changes: secularization, or the declining power of religious beliefs and institutions and the subsequent decline in religious practice. The ascendancy of secularism resulted from many factors but derived in large part from two of the century's greatest scientific achievements, in a new theory of earth's history and Darwin's theory of evolution by natural selection. It affected how a new generation studied the Bible itself, as part of a movement called *historical criticism*, and it drew intense and conflicted responses from all faiths across Europe.

THE VOYAGE OF THE BEAGLE, 1831–1836

ENGLAND

◀ **God Is Not Dead** Prayer card (1867) depicting pilgrims to the grotto at Lourdes, France, where a vision of the Virgin Mary occurred to St. Bernadette Soubirons. At top, Christ displays his Sacred Heart while bestowing a blessing on the church. Pilgrims look through a protective fence at the grotto—at the back of which stands the figure of Mary.

NIETZSCHE: A COSMOS WITHOUT GOD

The son, grandson, and great-grandson of Lutheran pastors, Nietzsche was steeped in Christian tradition—and like so many of his peers, he had left his faith behind by his mid-twenties. Yet rather than rejoicing in the power of the rational mind released at last, he saw only ruin and misery. In his 1882 book *The Gay Science*, he cast the dilemma as a parable.

> Have you heard the tale of the lunatic who lit his lantern early one morning and ran into the marketplace shouting out, "I want to find God! I want to see God!" Since many in the crowd around him did not believe in God, he stirred them to laughter.
>
> "Is God lost?" asked one.
>
> Another replied, "Maybe He has lost His way, like a little child?"
>
> "No, surely He is simply hiding, or has gone on holiday!"
>
> "Perhaps He emigrated instead!"
>
> They all jeered and laughed, but the lunatic stood his ground. Piercing them with his eyes he cried out, "Do you want to know where God has gone? I'll tell you: We have killed him! Yes, you and I—we murdered Him!... God is dead and will remain so, and we are the ones who killed Him. What comfort is there now for us—we, the worst of all murderers! The holiest and most powerful force ever to have existed has bled to death, cut open by our knives, and there is no one who can wipe the bloodstain from our hands. What water can possibly wash it away? What rites of atonement, what sacred mysteries would have to be invented [to purify us]? Is not the deed we have done too much for us to bear? Must we not become gods ourselves now, simply to appear worthy of our action?

At this, the crowd grows silent. They had not, Nietzsche saw, considered the implications of their unbelief or their mockery:

> At length the lunatic hurled his lantern to the ground, where it smashed into pieces and its light went out. Then the lunatic said, "I have come too early; it is not yet my time. News of the Great Event is still

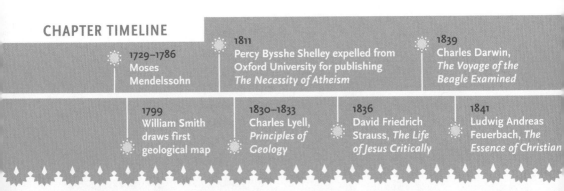

approaching, still on the move, and hasn't yet reached their ears. Just as lightning and thunder require time [to reach men's awareness], as starlight does too, so do deeds require time before men can perceive them and understand—and the meaning of this particular deed is still further from these men than even the most distant stars. And yet they themselves did it!"

It is said that the lunatic later pushed his way into several churches and struck up a funeral prayer, crying "May God rest in eternal peace!" Each time, when he was led outside and asked to explain himself, he replied only, "What are churches now but the tombs and mausoleums of the Lord?" *(The Gay Science, no. 125)*

A cosmos without God, Nietzsche understood, is purposeless and without meaning. The universe becomes a vast sprawl of indifference. An act of creation meant that life exists for a reason. If there is no Creator, all that exists is a random gathering of molecules—beautiful, perhaps, but in the end pointless and spiritually void. Worst of all, human life has no intrinsic value. I may be kindhearted and charitable, with love for everyone around me; or I may selfishly hoard material goods, seize whatever sexual pleasures I desire, and smash the skulls of anyone I wish to harm. It makes no difference at all. The world will continue on its way, and all my actions, whether "good" or "bad," will be forgotten. It certainly is "nicer" to be kind than to be selfish—but niceness is no substitute for God. If human existence is a mere crack of light between eternities of darkness, then why not take whatever pleasures one desires while one can? This is, after all, the only opportunity one will ever have to experience them.

> Nietzsche was not the first philosopher to consider the implications of a Godless universe, but he felt those implications so deeply that his writings still have the power to shock, enthrall, enrage, and horrify readers.

Nietzsche Friedrich Nietzsche (1844–1900), the philosopher of the death of God.

Nietzsche was not the first philosopher to consider the implications of a Godless universe, but he felt those implications so deeply that his writings still have the power to shock, enthrall, enrage, and horrify readers. He is one of the very few philosophers to whom people respond viscerally. But that was his aim—to shake us out of our intellectual complacency and force us to confront painful questions. If "God is dead," this is precisely why we have to start thinking harder than we have ever done. And without delaying a single instant.

The 19th century marks a watershed in European history, the period when Western culture began to turn decidedly secular. Since the dawn of Western history in 3000 BCE, religion had formed an essential part of the bedrock of its culture. Religious doubters, rebels, skeptics, heretics, and critics existed in every faith and every age, but genuine nonbelief was rare. How else could one explain the existence of the world than by a god? From ancient Greece forward, virtually all leading scientists—from Aristotle to Newton—were people of religious conviction. Philosophers from Plato to René Descartes (1596–1650), Baruch Spinoza (1632–77), Immanuel Kant (1724–1804), and Georg Friedrich Hegel (1770–1831) all retained passionate, if sometimes quirky, convictions about God. Even the most irreligious of the Enlightened, Voltaire, acknowledged the existence of a divine creator. **Atheism** existed, and indeed the word dates back to the 16th century, but its usage was limited to "godlessness" in the moral sense—of "godless" behavior.[1] Except for Nietzsche, almost everyone yet mentioned in this book accepted the existence of one or more deities—and based ethical behavior at least partly on that belief.

What, then, had happened? Why did the rejection, or mere absence, of religious belief suddenly become so prominent in European society? In 1811 the Romantic poet Percy Bysshe Shelley (1792–1822) was expelled from Oxford University when he was discovered to be the author of a pamphlet called *The Necessity of Atheism*. In 1877, however, the Russian writer Leo Tolstoy (1828–1910) could have one character describe another, in his novel *Anna Karenina*, as

> an odd, uneducated fellow, one of those wild "modern" people one meets so often these days, a "freethinker" raised from birth with notions of nonbelief, negation, and materialism. . . . It used to be the case that a

---

[1]   The words secularism, agnosticism, and atheism (in the sense of disbelief) were all coined in the second half of the 19th century.

"freethinker" was someone who had been brought up with the ideas of religion, law, and morality, and had reached the state of freethinking after long years of personal pain and struggle. But now there is this new kind of ready-made freethinker—the ones who grow up without ever even hearing that there once were such things as moral laws and religious convictions, and that these were the authorities in life. These new folks, now, simply grow up in a world where all this is rejected out of hand—which is to say, they grow up as savages. *(Anna Karenina 5.9)*

From the passionate and risk-taking rejection of God to a world in which it simply does not occur to many to wonder about God's existence is quite a leap into the dark. Or into the light, depending on one's point of view.

WHO KILLED GOD?

The decline of Christianity in 19th-century Europe resulted from a host of factors. Industrial capitalism figures large. The working class wrenched millions of Europeans from their rural parishes and deposited them in dense and wretched urban settings, in which there was little or no organized religious life. Forced to work twelve to fourteen hours a day in factories, six days a week, with few churches or clergy members available, many of the working poor simply lost the habit of attending church. And given widespread illiteracy, there was insufficient Bible reading or private devotions to compensate. In cities from Manchester to Milan, and from Oporto to Prague, thousands of gleaming new churches were built or revamped, yet these lay overwhelmingly in tidy middle-class precincts that few working-class people could reach—and those people would have felt distinctly out of place and unwelcome even if they could have reached them.

Another cause of unease was the institution of the "established church," meaning the legal proclamation of a specific Christian tradition as the official faith of a nation. United Italy designated Roman Catholicism as its state religion; England had its Anglican Church and Scotland its Presbyterian Church. Each of the provinces of united Germany had its own national church, and the alliances between governments and the Orthodox Churches in eastern Europe and Russia date back to the Middle Ages. Popular discontent with a government's policies frequently resulted in popular dissatisfaction with the church. Meanwhile the bourgeois classes that benefited most from the industrial economy came to represent the centers of power within each government.

Less directly involved, though still a factor, was prosperity itself. 19th-century Europe witnessed a proliferation of new department stores, exhibition halls,

Temple of Consumerism   The grand staircase at Le Bon Marché department store in Paris. The founder of the store was Aristide Boucicaut (1810-1877), who credited much his success to his promotion of his store as a place where proper bourgeois women could meet without chaperones.

The untimely death of deeply loved relations, friends, or romantic partners has proved through the centuries to be a powerful impulse to religious meditations. Without the painful presence of death, once a constant in life even with the best available medical care, it became easier to avoid thinking about it.

museums, sports venues, theaters, music halls, and restaurants.[2] All these challenged the traditional role of churches as centers of community. As church became a once-a-week, Sunday-mornings-only affair, religious enthusiasm waned. And for those millions who did not share in the prosperity of the age, taverns and bodegas provided some relief from their miseries. Meanwhile, many of the most enthusiastic believers, both Protestant and Catholic, lay or clerical, left Europe to pursue missionary work overseas, often in Africa or eastern Asia.

Another contributing factor to secularism may have been modern medicine. Physicians became able to treat and cure a broader array of ailments; vaccines mitigated the horrors of cholera and smallpox; and improvements in food production and distribution lessened famine. Child mortality decreased, life expectancy increased, and more and more people lived longer and healthier lives. These were undeniably positive developments, but they contributed to secularization by lessening the presence of death in peoples' lives. This is not a trivial point. Among the middle classes who had access to modern medical care, it was not uncommon to attend only a handful of funerals in a lifetime—usually later in life when older relatives died. For comparison, England's Queen Anne (r. 1702–1707) had eighteen pregnancies, thirteen of which ended in miscarriages; four children were born but died before the age of two. Her sole surviving child died just days after his eleventh birthday. The untimely death of deeply loved relations, friends, or romantic partners has proved through the centuries to be a powerful impulse to

---

[2]   The first two department stores were Bainbridge's in Newcastle-upon-Tyne and Le Bon Marché in Paris; both opened in 1838.

religious meditations. Without the painful presence of death, once a constant in life even with the best available medical care, it became easier to avoid thinking about it.

Until the late 19th century, too, religious houses had been the main providers of social services throughout Europe: they had run hospitals and orphanages, provided education, organized soup kitchens and almshouses, and offered palliative and charitable care for the elderly and destitute. The liberal nation-states, however, gradually took over most of these roles as the century progressed, which effectively marginalized the active presence of religious life in society. From the point of view of the disaffected, churches—especially established churches—were institutions that enjoyed their tax exemptions and government subsidies while apparently catering to the well-to-do middle and upper classes. But they played a constantly declining role in most people's lives and lost popular support.

The advance of liberalism, especially after 1848, also had an indirect philosophical effect. By promoting toleration of differing traditions and dissenting views as a civic virtue, it implicitly allowed and perhaps even encouraged the circulation of ideas that directly challenged religion's traditional position of cultural authority. By making a virtue of welcoming dissent, liberal society unintentionally added to the growing sense of distance from their religious roots felt by millions. And the religious and social debates of the age reached ever increasing numbers of people thanks to the proliferation of newspapers and magazines in the second half of the century. Finally, by inviting religious plurality, liberal Europe created a marketplace of ideas that provided encouragement to many but also fostered confusion when it came to people's religious convictions. The midcentury **Oxford movement** in England, for example, aimed to confront the problem of Anglicans who no longer adhered to the traditions of Anglican Christianity because they no longer really understood them. A parallel development in Protestant Germany was the so-called Neo-Lutheran movement. Denominational and nondenominational Sunday schools began to proliferate to combat religious ignorance or indifference.[3]

Toleration contributed to the rise of **secularism** by redefining civic virtues. The earliest secularists did not present themselves publicly as enemies of Christianity but rather as champions of nonpartisanship. George Jacob Holyoake (1817–1906), the most prominent early campaigner for civic secularism in England, described his position in this way:

> Secularism is not an argument against Christianity; it is one independent of it. It does not question the pretensions of Christianity; it

---

[3]   The first known Sunday school, at Surrey Chapel in London, opened around 1800 and enrolled as many as three thousand children by 1860.

advances others. Secularism does not say there is no light or guidance elsewhere, but maintains that there is light and guidance in secular truth, whose conditions and sanctions exist independently, and act forever. Secular knowledge is manifestly that kind of knowledge which is founded in this life, which relates to the conduct of this life, conduces to the welfare of this life, and is capable of being tested by the experience of this life. *(Origin and Nature of Secularism, 1896)*

Holyoake was briefly imprisoned for blasphemy in 1842. The secularist cause was given formal order by the creation of groups like England's National Secular Society, founded in 1866, and Germany's Freethinkers' League (*Freidenkerbund*), established in 1881.

The last person imprisoned for blasphemy in England was John William Gott (1866–1922), a salesman in the garment trade. Gott's crime was not rejection of Christianity but mockery of it. In 1921 he had published a series of crude pamphlets, one of which depicted Jesus dressed like a circus clown, standing on the backs of two donkeys as he entered Jerusalem. Condemned to nine months' hard labor, Gott completed his sentence but, his health broken, died shortly after his release.

THE THEORY OF CREATION

Secularism found a target in one of the most notorious false beliefs of its time— the date of Creation. It found new weapons, too—in science's attempts to trace history in the earth and in evolution by natural selection.

James Ussher (1581–1656) was a brilliant and saintly Anglo-Irish Protestant scholar, the archbishop of Armagh and primate of all Ireland who helped calm the Irish religious and political scene during the panicked violence of the English Civil War; unfortunately, he is remembered today chiefly for a single ridiculous idea. In 1648, the same year when the Peace of Westphalia put an end to the Wars of Religion and inaugurated the age of absolutist governments, Ussher published a lengthy study of biblical history entitled *The Annals of the Old Testament*, which attempted to work backward through the detailed chronologies given in the Hebrew Bible and thereby calculate the likely dates of the most important events it describes. The ancient Jews, Greeks, Romans, and early Christians all used different calendars, some lunar, some solar, and all originating at different points. This made the task immensely complex—especially since Ussher correlated their particulars with the astronomical tables of Johannes Kepler and the calendrical measurements used by the ancient Egyptians and Persians. After years of painstaking research, Bishop Ussher opened his *Annals* with the solemn announcement that God began his six-day labor of Creation, as related in the initial chapter of Genesis, at sunset on the evening preceding Sunday, October 23, in the year 4004 BCE—making the world around him exactly 5,652 years old.

His conclusion was remarkable more for its precision than for its originality; attempts to determine the date of Creation by means of the Bible's many genealogies and royal lists were as old as the Bible itself. The Jewish calendar's Year 1—the year *before* God began his work of Creation—corresponds to the year 3760 BCE, and the astronomer Johannes Kepler calculated Creation to have occurred in 3992 BCE. Isaac Newton himself, a half century after Ussher, concluded that the Creation took place in the year 4000 BCE. The belief that the world in the 19th century was approaching six thousand years old was surprisingly widespread, and Ussher's chronology was commonly printed inside editions of the Authorized (King James) Version of the Bible until the early 19th century.[4] In the United States an edition known as the Scofield Reference Bible, which included the King James Version and an annotated update of Ussher's chronology, appeared in the years immediately prior to the American entry into World War I. It sold more than two million copies before the middle of the 20th century and became the foundation of the Christian-fundamentalist challenge to the theory of evolution.

The theory of the 4004 BCE Creation never had official recognition from any of the mainstream Christian churches in the West, and it came under direct attack from the work of three British scientists: two geologists, William Smith (1769–1839) and Sir Charles Lyell (1797–1875), and the biologist Charles Darwin (1809–1882). Smith was the self-educated son of a village blacksmith; apprenticed to a surveyor working to map out canals for the great industrial boom then underway, he developed a passionate interest in geological formations and fossils. He taught himself map drawing and in 1799 produced a geological map of the area around the city of Bath in Somerset. It showed consistent relationships between the various strata of stone and their fossil remains, illustrating the development over time of the entire region.

The success of this map, and the enthusiasm it raised among other geologists, inspired Smith to his greatest project—a map of the entire geological structure of Britain, which he published in 1815. Smith's maps, and the detailed data he published along with them, pointed to rock strata composed of like materials and containing similar fossils. These can be connected to create a picture of the formation of the land. In other words, he provided clear evidence that the British

---

4   Ussher identified 2348 BCE as the date of Noah's Ark and the Great Flood and 1491 BCE as the year when Moses led the Exodus of the Jews from Egypt.

A Map that Changed the World   William Smith published his geological map of Britain in 1815, which made clear that the the island emerged gradually over time, rather than appeared whole from a single act of creation. Unfortunately, others plagiarized his map and subsequent books, and he fell into debt. He spent two years in debtors' prison, and afterward worked as a surveyor. Above is a detail of the map showing southwest England and part of Wales.

Isles emerged from sequential development over long periods of time rather than all-at-once creation.

Sir Charles Lyell was in many ways the antithesis of Smith. Born to a prominent Scottish family of lawyers and civil servants, Lyell went to Oxford University, traveled extensively, moved easily in society, married a famous beauty who was also a scientist, and held a professorship at King's College London. A gregarious, charming, and generous man, he made his career less by conducting field research (his eyesight was poor) than by synthesizing the investigations of others. His most important work was the three-volume *Principles of Geology* (1830–1833), which, surprisingly, became a bestseller.

Lyell's main contribution was the popularization of the theory called **uniformitarianism,** originally proposed by another Scottish geologist, James Hutton (1726–1797). The theory stated that geological change consists of the slow accumulation of smaller changes—and these changes continue to happen in the present. The idea seems self-evident today, but it was a radical challenge to a world that believed that the earth's entire history covered less than six thousand years. Lyell's theory demanded hundreds of thousands of years for the physical record to make sense. The fact that Lyell himself was known to be a deeply committed Christian gave his theory additional force; it was well known that he accepted his own theory only because the evidence for it was so overwhelming. And he continued to expand and revise this theory through twelve editions of *Principles* and through six editions of a subsequent study called *Elements of Geology*.

EVOLUTION BY NATURAL SELECTION

The young English naturalist Charles Darwin read Lyell's *Principles of Geology* while on a five-year voyage (1831–1836) aboard the HMS *Beagle*, exploring the coasts of South America and its outlying islands. Several papers that he delivered after his return to England, along with the publication of his travelogue *The Voyage of the Beagle* (1839), established his reputation as a scientist and writer of rare gifts. He and Lyell became lifelong friends, and their relationship grew ever closer despite Lyell's resistance to Darwin's great contribution—his **theory of evolution by natural selection**. Some of the fundamental ideas behind it had been around for several years; yet no one had pieced them together with as much geological support and analysis as Darwin. Moreover, although other scholars had suggested that species change over time, none had come up with an explanation for why they did so. Darwin supplied a powerful one, and it is the central idea behind the science of biology today.

Darwin's theory, worked out in detail in the years after his voyage, dealt wholly with the animal world, but it clearly implied that human beings evolved in a similar manner. Darwin posited natural selection as the means by which evolution occurs. First, nature produces a superabundance of offspring in each generation. A single grain of wheat, for example, produces a wheat shaft that contains dozens of new grains, or a single female salmon lays hundreds of eggs that are then fertilized by the millions of sperm cells produced by the male salmon. Second, this superabundance results in a contest among those offspring for the resources necessary for life. This contest will favor individuals who have a unique ability that gives them an advantage over their rivals. And third, this preferred characteristic, whatever it might be, is then passed on to its offspring. Eventually, this will allow the species to develop into a new form.

> As many more individuals of each species are born than can possibly survive; and as, consequently, there is a frequently recurring struggle for existence, it follows that any being, if it vary however slightly in any

manner profitable to itself, under the complex and sometimes varying conditions of life, will have a better chance of surviving, and thus be *naturally selected*. From the strong principle of inheritance, any selected variety will tend to propagate its new and modified form.   *(The Origin of the Species, ch. 1)*

Even though Darwin could observe the effects of natural selection, he did not have a scientific basis for explaining how it actually happened. Today, the science of genetics tells us how that inheritance takes place. All living things and all their organs are made up of tiny cells, and all cells carry within them genes—which they pass on to the next generation. However, this basic unit of heredity may change, and the accumulation of slow changes, as in geology, may change a species.

Darwin spent fifteen years working out the details of his theory—which he finally published as **On the Origin of Species by Means of Natural Selection** in 1859. Darwin ended the book with a plea that it be seen as a celebration of life rather than as an attack on cherished assumptions:

> Authors of the highest eminence seem to be fully satisfied with the view that each species has been independently created. To my mind it

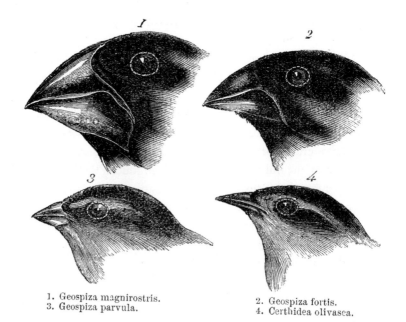

1. Geospiza magnirostris.
3. Geospiza parvula.

2. Geospiza fortis.
4. Certhidea olivasea.

Endless Forms Most Beautiful   Prints made from drawings by Charles Darwin (1809-1882) while on his trip to the Galápagos islands, published in his *Voyage of the Beagle* (1839). Here he shows some of the variation in the beaks of finches.

accords better with what we know of the laws impressed on matter by the Creator, that the production and extinction of the past and present inhabitants of the world should have been due to secondary causes, like those determining the birth and death of the individual. When I view all beings not as special creations, but as the lineal descendants of some few beings which lived long before the first bed of the Silurian system was deposited, they seem to me to become ennobled. Judging from the past, we may safely infer that not one living species will transmit its unaltered likeness to a distant futurity. And of the species now living very few will transmit progeny of any kind to a far distant futurity.... As all the living forms of life are the lineal descendants of those which lived long before the Silurian epoch, we may feel certain that the ordinary succession by generation has never once been broken, and that no cataclysm has desolated the whole world. Hence we may look with some confidence to a secure future of equally inappreciable length. And as natural selection works solely by and for the good of each being, all corporeal and mental endowments will tend to progress towards perfection.

It is interesting to contemplate an entangled bank, clothed with many plants of many kinds, with birds singing on the bushes, with various insects flitting about, and with worms crawling through the damp earth, and to reflect that these elaborately constructed forms, so different from each other, and dependent on each other in so complex a manner, have all been produced by laws acting around us. These laws, taken in the largest sense, being Growth with Reproduction; inheritance which is almost implied by reproduction; Variability from the indirect and direct action of the external conditions of life, and from use and disuse; a Ratio of Increase so high as to lead to a Struggle for Life, and as a consequence to Natural Selection, entailing Divergence of Character and the Extinction of less-improved forms. Thus, from the war of nature, from famine and death, the most exalted object which we are capable of conceiving, namely, the production of the higher animals, directly follows. There is grandeur in this view of life, with its several powers, having been originally breathed into a few forms or into one; and that, whilst this planet has gone cycling on according to the fixed law of gravity, from so simple a beginning endless forms most beautiful and most wonderful have been, and are being, evolved.

Within the scientific community, Darwin's theory of evolution carried the day. Even Lyell eventually endorsed it. His problem was not with evolution itself but with the idea of natural selection. It seemed to undermine the notion of a heavenly plan; it could even dismiss the need for a Creator altogether. Others, however, saw no reason why Darwin's work had to be regarded as an attack on religion. A popular novelist and historian of the day, Charles Kingsley (1819–1875), who was also an Anglican priest, sent Darwin a letter immediately after its publication:

> [It] is just as noble a conception of Deity to believe that He created primal forms capable of self development into all forms needful . . . as to believe that He required a fresh act of intervention to supply the lacunas which He Himself had made. I question whether the former be not the loftier thought.

Not only could the Anglican priest accept so "non-Christian a theory as evolution"; he delighted in it.[5]

A famous debate took place at the Oxford Association for the Advancement of Science in 1860 between Darwin's most vocal champion, Thomas Huxley (1825–1895), and Samuel Wilberforce (1805–1873), then the bishop of Oxford. Darwin did not attend. His work on *The Origin of Species* had been so all-consuming that his health broke down while he was completing it. Angry words flew across the stage, and the crowd roared and jeered; in the end, both sides declared victory. While inconclusive, this debate set the tone for the war of words that ensued in lecture halls, pulpits, newspapers and magazines, common rooms, and at dinner tables across England and the Continent.

For many people, opposition to evolution was visceral. By validating the notion of an earth that was hundreds of millions of years old, they felt, it removed God from the creation of life. It seemed not only to contradict biblical tradition but to be holding it up to ridicule. Darwin's later book *The Descent of Man* (1871) stated explicitly what *The Origin of Species* had only implied: human beings themselves were the product of evolution and had emerged from more primitive species.[6] Cartoonists rushed

---

5   "What can be more delightful to me," Kingsley is said to have replied at an aristocratic dinner, "than to know that Your Ladyship and I sprang from the same toadstool?"

6   Darwin never claimed that humans are descended from apes. Instead, humans and apes are descended from a remote common ancestor. 'Some ancient member of the anthropomorphous subgroup gave birth to man,' he writes in ch. 6 of *The Descent of Man*. This subgroup includes a variety of apelike creatures, such as the gorilla, chimpanzee, and orangutan (and their forebears).

to depict Darwin derisively as an ape-man. His bald head, strong facial features, and flowing white beard—which he had grown to cover some of the effects of his long illness—were well suited to caricature.

The notion of all earthly life as a struggle for existence seemed coldly harsh. That the fittest survive at the expense of the rest seemed irreconcilable with a loving Creator. The Bible's apparent evidence that the world was created in 4004 BCE could be set aside easily enough by interpreting its dates as merely symbolic. Abraham did not literally live to be 175 years old (Genesis 25.7), it might be said; the high number of years attributed to him simply symbolized great age and wisdom. However, Scripture repeatedly asserts that the loving God made the cosmos as a thing of supreme beauty and order, all set in motion according to his divine plan. This was tough to square with the arbitrary ruthlessness of Darwin's world-as-battlefield. If the Bible's most fundamental traditions and moral teachings can be set aside as mistaken, then what is left?

Ape-man   Darwin suffered from ill health most of his life adult life (he ultimately died of heart disease), and the intense exertion of writing his *Origin of Species* nearly killed him. During a long convalescence he grew out his beard, which together with his advancing baldness gave him a distinctive look that was easily and sometimes cruelly caricatured. Here he is shown as half man and half monkey, trying to teach another monkey about its identity.

THE BIBLE AND HISTORY

Can the authority of the Scriptures be salvaged? It all depends on how one reads them, answered a new group of biblical scholars on the Continent. These new scholars referred to their work as **higher criticism** or **historical criticism** in order to differentiate it from the type of literary work that seeks to establish improved editions of texts corrupted through faulty copying and printing. Instead, they sought to determine the origins of the biblical texts in time and place.

The Gospel of Matthew, for instance, places unique emphasis on proving how Jesus's acts fulfill Hebrew prophecy. For the new scholars, this suggests that Matthew wrote his book specifically for a Jewish audience—and further, that he may have originally written the text in Hebrew or Aramaic instead of the Greek in which we have it. Specific episodes of Jesus's life are repeated across the first three Gospels. This suggests not only that the Gospels borrowed from one another but hints at the existence of an otherwise unknown, missing collection of source material (now known to biblical scholars as "Q") from which they drew.

Some reevaluation of religion may have been expected after the convulsions of the Scientific Revolution and the Enlightenment, which had challenged so many aspects of religious tradition. But the goal of this new type of criticism was not mere appreciation. It was closer to forensic analysis—of a sort that one might find at the scene of a crime or in a courtroom.

The first great scholar of this sort was Friedrich Schleiermacher (1768–1834), a Lutheran pastor and professor of theology at the newly established University of Berlin. Schleiermacher did some early work in historical criticism, but he is best known for training the generation of critics that followed, many of whom became associated in one way or another with the University of Tübingen in southern Germany. His pupil David Friedrich Strauss (1808–1874) ignited a scandal when he published *The Life of Jesus, Critically Examined* (1836), in which he stripped Jesus's life of all its miraculous aspects. He argued that tales of Christ's astonishing deeds, and indeed his resurrection, were simply literary devices—magical set pieces drawn from centuries-old mythological tales.

In wanting to persuade readers that Jesus was in fact the Messiah promised in Jewish prophecy, Strauss argues, the writers of the Gospels simply invented episodes of spiritual derring-do, like plot devices in a film script, that echoed episodes from the Old Testament. Thus the scene of Jesus's walking on the water to join his disciples on their fishing boat never actually occurred; it is rather a fictional echo of both the Noah's Ark story and the tale of Jonah and the whale—but with salvation coming over the water's surface, instead of God's wrath. The tale of the Virgin Birth, according to Strauss, was nothing more than an effort to give Jesus as remarkable an entrance into history as they could muster.

More daring still, he insists that even the accounts of Jesus's resurrection from death are just adaptations of earlier legends, like the deaths and resurrections of Mithras or Osiris, that early Christian followers found useful in winning converts. While he professed to admire "the Jesus of history" even though he rejected "the Christ of faith," Strauss unsettled readers across Europe. A reviewer of the English translation, Lord Shaftesbury (1801–1885), called Strauss's volume "the most pestilential book, I think, ever vomited out of the jaws of hell."

Stripping away all supernatural elements to discover "the historical Jesus" became the rallying cry of the new scholarship. Five years later another German academic, Ludwig Andreas Feuerbach (1804–1872), published a dense volume called *The Essence of Christianity* (1841) that mounted an even more radical attack on biblical faith. To Feuerbach, the Christian God is little more than an exercise in wish fulfillment by the entire culture. Since we can imagine supreme virtues like justice, goodness, generosity, and love, he argues, we create a Being that unites these virtues and indeed personifies them. For most people, to deny the existence of the Being would be tantamount to denying the virtues themselves; and since we cannot live without believing in ideals, we create, out of our own need, the Supreme Ideal, which is God.

To long for something is to feel that it is necessary, and our sensibilities long for a personal God. But the longing for a personal God is genuine, heartfelt, and profound only when it is a longing for a single entity—only a single God can satisfy it.... Whatever we feel strongly enough is necessary we feel strongly enough to be real.... Our desire says, "A personal God must exist"—that is, it is unacceptable that God should not exist; our satisfied feeling [therefore] simply says, "He exists."... Our longing demands a crafted, sympathetic, personal God, a single One, and a historically true One. (*The Essence of Christianity, ch. 15*)

Supreme Ideal   William Blake (1757–1827) engraved and printed versions of this image numerous times. Called *The Ancient of Days*, it illustrates a biblical verse (Proverbs 8.25) and was used by Blake as the frontispiece to his work *Europe: A Prophecy* (1794). It depicts God in the process of forming the universe, holding out a compass to mark the perfection of his creation.

To Feuerbach, even the pared-down and demythologized Jesus of historical criticism is evidence of our instinctive need to believe and to seek some firm rooting for the belief.[7]

The next blow came from France. In 1863 Ernest Renan (1823–1892) published *The Life of Jesus*, the first full-scale attempt at a biography of the "historical Jesus." Renan had studied for the priesthood but lost his faith—as a result, ironically, of the curriculum at his seminary. As he came to master Biblical Hebrew, Renan saw that the traditional attributions of date and authorship for many of the Old Testament texts were incorrect. The five books of the Torah could not possibly have been written by Moses, for instance, since the books show countless

---

[7]   Strauss and Feuerbach were both translated into English by Marian Evans—who later gained fame as the novelist George Eliot (1819–1880).

Ernest Renan   Ernest Renan (1829–1892), author of *The Life of Jesus*.

signs of different authorship and of an anachronistic Hebrew vocabulary. Some texts, like parts of Deuteronomy, were clearly written many centuries after the earliest sections of Genesis. And the difficulties multiply as one progresses through the rest of the Hebrew Bible. Differences in vocabulary and grammar alone show that the book of Isaiah, for instance, has at least two and possibly three separate authors. The book of Daniel was written in its present form nearly four hundred years after the events to which it supposedly bears eyewitness.

The problem of multiple authorship challenged the tradition of accepting the Bible as the literal word of God. But even the faithful of a more liberal bent were puzzled. Would biblical books written centuries later than others therefore supersede the books that came before? If so, then why retain the earlier works at all? Worse still, historical criticism drew many similar conclusions about the New Testament. Renan's book became an international bestseller, and it has never been out of print down to the present day.

Higher criticism of the Bible quickly became a popular phenomenon, with books by new scholars (and by a few charlatans) appearing almost monthly, in every country in Europe. The German scholar (and close friend of Karl Marx) Bruno Bauer (1809–1882) declared half of the Epistles of Saint Paul in the New Testament to be forgeries. A Dutch scholar named Allard Pierson (1831–1896) declared Jesus's Sermon on the Mount to have been plagiarized from Jewish wisdom literature. Edwin Johnson (1842–1901), an Englishman, argued that there was no reliable evidence for the very existence of Jesus. Another German, Adolf von Harnack (1851–1930), perhaps the greatest Protestant theologian of the 19th century, announced that the Gospel of John should be disregarded altogether as a historical source, since "its author acted with the freedom of an absolute monarch, switching events around at will and showing them from perverse angles, inventing [Jesus's] speeches and dialogues out of whole cloth, and presenting [Jesus's] greatest thoughts in entirely fictive situations."

A French priest, Alfred Loisy (1857–1940), began his scholarly career teaching at one of France's most prestigious Catholic seminaries, the Institut Catholique de Paris, but quickly ran into trouble. A gifted professor of Greek and Hebrew, he put forth a fivefold argument: Moses did not write any of the Torah; the opening chapters of Genesis on the creation of the world must be read as allegory instead of history; the Old and New Testaments must be judged separately in regard to their historical accuracy; the religious teachings presented in the

Bible represent a development over time rather than a single, eternal doctrine; and, for purposes of determining historical truth, the Scriptures are no more authoritative or exempt from criticism than any other ancient texts. By 1893 he was compelled to resign from his seminary post and take up teaching at a public college. Loisy continued to publish, and to land in trouble. Finally, in 1908, Pope Pius X (r. 1903–1914) excommunicated him.

Historical Criticism by itself did not lead to the rapid development of secularism in Europe, but it followed on the heels of other major social upheavals and scientific challenges. Coming as it did after industrialism, modern geology, and evolutionary theory, its contribution to the spread of religious doubt appeared increasingly large and dire. Mainstream Christian churches encouraged the faithful to seek out biblical wisdom. But where does a believer turn when the churches, perhaps through no fault of their own, cannot keep pace with the age, and the Scriptures themselves are of uncertain authority? How does one balance a commitment to a tradition of revealed Truth with a willingness to explore new ideas and new ways of thinking? Even more fundamentally, was it still possible to be a Christian believer and remain intellectually honest?

> Historical Criticism by itself did not lead to the rapid development of secularism in Europe, but it followed on the heels of other major social upheavals and scientific challenges. Coming as it did after industrialism, modern geology, and evolutionary theory, its contribution to the spread of religious doubt appeared increasingly large and dire.

THE PROTESTANT CHURCHES' RESPONSE

Communities often respond to crisis by pulling in opposite directions: some in the community embrace new ideas, while others reaffirm established certainties. Depending on the circumstances, either reaction can make sense; and in some cases, both reactions might. The Christian churches of the 19th century, like the governments of the age, had to confront upheavals unlike anything they had dealt with previously. The wars of religion in the 17th century had been brutal, and yet they were conflicts over which version of Christian revelation was the true one. For all their horror, they were at least conflicts between groups of genuine conviction. But how does one deal with the explicit *denial* of revelation and the argument that there is no truth to be fought over? If the teachings of Christianity are not heaven-sent truths, does faith have a future? "Yes, indeed," answered the mainstream churches, both Protestant and Catholic. "No, not really," answered more and more Europeans as they sank comfortably into their increasingly secular lives.

Take just two examples of the resulting tug-of-war. In England, the Anglican reaction to the triple blow of industrialism, science, and historical criticism was slow and measured, for the most part, with occasional outbursts of energetic activity. Rural society felt relatively little impact. Small village parishes still formed the backbone of the community, and attendance at services remained high. But life in the cities was another matter altogether. As with the state, the church devoted a greater percentage of its resources to serving the fast-growing middle-class sections of the towns than to the downtrodden workers' slums. "Proper society" mattered more.[8]

A national census in 1851 revealed two surprising facts: for the first time ever, more people in England lived in towns than in the countryside; and second, attendance at religious services was in sharp decline. Of the country's 17.9 million people, 5.2 million identified themselves as active Anglicans, 4.5 million were "Dissenters" or "Non-Conformists" (the terms for anyone who was a Protestant Christian but not an Anglican), and a mere 380,000 were Roman Catholics. That meant more than 7.2 million English people, or 40 percent of the nation, effectively declared themselves either nonpracticing Christians or nonbelievers.[9] Only five years later, another survey showed, less than 20 percent of Londoners attended church. There is little evidence of overt hostility to religion among the workers and urban poor, since we have few records that come from them directly. (One Evangelical Christian reformer, Hannah More [d. 1833], had long advocated teaching the masses how to read but not to write, lest their unhealthy thoughts begin to circulate.) This suggests that their nonappearance at church resulted from either a lack of opportunity or indifference.

The Nonconforming churches and the more Evangelical sectors of Anglicanism did a better job of serving the urban poor than did the Church of England. Nonconformist denominations included the Baptist, Congregationalist, Methodist, and Presbyterian churches, as well as the newly established (1865) sect known as the Salvation Army. These denominations tended to place more emphasis on biblical teaching and puritanical morality, and less on institutional tradition and formal liturgy, than the Anglicans and Catholics, which made it easier for them to establish themselves in poorer districts. Group worship could take place in homes and meeting halls and did not rely to such an extent upon large church buildings as the centers of community. These denominations benefited somewhat from class antagonisms; the very fact that they were Nonconformist—that is, that they consciously disassociated themselves from the

---

8   In 1833, Parliament voted more money to maintain the royal stables at Windsor Castle than to provide elementary schools for the general public.

9   "It is not that the Church of God has lost the great towns," wrote one Anglican clergyman; "it has never had them."

Preaching the Gospel   An itinerant preacher in India, late 19th century. As Christianity began to lose place to secularism within Europe, missionaries focused more of their energies on spreading the Christian message abroad, in Africa and Asia.

Church of England—formed part of their appeal. By rejecting the established church, parishioners were in some ways declaring opposition to the middle class that made up most of its members and to the aristocracy that made up most of its highest officials. But popular participation in the Nonconformist churches declined in the second half of the 19th century at roughly the same rate as in the Anglican Church.

Being so strongly based on a tradition of biblical reading that tended toward the literal, these groups had particular difficulty with the intellectual challenges posed by historical criticism and the rise of modern science. For many of these people, the loss of unquestioned biblical authority meant the collapse of faith itself. The novelist George Eliot (Marian Evans), who was raised an Evangelical, identified her loss of faith precisely with her doubt of Scriptural inerrancy. Dissenters engaged energetically in missionary work in the fast-multiplying British colonies in Africa and India; yet that meant that many of their most talented and charismatic men and women were drawn away from the home front.

The Anglican Church itself was torn over the rise of secularism. To conservative Anglicans the answer lay in a rigid opposition to modern science and historical criticism. Samuel Wilberforce, the bishop of Oxford who had debated evolution with Thomas Huxley, dismissed Darwin's *Origin of Species* in one of the book's earliest reviews:

> Now we must say at once and openly... that such a notion [as evolution by natural selection] is absolutely incompatible not only with single expressions in the Word of God but with the whole representation of that moral and spiritual condition of man which is its proper subject matter. Man's derived supremacy over the earth; man's gift of reason; man's free-will and responsibility; man's fall and man's redemption; the incarnation of the Eternal Son; the in-dwelling of the Eternal Spirit,—all are equally and utterly irreconcilable with the degrading notion of the brute origin of him who was created in the image of God.... Man is not and cannot be an improved ape. *(Quarterly Review 108:258–260)*

The Church of England suffered greatly from the growing rift between "Low Church," "High Church," and "Broad Church" Anglicans. The Low Church consisted of the Evangelicals—those parishioners with the least interest in preserving strict liturgical and ritual tradition, basing their theology solidly on the literal meaning of the Scriptures. The High Church consisted of just the opposite—the Anglicans most dearly loyal to ritual, hierarchy, and tradition. The Broad Church was made up of the most liberal Anglicans, who remained most open to liturgical reform, evolutionary theory, and historical criticism. Wilberforce belonged to the High Church wing, but in his review of Darwin he championed unreservedly the authority of Scripture over any amount of scientific evidence to the contrary.

Secularism won out over each of the three branches in roughly equal amounts—though for different reasons. The Low Church lost numbers through its refusal to accept modern intellectual life; the High Church lost the working class that felt alienated from "proper society." And the Broad Church lost members precisely because its intellectual openness to evolution and historical criticism inadvertently helped the idea of a Godless universe to succeed.

In Germany the challenge to religion included an unexpected political element. A royal decree by Friedrich Wilhelm III (r. 1797–1840) known as the Prussian Union of 1817 had not only gathered the autonomous Lutheran Churches into a single national entity but had folded the Reformed (Calvinist) Churches into the mix. It thereby created a kind of Protestant superchurch called the Evangelical Christian Church. Coming as it did on the three hundredth anniversary of the start of the Protestant Reformation, the union aimed to breathe new life into Christian worship, but the move was controversial from the start. Many Calvinist ministers resisted their forced assimilation into what they regarded as a too-liberal Lutheran tradition. In turn, many Lutheran clergy objected that much of what was most distinctive about Lutheran worship was lost. But matters became even more dire as Prussian political power, led by Otto von Bismarck, overwhelmed the other German states and created a united Germany.

As opposition to the Reich became impossible, popular resentment found expression through opposition to the official Evangelical Church, usually through the simple choice not to attend Sunday services. Many thousands of Germans who found it impossible to accept the established church yet who refused to relinquish regular worship emigrated to the United States in the 1840s and 1850s. Among those who remained behind, many rallied to a reform movement they called **Neo-Lutheranism**, which aimed not only to reaffirm the distinctive Lutheran heritage but also to address the problems of Darwinian theory and historical criticism.

Neo-Lutherans were not a uniform theological bloc, and in fact they quickly divided into schools of thought that were roughly analogous to Low, Broad, and High Anglicanism. Since traditional Lutheranism placed such a high premium on the authority of Scripture, great numbers of the Neo-Lutherans insisted all the more strongly on the belief in Scriptural inerrancy and the body of Scriptural interpretation established in Martin Luther's *Book of Concord*; these became known as the Confessional Lutherans and most closely resembled the Scripturally-based Low Church wing of Anglicanism; they notably championed the rejection of modern science and textual criticism. Other Neo-Lutherans, however, were more analogous to the High Church Anglicans; they privileged the institutional tradition of Lutheranism and the need to remain united against a hostile world. Still others believed that traditional faith and the new sciences could be harmonized—or at least that harmony was worth attempting. These Neo-Lutherans became known as the Erlangen school—after the university where many of their leading scholars were trained—and parallel the Broad Church leaders in the Church of England.

Whatever their intellectual and moral merits, the three Neo-Lutheran groups failed to staunch the hemorrhage of Christians from communal worship. No book of Christian theology, traditional devotional literature, or biblical commentary published in German in the 19th century came close to selling as many copies as Strauss's *Life of Jesus, Critically Examined* or Feuerbach's *Essence of Christianity*.[10] Even within the Lutheran liturgies of the century, the slow advance of the

---

[10]   The German translation of Darwin's *Origin of Species* outsold Luther's *Book of Concord*.

secularist worldview could be seen. The Apostles' Creed had long been one of the foundational documents of Protestant Christianity. This ancient statement of faith was given special approbation by Martin Luther in the 16th century because it did not contain the declaration about the "one, holy, catholic, and apostolic Church" that was found in the Nicene Creed:

> I believe in God, the Father Almighty,
>   maker of heaven and earth.
> And in Jesus Christ, his only Son, our Lord,
>   who was conceived by the Holy Spirit,
>   and born of the virgin Mary,
>   suffered under Pontius Pilate,
>   was crucified, died and was buried.
>   He descended into hell.
>   On the third day He rose again from the dead.
>   He ascended into heaven
>   and sits at the right hand of the Father.
>   From thence He will come to judge the living and the dead.
> I believe in the Holy Spirit,
>   the holy Christian church,
>   the communion of saints,
>   the forgiveness of sins,
>   the resurrection of the body,
>   and the life everlasting. Amen.

But the Prussian Synod of 1846 authorized a revised version for the established Evangelical Christian Church. This version removed three elements deemed no longer acceptable, given the advances of modern science and critical analysis: the Virgin Birth, Christ's descent into hell, and the bodily resurrection of the saved on Judgment Day.

Arguments over these matters dominated church life in Germany through the middle decades of the century. In 1892 a Lutheran minister in Württemberg, Christoph Schrempf, caused an even greater scandal when he acknowledged from the pulpit that he could no longer, in good faith, recite any part whatsoever of the Apostles' Creed. When a group of offended university students complained to one of their divinity professors—Adolf von Harnack (1851–1930), a leader in historical criticism—about Schrempf's audacity, Harnack responded that, while the Creed deserves respect for its antiquity and historical significance, it could not and should not be believed by any educated Christian.

THE CATHOLIC COUNTERATTACK

Industrialism affected Catholic Christianity less than it did the Protestant variety. Catholics made up a high percentage of industrial workers across Europe and generally brought with them ingrained habits of communal identity. Irish immigrants, for example, filled many of northern England's largest factories, just as Polish, Czech, and Hungarian workers flocked into German manufacturing cities. And as immigrants, their minority status heightened their sense of solidarity. Catholic migrant workers tended to live in congregated clusters, which led easily to the development of full parish life. Moreover, the Catholic Church was relatively quick to condemn the excesses of industrial capitalism and the wealth disparities between the bourgeoisie and the working poor. That meant that fewer Catholics fell away from their faith because of their church's supposed association with the capitalist elite.

The supreme expression of the church's warnings about unchecked capitalism appeared in 1891 when Pope Leo XIII (r. 1878–1903) issued the encyclical **Rerum Novarum** ("Of New Things"). The Church recognized the intrinsic rights of private property but insisted on the equal right of workers to form labor unions. Without a system of collective bargaining, Leo argues, the industrial capitalist economy gives a morally unacceptable permanent advantage to the wealthy.

> Let workers and employers therefore make free agreements, and in particular let them agree freely as to wages; nevertheless, there remains

Noble Workers   Giuseppe Pellizza da Volpedo (1868-1907) was an artist who dedicated most of his short life to promoting the rights of the working class in Italy and advocating for socialism. His best-known work, *The Fourth Estate* (1901), commemorates a labor strike in Milan. The prominent role given to a woman in the picture was radical even among Italian progressives of the era.

a fundamental requirement of natural justice older and more authoritative than any arrangement between man and man—namely, that wages ought not be so low that a frugal and well-behaved worker cannot support himself or his family. When a worker is forced, by need or by fear of something even worse, to accept wages lower than this threshold by an employer who refuses to pay more, the worker is nothing more than a victim of violent injustice.

At the same time he insists, in a swipe at Marxism, that the relationship between workers and owners must not be and need not be one of conflict.

> The great error [of Marxists] is to insist on the idea that each class is inevitably hostile to the other, and that capitalists and workers are fixed by a law of nature in a state of perpetual conflict. This view is so wrongheaded and contrary to reason that in fact its exact opposite is true—for just as the harmony of the human body derives from the proper arrangement of its various parts, so too does nature ordain that in human society the various classes should dwell in harmonious accord. This is what produces the balance in a body politic. Each class needs the other, for capital cannot survive without labor, and labor cannot survive without capital.

The Catholic social movement, of which Rerum Novarum was merely one part, had begun in the 1820s as soon as industrialization took root on the Continent, which insulated the faith from the slow pull of involuntary secularism. **Social Catholicism** was founded on the idea that the challenge to Christian society under industrialism was structural rather than personal. The question, in other words, was not "How do we help the poor?" but "How do we combat poverty?" Liberal economics in the industrialized state did not merely fail to eradicate poverty but actually caused it—and hence the response had to be principled and ideological as well as activist.

Clergy in Belgium, France, and Germany preached steadily against the systemic flaw of unregulated capitalism. In 1825 the first full-length moral indictment of industrial society appeared: *Regarding the Faith and Its Relations with the Civil and Political Order*, by a French priest named Hugues de Lamennais (1782–1854). A German priest and later bishop of Mainz, Wilhelm Emmanuel (Baron von Ketteler, 1811–1877), entered the fray immediately after his ordination, preaching on workers' rights and the need for state regulation of the marketplace. He called for the legalization of labor unions throughout Europe. In 1869, at a bishops' conference in the ancient German city of Fulda, he argued passionately that the problem of industrial capitalism was vastly more significant than any of the intellectual conflicts then confronting Christian society. Poverty, he insisted, not Charles Darwin or David Friedrich Strauss, was the real scourge of the age. In England, Henry Edward Manning (1808–1892), a convert from Anglicanism, regularly preached sermons on the rights of laborers; in 1889 he helped negotiate a settlement to the dockworkers' strike that paralyzed commerce in London. After he was made a cardinal in the church, Manning became a close adviser to Pope Leo XIII and indeed helped him to write Rerum Novarum.

The Catholic Church had less success against political nationalism, especially in Italy. The campaigns to create a unified Italy found their main obstacle in the pope himself. Since the early Middle Ages the Roman pontiff had been not only the spiritual leader of all Catholics but also the political ruler of the Papal State—a large territory in the middle third of the Italian peninsula. Believing that its civil domain was vital to the financial support of the worldwide church, Pope Pius IX (r. 1846–1878) steadfastly opposed every effort to create an Italian nation. The longest-reigning pope in history (after Saint Peter himself), he became a virtual prisoner in the Vatican Palace when Vittorio Emmanuele II's soldiers seized Rome in 1860. Pius compensated for his loss of political sovereignty by summoning the First Vatican Council (1869–1870), the convocation best known for pronouncing the dogma of papal infallibility.

The infallibility of the pope had been a traditional assumption among Catholics since the Middle Ages, but it had never been formalized as an official teaching. The Vatican Council determined that the dogma of infallibility, already established by tradition, needed formal definition in order to provide a guarantee of the church's authority against the intrusion of new ideas upon Catholic faith. Here they were thinking not of the challenges of Darwinian evolution or modern physics but the implications of historical criticism.

Scholarly analysis of the Scriptures, they wanted to assert, can validly contribute to the appreciation of the biblical text but can never replace the interpretive authority of the church. The pope, as head of the church, must have recourse to the exercise of absolute authority over it in the definition of its central beliefs— at least in certain circumstances. Pius IX's political travails in Italy made him increasingly conservative, and although he remained revered for his piety and gentle nature, his last years in office were marked by a deepening isolation from the world outside the palace walls. The church seemed in these years to enter a period of withdrawal and retrenchment.

THE WAR ON MODERNISM

Pius's successor, Leo XIII, resolved to bring the church back into direct engagement with the world. Though no less conservative than Pius had been, Leo revitalized the church's campaign to secure the rights of workers and the poor. He introduced the idea of **subsidiarity**, by which he meant that problems ought generally to be resolved locally. This principle, which governed Catholic social teaching throughout the 20th century, had two aims. First, it sought to preserve the dignity of persons and to help them recognize their own moral responsibilities. And second, it sought to safeguard against an overreaching centralized government.

The church responded slowly to the scientific discoveries and Scriptural analysis of the century. Leo was a natural diplomat and had the gift of knowing his own intellectual limits, and so he set out not to respond to the intellectual assaults on Catholic tradition but to prepare the groundwork for such a response. His most important effort in this regard was the encyclical *Providentissimus Deus* ("The God of All Providence," 1893), which effectively established two guiding principles. First, the truths of science and Scripture can never contradict each other once they are fully known and understood. Since both are gifts from God, they must ultimately exist in harmony; apparent contradictions between them merely indicate where our understanding is imperfect. Second, the study of the Scriptures should be welcomed at all times. It merely requires an honest spirit that seeks a better understanding of God's word, rather than a malicious spirit that desires only to point out textual inconsistencies for their own sake.

Leo's successor would have none of it. Pius X (r. 1903–1914) railed against all forms of intellectual novelty—which he grouped under the heading **modernism**. He was kindly, pious, and generous but temperamentally ill-equipped to deal with innovations; he regarded any new idea as a direct threat to the faith and stubbornly refused to consider it. Soon enough, he would not allow new ideas to be considered. In two decrees issued in 1907, *Lamentabili Sane Exitu* ("With lamentable consequence") and *Pascendi Dominici Gregis* ("Feeding the Lord's flock"), he formally condemned sixty-five teachings that he deemed irredeemably anti-Catholic. Calling them a **Syllabus of Errors**, he ordered all clerics to swear a loyalty oath that explicitly rejected every tenet of modernism. The oath, which was required of all clergy until 1967, ran in part:

> I proclaim that God, Who is the origin and the end of all things, can be known with certainty by the natural light of reason; . . . that the teachings of the Faith have been handed down to us from the Apostles, through the orthodox Fathers, and always with exactly the same meaning and the same intent; . . . I declare my complete opposition to the

errors of the modernists, who claim that there is nothing divine in sacred tradition [of the church]. . . . I firmly maintain and shall maintain to my last breath the belief of the Church Fathers in the sacred gift of Truth— Truth which most certainly exists, has existed, and always shall exist in the apostolic succession of bishops. . . . And I vow that I will keep these promises faithfully, wholly, and sincerely, keeping them inviolate, and in no way ever deviating from them in teaching or any other way. . . . All these things I do promise and swear, so help me God.

He followed up by instituting a clerical purge. He recommended the establishment of oversight committees (called *sodalitia*, or "fellowships") in every diocese in the church worldwide. These he charged with the detection of modernism and empowered to censor all clerical publications, and he entitled them to work in complete secrecy.[11] Accordingly, scores of books were banned and dozens of priestly careers ended—some by expulsion from clerical orders and some even by excommunication. In time the entire École biblique in Jerusalem, founded by a Dominican priest in 1890, was condemned and briefly closed.

The effect of these measures was easy to imagine: much of Catholic intellectual life stagnated. It did not recover until after World War II, with the establishment of the Second Vatican Council (1962–1965). To many in the broader Western society, the church's war on modernism seemed a painful embarrassment, not merely a flat-out inability to understand modern scientific and textual thinking but a petulant refusal by pious ideologues to think or to allow others to do so. Victims of the purges under Pius X—like the French scholar Alfred Loisy (1857–1940), the English Jesuit George Tyrell (1861–1909), or the Austrian lay theologian Friedrich von Hügel (1852–1925)—became martyrs to intellectual freedom, for their supporters. Loisy was defrocked and excommunicated, while Tyrell was expelled from the Jesuit order and excommunicated. Both men were denied a Catholic burial. And the Roman Catholic Church entered the 20th century with a growing popular reputation as the enemy of thinking.

> To many in the broader Western society, the church's war on modernism seemed a painful embarrassment, not merely a flat-out inability to understand modern scientific and textual thinking but a petulant refusal by pious ideologues to think or to allow others to do so.

---

[11] Some censors went so far as to intercept private mail and to review a suspect's book purchases at local shops. Many kept notes in secret codes.

MODERNISM, SECULARISM, AND THE JEWS

In the 18th century, Jewish biblical scholars who worked to harmonize their tradition with the principles of the Enlightenment became known as **maskilim** ("the enlightened ones"). Their aims were twofold: to strain out irrationalities from Jewish observance, thereby broadening its appeal to the irreligious Enlightened society; and to revitalize Scriptural study among Jews for its own sake. The zenith of maskilic efforts was the publication of a new edition of the Torah by Moses Mendelssohn (1729–1786) between 1780 and 1783. Mendelssohn's edition included a parallel German translation (written, though, in Hebrew letters) and highly detailed technical notes on linguistic problems in the Masoretic text. What Mendelssohn left out of his edition were the rabbinical commentaries on legal and ritualistic issues raised by the text that had been traditionally included in Hebrew Bibles from the 13th century on. Mendelssohn's great work had many mistakes and shortcomings, but it nevertheless represented a major breakthrough—a Torah that aimed above all to be read as a text and not as a guide to daily observance.

After the Congress of Vienna imposed a new political order on Europe in 1815, Jewish excitement over the new Torah continued to grow. Soon new editions of the books of the Prophets (*Nevi'im*) and of the Writings (*Ketuvim*) appeared, all prepared along Mendelssohn's model. Dense scholarly books on the fine points of Hebrew grammar, synonyms, particles, and toponyms were published with surprising frequency; soon entire academic journals dedicated to the study of Hebrew philology and literature were founded. An entire new academic field began to emerge—in Germany, first of all—called the *Wissenschaft des Judentums* ("Jewish sciences"). It was not long before non-Jewish and non-German scholars took notice. When the historical development of the Hebrew language became better understood, the development of the biblical texts themselves over time became clearer—the phenomenon that triggered historical criticism and eventually the modernist crisis among Christians.

One of the greatest of the early Wissenschaft scholars was Abraham Geiger (1810–1874), a Reform rabbi from Frankfurt am Main who spent most of his scholarly career at Breslau, in Prussia (today's city of Wrocław, in Poland). Geiger founded two important journals (and filled the first volumes of each with many of his own researches). In his masterpiece, *The Biblical Text and Its Transmission* (*Urschrift und Übersetzung der Bibel*, 1857), he laid out the most detailed argument yet published on the development of the Bible over centuries. It addressed the presence of competing versions on the text, as well as the variations between the numerous translations and editions of it over time. To Geiger, the Bible and indeed all of Jewish tradition possess an unfixed, fluid nature: "Every age, every cultural movement, and every personality in our history has brought ideas of its own to bear on the Bible." Moreover, they will continue to do so. Geiger hoped that the efforts of historical criticism would lead the Jews on to the next phase of development, seeing in their tradition's adaptability the secret of its endurance. We do not know what Geiger thought of Darwinian theory, but his views on the evolution of Judaism are interestingly consonant with it, whether intentionally or not. A loose German translation of *Origin of Species* was published in 1860, with a much better version coming a decade later.

What was *not* part of Geiger's intention was the secularizing effect of his scholarship on many of Europe's Jews. Most of the new scholars were, or soon became, Reform Jews rather than Orthodox, and their work contributed directly to the firm establishment of the Reform tradition. The Wissenschaft school did not start the secularizing trend. The movement away from Orthodoxy had begun at least a century earlier, in the early 18th century. Yet Orthodox leaders failed to respond to developments effectively. It may be that they regarded the rise of anti-Semitism or the suffering of the industrialized poor as the more pressing problems; certainly nationalistic passions from one end of Europe to the other gave them reason to pause. But the fact remains that Jewish Orthodoxy by and large dug in its heels. Like Catholic conservativism, it fought against the new scientific understandings of religious tradition by simply saying no.

Surprisingly few Orthodox rabbis took on the Darwinian challenge, though. Instead, they just ignored it. Judaism had never accepted the notion of original sin and the Fall of Man—the idea that human life is a devolution from an earlier state of spiritual perfection. Thus, few Jews felt that mankind's arising from primitive beginnings threatened their tradition. Moreover, Orthodoxy had never insisted on a literal interpretation of the Six Days of Creation, which left the door open to accepting geological time.

Once again, social and economic changes led to the spread of secularism or nonobservance, but here the role of industrialization is less important than it was for Christian Europe. Over the course of the 19th century, Europe experienced two major waves of immigration—of Jews fleeing the troubled Ottoman Empire, and of Jews escaping the pogroms in Czarist Russia. The overall European population doubled to more than 400 million, and the number of Jews went from roughly 3 million to 8 million. Close to 5 million, however, lived specifically in eastern Europe, and most of them were poor—victims either of the weak economic development of the area, of their own refugee status, or of legal barriers to advancement.[12] Given their dire condition, many emigrated yet again, further west into cities like Warsaw (30,000 in 1800, 300,000 in 1900), Berlin (12,000 in

---

[12]   Most secondary schools at the time restricted Jewish enrollment to no more than 5 percent of the student body.

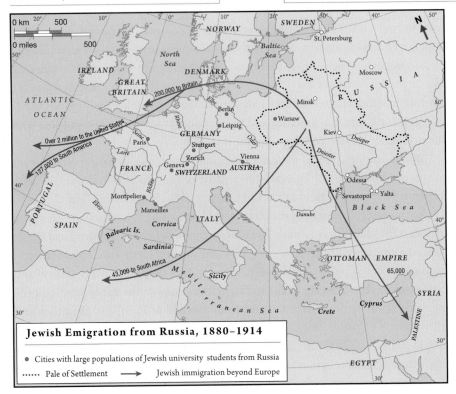

Jewish Emigration from Russia, 1880–1914

- Cities with large populations of Jewish university students from Russia
- ⋯⋯ Pale of Settlement   ⟶ Jewish immigration beyond Europe

MAP 20.1   Jewish Emigration from Russia, 1880–1914

1800, 140,000 in 1900), and Vienna (2,000 in 1800, 150,000 in 1900). There they followed the classic immigrant pattern of hard work, education, and advancement through subsequent generations to reach professional status—doctors, lawyers, journalists (see Map 20.1). Secularization, as a consequence, resulted from the drive to succeed and gain acceptance.

The family of Karl Marx fit this pattern, as did those of Theodor Herzl (1860–1904) and Sigmund Freud (1856–1939). What was unusual in their cases was simply the degree of secularism and assimilation that they had achieved. Describing the same phenomenon among Jewish immigrants to the United States, Moses Weinberger (1854–1940), a popular Orthodox writer, lamented in 1887:

> How awesome is the strength of America! In a single year it transforms "Rachel, wife of Reb Jaakov" into "Mrs. Jacobs" and "Reb Baruch, cobbler and shoemaker" into "Mr. Bennett, Shoe Manufacturer." The Enlightenments of Berlin and Europe put together did not accomplish as much in half a century.

A separate movement among 19th-century Jews is known variously as Secular Judaism, Secular Zionism, Humanistic Judaism, or Cultural Zionism. This was not, as it might sound, a vision of Jewish identity shorn of religious convictions. Rather, it emphasized a fundamental unity of identity across the religious lines that divided the multiple Jewish traditions—Orthodox, Reform, and Conservative Judaism, plus the many subgroups and outcroppings belonging to each. Among the early leaders of this mission was Asher Ginsberg (1856–1927), a Russian Jew better known by his pen-name Ahad Ha'am. Ahad Ha'am clashed with Theodor Herzl over the issue of establishing a Zionist state in Palestine, thinking it was impractical. But he did want to help organize and maintain a Jewish presence in Palestine, one that would symbolize for all Jews everywhere their ancestral linkage. It would establish, in his words, "a Jewish state and not merely a state made up of Jews." Seeing the growing divisions among Jews as a greater problem, for the moment at least, than the vulnerable position of Jews in Western society, Ahad Ha'am devoted his life to calling all Jews to recognize their fundamental and eternal connectedness.

THE ISLAMIC EXCEPTION

The rapid growth—imposition, really—of Wahhabism was the major development in Islam in the 19th century. Scientific study in the Muslim world had long since turned inward; it consisted of endless commentaries on codified bodies of knowledge, rather than in exploring new areas of investigation. Europe had pulled ahead of the Arabic-speaking world in science as early as the 13th century, and the Scientific Revolution of the 17th century widened the gap almost beyond bridging. Few of the advances and discoveries of the 19th century made much of an impact in the Islamic world, or indeed were even known there, and so they presented nothing like the threat to traditional faith they did in the West. Darwin's *Origin of Species* remained virtually unknown; it appeared in an Arabic translation for the first time only in 2009. The closest available version of Darwinian theory was an edition of Thomas H. Huxley's popularization, in English, in which certain key terms were printed in boldface, with Arabic footnotes at the bottom of each page. It was published in 2008.[13] The scientific vacuum this represented made it easier for Wahhabism's form of anti-intellectualism to take root.

> Few of the advances and discoveries of the 19th century made much of an impact in the Islamic world, or indeed were even known there, and so they presented nothing like the threat to traditional faith they did in the West.

Not all Muslim societies experienced the same distancing from modern science. Some embrace it wholeheartedly, at least in theory, while their actual

---

[13] A 2009 poll in Egypt found that only 9 percent of the adult population both knew of evolution and believed in it.

involvement is somewhat marginal. Others, however, remain staunchly opposed. They see the systematic structure of scientific thinking as an attempt to confound the complete freedom of action retained by Allah. In a few instances, opposition to science lasted until well into the 20th century. In Iran, for example, dissection of corpses remained forbidden in medical schools until the 1920s. And at the leading Islamic university in Egypt (al-Azhar) the Copernican heliocentric model was not officially accepted until 1961.

Historical Criticism found no friendlier audience among Muslims, although efforts began in Europe to apply its tenets to the Qur'an. In 1843 Gustav Weil (1808–1889), a German Jewish scholar of Arabic and Turkish who worked as the librarian of the University of Heidelberg, published *The Prophet Muhammad: His Life and Teaching*, the first-ever work to apply critical methods to the origins of Islam. Apart from the Qur'an and *hadith*, Weil had access only to a single other source—the life of the Prophet written by Ibn Hisham (d. 833), an edited version of an even earlier biography of the Prophet written by Ibn Ishaq (d. 767), whose text was then unknown in the West. He followed this with an even more ambitious volume titled *A Historical-Critical Introduction to the Qur'an* (1844) and an essay titled "Biblical Legends among the Muslims" (1849), which details the ways in which rabbinical writings influenced Islamic tradition.

Al-Azhar University, Cairo, ca. 1910   Founded in the 10th century, Al-Azhar is one of the oldest universities in the world. For nearly a thousand years its curriculum—Islamic law and jurisprudence, Arabic, grammar. logic, and philosophy—barely changed.

These works sparked enough interest that soon a fairly large corps of scholars, mostly German and British, ventured into the field, and a stream of editions, translations, and historical-critical analyses were published. Sir William Muir's (1819–1905) *Life of Mahomet and the History of Islam to the Era of the Hegira*, in four volumes, appeared between 1858 and 1864. It was followed by the *Prolegomena to the Historical Origins of Islam* by Julius Wellhausen (1844–1918), *Muslim Studies* by Ignaz Goldziher (1850–1921), the ten-volume *Annals of Islam* (1905–1907) by Leone Caetani (1869–1935), and the series of works by the controversial Belgian Jesuit scholar Henri Lammens (1862–1937). With the exception of Lammens, all of these scholars professed admiration for Islam and Arab culture, and they dissected the early Muslim texts to show how Islam evolved historically. Like the Gospels when it came to Jesus, they found, the earliest Islamic texts that discuss the Prophet come roughly a century after his death. They should hence be read not as authoritative contemporary evidence but as after-the-fact attempts to sculpt a narrative by those who had emerged as leaders of the movement. Most Muslims around the world heatedly rejected these ideas.

To many in the Islamic world most strongly opposed to the new science and criticism, their opposition was not merely a knee-jerk rejection of innovative thinking. Rather, it was a rejection of European political imperialism—which was beginning to take place precisely at the end of the 19th century as new scholarly texts were coming into print. Indeed, many Muslims regarded those works as the intellectual front of the imperialist war itself; many still do.

WHO, WHAT, WHERE

atheism

higher criticism

Historical Criticism

maskilim

modernism

Neo-Lutheranism

On the Origin of Species by Means of Natural Selection

Oxford movement

Rerum Novarum

secularism

Social Catholicism

subsidiarity

Syllabus of Errors

theory of evolution by natural selection

uniformitarianism

SUGGESTED READINGS

Primary Sources

Darwin, Charles. *The Descent of Man.*

———. *On the Origin of Species.*

Feuerbach, Ludwig. *The Essence of Christianity.*

Geiger, Abraham. *The Biblical Text and Its Transmission.*

Goldziher, Ignaz. *Muslim Studies.*

Leo XIII, Pope. *Rerum Novarum.*

Lyell, Charles. *Principles of Geology.*

Newman, John Henry. *Apologia Pro Vita Sua.*

Nietzsche, Friedrich. *The Gay Science.*

Renan. Ernst. *The Life of Jesus.*

Strauss, David Friedrich. *The Christ of Belief and the Jesus of History.*

———. *The Life of Jesus Critically Examined.*

Wellhausen, Julius. *Prolegomena to the Historical Origins of Islam.*

———. *Prolegomena to the History of Ancient Israel.*

Anthologies

Fritzsche, Peter, trans and ed. *Nietzsche and the Death of God: Selected Writings* (2011).

Guy, Josephine, ed. *The Victorian Age: An Anthology of Sources and Documents* (2001).

Herbert, Sandra. *Charles Darwin and the Question of Evolution: A Brief History with Documents* (2011).

Studies

Artigas, Mariano, Thomas F. Glick, and Rafael A. Martínez. *Negotiating Darwin: The Vatican Confronts Evolution, 1877–1902* (2007).

Bernardi, Peter J. *Maurice Blondel, Social Catholicism, and Action Française: The Clash over the Church's Role in Society during the Modernist Era* (2008).

Brown, Callum G. *The Death of Christian Britain: Understanding Secularisation, 1800–2000* (2009).

Browne, Janet. *Charles Darwin: A Biography.* (2003).

Burrow, J. W. *The Crisis of Reason: European Thought, 1848–1914* (2002).

Chiron, Yves. *Saint Pius X: Restorer of the Church* (2002).

Crews, Robert D. *For Prophet and Tsar: Islam and Empire in Russia and Central Asia* (2009).

Ford, Alan. *James Ussher: Theology, History, and Politics in Early-Modern Ireland and England* (2007).

Hill, Harvey. *The Politics of Modernism: Alfred Loisy and the Scientific Study of Religion* (2002).

Jodock, Darrell. *Catholicism Contending with Modernity: Roman Catholic Modernism and Anti-Modernism in Historical Context* (2010).

Koltun-Fromm, Ken. *Abraham Geiger's Liberal Judaism: Personal Meaning and Religious Authority* (2006).

Larsen, Timothy. *Crisis of Doubt: Honest Faith in Nineteenth-Century England* (2009).

———. *A People of One Book: The Bible and the Victorians* (2011).

McLeod, Hugh. *Secularisation in Western Europe, 1848–1914* (2000).

O'Connor, James, trans. *The Gift of Infallibility: The Official Relatio on Infallibility by Bishop Vincent Ferrer Gasser at Vatican Council* (2008).

Prusak, Bernard P. *The Church Unfinished: Ecclesiology through the Centuries* (2004).

Schultenover, David G., ed. *The Reception of Pragmatism in France and the Rise of Roman Catholic Pragmatism, 1890–1914* (2009).

Winchester, Simon. *The Map That Changed the World: William Smith and the Birth of Modern Geology* (2001).

Young, Julian. *The Death of God and the Meaning of Life* (2003).

———. *Friedrich Nietzsche: A Philosophical Biography* (2010).

For additional resources, including maps, primary sources, visuals, web links, and quizzes, please go to **www.oup.com/us/backman.**

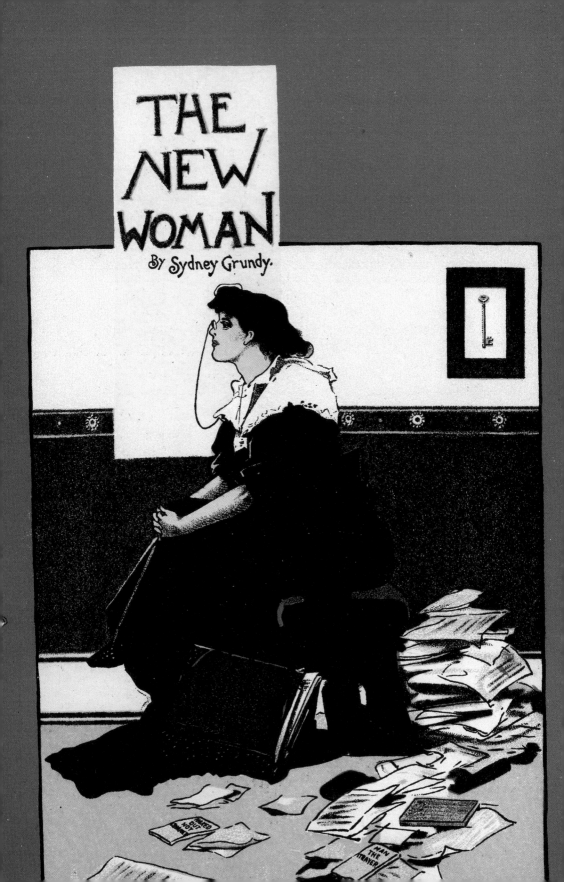

CHAPTER 21

The Modern Woman

1860–1914

Throughout the second half of the 19th century, ever-increasing numbers of women across the Greater West began to agitate for equal rights, most particularly the right to vote. Calls for better treatment of women date back to the 14th century at least, but usually from solitary voices. Now the issue of women's rights was the subject of more widespread expectation and demand.

WOMEN AND THE RIGHT TO VOTE

Women first enfranchised:
pre-1914 | 1921–45 | 1971–
1914–20 | 1946–70 | no suffrage

The first major step forward occurred in the labor protests of the early 1800s, when European women formed the majority of the workforce in certain industries. These women expected an improvement in their lot as part of the rise of workers' rights, but their hopes were beaten down for the most part and had to wait for another generation or two. The first bill before the British Parliament to extend suffrage (the right to vote) to women was presented in 1867 and defeated by an overwhelming vote of 194 to 74. Ironically, the very industrial system that had kept women down before 1860 gave them the means to press forward in the latter decades of the century. These changes in the workplace, during the Second Industrial Revolution (see chapter 22), combined with the development of political liberalism to enable the call for women's suffrage and ultimately the rise of broader demands for women's rights, in the **feminist movement**.

THE APPETITE FOR REFORM

◀ *The New Woman* Promotional poster for production of *The New Woman* (1894), a play by Sydney Grundy, in London.

The hunger for reform was acute. Popular attitudes regarding women's place in society ranged widely, but the majority emphasized their fundamental duty to maintain the family and household and insisted on the unnaturalness of their interest in civil society, politics, and intellectual life. As the popular London weekly newspaper *The Saturday Review* put it in 1871:

> The power of reasoning is so small in women that they need adventitious help, and if they have not the guidance and check of a religious conscience, it is useless to expect from them self-control on abstract principles. They do not calculate consequences, and they are reckless when they once give way, hence they are to be kept straight only through their affections, the religious sentiment, and a well-educated moral sense.[1]

The sanctity of the family as the fundamental unit of society, in this view, trumped any demand by women for civic equality. Hence opposition to female suffrage was primarily moral—which set it apart from the economic and class-based arguments levied against the demands of male workers and commoners. Hundreds, if not thousands or even more, of pamphlets, sermons, domestic guidebooks, novels, melodramatic stage-plays, sentimental popular songs, mawkish paintings, and family-oriented magazines pressed the point continually.

Industrialization had separated the work space from the domestic space, and among the middle class this led to a heightened popular vision of the home as a place of refuge. A wife, as overseer of the domestic safe haven, both supplied and tended to the essential emotional cohesion of family life; but until divorce laws were reformed she did so from a position of legal powerlessness. To those pressing for reform, both female and male, the liberal capitalist ideology that distinguished between the male-identified public sphere and the female-identified home front was the fundamental problem. The solution, therefore, was not merely to remove the barriers that excluded women from the man's world of commerce and government;

---

[1]   Another example: "No woman can or ought to know very much of the mass of meanness and wickedness and misery that is loose in the wide world. She could not learn it without losing the bloom and freshness which it is her mission in life to preserve."—*The Saturday Review*

CHAPTER TIMELINE

1869
John Stuart Mill, *The Subjection of Women*

1872
George Eliot, *Middlemarch*

1878
First international congress for women's rights meets in Paris

1867
First bill presented to British parliament to extend suffrage; Russia and Finland open their universities to women

1870
First commercially produced typewriters

1874
Women's labor and trade; unions legalized in France

Family Values   Queen Victoria (r. 1837-1901), Britain's longest reigning monarch, enjoyed huge popularity in the first half of her reign, but the death of her husband, Prince Albert, in 1861 sent her into a protracted seclusion and left her with an increasingly dour demeanor; her popularity surged again after 1876 when she assumed the title of Empress of India and stood as the resolute champion of British imperialism. In this early family portrait, Victoria and Albert watch affectionately over five of their children. They eventually had nine, before Albert's death.

it was to end the very notion of separate female and male spheres of belonging and action. As one Englishwoman recalled, in a biography of her suffragist mother published in the 1930s:

> To remain single was thought a disgrace and at thirty an unmarried woman was called an old maid. After their parents died, what could they do, where could they go? If they had a brother, as unwanted and

1880
Naphey, *The Physical Life of Woman*; France allows girls to attend secondary school

1903
Women's Social and Political Union formed in Britain

1913
"Cat and Mouse Act" passed in Britain

1893
Helene Stöcker, "The Modern Woman"

1906
Universal suffrage in Finland

1923
Huda'i Sha'arawi founds Egyptian Feminist Union

permanent guests, they might live in his house. Some had to maintain themselves and then, indeed, difficulty arose. The only paid occupation open to a gentlewoman was to become a governess under despised conditions and a miserable salary. None of the professions were open to women; there were no women in Government offices; no secretarial work was done by them. Even nursing was disorganized and disreputable until Florence Nightingale recreated it as a profession by founding the Nightingale School of Nursing in 1860.

This was Louisa Garrett Anderson (1873–1923), an early feminist whose mother, Elizabeth Garrett Anderson (1836–1917), had been Britain's first-ever female licensed physician.

The same point was made at greater length by the political philosopher John Stuart Mill (1806–1873) in his book *The Subjection of Women* (1869):

> There is no country of Europe in which the ablest men have not frequently experienced, and keenly appreciated, the value of the advice and help of clever and experienced women of the world, in the attainment both of private and of public objects; and there are important matters of public administration to which few men are equally competent with such women; among others, the detailed control of expenditure. But what we are now discussing is not the need which society has of the services of women in public business, but the dull and hopeless life to which it so often condemns them, by forbidding them to exercise the practical abilities which many of them are conscious of, in any wider field than one which to some of them never was, and to others is no longer, open. If there is anything vitally important to the happiness of human beings, it is that they should relish their habitual pursuit. This requisite of an enjoyable life is very imperfectly granted, or altogether denied, to a large part of mankind; and by its absence many a life is a failure, which is provided, in appearance, with every requisite of success. But if circumstances which society is not yet skilful enough to overcome, render such failures often for the present inevitable, society need not itself inflict them. The injudiciousness of parents, a youth's own inexperience, or the absence of external opportunities for the congenial vocation, and their presence for an uncongenial, condemn numbers of men to pass their lives in doing one thing reluctantly and ill, when there are other things which they could have done well and happily. But on women this sentence is imposed by actual law, and by customs equivalent to law. What, in unenlightened societies, colour, race, religion, or in the case of a conquered country,

nationality, are to some men, sex is to all women; a peremptory exclusion from almost all honourable occupations, but either such as cannot be fulfilled by others, or such as those others do not think worthy of their acceptance. Sufferings arising from causes of this nature usually meet with so little sympathy, that few persons are aware of the great amount of unhappiness even now produced by the feeling of a wasted life.

Mill never used eight words to say something when he could think of eighty; but his perception was sharp and his character essentially sympathetic. His argument throughout *The Subjection Is Women* is primarily **utilitarian**: women have proven themselves talented and resourceful in spite of the appalling constraints placed on them by centuries of cultural tradition, and therefore it can only benefit society to put these proven skills to full use by allowing women to participate in civic life. Mill was enough a man of his era to maintain that women ought not to enter the workplace, since that would remove them from their domestic responsibilities, yet he advocated full political rights for them and equality before the law. Early feminists like Anderson and Mill moved against the tide of their times. The cofounder of the magazine *The Economist*, Walter Bagehot

Dangerous Liaison *Interior*, by Degas (1869), presents a disturbing vision of male-female relations. The narrow bed, simple furnishings, and the prominent display of a sewing box suggest this is a scene of a prostitute and a customer in a hotel room. (In Paris at that time prostitutes often carried sewing boxes, both as an indicator of their profession but also, and more practically, so they could repair their clothing after a customer's rough assault.) The disheveled woman has turned her back on the man, who stands, dark and menacing, against the door.

(1826–1877), offered just one response, and Mill's advocacy for women's suffrage nearly caused a permanent rupture of his relations with his own father.[2]

Things were no better for women on the Continent. French law declared as a bedrock legal principle the notion that "a wife owes obedience to her husband." German law granted every husband the sole right to decide when the breastfeeding of his infant son by his wife should end. (The nursing of daughters, presumably, was not sufficiently important to merit regulation by the state.) As late as 1900, German law denied all parental rights over her children to any woman who remarried after her husband's death; her new husband, the children's stepfather, assumed sole legal authority over them. Social pressures limited the movements that proper middle-class women could make in the world, while allowing men to roam freely, with predictable results. By the end of the 19th century nearly 17 percent of all the children born in France annually were illegitimate, and nearly one-quarter of all adult female deaths either resulted directly from or were complicated by sexually trans-mitted diseases.[3] In nearly every major statistical category—life expectancy, education, employment, and income, above all—women on the Continent lagged behind men, especially in the working class; it was only a matter of time before calls were raised to do something about it. Reformers in Britain and the United States led the way, with Scandinavian activists close behind. In order to protect women's health and secure their rights under the law, they quickly realized, two things stood out as strategic necessities—suffrage and education.

> By the end of the 19th century nearly 17 percent of all the children born in France annually were illegitimate, and nearly one-quarter of all adult female deaths either resulted directly from or were complicated by sexually transmitted diseases.

WHOSE RIGHTS COME FIRST?

Opposition came in many forms and from many directions, some of them surprising. That most men in Europe opposed women's suffrage comes as no surprise. Neither does the opposition mounted by most of the mainstream churches, which dismissed ideas of the "modern woman" as an abrogation of the traditional roles of wife and mother. But large numbers of intelligent, talented, and ambitious women also refused to go along with the call to equal rights—such as the nurse and organizer Florence Nightingale (1820–1910) and the novelist Mary Ward (1851–1920). And often their reason was not so much lack of sympathy for women as passion for reform on behalf of others.

---

[2]   Bagehot: "The light nothings of the drawing room, and the grave things of the office, are as different from one another as two human occupations can be."

[3]   French law forbade unwed mothers to bring paternity suits against the fathers of their children.

Nightingale, whose opposition to the women's movement was particularly fierce, shared many of the attitudes of contemporary males about female abilities and weaknesses. She had served heroically in the Crimean War of the 1850s, tending to thousands of wounded British soldiers. After the war she established a school in London that launched modern nursing as a profession; she also helped raise funds for the grand Royal Buckinghamshire Hospital outside the city. A deeply pious and determined woman, she maintained throughout her life that the cause of women's rights paled in comparison with the world's other sufferings. In fact, as she wrote to a friend in December 1861, it seemed to be nothing more than middle-class self-absorption:

> Now just look at the degree in which women have sympathy—as far as my experience is concerned. And my experience of women is almost as large as Europe. And it is so intimate too. I have lived and slept in the same bed as English countesses and Prussian *Bauerinnen* [peasant girls]. No Roman Catholic *Supérieure* [mother superior] has ever had charge of women of the different creeds that I have had. No woman has excited "passions" among women more than I have. Yet I have no school behind me. My doctrines have not taken hold among women.... No woman that I know has ever *appris à apprendre* [attempted to understand]. And I attribute this to want of sympathy.... It makes me so mad, the Women's Rights talk.... Women crave for being loved, not for loving. They scream out at you for sympathy all day long, [but] they are incapable of giving any in return, for they cannot remember your affairs long enough to do so.... I am sick with indignation at what wives and mothers will do [out] of the most egregious selfishness. (Quoted in Cook, *The Life of Florence Nightingale, 1820–1910*, 1913)

To Mary Ward—who published two dozen novels under her married name, Mrs. Humphrey Ward—suffrage represented a perversion of female character. As she wrote in a magazine editorial in 1889, suffrage reform was an effort to fit women into roles to which they were not suited by nature or by Christian faith:

> As voters for or members of School Boards, Boards of Guardians, and other important public bodies, women now have opportunities for public usefulness which must promote the growth of character, and at the same time strengthen among them the social sense and belief. But we believe that the emancipation process has now reached the limits fixed by the physical constitution of women, and by the fundamental difference which must always exist between their main occupations and those of men.... Nothing can be further from our minds than to seek to depreciate the position or the importance of women. It is because we are

keenly alive to the enormous value of their special contributions to the community, that we oppose what seems to us likely to endanger that contribution. We are convinced that the pursuit of a mere outward equality with men is for women not only vain but demoralizing. It leads to personal struggle and rivalry, where the only effort of both the great divisions of the human family should be to contribute the characteristic labour and the best gifts of each to the common stock.

The first significant gains in women's rights, ironically, appeared in states along the European periphery, although these were rights separate from suffrage itself. Tsarist Russia opened its universities to women in 1867, for example, as did Finland. The United States formally allowed women to enroll in its universities the following year, and Sweden did so the year after that.[4] In 1872 Sweden

Female Physician   Emily Shanks (1857-1936), a British-Russian painter who lived in Moscow until 1914, painted this scene of a female physician conducting an ear exam. Women were allowed to study medicine informally in Russia as early as the 1850s, but the first MD degree was not granted until 1867 when Nadezhda Suslova (1843-1918) became the country's first licensed female physician.

---

4   By 1880 fully one-third of all university students in the United States were women.

outlawed arranged marriages that did not have the expressed consent and agreement of the bride. The first women's labor and trade unions in France were
legalized in 1874, and by 1900 the law allowed women to practice law. In Russia,
roughly one of every ten licensed physicians was female by 1914.

An obvious questions arises: Why were the dominant European states—the
states with the most developed economies, highest literacy rates, most established
democratic systems, and most elaborate and sophisticated networks of communication—the last states to extend suffrage to women? The women's rights movement,
after all, had actually arisen originally in those leading nations. Calls for women's
full legal and political equality date back to the Enlightenment of the 1700s in
England and France. To pick just a sampler, Jeremy Bentham's *Introduction to the
Principles of Moral and Legislation* (1781), the Marquis de Condorcet's *In Support of
the Rights of Citizenship for Women* (1790), and Mary Wollstonecraft's *Vindication
of the Rights of Women* (1792) all called for universal suffrage, equity in property
rights, and reform of marriage and divorce laws. And the leading feminist writer
in Sweden, Hedvig Nordenflycht (1718–1763), was calling, more tamely, for improved education for females. Many women of the 19th century in fact agreed with
Florence Nightingale's opinion that the world had far more pressing issues to deal
with than the plight of European women.

Harriet Martineau (1802–1876), for example, one of the founders of modern
sociology, thought the feminist leaders of her time to be downright dangerous;
her political passions focused on abolishing the slave trade, extending suffrage to
working-class men, and improving educational opportunities for women. Public
health issues and poor relief, not political rights for middle-class women, were
what mattered. Martineau's first two books, *Illustrations of Political Economy*
(1832) and *Poor Laws and Paupers Illustrated* (1834), focused on the economic
injustice of industrial capitalism and became bestsellers, ironically leaving her financially secure for life. She never married (although she nearly wedded Charles
Darwin's brother, Erasmus). Her three-volume study *Society in America* (1837)
is one of the classic works of early sociology. The result of two years of travel
in the United States, it offers a sharp critique of American values and practices.
The chapter "The Political Non-Existence of Women" describes how American
women are given "indulgence rather than justice" and have few prospects in life
other than marriage. Toward the end of her life, Martineau signed petitions calling for female suffrage but refused to call herself a suffragist.

The delay in bringing female suffrage to Belgium, Britain, France, Germany,
Holland, and Italy was due not only to stubborn male opposition. For many
passionate reformers, the problems of the working poor were simply more dire.
Not everyone agreed, and certainly not Beatrice Webb (1858–1943), coauthor
with her husband, Sidney, of *The History of Trade Unionism* (1894) and *Industrial Democracy* (1897) and a founder of the socialist Fabian Society. To her, the

prospect of two oppressed individuals, one denied the vote and the other dying of starvation, created an obvious moral choice for action. A noted German activist of the era, Anna Maier, in her autobiography (1912) described the plight of her life in distinctly economic rather than sexual terms. To Maier, economic oppression trumped sexual prejudice and had to be dealt with first:

> My father was a weaver and my mother a spooler, although whenever necessary they did any work they could find. I was the youngest of twelve children and learned at an early age what it is to work. . . . [From the age of six] I had to get up at five o'clock every morning to do some spooling before running off to school. My clothes were rags. After a morning at school I hurried home to do some more spooling before having lunch, and then I returned to school for the afternoon lessons, after which I went back to more spooling. . . . When I was thirteen my mother took me by the hand and we went to the manager of a nearby tobacco factory, to see if he would give me a job. He refused, but my mother begged him to take me on since my father had recently died and we were desperate, and so he hired me. . . . The way workers were treated at the factory was hellish. The older women berated the young girls and sometimes even beat them. . . . Years went by, and eventually a new newspaper, the *Arbeiterinnen Zeitung* ["Women Workers' Daily"], started to be published; one of the older women smuggled a few copies into the factory. . . . When a friend loaned me a copy I had to hide it at work and could not even let my mother see it at home. I learned many new things and met many new people. . . . When some men founded a workers' organization they said women could not join, but when a party agent came . . . I asked him if I wasn't enough of an adult worker to be a member. I remember that he was embarrassed at first, but he finally spoke up: "When do you want to start?" I joined, and remain a member to this very day.

The gradual success of antipoverty programs and the legalization of labor unions indirectly helped the cause of women, for as they alleviated the sufferings of the working poor, they freed up energies to pursue other goals.

SUFFRAGISTS AND SUFFRAGETTES

Suffragists and suffragettes were not the same thing. They pursued the same end—women's right to vote—but their methods differed. In simplest terms, **suffragists** worked peaceably and within the legal system for women's rights, whereas

suffragettes favored confrontation, aggressive action, and, whenever they thought it necessary, even violence in order to change society. Britain's National Society for Women's Suffrage formed in 1867 and provided a model for similar groups that sprung up quickly on the Continent—like the VVV (*Vereeniging voor Vrouwenkiesrecht*, or "Society for Women's Legal Rights") in Holland. In 1878 a loose network of these associations convened the first international congress for women's rights in Paris, where they embraced the terms feminist and suffragist and charted out strategies for their cause. These drew heavily on their observations of (male) electoral politics of the age, which included fostering political alliances and courting sympathetic members of the press. Earlier campaigns by women to promote the abolition of slavery and alcohol had given them vital experience at shaping public opinion. But in the end these early feminist organizations proved more successful in enrolling members than in bringing about significant reform. Constitutional change is a slow-moving business, especially when it faces entrenched resistance.

The denial of female suffrage lingered into the 20th century, which resulted in a dramatic change in some reformers' tactics. Led by the redoubtable Emmeline Pankhurst (1858–1928) and her three daughters, Christabel (1880–1958), Sylvia (1882–1960), and Adela (1885–1961), the new group called themselves suffragettes. These activists broke away from the main suffragist association in Britain in 1903 and established the Women's Social and Political Union (WSPU). The WSPU was a distinctly more militant organization; its motto was "Deeds, not words." The suffragettes provoked anger and outrage everywhere they went. Unaffiliated with any political party, they nevertheless attended and intentionally disrupted political

Redoubtable Suffragette   Emmeline Pankhurst addressing a crowd of men.

meetings by the score; they protested outside Parliament and sometimes chained themselves to its doors; some vandalized shop windows and churches.[5]

Pankhurst herself engaged in little overt violence other than trying to force her way into Parliamentary meetings (for which she was imprisoned for six weeks)—and once slapping a policeman in order to be arrested. But she declared that "the condition of our sex is so deplorable that it is our duty to break the law in order to draw attention to the reasons why we do so." In a speech in the United States in 1913, she described her experience and the WSPU's tactics:

I do not come here as an advocate, because whatever position the suffrage movement may occupy in the United States of America, in England it has passed beyond the realm of advocacy and it has entered into the sphere of practical politics. It has become the subject of revolution and civil war, and so tonight I am not here to advocate woman suffrage. American suffragists can do that very well for themselves. I am here as a soldier who has temporarily left the field of battle in order to explain—it seems strange it should have to be explained—what civil war is like when civil war is waged by women. . . . I am here [also] as a person who, according to the law courts of my country, . . . is of no value to the community at all; and I am adjudged because of my life to be a dangerous person, under sentence of penal servitude in a convict prison. So you see there is some special interest in hearing so unusual a person address you. I dare say, in the minds of many of you—you will perhaps forgive me this personal touch—that I do not look either very like a soldier or very like a convict, and yet I am both. . . . We have brought the government of England to this position, that it has to face this alternative: either women are to be killed, or women are to have the vote. I ask American men in this meeting, what would you say if in your State you were faced with that alternative, that you must either kill them or give them their citizenship,—women, many of whom you respect, women whom you know have lived useful lives, women whom you know, even if you do not know them personally, are animated with the highest motives, women who are in pursuit of liberty and the power to do useful public service? Well, there is only one answer to that alternative; there is only one way out of it, unless you are prepared to put back civilization two or three generations; you must give those women the vote. Now that is the outcome of our civil war.

---

[5]   One suffragette committed suicide by running into the path of a racehorse owned by the royal family, to draw attention to the plight of women.

Ultimately, she was arrested several dozen times before Parliament finally granted unrestricted women's suffrage in 1928.

Suffragettes on the Continent followed similar measures. In France, Hubertine Auclert (1848–1914) became infamous, and triggered a wave of copycat protests, when she smashed a ballot box in a municipal election in Paris to express her disgust at being unable to vote. Madeleine Pelletier (1874–1939), a physician and France's first female licensed psychiatrist, made her mark by agitating not only for suffrage but for women's rights to contraception and abortion (then a taboo subject) and by protesting the normative ideas of femininity by dressing as a man, complete with cane and bowler hat.[6] Moreover, she continued to provide abortion services despite their illegality. A German socialist, Clara Zetkin (1857–1933), edited a radical newspaper (*Die Gleichheit*, "Equality") and invited arrest by taking a public position against World War I.

Many imprisoned suffragettes protested their arrests by going on hunger strikes, hoping to win sympathy for their cause by sacrificing themselves even to the point of death. Governments quickly responded by ordering forced feedings, a brutal process in which the woman was bound to a chair, had rubber tubing pushed down her throat or through her nostrils and into her stomach, and then had a loose porridge poured into her. Worse still, the British government passed the "Cat and Mouse" Act (officially, the Temporary Discharge of Prisoners for Ill Health Act) in 1913. This ordered police to release from prison any hunger-striking suffragette, only to rearrest her after she had regained her health on the outside. The forced feedings and repeated arrests swung public sympathy toward the women prisoners—especially when their sufferings were made public. In her memoir (1914), Lady Constance Bulwer-Lytton (1869–1923) wrote of disguising herself as a poor seamstress in order to avoid receiving preferential treatment because of her noble status. The harsh treatment she received in prison resulted in a stroke that left her right

Rallying for Women's Suffrage
German poster in support of Women's Day (March 8, 1914), a rally on behalf of women's suffrage. The German government banned this poster soon after its appearance, and most copies have been destroyed.

---

6   Asked once why she dressed as a man, Pelletier responded, "I'll show my breasts when men start wearing pants that show their pricks."

arm paralyzed. She taught herself to write with her left hand and produced *Prisons and Prisoners* in a year.

But extreme actions, even terrorist ones, cost the movement public sympathy, too. To chain oneself to the houses of Parliament was one thing; to set fire to the homes of Parliamentarians was another. In February 1913 a group of WSPU members burned down the home of David Lloyd George, then the chancellor of the exchequer. Lloyd George privately supported women's suffrage but officially opposed it in 1913, for fear that it might disrupt preparations for the coming World War. The following year another suffragette took an axe to a painting of Venus by Diego Velázquez (1599–1660) in the National Gallery in London. She claimed that she was merely doing to one beautiful woman what society was doing to all.

As dedicated as the suffragists were, and as brave and selfless as at least many of the suffragettes were, winning the vote ultimately resulted more from the economic conditions in Europe after World War I. Before that, only Finland (1906) and Norway (1913) had universal suffrage; Denmark passed it in 1915. After the war, women were enfranchised in half of Europe (see Map 21.1).

LOVE AND THE "MODERN WOMAN"

Helene Stöcker (1869–1943) was a leading German feminist who advocated suffrage but devoted most of her prodigious energy to women's sexual health. That issue turned out to be an increasing part of redefining a woman's role. It also went hand in hand with the growing availability of information about sex throughout society—and growing controversies over birth control. It was also just one part of the redefinition of female identity—in literature, education, and public perception.

Stöcker founded the Society for the Protection of Mothers in 1905 (later renamed the German Society for the Protection of Mothers and for Sexual Reform) and edited two journals—*Mutterschutz* ("Care for Mothers") and *Die neue Generation* ("The New Generation"). Through these she campaigned for publicly available sex education, including contraception and abortion, and advocated for the legal rights of children born out of marriage. In 1906 she published *Women and Love: A Manifesto for Emancipating Women and Men in Germany*, which described her plan to reinvent male-female relationships, preferably within marriage but not necessarily so. Her goal, she insisted, was not just to pursue equality for its own sake; it was to help relationships between men and women to become more true, more intimate, and more rich. The greatest harm of the gender inequity of the age was not the legal injustice of it, she argued, but the emotional aridity of the relationships it fostered and even encouraged.

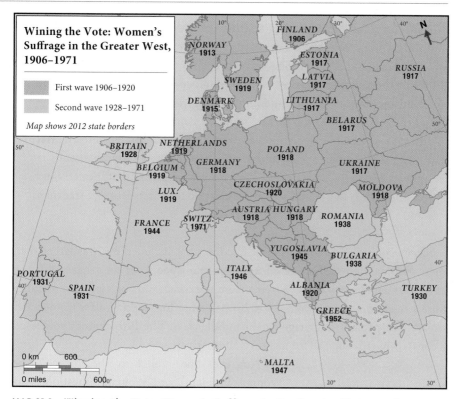

Wining the Vote: Women's Suffrage in the Greater West, 1906–1971

First wave 1906–1920

Second wave 1928–1971

Map shows 2012 state borders

FINLAND 1906

NORWAY 1913

ESTONIA 1917

RUSSIA 1917

SWEDEN 1919

LATVIA 1917

DENMARK 1915

LITHUANIA 1917

BELARUS 1917

BRITAIN 1928

NETHERLANDS 1919

POLAND 1918

GERMANY 1918

UKRAINE 1917

BELGIUM 1919

LUX. 1919

CZECHOSLOVAKIA 1920

MOLDOVA 1918

AUSTRIA 1918

HUNGARY 1918

ROMANIA 1938

FRANCE 1944

SWITZ. 1971

YUGOSLAVIA 1945

BULGARIA 1938

PORTUGAL 1931

SPAIN 1931

ITALY 1946

ALBANIA 1920

TURKEY 1930

GREECE 1952

0 km   600

0 miles   600

MALTA 1947

MAP 21.1   **Winning the Vote: Women's Suffrage in the Greater West, 1906–1971**

Stöcker envisioned a world in which any woman who wanted to do so could rise above the traditional path of being a dutiful daughter, then a quiet, uncomplaining wife, and then a loving selfless mother. If a woman wanted, she could pursue an independent life filled with emotional, intellectual, and sexual richness. Stöcker's essay "The Modern Woman" (1893) put the case with her typical candor:

> I am describing a unique species, . . . the modern woman, . . . who sets out from the shelter of her father's household . . . in order to gain financial independence, the prerequisite of every freedom. . . . The modern woman does not wish to become man-like but only to become a happier, because a more free, person, one who continues to grow in her unique womanly way. She long ago gave up the childish complaint that she was not born male; rather, she has learned to appreciate her unique feminine strength as a rare gift, a thing set apart, something beyond traditional categories. . . . [The modern woman] is born for love. With the fires of her nature—with all her heart, soul, and sensuality—she craves

intimacy, and she needs it more than a man does.... She yearns to give and receive love as a woman, not simply to sit quietly by while clever men talk to one another.... She craves freedom too, and just as intensely. Only these two things, love and freedom, combined, can grant her the kind of inner peacefulness found among truly liberated people. She therefore maintains a critical distance, a composure, in order to avoid being overwhelmed by her intense youthful sensuality, lest, after a brief thrill, she end up making herself and another truly miserable. But she knows one thing all too well: The greatest happiness that life can offer develops only in a relationship between two fully free people, a free man and a free woman. Of this there is no doubt.

Stöcker's concern was for a kind of freedom that included but was larger than mere political rights. She wanted, as did so many people of her generation, to redefine sexual identity so as to free it from the constraints of Victorian morality. Surely there must be alternatives to brutish labor for working-class women and dreary if respectable marriage for the middle class. The 19th century witnessed a constantly growing call for just such alternatives.

Not everyone joined in the chorus. The "Woman Problem" or "Woman Question" was analogous to nationalism: just as the air was filled with passionate discussions of the "Englishness" of the English, the "Germanness" of the Germans, or the "Spanishness" of the Spaniards, so too were many people intent to define the essential qualities of womanhood. Advances in science were of little help here, since Darwinian evolution appeared to reduce human life to a set of predetermined biological functions. And related sciences did not seem any more enlightened.

> Stöcker's concern was for a kind of freedom that included but was larger than mere political rights. She wanted, as did so many people of her generation, to redefine sexual identity so as to free it from the constraints of Victorian morality.

A popular American medical guide of the 1880s, *The Physical Life of Woman: Advice to the Maiden, Wife, and Mother,* by Dr. George Napheys, asserted that "the vast majority of women" possess only "moderate" sexual appetites, and "only in very rare instances do women experience one tithe of the sexual feeling which is familiar to most men. Many of them are entirely frigid, and not even in marriage do they ever perceive any real desire." A German gynecologist, Dr. Otto Adler, estimated in 1904 that "as many as forty percent" of all women experience no sexual desire in their lifetimes. Anatomists who studied the brain announced confidently that men are by nature between 12 and 20 percent more intelligent than women. Intellectual work, they proclaimed, when performed by women, diverts bodily energies away from their natural reproductive mission. An Englishwoman studying medicine at Girton College in 1888 summarized the attitude of physicians around her, in an anonymous article in the *Westminster Review*, as a sarcastic warning:

> Women, beware! Beware! You are on the brink of destruction! You have hitherto been engaged only in crushing your waists [by wearing corsets], now you are attempting to cultivate your minds! You have been merely dancing all night in the foul air of ballrooms; now you are beginning to spend your mornings in study. You have been incessantly stimulating your emotions with concerts and operas, with French plays and French novels; now you are exerting your understanding to learn Greek and solve propositions in Euclid. Beware! Oh, beware!! Science pronounces that the woman who studies—is lost!

Knowledge of sex, and confusion about it, abounded. Condoms, which had been used in Europe at least since the early 18th century, were readily available at taverns, pharmacists, and outdoor markets.[7] Other methods of contraception included cervical caps and diaphragms (made of vulcanized rubber after 1850), and herbal abortifacients like Queen Anne's lace, which consisted of the crushed seeds of flowering wild carrots. The most commonly used methods were presumably coitus interruptus and what is known today as the "rhythm method." Abortion was illegal everywhere in Europe but was generally available—at a high price and at considerable risk to health. Christian churches, too, felt the need to determine and enact official positions on contraception. Most had always condemned abortion, but doctrines on contraception were another matter. Until such measures became widely available, starting in midcentury, the churches had felt no need to take a definitive position except to condemn coitus interruptus as the "sin of Onan"—a reference to the tale in Genesis 38. Onan was the brother of Judah, and according to the custom of the times Onan had a responsibility, after Judah's early death, to wed and provide offspring for Judah's childless widow. When Onan instead "spilled his seed on the ground" by interrupting the sexual union with his sister-in-law, God condemned him to death for disobedience to the Law. Whatever the cause, birth rates among the middle class declined significantly between 1850 and 1914. In Britain, for example, one-quarter of all families

---

[7]   Condoms occasionally were sold at concession stands in theaters. The German army after 1870 handed them out to soldiers when they were about to go off duty.

had eight or more children in 1825. By 1925 fully one-half of all families had only one or two children each, while one family out of every six was childless.

The distribution of information about birth control ("family management" or "family limitation," as it was known at the time) was highly contentious. Western countries struggled with the tension between traditional morals and the free exchange of scientific knowledge. In the United States, President Theodore Roosevelt (r. 1901–1909) spoke for many when he called family limitation "one of the most unpleasant and unwholesome features of modern life." But women's demand for reliable contraception continued to grow. Dr. Aletta Jacobs (1854–1929), Holland's first female physician, established Europe's first birth control clinic in Amsterdam in 1882, dispensing information about contraception and the materials for it. A German physician in Breslau (today's city of Wrocław, Poland), Dr. Richard Richter, published the first treatise on the use of intrauterine devices in 1909. Alarmed by this proliferation of materials, social critics in Germany began to express concern that the ensuing labor shortage would invite immigration by "alien people—especially Slavs and perhaps the eastern European Jews too."

Ignorance of sexual matters was nevertheless widespread and, to an extent, deliberately imposed. If the moral code of "proper society" forbade the discussion of sex and tried to control the distribution of scientific knowledge about it, then it is not surprising that many men and women began their sexual lives without any accurate understanding of what they were beginning. Experts still warned that masturbation was medically harmful to both men and women, since it depleted the body of "vital fluids and energies." That depletion supposedly left the body, according to a medical guide of the time, more vulnerable to "seminal weakness, impotence, dysury [painful urination], *tabes dorsalis* [syphilitic myelopathy], pulmonary consumption, dyspepsia, dimness of sight, vertigo, epilepsy, hypochondriasis, loss of memory, manalgia [catatonia], fatuity [dementia], and death."

Much of Western society held two contradictory beliefs at once—in the sexual rapaciousness

Male Antimasturbation Device
Masturbation had long been criticized in European culture as a sin or a personal failing, but it only became regarded as clinically unhealthy in the early 18th century, when a series of pseudo-scientific works warned of its supposedly harmful effects. In Victorian times, concerns about the dangers of masturbation grew so extensive that many parents began to employ physical methods to prevent their sons from indulging in the fearful practice. This piece dates to 1880. Made of copper, it was worn on a belt to protect boys both from masturbation and from unintentional nocturnal emissions.

of women and in their natural sexlessness. The explanation lay in the widespread view that there are two types of women.[8] Assuming that most women—proper women, in society's eyes—had no interest in sex, many felt there was no need to educate them about it, and the consequence was entrenched ignorance.

Many of the era's greatest works of literature are dedicated to exploring female identity in both its generalized essentials and its individual quirks. These are great works of art—and their authors are all male. Women writers also explored female character in depth, but generally with less of a singular focus on a specific woman, as in the works written by men, and generally with less artistic success. George Eliot's *Middlemarch* (1872) was undeniably the greatest novel written by a European woman in the late 19th century; the first in the 20th century by a woman to have truly changed the very shape of the novel was Virginia Woolf's *Mrs. Dalloway* (1925). No doubt the more modest growth in the intervening fifty years has many causes—and no doubt the underappreciation of novels and plays written by women in their time has contributed to our ignorance in our own.

Literature of Female Identity: A Sampler
Madame Bovary (1857), by Gustave Flaubert
Anna Karenina (1878), by Leo Tolstoy
The Portrait of a Lady (1881), by Henry James
Fortunata and Jacinta (1887), by Benito Pérez Galdós
Hedda Gabler (1890), by Henrik Ibsen
Tess of the d'Urbervilles (1891), by Thomas Hardy
The New Woman (1893), by Bolesław Prus
Effi Briest (1894), by Theodor Fontane.

In the intervening fifty-plus years, women in every Western country continued to produce excellent fiction (Willa Cather and Edith Wharton in the United States, for example) but were their aims any less revolutionary, and if so, why? It is an important question. Why, at the very time when the status of women in Western society was being most passionately and universally debated, were women novelists, poets, and playwrights stimulating any less of a debate? No doubt the deep involvement of so many women in suffragist and suffragette

---

[8]   As one medical writer in Oxford put it: "Nine out of ten women are indifferent or actively dislike [sex]; the tenth, who enjoys it, will always be a harlot."

work partially explains the lack; the times called for action, not novels or poems. Moreover, political themes seldom make for enduring literature.

Sex itself may provide another explanation. Not gender, but actual sex. European fiction and drama from 1850 to 1914 was dominated by the **realist** and **naturalist** schools, which aimed for a fuller and more detailed depiction of daily life. It lingered on its characters' gritty surroundings, the sounds and smells of the cities they inhabited, the sense of despair and misery created by wretched food, hard labor, and oppressive social mores. A goal of these writers was to depict the whole array of pressures, demands, irritations, and longings that shape human lives. One of the greatest naturalist writers in France, Émile Zola (1840–1902), wrote a series of twenty novels with interlocking characters, families, settings, and events in an effort to portray the entire panorama of French life during the Second Empire. His descriptions of social snobbery, grueling manual labor, inadequate housing, the ruin of alcoholism, prostitution, marital bliss, and marital despair are often unnervingly vivid.

Nana   *Nana*, by Edouard Manet (1832-1883). Painted for the 1877 Salon at Paris but rejected for its immoral character, Manet's large canvas (almost nine feet tall) presents another scene of a prostitute and her client. What offended viewers about this picture was not its subject-matter (which was fairly common by that time) but the fact that the young woman appears to have no shame about her profession; indeed, she has turned toward and is smiling prettily at the viewer. The fact that her customer, though only half shown, is clearly a member of respectable bourgeois society probably did not help either.

Many realist and naturalist writers depicted sexual relations with a candor that often set the Victorians' teeth on edge. Though tame by 21st-century standards, the frank sexuality in European literature from 1850 to 1914 may have been off-putting to women writers—something they did not wish to attempt, or felt that they could not do. Even Virginia Woolf, as late as her death in 1944, allowed no sex to enter any of her books.[9] Women writers already worked in the face of enough social prejudices. Did they feel that writing frankly about sexual feelings might be too much? No one can say for sure.

---

[9]   Woolf's most subversive novel, the time-shifting, gender-bending fantasy *Orlando*, published in 1928, was inspired by her lesbian affair with Vita Sackville-West. But it contains no trace of eroticism.

> **Literature of Sexuality: A Sampler**
> *L'Assommoir* (1877), by Émile Zola
> *Ghosts* (1881), by Henrik Ibsen
> *Miss Julie* (1888), by August Strindberg
> *The Kreutzer Sonata* (1889), by Leo Tolstoy
> *Jude the Obscure* (1895), by Thomas Hardy.
> *Sister Carrie* (1900), by Theodore Dreiser
> *The Sacred Fount* (1901), by Henry James

SCHOOL, WORK, AND THE NEW WOMAN

As the European industrial economy continued to expand, the late 19th century saw explosive growth in public education across the West. Even factory workers at the low end of the pay scale needed to be functionally literate and numerate, if only so that they could read the regulations governing the shop floor. Prior to the revolutions of 1848, most Western states had established only public secondary schools. Elementary education was thought to be needed only by the relatively well-to-do, who hired private tutors for their young children, which left poor working-class youths free to be exploited in the factories. When the 19th century began, only Germany had a system of state-run primary schools; France created its system in 1833. For most working-class girls, formal education ended there. France did not open its secondary schools to girls until 1880, and by the end of the century there were only three dozen such schools for girls in the entire country, and the schooling was not made compulsory until a few years later. Germany's first secondary school for girls appeared in 1872. In Britain, primary schooling became compulsory in 1880 but was not run by the state until 1902. In the Netherlands compulsory state-run schools did not exist for either boys or girls before 1901, but private primary and secondary education had long been among the best in Europe. Usually the creation of public primary education systems followed within a decade of the outlawing of child labor.

Secondary education expanded rapidly too, as the economy created a demand for better-educated workers. Careers in civil service, law, and medicine opened up too. New careers as railway engineers, train staff, postal workers, shipping clerks, harbormasters, civil servants, accountants, public works supervisors and staff, secretaries, teachers, journalists, and legal aides all appeared in the late 19th century—and all needed preparation. Public schools provided new opportunities for women, since the education of children seemed to many to be a natural extension of women's traditional role as caregivers. The United

States led the way, with fully two-thirds of all primary and secondary school teachers being female by 1890. Europe's figures did not measure up, but the majority of primary school teachers in each country were women. So great was the demand, in fact, that entire colleges for training teachers were created; along with special colleges for medical training, they were the first cracks in the walls that kept women out of the university system. Aside from professional colleges, the first colleges for women were established in the 1870s and 1880s—such as Newnham College in Cambridge or Lady Margaret Hall in Oxford—but were not formally accepted into their university systems until well into the 20th century. Overall, the numbers of women in all areas of education continued to grow until, on the eve of war in 1914, perhaps as many as 12–15 percent of European undergraduate students were female.

A different and special chapter in the development of education opened with the career of Maria Montessori (1870–1952), the first female licensed physician in Italy. Her training in psychology led to an interest in the education of mentally handicapped children. In 1896, with the support of the Italian minister for education, she worked with a group of special-needs children whom the state schools had dismissed as uneducable. Using her own experimental methods, she produced an impressive result: within three years, her eight-year-old students outscored public school students in reading and writing. This led to her opening a new elementary school in a rough neighborhood in Rome in 1907, where she wanted to see what effect her methods would have on mainstream students.

Montessori's methods were controversial among educators, and remain so today, but produced consistently superior performance in every category, including social behavior, up to the age of twelve. Her method was based on the notion of self-directed education, or "spontaneous self-development." She believed that children, being naturally inquisitive, learn better by being allowed to explore at their own rate than by being drilled with data according to a state plan. As she wrote in *Education for a New World*, the teachers in her schools thus acted more as facilitators or guides than as deliverers of knowledge:

Maria Montessori (1870–1952)
Educational reformer and the first woman to receive a medical degree in Italy.

Scientific observation has established that education is not what the teacher gives; education is a natural process spontaneously carried out by the human individual, and is acquired not by listening to words but by experiences upon the environment. The task of the teacher becomes that of preparing a series of motives of cultural activity, spread over a specially prepared environment, and then refraining from obtrusive interference. Human teachers can only help the great work that is being done, as servants help the master. Doing so, they will be witnesses to the unfolding of the human soul and to the rising of a New Man who will not be a victim of events, but will have the clarity of vision to direct and shape the future of human society.

Schools using her methods, whether officially affiliated with the International Montessori Association or not, began to spring up across Europe and especially in the United States.

Meanwhile, the numbers of women in the workplace also increased. The development of the telegraph and telephone systems created a need for well-trained operators, while machines like the typewriter (invented in 1829, with the first commercially produced typewriter appearing in 1870) virtually created the modern business office, with its attendant pools of secretaries, clerks, and administrative managers. Women thus became essential, if "inferior," elements of the modern commercial economy. Newspapers and magazines dedicated to them multiplied exponentially. Hundreds of popular songs, plays, and paintings focused on the **new woman** of the start of the century, whether to celebrate, lampoon, or pillory her. Some were gently playful, as in the popular stage play *The New Woman* by Sydney Grundy, or in this anonymous poem of 1898:

> Rock-a-bye baby, for father is near.
> Mother is "biking"—she never is here!
> Out in the park she's scorching all day
> Or at some meeting is talking away!
>
> She's the king-pin at the women's rights show,
> Teaching poor husbands the way they should go!
> Close then your eyes; there's dishes to do.
> Rock-a-bye baby, 'tis Pa sings to you!

The reference to "biking" alludes to a popular new invention: the chain-driven bicycle. Earlier bicycles had employed direct drive—that is, the pedals were attached directly to the hub of the large front wheel. Though capable of significant speed, these early bicycles were notoriously unstable and required a man's strength to pedal. Chain-driven bicycles, however, suited women and were quickly adopted as a new means of locomotion that was doubly important. They enabled, in those pre-automobile days, a wider degree of maneuverability, and they symbolized, in their very propulsion, the spirit of independence shown by the new woman.[10]

Free to move her own person, to control her own sexual life, to attend school, to pursue a career, and to seek a new kind of fulfillment in life, the New Woman entered the 20th century full of hope.

The finest achievement of the new woman has been personal liberty. This is the foundation of civilization; and as long as any one class is watched suspiciously, even fondly guarded, and protected, so long will that class not only be weak, and treacherous, individually, but parasitic, and a collective danger to the community. Who has not heard wives commended for wheedling their husbands out of money, or joked because they are hopelessly extravagant? As long as caprice and scheming are considered feminine virtues, as long as man is the only wage-earner, doling out sums of money, or scattering lavishly, so long will women be degraded, even if they are perfectly contented, and men are willing to labor to keep them in idleness! Although individual women from prehistoric times have accomplished much, as a class they have been set aside to minister to men's comfort. But when once the higher has been tried, civilization repudiates the lower. Men have come to see that no advance can be made with one half-humanity set apart merely for the functions of sex; that children are quite liable to inherit from the mother, and should have opportunities to inherit the accumulated ability and culture and character that is produced only by intellectual and civil activity. The world has tried to move with men for dynamos, and "clinging" women impeding every step of progress, in arts, science, industry, professions, they have been a thousand years behind men because forced into seclusion. They have been over-sexed. They have naturally not been impressed with their duties to society, in its myriad needs, or with their own value as individuals. The new woman, in the sense of the best woman, the flower of all the womanhood of past ages, has come to stay— if civilization is to endure.

So declared *The New Womanhood*, a best-selling manifesto of 1904 by Winnifred Harper Cooley. This hymn of victory to come is likewise expressed in fictional

---

[10] Bicycles helped get rid of the Victorian corsets and stays that had for so long restricted and deformed women's movements.

form in *The New Woman* (1893), by one of Poland's greatest novelists, Bolesław Prus (1847–1912).

WOMEN, ISLAM, AND NATIONALISM

Yet another book championed the rights of women and called for an end to their social seclusion, free access to education, and a guarantee of full political equality. In fact, it was also entitled *The New Woman* and appeared between Prus's novel and Harper Cooley's manifesto. It was *Al-Mar'a al-jadida*, published in Cairo in 1901, by Kasim Amin (1863–1908). His call was not alone, but it quickly ran into struggles over Arab nationalism and the Ottoman decline.

Amin's father was a Kurd and his mother an Egyptian; apart from four years in France in the 1880s, he spent the whole of his brief life in Egypt.

Spirit of Independence   Advertisement for the Grand Manège Central, a popular bicycling track and park in Paris, ca. 1890. The American suffragist Susan B. Anthony (1820-1906) once declared: "I think [the bicycle] has done more to emancipate women than anything else in the world. It gives women a feeling of freedom and self-reliance. I stand and rejoice every time I see a woman ride by on a wheel. . . the picture of free, untrammeled womanhood."

An aristocrat, and wealthy, he worked for a time as a lawyer and was one of the cofounders of Cairo University, which he served as vice president and secretary general. While in Paris, Amin had made contact with the great Islamic reformer Muhammad Ali, who inspired his conviction that Islam needed to remake itself in order to adapt to the modern world. Otherwise, it risked losing out to the conservative Wahhabi movement, which regarded every social innovation as an affront to sacred tradition.

To Amin (more so even than to Muhammad Ali himself) the most urgently needed reform was to improve the social status of women in Muslim society. He called for four essential changes—allowing women's access to education, a constitutional guarantee of political equality, abolition of the customary wearing of the veil, and reform of marriage laws in order to deny husbands their right to repudiate a wife at will and to take multiple wives. To make his full argument required two books, and *The New Woman* had been preceded in 1899 by the legal treatise *The Emancipation of Women* (*Tahrir al-mar'a*). These were bold positions to take even in the Islamic Enlightenment atmosphere of turn-of-the-century Egypt, and Amin stirred up considerable opposition (although he was ultimately admired within Europe after *The Emancipation of Women* appeared in a German translation in 1928). For several years he engaged in a public debate with conservative jurists on these issues, but he soon devoted the bulk of his time to the establishment of Cairo University (1908), which Amin and his cofounders intended to be a Western-style university emphasizing liberal thought. It could therefore serve as a complement, even a counterbalance, to the religiously based al-Azhar University, which dated back to the year 972.

For conservative Muslims, especially those of Arab ethnicity, modernization violated both the spirit of the faith and the dictates of nature; authentic Islamic identity and Western notions of human rights, democracy, and social progress, they insisted, were fundamentally incompatible.

As in Europe, the question of women's status in the Islamic world was related to the issue of nationalism. Tanzimat efforts (1839–1876) to modernize the Ottoman superstate proved in the end to be impossible. For conservative Muslims, especially those of Arab ethnicity, modernization violated both the spirit of the faith and the dictates of nature; authentic Islamic identity and Western notions of human rights, democracy, and social progress, they insisted, were fundamentally incompatible. For many others, especially those who welcomed the socially liberalizing aspect of Tanzimat but rejected its insistence on the continuation of Ottomanism, the future lay in local autonomy, independence from both the universalizing claims of Ottoman political overlordship and ethnically Arab religious supervision. They wanted to break free of both constraints and establish instead new provincial societies that were free to define their own Islamic and national identities. Abu al-Qasim al-Shabbi (1909–1934), a Tunisian poet and social critic of the era, put it bluntly: "Everything the Arabs have produced throughout all the long centuries of their history is colorless and utterly devoid of inspiration."

Writers experimented with new literary forms, especially the novel, because of its ability to express criticism of social ills and depict the struggles of individuals against various forms of oppression. As in Europe, the travails of women were a theme for many novelists and playwrights, including Taha Husayn (also spelled Hussein; 1889–1973), Mahmud Taymur (1894–1973), and Tawfiq al-Hakim (1898–1987). In al-Hakim's 1934 play based on *A Thousand and One Nights*, Scheherazade's storytelling helps her survive her murderous husband, and she achieves a mystical union with the ancient goddess Isis.

The reformers pressed especially for girls' rights to education and the reform of marriage practices to prohibit forcing girls into arranged marriages against their wills. Namik Kemal (1840–1888), an Ottoman court official turned playwright and journalist, championed girls' education in countless articles and essays. Ahmed Midhat (generally known as Midhat Pasha; 1822–1884) edited a daily newspaper in Istanbul, *Tercüman-ı Hakikat* ("The Interpreter of Truth"), that promoted social reform and distributed a weekly supplement designed especially for schoolchildren. Midhat also wrote over one hundred

Huda'i Sha'arawi Sha'arawi was a social reformer and founder of the feminist movement in Egypt, and author of *Harem Years: Memoirs of an Egyptian Feminist.*

books of history, popular science, and social reform, reaching an enormous audience. But the best-known feminist of her time was the Egyptian reformer Huda'i Sha'arawi (1878–1947), who organized a women's self-help society and the Union of Egyptian Women-Intellectuals. She also founded the Egyptian Feminist Union, in 1923, and served as its president until her death. Sha'arawi focused her prodigious energies on political involvement, speaking at conferences across Europe and organizing feminist demonstrations throughout Egypt. In addition to her *Memoirs,* she published two feminist journals called *The Egyptian Woman*—one in French (*L'Égyptienne*) and one in Arabic (*al-Misriyya*).

A few schools for girls opened in the 1880s and 1890s and received public funds, but more girls were probably enrolled in private or missionary schools than in the state-run system. Illiteracy remained a problem for both boys and girls, however; as late as 1914 perhaps only 10 percent of the Ottoman population could read and write. In general, reforms were most successful in those countries that had both close commercial and diplomatic relations with Europe and a higher percentage of non-Muslims among their populations: Egypt, Lebanon, Palestine, and what would eventually become the nation of Turkey. The countries of the Arabian Peninsula, Iraq, and Iran, however, saw little change. In Bengal, in the northeastern corner of India, a woman named Rokeya Sakhawat Hussein (1880–1932) opened the first high school for Muslim girls in 1909. At the same time, conservative ways remained deeply entrenched. As late as 1908, in fact, the slave trade remained legal throughout much of Ottoman society, so long as the slaves in question were non-Muslim females. The American ambassador to Constantinople during World War I famously noted that Armenian girls could be purchased in Turkish cities for as little as eighty cents apiece.

HONOR KILLING AND GENITAL CUTTING

As nationalist aspirations among peoples long ruled by the Ottomans rose, certain ethnic and cultural practices not formally part of Islamic teaching began to revive. Two of these are significant in regard to women: honor killing and genital cutting. Neither is accepted by mainstream Islamic tradition today, whether Sunni or Shi'ite. Both, however, were widely practiced in the Islamic world and experienced a resurgence during the Ottoman breakup.

Honor killing has a long history in many parts of the Islamic world, dating back to well before the arrival of the Prophet, but it is hardly a custom unique to Arab culture. The ancient Romans practiced it: the paternal authority (*patria potestas*) of the head of a family entitled him, and in fact demanded of him, that he preserve the good honor and repute of his household by eliminating those whose licentiousness brought dishonor to the clan. Many of the pre-Christian Germanic tribes demanded that families protect the moral uprightness (*mundium*) of their clans by killing those unmarried females who lost their virginity.[11] To the Arabs, Egyptians, and Kurds who followed the practice, two distinct concepts of honor predominated. Male honor (*hasab*) was both

Modern but Pure   Some unliberated women sunbathing near Istanbul, ca. 1900. The modernizing Tanzimat reforms of the mid-nineteenth century paid little attention to promoting the rights of women in the Ottoman state. As late as 1908 there was still an active slave-trade in females, even though slavery had been officially abolished in the 1840s and 1850s.

---

[11]   The Salian Franks allowed any member of the family to kill a wayward female. Early Burgundians ruled that a woman who had sex outside of marriage was to be drowned in a swamp.

hereditary and personal, the reputation held by virtue of one's birth and family status as well as one's personal integrity; like a bank balance it could increase or decrease according to one's behavior and the actions of the family one headed. Female honor ('**ird**), by contrast, was solely personal. More akin to the English-language concept of "purity" than "honor," moreover, it was a quality that a woman either possessed or did not, and its value only decreased. Once lost, it was lost forever. But the moral stain of the loss of 'ird spread to the members of the woman's family—which justified the action needed to restore the family's hasab: the killing of the sinner. Honor killings in the last decades of Ottoman rule remained hidden from view and difficult to quantify. Those who perpetrated or witnessed such killing did not consider it a crime, and hence they saw no need to report it to authorities. The Turks themselves, to whom honor killing was more culturally foreign, did not wish to stir up the anger of their non-Turkish subjects by investigating such deaths too intently.

Female circumcision was most widely and openly practiced in the northeastern quadrant of Africa—Egypt, Ethiopia, Somalia, and Sudan—and in many parts of the Middle East. The custom was publicly condemned but long remained a secret practice in northern Arabia, southern Jordan, and the Kurdish regions of Iran, Iraq, Syria, and Turkey. Secret, but not rare. As many as 80–90 percent of females in some of these regions either submitted or were forced to submit to some form of circumcision. Men who frequently went off on lengthy trading journeys relied on circumcision as a way of guaranteeing their wives' fidelity. In the most extreme cases nearly the entire vaginal opening was sewn shut, in addition to the more customary removal of the clitoris.

The practice predates Islam and probably originated from a mixture of motives—hygienic, aesthetic, and moral. The hygienic argument held that circumcision allowed for easier and fuller cleansing of the body after menstruation or childbirth; the aesthetic argument maintained that the procedure enhanced the beauty of the female form. The moral argument was the most nefarious, as it remains today. The moral motive insisted that circumcision promoted chastity before marriage and fidelity within marriage. Because it denied women the ability to experience pleasure, it thus removed temptation. The Islamic position on genital cutting is open to interpretation. A verse in one collection of the hadith of the Prophet Muhammad relates that when Muhammad encountered a woman in Medina who worked as a ritual circumciser, he said to her. "But do not mutilate— it is better for the woman and more desirable for her husband [to cut less rather than more]." This would seem at least to permit the practice, but legal scholars have long debated the authenticity of the verse.[12]

---

[12] Most Islamic scholars today soundly reject female circumcision, yet the practice remains widespread.

The call for the emancipation of women in the Islamic world, then, required bravery and countercultural determination unlike anything faced by women in western Europe. But in both cases the call was met with considerably more indifference and hostility than sympathy. To alter the position of women in society meant to change the definition of the nation itself at a critical moment. In Europe, the ideological dream of the nation was about to be realized in global empire. In the Islamic world, the dream of national independence, after four hundred years of political subjection to the Turks, seemed about to end. The call for emancipation arose at the same time across the Greater West but was heard only in Europe—and only after its imperial dreams had set the world afire.

WHO, WHAT, WHERE

feminist movement	realist
'ird	suffragettes
naturalist	suffragists
new woman	utilitarian

SUGGESTED READINGS

Primary Sources

Bulwer-Lytton, Constance. *Prisons and Prisoners.*

Martineau, Harriet. "The Political Non-Existence of Women," in *Society in America.*

Mill, John Stuart. *The Subjection of Women.*

Norton, Caroline. *English Laws for Women in the Nineteenth Century.*

Reid, Marion Kirkland. *A Plea for Woman.*

Shaarawi, Huda. *Harem Years: The Memoirs of an Egyptian Feminist.*

Stöcker, Helene. *Women and Love: A Manifesto for Emancipating Women and Men in Germany.*

Verbitskaya, Anastasia. *The Keys to Happiness.*

Source Anthologies

Badran, Margot, and Miriam Cooke, eds. *Opening the Gates: A Century of Arab Feminist Writing* (2004).

Nelson, Carolyn Christensen, ed. *A New Woman Reader: Fiction, Articles, and Drama of the 1890s* (2000).

Patterson, Martha H., ed. *The American New Woman Revisited: A Reader, 1894–1930* (2008).

Studies

Ali, Kecia. *Sexual Ethics and Islam: Feminist Reflections on Qur'an, Hadith, and Jurisprudence* (2006).

Bartley, Paula. *Emmeline Pankhurst* (2003).

Bush, Julia. *Women against the Vote: Female Anti-Suffragism in Britain* (2007).

Capaldi, Nicholas. *John Stuart Mill: A Biography* (2004).

Friedmann, Yohanan. *Tolerance and Coercion in Islam: Interfaith Relations in the Muslim Tradition* (2003).

Haeri, Shahla. *Law of Desire: Temporary Marriage in Shi'i Iran* (2002).

Hatem, Mervat F. *Literature, Gender, and Nation-Building in Nineteenth-Century Egypt: The Life and Works of 'A'isha Taymur* (2011).

Keddie, Nikki R. *Women in the Middle East: Past and Present* (2006).

Kertzer, David I., and Marzio Barbagli, eds. *Family Life in the Long Nineteenth Century, 1789–1913.* (2002).

Logan, Deborah Anna. *Harriet Martineau, Victorian Imperialism, and the Civilizing Mission* (2010).

———. *The Woman and the Hour: Harriet Martineau's "Somewhat Remarkable" Life* (2002).

Malone, Carolyn. *Women's Bodies and Dangerous Trades in England, 1880–1914* (2003).

Marchand, Suzanne, and David Lindenfeld, eds. *Germany at the Fin de Siècle: Culture, Politics, and Ideas* (2004).

Offen, Karen M. *European Feminisms, 1700–1950: A Political History* (2000).

Phillips, Melanie. *The Ascent of Woman: A History of the Suffragette Movement and the Ideas behind It* (2003).

Pugh, Martin. *The Pankhursts: The History of One Radical Family* (2008).

Roberts, Mary Louise. *Disruptive Acts: The New Woman in Fin-de-Siècle France* (2002).

Stansell, Christine. *The Feminist Promise: 1792 to the Present* (2010).

Tosh, John. *A Man's Place: Masculinity and the Middle-Class Home in Victorian England* (2007).

For additional resources, including maps, primary sources, visuals, web links, and quizzes, please go to **www.oup.com/us/backman**

Midi le jour, Minuit la nuit.

CHAPTER 22

The Great Land Grab

1880–1914

EUROPEAN COLONIES AND
PROTECTORATES, 1914

There is, it seems, no end to empires. To individual megastates, yes—but to empires themselves, no. We have already had a parade of them: the Akkadians, the Midians, the Hittites, the Assyrians, the Babylonians, the neo-Babylonians, and the Persians—empires all, and all only by the end of our first chapter. Subsequent chapters presented the Athenian, the Alexandrian, the Roman, the Parthian, the Byzantine, the Umayyad, the Carolingian, the Ottonian, the Abbasid, the Seljuk, the Mamluk, the Mongol, and the Ottoman empires. Then came the empires of Tamerlane and Charles V. The Venetian Empire in the Mediterranean. The Aztec, Incan, and Mayan Empires of the pre-1492 New World. The Spanish Empire in the Americas. The Safavid Empire in Iran. The Mughal Empire in India. The Polish-Lithuanian Empire. Napoleon's Empire. The Austrian-Hungarian Empire. France's Second Empire. Russia's Romanov Empire. Until one begins to list them, one hardly realizes the extent to which Greater Western history appears to be dominated by them.

Is it possible that this is not accidental? Might empires, in fact, be the norm of human political life—the default position, so to speak? Many have thought so. Especially at the dawn

◀ **The White Man's Burden**
A French colonial officer in West Africa attempts to teach his pupils how to tell time by a watch. Several girls are attentive, but the boys present are happily distracted by a playful monkey. The cartoon is uncritical, even affectionate, and exudes an atmosphere of patience on the part of the officer. The children are like school-children everywhere—some studious, some mischievous. But no sign of oppression or resentment is visible. Neither are any African adults, who presumably are somewhere else, working for colonial masters who are far less kindly and patient.

of the 20th century, this thought seemed to drive the European nations and others as well into headlong competition to cover and to covet the earth. Belgium, Britain, France, Germany, and Italy all took part. So, more modestly, did Japan and the United States. Ever since, it has been commonplace to condemn Europe and America for the global landgrab they indulged in. **Imperialism**, say critics, is evil, a harsh and soulless crushing of cultures considered "Other"—and European and American imperialism, by virtue of those territories' technological advantages over their victims, are uniquely evil. Racism and exploitation, a greed that flat-out ignored the peoples and interests of the rest of the world, is what lay behind the Western feeding frenzy. There is much to say for this view. Critics of European imperialism can literally point to the graves of millions who died in the mad dash to make rich Europe even richer. But the period from 1880 to 1914 was also a time of resistance to empire, as reformers, activists, politicians, journalists, writers, critics, and commoners of all stripes cried out in horrified dismay at what their society was becoming or had already become. It was the time of a Second Industrial Revolution and the Gilded Age it enabled.

"THE WHITE MAN'S BURDEN"

Karl Pearson (1857–1936), a prominent British mathematician and ardent champion of the British Empire, saw imperialism as simply the best use of the earth's resources. In an essay called "National Life from the Standpoint of Science" (1900), he wrote:

> History shows me one way, and one way only, in which a high state of civilization can be produced—namely, the struggle of race with race, and the survival of the physically and morally fitter race. If you want to know whether the lower races of man can evolve a higher type, I fear the only course is to leave them to fight it out among themselves.... Let us suppose that we could prevent the white man, if we liked, from going to lands

CHAPTER TIMELINE

1869
Completion of
the Suez Canal

1880
Beginning of mass
European emigration

1884–1885
Congress of
Berlin

1898–1901
Boxer Rebellion,
China

1870
Population of Europe
is 295 million

1884
First gasoline-powered
automobile patented

1898
Battle of Omdurman,
Sudan

of which the agricultural and mineral resources are not worked to the full; then I should say, "A thousand times better for him that he should not go, than that he should settle down and live alongside the inferior race."

Aside from its obvious racism, Pearson's argument was essentially amoral, and supporters of any of the empires mentioned above would likely have agreed. It runs something like this. The earth offers only finite amounts of natural resources, but the constantly increasing human population has constantly increasing needs. Given those needs, the right to access and exploit resources belongs to whoever is in the best position to get the most value from them. A society that has failed, for whatever reason, to put its resources to proper use has effectively renounced its right to control them. And any foreign group that exploits those materials for productive gain is not only right to do so but also benefits the society shunted aside. Imperialism is therefore best understood as a vital instrument in the evolution of human civilization, and its benefits far exceed any harm it causes. Pearson again:

> The struggle for existence between the white man and the red man in America, painful and even terrible as it was in its details, has given us a good far out-balancing its immediate evil. In place of the red man, who contributed practically nothing to the work and thought of the world, we have a great nation, mistress of many arts, and able, with its youthful imagination and fresh, untrammeled impulses, to contribute much to the common stock of civilized man.
>
> The great function of science in national life is to show us what national life means, and how the nation is a vast organism subject to the great forces of evolution. . . . Is it not a fact that the daily bread of our millions of workers depends on their having somebody to work for? That if we give up the contest for trade routes, free markets, and waste lands, we indirectly give up our food supply? Is it not a fact that our strength depends on these and upon our colonies, and that our colonies have been

1899
Rudyard Kipling, "The White Man's Burden"

1901
Naoroji, *Poverty and Un-British Rule in India*

1903
Ford Motor Company founded

1904–1905
Russo-Japanese War

1911
Taylor, *Principles of Scientific Management*

1914
Population of Europe is 450 million; over 90 percent of Africa partitioned among European states

won by the ejection of inferior races, and are maintained against equal races by respect for the present power of our empire?.... The path to progress is strewn with the wreck of nations; traces are everywhere to be seen of the slaughtered remains of inferior races, and of victims who found not the narrow way to perfection. Yet these dead people are, in very truth, the stepping-stones on which mankind has arisen to the higher intellectual and deeper emotional life of today.

The thought is odious, even vile. But does that mean it is incorrect?

To believe in the innate superiority of one's race or culture is nothing new. The ancient Persians had no doubt about the inferiority of every culture they overran. To the ancient Greeks the word for "barbarian" (*barbaroi*) applied to any non-Greek ethnic group; neither Charlemagne nor Tamerlane considered any of his conquered peoples to be his equal. And Napoleon was confident in France's divine mission to lead the world. The nations that set out after 1880 to dominate the globe shared the same confidence in their rights to rule others. But a new element crept into their thinking. The imperialism of the late 19th and early 20th centuries differed from earlier imperial adventures in this one important regard: the European champions of imperialism thought of their actions in Darwinian terms—as a necessary step in the evolutionary development of the entire human species. This was **social Darwinism**, the misuse of Darwin's theory of evolution by natural selection to justify competition among societies. It was all the more self-confident because of what many Europeans regarded as its scientific certitude. Belief in the "survival of the fittest" justified their actions as morally necessary—the best, or even perhaps the only, means by which human civilization itself could advance.

In the words of Rudyard Kipling's most famous poem (1899), imperialism was "The White Man's Burden":

> Take up the White Man's burden—
> No tawdry rule of kings,
> But toil of serf and sweeper—
> The tale of common things.
> The ports ye shall not enter,
> The roads ye shall not tread,
> Go mark them with your living,
> And mark them with your dead!

The imperialism of the late 19th and early 20th centuries differed from earlier imperial adventures in this one important regard: the European champions of imperialism thought of their actions in Darwinian terms—as a necessary step in the evolutionary development of the entire human species.

Take up the White Man's burden—
And reap his old reward:
The blame of those ye better,
The hate of those ye guard—
The cry of hosts ye humour
(Ah, slowly!) toward the light:—
"Why brought ye us from bondage,
Our loved Egyptian night?"

Take up the White Man's burden—
Ye dare not stoop to less—
Nor call too loud on Freedom
To cloak your weariness;
By all ye cry or whisper,
By all ye leave or do,
The silent, sullen peoples
Shall weigh your Gods and you.

THE SECOND INDUSTRIAL REVOLUTION

An empire is a machine—an ordered system of tools, institutions, and communications to govern people and administer goods. And that is a much more difficult thing to accomplish than the military conquests that lead up to it. Military conquest, after all, is nothing more than a bloodstain on a map, however great or small the area. An empire is so much more. Genghis Khan butchered millions of people in the process of getting tens of millions more to obey him out of sheer terror, but what he "created" was no more an empire than the atomic bombing of Hiroshima was an urban-development plan. True empires require engineers, jurists, civil officials, industrialists, financiers, teachers, missionaries, skilled laborers, and the infrastructures that can connect them efficiently and reliably. From 1870 to 1914 western Europe developed an abundance of all these, in what is known as the **Second Industrial Revolution**. And the natural resources needed to fuel and feed that revolution lay increasingly overseas—as did the new shape of empire.

The first wave of industrialization had focused on the production of consumer goods—textiles and food, especially, with housewares and furniture running second. All were fueled by the new energy technologies of coal and by high-grade refined iron. The Second Industrial Revolution was essentially a continuation of the earlier process but with a focus instead on producing capital goods—goods used to produce other goods, such as steel, heavy machinery, chemicals, electrical power, and refined petroleum. Many of these are the "capital"

Industrial Warfare "If you want to make a pile of money, invent something that will enable these Europeans to cut each others' throats with greater facility," was the advice given by a friend to Hiram Stevens Maxim (1840-1916), an American inventor who patented his Maxim Gun, the first portable automatic machine gun, in 1884. Capable of firing ten rounds per second, it gave an incalculable advantage to the British in their imperial expansion. In its first battlefield use, in southern Africa in 1893, a mere four British gunners were able to repel an attack by three thousand African warriors.

of industrial capitalism, or resources in the hands of factory owners. Many are also public goods, like automobiles and radios, open to everyone and bringing people together. Other key developments of this period were the telegraph and telephone, lighter and stronger steamships and railroads, subways, the internal combustion engine, the airplane, and modern weaponry—like repeating rifles, artillery, and machine guns. The chemical industry produced soaps, detergents, dyes, photographic plates and films, medicines, gasoline and other petroleum products, synthetic textiles, paints, fertilizers, and explosives.

When the French chemist Louis Pasteur (1822–1895) discovered germs—the microorganisms that cause many diseases—he established an entire new science, which in turn led to two critical innovations. One was *pasteurization*, in which foodstuffs are heated to destroy the bacteria that cause spoilage. The other was *immunology*, the study of vaccines and other means to protect people from disease. He perfected a vaccine against rabies by 1885, and by the end of the century scientists had developed vaccines against cholera, diphtheria, and typhus. Joseph Lister (1827–1912), an English chemist, developed the first successful antiseptic and the process of disinfection.[1] Their work helped launch modern medicine, as did Madame Marie Skłodowska-Curie (1867–1934). Curie, who won the Nobel Prize in physics (1903) and again in chemistry (1911), established radiology, the study of radioactivity, and her work led to the development of X-rays.

While railroads had been in use for decades, it wasn't until the 1880s that they overtook canals as the dominant means of transporting cargo in Europe. Once advances in steel production dramatically reduced the cost of laying and maintaining rail lines, the cost of shipping cargo along those lines decreased as well, which spurred further production of goods. The development of electrical grids, telegraph and telephone networks, and radio systems enabled communication at speeds never before known. It felt like a whole new era in human development. "The economic changes that have occurred during the last quarter of a century— or during the present generation of living men—have unquestionably been more important and more varied than during any period of the world's history," crowed an enthusiastic American economist, David Ames Wells (1828–1898).

Karl Friedrich Benz (1844–1929) patented the first gasoline-powered automobile in 1884, but it was Henry Ford who revolutionized personal transportation. He founded the Ford Motor Company in 1903, with its innovative assembly-line model. Mass production became the norm, or at least the desired one. With plentiful cheap oil, high-grade steel machinery, and endless quantities of electrical power, goods could be produced literally around the clock. By 1900, the half dozen leading European nations produced two-thirds of all the manufactured goods on the planet. Modern transportation and communication allowed these goods to reach markets around the world, and they brought back to Europe the resources to produce more goods, which in turn stimulated new cycles of production and consumption (Map 22.1).

New technologies appeared with stunning rapidity. In the United States alone nearly a million patents were issued for inventions between the end of the Civil War (1865) and the start of World War I—everything from pneumatic braking systems (1872) and the phonograph (1877) to the telephone (1879), light bulb (1880), jackhammer (1890), radio (1893), semiautomatic rifle (1898), safety razor and electric vacuum cleaner (1901), airplane (1903), helicopter (1907), dental braces (1910), and the backless bra (1914). So quickly were new industries created that in a single five-year period, 1896–1901, the volume of stocks sold on the New York Stock Exchange increased by a factor of six. Not only did new technologies appear constantly, the amount of time taken to bring those technologies to general use shortened dramatically. The telephone, invented in 1879,

---

[1]   Listerine, the antiseptic mouthwash named for Joseph Lister, was originally marketed as a floor cleaner and a treatment for gonorrhea.

MAP 22.1   Industrialization and Manufacturing, 1870–1914

had become a standard business necessity across Europe and the United States by 1900. The automobile was a novelty item at first, but with the development of the petroleum industry it was soon transforming entire cities. Petroleum also supplied the asphalt on which automobiles ran.

Charting a New Course   The first automobile maps appeared in 1900 in both France and Germany. In both countries, bicycle tire manufacturers, all of whom quickly started manufacturing tires for cars, sponsored or created automobile maps to encourage people to buy their new products. In 1910, the French tire company Michelin published its first road map of France, which included information on local attractions and restaurants.   Shown above is the cover of this early Michelin Guide, bearing an advertisement for Renault automobiles.

Modern management techniques must be counted among the innovations of the era. Called **scientific management** by its founders, this set of ideas aimed at a single goal: to improve the efficiency of the manufacturing workplace by increasing the productivity of labor. Machines, after all, could be set to function at a constant rate for as long as they were fueled and maintained, but workers were less predictable. Some were more intelligent and skillful than others, some more energetic and diligent, and some more highly motivated and determined; still others were lazy, inconsistent, awkward, and slow. To even out these differences, scientific management sought to break down manufacturing into small, distinct steps. Rather than have a hundred furniture makers each build an entire dining table, one worker could plane lumber for the tabletop, the next join the pieces, the third trim the edges, the fourth shape the table legs on a lathe, and so on, step by step, over and over, again and again. Finally, the finished dining tables emerged from the assembly line—identical, at a steady pace, and with maximum efficiency. In *The Principles of Scientific Management* (1911), Frederick Winslow Taylor (1856–1915) called for the minute study of workers' physical movements in order to design steps with perfect efficiency. The point was to get workers to adapt themselves to the machines they operated.

This was time management: the efficiency of the machines set the pace of manufacture. It still sometimes called for intelligent, highly skilled workers, but Taylor also saw that many tasks could be performed by any worker regardless of skill, intelligence, or motivation. At times, in fact, industry could exploit workers' lack of education or intellectual sharpness. The booming steel industry, he

Unscientific Management   This still from Charlie Chaplin's masterpiece "Modern Times" (1936) illustrates how human labor was made to accommodate the workings of machines in industrial manufacture. The machine itself became the workers' boss, and occasionally (as here, with Chaplin trying to rescue a fellow worker trapped in the gears) it not only directed the workers' lives, but it consumed them.

noted, had a particular need for dullards, since the handling of pig iron (iron ore at the intermediate stage of the smelting process) called for more brawn than brains:

> Now one of the very first requirements for a man who is fit to handle pig iron as a regular occupation is that he shall be so stupid and so phlegmatic that he more nearly resembles in his mental make-up the ox than any other type. The man who is mentally alert and intelligent is for this very reason unsuited to what would, for him, be the grinding monotony of work of this character. Therefore the workman who is best suited to handling pig iron is unable to understand the real science of doing this class of work. He is so stupid that the word *percentage* has no meaning to him, and he must consequently be trained by a man more intelligent than himself into the habit of working in accordance with the laws of this science before he can be successful. The writer trusts that it is now clear that even in the case of the most elementary form of labor that is known, there is a science, and that when the man

best suited to this class of work has been carefully selected, when the science of doing the work has been developed, and when the carefully selected man has been trained to work in accordance with this science, the results obtained must of necessity be overwhelmingly greater than those which are possible under the [traditional] plan of "initiative and incentive."

The condescending tone is on display throughout the book. Even Taylor balked at calling workers mere appendages to machinery, but that is the essence of his management science and the key to his vision of efficiency.[2]

One of the chief problems with improved industrial capacity was overproduction. When manufactures outpaced consumption, prices tumbled and profits slumped or even disappeared. The problem was noted as early as the 1820s, when the word "depression" was used for the first time in its economic sense.

The Suez Canal   Crowds watch the first ships to sail through the Suez Canal on November 17, 1869, in this print from a German magazine. The canal was designed by a French engineer, Ferdinand de Lesseps (1805-1894), the same man who later formally presented (though he did not design or build) the Statue of Liberty, to President Grover Cleveland of the United States.

---

[2]   At Harvard Business School, founded in 1908, *The Principles of Scientific Management* was the core textbook until the start of the Great Depression in 1929.

Every advance in technology, it seemed, only made the problem worse by making it easier to produce and deliver more goods. Modern railroads and steamships could cross continents, oceans, and soon even the most daunting natural barriers. The Transcontinental Railroad crossed America in 1869, the same year the Suez Canal was completed, cutting in half the time needed for ships to sail from Europe to India. The twelve-mile-long Simplon Tunnel through the Alps, along the Swiss-Italian border, sped people and goods between northern and southern Europe. Never before in Western history were so few people able to feed so many, with less than 10 percent of the population engaged in farming. This freed more workers to seek employment in cities, which pushed wages down, but production levels remained so high that food prices fell even faster.

A growing population lessened the risks of a rapid fall in prices, or deflation. The birthrate in most of western Europe declined sharply between 1870 and 1914, especially among the bourgeois and skilled-labor classes. This decline was due in part to the availability of contraception but probably even more to the (slowly) growing alternatives to motherhood available to women. Advances in medicine brought about an even sharper decline in mortality, with the net result that a European population of 295 million in 1870 ballooned to over 450 million by the start of World War I—a gain of 60 percent in a single generation. Such impressive growth ensured steadily expanding markets for goods of all sorts. Even this was not enough, however. Markets, like the homes they supplied, filled to bursting with a seemingly never-ending stream of household goods, foodstuffs, appliances, tools, and decorative objects. As production grew in pace, the only solution to declining profit margins was to find ever more markets to flood with commodities. That meant looking overseas.

LOOKING OVERSEAS

Overseas resources were definitely within reach. Commercial contacts with Africa, India, eastern Asia, and the South Pacific islands had continued since the late 16th century, so the routes, harbors, and geography were mostly familiar. Now the telegraph, radio, and telephone enabled regular contact with far-flung territories, and modern weaponry gave Europeans a decisive battlefield advantage. The West seized roughly one-quarter of planet Earth (and roughly one-third of its human population) in an astonishingly short span of time.

The unification of Germany in 1870 was the trigger event. German industrial capacity had grown rapidly under Bismarck's leadership—so quickly that even the expense of a large military and extensive social programs did not slow economic expansion. Moreover, since Germany had been a comparative latecomer to industrialization, its factories benefited from newer technologies. Germany was also one of the few countries in Europe to have a rising birthrate, which meant that the population was younger than in Britain, France, or Italy. The rush of youthful energy and optimism seemed to be on Germany's side. All it lacked was overseas connections.

News from Around the World The White House became wired for telegraph and telephone in the 1880s. (Computers were introduced during President Jimmy Carter's term.) Here a trio of engineers monitor the telegraph system bringing news of the Spanish-American War in 1895.

A second trigger was Reconstruction, the remaking of the American South after the Civil War. The South had long been among the principal suppliers of raw cotton for European textile factories, but the catastrophic Civil War (1861–1865) had essentially cut off those supplies. In the postwar decades American policy aimed primarily at developing domestic industry, and this inward turn not only meant a decrease in the export of raw materials; it also increased competition on world markets by introducing American finished goods. Like Germany, America was a young nation filled with energy and ambition, and it soon became a major producer of everything from textiles and foodstuffs to steel, machinery, weapons, automobiles, and electrical appliances.

America also invested in education. The Morrill Act of 1862 (renewed and expanded in 1890) granted states the right to sell or develop federal lands for the creation of colleges and universities. These land-grant colleges meant continued innovation in arts, engineering, and sciences.[3] America's growing military might was also a factor. Though still recovering from the Civil War, American fighting forces, once fully modernized, had the potential to rival the great European powers, especially on the sea-lanes. In response, Europe had to seize the moment.

> Though still recovering from the Civil War, American fighting forces, once fully modernized, had the potential to rival the great European powers, especially on the sea-lanes. In response, Europe had to seize the moment.

The British led the way by transforming their long commercial domination of India into full-scale exploitation, led by the privately held British East India

---

3   The first land-grant university created from scratch was Kansas State University in 1863.

Company. India produced cotton on a massive scale, which compensated for the loss of American cotton, while its enormous population was a potential market. An uprising against British control in 1857 led to a sharp military crackdown, after which the entire subcontinent was formally declared a colony (1858) of Her Majesty Queen Victoria (r. 1837–1901). So great a prize was India that for nearly a dozen years the British scarcely looked elsewhere for further colonial adventures. With Germany's and Italy's unifications, however, that had to change. The Continent was now awash with goods, and prices plummeted. The Long Depression (1873–1896), known in its time as the Great Depression until a still greater one struck in 1929, was marked by severe deflation and loss of profits. In the United States the price of cotton fell by 50 percent; grain fell to only a third of its previous value. Declines in Europe were at times even worse, owing to panics on the Vienna, Paris, and London stock exchanges. Since decreasing production was unthinkable, the answer was two-pronged. First, increase access to markets abroad by seizing them; and second, seek protection by discouraging competition within an industry and by government subsidies. Firms joined or cooperated, forming cartels, to thwart the natural workings of the market.

Until the 1870s few governments, whether Liberal or Conservative, favored outright colonialism. In 1852 the British prime minister Benjamin Disraeli, a Conservative, had dismissed England's handful of colonies as "a millstone around our necks" that cost far more to protect and maintain than they produced.[4] But by the mid-1880s newspapers were describing the race to extend Western industrial might throughout the entire world. "When I left the Foreign Service in 1880," wrote one British diplomat, "nobody thought about Africa. When I returned to it in 1885, the nations of Europe were almost quarreling with each other as to the various portions of Africa which they should obtain." A contemporary French official expressed his amazement, saying, "We are witnessing something never before seen in history—the actual partition of a foreign continent [Africa] by a handful of European countries." He quickly added, however, that "France, of course, is entitled to the largest share in these spoils."

An international congress met in Berlin in 1884–1885 to lay out the legal framework for European expansion into Africa. Organized by Otto von Bismarck, the **Conference of Berlin** included Austria-Hungary, Belgium, Denmark, France, Germany, Italy, the Netherlands, the Ottoman Empire, Portugal, Russia, Spain, and Sweden (in union with Norway at the time). The United States was invited

---

4   William Gladstone, a Liberal, declared that "the lust-love of territory have been among the greatest curses of mankind."

Repulsing the Europeans   Italy was a latecomer to European imperialism. The Italians invaded Ethiopia (one of the few parts of Africa not yet taken) in 1895. In a decisive battle at Adowa, at the northernmost point of the country, an Ethiopian army, armed with the latest Western military technology, crushed the ill-placed and ill-trained Italian forces. This painting by an unknown Ethiopian artist, depicts the victory over the Italian soldiers—identifiable here by their red headgear.

but did not attend. Of course, no African countries were invited; none, in fact, were even informed of the congress' intentions. The conference did not actually divide Africa among the European powers. It merely established the standards by which any European country could claim an African territory against another European rival. Yet its effect was immediate: in the ensuing scramble, France extended its traditional hold over central North Africa by seizing the territory of French West Africa (today's Benin, Burkina Faso, Ivory Coast, Guinea, Mali, Mauritania, Niger, and Senegal) in 1895. Italy invaded Ethiopia in the same year, but was beaten off; a few years later, however, the Italians captured Somalia and eventually Libya. With government backing, a British businessman and diamond merchant, Cecil Rhodes (1853–1902), used his position as prime minister of the British Cape Town Colony in southern Africa to instigate the Boer War (1899–1902), a conflict with the then Orange Free State and the Transvaal Republic (forerunners of the Union of South Africa), where a large deposit of diamonds had recently been discovered.[5] One result was the extension of British sovereignty northward into what came to be called Rhodesia (today's Zambia and Zimbabwe). Portugal seized Angola and Mozambique. Germany secured Cameroon, Namibia, and Tanzania. By 1902, fully 90 percent of Africa had been

---

[5]   Rhodes, an ardent imperialist, once declared, "If I could, I would annex other planets."

partitioned among the dominant European states; only Ethiopia and Liberia remained independent (see Map 22.2).

The rush to carve away parts of Asia was no less feverish or violent, but generally not as successful. Direct commercial relations, circumventing the Ottoman middleman, had gone on since the 16th century with permanent trading posts established from India to the Malay Peninsula and from southern China to Japan. The Dutch were the first, and periodically among the most vicious, European nation to take full political control of an Asian country. The government-chartered Dutch East India Company had been established in 1602 with an awarded monopoly on the movement of goods into and out of Indonesia. The British East

MAP 22.2   **The Scramble for Africa**

India Company held sway over most of India, by grant of Parliament, from the second half of the 18th century onward. In the early 19th century Britain then expanded further east and seized control of Burma before turning south and taking Malaya.

The Europeans sometimes turned to even nastier measures, as when the British forced the Chinese to accept India-grown opium in lieu of money to pay for Chinese silks and tea. By 1840 opium addiction was so widespread in China that the emperor attempted to deny the British entrance to Chinese harbors, which prompted so-called gunboat diplomacy to force the opening of the ports. The First Opium War (1839–1842) ended with China forced to cede to Britain permanent control of the harbor at Hong Kong.[6] France moved aggressively into Southeast Asia in the 1850s and 1860s, using the murder of a Spanish missionary by a group of resentful Vietnamese as an excuse to colonize much of southern Vietnam. By 1883 France was in control of the northern regions of Vietnam, along with much of Cambodia. Ten years later it added Laos to French Indochina (see Map 22.3).

All that remained up for grabs by 1890 were the outlying islands of the South Pacific. Britain snatched up Fiji and a few surrounding sites, while Germany seized the Marshall and Samoan Islands. France moved into Tahiti and into New Caledonia, an archipelago off the eastern coast of Australia. The biggest prize in the Pacific, however, was the widespread group of Philippine Islands. These had long previously belonged to Spain, but a successful revolution in 1898 brought about a short-lived period of independence. In that year the United States ended its brief but bloody conflict with Spain—the Spanish-American War of 1898, fought over the issue of control of Cuba and Puerto Rico. Among other things, the peace treaty gave the Philippines to America. Not all Americans were enthusiastic about taking up colonial responsibilities so far from home. Rudyard Kipling composed "The White Man's Burden" at this time precisely to rouse Americans to imperialist action. The United States and the Philippine Republic signed a peace treaty after three years of fighting (1899–1902); warfare continued in some of the outer islands, however, as late as 1913. In 1934, Congress guaranteed Philippine self-rule in ten years. World War II intervened, however, and Philippine independence did not become a reality until 1946.

Only Japan managed to retain full independence, which it did largely by becoming an imperialist power itself. Rapid industrialization had begun in 1868 after the Meiji Restoration overthrew a backward-looking network of feudal

---

[6]   Hong Kong remained the last outpost of the British Empire in Asia; it was not restored to Chinese control until 1997.

MAP 22.3   The Carving Up of Southeast Asia

regimes and restored the imperial dynasty, but the new government was intensely aware of Japan's weakness: it had no modern navy. Moreover, Japan had ample agricultural land but virtually no metal ore for mining. That meant that the nation could industrialize only by importing raw materials and exporting finished products, and it had to unload its ships in reliable markets. With so many of the Pacific and East Asian markets snapped up by Europe, Japan had to carve out its own colonial zones, which brought it into conflict with Russia.

The Russo-Japanese War (1904–1905) was fought for control of Manchuria, Korea, and the island of Sakhalin. The first two were prized as rich in resources and heavily populated; the latter was the sole major source of petroleum in East Asia. This was primarily a naval war, with a handful of battles for control of ports. Japan's victory surprised most observers, but the treaty that ended the war awarded Japan no territory and released Russia from having to pay for the costs of the conflict.[7] Riots erupted across Japan in response to the news and fostered a powerful sense of

---

[7]   President Theodore Roosevelt won the Nobel Peace Prize for helping to negotiate a peace treaty between Japan and Russia.

Japanese Victory   Japanese victory at the Battle of Tsushima, the decisive naval battle of the Russo-Japanese War (1904-1905). Japan's forces annihilated two-thirds of the Russian imperial fleet.

betrayal. Doubting that it would ever receive a fair hearing on the international scene, the imperial government, with popular backing, decided to turn aggressive. Five years after the war, Japan annexed the Korean peninsula; Russia agreed to withdraw from Manchuria, opening the way for further Japanese expansion. Japan continued to develop its military might, and when World War I ended in 1918 the Japanese quickly seized Germany's Asian colonies.

JAPANESE EXPANSION
IN NORTH ASIA, 1870–1905

■ Japanese Empire, 1870
■ Territory acquired, 1874–1910
■ Japanese sphere of influence from 1905

MISSIONARY EUROPE

Western Europe's global land grab was without precedent in history. The political and economic factors behind it, importantly, were buttressed by an often convoluted set of religious and humanitarian motives. Armies of missionaries traveled before, with, and after the troops, spreading Christianity and attempting to quell the long-standing tribal hatreds and class and ethnic rivalries that they encountered wherever they went. With their various Christian moralities in tow, missionaries confronted a parade of cultural practices they found not only foreign but authentically horrifying. In much of east Africa, for example, the tradition of female genital cutting aroused particular disgust. The stoning of women for alleged adultery or the enslavement of children elicited a special sympathy. The Hindu folk practice of *sati* also demanded some sort of response: in parts of old India, a widow was thrown alive onto the burning funeral pyre of her deceased

Doing God's Work   Missionaries conducting a baptism ceremony in the Congo. By 1900 there were approximately nine million Christians in Africa; by the year 2000 that number had grown to nearly four hundred million. The continent's traditional religions have declined dramatically. Africa north of the Sahara Desert is now overwhelmingly Islamic, but south of the desert it is chiefly Christian.

husband so that she could accompany him into the life beyond. If imperialist subjugation was the price of putting an end to such practices, missionaries preached, then it was a price worth paying.

Writing a quarter century later about Britain's seizure of Egypt in 1882, Sir Evelyn Baring (1st Earl of Cromer, 1841–1917), Britain's first colonial governor of that country, offered a classic defense of imperialism. It needed to be done as much for Egypt's benefit as for Britain's, since the Egyptians had proven themselves to be incapable of running their own affairs. And if it needed doing, then better the British than anyone else:

> Egypt may now almost be said to form part of Europe. It is on the high road to the Far East. It can never cease to be an object of interest to all the powers of Europe, and especially to England. A numerous and intelligent body of Europeans and of non-Egyptian orientals have made Egypt their home. European capital to a large extent has been sunk in the country. . . . In addition to these peculiarities, which are of a normal character, it has to be borne in mind that in 1882 the [Egyptian] army was in a state of mutiny; the treasury was bankrupt; every branch of the administration had been dislocated; the ancient and arbitrary method,

under which the country had for centuries been governed, had received a severe blow, whilst, at the same time, no more orderly and law-abiding form of government had been inaugurated to take its place.... History, indeed, records some very radical changes in the forms of government to which a state has been subjected without its interests being absolutely and permanently shipwrecked. But it may be doubted whether any instance can be quoted of a sudden transfer of power in any civilized or semi-civilized community to a class so ignorant as the pure Egyptians, such as they were in the year 1882. These latter have, for centuries past, been a subject race. Persians, Greeks, Romans, Arabs from Arabia and Baghdad, Circassians, and finally, Ottoman Turks, have successively ruled over Egypt, but we have to go back to the doubtful and obscure precedents of Pharaonic times to find an epoch when, possibly, Egypt was ruled by Egyptians. Neither, for the present, do they appear to possess the qualities which would render it desirable, either in their own interests, or in those of the civilized world in general, to raise them at a bound to the category of autonomous rulers with full rights of internal sovereignty. If, however, a foreign occupation was inevitable or nearly

Slaves in Chains   Slavery was officially abolished in Zanzibar in 1873. Until then it had been the busiest slave market in eastern Africa, with as many as fifty thousand slaves a year passing through its ports; most of these were sent to the Persian Gulf region.

inevitable, it remains to be considered whether a British occupation was preferable to any other. From the purely Egyptian point of view, the answer to this question cannot be doubtful. The intervention of any European power was preferable to that of Turkey. The intervention of one European power was preferable to international intervention. The special aptitude shown by Englishmen in the government of Oriental races pointed to England as the most effective and beneficent instrument for the gradual introduction of European civilization into Egypt. *(Lord Cromer, Modern Egypt, 1908)*

At the same time, one can argue that imperialism simply replaced one form of slavery with another. Perhaps no number of schools, hospitals, railroad systems, newspapers, and democratic institutions—all legacies of European rule—can offset cultural murder.

Nothing can justify the orgies of violence and theft that attended empire building, yet European control did put an end to the international slave trade. It also attempted to halt practices like female circumcision in Africa, sati in India, and foot-binding in China. At the same time, one can argue that imperialism simply replaced one form of slavery with another. Perhaps no number of schools, hospitals, railroad systems, newspapers, and democratic institutions—all legacies of European rule—can offset cultural murder.

A GILDED AGE

The Europeans' technological superiority gave them the most lopsided military victories in human history. Some of them had nearly a carnival atmosphere, resembling nothing so much as our modern video games. And once in power around the globe, the Europeans instituted many of the practices of **command economies**—economies that aim to provide the highest possible yield for whoever held the raw materials and captive markets. It brought at home the chilling self-confidence of a "gilded age."

Shooters simply mowed down the resistance with seemingly endless numbers of clicks—except that Europe's remote controls consisted of real weapons. Remington and Winchester breechloading rifles, elephant guns, Jarmann M1884 repeating rifles, Kropatschek 11-millimeter carbines, Maxim and Gatling machine guns, and seven-pound field artillery—all these squared off against warriors armed with little more than spears and arrows. The results were horrifying and became horrifyingly familiar.

In 1897 a French force of only 32 Europeans and 507 African mercenaries massacred a native army near Sokoto, in today's Nigeria, that numbered more than 30,000. Two years later only 320 Senegalese fighters, under French command, wiped out over 12,000 Sudanese troops. And in 1908 a company of 389 French soldiers annihilated a 10,000-man army from the kingdom of Ouaddai, near today's province of Darfur along the Chad-Sudan border in east-central Africa.

The British scored their one-sided victories as well, including the campaign to conquer Sudan in 1898. Sudan itself was of relatively little value to the British in terms of natural resources. The country, upriver from Egypt, mattered principally for strategic purposes: those who controlled Sudan could impede traffic along the Nile. The Sudanese fighters, known as Dervishes, numbered over 50,000 and met the English at Omdurman, now a suburb of the Sudanese capital of Khartoum. The well-armed British were aided by a flotilla of gunboats that had steamed up the river. Winston Churchill (1874–1965), the future prime minister, served there as a second lieutenant and described the battle in an 1899 memoir:

> [The infantry] fired steadily and stolidly, without hurry or excitement, for the enemy were far away and the officers careful. Besides, the soldiers were interested in the work and took great pains. But presently the mere physical act [of repeated firing] became tedious.... But at the critical moment the gunboat arrived on the scene and began suddenly to blaze and flame from Maxim guns, quick-firing guns, and rifles. The range was short; the effect tremendous. The terrible machine, floating gracefully on the waters—a beautiful white devil—wreathed itself in smoke. The river slopes of the Kerreri Hills, crowded with the advancing thousands, sprang up into clouds of dust and splinters of rock. The charging Dervishes sank down in tangled heaps. The masses in the rear paused, irresolute. It was too hot even for them.... And all the time out on the plain on the other side bullets were shearing through flesh, smashing and splintering bone; blood spouted from terrible wounds; valiant men were struggling on through a hell of whistling metal, exploding shells, and spurting dust—suffering, despairing, dying.

The carnage lasted for five hours and left ten thousand Dervishes dead, fifteen thousand wounded, and another five thousand captured; the British lost fewer than fifty men. Churchill's vivid memoir mentions, but does not quantify, how many British gunmen suffered the effects of carpal tunnel syndrome from pulling the triggers of their weapons so many times.

Industrial Warfare Lord Kitchener, major-general of Britain's imperial troops in Africa, defeated the Mahdist forces (an Islamic messianic group) in battle at Omdurman, in Sudan, in 1898. The British killed over ten thousand Mahdists and wounded another thirteen thousand, while suffering only forty seven losses themselves. According to an eyewitness: " . . . It was not a battle but an execution . . . The bodies were not in heaps—bodies hardly ever are; but they spread evenly over acres and acres. Some lay very composedly with their slippers placed under their heads for a last pillow; some knelt, cut short in the middle of a last prayer. Others were torn to pieces."

Lopsided advantages like this did more than ensure battlefield success; they altered the perceptions of warfare itself and of the participants as well. The Europeans appeared not simply as the victors. Rather, a society that could engineer such stunning conquests must in some sense be superior. As for its victims, a nation that clings to spears and arrows in an age of steel and gunpowder may not deserve massacre and foreign oppression, but it can hardly be surprised when they result. Such, at any rate, was the attitude of many in the West. An officers' manual for British forces fighting in Sierra Leone described "the weird and treacherous surroundings, and the nerve-wracking effects of the climate" in the region. It contrasted the "cunning savages . . . like the wild animals of [their] own forests" with "the stern discipline and enthusiastic *esprit de corps* of the British army" under the command of "that indispensible factor in the machine of West African warfare—the British officer." European readers more often felt wonder and pride than revulsion.

Even the Europeans, however, were disgusted by the excesses of King Léopold II of Belgium (r. 1865–1909). Léopold, who had long been keen to develop colonial holdings in Africa, cast his eye on the vast natural wealth of the Congo: "To open to civilization the only part of the globe where it has not yet penetrated, to pierce the darkness which envelops whole populations, is a crusade, if I may say so, a crusade worthy of this century of progress." Unable to stir the Belgian parliament into action, he hit on the idea of establishing instead a private company, the International African Association, to help the Congolese "develop." He hired the scurrilous British explorer Henry Morton Stanley (1841–1904) to represent the Association and get local tribal rulers to sign

The Horror A photo of Congolese with their hands chopped off, the common punishment for failure to meet rubber-collection quotas. "The baskets of severed hands, set down at the feet of the European post commanders, became the symbol of the Congo Free State. . . . The collection of hands became an end in itself. Force Publique soldiers brought them to the stations in place of rubber; they even went out to harvest them instead of rubber. . . They became a sort of currency. They came to be used to make up for shortfalls in rubber quotas, to replace. . . the people who were demanded for the forced labour gangs; and the Force Publique soldiers were paid their bonuses on the basis of how many hands they collected."

friendship pacts with it, but the pacts turned out to be sales contracts—giving ownership of the entire region to Léopold. He found himself in possession of thirty million people and an area of 900,000 square miles (2.3 million square kilometers). The Congolese were brutally whipped and beaten, forced to harvest rubber, palm oil, and ivory (the three most profitable products of the region). Workers who failed to meet their quotas were punished by having their hands chopped off.

Léopold's thugs were organized into the "Force Publique," whose savagery was so methodical that they kept accounts of the number of hands they had severed. They were expected to produce a hand for every bullet they fired, lest they be charged with wasting military resources. Hands became, in fact, a form of currency, redeemable for bonus payments at the end of each month.[8] An estimated five to eight million Congolese were murdered during Léopold's reign, with an equal number dying of starvation and disease.

In 1908, after proof of the Belgian cruelties was published (1904) by a British diplomat, the Belgian Parliament forced Léopold to relinquish control of the Congo and placed it under the authority of the Belgian state. Yet Léopold was among the wealthiest people in the Western world and remains a popular

---

[8] Severed hands were delivered to officials throughout the 1890s at nearly a metric ton per day.

figure in Belgian history. Among Belgians today, he is remembered for the large number of public buildings he constructed with his wealth, including the Musée de Congo in Tervuren. Now known as the Royal Museum for Central Africa, it contains thousands of artifacts of Congolese life. It makes no mention, however, of the savagery that brought them to Belgium and reduced the Congolese population by one-half. To this day, the museum's website states only that "to promote Belgium's work of 'development and civilization' in Congo . . . Léopold II hoped to build some form of museum or 'showcase.'"

On the last day of December in the year 1900 Mark Twain (Samuel Clemens; 1835–1910) penned a brief "Salutation-Speech from the 19th Century to the 20th," which appeared the next day in the *New York Herald*. Like most of the American writer's late work, this piece is marked with a sharp, bitter humor. In it, he regrets the era he has lived through and holds little hope for the century to come:

> I bring you the stately matron named *Christendom*, returning be-draggled, besmirched, and dishonored from pirate-raids in Kiaw-Chow, Manchuria, South Africa, and the Philippines, with her soul full of mean-ness, her pocket full of boodle, and her mouth full of pious hypocrisies. Give her soap and a towel, but hide the looking-glass.

Western society needed a thorough cleansing, and a younger Mark Twain might have hoped one was possible. But the imperial, gilded, rapacious world he lived in offered no reason for optimism.

Government and chartered companies "expropriated" (that is, stole) lands, crop fields, mines, flocks, and businesses at will. They forced locals to work at reduced wages, and they seized mineral rights and monopolized control of imports and exports. They dismantled support for centuries-long commercial routes, since neighboring territories were likely to be subjects of a rival European power. They also built tariff barriers that kept competitors' goods out of domestic markets. They ensured that their colonies sold only the goods produced by their imperialist masters, at whatever price those masters set.

Their goal was clear: to maximize profit for the European power in control of each region, its government, its officials, and its merchants. The imperial age thus strongly resembles the absolutist era—but with a difference. Compared to mercantilism, it worked better, because it covered a broader area and its tools of oppression were more deadly. The larger the empires grew, too, the greater was the need to protect business interests. Mining and manufacturing, and the banks used to back them, were seen as too big to allow to fail.

England's industries found it difficult to compete with Continental rivals, but no matter: they simply consolidated into larger and larger corporations in the hopes of improving profits. Many banks and investment houses consolidated as well and worked out special relations with the government-led Bank of England. In this way, Britain gradually exposed itself to crushing debts, and the shakiness of the entire structure increased the need for government manipulation. In fact, it was partly in order to write off debt from the construction of the Suez Canal that the British decided in 1882 to annex it.

The command economies of imperialism and its repeating cycles of boom and bust effectively locked out underdeveloped nations within Europe from international markets. Unable to compete or secure funding for their own industrialization, many of these countries—Greece, Ireland, Italy, Norway, Poland, Sweden most notably—lost tens of millions of their people through emigration between 1880 and 1914. Approximately one-half of these emigrants made their way to the United States, with the other half divided between Australia, Canada, and Latin America (see Map 22.4).

> The imperial age thus strongly resembles the absolutist era—but with a difference. Compared to mercantilism, it worked better, because it covered a broader area and its tools of oppression were more deadly.

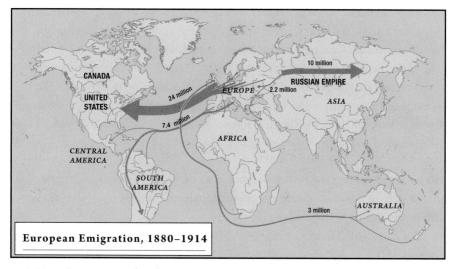

European Emigration, 1880–1914

MAP 22.4   European Emmigration, 1880–1914

WESTERN WAYS: EMULATION AND RESISTANCE

Once in control of their colonies, the Europeans encountered consistent but relatively minor unrest. Their technological edge made resistance seem futile to most of their subjects, many of whom were accustomed to rule by small numbers of tribal elites. Although they smarted under European oppression, they nonetheless benefited from the disappearance or at least the neutralization of longstanding tribal and clan conflicts.

Some colonial subjects emulated Western ways as a means to modernize their societies. They prized Western education, technology, and civil government, and they sought to promote improved understanding between rulers and ruled, even though the treatment they received from their European governors was shoddy. "However well-educated and clever a native might be," wrote a British military officer in India, "and however brave he may prove himself, I believe that no rank we can bestow on him would cause him to be considered an equal of the British." Contrast that with an 1871 speech by Dadabhai Naoroji (1825–1917), an Indian statesman who served in the British Parliament from 1892 to 1895:

> The introduction of English education, with its great, noble, elevating, and civilizing literature and advanced science, will for ever remain a monument of good work done in India and a claim to gratitude upon the Indian people. . . . Britain may well claim credit for law and order, which, however, is as much necessary for the existence of British rule in India as for the good of the Indian people; for freedom of speech and press, and for other benefits flowing therefrom. . . . [But] the benefits are more than counterbalanced by evils inseparable from the system of a remote foreign dominion. . . . Commonsense will suggest this to any thoughtful mind. These evils have ever since gone on increasing, and more and more counterbalancing the increased produce of the country, making now the evil of the bleeding and impoverishing drain by the foreign dominion nearly or above £30,000,000 a year. *(Poverty and Un-British Rule in India, 1901, pp. vi–viii)*

His book *Poverty and Un-British Rule in India* (1901) brought to popular attention within Britain the devastating effect of colonialism on the Indian people, while still expressing hope for a shared prosperity.

The case of Mohandas Gandhi (1869–1948) is instructive.[9] Born to a prominent provincial Hindu family near Bombay (today's city of Mumbai), he traveled to London

---

9   Mahatma, as Gandhi is also known, is a Hindu honorary title meaning "Great Soul."

in 1888 and studied law at University College London for three years. He spoke fluent English, adopted Western dress and manners (though he hated British cooking), and hoped to make a living as a barrister back in British India. His career faltered, however, and he took a position in British South Africa, where his encounters with racism and discrimination turned him gradually against the empire. For a time, Gandhi exhibited a measure of Western-style race prejudice, too: "Kaffirs [a derogatory term for black South Africans] are as a rule uncivilized.... They are troublesome, very dirty, and live almost like animals," he wrote in the newspaper he founded while in South Africa, the *Indian Opinion*. On another occasion he asserted, "We believe as much in the purity of race [as white South Africans do].... We believe also that [whites] should be the predominating race." He finally returned to India in 1915, renounced Western dress, embraced strict Hindu asceticism (for example, taking a vow of lifelong celibacy), and began the nonviolent protest campaign against British rule in India for which he became famous.

The Young Gandhi   Mohandas Gandhi (1869-1948) seen here as a barrister in South Africa. Remembered, of course, as the champion of India's independence from Britain and as the apostle of non-violence, Gandhi also campaigned tirelessly for the rights of women. He wrote in *Young India* (1930), a newsweekly he published from 1919 to 1932: "to call woman the weaker sex is a libel; it is man's injustice to woman. If by strength is meant brute strength, then, indeed, is woman less brute than man. If by strength is meant moral power, then woman is immeasurably man's superior. Has she not greater intuition, is she not more self-sacrificing, has she not greater powers of endurance, has she not greater courage? Without her, man could not be. If nonviolence is the law of our being, the future is with woman. Who can make a more effective appeal to the heart than woman?"

The largest sustained rebellion against the Europeans, the **Boxer Rebellion** (1898–1901), occurred in China. It began when a millennial Buddhist sect from northern China opened a campaign of violence against European missionaries and native Chinese who had converted to Christianity. The rebels came largely from the peasantry and called themselves the society of the Yihequan, meaning "Righteous and Harmonious Fists." They believed themselves the sanctified saviors of China from foreign imperialism, fighters whose religious rituals made them invulnerable to Western guns and cannon. The Yihequan believed they would be reincarnated as "spirit warriors"—an entire ghost army that would rout the Western corrupters of China's world. They opposed Western culture as much as Western colonial rule and hence had much in common with other nationalist movements around the globe.

Later Chinese nationalists were ambivalent about the Boxers and remain so today. They admired the patriotism the rebels evinced but wanted to distance themselves from both the Boxers' low origins and unorthodox religious convictions. After uprisings in the countryside, the Boxer forces, perhaps a quarter million strong, moved into Beijing and other cities, in order to target missionaries, merchants, and diplomats. They killed several hundred Westerners, along with several thousand Chinese Christian converts. The empress dowager of the weak Qing dynasty was personally sympathetic to the Boxers but was compelled by her treaties with the Europeans to help put them down. In the end, the Boxers were routed by an alliance of soldiers from the five leading European states (Austria-Hungary, Britain, France, Germany, and Italy) plus forces from Japan, Russia, and the United States. To avenge the murdered missionaries and converts, the Eight Army Alliance committed widespread atrocities, including murder, rape, and arson, against civilians.

Mark Twain again: Soon after his toss-away "Salutation to the 20th Century," he wrote a parody of the "Battle Hymn of the Republic." In it he curses the imperialist greed that, he believed, had overtaken Western society. It had made his whole working life nothing but an "era of incredible rottenness." The aftermath of the Boxer Rebellion—which he had publicly supported—was particularly galling to him.

> Mine eyes have seen the orgy of the launching of the Sword;
> He is searching out the hoardings where the stranger's wealth
>   is stored.
> He hath loosed his fateful lightnings, and with woe and death
>   has scored;
> His lust is marching on.
>
> I have seen him in the watch-fires of a hundred circling camps,
> They have builded him an altar in the Eastern dews and damps;
> I have read his doomful mission by the dim and flaring lamps—
> His night is marching on.
>
> I have read his bandit gospel writ in burnished rows of steel:
> "As ye deal with my pretensions, so with you my wrath shall deal;
> Let the faithless son of Freedom crush the patriot with his heel;
> Lo, Greed is marching on!"

We have legalized the strumpet and are guarding her retreat;
Greed is seeking out commercial souls before his judgment seat;
O, be swift, ye clods, to answer him! Be jubilant my feet!
Our god is marching on!

In a sordid slime harmonious, Greed was born in yonder ditch,
With a longing in his bosom—and for others' goods an itch—
As Christ died to make men holy, let men die to make us rich—
Our god is marching on.

His daughter advised him that this scornful rendition of a much-loved hymn was too bitter and was certain to offend his readers. He never published it.

WHO, WHAT, WHERE

Boxer Rebellion
command economies
Conference of Berlin
imperialism
scientific management

Second Industrial
Revolution
social Darwinism

SUGGESTED READINGS

Primary Sources

Baring, Evelyn. *Modern Egypt.*

Gandhi, Mohandas. *An Autobiography: The Story of My Experiments with Truth.*

Hobson, J. A. *Imperialism: A Study.*

Taylor, Frederick Winslow. *The Principles of Scientific Management.*

Anthologies

Bowman, William D., Frank M. Chiteji, and J. Megan Greene, eds. *Imperialism in the Modern World: Sources and Interpretations.*

Brown, Judith M., ed. *Mahatma Gandhi: The Essential Writings.*

Fischer, Louis, ed. *The Essential Gandhi: An Anthology of His Writings on His Life, Work, and Ideas.*

Martin, Susan K., Caroline Daley, Elizabeth Dimock, Cheryl Cassidy, and Cecily Devereaux, eds. *Women and Empire, 1750–1939: Primary Sources on Gender and Anglo-Imperialism.* (2009).

Naoroji, Dadabhai. *Poverty and Un-British Rule in India* (1901).

Smith, Bonnie G., ed. *Imperialism: A History in Documents* (2000).

Studies

Appleby, Joyce Oldham. *The Relentless Revolution: A History of Capitalism* (2010).

Bickers, Robert, and R. G. Tiedemann, eds. *The Boxers, China, and the World* (2007).

Broadberry, Stephen, and Kevin H. O'Rourke, eds. *The Cambridge Economic History of Modern Europe* (2010).

Cannadine, David. *Ornamentalism: How the British Saw Their Empire* (2002).

Curtin, Philip D. *The World and the West: The European Challenge and the Overseas Response in the Age of Empire* (2002).

Delmendo, Sharon. *The Star-Entangled Banner: One Hundred Years of America in the Philippines* (2004).

Deringil, Selim. *The Well-Protected Domains: Ideology and the Legitimation of Power in the Ottoman Empire, 1876–1909* (2011).

Drayton, Richard. *Nature's Government: Science, Imperial Britain, and the "Improvement" of the World* (2000).

Ferguson, Niall. *Colossus: The Rise and Fall of the American Empire* (2004).

———. *Empire: The Rise and Demise of the British World Order and the Lessons for Global Power* (2003).

Gelber, Harry G. *Opium, Soldiers, and Evangelicals: Britain's 1840–42 War with China and Its Aftermath* (2004).

Hanioğlu, M. Şükrü. *Preparation for a Revolution: The Young Turks, 1902–1908* (2001).

Harrington, Peter. *Peking, 1900: The Boxer Rebellion* (2001).

Jasanoff, Maya. *Edge of Empire: Lives, Culture, and Conquest in the East, 1750–1850* (2006).

Karabell, Zachary. *Parting the Desert: The Creation of the Suez Canal* (2004).

Kern, Stephen. *The Culture of Time and Space, 1880–1918* (2003).

Lelyveld, Joseph. *Great Soul: Mahatma Gandhi and His Struggle with India* (2012).

Linn, Brian McAllister. *The Philippine War, 1899–1902* (2000).

Meyer, Karl E., and Shareen Blair Brysac. *Tournament of Shadows: The Great Game and the Race for Empire in Central Asia* (2006).

Pomeranz, Kenneth. *The Great Divergence: China, Europe, and the Making of the Modern World Economy* (2001).

Silbey, David J. *A War of Frontier and Empire: The Philippine-American War, 1899–1902* (2007).

Watts, Sheldon. *Epidemics and History: Disease, Power, and Imperialism* (2000).

Wesseling, H. L. *The European Colonial Empires, 1815–1919* (2004).

Xiang, Lanxin. *The Origins of the Boxer War: A Multinational Study* (2002).

For additional resources, including maps, primary sources, visuals, web links, and quizzes, please go to **www.oup.com/us/backman.**

CHAPTER 23

From Nihilism to Modernism

1880–1939

N ot all Westerners at the start of the 20th century were greedy, grasping imperialists, and not all believed in their historical destiny and in social Darwinism. What Mark Twain called an "era of incredible rottenness" also had some of the most intense soul-searching and self-criticism the West had seen since the 17th century. The analysis was thoroughgoing and biting: it was creative, scientific, poetic, religious, and philosophical. At times it bordered on being obsessive. No single outlook or set of ideas defined it, although elements of confusion and doubt, and of the loss of old certainties, were predominant. It took the form of new styles in painting and sculpture, bold experiments in music, even bolder dissections of the human mind, and innovations in fiction and drama. It also challenged basic assumptions about truth and value.

THE GREATER WEST IN A TIME OF UNCERTAINTY, 1880–1939

Even the sciences discovered that some of their most fundamental beliefs about space, time, and motion were doubtful if not flat-out wrong. In philosophy the confident idealism of midcentury, as evidenced by a writer like Georg W. F. Hegel (1770–1831), gave way to thoroughgoing uncertainty about the nature of reality, a more radical individualism, and a renewed interest in logic and language. And both developments suggest a turning away from the world and toward the self, in philosophy's attempts to produce order. Even

◀ **A Certain Horror** *The Scream*, by Edvard Munch (1893). Munch's diary described the picture's origins: "I was walking along a path one evening, the city [of Oslo] was on one side, the fjord on the other. I was tired and felt ill, so I stopped and looked over the fjord. The sun was setting and the clouds were as red as blood. I felt a scream passing through the world, and could even hear it, or so it seemed. So I painted this picture."

architecture and home decoration visibly rejected 19th-century mass production and imperial grandeur and gave way to arts-and-crafts movements that emphasized individuality, originality, and personal expression.

SICKNESS UNTO DEATH

In politics, socialists, anarchists, feminists, commonsense democrats, isolationists, and even some conservatives loudly protested the imperialist frenzy. Many had seen the march to empire coming as early as midcentury, with developments like the Crimean War and the Louis-Napoleon's proclamation of the Second French Empire. Karl Marx, in 1852, saw the new aggressiveness as an effort to emulate the glories of 1805–1812, but its heart was nothing more than the pursuit of money. Bonaparte, Marx sneered, at least could have claimed some sort of justification for his violence. Europe's new aggressors were marked by nothing more than "passions with no truth in them; truths with no passion in them; unheroic pseudo-heroes; history without events; [and] a series of developments driven forward by nothing more than the calendar."

Not all opponents of imperialism were revolutionaries like Marx. George Bernard Shaw (1856–1950) denounced empire building in essays, lectures, pamphlets, and plays like *The Man of Destiny* (1895, about Napoleon), *Caesar and Cleopatra* (1898), and *John Bull's Other Island* (1904, about the Irish Question). Shaw was no democrat; he was far too skeptical about the intelligence of common people. Yet he championed a moderate form of socialism that would free people from the concern for wealth that drove imperialism.

In the United States, the Anti-Imperialist League formed in 1898 to oppose annexation of the Philippines. To the League, this violated the principle of government by consent of the people, enshrined in the Declaration of Independence. Otto von Bismarck, ever eager to expand Germany's power within Europe, had no interest in imperialist adventures outside the Continent and resisted them with all his might—which led to his dismissal by Emperor Wilhelm.

CHAPTER TIMELINE

1881 Ibsen, *Ghosts*

1885 Haggard, *King Solomon's Mines*

1886 Nietzsche, *Beyond Good and Evil*

1889 Van Gogh, *Starry Night*

1891 Wilde, *The Picture of Dorian Gray*

1899 Freud, *Interpretation of Dreams*

1900 Max Planck formulates quantum theory

1901 Husserl, *Logical Investigations*

Many leading intellectuals, too, like the classical scholar and parliamentarian Theodor Mommsen (1817–1903), denounced imperialism as simply a waste of time and energy.

Industry still demanded more materials, more products, and more markets. Yet to critics it seemed to cheapen people's lives. Oscar Wilde (1854–1900), the playwright and novelist, dismissed as a cynic someone "who knows the price of everything, and the value of nothing." Mass production meant crass production. It was fine to devote a nation's talent and treasure to spreading literacy and scientific knowledge among the masses. What good was it, however, if those skills went only to produce cheap housewares, kitschy art, and shallow pulp fiction?

Books became the dominant form of popular entertainment, with novels surpassing poetry as the favorite genre. Max Pemberton (1863–1950) wrote many adventure stories aimed at working-class audiences. His most successful was *The Iron Pirate* (1896), about a steam-driven frigate that terrorizes the Atlantic. H. Rider Haggard (1856–1925) was even more successful, with novels like *King Solomon's Mines* (1885) and *She* (1887).[1] The latter tells of an English scholar of antiquities who travels to an uncharted kingdom "in darkest Africa," ruled by a mythical immortal beauty. "God help English literature," wrote one critic of the time, "when English people lay aside . . . the works of Defoe, Swift, Thackeray, Charlotte Brontë, [and] George Eliot . . . for the penny-dreadfuls of Mr. Haggard."[2] The pressure of the marketplace drove down standards in popular music as well. The invention of the phonograph and radio, while good things in themselves, meant that people no longer had to learn to play instruments in order to have music in their lives. They could simply turn on the machine to hear whatever they wished. Light popular songs crowded out more serious and

---

[1]   H. Rider Haggard's novels later became the models for the Indiana Jones movies.

[2]   Cheap adventure novels were called penny dreadfuls, because they appeared in magazine installments costing only a penny.

1905	1907	1911–1913	1920	1938
Einstein publishes special theory of relativity	Picasso, *Les Demoiselles d'Avignon*	Russell and Whitehead, *Principia Mathematica*	Freud, *Beyond the Pleasure Principle*	Sartre, *Nausea*

1906	1910	1915	1924
First performance of Schoenberg's Chamber Symphony No. 1	Kandinsky, *On the Spiritual Element in Art*	Einstein puts forward general theory of relativity	Mann, *The Magic Mountain*

Low Culture   A group of friends listening to a gramophone, Béziers, France, ca. 1910.

challenging music. Culture, it seemed, was being split into high and low—and low culture was winning out.

Many writers, critics, and artists at the end of the 19th century therefore reacted by championing the high. "Art for art's sake" became their rallying cry. Art had to be dedicated to nothing but itself; it had to pursue beauty, truth, and deep feeling on their own terms, without any concern for the masses. "Nothing is truly beautiful unless it is useless," wrote the French critic Théophile Gautier (1811–1872). "Everything that is useful is actually ugly since its usefulness derives from its answering to a human need—and human needs are ignoble and disgusting. . . . The most useful thing in a house [after all] is the toilet."

The preface to Oscar Wilde's novel *The Picture of Dorian Gray* (1891), served as a manifesto for this passionate aestheticism:

> The artist is the creator of beautiful things. To reveal art and conceal the artist is art's aim . . . .
>
> Those who find ugly meanings in beautiful things are corrupt without being charming . . . . Those who find beautiful meanings in beautiful things are the cultivated. For these there is hope . . . .
>
> There is no such thing as a moral or an immoral book. Books are well written, or badly written. That is all.

... It is the spectator, and not life, that art really mirrors. Diversity of opinion about a work of art shows that the work is new, complex, and vital.... We can forgive a man for making a useful thing as long as he does not admire it. The only excuse for making a useless thing is that one admires it intensely.

All art is quite useless.

Wilde's career reached its zenith in his stage comedy *The Importance of Being Earnest* (1895); but his fall, after a conviction for "gross indecency" with his homosexual lover, inspired a keen self-investigation. Written in 1897 while in his prison cell, his *De Profundis* ("Out of the Depths") recognizes the need for moral seriousness and the pursuit of goodness in life. This farewell letter/essay was not published until 1905—five years after his death in Paris. Without this sense of spiritual purpose, life is cast adrift. And this very aimlessness permits the greed, power wielding, and self-serving hypocrisy of late Victorian society. In the words of the Danish philosopher Søren Kierkegaard (1813–1855), it was "the sickness unto death" and the principal curse of modern European life.

Wilde ends *De Profundis* with a resolve not to despair of his fall from fame and fortune but to live henceforth transforming every experience of life into goodness—the truth of beauty lies in the determination to ennoble life with meaning, rather than merely to adorn it, as before, with cleverness and wit:

> Religion does not help me. The faith that others give to what is unseen, I give to what one can touch, and look at.... When I think about religion at all, I feel as if I would like to found an order for those who cannot believe.... And agnosticism should have its ritual no less than faith. It has sown its martyrs, it should reap its saints.... Its symbols must be of my own creating. Only that is spiritual which makes its own form. If I may not find its secret within myself, I shall never find it. If I have not got it already, it will never come to me. Reason does not help me.... But, somehow, I have got to make both of these things just and right for me.

Wilde accepts the challenge to make one's own meaning, one's own beauty, one's own truth, since he sees that the soul is made stronger by the effort itself. But Meaning, Beauty, and Truth—all capitalized—will never actually be achieved or attained. And for a very simple reason: because they do not exist.

A WAVE OR A PARTICLE?

Many intellectual currents accepted, or even urged, the notion that there were no fixed moral or material truths. They rejected the solid bourgeois certainties of the 19th century—belief in a rational, coherent, material universe, in nationalism and progress, in philosophical idealism, and in universal moral and aesthetic values. But they did not reject these assumptions carelessly or out of pique. Years of grinding work in laboratories, libraries, studies, and artists' studios lay behind this radical and seemingly abrupt break with the past. And the first signs of major change occurred in the sciences.

Europeans in the 19th century commonly regarded physics as the least interesting of all sciences. It seemed a professional dead end; after Sir Isaac Newton, all that remained to do was to clear up a few minor things or add a few points to the general picture. Newton's three laws of motion, as laid out in the *Principia Mathematica*, had established classical mechanics (the movement of matter); his law of universal gravitation explained nature's fundamental force. The cosmos operated according to fixed laws and mathematical formulas. Alfred North Whitehead (1861–1947), the great British mathematician and philosopher, described the start of his career as "an age of successful scientific orthodoxy, undisturbed by much thought beyond the conventions ... [and] one of the dullest stages of thought since the time of the First Crusade." The discovery of a new energy, electricity, stirred things up for a while, but James Maxwell (1831–1879), a Scottish physicist, soon calmed things down again. Maxwell showed how electricity, magnetism, and light are all manifestations of the same force—electromagnetism. The rest of physics, it seemed, was merely a matter of adjusting a few details.

But then a spate of new discoveries popped up, discoveries that could not be fitted into the Newtonian framework. In fact, they seemed to attack it. On November 8, 1895, Wilhelm Röntgen (1845–1923) discovered X-rays while experimenting with electrical current passing through a vacuum tube.[3] These rays were yet another elemental force, but they could not be explained by the standard model. Then came the electron, discovered by 1897 by J. J. Thomson (1856–1940) at Cambridge University in England. Before Thomson, atoms were believed to be the smallest particles in nature—the fundamental building blocks. As Thomson deflected cathode rays through electromagnetic fields, he found subatomic particles less than 0.0005 times the mass of the smallest atom, hydrogen. The very next year Madame Curie discovered another element, radium, that somehow emitted radiation—and with it another new form of energy, radioactivity. Suddenly the universe, at

---

[3]   The "X" in X-rays derived from the mathematical sign for an unknown. Röntgen received the first ever Nobel Prize in physics, in 1901.

X-ray Vision   Cartoon of a "beach idyll" when seen via the new technology of X-rays, discovered by Wilhelm Röntgen in 1895. Certainly not what most of us were thinking of when as youngsters we longed to have X-ray vision.

the smallest of levels, looked stranger than it had since the time of Copernicus, Kepler, and Galileo.

These discoveries showed the universe to be immensely more complex than anyone understood. But they were nothing compared to what came next. All of classical physics, and even the newer discoveries, had relied on the *ether*. This medium had neither mass, nor weight, nor color; it was uniform, odorless, and tasteless; it was imperceptible to touch or measurement; it offered no physical resistance. Yet it had to exist, because all of those atoms and energies had to move *through something*. Otherwise atoms and energies could not interact, just as swimmers rely on water in order to move through the sea or a pool. The ether ensured that all movement, all changes in momentum and direction, and all interactions of force and counterforce would proceed smoothly and perfectly. But then came Max Planck (1858–1947) and Albert Einstein (1879–1955), and our understanding of the universe would never be the same.

Planck and Einstein seldom performed experiments; they both preferred to work out on paper the theories behind other people's data. Planck's first breakthrough came in 1900, after a group of physicists who were trying to coax the maximum brightness out of light bulbs with the least possible electricity sent the accumulated data of their experiments to him. He came up with an astonishing conclusion: the data could be explained only by introducing into the calculations a fixed unit of energy—a kind of packet of light energy, called a *quantum*. One could have x amount of light energy, or $2x$, or $3x$, and so on, but nothing in between. Light was not, therefore, a continuous wave of energy but instead a torrent of finite bits.

To make matters even more confusing, these quanta of light (the plural of quantum) behaved like physical particles possessing mass, even as they also had the characteristics of waves. Planck turned to this conclusion, he later wrote, "as an act of despair." It was the only way to make mathematical sense out of the data, even though it upset the foundations of all of physics. In this he was remarkably like Copernicus four hundred years earlier, who had to wreck the system he had inherited in order to make his numbers crunch better. Planck had reluctantly invented a new physics based on quanta, a **quantum theory**. Most physicists rejected his claims at first, even though they could find no fault in his reasoning. Once Einstein confirmed Planck's theory, however, most fell into line.[4]

Not even Einstein, however, was prepared for the next step. Matter, too, appeared to behave as both wave and particle. That is the basis of how quantum developed over half a century or more, to reveal the inner workings of atoms and molecules. Scientists could make sense of the properties of the different chemical elements that, before, had just seemed handed down like a table in a reference book. They could better understand reactions between atoms and molecules, unleashing a new scientific revolution in chemistry, physics, and biology—to the point that we can now look deep into the brain or hold entire computers in our hands. Yet they could make predictions about only the *probability* that any one particle would be anywhere. That "wave-particle duality" is also the basis of the *uncertainty principle*, which sets limits on what one can know about a particle at a given moment. If uncertainty has become as powerful a metaphor as relativity, no wonder Einstein rebelled against quantum theory. Besides, he had made some sweeping and precise predictions of his own.

European culture had earlier periods of uncertainty about how to know what was true, but now the very idea of fixed truth seemed to be false. Nothing quite like this had happened before, and it crossed scientific and artistic lines.

RELATIVITY AND SPACE-TIME

Einstein finished the task of reinventing physics in 1905 when he published what came to be known as his special theory of relativity. His general theory of relativity followed in 1915. They are difficult, but it is important to understand the basics—and not solely in order to appreciate the science. **Relativity** could in fact stand for the entire cultural and intellectual ferment of the early 20th century. It could stand for the relativity of aesthetic values, of philosophical terms, and of literary judgments. Artists and poets did not derive their ideas from Planck and Einstein, although many were keenly aware of them, but there are parallels all the

---

4   Speaking of one holdout against quanta, Plank recalled, "He's a perfect example of the type of theorist we do not need . . . the kind who says 'The facts don't fit my theory; too bad for the facts.'"

same. European culture had earlier periods of uncertainty about how to know what was true, but now the very idea of fixed truth seemed to be false. Nothing quite like this had happened before, and it crossed scientific and artistic lines. As the American historian, political writer, and novelist Henry Adams (1838–1918) wrote in a letter (1903) to a British friend (Charles Gaskell):

> Forty years ago, our friends always explained things and had the cosmos down to a point, [with] Darwin and Charles Lyell. Now they say they don't believe there is any explanation, or that you can choose between half-a-dozen, all correct.... Every generalisation we settled forty years ago is abandoned.... Science has given up the whole fabric of cause and effect. Even time-sequence is beginning to be threatened. I should not at all wonder if someone should not upset time. As for space, it is upset already. We did that sixty years ago, with electricity.

The **special theory of relativity**, or special relativity, maintains that all measurements of space and time are relative. This is not just a matter of perspective, like looking at a draftsman's ruler or waiting in line. A ruler may be twelve inches in length, but if one looks at it from a distance or at an angle it appears considerably shorter. An hour spent waiting at the Registry of Motor Vehicles seems infinitely longer than an hour spent listening to Mozart. Einstein's results are something else again. Consider a man bouncing a basketball. Suppose it moves with perfect regularity and in a perfectly vertical line—three feet down, three feet up, over and over, exactly one bounce per second. The ball therefore travels a total of six feet per second. But now imagine that the man is standing on a flatcar on a train that is moving down the track as he bounces the basketball. To an observer watching from a platform thirty feet away, the ball moves not in a vertical line but at an angle to the vertical because of the horizontal movement of the train. Moreover, the ball turns out to travel at a different speed—say, five feet diagonally down and five feet diagonally up, for a total of ten feet per second.

The special theory shows that this is not simply a difference of perspective. The ball does not just "seem" to be traveling at one speed and not the other; the special theory holds that the ball is actually traveling six feet per second *and* ten feet per second, depending on the observer, *at the same time.* Time and space are elastic and should be conceived as different facets of a single dimension that Einstein called **space-time.**[5]

---

[5]   Einstein's special theory of relativity is the basis of the idea that nothing can go faster than the speed of light.

Space-time   A photo of the Andromeda galaxy (also known as M31) taken through a Celestron 80ED telescope with a one-hour exposure. Andromeda is a spiral galaxy roughly 2.5 million light-years from Earth and contains over a trillion stars. Andromeda and our own Milky Way galaxy are drawing nearer to one another and will collide in about 4.5 billion years.

The **general theory of relativity**, or general relativity, describes gravity's relationship to space-time. Newton had posited gravity as an attraction between all particles with mass, but he offered no insight into what gravity actually is. After all, why would two bodies hundreds of billions of miles apart feel attracted toward each other? Newton admitted defeat on this question and happily returned to his calculations on how great the force would be. To Einstein, gravity is not a force at all. It is simply the name we give to an experience we have of space-time. A person in a stationary elevator can "feel gravity." It is the sensation of the floor of the elevator, preventing him from falling into the Earth's core (or at least into the basement). But if now the elevator began to accelerate upward, even if there were no Earth below pulling the person down, he would feel the exact same sensation of the floor pushing upward. In fact, he could not tell if the elevator was moving or not. Einstein called this relationship of motion to gravity the *equivalence principle*.

In general relativity, every vantage point in the universe, whether moving or stationary, is as valid as every other vantage point. The laws of physics will look the same in each. There is no fixed and absolute center to anything: to space, to motion, to "gravity," to time. Everything is relative. From the point of view of a spectator, a football thrown by a quarterback appears to arch smoothly upward, reach a zenith, then arch smoothly downward into the receiver's arms. That is true, says Einstein—but it is also true that the ball travels in a straight line through a space-time that is curved. It is the curvature of space-time that gives the impression of the ball's rising and falling. Adding to the wonder and confusion of it all, adds Einstein, it is also true, from a different vantage point, that the ball is not moving at all. The curved space-time of the universe rushing past it gives the impression of the ball in flight. Each observation is equally valid.

Planck received the Nobel Prize in Physics in 1918, Einstein in 1923. Their ideas have been confirmed by thousands of experiments and to unimaginable degrees of precision. They were sufficient to upend the entire scientific understanding of the cosmos, but taken together they add yet another level of confusion: quantum theory and general relativity, as we currently understand them at least, cannot both be true—or at least they have so far resisted the unity of a single theory that gives the right answers. Much of the research done in the hundred years since Planck and Einstein has been devoted to reconciling them. Einstein himself spent the last twenty years of his life trying to determine a "unified field theory" that would harmonize these theories. Efforts continue in ways more open to the paradoxes of quantum theory than Einstein himself ever was, with string theory today.

While immensely sophisticated and mathematically complex, these ideas quickly entered 20th-century culture. Everything thought by scientists for three thousand years had been shown to be false, and the two new truths that prove it actually conflict with one another. A story like that is hard to keep secret. What people took away from the new physics was the broader idea of relativity—no fixed points, no absolute time, no absolute space. And the more we learned about the universe, the more immense, confusing, unexpected, and for some more frightening it seemed to be. An English physicist, Paul Dirac (1902–1984), described the instant popularity of Planck's and Einstein's work this way:[6]

> What people took away from the new physics was the broader idea of relativity—no fixed points, no absolute time, no absolute space. And the more we learned about the universe, the more immense, confusing, unexpected, and for some more frightening it seemed to be.

> It is easy to see the reason for this tremendous impact. We had just been through a terrible and very serious war.... Everyone wanted to forget it. And then relativity came along as a wonderful idea leading us to a new domain of thought. It was an escape from the war.... Relativity was a subject that everybody felt himself competent to write about in a general philosophical way. The philosophers just put forward the view that everything had to be considered relative to something else, and [then] they rather claimed that they had known about relativity all along.

Dirac was being ungenerous to philosophers, but he was right to point to the similarities between modern science and contemporary philosophy. There too, the focus was on the futility of finding absolute and permanent truth. Unlike the physicists, though, the philosophers simply gave up.

---

[6] Dirac was also the first physicist to put forth the idea of antimatter.

THE WILL TO POWER

Like physics, philosophy in the 20th century was insightful and brilliant. Like physics, too, it has often been exceedingly difficult to understand. Often, however, it has been depressing, and that is not an unfortunate side effect. It is the work's very point. Coming down from the heights of idealism, its thrust has been the randomness, contingency, and disorder of life. Modern philosophy has argued for the inability of our minds to comprehend reality—and the slipperiness of language in trying to discuss it. It is not a pretty picture.

The fundamental division is between analytic and rationalist philosophies. **Analytic philosophy** stresses the need for close and careful reasoning. Analytic philosophies have had a dizzying array of names, including symbolic logic, logical positivism, functionalism, and eliminative materialism. **Rationalist philosophy** stresses instead the movement of the human mind itself. Rationalist philosophies, too, have splintered into a vast number of specialties, including phenomenology, existentialism, hermeneutics, neo-Marxism, structuralism, and post-structuralism. In general, the analytic philosophers have been English speaking, while rationalist philosophy has dominated Continental thought. What they share is a 19th-century inheritance—a purposeless universe and a view of human life that is, in the absence of a divine Creator, without essential function or meaning.

The key figure in the new bleakness was Friedrich Nietzsche (1844–1900), the prophet of God's death. Although little known in his lifetime, Nietzsche's work advanced the nihilistic philosophy of the age, even though he himself rejected the extreme skepticism known as **nihilism**. To Nietzsche, human life without God is tragically meaningless. Every individual's existence is a cold crack of light between two eternities of darkness, and nothing that happens during that brief crack matters in any absolute sense. We are simply random gatherings of molecules that cohere and experience consciousness for a short time before dissolving again into nothingness. Not a very sunny view. "Hope in [a supposed] reality is the greatest evil that can befall anyone," he writes, "for all it does is prolong one's agony." But Nietzsche's point is to rouse us to action, not to drive us to collapse in despair. This is exactly where he parts company with the nihilists: we should not simply accept the world's randomness but actually do something about it. Let's not make the agony of our existence even worse by being stupid while we are here. Let's not tell ourselves comforting lies or live by values we do not genuinely believe in. Instead, we should have the courage to face awful reality as it is and live authentically while we live.

> To Nietzsche, human life without God is tragically meaningless. Every individual's existence is a cold crack of light between two eternities of darkness, and nothing that happens during that brief crack matters in any absolute sense.

How do we know what is authentic? As usual, it is easier to identify what is false than what is true. One thing that is clearly false, Nietzsche argues, is the Western belief in democracy and the equality of mankind. In our heart of hearts, he demands, we know that we do not believe in this idea. One has only to look around—at one's coworkers, at crowds on a bus, at the people lined up in grocery stores, at mobs gathered at a ball game. If we are honest, we will admit to ourselves that most people are stupid. In contrast, democracy makes sense only if one assumes that people are all equally capable of making intelligent decisions about how to govern society. We should therefore throw democratic ideas and institutions on the trash heap. Go ahead and admit it, Nietzsche urges. Life is already brief, purposeless, and meaningless. Why spend the little time we have living in a political system that gives fools an equal share of influence? Why should we refuse to acknowledge what we all actually think? Just to be nice? That sounds pleasant, he says, but niceness is no basis for a philosophy, except to fools:

Believing in Democracy   A group of night-school students, many of them new immigrants, saluting the American flag. Note that the flag has only forty-eight stars; Alaska and Hawaii both gained statehood in 1959. (Arizona became the 48th state in 1912.) Roughly a quarter-million immigrants received citizenship per year through the 1920s and the first half of the 1930s. Fear of Fascist and Communist infiltration drove down the number to a fifth of that from 1935 to 1945, but by 1950 that number rose to a quarter-million per year again. The number of new citizens per year then held steady at that level until 1970, when it began another period of rapid growth.

> What bizarre distortions and lies people put up with! It never ceases to amaze anyone who has eyes to see. "Oh, look! Isn't everything around us so cheery and free, so easy and simple! Isn't it wonderful how we have given ourselves a free pass to experience everything that is superficial! . . . And oh! how we figured out from the dawn of time how to keep ourselves ignorant so that we might enjoy a degree of freedom and escape from care, feel ourselves to be brave and cheerful, and to actually enjoy existence!" *(Beyond Good and Evil [1886])*

What is another idea to reject? Christianity. All religions to Nietzsche (the child of a family of Lutheran ministers) are just emotional security blankets.

And Christianity—at least in what he saw it in its late 19th-century form—is particular guilty because of its very niceness. The Christianity of his time, he finds, preaches what he terms a "slave-morality" of meekness and passivity, of self-denial and contempt for strength. As he put in a late book,

> I say that [this] Christianity is the greatest single curse on mankind, [its] most gargantuan and deep-seated depravity, . . . the most enduring blemish on the human race, . . . for it favors everything that is weak, base, and malformed . . . . Some call it the "religion of compassion,"' but I say that compassion negates all the fundamental instincts that contribute to the vitality and meaning of life! (*The Twilight of the Idols* [1888]).

Nietzsche was not as resolutely anti-Christian through most of his life as most people think. He hated Victorian piety as intellectually soft, but he retained an emotional attachment to, though not an actual belief in, the intellectually and morally rigorous Christianity he had grown up with.[7] His rants on the need to annihilate every vestige of Christianity date to the last two years of his life, when the onset of his mental illness was undeniable: he signed letters as "Nietzsche Caesar," filled wastebaskets with torn up money, declared his intention to establish a world government, and vowed to murder all anti-Semites.

Regardless, reading Nietzsche is a visceral experience. He shouts, curses, and ridicules. He uses coarse language and offers ugly analogies. He aims to shock. His books offer no calm, rational arguments; instead they consist of series of independent passages, each written at a white heat and usually in a single burst of inspiration. He writes in a confrontational and emotional style, like a firefighter trying to hurry people out of a burning building that is on the brink of collapse. Life is a state of continual emergency, and Nietzsche understood that we are our truest selves during emergencies. We may not be our best selves, but we are truest to what we value most. We are willing to be selfish if selfishness is called for and ready to bark out orders if necessary. We are focused on what has genuine meaning to us.

Life is a state of continual emergency, and Nietzsche understood that we are our truest selves during emergencies. We may not be our best selves, but we are truest to what we value most.

Nietzsche offers no solace to his readers and insists that we stop pretending that everything is fine. We must stop telling ourselves that everything is in God's hands, that history is progress, that democracy and capitalism will make the world better, that all people are created equal, and that Christian platitudes can relieve

---

7   Nietzsche, the prophet of the death of God, it turns out, was sentimentally fond of Christmas trees.

human suffering. We must stop saying that the West is right to bring "civilization" (not to mention schools, electricity, and railroads) to the savages around the earth. The only things he recognizes as absolutely good are the desire for life and the urge to create. There is hope of an ennobling life, with purpose, only in the instinctive human yearning to renew existence.

Thus he champions the **will to power**—the passionate striving to make meaning and leave a mark on the world. The phrase sounds ominously like a prelude to 20th-century fascism—and it has often been interpreted that way. Yet Nietzsche, despite his love of violent vocabulary and strident prose, was neither a fascist nor a sadist. (As a medical orderly during the Franco-Prussian War he regularly fainted at the sight of blood.) By the will to power, he meant the *creative drive* or *creativity*. In one of his notebooks, he discusses his philosophical ideas in relation to recent discoveries in physics:

> The triumphant idea of force—namely, the thing by means of which our physicists have invented God and God's invention of the world—needs elaboration. It needs an interior element, one I call "the will to power." An insatiable desire to enact power, to wield it and use it, to spur creation.

Nietzsche envisions a world in which those with the will to power would emerge as natural leaders, whether in politics, intellectual life, or art. These **supermen** (*Übermenschen*) would do a better job of it than the general masses. They would also provide inspiration and models for people everywhere to tap into their own creative drives. Such a scheme might make for a messy, conflict-prone world—but, Nietzsche asks, isn't that the world we live in now? In the world of supermen, the conflicts would at least be noble ones. We could set aside the shameful struggles over wealth and social status and the hypocritical moralism of Mark Twain's era of incredible rottenness.

THE RHODES COLOSSUS
STRIDING FROM CAPE TOWN TO CAIRO.

Super-man? Cecil Rhodes (1853-1906) as viewed by Punch magazine (December, 1892) as the colossus of British imperialism in Africa, from Cairo to Cape Town. "I would colonize the moon, if I could," he once said.

LOGIC AND LANGUAGE

Western philosophers after Nietzsche had experienced the death of God and of classical physics. They had witnessed the unnerving strangeness and relativity of the universe develop from a rarified scientific theory to a general world view. Many, too, were disgusted by the aggressive, industrial, and imperialistic culture around them. This seemed, on the whole, to be the greatest and most thorough fracturing of the European mind since the 17th century, when John Donne complained, "'Tis all in pieces, / All coherence gone." What were they to do? In general, they turned their gaze away from the world and toward the inner tools we use to try to make sense of it. If the world makes no fixed sense, they argued, then we should turn attention to the question of how logic and language ever made us think there was a real order to the cosmos in the first place. The very word "reality" in 20th-century culture, both high and low, started regularly to appear inside quotation marks.

In the Anglophone tradition, major Analytical philosophers, such as Bertrand Russell (1872–1970) and his student Ludwig Wittgenstein (1889–1951), focused on the structures and functions of logic and language.[8] These are, after all, the

Making Sense out of the Shards of Reality   *Logicomix: An Epic Search for Truth* is a graphic novel by Apostolos Doxiadis, published in 2009, that narrates and illustrates Bertrand Russell's attempt to find some form of absolute truth in the philosophical foundations of mathematics. Here he debates (and as in real life, was tormented by) his most brilliant student, Ludwig Wittgenstein.

---

8   Wittgenstein was an Austrian Jew who wrote most of his work in German; but since he both studied and later taught at Cambridge University, lectured in English, and wrote at least some of his work in English, I include him among the Anglophone philosophers. Certainly his lifelong emphasis on the relationship between logic and language places him in that tradition. Indeed, he is one of its main shapers.

tools with which humans try to create a reality out of a messy universe. Idealism had regarded the world, much like Newtonian physics, as a vast, comprehensive, interlocking system. Analytical philosophers, by contrast, approached the topic more modestly. Given that there is no grand system, what sense can we make out of the shards of reality within our grasp? If, for example, there are no universal standards of goodness, justice, or beauty, is there any legitimacy in holding simple beliefs about them? If goodness is relative, then why is it good to offer help to people in need? Why is it just to punish harshly someone who commits a violent crime but to punish less severely someone who commits a nonviolent one? If beauty is a relative construct, then can it be said that a piano sonata by Beethoven is "better" than a tune by a Dixieland jazz band? To answer these questions, the analytical philosophers insisted, one must not investigate the ideal concepts of Goodness, Justice, and Beauty—a hopeless activity, in any case. Instead, one should analyze specific propositions about people in need, about behavior (and misbehavior), and about art.

Take those sentences again. What do they propose? Does goodness consist in the help *given* to people in need or simply in *offering* help? Must the people receiving help *know* that they need it? Suppose they need help but do not know it, or do not desire it. Can any assistance offered them still be considered good? If so, under what conditions, and why? The only way to understand an act of goodness, then, is to wrestle with meanings. In the second proposition, about crime, one must wrestle not only with the adjective *just* (as in "it is just to punish violent offenders") but also with the phrase *it is*. What do we mean when we say that something "is" something else? For example, when we say, "Snow is white," are we stating that snowness and whiteness are identical? If so, then is it also true that the white sheets on my bed are made of snow? Or are we saying that snow uses whiteness, possesses it, shares it, or enacts it? What, exactly, *is* the meaning of *is*?

Methods like these use language in order to understand language, which risks philosophy itself becoming a kind of mere wordplay. To avoid that, many analytical philosophers turned instead to the tools of mathematics and symbolic logic. Reduce language whenever possible to sets of mathematical symbols and turn sentences into formulas. Their philosophical writings became highly technical. For example, Wittgenstein describes a relation between two hypothetical statements (*propositions* in the preferred analytical term to use) in this way:

> We must not say, "The complex sign '*aRb*' says '*a* stands in relation R to *b*;'" but we must say, "That '*a*' stands in a certain relation to '*b*' says that *aRb*."

Such thinkers sought greater precision in philosophical thinking, but precision usually came at the expense of accessibility. In Russell's 1905 essay "On

Denoting," to choose another example, he defined the proposition "x is a mountain" as the symbol Mx, and the proposition "x is golden" as the symbol Gx. He could then confidently state "A golden mountain does not exist" in this way:

$$\sim[(\exists x)(Mx \ \& \ Gx) \ \& \ \forall y((My \ \& \ Gy) \rightarrow y = x)]$$

This may be correct, but who can tell? Russell also wrote, along with Alfred North Whitehead (1861–1947), a three-volume work on the foundations of mathematics. Titled *Principia Mathematica* (1911–1913) after the great work by Sir Isaac Newton, it uses just this type of symbolic logic throughout more than a thousand dense pages in order to come to the conclusion—now logically proven as never before—that one plus one equals two.[9] Analytical philosophy did not intentionally keep common people at a distance, but it often came across as disdainful of nonspecialists. These philosophers employed a highly technical style because they saw themselves as scientists rather than humanists.

FROM PHENOMENOLOGY TO EXISTENTIALISM

Continental philosophers could be just as brilliant and just as opaque, but in a very different way. They studied the ways in which we experience things—a method known as **phenomenology**. While there may or may not be a universal ideal called Beauty, we have all experienced beautiful things—a sunset, a Bach cantata or a favorite song, a poem, whatever. Analytical philosophers might busy themselves dissecting the phrase "Cantata 199 by Bach is beautiful." Phenomenologists instead set out to study how we experience the music. What physiological effects does it produce as we listen? What memories does it invoke? What thoughts do we have during its performance? What is the flow of our emotions as one passage leads into another—or our sensation(s) after the music stops?

Phenomenology is based on the belief that, whereas the world may or may not be rationally ordered, our reactions to it are—or at least they can be. Phenomenology is *subjective*, meaning that it begins from the point of view of someone's experience. It is also *intentional*, meaning that it examines the how and why of the experience. The great figure at the turn of the century was Edmund Husserl (1859–1938), a German-speaking Jew born in what is now the Czech Republic. He spent his career at the universities of Göttingen and of Freiburg. His two-volume *Logical Investigations* (1900–1901) set the tone for Continental philoso-

---

9   As Russell dryly put it on the last page of the third volume of his master work, this now-certain truth that 1 + 1 = 2 "may prove useful."

phy for the entire century. Among those who were either directly or indirectly his students were Martin Heidegger (1889–1976), Edith Stein (Saint Teresa Benedicta of the Cross, 1891–1942), Jean-Paul Sartre (1905–1980), Hannah Arendt (1906–1975), Karol Wojtyła (Pope John Paul II, 1920–2005), and Jacques Derrida (1930–2004).

As Husserl described it, phenomenology was based on two key ideas. First, we can only truly know our perceptions of things rather than the things themselves. Perhaps the thing itself may not exist; all we can say for certain is that we have a perception of it.[10] Second, our perceptions have a structure. With phenomenology, therefore, we no longer philosophize about the world but about ourselves only. Nevertheless, it turns out we are pretty fascinating. Our perceptions, emotions, memories, intuitions, and modes of thinking are endlessly complex, but they betray hitherto unknown structures and patterns. Phenomenology emphasizes the ways in which humans are hardwired to interpret experience. Our minds, to borrow a somewhat dated computer analogy, are not blank disks that the world fills with data; rather our mental disks are formatted in particular ways that determine how the data will be stored, reclaimed, and used. Husserl's ideas led in time to the notion of **structuralism**: our lives occur within sets of structures that shape our every experience. These structures can be biological, cultural, economic, geographical, historical, linguistic, political, psychological, religious, or even sexual. Together, they provide a kind of scaffolding from which we view and participate in the world.

Another philosophy to develop from phenomenology is **existentialism**. Existentialists agree with the structuralist foundation of phenomenology. However, they believe, this does not by itself explain everything about human nature—or even about any individual human's nature. We still have choices. As a white, male, middle-aged, middle-class, Christian, university-educated, Midwestern-born but now Boston-based, heterosexual, politically liberal, suburban, American, married history professor, I might be predisposed to react in a predictable way in any new situation. Yet I still have unique personal desires and inclinations, and I can exert a free will. I can make of my life what I want of it, to a degree. The structures into which I was born, or into which I have grown, determine probabilities, not certainties. My lived life, my "reality" (those quotation marks again), is whatever I make of my existence. In the formula made famous by Jean-Paul Sartre, "existence precedes essence": my nature is the product of

---

[10] Husserl's insight harmonizes with Einstein's: all that exists is our perception of space-time.

my choices in life, not vice versa. It is easy to trace these ideas back to Nietzsche, the great champion of the creative will, and it is easy to see, ironically, how the existentialist view proved so attractive to religious thinkers of the 20th century, especially Protestant Christian ones. Karl Barth (1886–1968), Rudolf Bultmann (1884–1976), Paul Tillich (1886–1965), and Reinhold Niebuhr (1892–1971) are leading examples.

To Sartre, however, the existentialist view of life entails a certain horror. Life is contingent and depends on our choices and actions in order to come into being; reality is what we make. And awareness of that inspires an overwhelming sense of moral duty that he described as a philosophical nausea. *Nausea* is, in fact, the title of Sartre's best-known novel, published in 1938. Written in the form of a diary, it relates the anxieties of a young historian trying to finish a book about an 18th-century political figure. The novel contrasts the Enlightenment era that he studies—with its confidence in reason, order, and progress—and the directionless confusion of the young historian's personal life in the 20th century. The result is anxiety and despair. The awareness of having to create his own reality is too much for him.

> I live alone, absolutely alone, never speaking to anyone.... When living alone, one forgets what it is to speak. Possibilities in life disappear along with one's friends. Events float past one; sometimes someone suddenly appears, says something, then goes away.... All I can get out of these tragic solitudes of mine is a small amount of a kind of empty purity.

He admires but is frightened by people who live in the world.

> People who live in the world have figured out how to look at themselves in the mirror and see themselves as they appear to their friends.... The Nausea isn't inside me—it's out there. I can feel it, in the walls, in my suspenders. It's everywhere around me.... Nothing really happens in life. Scenes changes, people come and go, that's all. Days follow one another, days after days, with no rhyme or reason, an endless, monotonous sequence.... Everything changes, though, when you talk about life, though hardly anyone notices, because people think we speak the truth. As though there was a single true story in life! Things happen the way they happen, but we talk about them altogether differently.

Toward the end, the narrator starts to recognize that life's meaninglessness can present an opportunity to create a meaning of his own. He can choose to think, to act, and to feel. "The feeling of Nausea hasn't left me," he concludes, "and I don't

Sartre Demonstrating against Racism   After 1945 Sartre became a political activist in the Marxist vein, and although he never formally joined the Communist Party he was nevertheless an ardent, if naïve, supporter of Stalin, China's Mao Zedong, and Cuba's Fidel Castro. Here he joins a group of youths protesting discrimination against France's growing immigrant population.

expect it to; but it's no longer a burden, a sense of sickness, or a passing spasm. It is me."

Existentialism is a call to duty. It demands that we take action and make something of the world, or at least of our lives in it, and many of the leading existentialists led lives of deep commitment to political and social causes. On the other hand, it could also be used to lend an aura of faux sophistication to lives of shallow languor; to do nothing intentionally, like the narrator in *Nausea*, as an expression of one's philosophical depth.

> Existentialism is a call to duty. It demands that we take action and make something of the world, or at least of our lives in it, and many of the leading existentialists led lives of deep commitment to political and social causes.

THE ILLNESS OF WESTERN SOCIETY

Sartre's novel appeared in 1938, but its anxiety had roots in Western society back at least to the 1880s. Crowded into industrial cities, choking on coal smoke and chemical fumes, urban Europeans began to show a new degree of concern simply for their health. They spent long hours at hard physical labor or hunched over desks in clerical offices. Governments churned

A Scout Is Clean   "A scout is clean" in mind, body, and deed, according to the regulations of the Boy Scouts organization founded by Robert Baden-Powell (1857-1941), a retired lieutenant general in the British Army. His *Scouting for Boys: A Handbook for Instruction in Good Citizenship* (1908) was one of the bestselling books of the 20th century. The rapid rise of the Boy Scouts and the Girl Scouts (Girl Guides, in Britain and Canada) illustrates the patriotic passions of the era. This trading card—distributed, ironically, in packages of cigarettes—comes from 1929.

out hundreds of reports on public health; newspapers reported on outbreaks of diseases. Public schools began to distribute milk and lunches to students; they more often included physical exercise in their daily curricula. The movement to create public parks and sporting fields grew; so did amateur leagues for soccer, rowing, boxing, and racing. Popular guides like *Mrs. Beeton's Book of Household Management* (see chapter 18) covered hygiene, first aid, nutrition, and exercise. New associations like the Boy Scouts and Girl Scouts promoted fitness and outdoor activity, while bicycling clubs and gymnasia promoted new sports like basketball and tennis. The better-off paid equal attention to mental health. Spas dotted the map, and the new field of psychology burgeoned.

Many critics of turn-of-the-century culture used the imagery and language of illness to describe what they saw around them. European society was "disintegrating, corroding, as a result of the decay of civilized life," proclaimed the first edition of *Le Décadent*, published in Paris in 1886. Henrik Ibsen's drama *Ghosts* (1881) suggested a moral rot in European culture analogous to advanced syphilis, prompting one critic to describe the play as an open sewer. Arthur Schnitzler used the same metaphor in his 1900 play *La Ronde* ("A Circle Dance"), in which pairs of lovers meet in various locales around Vienna, before or after their sexual encounters. Schnitzler's lovers come from every social class, from the Austrian aristocracy to lowly prostitutes, and they portray the moral decadence that so many thought endemic to the time. The novels *Against the Grain* (*À rebours*,

1884) by J. K. Huysmans and *The Picture of Dorian Gray* (1890) by Oscar Wilde both chronicle, in lushly lurid language, the physical and spiritual decay of their protagonists. The popular Welsh writer Arthur Machen (1863–1947) exploited themes of degeneration and sickness in horror stories like "The Great God Pan" (1894) and fantasy novels like *The Hill of Dreams* (1907). Tuberculosis—generally known as "consumption" at the time—appeared time and again in novels, plays, and operas whose heroes, antiheroes, and love interests waste away in settings of physical and emotional rot. *La Bohème* "The Bohemian Girl"; 1896), an opera by Giacomo Puccini (1854–1924), traces the doomed love of a consumptive artist in a Parisian garret in sumptuous music. The novel *Buddenbrooks* (1901), by Thomas Mann (1875–1955), chronicles the decline of German society through several generations of a physically and spiritually sickly mercantile family. Mann's *Tristan* (1903) and *The Magic Mountain* (1924) are set in a tuberculosis sanatorium.

European medicine identified women as vulnerable to hysteria. This supposed female disorder—named after the Greek word for the uterus—accounted for everything from nervousness and loss of appetite to general irritability and abdominal pain. Several medical journals reported that as many as one-quarter of all women were afflicted. Plays and novels of the time are filled with scenes of female fainting and otherwise inexplicable discontent. Along with rest and avoiding any activity that might rouse emotions, one common treatment was a "pelvic massage." (The physician would keep this up until the women experienced a "hysterical paroxysm," to rebalance their nervous energies.)[11]

One of the chief causes of hysteria, experts announced, was the tendency of women to veer from their traditional roles as wives and mothers. The development of a woman's mind through education redirected the natural energies and fluids that kept the womb healthy, causing it to atrophy. "If we wish woman to fulfill the task of motherhood, she cannot possess a masculine brain," wrote the eminent German neurologist Paul Julius Möbius (1853–1907). "If a woman's female abilities were developed in the same way as those of the male, her maternal organs would suffer and [she would] end up as a repulsive and useless hybrid."

With so many voices bearing witness to the illness of Western society, it is not surprising that other voices answered—with some unexpected diagnoses and treatments all their own. Political and social critics denounced the policies that had given the West control of much of the world but had cost it its soul. Chemistry had to reinvent itself after the discovery of new particles and new forms of energy. Physics replaced the Newtonian order with two new systems, quantum

---

[11] Doctors turned eagerly to electric vibrators to treat more patients with hysteria per day. "Aids that every woman appreciates," ran the slogan in a catalog that sold the devices.

theory and relativity, that seemed to contradict one another. Philosophy almost gave up on the external world to focus on our modes of perception, and literature described a culture suffering from terminal illness. And a new science of the mind emerged: psychology.

SEXUALITY AND PSYCHOANALYSIS

Where there is illness, there will be physicians, or those acting as such, to treat the afflicted. Psychology emerged in the 1870s and grew rapidly both in sophistication and in popularity. The existence of an unconscious or subconscious mind dates at least to 1889, with the work of the French psychologist Pierre Janet (1859–1947), and allusions to a mind within the mind can be traced back to the Enlightenment. But the idea gained new power with the work of Sigmund Freud (1856–1939).

After completing his medical studies, Freud specialized as a neurologist and general psychologist. In 1886 he married and set up a private practice in his hometown of Vienna. Freud first used hypnosis as a means to access the inner thoughts of his patients, but he noticed that its effects were temporary; besides, most of his patients spoke quite freely without it. He developed instead **psychoanalysis**, the technique of encouraging free association, and he saw meaningful patterns not only in what his patients said but also in what they avoided saying. From this he developed the concept of *repression*: certain thoughts were being held back not only from open expression but even from the patients' conscious thinking. And many of these repressed thoughts turned out to be sexual. Freud hypothesized that neuroses resulted from the patient's inability to address basic erotic instincts.

By the late 1890s, Freud had begun to elaborate a new theory of consciousness. For Freud, our waking minds are in continual dialogue with our unspoken urges, and equally powerful social and cultural norms regulate those instinctive drives. In Freud's terminology, one's conscious mind, the *ego*, was a product of and a counterbalance to two additional processes. One was our biological instinct for sexual pleasure, the *id*. The other was the ethical conscience, the *superego*—consisting of social norms, religious teachings, and cultural values. Freud realized that he could test his theory by studying not only his patients' free-associative ramblings but also their unconscious ones—in their dreams. What is a dream, after all, but our minds still thinking and talking while our bodies rest?

In 1899 he published what he considered his greatest work, *The Interpretation of Dreams*, which argues that dreams originate as wish fulfillment. Common moral standards dictate that one ought not to act on every sexual impulse. In response, our superegos repress these feelings without our conscious effort. To Freud, however, these impulses are never annihilated; they simply find expression

Freud's Couch   This is the original couch used in Sigmund Freud's psychoanalytic practice in Vienna, where much of the clinical work was done that led to the formulation of his theories of the human mind.

in indirect ways—chiefly through our dreams. But even in the dream state, our superegos remain active, which explains why erotic desires are often expressed in our dreams through disjointed images, dialogues, or sensations. Our ids also find delight and release in racy jokes (when in safe company) and "Freudian slips" of the tongue. (The formal term is *parapraxis*—plural *parapraxes*.)

Freud's *Three Essays in the Theory of Sexuality* in 1905 insisted on sex as the primal and primary human instinct, and it provoked a storm of protest. Victorian society was never as prudish as people often think it was; polite society did not relish open discussions of sexual matters, but it permitted them within the limits of propriety. *Three Essays* rankled not simply because it dealt with sexuality but because of what it said about sex.

Freud describes infantile sexuality as progressing through stages. The first is an intense focus on the delight derived from bodily contact with one's parents, in nursing or cuddling. The second, the "anal stage," finds relief in control of the lower digestive tract. In the third stage, the child becomes fascinated with the genitals. This "Oedipal stage,"

> To a class-obsessed world like Freud's, the notion that a duke experiences the same mental processes as a ditch-digger was unpardonable.

however, was the most shocking of all. In Freud's theory, when a child becomes aware of genital pleasure, a complex chain reaction sets in—culminating in a son's desire to supplant his father as the object of his mother's attention. In the parallel "Electra" stage, a daughter desires to supplant her mother in her father's affection. It is not that all children desire to have sexual intercourse with their parents. Rather, at some basic level, one's parents are the source of physical pleasure from the moment of one's birth, and hence we associate body pleasure with our parents. At puberty, however, our bodies begin to feel an entirely new type of pleasure stimulus, one which our species is hardwired to dissociate from our parents. (This is what he meant as a taboo.) Learning to accept this new body pleasure as something wholly distinct from the body pleasure we associate in our minds with our parents is part of the inner conflict of adolescence.

Freud labored for years to earn acceptance of his theories. Despite his growing clinical practice and dedicated disciples, the psychological world resisted his focus on the role of sex in shaping human nature. Most people are still uncomfortable with his model. Freud is saying, after all, that everyone is driven by instinct; everyone's conscience represses true nature; everyone's consciousness has the same fundamental structure. To a class-obsessed world like Freud's, the notion that a duke experiences the same mental processes as a ditchdigger was unpardonable.

The turning point came in 1909, when Freud accepted an invitation to deliver a series of public lectures in the United States, later published as *Five Lectures on Psychoanalysis.* They helped correct the popular image of him as a sex-obsessed madman. His *Introductory Lectures on Psychoanalysis* (1917) also secured his reputation. His polite manner and the straightforward, accessible rigor of his thinking won people over and made them willing at least to consider his approach.

Many people wrote to Freud, from this time on, with questions or entreaties. One of his most famous letters (1935) was this response, in English, to an American woman's inquiry about her son:

> Dear Mrs. [X].
> I gather from your letter that your son is a homosexual. I am most impressed by the fact, that you do not mention this term yourself in your information about him. May I question you why you avoid it? Homosexuality is assuredly no advantage, but it is nothing to be ashamed of, no vice, no degradation, it cannot be classified as an illness; we consider it to be a variation of the sexual function produced by a certain arrest of sexual development. Many highly respectable individuals of ancient and modern times have been homosexuals, several of the greatest men among them (Plato, Michelangelo, Leonardo da Vinci, etc.). It is a great

injustice to persecute homosexuality as a crime and cruelty too. If you do not believe me, read the books of Havelock Ellis.

By asking me if I can help, you mean, I suppose, if I can abolish homosexuality and make normal heterosexuality take its place. The answer is, in a general way, we cannot promise to achieve it. In a certain number of cases we succeed in developing the blighted germs of heterosexual tendencies, which are present in every homosexual; in the majority of cases it is no longer possible. It is a question of the quality and the age of the individual. The result of treatment cannot be predicted. What analysis can do for your son runs in a different line. If he is unhappy, neurotic, torn by conflicts, inhibited in his social life, analysis may bring him harmony, peace of mind, full efficiency, whether he remains a homosexual or gets changed. If you make up your mind he should have analysis with me—I don't expect you will—he has to come over to Vienna. I have no intention of leaving here. However, don't neglect to give me your answer.

Sincerely yours with kind wishes,

Freud

P.S. I did not find it difficult to read your handwriting. Hope you will not find my writing and my English a harder task.

BEYOND THE PLEASURE PRINCIPLE

As his fame grew, Freud continued to revise his conclusions. Most significantly, he argued that an instinct toward aggression challenges sex for primacy. Aggression originates as the instinct for self-preservation. In a life-or-death situation, people will resort to violence. Aggression also represents an expression of the sexual instinct: to secure access to a mate, human behavior ranges from competitive mating rituals to actual violence. Every act of creation is also an act of destruction. To grow a crop, one must first rip out existing plant life.

In 1920 he published *Beyond the Pleasure Principle,* a treatise on what he called the "death drive." This drive represents the counterweight to the life-generating sexual impulse, but is also in some ways just another expression of it. Sexual enjoyment involves stimulation of our physical senses and mental energies—and yet there is a countervailing pleasure in the calming of the senses after great excitement. We experience the pleasure of relaxation not only after a bout of sex but also after a hectic day's work or battling heavy traffic. The desire for death is the purest and most complete craving for calm after the strain and clamor of life. It is a longing to return to the inanimate state from which we all originate.

Freud came slowly to the theory of aggression. In fact, it took a world war to convince him of humanity's innate barbarism. His work challenged, thrilled, amused, and revolted people, and it still does. Psychologists today have moved far beyond Freud's original model and have rejected much of it; it is seldom taught in psychology departments. However, the effect of his ideas is still felt throughout Western culture. He stands with Darwin, Marx, and Einstein as one of the most influential thinkers of the last two hundred years. (Imagine *that* conversation!) He can even be called a structuralist, since he believed that human consciousness has an order. We think, react, value, and believe according to principles whose workings follow logical patterns. At the same time, he is an irrationalist, since he sees human nature as at the mercy of forces it can neither understand nor control. We are masses of sensation, fear, longing, and anger. What we call reason—even civilization itself—is only the imperfect casing we have erected to contain and control these instincts.

Freud insisted that Western civilization was sick—literally, clinically sick. He saw neuroses all around him, in depressions, phobias, anxiety disorders, and psychoses. He began by analyzing and treating individual cases, but the horrors of the new century led him to psychoanalyze the culture itself. His late book-length essay titled *Civilization and Its Discontents* (1929) could with justice be called "Civilization and Everyone in It." It argues that to be civilized *is* to be unhappy. Civilized behavior begins in not giving expression to our most fundamental instincts. It means not having sex with every attractive person we encounter, not striking every person who raises our anger, and not always saying what we feel. It is the superego given social form. But no degree of civilized conduct can extinguish our creative and destructive instincts:

> Civilization exacts a heavy toll on man's sexuality and his instinct for aggression.... [Our natural instincts] are not to love our neighbor but to indulge our aggressive impulses upon him—whether, that is, to hurt him for labor, to use him to satisfy our sexual desires, to seize his possessions, to humiliate him, hit him, torture him, kill him.

And then the cage door snaps shut:

> Who has the audacity to deny this, in the face of all the facts of history?

For Freud, civilization cannot bring happiness. After five thousand years of effort, mankind appears no less unhappy than in the days of Hammurabi

The Death-Drive   Freudian theory had long insisted that Eros—the sexual drive—was the main motivating force in human life, but the experience of World War I led Freud to posit the existence of a second fundamental instinct—Thanatos, the death drive, by which he meant both the instinct of aggression toward others and the innate desire for the thrill of risk. This 1915 painting, *The Charge of the Lancers*, is by Umberto Boccioni, a leading artist of the Futurism movement.

the Babylonian. We are better fed, better educated, and possess more creature comforts, but could such things mask our true desires and our truest selves? Civilization itself seems an example of the comforting lie that Nietzsche warns against. Freud hardly wants to see a return to barbarism—although he lived to see it, with the rise of the Nazis and his subsequent escape to London. He wants only to relieve as much of the pain of civilized life as possible. And the only way to do so was to alleviate the crushing control of the superego. To Freud, the end of the 19th century saw the West trapped in a hypocritical sexual morality, an outworn religious culture, a decayed social structure, brutal imperialist governments, and callous capitalism. Society itself suffered from a neurosis that was to develop in the mid-20th century into a full-blown case of mass psychosis.

MODERNISM AND IRONY

Modernism was a movement from roughly 1860 to 1950 that began with the visual arts in Europe, with the group known now as the postimpressionists. It spread to literature, architecture, and finally to music. Like the Romanticism that characterized the start of the century, **modernism** resists easy definition since it reached so many different spheres. The sheer number of figures who made up the movement sets it apart from the past. Unlike other cultural eras and movements— art for art's sake, classicism, decadence, Enlightenment, impressionism, Romanticism, symbolism—the term modernism offers no hint of its core ideas or values. After all, it means nothing more than "the new." That, already, however, was a distinctive cry. The American poet and critic Ezra Pound (1885–1972) coined a slogan for a generation he called upon them to "make it new."

The closest thing to a manifesto of modernism appeared in 1863, in "The Painter of Modern Life," an essay by the French poet Charles Baudelaire (1821–1867) that defended Constantin Guys (1802–1892). Guys, as Baudelaire sees it, is determined to cast off old ways of expression and would demand radically new responses from viewers as well. Shock is part of the point, Baudelaire is honest enough to admit, but only a part. New techniques, expertly employed, will also produce new perspectives on truth and beauty: "He is in search of something indefinable—something we may perhaps term *modernity*." Many artists of the time painted even contemporary scenes with figures cloaked in medieval dress or Asian finery (then a popular fashion). "This is, on the face of it, utter laziness— pure and simple!"

The craft of art lies not in perpetuating old standards of beauty but in seeking out new ones. It risks mistakes of judgment in the quest to find new pleasures and new insights. Baudelaire cannot resist an example sure to offend his readers—an image of a common prostitute. To produce that image, painters would be false to their artistic calling if they used the same techniques as a Renaissance artist painting fabled Greek and Roman courtesans. The result would be more than historically inaccurate; it would be an artistic abomination.

Modernism demands the new, but it also rejects modernity. It rejects the inherited attitudes about how artists should work—in structure, technique, and presentation. And yet it also rejects the impersonality of conformist, mass-produced, and mass-consumed culture. The same ambivalence applies to the public at large. While nearly every leading modernist desired a wider following, most of them also railed at popular taste. They wanted an art and literature that could be understood and appreciated not just by the wealthy or the aristocracy, but they often dismissed the very audiences who viewed, read, or listened to their art.

The vogue of the misunderstood genius has a long history, and a great many modernists did not fit the image at all. However, they often set themselves apart

TABLE 23.1 **Modernism: Leading Artists**

VISUAL ARTISTS	LITERATURE	MUSIC
Paul Cézanne, 1839–1906		
Henri Rousseau, 1844–1910		
Paul Gauguin, 1848–1903		
Vincent van Gogh, 1853–1890	Joseph Conrad, 1857–1924	
Georges Seurat, 1859–1891	Constantine Cavafy, 1863–1933	
Gustav Klimt, 1862–1918	William Butler Yeats, 1865–1939	
Wassily Kandinsky, 1866–1944	Luigi Pirandello, 1867–1936	Claude Debussy, 1862–1918
Henri Matisse, 1869–1954	Marcel Proust, 1871–1923	Aleksandr Scriabin, 1872–1915
Piet Mondrian, 1872–1944	Hugo von Hofmannsthal, 1874–1929	Arnold Schoenberg, 1874–1951
Pablo Picasso, 1881–1973	Rainer Maria Rilke, 1875–1926	Charles Ives, 1874–1954
Georges Braque, 1882–1963	Thomas Mann, 1875–1955	Maurice Ravel, 1875–1937
Amadeo Modigliani, 1884–1920	E.M. Forster, 1879–1970	Béla Bartók, 1881–1945
Marcel Duchamp, 1887–1968	Robert Musil, 1880–1942	Igor Stravinsky, 1882–1971
Juan Gris, 1887–1927	James Joyce, 1882–1941	Anton Webern, 1883–1945
Giorgio de Chirico, 1888–1978	Virginia Woolf, 1882–1941	Alban Berg, 1885–1935
	Franz Kafka, 1883–1924	Sergei Prokofiev, 1891–1953
	William Carlos Williams, 1883–1963	Leo Ornstein, 1893–2002
	D. H. Lawrence, 1885–1930	Paul Hindemith, 1895–1963
	Ezra Pound, 1885–1923	Virgil Thomson, 1896–1989
	Aaron Copland, 1900–1990	Fernando Pessoa, 1888–1935
	T.S. Eliot, 1888–1965	Dmitri Shostakovich, 1906–1975
	H.D. [Hilda Doolittle], 1886–1961	Olivier Messiaen, 1908–1992
	Djuna Barnes, 1892–1982	John Cage, 1912–1992
	Federico García Lorca, 1898–1936	Benjamin Britten, 1913–1976
	Bertold Brecht, 1898–1956	
	Ernest Hemingway, 1899–1961	

from and sometimes at odds with mainstream popular culture. One can count on a single hand the leading modernists who came from working-class origins, although a few others pretended to have humbler backgrounds than they actually did.

Disdain for mainstream culture was felt passionately. To Baudelaire, respectable European society was "utterly worn out, brutalized, and greedy" and incapable of genuine feeling. The playwright Bertolt Brecht, too, complained:

> Whenever anyone goes to conventional stage drama, he says of it, "Oh yes, I've felt that way too; that just how I experience things; that's real life .... That's what great art is. Everything is so clear and self-evident. I cry when everyone else cries and laugh when everyone else laughs."

He wanted to create a new type of drama that solicits a very different reaction:

> "Who ever would think that way? You can't do that! It's too strange; it's beyond belief; and it has to stop!"

James Joyce, the author of *Ulysses* (1922), summed up his own attitude in a letter: "Writing in English is the most ingenious torture ever devised for sins committed in previous lives. The English reading public explains the reason why."

THE ARTISTIC TRUTH WITHIN

There was more to modernism than contrariness. In the visual arts, painters and sculptures aimed to reproduce the "truth within" rather than just external appearance. They sought personal visions of the realities beneath the surface. Art became less representational and more intuitive, symbolic, and impressionistic—more expressive of the artist's response to the world than of the world itself. It parallels the philosophical currents of the age, sometimes consciously so. The composer Arnold Schoenberg pronounced that the purpose of art was "to express oneself *directly*—not one's taste or upbringing, or one's intelligence, knowledge, or skill. Not all the *acquired* characteristics, but that which is *inborn* [and] *instinctive*."

The primitive self, driven by passion and instinct, is the only self that matters to art—because it is the source of art. Most of the modernists felt naturally drawn to the irrational, intuitive, and primitive. Paul Gauguin abandoned Europe (not to mention his wife and five children) to live in Tahiti and to create a new art. Pablo Picasso was fascinated with tribal African masks. Such writers as Constantine Cavafy and Rainer Maria Rilke shared a passion for ancient Greek mythology. Mann's four-volume novel *Joseph and His Brothers* (1930–1943) reimagined the very roots of mythology in the Biblical tale. Schoenberg, Igor Stravinsky, and Sergei Prokofiev drew for their music on ancient folktales and songs.

Modernism broke with established forms in the quest to express subjective experience. Painters and sculptors abandoned the representational art they had inherited in favor of highly personal expression. Vincent van Gogh's *Starry Night* (1889) draws its power from its refusal to portray the sky as it appeared outside his asylum window, so that he could express instead the state of his troubled mind. Picasso could paint exquisite representational art, but representational painting did not allow him to express what he wanted. His breakthrough, *Les Demoiselles d'Avignon* ("The Young Ladies of Avignon," 1907), portrays naked prostitutes along the Carrer d'Avinyó, a street in Barcelona then notorious for its sordid nightlife. Two of the women wear African masks and savage expressions while the remaining three scowl. All five stare blankly and disdainfully at the viewer—presumably their next customer—as though challenging his right to be there. Their bodies are shown from at least two separate perspectives, which breaks their forms into geometric shapes and flat fields of color. The painting makes viewers feel as though they are under attack. No wonder so many people hated it, starting when it was first exhibited, in 1916.[12] Picasso knew he had produced a masterpiece and so kept it in his private collection.

The Russian-born émigré Wassily Kandinsky (1866–1944), who spent most of his adult life in Germany and France, was the most direct and eloquent theorist

Four Modernist Works   *Left: Les Demoiselles d'Avignon* (1907) and *Sketch of Igor Stravinsky* (1922) by Pablo Picasso, *Right: Composition No. 4* by Wassily Kandinsky, and *Starry Night, Saint-Rémy* (1889) by Vincent van Gogh.

---

[12]   The painter Henri Matisse reportedly flew into a rage at Les Demoiselles d'Avignon, feeling that Picasso was mocking Modernism.

of Modernism after Baudelaire. At the age of thirty he gave up a successful career as an economist, after being moved by an exhibit in Munich of paintings by Claude Monet, the impressionist. (Kandinsky had been offered a prestigious professorship at the leading university in Estonia.) He decided almost instantaneously to enroll instead in art school. His 1910 book *On the Spiritual Element in Art* has never been equaled as a meditation on art by a practicing artist. Kandinsky wrote about art so well because, as a late convert to it, he had thought about it so much. He asked why it matters, why it is worth giving up a profitable career for, and why it can elevate the soul even in a time of deepening confusion and despair. Art, to him, is as much religion as aesthetics, in a world that no longer has a place for metaphysics:

> The spirit strengthens itself and develops itself just as the body does; and just as a body can weaken and become worn out, so too can the spirit. The essential, life-generating force within every artist is precisely like the "talent of gold" described in the Gospel story—it is the priceless thing that must not be buried away, and any artist who lets his talents decay without putting them to use is like the "lazy servant" of the story.... Art is a force that has a goal: it must be made to serve the development and refinement of the human soul.

Art, in other words, supplants religion (as Nietzsche had already insisted); it is the only remaining means of achieving anything like spiritual salvation:

> An artist must train his soul as much as he trains his eye.... And above all he must have something to say; to master a technique, to gain control over physical form is not the goal of art. Art's only real goal is to adapt form to spiritual meaning.

This is precisely why abstraction is not only acceptable but necessary. The only eternal realities that the spirit can attain and understand, the only transcendent truths available to us, are those experienced through aesthetic bliss. And that art follows no rules but its own:

> Abstract forms, or representational forms that have been partially abstracted, can take the place of determinedly physical objects in almost any painting.... For "beauty" in art is nothing more nor less than the expression of the soul's desire. Whatever seems beautiful to our souls is beautiful in art.

Modernists like Kandinsky thought of art as the only substitute for religious faith, the only spiritual lifeline available in a world otherwise devoid of hope or meaning beyond our meager selves.

Composers like Arnold Schoenberg, Igor Stravinsky, and Alban Berg jettisoned tonality—the basis of 18th- and 19th-century music in familiar chords. They developed instead twelve-tone music, which treated equally the notes of the scale. The result was an intentional dissonance that struck many new listeners as an assault. Fistfights broke out at the first performance of Schoenberg's Chamber Symphony No. 1 (1906), and rioting crowds sometimes spilled out into the streets.[13]

Modernists like Kandinsky thought of art as the only substitute for religious faith, the only spiritual lifeline available in a world otherwise devoid of hope or meaning beyond our meager selves.

Poets like Rilke and William Butler Yeats experimented with blank verse and unmetered rhythms, but they still mostly adhered to traditional forms until the start of World War I. And the novel was among the last literary genres to undergo transformation. As early as 1900, Henry James focused more on the interior lives of the characters than on their explicit actions. In *The Ambassadors* (1903) and *The Golden Bowl* (1904), he carefully dissects their characters' motives and reactions. Luigi Pirandello, from the novel *The Late Mattia Pascal* (1904) to his plays *Six Characters in Search of an Author* (1921) and *Henry IV* (1923), explores the uncertain nature of individual identity and morality. The character of Pascal, trapped in a loveless marriage and a dead-end job, trudges through existence only for the sake of his twin daughters. When they unexpectedly die, he sets off alone on a holiday to deal with his mourning—only to find out that his shrewish wife (and her own shrewish mother) have declared him missing and, later, dead. Freed at last from his old existence, Mattia changes his name, acquires a fortune through gambling, and travels across Europe enjoying life for the first time. But feelings of guilt creep in. He fakes his assumed character's death and returns home—only to find that his wife has remarried and is now happy. He can longer exist either as Mattia or as his alter ego.

In 1906 the Austrian writer Robert Musil published *The Confessions of Young Törless*, about psychological and sexual sadism in a military academy. It

---

[13]   The riot at the premiere of Stravinsky's Rite of Spring (1913) resulted from the crowd's anger at what they considered the brutish choreography of the ballet, not just the music.

was one of the first novels to explore explicitly Freud's ideas about the conflict between the irrational instinct and the conscious mind. As with poetry, however, the main break with the novel's past occurred after the start of the war in 1914. Writers like James Joyce, Virginia Woolf, and Ford Madox Ford now introduced stream-of-consciousness narratives, a nonchronological order of events, and unreliable narrators.

Modernist art emerged from a perceived need for a rupture with tradition, in order to explore the disordered inner reality of existence. Little of it is comic, since the turn-of-the century generation did not find much that was funny in instinctive drives or in the impossibility of permanent meaning. For T. S. Eliot, the poet and critic, the artist actually has to quell all emotion when creating art: "Poetry is not a turning loose of emotion, but an escape from emotion; it is not the expression of personality, but an escape from personality. But, of course, only those who have personality and emotions know what it means to want to escape from these things." The artistic and intellectual life of the 20th century began in uncertainty, aimless yearning, and despair. And it got worse.

WHO, WHAT, WHERE

analytic philosophy	rationalist philosophy
existentialism	relativity
general theory of relativity	space-time
modernism	special theory of relativity
nihilism	structuralism
phenomenology	supermen
psychoanalysis	uncertainty principle
quantum theory	will to power

SUGGESTED READINGS

Primary Sources

Baudelaire, Charles. "The Painter of Our Time."

Eliot, T. S. "Tradition and the Individual Talent."

Freud, Sigmund. *Civilization and Its Discontents.*

———. *The Interpretation of Dreams.*

Kandinsky, Wassily. *On the Spiritual Element in Art.*

Rilke, Rainer Maria. *New Poems.*

Sartre, Jean-Paul. *Nausea.*

Shaw, George Bernard. *Caesar and Cleopatra.*

———. *John Bull's Other Island.*

Wilde, Oscar. *De Profundis.*

———. *The Importance of Being Earnest.*

Anthologies

Marino, Gordon, ed. *Basic Writings of Existentialism* (2004).

Otis, Laura, ed. *Literature and Science in the Nineteenth Century: An Anthology* (2009).

Rainey, Lawrence, ed. *Modernism: An Anthology* (2005).

Studies

Fawaz, Leila Tarazi, and C. A. Bayly, eds. *Modernity and Culture: From the Mediterranean to the Indian Ocean* (2001).

Garff, Joakim. *Søren Kierkegaard: A Biography* (2007).

Gay, Peter. *Modernism: The Lure of Heresy from Baudelaire to Beckett and Beyond* (2010).

———. *Schnitzler's Century: The Making of Middle-Class Culture, 1815–1914* (2002).

Holmes, Deborah, and Lisa Silverman, eds. *Interwar Vienna: Culture between Tradition and Modernity* (2009).

Jodock, Darrell. *Catholicism Contending with Modernity: Roman Catholic Modernism and Anti-Modernism in Historical Context* (2000).

Kragh, Helge. *Higher Speculations: Grand Theories and Failed Revolutions in Physics and Cosmology* (2011).

———. *Quantum Generations: A History of Physics in the Twentieth Century* (2002).

Paret, Peter. *German Encounters with Modernism, 1840–1945* (2001).

Perelberg, Rosine Jozef, ed. *Freud: A Modern Reader* (2005).

Pippin, Robert B. *Nietzsche, Psychology, and First Philosophy* (2011).

Porter, Bernard. *The Absent-Minded Imperialists: Empire, Society, and Culture in Britain* (2006).

Preston, Aaron. *Analytic Philosophy: The History of an Illusion* (2010).

Singer, Barnett, and John Langdon. *Cultured Force: Makers and Defenders of the French Colonial Empire* (2008).

Weller, Shane. *Modernism and Nihilism* (2011).

Young, Julian. *Friedrich Nietzsche: A Philosophical Biography* (2010).

Zahavi, Dan. *Husserl's Phenomenology* (2003).

For additional resources, including maps, primary sources, visuals, web links, and quizzes, please go to **www.oup.com/us/backman.**

CHAPTER 24

The World at War (Part I)

(1914–1918)

The day after the signing of the armistice that ended World War I, the British novelist D. H. Lawrence (1885–1930) wrote to a friend with a gloomy warning:

THE WORLD AT WAR, 1914–1918

Major clashes, 1914-1918

> I suppose you think the war is over and that we shall go back to the kind of world you lived in before it. But the war isn't over. The hate and evil is greater now than ever. Very soon war will break out again and overwhelm you.... The crowd outside thinks that Germany is crushed forever. But the Germans will soon rise again. Europe is done for.... The war isn't over. Even if the fighting should stop, the evil will be worse because the hate will be dammed up in men's hearts and will show itself in all sorts of ways.

He had good reason to be pessimistic. The war that ended in November 1918 had been the cause of more bloodshed and horror than any conflict in Western history—and of more than in all human history after the psychotic conquests of Genghis Khan seven hundred years earlier. Three empires—the Austrian-Hungarian, the German, and the Ottoman—lay in ruins. Two others—the British and the American—had been knocked staggering.

Along the war's three hundred-mile-long western front, in northern and eastern France, entire towns and villages had been obliterated, crop fields and mines devastated, and roads

◀ **Armed to the Teeth** The Krupp armaments factory in Essen, Germany, 1912.

and bridges ruined. Millions of corpses lay buried or rotting in the sun. Some sixty-five million soldiers had taken part. By the time the war ended, ten million of them lay dead, another twenty-one million of them had been wounded, and still another million remained missing. The deaths were shared by all: on the side of the Axis powers, 1.8 million Germans and 1.2 million Austrian-Hungarians; on the side of the Allies, 1.7 million Russians, 1.4 million French, and nearly a million British. The late-coming Italians lost 460,000 soldiers, and the even later-coming Americans lost 115,000. The rest of the dead consisted primarily of Serbs, Turks, Romanians, Poles, Czechs, Slovaks, and Arabs.

By the war's end, the political map of the West had already changed, with America's entry into a European war, a revolution in Russia, and the birth of what would become the Soviet Union. It was to change still more after the war, with a harsh peace treaty, the resentment of the losers, and the end of the Ottoman Empire.

THE RUN-UP TO WAR

With hindsight, one can see the war coming as early as 1905, but not as the result of any presumed inevitable march of political events or economic developments. The popular demand for war simply rose continually. World War I was willed into being by a Europe drunk with nationalistic pride, with each nation eager to claim its victor's cup in the social Darwinian battle of life. Militarism had been on the rise across Europe ever since German unification in 1870, and it had to be. The "balance of power" codified by the Treaty of Vienna in 1815 had presupposed a permanently fragmented German people, but unification had tipped the scale heavily in Germany's favor. Some sort of direct action was necessary, and that action found expression in the rapid development of

> World War I was willed into being by a Europe drunk with nationalistic pride, with each nation eager to claim its victor's cup in the Social Darwinian battle of life.

CHAPTER TIMELINE

1899–1902 Boer War	1905 Failed revolution in Russia	1914 Beginning of World War I
1900–1914 Fifteen million Europeans emigrate overseas	1908 Young Turks lead constitutional reform in Turkey	1915 Germany sinks Lusitania; beginning of Armenian genocide

military might—put to use in the colonization of Africa and much of Asia. And once the imperialist land grab was completed, the massive military remained.

Europe around 1900 was armed to the teeth, much as in the Age of Absolutism by 1715. As armies swelled and stockpiles of weapons ballooned, pressure built up to put them to use. In capitalist terms, unexercised muscle was a wasted resource. In Germany the Colonial Society, a nationwide group that championed imperialism, issued vague but insistent calls for war. "Peace is rotten," declared the Berlin-based poet Georg Heym (1887–1912) in a private notebook. He hoped for a war, "any war, even an unjust one," and in that same year (1912) he published a disturbing paean to it. Opening "He is risen that was long asleep," the poem describes the awesome, mythic power of War as it sweeps across the countryside, smashing towers, obliterating cities, devouring woods and fields. The nightmarish effect of "War," however, derives not from Heym's powerful description of War's terrible strength, but from his admiration of it.[1]

The popular journalist-lawyer Heinrich Class (1868–1953) was a member of another patriotic group, the Pan-German League. He wrote in the same year:

> If any nation has just cause to seek to expand its sphere of influence, it is the German one, whose population is rapidly growing, whose industry needs new markets, and whose overall economy needs new land from which to derive new resources.... We need these things and we need them now, and we need to acquire them by any means whatsoever.... We must engage in a proactive politics abroad—in fact, let us state it bluntly: we must be aggressive.... To begin with, any expansion within Europe can only come from direct conquest since neither France nor Russia will be so obliging as to give away part of their territories to us.... Another consideration is whether or not southeastern Europe might do

---

[1] He is risen that was long asleep, Risen now from caverns deep, He stands in the twilight, unknown, and grand, And crushes the moon in His black hand.

1916	1918	1920
Start of Arab revolt	End of World War I	Treaty between Allied powers and Turkey abolishes Ottoman Empire

1917	1919
Bolsheviks assume power in Russia	Paris Peace Conference; Treaty of Versailles

for us, specifically the parts of the Austrian Empire and of the Balkans generally where the Slavic peoples (a "sub-German people," if I may put it thus) currently reside.

The Germans were not alone in their ardor for conflict. French politicians, writers, university students, and workers smarted from their defeat in the Franco-Prussian War of 1870. Demoralized by the Dreyfus Affair, they urged restoration of the country through military glory.[2] Only victory on the field, they declared, could restore national honor. In Britain, too, many people looked eagerly forward to a contest that would settle, once and for all, the intense competitions begun with the founding of the German Reich. British confidence ran at high level. After all, the country had not had a serious military setback since the American Revolution. British forces in the last twenty years had put over three hundred million people around the world under their control.

Not everyone had war fever, of course. Trade unionists and socialist reformers in all countries were among the loudest voices condemning the march to conflict. Members of the clergy also spoke up frequently against the militarist wave. One of the best known opponents of war was Norman Angell (1872–1967), the Paris-based editor of the *Daily Mail,* who in 1909 published a pamphlet called *Europe's Optical Illusion.* (It appeared in expanded form the following year as *The Great Illusion.*) Angell speaks the language of business. He argues that, aside from purely moral issues, a European war would be disastrous simply because the economies of the countries had become too interdependent. Unlike manufacturing, the finance industry crossed too many international borders to survive a conflict. Credit was extended in such an extended web, he argues, that any prolonged disruption to a single commercial sector would be felt everywhere (see Map 24.1). Angell sees an appeal to economic interests as the only argument that might succeed in a society that so romanticizes bloody conflict:

> War has no longer the justification that it makes for the survival of the fittest; it involves the survival of the less fit. The idea that the struggle between nations is a part of the evolutionary law of man's advance involves a profound misreading of the biological analogy. . . .

---

[2]   Alfred Dreyfus (1859–1935) was a French army captain unjustly accused of passing military secrets to the German embassy in Paris in 1894. His two trials, both of which ended in his conviction, were the cause of intense national debate and scandal since Dreyfus was a Jew and the charges against him were at least partially motivated by anti-Semitic hatred. He was fully exonerated in 1906 and reinstated in the army with the rank of major. Nevertheless, he had already endured five years of imprisonment in solitary confinement at the penal colony on Devil's Island in French Guiana and after his exoneration he was wounded in an assassination attempt. He retired from the army in 1907 but re-enlisted when World War I broke out and served throughout the conflict, earning promotion to the rank of lieutenant colonel.

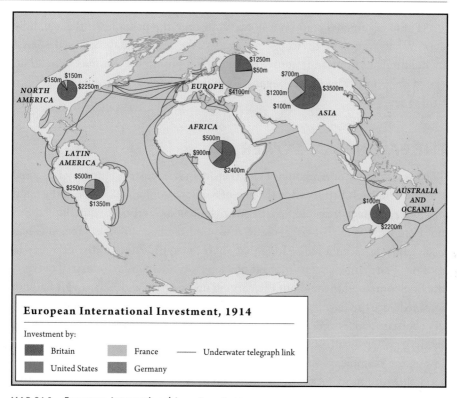

European International Investment, 1914

Investment by:

Britain   France   —— Underwater telegraph link

United States   Germany

MAP 24.1   European International Investment, 1914

Are we, in blind obedience to primitive instincts and old prejudices, enslaved by the old catchwords and that curious indolence which makes the revision of old ideas unpleasant, to duplicate indefinitely on the political and economic side a condition from which we have liberated ourselves on the religious side? Are we to continue to struggle, as so many good men struggled in the first dozen centuries of Christendom— spilling oceans of blood, wasting mountains of treasure—to achieve what is at bottom a logical absurdity, to accomplish something which, when accomplished, can avail us nothing, and which, if it could avail us anything, would condemn the nations of the world to never-ending bloodshed and the constant defeat of all those aims which men, in their sober hours, know to be alone worthy of sustained endeavor?

Back in England, Angell continued to campaign against the slaughter. He later served briefly as a member of Parliament, was knighted in 1931, and in 1933 received the Nobel Peace Prize.

These arguments could not hold out against the passions of the age, however. What argument could prevail against the sentiments expressed shared by hundreds of thousands across Europe? As a prominent German general declared once hostilities in fact began, "Even if it all ends in ruin, it has been beautiful to see."

THE BALANCE OF POWER

The assassination of Archduke Franz Ferdinand of Austria-Hungary triggered the catastrophe. It happened in the city of Sarajevo, on June 28, 1914, at the hand of a bitter nineteen-year-old Serb nationalist named Gavrilo Princip. But if it had not been this event that triggered it, it would have been another. Tensions had been running so high for so long that anything could have set the calamity in motion. The main elements in these tensions were economic. Industrial overproduction continued throughout the carving up of Africa and Asia, and it had not lessened once the European empires had achieved full size. The result was a cycle of economic booms and busts between 1885 and 1914 that was made even worse by the growing availability of cheap transportation. Petroleum and electricity allowed, for example, massive imports of American, Argentinean, and Canadian foodstuffs to Europe. Against this threat, Europeans could either erect punitive tariff barriers or prop up their native industries with subsidies. To varying degrees, they did both. Manufacturers formed cartels to regulate output and fix prices. Banks organized themselves into consortia to set interest rates and control the movement of capital.

Not Looking Back   A photo of European immigrants on a dock in New York Harbor around 1900. The father points to the land that will be their new home.

State interventions and cartel manipulations not only distorted markets but solidified the divide that separated Europe's rich, developed nations from its poorer, undeveloped ones. Ireland, Greece, Portugal, Poland, and the Scandinavian countries could not compete internationally, and their sharp economic declines drove more and more of their populations abroad. Between 1815 and 1900 over forty million people had already emigrated from Europe—primarily to the United States, Canada, Argentina, Brazil, and Australia. Almost fifteen million more did so between 1900 and 1914 (see chapter 23). Only Belgium and the Netherlands experienced a net gain in population through migration. Artificial controls in the markets also hardened the distinction between the wealthy and the poor within each industrialized country. With little capital available for smaller businesses, labor wages stagnated from 1900 to 1914, while prices for most consumer goods rose.

The widening gap between rich and poor led to the rise of trade unions and the creation of the Labour Party in Britain, which by 1906 held twenty-nine seats in Parliament. Germany, in contrast, avoided strong labor unions by initiating a broad network of social welfare programs, like workman's compensation and retirement pensions. These programs lured workers away from radicalizing, but they were expensive. Coupled with the huge new military expenditure and generous subsidies to industrialists, they left the central governments of the European empires increasingly vulnerable. Each boom-and-bust cycle after 1900 only made matters worse, until the system practically cried out for resolution.

The leading states created alliances that they hoped would preserve economic and military balance. These alliances often changed, as each boom-and-bust cycle altered the relative strengths of each partner. One year's ally might be next year's diplomatic and commercial rival (see Map 24.2). But the alliances generally tried to counterbalance the economic and military weight of the German Empire. Britain aimed above all to secure its naval superiority. It wanted to maintain sufficient

MAP 24.2   European Alliances, 1878–1914

Gold Miners, South Africa   South Africa has rich natural deposits of diamonds and gold, the desire for which lured the British to wage the two Boer Wars (1880-1881, 1899-1902). A recent geological survey reports that the country has as much as 50 percent of the world's known gold reserves.

strength to battle any two European nations combined—usually Germany and any country with which it could be allied. In the Anglo-French Entente of 1904, also known as the Entente Cordiale, for example, France recognized British interests in Egypt and Suez in return for British recognition of French interests in Morocco. The Anglo-Russian Entente of 1907 (sometimes erroneously called the Triple Entente) settled border disputes between British and Russian zones of influence in Afghanistan and Persia. These agreements, and others like them, did not create actual military alliances, yet they did pave the way to them by preemptively removing points of contention. Germany, for its part, responded to these ententes by forming pacts of its own with Austria-Hungary and the Ottoman Empire. Surging nationalism among many of the Slavic and Arab peoples living under Habsburg and Ottoman rule, respectively, weakened those empires dramatically. And the cost of putting down their rebellions helped to keep the two states near bankruptcy as the century began.

Relations between Britain and Germany had grown especially strained during the Boer War (1899–1902). The Germans took the side of the Afrikaners against the British, who were determined to extend their colonies in South Africa, once huge deposits of gold were discovered in the Afrikaner Orange Free State. Britain won a modest victory in the war, but it came at a heavy price in men, material, and prestige. Germany enjoyed the Britons' embarrassment and the apparent vulnerability of British forces.

Relations worsened several years later, thanks to the blundering of Kaiser Wilhelm II, who had a long track record of putting his foot in his mouth. In an interview with England's *Daily Telegraph* on October 28, 1908, he described the British people as "mad as March hares." He claimed to have personally drawn up the battle plan that helped the British win a campaign against the Afrikaners and to have forwarded it to his "revered grandmother" Queen Victoria. Public opinion in Britain was outraged, and the German Reichstag took action to limit the emperor's authority on the international scene. Subsequent crises in North Africa and the Balkans, in the context of the fast-decaying Habsburg and Ottoman Empires, brought matters to a fever pitch.

In 1905 the German chief of general staff, Alfred Graf von Schlieffen (1833–1913), had developed a detailed battle plan in the event of a two-front war with France and Russia. Kept secret for nine years, the **Schlieffen Plan** called for a rapid strike at France via Belgium and Luxembourg, in order to circumvent French defenses. It would attack Paris from the north and score a quick victory before Russian forces could marshal in the east. When the Austrian archduke was assassinated in June 1914, the Habsburg state declared war on Serbia, which called in its ally Russia, which in turn prompted Austria to summon its ally Germany. Dreading its two-front vulnerability, Germany took preemptive measures by declaring war on France and putting the Schlieffen Plan into effect. Belgium, however, was a neutral country without any alliances at all.[3] To aid this innocent victim and to uphold international law, Britain, on September 4, 1914, declared war on Germany. Within a matter of three months, a provincial crisis in the Balkans had swelled into a global conflict.

World War I pitted the Axis powers of Germany, Austria-Hungary, the Ottoman Empire, and Bulgaria against the Allied forces of the British Empire, France, Russia, Serbia, Belgium, and Luxembourg. Eventually Japan (1914), Italy (1915), Romania and Portugal (1916), Greece, and the United States (1917) joined the fray, on the side of the Allies. The empires drew on all their dominions for soldiers and material support, leading to further conflict around the globe. Casualties mounted quickly, and colonial subjects seized the opportunity to rise up against their imperial masters. By 1916 the Axis and Allied powers both resorted to forced conscription. And resistance to the draft, combined with events in the colonies, shook up societies far from the war's center in Europe.

---

[3]   In fact, the 1831 treaty that established Belgium as an independent nation had explicitly forbidden it to form alliances.

TABLE 24.1 **World War I (1914–1918)**

June 28, 1914	Archduke Ferdinand of Austria-Hungary murdered in Sarajevo.
August 4	Germany invades Belgium.
August 26–30	Russia invades Germany and is defeated at battle of Tannenberg.
September 4–10	German advance on Paris halted at 1st battle of the Marne.
October 18	Trench warfare begins.
February 19, 1915	Allied campaign against Gallipoli begins (lasts until January 1916).
May 7	Germany sinks the *Lusitania*.
May 23	Italy enters war, joining the Allies; German counter-offensive drives Russians from most of Poland.
October 3–5	Allied troops land at Salonika.
February 21, 1916	Battle of Verdun begins. Lasts until 15 December.
April 23	Start of Easter Rebellion in Dublin.
June 6	Arab Revolt begins.
June	Russian forces against Austria suffer one million casualties.
July 1	Battle of the Somme (lasts until 18 November). Allies lose 600,000 soldiers.
August 27	Romania enters the war.
November 28	First German air-raid on London.
February 1, 1917	German U-boats begin unrestricted attacks.
March 11	British forces capture Baghdad.
March 15	Russian tsar is overthrown, forced to abdicate.
April 6	U.S. enters the war on the Allied side.
November 16	Vladimir Lenin and his Bolsheviks come to power in Moscow.
December 9	British capture Jerusalem.
January 8, 1918	President Wilson announces his 14 Points.
March 3	Treaty of Brest-Litovsk: Russia withdraws from the war.
June	Re-unified German army advances to within 60 miles of Paris.
August	British victory at Amiens.
October 30	Ottoman Empire and Austrian-Hungarian Empire surrender.
November 11	Austria and Germany sign armistice agreements with Allies, ending the war.
January 12, 1919	Paris Peace Conference begins.
June 28	Treaty of Versailles is signed.

A NEW MAP OF HELL

The narrative of the war is dismal to recount. Most Western accounts of the war emphasize the importance of the western front—the long, entrenched line along the French-German border, from Belgium to Switzerland—but other fronts proved equally as significant and deadly. World War I was fought in seven separate arenas: on the western front, on the eastern front with Russia, in northern Italy, in the Balkans, along the periphery of the Ottoman Empire, in the European colonies, and at sea. Each had its own unique horrors. And each left nations obliged to mobilize "the home front" to share those horrors (see Map 24.3).

On the western front, the initial German advance through the Low Countries was halted a few miles short of Paris at the First Battle of the Marne (1914). More than two million soldiers took part in all, roughly one-quarter of whom died or were wounded. After this defeat, the Germans withdrew to a line that ran in a rough arc from Ypres in Belgium, through Soissons in northern France, and down to Verdun in northeastern France. This line moved little over the years and became a site of trench warfare that claimed over three hundred thousand French and German lives before the war's end. More than a half million more were wounded. Both sides tried to break the deadlock by mounting major offensives—most notably at Verdun (1916), at the Somme (1916), and at Passchendale in Belgium (1917). These gained little territory but left hundreds of thousands of corpses lying on the muddy fields. A final effort to break the standoff came in 1918, with the Second Battle of the Marne, when German forces made a last-ditch effort to get through Allied lines and seize Paris. This too resulted only in more slaughter—a quarter-million dead, all told.

The eastern front saw a handful of initial Russian victories, as they rushed forward while German forces became mired in the west. Before long, however, Germany repelled the Russian advance, and by the end of 1915 a German and Austrian counteroffensive drove the Russians out of Poland. Fighting in 1916 pummeled Russia's forces with extremely heavy losses, and 1917 brought another shock—the Russian Revolution and the fall from power of the tsar. This led to Russia's formal withdrawal from the war. The Treaty of Brest-Litovsk, formalized on March 3, 1918, freed Vladimir Lenin's Bolshevik forces to concentrate on securing their control over Russia itself.

The war in northern Italy was fought primarily between the Italians and Austrians. This third front, along Italy's northeastern border with Austria, did not open until Italy joined the war in 1915, and Allied hopes that it might break the deadlock elsewhere were soon dashed. No fewer than a dozen fierce campaigns were fought near the Isonzo River in the Italian Alps. Fighting ended with an Austrian surrender in October 1918.

The Axis armies marched into the Balkans early in the war, and by October 1915 they routed the Serbian forces and seized the Serb capital of Belgrade. They then joined with Ottoman and Bulgarian forces and took Romania. An effort to conquer Greece failed, and the last years of the war were spent in trying to quell rebellions among the Serbians and Bosnians.

For decades, the Ottoman Empire had been dismissed as "the sick man of Europe." However, despite predictions of its speedy collapse, Ottoman forces surprised the Allies with their resilience. The Turks held off a major Allied

MAP 24.3   World War I, 1914–1918

invasion (composed largely of soldiers from Australia, New Zealand, Canada, and South Africa) at Gallipoli, on the Dardenelles straits, for eight months in 1915. In the plain between the Tigris and Euphrates rivers, the British hoped to launch a sudden strike straight into Baghdad; the Turks stopped the Allies at Kut al-Amara. More than 20,000 British soldiers died in the siege of Kut and another

World War I, 1914–1918

	Axis Powers
1915	Neutral state that joined Axis Powers, with date
	Allied Powers (including colonies)
1914	Neutral state that joined Allied Powers, with date
	Country that remained neutral
	Furthest advance by Axis Powers on date marked
	Furthest advance by Allied Powers on date marked
▷	Allied convoy routes
- - -	Naval blockade of Central Powers
——	Borders in 1914
⚓✕	Naval battles

10,000 were marched off across the desert as prisoners of war, two-thirds of them dying along the way.

The Turkish economy, however, could not keep Ottoman forces supplied, which left the empire severely weakened. The Allies capitalized on this by organizing the **Arab Revolt**, an uprising of Middle Eastern Arab tribes against Turkish rule.

Colonial Troops   Many of the combatants in World War I came from the European colonies. Here, for example, is a photo of a Ugandan color guard on march (under a British officer, of course).

Lieutenant Colonel T. E. Lawrence (1888–1935), the British officer popularly known as Lawrence of Arabia, played a pivotal role. The revolt aimed to replace Ottoman imperial rule with autonomous Arab countries. Unknown to Lawrence, however, the British and French governments had already agreed secretly to divide up the Middle Eastern dominions between themselves. This pact, known as the **Sykes-Picot Agreement** (1916), arranged for Britain to receive what is today southern Iraq, Jordan, and most of what is now Israel. France received northern Iraq, today's Syria and Lebanon, and the southeastern corner of today's Turkey. Imperial Russia, a junior partner in the arrangement, was to receive the city of Istanbul (Constantinople) and the Bosporus—but Russian claims were nullified by the Bolshevik Revolution of 1917.

A small amount of fighting took place in the German colonies in Africa and Asia, but few troops were available to defend these far-flung territories, and imperial Germany surrendered most of its colonies shortly after the war began. Only the colony at German Southwest Africa, today's Namibia, held out until 1918.

There was only one pitched naval battle in the entire war. At the Battle of Jutland in June 1916, British and German naval forces fought to a draw, leaving the British in control of the North Sea. More significant were the attacks of German submarines, or U-boats, on international shipping. German strategy was to cut off the resupply of Britain: it imposed an embargo on all ships, of whatever origin, carrying any civilian or military goods to the United Kingdom. In practice, this meant attacking British and American ships. The U-boats proved highly effective, but at the cost of slowly drawing America into the general conflict.

In 1917, Germany declared its intent to engage in unrestricted maritime attacks; Russia withdrew from the war, and Germany reallocated its hitherto split forces along the single western front. All this brought America into the war in April 1917. When it became clear that the American entry would only prolong the slaughter, all sides agreed to an armistice. The Treaty of Versailles formally ended the war on June 28, 1919—five years, to the very day, after the assassination of the Austrian archduke in Sarajevo.

THE WAR IN THE TRENCHES

The narrative of the war and its strategies is important. So are the political wrangling and diplomatic schemes surrounding them. One can view the entire century as a long, drawn-out consequence of the Great War. But two elements of the war deserve special notice—the experience of common soldiers and the customs of the military officers who commanded them.

Along most of the western, eastern, and Italian fronts, the war quickly devolved into a brutal war of attrition. Battlefronts moved little, which meant that the physical desolation of these areas was severe. The western front especially was dominated by trench warfare—parallel lines of muddy ditches, separated by a "no man's land" of landmines and barbed wire. From these ditches, soldiers fired machine guns, threw grenades and canisters of poison gas, tended mortar batteries, and occasionally charged one another with bayonet-fitted rifles. Most trenches were between seven and eight feet deep and perhaps four feet wide. Proper drainage was not possible under such conditions, so soldiers lived daily in water-and-urine soaked mud up to a foot deep. Worse still, trenches ran in zigzag patterns rather than straight lines, in order to minimize the damage from grenades and artillery shells. The patterns also limited a sniper's ability to fire down a long line of crowded men. Yet they meant that most soldiers lived day in and day out seeing only walls of mud on all sides. The mounds of filth and piles of corpses encouraged a large rat population, which spread disease. Well behind the trenches were various supply camps; even further behind was the heavy artillery. Most higher-ranking officers took up stations somewhere behind the artillery, often separated from the fighting by several miles.

> Most trenches were between seven and eight feet deep and perhaps four feet wide. Proper drainage was not possible under such conditions, so soldiers lived daily in water-and-urine soaked mud up to a foot deep.

All Dead on the Western Front   "The Price of Victory" reads the original caption to this candid news photo of French soldiers in a trench near Argonne, in northern France, in June 1915. The pipe-smoking central figure steps casually over a wounded comrade as he helps to carry out a corpse.

It was too much heavy firepower in too concentrated an area. Opposing trenches were sometimes so close that enemy soldiers could converse with one another. Artillery barrages intended to weaken the enemy's position fell all too often on the gunners' own comrades, and clouds of poison gas needed only the mildest of breezes to bring the fumes on the very soldiers who had released them. By 1916 cheaply made gasmasks were standard issue for all soldiers, but they never provided any real protection. Chlorine gas left countless soldiers blinded, with permanently blistered faces and scarred lungs.

Siegfried Sassoon (1886–1967), one of the greatest of World War I poets, famously described the horrors of trench warfare in his poem "Attack":

> At dawn the ridge emerges massed and dun
> In the wild purple of the glow'ring sun,
> Smouldering through spouts of drifting smoke that shroud
> The menacing scarred slope; and, one by one,
> Tanks creep and topple forward to the wire.
> The barrage roars and lifts. Then, clumsily bowed
> With bombs and guns and shovels and battle-gear,
> Men jostle and climb to, meet the bristling fire.
> Lines of grey, muttering faces, masked with fear,
> They leave their trenches, going over the top,
> While time ticks blank and busy on their wrists,
> And hope, with furtive eyes and grappling fists,
> Flounders in mud. O Jesus, make it stop!

The heavy weaponry—giant howitzers and concrete machine-gun pillboxes, especially—was designed for defensive rather than offensive purposes. That left both sides unable to move forward even if they did score an occasional victory.[4] Small wonder that photographs of battlefields often look like blasted moonscapes.

Small wonder too that officers' reports on both sides, trying to show evidence of progress for their home offices, rarely spoke of strategic gains. Instead of territory, they used a grim tally of corpses as indices of achievement. On the eastern front, woefully ill-equipped Russian soldiers faced unending volleys of

---

4   At Verdun, in 1915, 1.5 million Allied soldiers died to advance the battlefront a mere three miles—thirteen deaths for every inch of ground gained.

Ghostly Battlefield Soldiers of the 10th Field Artillery Brigade, Australian 4th Division, on march near Ypres, France, in October 1917.

Axis artillery shells and machine-gun fire. The tsar's officers could respond only by ordering wave after wave of soldiers into the barrage, in the hope that, eventually, the Germans and Austrians would run out of ammunition. Russian losses mounted so quickly that when rebels rose up against the tsar, in 1917, the army joined with them. At the time of the Treaty of Brest-Litovsk, the truce between Russia and the Axis, nearly four million Russian soldiers were held as prisoners of war by Germany and Austria.

In the face of these grim realities, it became more and more difficult to sustain popular support for the war effort. The war was, after all, initially touted everywhere as certain to be over by Christmas 1914, a mere six months after it began. In reality, as November's freezing rains gave way to a gray and bitter December, all that had happened was over a million senseless deaths. At the same time, the playwright George Bernard Shaw published a pamphlet, "Common Sense about the War." He argued that it was every patriotic British soldier's duty to rise from the trenches, turn about-face, and shoot his own officers for their incompetence and moral idiocy.

Shaw's outrage stemmed in part from how officers were placed in command. At the start of the war, only 250 of the more than 12,000 officers in the British regular army had earned their positions by promotion from within the ranks. The rest had acquired their posts thanks to aristocratic status, family connections, or

British public school ties. They had little military experience or knowledge of military affairs, but the social elite was supposedly better suited to command. No wonder their blunders brought on so many deaths. In March 1915 an army study reported with concern that twelve thousand members of the upper classes or graduates of elite schools were actually serving as common soldiers. By the end of the year, almost all had been reappointed to the officers' corps.

Soldiers captured in battle became prisoners of war, held according to standards set by the Hague Conventions of 1899 and 1907. These international agreements called for prisoners to receive the same standards of housing, diet, medical attention, and general treatment as soldiers serving the host country. Not all prisoners were so lucky. When the war ended, Germany held roughly 2.5 million prisoners, while Britain and France each held approximately three-quarters of a million. The United States had about 50,000 in its possession. Most of these received adequate to fair treatment. But prisoners in the non-European theaters of the war fared far worse. At least one-third of the Allied soldiers captured by the Ottomans died during their imprisonment. Disease, malnutrition, thirst, and forced labor were the main causes. The Turks generally established their prisoner-of-war camps far from the battlefronts—in the Balkans, the Middle East, or

Armenian Genocide Starvation, dehydration, exposure, and forced marches killed most of the victims of the Armenian tragedy, 1915–1916. The government of Turkey does not deny the deaths of 1.5 million Armenians; it insists rather that they were the result of wartime happenstance instead of an intentional policy.

in Mesopotamia. And they forced their prisoners to march hundreds of miles to the camps—ostensibly to reserve transport vehicles and fuel for the war effort. But the forced march of prisoners across mountains and through deserts, without enough food and water, produced predictable results.

The worst single chapter of this grim history was the death of as many as 1.5 million Armenians—victims of massacre, deportation, forced march, and starvation. This Armenian genocide began with the arrest in Istanbul of 250 leaders of the Armenian community in April 1915, right after the Allied raid at Gallipoli. They were suspected of complicity in a plot to bring down the Ottoman state. From that point on, Armenian populations across eastern Anatolia were subject to torture, burnings, drownings, and even injections with morphine and typhoid fever. No official record has ever been found in the Ottoman archives directing a conscious campaign of annihilation. To this day, the Republic of Turkey denies the accusation of genocide, although Turks do not dispute the deaths of the Armenian people. But the evidence is overwhelming.[5] Hundreds of thousands of corpses lay strewn along the roads and tracks from the Armenian highlands to the Syrian desert.

THE HOME FRONT

Mobilizing the home front was every bit as vital as mobilizing the military, especially since none of the countries were prepared for a long war. France had entered the conflict with only a one-month supply of ammunition. The Germans, confident of a quick victory, never bothered to requisition winter boots and coats for their infantrymen until winter had set in.[6] Retooling the industrial economies for war thus became a top priority. The transition involved nationalizing industries, rationing most consumer goods, forbidding labor strikes, and raising capital by selling war bonds. To keep society in line, most states instituted some form of censorship and mounted extensive propaganda campaigns. Britain's Defense of the Realm Act (1914), for example, empowered the government to censor newspapers, read private mail, search homes without a warrant, and imprison or deport anyone guilty of unpatriotic utterances.

In every country the compulsory military draft left a severe shortage of laborers in fields and factories. The German Reichstag not only forbade labor strikes but even made it illegal for any able-bodied man to be unemployed. Women had to step in to keep domestic production going. Food shortages

---

[5]   As early as August 18, 1915, the *New York Times* reported that Turkish acts were "a plan to exterminate the whole Armenian people."

[6]   The winter of 1914–1915 was a bad one on the western and eastern fronts. Soldiers complained that even grenades froze together in their supply crates.

became common; in Germany alone over 750,000 civilians perished from starvation or complications from malnutrition. State investment in manufacturing, however, tended to go to the same large industrial and agricultural firms as before the war began. At least, it was thought, they could operate on a large enough scale to meet wartime needs. But the close relationships between them and the government raised alarms about war profiteering at the expense of small businesses and common workers.[7]

Women's Work   Workers taking inventory in a British munitions factory during World War I. The extraordinary amount of munitions used in the war necessitated continuous production. As millions of men went into active service, women in all the involved countries stepped up to fill the factory positions.

---

[7]   The so-called Spanish Flu epidemic that spread across the entire world between January 1918 and December 1920 was the worst natural disaster since the Black Death in the mid-14th century and the smallpox pandemic in the New World in the 16th century. The origin of the flu virus is thought to have been somewhere in north-central Kansas. From a military installation there, Fort Riley, it likely spread among American soldiers who brought the virus into Europe. By the time the virus ran its course, the disease had spread globally, even into the Arctic, and may have killed as many as one hundred million people—approximately 5 percent of the global population. Despite its name, there was nothing Spanish about the flu. The virus received its name because Spain's non-involvement in World War I meant that it was the only European country not to be under news-censorship, and so the first detailed reports of flu appeared in that country.

The steady war propaganda kept the public in support of the war for quite some time, even in the face of mounting fatalities. In fact, the longer the war dragged on, the greater the effort was to rally support. Only the nature of the propaganda changed—from early enthusiastic posters to cartoon depictions of the enemy as bloodthirsty savages.[8] However, thousands on all sides took public stances against the conflict. Their reasons differed. Some argued along class lines, others along economic or racial lines; still others staked out a moral position against all forms of militarism. In Britain, over fifteen thousand individuals officially registered for "conscientious objector" status, as permitted by the Hague Conventions, risking social ostracism and even imprisonment.

By 1917 tens of thousands of French soldiers mutinied against directives to begin another frontal assault on German trenches. They objected to a new tactic called a "creeping barrage." Soldiers were to charge forward just a few feet behind successive waves of artillery shells, which would give them cover. Instead, the barrages killed the very troops they were supposed to be helping. In the end, roughly 25,000 soldiers underwent courts-martial for mutiny, and roughly one-tenth were convicted. Most of these received harsh imprisonments, and several hundred were executed.

In November 1914 a group of 101 British suffragists signed their names to an "Open Christmas Letter" addressed to "the Women of Germany and Austria":

> Sisters,
> Some of us wish to send you a word at this sad Christmastide, though we can but speak through the Press. The Christmas message sounds like mockery to a world at war, but those of us who wished and still wish for peace may surely offer a solemn greeting to such of you who feel as we do. Do not let us forget that our very anguish unites us, that we are passing together through the same experiences of pain and grief.
> Caught in the grip of terrible circumstance, what can we do? Tossed on this turbulent sea of human conflict, we can but move ourselves to those calm shores whereon stand, like rocks, the eternal verities—Love, Peace, Brotherhood.
> We pray you to believe that come what may we hold to our faith in Peace and Goodwill between nations; while technically at enmity in obedience to our rulers, we owe allegiance to that higher law which bids us live in peace with all men.

---

[8]   A poster announced the start of war: "The Great Game Has Begun!"

Though our sons are sent to slay each other, and our hearts are torn by the cruelty of this fate, yet through pain supreme we will be true to our common womanhood. We will let no bitterness enter in this tragedy, made sacred by the life-blood of our best, nor mar with hate the heroism of their sacrifice. Though much has been done on all sides you will, as deeply as ourselves, deplore, shall we not steadily refuse to give credence to those false tales so freely told us, each of the other?

We hope it may lessen your anxiety to learn we are doing our utmost to soften the lot of your civilians and war prisoners within our shores, even as we rely on your goodness of heart to do the same for ours in Germany and Austria.

Do you not feel with us that the vast slaughter in our opposing armies is a stain on civilization and Christianity, and that still deeper horror is aroused at the thought of those innocent victims, the countless women, children, babes, old and sick, pursued by famine, disease, and death in the devastated areas, both East and West?

As we saw in South Africa and the Balkan States, the brunt of modern war falls upon non-combatants, and the conscience of the world cannot bear the sight.

Is it not our mission to preserve life? Do not humanity and common sense alike prompt us to join hands with the women of neutral countries, and urge our rulers to stay further bloodshed?

Relief, however colossal, can reach but few. Can we sit still and let the helpless die in their thousands, as die they must—unless we rouse ourselves in the name of Humanity to save them? There is but one way to do this. We must all urge that peace be made with appeal to Wisdom and Reason. Since in the last resort it is these which must decide the issues, can they begin too soon, if it is to save the womanhood and child-hood as well as the manhood of Europe?

Even through the clash of arms we treasure our poet's vision, and already seem to hear:

A hundred nations swear that there shall be
Pity and Peace and Love among the good and free.

May Christmas hasten that day. Peace on Earth is gone, but by re-newal of our faith that it still reigns at the heart of things, Christmas should strengthen both you and us and all womanhood to strive for its return.

We are yours in this sisterhood of sorrow.

The author of the letter was Emily Hobhouse (1860–1926), a longtime social activist. Hobhouse got her start in public life when she campaigned against the brutal conditions that she had witnessed in British concentration camps in South Africa during the Boer War. The Christmas Letter created a rift among suffragists, since many of them supported the war. Despite their differences, however, most suffragists agreed to set aside the issue of women's rights until the war was over and to dedicate themselves to humanitarian work in the meantime.

A group of 150 German suffragists responded in March 1915 with an open letter (in English) of their own:

> To our English sisters, sisters of the same race, we express in the name of many German women our warm and heartfelt thanks for their Christmas greetings, which we only heard of lately.
>
> [Your] message was a confirmation of what we foresaw—that women of the belligerent countries, with all faithfulness, devotion, and love to their country, can go beyond it and maintain true solidarity with the women of other belligerent nations, and that really civilised women never lose their humanity.

OFFICERS AND GENTLEMEN

Every war introduces new weapons and new technologies of communication and transport and confronts new and usually unforeseen challenges. However, it takes time to understand the innovations and translate them into military tactics. As the saying goes, commanders are always fighting the last war. When World War I began, none of the top officers on either side of the conflict was familiar with trench warfare, submarine warfare, or aerial warfare. None had experienced poison gas or the gargantuan howitzers of modern artillery. Joseph Joffre (1852–1931), the French commander in chief at the outbreak of hostilities, had never even commanded an army before. His entire career up to that point had consisted of working as a military engineer. King George V read concerned reports from his general staff about the incompetence of the chief commander of the British Expeditionary Force, General John French. The leading commanders on all sides

> When World War I began, none of the top officers on either side of the conflict was familiar with trench warfare, submarine warfare, or aerial warfare. None had experienced poison gas or the gargantuan howitzers of modern artillery.

had inherited a tradition that still mimicked the military strategy and tactics used by Napoleon Bonaparte—a fast-moving infantry, pressing ever forward, complemented by portable artillery. This had worked brilliantly for Bonaparte at Austerlitz in 1805—but not in 1915, when the German field commander, Erich von Falkenhayn, earned the nickname "the Blood Miller of Verdun."

Mistakes in command, even elementary ones, marked the war effort on all sides. Miscommunication between the German and Austria-Hungarian leaders, for example, left their realms exposed to Russian advance. Each had expected the other to protect the Russian front while they pressed ahead in Belgium and Serbia, respectively. The confusion allowed Russia's forces to advance through all of Poland before they were stopped. At the eight-month siege of Gallipoli (1915–1916), civilians were assigned to the minesweepers that were supposed to clear the waterways in preparation for the Allied attack—crews that, unsurprisingly, fled once they came under heavy Ottoman artillery fire. As a result, one-third of the Allied battleships were sunk. On the Italian front officers launched twelve direct assaults against dug-in Austrian alpine units that held a clearly superior uphill position—protected by minefields, barbed wire, machine-gun nests, and artillery units. Fully one-half of all of Italy's 600,000 casualties in the war were suffered right here.

Just as sobering were the losses in the air and at sea. Both the airplane and the submarine made their military debut and proved vital to the outcome of the

Flying above the Pyramids   Airplanes were used almost entirely for reconnaissance in the first year of the war, since their engines could not carry the additional weight of bombs. Pilots were not even issued parachutes, at first, since those too proved too heavy for most engines. Guns were of little use until they could be synchronized with the propellers, lest they shoot off their own blades.

conflict. France put 68,000 airplanes into service; 52,000 were destroyed in battle. The design of the planes had to be kept simple, since many pilots went into battle after as little as a single week's instruction. Airplanes and airships were used initially for surveillance, but commanders quickly got the idea of dropping explosives. However, early airplanes did not fly at high altitudes, which left them vulnerable to enemy ground fire. Airplanes had their most dramatic effect in the Arab Revolt against the Turks, since the Ottomans had little heavy artillery and had dedicated it to other theaters. T. E. Lawrence described a battle at Megiddo in Palestine toward the end of the war, when British and Australian forces trapped a division of Turkish soldiers in a narrow defile, then strafed them from the air:

> When the smoke had cleared it was seen that the organization of the enemy had melted away. They were a dispersed horde of trembling individuals, hiding for their lives in every fold of the vast hills. Nor did their commanders ever rally them again. When our cavalry entered the silent valley the next day they could count ninety guns, fifty lorries, and nearly a thousand carts abandoned with all their belongings. The RAF lost four killed. The Turks lost a corps.

Despite Allied victories, lives were seen as wasted. Americans were reluctant to join a war that the officer and political class either was not trying to win or was too incompetent to lead. More than that, complaints ran, members of the labor and rural classes were regularly ordered into the worst of the fighting; so were recruits from colonial territories. In Australia today, commemoration of the slaughter at Gallipoli is a more emotionally powerful holiday than Armistice Day itself. The French mutinies of 1917 resulted from the officers' belief that they could pinpoint artillery barrages, from miles away, to provide cover for advancing infantrymen—which was absurd on the face of it.

Siegfried Sassoon, the soldier-poet, protested the war with a letter read in Parliament on July 30, 1917, published subsequently in the *Times* of London:

> I am making this statement as an act of willful defiance of military authority because I believe that the war is being deliberately prolonged by those who have the power to end it. I am a soldier, convinced that I am acting on behalf of soldiers. I believe that the war upon which I entered as a war of defense and liberation has now become a war of aggression and conquest. I believe that the purposes for which I and my fellow soldiers entered upon this war should have been so clearly stated as to have made it impossible to change them and that had this been done the objects which actuated us would now be attainable by negotiation.

I have seen and endured the sufferings of the troops and I can no longer be a party to prolonging these sufferings for ends which I believe to be evil and unjust. I am not protesting against the conduct of the war, but against the political errors and insincerities for which the fighting men are being sacrificed.

On behalf of those who are suffering now, I make this protest against the deception which is being practiced upon them; also I believe it may help to destroy the callous complacency with which the majority of those at home regard the continuance of agonies which they do not share and which they have not enough imagination to realize.

Despite government censorship, news about the war and its horrors circulated widely. After the initial elation in 1914, a popular attitude of grim resignation and determination set in. The war was no longer popular, but few saw any alternative, once it had begun, except victory. When Russia pulled out of the conflict and American entered it, in late 1917, fear arose that the war would drag on interminably. After the Allied victory at the Battle of the Somme, the exhausted Germans were ready to submit.

RUSSIA'S REVOLUTION

Reaching from Germany and Poland in the west to China and Japan in the east, Russia comprises one-sixth of the world's land mass. It is an enormous territory, made up largely of flat grassland with an icy northern fringe and no natural internal boundaries in its western reaches and of forests, steppes, and fertile valleys interspersed with mountainous stretches in its eastern expanses. It is also vast, open, and despite its large population chiefly an empty space. It is a land of extensive ethnic and cultural diversity, marked by long distances, poor communication, an adverse climate, and above all defensiveness and vulnerability. It lacked both an effective government and any natural borders to keep enemies out.

Despite reformist victories, autocratic ineptitude and the miseries of World War I brought an end to tsarist rule and the start of civil war. By 1920 Vladimir Lenin (1870–1924) and his Bolshevik party had won and established a Communist rule that would govern Russia until 1991.

For long centuries the people of Russia suffered waves of invasion from all sides. According to tradition, Russia's history begins with an invasion of Swedish Vikings who established the first Kingdom of Kievan Rus' in the ninth century. Subsequent invaders included the Kumans, Pechenegs, Khazars, Slavs, Byzantines, Poles, Lithuanians, Germans, and French. Still other attackers included the Huns, Chinese,

Mongols, and Turkish peoples of the east. Without adequate means to defend themselves, Russia's rulers traditionally relied on two tactics. One was to relinquish territory by retreating; this forced invaders to maintain long supply lines while exposing them to often brutal winters. The other tactic was to hurl wave after wave of common soldiers at the attackers, in order to use up the invaders' stores of ammunition.

With a few exceptions, the Romanov rulers held tight to autocracy and resisted efforts to reform. The development of democratic traditions, capitalist economies, industrialization, and liberal societies in the West frustrated and frightened Russia's rulers more than they inspired them. If Bonaparte had not been enough to convince Russia of Europe's dangerousness and untrustworthiness, the Crimean War in the 1850s was. Through the second half of the 19th century, nevertheless, pressure for reform did increase. The question was how to reform. Many Russians supported Western-style reforms like human rights, democracy, and economic development; others hoped for a uniquely Russian version of change, something homegrown and rooted in tradition. The tension between these competing notions of change underlay much of Russia's social and cultural development of the era. It provides the backdrop for the parade of great literary artists Russia produced: Aleksandr Pushkin (1799–1837), Nikolai Gogol (1809–1852), Mikhail Lermontov (1814–1841), Ivan Turgenev (1818–1883), Fyodor Dostoevsky (1821–1881), Leo Tolstoy (1828–1910), and Anton Chekhov (1860–1904).

Bloody Sunday   Tsarist soldiers firing on demonstrators at the Winter Palace in Saint Petersburg, Russia, on "Bloody Sunday," January 9, 1905.

Calls for reform gained momentum in the 1860s and 1870s. Serfdom was abolished in 1861, and independent judiciaries with trials by jury were established. But in 1881 a terrorist assassinated Tsar Aleksandr II, which led his successor, Aleksandr III (r. 1881–1894), to strengthen the police state. He reached out for popular support by promoting a **Pan-Slavism** that masked an obsessive hatred of Jews, with the result that anti-Jewish pogroms became common and vicious. Aleksandr also tried to force rapid industrialization; his signature project was the Trans-Siberian Railroad, begun in 1891. Russia's loss in the war with Japan in 1905, combined

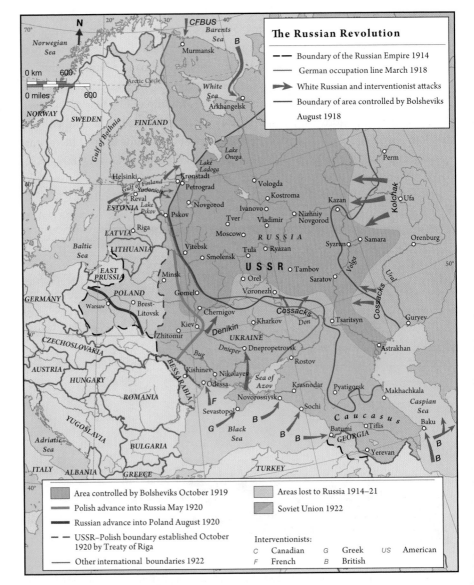

MAP 24.4   The Russian Revolution

with a failed attempt at revolution in Moscow and Saint Petersburg, led the next tsar, Nikolai II, to dismiss the Russian parliament.

The deaths of millions of poorly trained and ill-equipped soldiers, several years of horrendous crop failures, and the collapse of the currency led to a wave of food riots and labor strikes in early 1917. Unlike in 1905, the army supported the rebels this time, and the government fell. But as with revolutions elsewhere, most notably in France in 1789, the people could not agree on what government would replace the old administration. They were united only in their opposition to the tsar and to World War I. A dizzying array of rival parties quickly formed, and each party was just as quick to raise an army of its own. For two years a civil war raged across Russia. Liberals fought against Socialists against pro-tsarist Whites against pro-peasant Greens against Anarchists against Mensheviks against Bolsheviks (see Map 24.4).

The **Mensheviks** and Lenin's **Bolsheviks** were factions within the Communist movement behind rival leaders. The Bolsheviks won in part because they understood the depth of the popular desire for radical agrarian reform—how desperately the peasants wanted Russia's farmland redistributed. They won, too, because they believed unapologetically in the use of violence and terrorism to achieve their ends.

BOLSHEVISM AND THE LAWS OF HISTORY

Lenin possessed the unwavering drive and personal discipline of a true zealot.[9] Lenin's real name was Vladimir Ilyich Ulyanov, and his father had worked for the imperial bureaucracy as a provincial school inspector. He converted to radicalism as a youth and spent much of his young adulthood in Europe, where he made contacts with a network of dedicated reformers. (He became a Marxist in 1890 or 1891, during his study of the law as an extramural—that is, nonmatriculating—student at the University of Saint Petersburg.) Lenin sympathized with poor workers and farmers but never identified with them. He saw himself instead as a Romantic leader of the masses, a passionate intellectual superior to those whom he led.

His elitism carried over into his political thinking as well. Lenin's party positioned itself as a vanguard party: they held all authority and ruled the masses directly, rather than, as some Marxist groups had called for, establishing a government by public referendum. He championed a separate group of professional revolutionaries whose ideological purity would ensure the success of the revolution. It would also conveniently legitimize whatever tactics the party elite chose

---

[9] Lenin's older brother was executed in 1887 for a failed attempt to assassinate Tsar Aleksandr III. The hanging of his brother turned Lenin against the tsarist state.

to employ. The incorruptibility of the Bolshevik leaders, he was convinced, would prevent them from being seduced by the trappings of the power they so ruthlessly reserved for themselves.

Lenin had to alter Marxist theory in order to make it fit the Russian situation, and the changes he made helped set the tone for much of the 20th century's international politics. Marx had argued that the inevitable transfer of wealth and power to the working class would and could happen only in an industrial society. Industrial capitalism as he saw it, for all its evil, was a necessary stage en route to Communist freedom. The proletarian class who would inherit the earth consisted first and foremost of urban laborers. Russia by 1920, however, had not become an industrialized society by any stretch of the imagination. Dirt-poor farmers and unskilled laborers still made up easily 80 percent of the population. Lenin as an intellectual needed to tweak the Marxist formula so that historical development could leapfrog over the industrial stage and straight to socialism.

Lenin wrote his most interesting books during his two-decade European exile before coming to power, when he was trying to establish himself among the revolutionary elite. His first significant publication was *The Development of Capitalism in Russia* (1899). Stuffed with statistics and charts, it is his most technical and forbidding work, but it is an important one. It is here that he reworks Marxist theory by arguing that Russia's agricultural production already had all the labor specialization, class structure, and market competition called for by Marx. Lenin also extends his argument against **populism**. Populism, as he sees it, is moral compromise dressed up as common sense. True reform means centralizing all authority among professional revolutionaries, for the servitude of the masses allows them to be co-opted by capitalist landowners.

In the 1890s there were widespread calls within Russia for land reform—all within a structure of social democracy that would preserve the rights and citizenship of the elite. Lenin would have none of that. He insisted that only the

Russian Peasants   Russian villagers pose for a photographer in this picture from the 1890s. Their wooden huts with thatch roofs can be seen, as well as the simple dirt roads that were the norm. In spring these became nearly impassable as the melting snow turned them into rivers of mud.

revolutionary caste can lead the masses to freedom, and it can do so only by ignoring the opinions of those they lead. As he put it in *What Is to Be Done?* (1902):

> The history of the world shows that workers by themselves can achieve nothing more than a trade-union level of consciousness.... Socialist theory, however, emerged from the coalescence of the philosophical, historical, and social theorizing of the intellectual classes, those educated members of the propertied classes. In terms of their social backgrounds, both Marx and Engels, the very founders of modern scientific socialism, belonged to the educated bourgeoisie. In Russia too the theoretical foundations [of revolutionary Marxism] were established independently of the labor movement, as an organic, inevitable consequence of the thought trajectory of the revolutionary socialist intelligentsia.

The leaders of the revolution, in other words, are of not the same stock as the workers they control, and they should not apologize for it.

Lenin's next major publication was *Materialism and Empiriocriticism: Critical Comments on a Reactionary Philosophy* (1909). It represents Lenin's only attempt at genuine philosophical writing. A number of Russian thinkers living in Europe had fallen away from Marxism after 1900, seeing it as too dependent on a materialist and determinist view of the world. Surely there is more to human existence than objective economic forces and inexorable laws of historical inevitability. What about human individuality? Human will? The power of instinct and passion? The human tendency to irrational longing and the desire for beauty? Is there, in the end, no room for the human spirit in philosophizing about human life? Lenin responds with an emphatic *no*.

No other book betrays more of Lenin's thin, hard, and brittle personality. He argues that there are only two real possibilities in a philosophical view of the world—materialism and idealism. There is the world of objects, things, bodies, atoms, molecules, and natural forces on the one hand, and there is the world of theories, Platonic forms, abstract ideas, and impersonal notions on the other. Any philosophy that attempts a middle position or claims somehow to transcend the poles is either short-sighted or just plain verbal tomfoolery. His point is reminiscent of Thomas Hobbes in *Leviathan*: a society can consist only of absolute chaos or absolute order, and any position in between is simply the sweep of the pendulum on its way from one extreme to the other. Materialism, Lenin concludes, must be the truth, since it alone is supported by modern science. Physical reality exists outside of human thought for the simple reason that the universe existed before human beings did—millions of years before, in fact. Moreover, human thought emerges from the human brain, which is itself a physical object. No brain, no thought; materialism alone has verifiable existence.

Lenin's argument is neither elegant nor original, but he presents it with evangelical intensity. The theory of **dialectical materialism**, or of the pendulum swings of history in a firmly materialist world, is actually a fairly minor aspect of Marx's own thought. But with Lenin it appears front and center as the force driving history forward—to the confrontation of the proletariat and the bourgeoisie. There is no way for human beings to avoid this force, any more than they can avoid Newton's universal laws. Just as all molecules are subject to gravity, all humanity is driven by dialectical materialism.

> Materialism, Lenin concludes, must be the truth, since it alone is supported by modern science. Physical reality exists outside of human thought for the simple reason that the universe existed before human beings did—millions of years before, in fact.

Most of Lenin's contemporaries lambasted the book as cold, crude, and shallow. He seemed determined to ignore anyone else's ideas, even Marx's. Although the book quickly sank from view, it was revived in the 1930s by a new leader of the Bolshevik regime, Josef Stalin—whose ability to regard people as mere objects was even more pronounced than Lenin's.

EXPORTING REVOLUTION

Lenin's most interesting book was inspired by the experience of World War I. *Imperialism, the Highest Stage of Capitalism* was published in Saint Petersburg in 1917. Lenin wrote it while living in Zurich in 1916, as he watched World War I unfold in all its tragedy from a safe distance in neutral Switzerland. Lenin here confronts a significant problem: Karl Marx had not foreseen imperialism. According to Marx, industrial capitalism would result in a consolidation of economic power among the most prominent members of the bourgeoisie. Once this institutional lock on further economic development was in place, the proletarian revolution would take place.

Lenin had to address why a revolution had not occurred to stop imperialism before it began. His adroit answer also buttresses his earlier contention—that agrarian Russia could bypass the industrial stage and still effect a Marxist revolution. In late capitalism, he argues, finance and industry form a union of their own that shuts out all competition. Once it has taken over an entire national economy its profits become stagnant, which drives the cartel overseas in search of new markets and larger profits. By investing its capital abroad, the cartel divides the world between the imperialist industrial nations and the colonized countries that are locked out of industrial development. Because the undeveloped nations depend on monopolistic capital, they assume the role of the proletariat as the actors in the revolution. Lenin asserts that imperialism is neither an aberration nor an accidental consequence of capitalism; it is actually the *goal* of capitalist societies, and the Great War of 1914 is the initial stage of the revolution yet to come. And the agents of the revolution will be the agrarian workers of the undeveloped periphery—meaning Russia.

Once the Bolsheviks took control of the government, Lenin and his comrades indeed led the country as a vanguard. He introduced two final major revisions of Marx's thought. First, he insisted on violent action in order to bring the revolution to fruition. And second, he insisted on the need to export the revolution to the colonized nations living under capitalist rule. Just as Bonaparte had believed that absolutism had to be crushed everywhere in order to preserve the revolution in France, Lenin concluded that revolutionary Russia needed to promote the rising up of oppressed rural workers everywhere.

> Just as Bonaparte had believed that absolutism had to be crushed everywhere in order to preserve the revolution in France, Lenin concluded that revolutionary Russia needed to promote the rising up of oppressed rural workers everywhere.

For the time being, however, that was not possible, Lenin declared. The Bolsheviks had to get Russia in order first. In 1920 they instituted a complete state takeover of the land and whatever manufacturing base the country possessed. They conscripted labor, confiscated all foodstuffs and goods, and began an emergency redistribution of provisions. The following year, however, Lenin announced a new policy of state socialism. Now the government retained control of finance, transportation, and industrial output but allowed the rest of the economy to return to a modest degree of private enterprise. Peasants contributed a certain percentage of their crops to the state, but they were free to sell the rest on an open market. Traders were allowed to buy and sell as they pleased. In essence, Lenin throughout the 1920s introduced a "mixed" system—socialism in the large-scale economy and capitalism in the small, local economies.

Politically, Communist Russia was a dictatorship led by a Bolshevik party of some half million members, and Lenin himself reigned supreme. He maintained the "ideological purity" of the party—by which he meant keeping the party subservient to his authority—by instituting regular purges. Spying and terrorism began on a massive scale, along with a network of forced labor camps. "Let us cleanse the Russian land of every type of harmful insect . . . by which I mean the

Lenin in the Vanguard   Lenin addresses a Moscow crowd in 1918.

rich, the miscreants, the lazy—all those not dedicated entirely to the revolution-ary cause."[10]

The Bolsheviks wiped out, by imprisonment, extermination, or both, the entire professional class of financiers, entrepreneurs, civic officials, engineers, and administrators, seeing them as unreliable. They abolished the Russian Orthodox Church, confiscated its possessions, and forbade all religious ceremonies and religious education. An internal security bureau, the forerunner of the KGB, strictly censored all publications, broadcasts, and public addresses. Mandatory public education introduced the new generation to socialist ideals and the correctness of the Leninist model of communal existence. Lenin himself remained in complete control until his death in 1924, but he seemed diminished as a personality. His strength was as a firebrand, attacking old systems, rather than as the administrator of a bureaucracy, even a ruthless one. His final four years are filled with complaints: "Russians are lousy workers compared to those in the West." "Treat the Jews in the Ukraine with an iron rod . . . . Transfer them to the front, and never let them into government offices." "Tell every member of the Security Bureau to kill anyone who does not show up to work because he wants a stupid Christmas celebration."

---

[10]   "One out of every ten lazy workers," Lenin proclaimed, "should be shot on the spot."

Still, despite the horrors of the civil war and of Lenin's brutal governance, daily life for most Russians was probably better in the 1920s than it had been under the tsars. Food and shelter become more available, as did some forms of education and medical care. This says more about the miserable failure of the Romanovs than about the success of the Bolsheviks, but the fact remains. Visitors from the West brought back to Europe breathless reports about Marxism as a new path of development. The West could and should consider that path, they said, as it rebuilt from the ruins of World War I. The spike in Western interest in Marxism came immediately after the conflict ended in 1918, and it helped set the stage for the misery that followed.

Emancipated Women   A Soviet propaganda poster in honor of the heroines of socialist labor. It proclaims, "What the October Revolution brought to the female worker and the peasant woman."

HOW NOT TO END A WAR

The United States entered World War I on April 6, 1917, "to make the world safe for democracy," in the words of President Woodrow Wilson (r. 1913–1921). Wilson had recently won election to a second term, largely on the platform of having kept America out of the conflict, though in a state of "armed neutrality." In reality, the country had never been altogether neutral. Between 1914 and 1916, American trade with the Allies had increased fourfold, and most of the goods sold had been war material—weapons and ammunition, military rations, and supplies like tents, boots, and uniforms. U.S. banks had extended the Allies more than two billion dollars in loans and credits, which meant that only an Allied victory would ensure repayment. Britain and France's debt alone equaled $45 billion in today's dollars. When the British imposed a naval blockade on Germany's Baltic coast, American ships never even attempted to challenge it.

Germany launched its U-boats into the Atlantic primarily to interdict American supplies to the Allies, an action that provoked American anger but failed to rouse the country to join the fight. Even when a German U-boat, in May 1915, sank the *Lusitania*—a British transatlantic passenger liner that had 128 Americans on board—and Germany refused to apologize, the U.S. position

Creating a New World Order   The main protagonists at the Paris Peace Talks: Vittorio Emanuele Orlando of Italy, Britain's David Lloyd George, Georges Clemenceau of France, and U.S. president Woodrow Wilson.

did not change.[11] An intercepted telegram from Berlin to the German ambassador in Mexico City, in January 1917, added fuel to American outrage. The Zimmermann telegram (named for the diplomat who had sent it) showed that Germany had offered military aid if Mexico was willing to declare war, in order to regain the territories lost in 1845 when the United States annexed Texas. One month later, when the Russians overthrew the tsar and pulled out of the conflict, Germany was able to gather its forces for a single massive campaign against the western front. America finally stirred to action.

After armistice was declared on November 11, 1918, the difficult work of ironing out a permanent peace settlement began. The actual settlement punished the losers, angered both sides, and practically ensured anything but permanent peace. The collapse of the Ottoman Empire was just one more sign that although the old order was gone for good, the grounds for resentment still simmered.

The Allied leaders—President Wilson, British prime minister David Lloyd George, French prime minister Georges Clemenceau, and Italian prime minister Vittorio Orlando—met in Paris along with teams of diplomats, historians, lawyers, and economists amid high hopes. Negotiations deadlocked almost instantly. The United States maintained that no single country had caused the war and so

---

[11]   Germany claimed that the *Lusitania* was carrying war supplies to Britain—and, as it turns out, it was.

every participant shared responsibility; all, therefore, had to compromise on territorial concessions. Wilson pressed especially hard for a political redivision of central and eastern Europe to respect ethnic nationalities. The French, however, considered themselves the victims of German aggression. The overwhelming bulk of the fighting on the western front, after all, had taken place on French soil. The only acceptable option was to punish Germany so that she could never again threaten France. The British took a position somewhere between the two. After months of talks and no progress at all, the governments finally agreed out of exhaustion and frustration to France's demands.

The **Treaty of Versailles** (1919) actually consists of five separate treaties, one with each of the Axis powers (Germany, Austria, Hungary, Bulgaria, and Turkey), and each one created as many problems as it resolved. The treaty with Germany—the Treaty of Versailles proper—proved the most controversial. France insisted on, and won, vast concessions. Germany was stripped of all overseas colonies and internationally held funds, which were duly reapportioned among Belgium, Britain, France, and Italy. The regions of Alsace and Lorraine were ceded to France, and the rest of Germany west of the Rhine River was given over to a new international body dedicated to world peace and cooperation, the League of Nations. Germany's borders were in essence pushed back to what they had been in 1871. The German military was limited to one hundred thousand soldiers and was denied aircraft, heavy artillery, and warships.

Most galling of all to the Germans were articles 231 and 232 of the treaty, which forced Germany to accept guilt for the entire war:

> Article 231: The Allied and Associated Governments affirm and Germany accepts the responsibility of Germany and her allies for causing all the loss and damage to which the Allied and Associated Governments and their nationals have been subjected as a consequence of the war imposed upon them by the aggression of Germany and her allies.

> Article 232: The Allied and Associated Governments recognize that the resources of Germany are not adequate, after taking into account permanent diminutions of such resources which will result from other provisions of the present Treaty, to make complete reparation for all such loss and damage. The Allied and Associated Governments, however, require, and Germany undertakes, that she will make compensation for all damage done to the civilian population of the Allied and Associated Powers and to their property during the period of the belligerency of each as an Allied or Associated Power against Germany.

These articles obliged Germany to make reparations for all civilian losses to the Allied powers, which a separate commission reckoned at a sum of 226 billion reichsmarks (roughly $680 billion in today's currency). This was an impossible sum, since so much of Germany's accumulated wealth had been confiscated. The treaty, after all, had taken away territories that supported most of the nation's industrial capacity—75 percent of its iron ore deposits, 30 percent of its steel production, and nearly 30 percent of its available coal.

As stringent as it was, the treaty represented far less than France had originally wanted. Criticism of the pact emerged almost instantly. The British Parliament and the U.S. Congress refused to ratify it, which left France feeling exposed, with unreliable allies. A leading British economist who had in fact been a delegate to the peace conference, John Maynard Keynes (1883–1946), repudiated the treaty. In his *Economic Consequences of the Peace* (1919), Keynes had a gloomy prediction not only for Germany but for the entire Continent:

> The essential facts of the situation, as I see them, are expressed simply. Europe consists of the densest aggregation of population in the history of the world. This population is accustomed to a relatively high standard of life, in which, even now, some sections of it anticipate improvement rather than deterioration. In relation to other continents Europe is not self-sufficient; in particular it cannot feed itself. Internally the population is not evenly distributed, but much of it is crowded into a relatively small number of dense industrial centers. This population secured for itself a livelihood before the war, without much margin of surplus, by means of a delicate and immensely complicated organization, of which the foundations were supported by coal, iron, transport, and an unbroken supply of imported food and raw materials from other continents. By the destruction of this organization and the interruption of the stream of supplies, a part of this population is deprived of its means of livelihood. Emigration is not open to the redundant surplus. For it would take years to transport them overseas, even, which is not the case, if countries could be found which were ready to receive them. The danger confronting us, therefore, is the rapid depression of the standard of life of the European populations to a point which will mean actual starvation for some (a point already reached in Russia and approximately reached in Austria). Men will not always die quietly. For starvation, which brings to some lethargy and a helpless despair, drives other temperaments to the nervous instability of hysteria and to a mad despair. And these in their distress may overturn the remnants of organization, and submerge civilization itself in their attempts to satisfy

desperately the overwhelming needs of the individual. This is the danger against which all our resources and courage and idealism must now co-operate.

Europe after the war did indeed have difficulty feeding itself, and not just Germany. For a time the Allied countries could draw on the resources of their colonies. Now, however, the collapse of the Ottoman and Habsburg Empires gave fresh hope to colonized peoples throughout the world. They might finally achieve freedom from all European control. Germany, meanwhile, was forced to swallow a humiliating treaty that left a legacy of resentment and betrayal.

> Now, however, the collapse of the Ottoman and Habsburg empires gave fresh hope to colonized peoples throughout the world. They might finally achieve freedom from all European control.

The settlement with Austria was not as punitive as that with Germany, although the Austrians felt that it was. Austria and Hungary became separate countries, much to the rejoicing of the Hungarians, and an autonomous Czechoslovakia was established. A short-lived kingdom of Serbia, Croatia, and Slovenia soon evolved into the federated state of Yugoslavia; smaller territorial concessions were made to Italy and Romania. Austria itself was thus reduced to a landlocked republic and was forbidden to unite with Germany into a larger German state. The Hungarians celebrated independence from Vienna and were left with an ethnically cohesive state. However, they resented losing control of the Slovak, Slovenian, and Balkan peoples—who had at one time made up 60 percent of their subjects (see Map 24.5).

YOUNG TURKS

The demise of the Ottoman Empire both was and was not a consequence of the war. The revolt in 1908 of a faction called the **Young Turks** had already led to a constitutional reform that reinstated the Turkish Parliament and severely limited the power of the monarchy. A number of peripheral territories, primarily in the Balkans and much of today's country of Libya, had already taken advantage of the political disorder and managed to win independence from Istanbul. While the rebellion contributed to a shrinking of the empire, it nonetheless produced a more stable and reform-minded government.

The Young Turks were not democrats, although they posed as such when negotiating with the Western powers. Interested above all in promoting pan-ethnic Islamic nationalism, they overthrew the sultan Abdul Hamid II in 1909 and replaced him with his half brother Mehmed V (r. 1909–1918). The Young

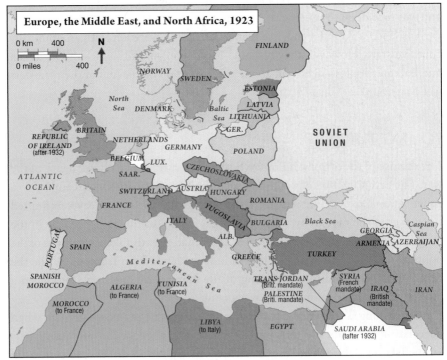

MAP 24.5   Europe and the Middle East in 1914 and 1923

Turks had modernizing ambitions, and some of them, at least, hoped to govern a united Islamic world under a secular regime, seeing this as the best hope of resolving the religious sectarianism among Muslims. The position of non-Muslims under Young Turk rule was uncertain. Indeed, the policies of the Young Turks were contradictory, which prompted groups like the Armenians and Jews to seek to break away from Turkish rule altogether. The Young Turk administration, not the sultan, entered the war on the Axis side.

The Arab Revolt had weakened Turkish power even further, by causing most of the Middle East to rise up against Istanbul. Defeat in the war meant the effective end of the empire, and the ensuing political confusion meant that it took until 1920 to formalize a peace treaty with the Allies. The treaty cut away even further at the Turkish dominion. Greece was awarded sites in Thrace, while Italy received control of Rhodes and the Dodecanese Islands. Independent republics of Armenia and Kurdistan were carved out of the eastern reaches of the empire (although all three were short-lived), and all the Arab territories were given over to the Allies. Syria became a French Mandate, while Iraq, Palestine, and Transjordan became a British Mandate.

Arab Delegates to the Paris Peace Conference   Prince Faisal stands in the foreground; just over his left shoulder, in Arab headdress, is Col. T.E. Lawrence (Lawrence of Arabia). Contrary to promises of independence made earlier to the Arabs, Britain and France retained control of much of the Middle East after the collapse of the Ottoman state.

Turkey was left, in essence, with only those territories that were primarily Turkish in population. The settlement hurt Turkish pride, which was further harmed by international accusations of guilt for the Armenian genocide. A new leader, Mustafa Kemal Atatürk (1881–1938), took advantage of wounded Turkish nationalism to promote a new Republic of Turkey with a curious blend of liberal and reactionary elements. He was committed to secularism and republican government, but rigidly determined to defend Turkey against any criticism from outside.

The Great War ended, at last, with bristling resentment, constrained economies, and damaged national pride on all sides. The coming years did not look hopeful.

WHO, WHAT, WHERE

Arab Revolt	populism
Bolsheviks	Schlieffen Plan
dialectical materialism	Sykes-Picot Agreement
Mensheviks	Treaty of Versailles
Pan-Slavism	Young Turks

SUGGESTED READINGS

Primary Sources

Angell, Norman. *The Great Illusion: A Study of the Relation of Military Power to National Advantage.*

Graves, Robert. *Goodbye to All That.*

Jünger, Ernst. *Storm of Steel: From the Diary of a German Shock-Troop Officer on the Western Front.*

Keynes, John Maynard. *The Economic Consequences of the Peace.*

Lenin, Vladimir. *Imperialism, the Highest Stage of Capitalism.*

———. *The State and Revolution.*

———. *What Is To Be Done?*

Shaw, George Bernard. *Common Sense about the War.*

Anthologies

Neiberg, Michael S., ed. *The World War I Reader: Primary and Secondary Sources* (2006).

Shevin-Coetzee, Marilyn, and Frans Coetzee. *World War I: A History in Documents* (2010).

Weinberg, Robert, and Laurie Bernstein. *Revolutionary Russia: A History in Documents* (2010).

Studies

Akçam, Taner. *A Shameful Act: The Armenian Genocide and the Question of Turkish Responsibility* (2007).

Azak, Umut. *Islam and Secularism in Turkey: Kemalism, Religion, and the Nation State* (2010).

Bass, Gary Jonathan. *Stay the Hand of Vengeance: The Politics of War Crimes Tribunals* (2002).

Bein, Amit. *Ottoman Ulema, Turkish Republic: Agents of Change and Guardians of Tradition* (2011).

Bloxham, Donald. *The Great Game of Genocide: Imperialism, Nationalism, and the Destruction of the Ottoman Armenians* (2007).

Campos, Michelle. *Ottoman Brothers: Muslims, Christians, and Jews in Early Twentieth-Century Palestine* (2010).

Ceadel, Martin. *Living the Great Illusion: Sir Norman Angell, 1872–1967* (2009).

Englund, Peter. *The Beauty and the Sorrow: An Intimate History of the First World War* (2011).

Fitzpatrick, Sheila. *The Russian Revolution* (2008).

Hanioğlu, M. Şükrü. *Atatürk: An Intellectual Biography* (2011).

Herwig, Holger H. *The First World War: Germany and Austria-Hungary, 1914–1918* (2009).

Kévorkian, Raymond. *The Armenian Genocide: A Complete History* (2011).

Kramer, Alan. *Dynamic of Destruction: Culture and Mass Killing in the First World War* (2009).

McMeekin, Sean. *The Berlin-Baghdad Express: The Ottoman Empire and Germany's Bid for World Power* (2010).

———. *The Russian Origins of the First World War* (2011).

Philpott, William. *Three Armies on the Somme: The First Battle of the Twentieth Century* (2011).

Sharp, Alan. *The Versailles Settlement: Peacemaking after the First World War, 1919–1923* (2008).

Strachan, Hew. *The First World War*. Vol. 1, *To Arms* (2003).

Suny, Ronald Grigor, Fatma Müge Göçek, and Norman M. Naimark, eds. *A Question of Genocide: Armenians and Turks at the End of the Ottoman Empire* (2011).

Thompson, Mark. *The White War: Life and Death on the Italian Front, 1915–1919* (2010).

Zürcher, Erik J. *The Young Turk Legacy and Nation Building: From the Ottoman Empire to Atatürk's Turkey* (2010).

For additional resources, including maps, primary sources, visuals, web links, and quizzes, please go to **www.oup.com/us/backman.**

CHAPTER 25

Radical Realignments

1919–1939

The Greater West entered the postwar era with little confidence and many worries. Europe remained politically unstable and economically vulnerable, and the Middle East churned with new turmoil and resentment toward Europe. America largely wanted to wash its hands of "foreign entanglements," to quote an old warning from George Washington in his presidential farewell address, and a new government in Moscow declared its goal of liberating the world from capitalist oppression. Desolation and confusion reigned. The immediate crisis, however, was economic. Most of Europe emerged from the war either bankrupt or perilously close to it. "The military crisis may be over," wrote the French poet Paul Valéry (1871–1945) in 1919, "but the economic crisis is still here with us in all its ferocity."

THE GREAT DEPRESSION IN THE GREATER WEST

Decline in industrial production of over 30%
Decline in industrial production of up to 30%

Apart from the dislocation of their overseas colonies, the European countries had lost their dominance in many international markets to relative newcomers—Australia, Canada, Japan, and the United States. Even worse, most of Europe's governments were deeply in debt. They had financed the war by selling billions of dollars in bonds and by borrowing both public and private funds from the United States. England and France responded to their debt problem, initially, by simply printing more money; but when bondholders objected to receiving repayment in devalued currency, they stopped. The United States, for its part, refused to accept the

◀ Force of Will Never a great orator, Mussolini compensated by being a passionate one. His expressive nature came across to many as buffoonish and insincere. An egoist who despised democracy and Christianity as refuges for the weak, he likened himself to a Nietzschean "superman" but lacked the positive qualities Nietzsche had expected in such a figure.

new currency, too. The United States emerged from the war in better economic and political shape than any other participant. Even so, America found it difficult to convert back to a peacetime economy and struggled with inflation that reached as high as 18 percent in 1919–1920.

Everything seemed in flux even before the beginning, in 1929, of the great economic crash called the Great Depression. Educators were revisiting the entire history of Western civilization. Attempts to create an international League of Nations foundered; national aspirations were emerging on the peripheries of Europe and in the Middle East; and runaway inflation set the stage for economic unrest. The tyrannies of Fascism and totalitarianism further threatened peace. Amid all this, modern literature entered a new stage with its own experiments and trauma.

HISTORY FOR BEGINNERS

People across Europe and America cried out for an explanation, which resulted in a growing popular interest in history. American colleges and universities responded with what came to be called "Western civilization" courses that followed the story from Mesopotamia to the Treaty of Versailles.

How on earth had the Western world got itself into such a mess? Europe, after all, was the cradle of democracy, modern science, Western Christianity, and philosophy. It had given birth to Michelangelo, Leonardo da Vinci, Shakespeare, Cervantes, Rembrandt, Bach, Mozart, Goethe, Voltaire, Pushkin, and Tolstoy. It had produced both industrial genius and the most trenchant criticism of industrialization. Europe had the world's highest literacy rates and standards of living. Its technological development was unmatched. Though still hampered by legal and social prejudices, women played a larger public role in it than in any other society on the globe. A vigorous and determined press enabled citizens to stay informed. Yet this civilization had now sunk to an extraordinary depth of savagery.

CHAPTER TIMELINE

1917 Balfour Declaration

1918 Oswald Spengler, *Decline of the West*

1919 Massive labor strikes in the U.S.A.

1922 Publication of *Ulysses* and "The Waste Land"; Fascists march on Rome

1923–1924 France occupies the Ruhr Valley

1924 Hyperinflation in Germany

1925 Virginia Woolf, *Mrs. Dalloway*; Publication of *Mein Kampf*

1928 Women receive full suffrage in Britain

People across Europe and America cried out for an explanation, which resulted in a growing popular interest in history. American colleges and universities responded with what came to be called "Western civilization" courses that followed the story from Mesopotamia to the Treaty of Versailles. While these courses did not shy away from the horrors of war, they emphasized the positive achievements of three millennia—monotheism, democracy, education, and prosperity. At the same time, literature and philosophy departments crafted "great books" and "great ideas" surveys of Western culture. Such courses presumed that the Western way of life still offered the best chance for a bright future. Before long, the courses created at the University of Chicago and at Columbia University established models that were quickly adopted by other schools around the country. The fundamental problem, they urged, was not with Western values themselves but with the perverting radical misrepresentations of them. Capitalism is not at fault; only the most unchecked and rapacious form of it. Democracy is not the culprit either; if anything, it was the too-limited and constrained versions of it that led to the trouble. The answer, therefore, was to pursue more and better capitalism, more and better democracy.

Survey courses of this type did not appear in Europe's universities, principally because Europeans already knew their history better than most Americans knew theirs; but European curricula moved sharply away from the nation-based focus of their history departments and placed new emphasis on the histories of other countries and cultures. Still, a two-volume history by a sickly German loner became almost overnight the most talked-about book in Europe. In universities, coffeehouses, public libraries, and private studies everywhere, everyone read it and debated it. The book was *The Decline of the West*, by Oswald Spengler; a first volume appeared in 1918, a second four years later. In it, Spengler identifies ten different morphological types of cultures, of which three are at work in the three thousand years of Western history. He argues that Western civilization has evolved through these three major phases of development—the Magian, the Apollonian, and the

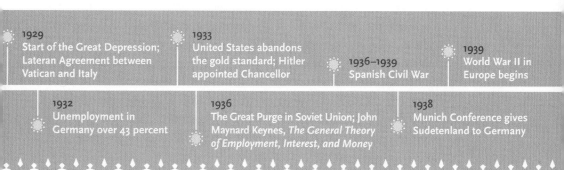

1929
Start of the Great Depression; Lateran Agreement between Vatican and Italy

1933
United States abandons the gold standard; Hitler appointed Chancellor

1936–1939
Spanish Civil War

1939
World War II in Europe begins

1932
Unemployment in Germany over 43 percent

1936
The Great Purge in Soviet Union; John Maynard Keynes, *The General Theory of Employment, Interest, and Money*

1938
Munich Conference gives Sudetenland to Germany

Faustian. Spengler describes these, respectively, as the belief in magic (including the major religions), the striving for order (classical Greece and Rome), and the pursuit of power and knowledge (the modern West). For him, Europe in the early 20th century had reached the end of its Faustian period, after which life ceases to be creative and vital and becomes bureaucratic and superficial.

His argument is not wholly original; an earlier form of it had been made by an Italian scholar named Giambattista Vico (1668–1744) in the 18th century. Vico, however, had emphasized the cyclical nature of civilizations: after the inevitable collapse of any society, it begins a new cycle by a return to another, though different, primitive stage. Spengler, in contrast, sees no necessary relationship between phases; when one phases ends (usually after a period of roughly one thousand years) a new one begins; but no one can predict which phase will succeed any previous one. History is a constant and random reconfiguration of cultural types around the globe.

Spengler's book proved popular not for the strength of its arguments but for the resonance of its gloomy outlook with the prevailing mood of postwar Europe. Indeed, once Europe recovered some stability in the 1920s, interest in Spengler evaporated until the gloom of yet another postwar era (in the late 1940s this time) made him once again a figure of interest.

Rival visions of history were quick to appear. For H. G. Wells (1866–1946), a popular novelist and science-fiction writer, hope for the future remains—so long as we remain dedicated to educating all people.[1] Catastrophes like the Great War occur only when ignorance and prejudice reign supreme, he assured readers. Wells published *The Outline of History* in 1920. In its 1,300 pages he argues for an evolutionary view of history. Mankind, he says, is in a continual state of adaptation. Although periods of crisis and ruin may occur, human history progresses upward—or it will if we let it:

> The need for a common knowledge of the general facts of human history throughout the world has become very evident during the tragic happenings of the last few years. Swifter means of communication have brought all men closer to one another for good or for evil. War becomes a universal disaster, blind and monstrously destructive; it bombs the baby in its cradle and sinks the food-ships that cater for the non-combatant and the neutral. There can be no peace now, we realize, but a common peace in all the world; no prosperity but a general prosperity. But there can be no common peace and prosperity without common historical ideas. Without such ideas to hold them together in harmonious co-operation, with nothing but narrow, selfish, and conflicting nationalist traditions, races and peoples are bound to drift towards conflict and destruction. This truth, which was apparent to

---

[1]   "Human history becomes more and more a race between education and catastrophe."—H. G. Wells.

that great philosopher Kant a century or more ago—it is the gist of his tract upon universal peace—is now plain to the man in the street. Our internal policies and our economic and social ideas are profoundly vitiated at present by wrong and fantastic ideas of the origin and historical relationship of social classes. A sense of history as the common adventure of all mankind is as necessary for peace within as it is for peace between the nations.

Even more massive works appeared, too. Arnold Toynbee's (1889–1975) *A Study of History* (twelve volumes, starting in 1934) and Will Durant's (1885–1981) *The Story of Civilization* (eleven volumes, starting in 1935) made bookshelves groan across the world.

The war was only one reason for the sudden fascination with history. The other was fear of Marxism. To many oppressed laborers and struggling émigrés, the Bolshevik success in Russia gave a jolt of encouragement, just as the American Revolution had inspired reformers in 18th-century France. Radical change seemed within grasp and worth pursuing. Across Europe workers' rights had been rolled back during the war, including the right to unionize, and that convinced many workers that the labor struggles of the previous century had to be fought anew. Capitalism, it seemed to them, was as likely to regress as to reform. Labor strikes across Europe and America prompted a broad array of legal and extralegal crackdowns by Western governments.

Concern about the "Red Menace" was especially strong in the United States, where fears of Bolshevism reached near-panic levels. In 1919 alone came the Seattle General Strike, the Boston Police Strike, the Pennsylvania Steelworkers' Strike, and the United Mineworkers' Strike. It is easy to see why Western civilization courses placed such emphasis on the rise of modern democracy and the strength of economic liberalism. They displayed a special fascination with the American and French Revolutions, as twin birthplaces of freedom, and they focused on capitalism's self-correcting powers, as guarantors of prosperity and justice. The pure "Western tradition," they argued, still represented humankind's best hope as long as it was allowed to work.

A renewed passion for history also characterized Arab society. While Arab chroniclers and memoirists had always been numerous,

Worker's Paradise   Bernard Shaw's faith in human nature was bitterly shaken by World War I, and in the mid 1920s he lost faith in democracy and drifted into admiration for strong leaders. An early enthusiast for Mussolini, he visited Russia in 1931 and returned full of enthusiasm for Stalin.

and some had earned a wide readership, no Arab historian of any note had emerged since Ibn Khaldun in the 14th century. The breakup of the Ottoman world, however, coupled with the surging nationalism of the ethnic Arabs seeking independence, inspired an energetic new wave of historical writing. Most of these works say more about the time in which they were written than about the eras they ostensibly discuss, though, since they tend to view earlier ages through the prism of 19th-century imperialism and colonialism. The medieval Crusades, for example, had been regarded for centuries in the Muslim world as a series of bitter but local frontier wars of relatively minor importance. No full-length Arab-language history of the Crusades, in fact, had ever even been written; the wars for the Holy Land had always taken a backseat to the conflicts that really mattered—those between the Arabs and the Turks, between the Arabs and the Persians, and between the Arabs, Persians, and Turks combined against the Mongols. In the aftermath of 19th-century imperialism and global conflict, however, Arab writers reinterpreted the Crusades dramatically. Suddenly these frontier skirmishes stood out as the first of Western Christianity's war upon Islam, the start of a determined crime spree to strangle Islam in its crib and seize control of the Arab lands.

PARCELING OUT NATIONS

President Woodrow Wilson had arrived at the Paris Peace Conference with an outline of how to structure the peace settlement and lay the foundations for postwar rebuilding. But the plan, known as the **Fourteen Points**, quickly proved unworkable. So, it soon proved, did Europe's economy.

Wilson's main ideas—apart from preserving free movement on the seas and free trade between countries—were to redraw Europe's political boundaries. After the collapse of the Habsburg, Ottoman, and Romanov Empires, he sought to recognize the ethnic and nationalist aspirations of the peoples in central and eastern Europe. He also hoped to create an international **League of Nations** that would arbitrate disputes, oversee demilitarization, and provide for collective security. But creating new borders faced two difficulties. First, the movement of peoples in the preceding hundred years made it impossible to establish countries without ethnic minorities. Europe's populace was now intermixed (see Map 25.1). Second, political rivalries between the dominant nations frustrated efforts to build stable new countries. The contours of Poland, for example, resulted from a desire to establish a buffer zone between Russia and Germany. Byelorussian, German, Jewish, and Ukrainian minorities made up at least a third of the new country's population, and no fewer than twenty-five political parties formed, each with a different constituency and a different vision of Poland's future. Similar problems confronted the newly created Bulgaria, Czechoslovakia, Hungary,

MAP 25.1   Ethnic Minorities in East-Central Europe, 1930

Romania, and Yugoslavia. Compounding their problems, the new states of eastern Europe were industrially undeveloped. Anywhere between 60 and 80 percent of their populations was still engaged in primitive farming.

Many of the same problems existed outside of Europe. The League of Nations had parceled out the former Ottoman Empire to Britain and France, since it judged the Middle East to be unready to stand on its own. Britain took control of Iraq, Palestine, and Transjordan, while France was given Lebanon and Syria. Britain also oversaw Arabia, Egypt, and Iran. The creation of these not-quite independent states, or **mandates**, outraged their inhabitants. Not only did they violate promises made by the Allies during the war, they seemed simply to substitute one form of foreign imperialism for another. Moreover, the Western powers took little notice of local conditions, including culture and religion. The Turks had at least understood the difference between Shi'a and Sunnis; between ethnic Arabs, Armenians, Kurds, Palestinians, Syrians, and Turkmen; and between the various tribes. In establishing a unified British Iraq, for example, the League of Nations fused distinct territories that the Ottomans had governed as independent provinces.

Global politics and dynastic rivalries within the Arab world complicated matters. Britain, for example, had established close ties with the Hashemite clan, a prominent Arab family said to be the last direct descendants of the Prophet Muhammad, and planned to install its leader, Faisal ibn Ali, as ruler of a unified Palestine and Transjordan. The **Balfour Declaration** in 1917, however, bound Britain to support a national Jewish homeland in Palestine. Caught between opposing allegiances, Britain divided Palestine and Transjordan as autonomous units, installed Faisal as king of Iraq (r. 1921–1933), and placed Faisal's brother Abdullah ibn Hussein on the throne as ruler of Transjordan (r. 1921–1951). Meanwhile a descendant of the 19th-century tribal emir Muhammad ibn Saud emerged as the leader in Arabia itself. This was Abd al-Aziz ibn Saud (emir from 1915 and king of Arabia from 1926 to 1953).

The Palestinian Mandate roiled with tensions between the native population (mostly Palestinian Arabs, but with sizable Jewish and Christian communities) and Zionist immigrants from Europe. Thousands of Jews migrated to Palestine in the postwar years, most of them settling on lands that they had purchased from departing Turks or Palestinian landowners pursuing a better life under one of the Hashemite rulers or the Saudi dynasts; others wanted simply to get away from the British. Although these transfers were legal, it did not take long for concern to arise about Jewish "displacement" of the Palestinians. By 1922 Britain decided

White City   Ben-Yehuda Street in Tel Aviv was famous for its Bauhaus-style architecture, which was used during a construction boom in the 1930s when thousands of Jewish refugees poured into the city. The neighborhood takes its nickname from the local practice of covering the exteriors of buildings with heat-reflecting white plaster.

to slow the migration of Jews into the region, in order to appease its millions of Muslim subjects. The Arabs opposed Jewish settlement (at this stage, at least) less out of resistance to the idea of Zionism than as a cudgel with which to beat the British. These developments pleased no one and set the stage for decades of turmoil.

NEW RIGHTS AND NEW ECONOMIES

Most European countries received new constitutions or significantly revised existing ones, and the most significant revision was the extension of the vote to women. The campaigns for female suffrage had taken a backseat to the war, but calls for the vote rose anew before the ink on the peace treaty was dry. Women received the right to vote in the new Czechoslovakia in 1918, in Germany in 1919, in Austria and the United States in 1920, and in Poland in 1921. Limited rights of suffrage were introduced in Britain and Hungary in 1918 and 1925, respectively; British women received full rights in 1928. Women in France and Italy were denied the vote until 1945, however, and Switzerland rejected female suffrage until 1971. Delays were largely the fault of the Liberal parties, who warned that women would vote overwhelmingly for Conservatives.

Economic concerns dominated the postwar years. Except for the regions around the old western front, the war had left most of Europe's factories intact. These factories needed to be retooled for commercial manufacture from their wartime activities, but they did not need to be rebuilt from the ground up. Industrial production could therefore begin again as soon as capital and raw materials became available. France, for the moment, was almost entirely dependent on German reparations and American credit for capital. Britain and Belgium also relied heavily on German payments but were better prepared to relaunch their manufacturing base. A problem blocked their path, however. Republican president Warren G. Harding (1921–1923) placed high tariffs on imports in order to protect American businesses. This meant that Europeans could not sell their products and

Selling the Empire Paris hosted the International Colonial Exposition in 1931, one of the last large-scale celebrations of imperialism. This poster invites visitors to delight in the colorful costumes and quaint handcrafts of France's happy underlings.

thereby earn the money they needed to pay off their American creditors. For Britain and Belgium, it also meant a greater reliance on their colonies and Middle Eastern mandates, while Germany turned instead to trade with eastern Europe and Communist Russia.

Inflation set in as governments let their currencies depreciate in order to make their goods cheaper and more competitive. The tactic worked, to an extent, but the falling currencies made it harder for Europeans to purchase American goods—which in turn triggered concerns for U.S. growth. Instability in the markets threatened to impede economic recovery. When Germany failed to make a reparation payment to France in 1923, the French took drastic action. Fearing that its ties with Russia might enable Germany to recover its prewar economic dominance on the Continent, and worried that America and Britain never ratified the Versailles Treaty and thus were unreliable allies, the French sent an army into the Ruhr Valley. There it seized German factories and effectively held the German workers and their families for ransom, while demanding payment in full of Germany's entire reparations debt.

Germans everywhere were outraged, and the Weimar government urged Ruhr citizens to stay at home and refuse to work for the French. When talks failed to resolve the dispute, Berlin responded by wildly printing trillions of marks—and declared the reparations bill "paid" with worthless currency. Feverish hyperinflation followed.

A single U.S. dollar in January 1924 purchased four German marks; by September a dollar equaled nearly 4.5 *trillion* marks. Personal savings, life-insurance policies, bond holdings, and pensions were wiped out instantaneously. Germans who received their pay in cash found that it lost half its value by the time they reached a shop in which to spend it. In October 1923, Betty Scholem, a woman living in Berlin, wrote to her son, the famous Jewish scholar Gershom Scholem, then living in Switzerland, describing conditions:

Play Money By November of 1923 hyperinflation had made German currency worthless. At more than four trillion marks to the U.S. dollar, the money had more value as fuel for kitchen stoves and fireplaces than as currency.

Streetcar fare is twenty million marks, and tomorrow it will probably be fifty. You can't even imagine what it is like. My God, it's like witnessing a witches' Sabbath, only a million times more wicked. As you know, we sell women's magazines to [a certain friend]. A few days ago her husband sent us a cashier's check for five million marks—but when we went to the local branch of their bank, here in Berlin, to pick it up, they charged us forty million marks in transfer fees! . . . [Some other friends of ours] went out to lunch and had rabbit. It cost 1.75 *billion*.

One needed a wheelbarrow full of marks to purchase a single loaf of bread.

The United States responded to the crisis with a plan created by the director of the federal Bureau of the Budget, Charles G. Dawes—who won the Nobel Peace Prize in 1925 and became vice president under President Calvin Coolidge. This massive bailout restructured reparations—which of course had not really been paid at all—so that Germany had a chance to meet its obligation without crippling its own economic development. The currency was stabilized within a year, but the issue of reparations and the moral stain of responsibility for the war continued to rankle Germans. Even as the economy improved, voters responded to candidates who announced their determination to do something about the "guilt payments" and restore Germany's honor.

Several years of impressive growth across Europe began in 1925. With order restored to markets and the threat of new French-German hostilities removed, relief and hope filled the air. Within four years, in fact, western Europe reached its prewar levels of industrial production. Radios, telephone systems, automobiles, phonographs, tractors, motion pictures, televisions, and gas lighting were manufactured. A new era was dawning, with an infinite number of new technologies and products on the horizon. Or so it seemed to governments and private banks, which lent money for new businesses at previously unimagined rates. Entrepreneurs drew investment from all quarters. But two underlying economic problems festered. First, machines like gasoline-powered tractors and combine harvesters, together with new chemical fertilizers, made agriculture more productive than ever. But that meant that prices could easily collapse just when farmers were taking on debt to purchase the machinery. Second, the rush of investment in new technologies and manufactures left less capital for established industries. For the time being, these were potential problems only. All they needed, however, was the right jolt, or series of jolts, to become a full-blown catastrophe.

THE GREAT DEPRESSION

Not everyone shared in the economic growth of the mid-1920s. In the United States, which was by then the largest and most influential economy in the world, the top 5 percent of the population received nearly 35 percent of all income, while 70 percent of the nation lived in or near poverty. Disparities in total wealth were even more lopsided. In Europe, matters varied from country to country. France, for example, had traditionally championed small and medium-sized companies over large firms, and so it was less at risk from stock-market fluctuations. Britain, too, had a less inequitable concentration of wealth than the United States, because it had had an income tax since 1798. Germany did not yet have one, since the Kaiser had preferred to fund the Great War on debt, fearing that a tax on wealth would anger the wealthy.

The web of debt nevertheless ensnared every Western country: governments owed other governments, banks owed other banks, and companies owed other companies. And the web grew more dangerous as people became more hopeful for the future. With so many exciting new products, people felt that the potential for riches was almost limitless. Urged on by zealous stockbrokers, they were therefore willing to invest their entire savings—and to borrow more in order to invest. For a while, all that cash did prompt growth; but rising stock prices quickly turned into a bubble, and when the bubble burst, stocks and bonds lost value, and credit dried up.

On Black Tuesday, October 29, 1929, on the New York Stock Exchange, prices tumbled. It was the beginning of the **Great Depression**. Banks and companies failed by the tens of thousands, throwing millions of people out of work. Farmers who had invested in new machinery only to see the agricultural prices fall could not make their loan payments and lost their farms. In order to staunch the flow of red ink, American banks all but stopped lending to Europe. This meant that credit-dependent countries like France and Germany could not purchase American goods, which in turn added to America's woes. Popular culture demonized bankers and portrayed them as incompetent, self-serving, soulless, or corrupt tricksters—or a combination of all four.[2]

The largest commercial bank in Austria came close to liquidation, which triggered a panic among European banks. Assets were frozen, which meant that depositors could not access their own savings, and lines of credit were cut off. Fearing a repeat of the miseries of the early 1920s, governments made the mistake of trying to stabilize currency rates rather than stimulating consumption and production by injecting new money into the system. Pressure placed on currencies by the Depression led most Western countries to abandon the **gold standard** (see Map 25.2). This monetary system, introduced in the West by Britain in 1821 (and adopted by the United States in 1873), pegged a currency to the price of gold, so that a British sovereign, a German mark, or an American dollar always bought the same amount of the precious metal. Since worldwide supplies of gold, and the demand for it, were relatively constant through the 19th century, currency values and exchange rates remained stable. The problem with the gold standard, though, was that gold prices alone did not reflect any given currency's actual value at any particular time: inflation and interest rates also played a part. In the run-up to World War I most Western governments needed to print money rapidly in order to cover their military costs—and this

---

[2]   Bank robbers like Pretty Boy Floyd (Charles Arthur Floyd) or Bonnie and Clyde (Bonnie Parker and Clyde Barrow) became popular-culture heroes.

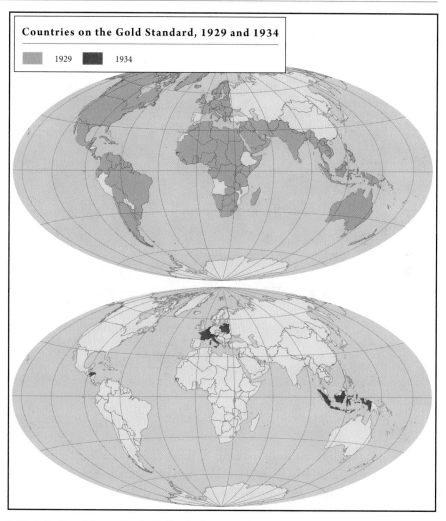

MAP 25.2   **Countries on the Gold Standard, 1929 and 1934**

forced up both interest rates and the inflation rate. The United States abandoned the gold standard in 1933.[3]

The statistics are grim. Banks failed; many of these were purchased, at bargain prices, by larger banks—which recouped their expenses by confiscating the homes, farms, and businesses of the failed banks' borrowers. Millions of Americans lost their homes, their farms, and their jobs. Unemployment reached as high as 25 percent, three years into the crisis. In Europe, the numbers were even worse. Over 40 percent of the German workforce was unemployed. In France, where

---

[3]   By 1933, in the United States alone more than five thousand banks failed.

Hunger Marchers   A series of protests against food shortages occurred throughout Britain during the Depression of the 1930s. The largest single demonstration took place in 1932. A group of three thousand protestors set out from Glasgow in Scotland, and by the time the march reached London there were as many as one hundred thousand involved. The metropolitan government summoned a police force of seventy-five thousand to break up the crowd before it could reach Parliament.

three-fourths of all farms were less than 25 acres (10 hectares) in size, farmers had no way to produce enough to meet their debt payments and often were lucky to be able to feed their families. In Poland roughly three-quarters of a million farmers lost their farms to debt.

The decline in international trade hit the shipping industry especially hard. The Dutch shipping industry declined by two-thirds in three years, while parts of coastal northern England and Scotland had unemployment rates of 90 percent or more. With tax revenues plummeting and the need for social services rising, Western governments leaned harder on their colonies. They cut salaries and wages for foreign workers, increased rents and taxes, and cut back on expenditures like road building, schools, health care, and a host of social services. Local resentments flared.

Manufacturing output declined by nearly 40 percent worldwide between 1929 and 1933. The effects were felt everywhere, but as always they were felt most stingingly among the urban and rural poor. Unemployment was particularly high among young people, those aged sixteen to twenty-six, who had little to do except sit idly in cafes and parks and nurse their resentment. Many of these made easy

TABLE 25.1   **Unemployment Rates during the Great Depression, 1929–1936**

	BRITAIN	GERMANY	SWEDEN	USA	NETHERLANDS
1929	10.4	13.1	10.7	3.2	5.9
1930	16.1	22.2	12.2	8.7	7.8
1931	21.3	33.7	17.2	15.8	14.8
1932	22.1	43.7	22.8	23.6	25.3
1933	19.9	26.3	23.7	24.9	26.9
1934	16.7	14.9	18.9	26.7	28.0
1935	15.5	11.6	16.1	20.1	31.7
1936	13.1	8.3	13.6	16.9	32.7

targets for recruiters from radical and reactionary political groups. Both Communist and Fascist parties relied on these feelings to gain followers.

THE SEARCH FOR SOMEONE TO BLAME

Ideology and its appeal are a recurring theme in fiction of the 1920s and 1930s. The German writer Thomas Mann (1875–1955) powerfully depicted this sort of seduction in two novellas; both "Disorder and Early Sorrow" (1925) and "Mario and the Magician" (1929) illustrate this bitter hopelessness. Less well known in the English-speaking world is the novelist Hans Fallada (1893–1947), whose *What Now, Little Man?* (1932), *A Wolf among Wolves* (1937), and *Iron Gustav* (1938) present the miseries of life in Depression-era Germany with unforgettable power. Fallada's books gave such a powerful description of life in the Weimar Republic that later the Nazi propaganda minister, Josef Goebbels, took an interest in using them as a way of justifying the Nazi regime; Goebbels tried to blackmail Fallada into writing an anti-Semitic and pro-Nazi novel. Fallada, who detested the Nazis and their anti-Semitism, avoided filling the request for a few years. In 1944, however, Goebbels had Fallada arrested and placed in an insane asylum until he produced. *The Drinker*, published ultimately in 1950, was instead an autobiographical work criticizing Fallada's own difficulties with drug and alcohol addiction. He died in 1947, leaving behind the manuscript of his greatest novel, *Every Man Dies Alone*, his indictment of the entire Nazi era. It was published shortly after his death.

A journey through the Congo turned André Gide (1869–1951), the French writer, against Western imperialism and led him to become, briefly but passionately, a Communist. "Communism," he wrote, "is the only promise for the salvation of mankind; I would lay down for it in an instant, to make it succeed." Membership in Britain's Communist Party (the CPGB) increased dramatically after the 1929 crash, especially in the heavily hit industrial towns and coalfields of the north and west, where local newspapers began to refer to certain locali-ties as "Little Moscows" because of their active Communist groups. Another site popularly regarded as a haven of Communism was the Jewish neighborhood in the East End, in London.

Popular and official attitudes toward Europe's Jews worsened. Jews were sin-gled out either as presumed leaders of socialist cells or as corrupt merchants and fi-nanciers. In Poland, employers were ordered to test their workers and apprentices for their knowledge of Polish—and thus to root out Yiddish-speaking Jews. The gov-ernment of Austria forced all Jewish-owned banks to close, while the government in Romania ordered Jewish companies of any sort to take on Christian partners or else forfeit their ability to obtain credit. The Greek state rescinded its contracts with Jewish businesses. In Britain, formal actions regarding Jews were confined to policy debates over Zionism and Palestine, but the tone of those debates was often ugly. According to the *Times* of London Zionist Jews were "pushing, grasping, and domi-neering," while the *Morning Post* bemoaned the fact that British citizens were being "compelled to pay for establishing a national home" for Jews. An Anglican clergyman

"The Biggest Rogue in All the Land"   As Nazi anti-Semitic racism goes, this cartoon is relatively mild. It contrasts the upright, healthy, hardworking, and noble Aryan youth with the supposedly decrepit, slovenly, money-grubbing Jew.

observed in 1920 that nearly all the British then living in Palestine were "obsessed by the notion that Zionism is incipient Bolshevism."[4]

Among the charges leveled against Jews everywhere was the rumor that they were benefiting from a crisis: birthrates across Europe fell sharply after 1929, as married couples feared they could not feed many mouths. But fewer children— who previously had worked on family farms, in factories, or in odd jobs—meant lower incomes for poor families. Some political circles saw the decline as part of the decline of the nation, and they singled out the Jews as a factor in both developments. Regarded as a race of financiers and merchants, they were blamed for economic woes everywhere, and as one of the few groups with population growth, they were seen as "taking over" society by biological means. Not everyone felt this way, of course, but complaints remained widespread throughout the Depression.

Henry Ford (1863–1947), founder of the Ford Motor Company, spoke for many when he wrote about the supposed dangers of "the International Jew" (1920) in the Michigan newspaper he owned, *The Dearborn Independent*:

> In Russia [the Jew] is charged with being the source of Bolshevism, an accusation which is serious or not, according to the circle in which it is made; we in America, hearing the fervid eloquence and perceiving the prophetic ardor of young Jewish apostles of social and industrial reform, can calmly estimate how it may be. In Germany he is charged with being the cause of the Empire's collapse and a very considerable literature has sprung up, bearing with it a mass of circumstantial evidence that gives the thinker pause. In England he is charged with being the real world ruler, who rules as a super-nation over the nations, rules by the power of gold, and who plays nation against nation for his own purposes, remaining himself discreetly in the background. In America it is pointed out to what extent the elder Jews of wealth and the younger Jews of ambition swarmed through the war organizations—principally those departments which dealt with the commercial and industrial business of war, and also the extent to which they have clung to the advantage which their experience as agents of the government gave them.
>
> In simple words, the question of the Jews has come to the fore, but like other questions which lend themselves to prejudice, efforts will be made to hush it up as impolitic for open discussion. If, however, experience has taught us anything it is that questions thus suppressed will sooner or later break out in undesirable and unprofitable forms.

---

[4] As late as 1938 the *Weekly Review* declared that the goal of Zionism "though not definitely avowed, is to secure world domination for the members of its race."

Ford's warning seems unnervingly prescient, although not in the sense he meant it:

> The Jew is the world's enigma. Poor in his masses, he yet controls the world's finances. Scattered abroad without country or government, he yet presents a unity of race continuity which no other people has achieved. Living under legal disabilities in almost every land, he has become the power behind many a throne. There are ancient prophecies to the effect that the Jew will return to his own land and from that center rule the world, though not until he has undergone an assault by the united nations of mankind.

The agonies of the Depression, in sum, added to concerns for Western decline left over from the war. A new generation, raised to believe in the unique injustice of their suffering, came of age determined to rescue their honor as well as their livelihoods. And they were willing to take desperate action.

A new generation, raised to believe in the unique injustice of their suffering, came of age determined to rescue their honor as well as their livelihoods. And they were willing to take desperate action.

MODERNISM, EXPERIMENT, AND TRAUMA

The war, the wretched peace treaty, a revolution and a civil war, the Red Menace, the Ruhr Valley disaster, hyperinflation, the Depression—all these traumas strengthened modernism in the arts, which now seemed prophetic (see chapter 23). The Irish poet William Butler Yeats (1865–1939) summed up the atmosphere in "The Second Coming" (1920):

> Things fall apart; the centre cannot hold;
>   Mere anarchy is loosed upon the world,
> The blood-dimmed tide is loosed, and everywhere
>   The ceremony of innocence is drowned;
> The best lack all conviction, while the worst
>   Are full of passionate intensity.

The proud confidence of the imperial age had given way to anxious doubt. Without a fixed center, life's only point of reference becomes the personal, but individual weaknesses and quirks leave its viewpoint uncertain. Still, if our consciousness is all we have, we would be wise to investigate it. Interwar modernism did precisely that, in complex, enduring art characterized by innovations and experiment.

This second generation of modernists was born after 1880 and therefore reached intellectual and artistic maturity during or after the war. For them, Freud's theories about human nature being driven by forces we imperfectly control resonated loudly. These impulses for creation and destruction, Eros and Thanatos (death), helped shape the literary and artistic culture of the 1920s and 1930s.

Paul Valéry, the French Symbolist poet and essayist, described the crisis of his generation in 1919 as "A Crisis of the Mind":

> No one can say what [ideas or values] will be alive or dead tomorrow, whether in literature, philosophy, or art; no one knows what ideas or forms of expression will be inscribed on [our culture's] casualty list, or what new things will take their place. Hope remains, of course.... but Hope is merely what we call the mistrust of what is obvious to any mind that thinks.... The facts are clear and pitiless: thousands of young writers and artists have died; the dream of a united European culture is lost; knowledge has been shown to be unable to save anyone or anything; science is gravely wounded, and what we might call its moral ambitions are shamed by the brutal applications to which we put it. Idealism barely survives,... realism lies hopeless and defeated,... faith has lost its way,... even the skeptics have lost their doubts,... and there is no one left who is the master of his own thoughts.

Valéry's gloom was characteristic of the postwar movement. The modernists, for all their playfulness, produced little work that can be called comic. Art's break with the past, combined with a loss of enthusiasm for the future, led to a fascination with the present moment. Literature kept returning to the inner thoughts of actors and viewers as they struggle, usually in vain, to free themselves from the horrors of the world.

A high point in modernism occurred in 1922, when three artistic masterpieces appeared: the novel *Ulysses*, by James Joyce (1882–1941), the poem "The Waste Land," by T. S. Eliot (1888–1965), and the film *Nosferatu*, by Friedrich W. Murnau (1888–1931). *Ulysses* depicts the events of a single crucial day in the life of Leopold Bloom, an assimilated Irish Jew living in Dublin. He visits the post office, attends the funeral of a friend, stops in the National Library, attends to a business errand, eats lunch, walks along the beach, and visits a friend who is giving birth in a hospital. Along the way Bloom encounters a young aspiring writer named Stephen Dedalus, with whom he forms an unexpectedly close bond. They drink together in a pub; Bloom then follows a drunken Stephen into a brothel in order to watch over him, and helps him after Stephen gets into a scuffle with a policeman. After he and Stephen part, Bloom returns home to his wife, Molly, who has spent the afternoon with her lover, and collapses into bed. A magnificent long stream-of-consciousness monologue by Molly closes the novel.

Joyce narrates this day with a riot of innovations. Patterned on Homer's epic *The Odyssey*, the novel presents Bloom as a modern-day Odysseus (Ulysses in Latin), with Stephen as his son Telemachus, and the unfaithful Molly as his ever-faithful wife, Penelope. Each chapter employs a different style and a new set of motifs and imagery. One chapter—the visit to the brothel—is written as a play, complete with stage directions. It enacts not only the two men's activities but also their thoughts and fears. Another section appears in the dry question-and-answer form of a Catholic catechism. A third episode shatters the narrative into nineteen vignettes of minor characters, who function as a chorus commenting on the main action. Yet *Ulysses* tells a traditional, or indeed mythical, tale of middle-aged loss, sadness, and longing. Stephen, Bloom's symbolic spiritual son, is a frustrated artist

James Joyce The greatest of the Modernist literary artists, Joyce was denigrated by many of his more elitist peers as a mere commoner trying to mingle with his betters. Virginia Woolf admired aspects of Joyce's talent but decided in the end that his work was too filled with low, tawdry realities. His novel *Ulysses* is "an illiterate, underbred book it seems to me," she sniffed; "the book of a self-taught working man, [and] we all know how distressing they are, how egotistic, insistent, raw, striking, [and] ultimately nauseating."

who rails against the political and religious bonds that shackle Irish society.[5] Molly, meanwhile, reawakened to sexuality after her afternoon love affair, meditates on the role that love and loneliness have played in her life. She claims in her soliloquy that she and Leopold have not had intercourse in a decade, but she resolves to tell Bloom in the morning about her infidelity and to renew their marriage.

Ulysses is a virtuoso performance and, for many, the supreme modernist novel. Its technical experimentations are not merely vehicles for displaying Joyce's talent; they are part of the point. The realist novel is dead, *Ulysses* proclaims. It is dead not only because nothing new can be done in that genre but because there is no reality to portray outside the perspectives of each individual character. Even those perspectives, however, cannot be fully trusted. Stephen and Leopold's states of mind are continually interrupted by impulses, hallucinations, visions, and suppressed memories; Molly's musings on the decade-long absence of sex in her marriage (a consequence of the trauma of their son's death) may just as

---

[5] For Stephen in *Ulysses*, "History is a nightmare from which I am trying to awake."

likely be self-delusion as self-confession, a way of justifying to herself her infidelity. One cannot be sure. And that is one of the book's many hidden revelations.

Following hard on *Ulysses*'s footsteps was T. S. Eliot's "The Waste Land." Like many of Eliot's poems, it was composed in fragments over the course of many months and possibly several years. Shifting between different voices, multiple situations, and abrupt jumps in time, it is filled with obscure literary, historical, and mythical allusions. The poem makes for difficult reading, and its overall effect is of collage.

> The realist novel is dead, *Ulysses* proclaims. It is dead not only because nothing new can be done in that genre but because there is no reality to portray outside the perspectives of each individual character.

> April is the cruelest month, breeding
> Lilacs out of the dead land, mixing
> Memory and desire, stirring
> Dull roots with spring rain.
> Winter kept us warm, covering
> Earth in forgetful snow, feeding
> A little life with dried tubers.
> Summer surprised us, coming over the Starnbergersee
> With a shower of rain; we stopped in the colonnade,
> And went on in sunlight, into the Hofgarten,
> And drank coffee, and talked for an hour.
> Bin gar keine Russin, stamm' aus Litauen, echt deutsch.
> And when we were children, staying at the archduke's,
> My cousin's, he took me out on a sled,
> And I was frightened. He said, Marie,
> Marie, hold on tight. And down we went.
> In the mountains, there you feel free.
> I read, much of the night, and go south in the winter.

Imagine a vast museum filled with all the treasures of Western art, literature, and music. Imagine video clips of all the major historical events, plus newspapers, music hall songs, excerpts of autobiographies, and recordings of burlesque performances. "The Waste Land" is what you might have if you picked through the ruins of such a museum after a catastrophic explosion and fire—shards of memories, bits of newsprint, fragments of sculptures, scraps of painted canvas, torn pages from volumes of verse. After the wreck of civilization, the poem suggests, the artist must piece together his own set of references and touchstones, to create his own ordering of the world. The reader does not "understand" the poem in the traditional way, since no one can recognize without help the origins of all the bits of charred ruin, but one knows that a catastrophe has occurred and that the museum will never again exist as it once did. Even the jumble of oddments, though, stirs deep emotions. Reading "The Waste Land" is astonishing. How can something that seems at first to make so little sense have such overwhelming power?

Nosferatu, also released in 1922, revises the legend of the vampire Dracula as it had been popularized in the 1897 novel by Bram Stoker. The film relocates the story from Stoker's contemporary England to a fictional Baltic port city in northern Germany in the 1830s. A representative of a German manufacturing firm is sent to Transylvania to meet with a new client, one Count Orlok, who of course turns out to be a vampire. He attacks the businessman in his sleep but does not kill him, as he usually does with his victims. Why? The businessman had shown Orlok a portrait of his wife back in Germany, and the vampire is smitten. He follows the businessman back to Germany and purchases the house directly across the street from the happy couple—all the while planning his attack and satisfying his bloodlust by kill-

Count Orlok The role of Count Orlok, the vampire in *Nosferatu* (1922), was played by Max Schreck (1879–1936). A favorite of playwright Berthold Brecht's, Schreck spent most of his career in theater, but he also appeared in a silent film version of Shakespeare's *Merchant of Venice* (1923).

ing dozens of other innocents. The wife, suspicious of her new neighbor, realizes what Orlok is when she reads a book on vampires. It informs her that the only way to kill a vampire is for a virtuous woman to offer herself to him as a sacrifice. One night she does so, for the sake of humanity, and Orlok, in his orgiastic enjoyment of her blood, fails to notice the rising of the sun. It vaporizes him.

Visually stunning, the film can still enthrall. Its distorted physical sets, unnatural lighting (white trees against a black sky, for instance), and oblique camera angles give it an unsettling awkwardness. These mirror and heighten the psychological discomfort felt by the film's protagonists but also by its viewers. As with *Ulysses* and "The Waste Land," the formal technique not only propels the story but is an intrinsic element of it. Orlok represents the unfulfilled human soul, condemned to an existence it did not choose and in pursuit only of its own desire. What it desires most is what will kill it. The Freudian echoes may or may not be intentional on the filmmakers' part. Either way, the film shows how much the interwar modernist movement had absorbed Freud's theories and made them its own. Orlok neither understands nor controls his impulse to bloodlust. On his first evening with the businessman in Transylvania, he nearly gives the game away when he leaps out of his chair to lick the blood when his guest accidentally cuts his hand while slicing bread. When the man's wife willingly submits to the vampire's attack, she sets the scene for Orlok's rapturous acquisition of both Eros and Thanatos.

Nosferatu is in large part an allegory of the rise of modern capitalist Germany, a society expanding its borders and pursuing its dream of wealth. It is the Germany that marched headlong into the Great War.

The fact that the film relocates the novel's setting to northern Germany in the 1830s is significant. The fictional city is an amalgam of two Hanseatic port cities that were vital to German trade. Germany in the 1830s had just established the Customs' Union (*Zollverein*), which presaged the German Empire under Bismarck. The seed of industrial capitalism, in other words, had just been planted. *Nosferatu* is in large part an allegory of the rise of modern capitalist Germany, a society expanding its borders and pursuing its dream of wealth. It is the Germany that marched headlong into the Great War.

These masterpieces aside, the second wave of modernism proved to be more varied, inclusive, and popular than the first. The most visible change was the prominence of women writers and artists among the avant-garde. Freed from the struggle for the right to vote, women emerged as important figures in modernist cultural life. Among all women modernists, however, pride of place belongs to Virginia Woolf (1882–1941), one of the 20th century's greatest writers.

Woolf was born into a prominent and famously complicated family; privately educated, she grew up in an atmosphere of extraordinary intellectual stimulation.[6] The death of her mother in 1895, when she was thirteen, was the first great emotional shock in Virginia's life and triggered an inward turn in her consciousness and behavior. The death of her father in 1904 resulted in a full-blown nervous breakdown; she recovered gradually but spent the rest of her life on the

---

6   Woolf's father, Sir Leslie Stephen (1832–1904), a well-regarded author and journalist, was the chief editor of the *Dictionary of National Biography*.

TABLE 25.2   **Women in Modernist Cultural Life**

Editors, Publishers, Critics	Painters and Sculptors
Sylvia Beach (1887–1962)	Camille Claudel (1864–1943)
Adrienne Monnier (1892–1955)	Natalia Goncharova (1881–1962)
Rebecca West (1892–1983)	Georgia O'Keefe (1887–1986)
Poets	**Short–story Writers**
H.D. (Hilda Doolittle, 1886–1961)	Katherine Mansfield (1888–1923)
Marianne Moore (1887–1972)	
Novelists	**Composers**
Djuna Barnes (1892–1982)	Alma Mahler (1879–1964)
Ivy Compton-Burnett (1884–1969)	Nadia Boulanger (1887–1979)
Edith Södergran (1892–1923)	Germaine Tailleferre (1892–1983)
Virginia Woolf (1882–1941)	Lili Boulanger (1893–1918)

edge of mental instability. She attempted suicide at least once, in 1913. She killed herself in 1941, when World War II and a resurgence of manic depression made her fear losing her mind once and for all.

Woolf's greatness as a novelist lay in her unique combination of technical virtuosity and intense emotion. Starting with her third novel, *Jacob's Room* (1922), and through to her two masterworks *Mrs. Dalloway* (1925) and *To the Lighthouse* (1927), she employs stream-of-consciousness monologues, unpredictable shifts in time and perspective, unreliable narrators, and at times a complete absence of plot. In this way, she focuses instead on the inner lives and intricate, unspoken bonds between her characters. Very little ever "happens" in a Woolf novel. The plot of *Mrs. Dalloway* consists simply of the preparations over a single day, in an upper-middle-class London family, for a dinner party that evening. Yet Woolf captures an astonishing range of emotions, impressions, memories, and longings among various family members. And these inchoate threads of feeling intertwine in intricate patterns. Few novels depict such emotional richness so quietly and yet so successfully.

Virginia Woolf One of the great writers of the 20th century, Woolf had produced most of her best writing before the start of the Great Depression: *Jacob's Room*(1922), *Mrs. Dalloway* (1925), *To the Lighthouse* (1927), among her novels, and *The Common Reader*(1925) and *A Room of One's Own* (1929) among her non-fiction.

Yet Woolf's novels can leave the reader with a feeling of incompleteness. Emotional life ends only when life itself ends, and the close of each Woolf novel does not feel like an ending at all. The same characters will awaken the next morning, and their inner maelstroms of sensation, regret, delight, and doubt will begin all over again. That, of course, is part of the modernist point: we are *beyond* ideas, plans, beliefs, and convictions. Life is by definition aimless, since no one can be certain of the target at which we should aim. Woolf skillfully depicts the emotionally corrosive effects of prejudice against women, but nowhere does she propose a specific idea of how to combat it. Woolf occasionally allowed her name to be added to petitions and helped her husband, Leonard Woolf, with some of his correspondence in his own political career. Otherwise, her political activities extended no further than conversation among her writer friends. Despite her professed admiration for the suffragists and the urgency of the political issues of the 1920s and 1930s, there is no evidence that she ever bothered to cast a vote in any election.

> The generation that came of age during those horrendous times, however, felt modernism's creative aimlessness and self-exploration to resonate profoundly with their own aching uncertainty.

But then neither did Joyce nor Eliot. Second-generation modernism emphasized the unfixed, shifting nature of reality. They viewed most systems of belief and intellectual constructs with ironic detachment. Before the Great War and the Great Depression, modernism found few avid supporters and was at best an interesting marginal culture phenomenon. The generation that came of age during those horrendous times, however, felt modernism's creative aimlessness and self-exploration to resonate profoundly with their own aching uncertainty.

THE RISE OF FASCISM: ITALY AND SPAIN

Fascism is the cult of power—the belief that force, directly applied to achieve a specific end, is the best form of government. Of course, all governments are in the business of reining in the actions of the people they govern; governments place limits on our daily activities, our business dealings, the ways in which we pass estates on to our heirs, the substances we are permitted to eat, drink, smoke, or inject, the people we are allowed to marry. We agree to controls on our personal freedom in return for the stability and order of communal life. But *control* implies *force*, and no government can long survive without possessing the ability to make the populace feel its sting. Good government therefore consists of knowing the right amount of force to apply, and when, and towards what end.

For an astonishing number of Europeans in the 1930s the best form of government, and perhaps the only form of government possible, considering the enormity of the West's troubles, was one in which the state abandoned any pretence of moderation, shared authority, or the consent of the governed and simply assumed the direct, open, and unchallenged exercise of its own will. This was *Fascism*—a word that derives from the name of one of the ancient symbols of

Roman power, the *fasces*: a long, tightly bound bundle of birch rods, from which the blade of a battle-ax emerges toward the upper end. It was not a weapon but the symbol of one.[7]

——————— ✦ ———————

As an ideology, Fascism differed in several ways from earlier forms of authoritarian government like royal absolutism, although the differences probably did not matter much to its victims; prisoners getting their faces crushed against stone walls have other things on their minds. Absolutism had been founded on the simple conviction that *someone* had to exert absolute external control on society; the absolute control mattered more than the identity of the person wielding it. Neither did it matter, in theory at least, what the absolute ruler did with that power: whatever the ruler wanted to do was the right thing to do.

In Fascism, however, the identity of the dictator was everything, for Fascism embraced the Romantic notion of the collective soul of a national group—the mystical shared spirit (or *genius*, in the 19th-century sense of the term) of a people that expressed their deepest needs and longings. As the living embodiment of that spirit the Fascist leader knew—in his blood and sinews as much as in his mind—what his people desired, needed, hoped for, and feared, and for that reason his actions *were* the nation's actions. He did not impose his will on the people, as in absolutism, but rather expressed their will—and the more forcibly, the better. Fascist leaders emphasized their mystical connection with the nation and presented their rule as the organic expression of the general will.

> Fascist leaders emphasized their mystical connection with the nation and presented their rule as the organic expression of the general will.

Italy's Benito Mussolini (r. 1922–1943) was Europe's first Fascist leader, coming to power after he and a large band of his followers staged a "March on Rome" in opposition to the rise of socialist parties across Italy. The war had displaced millions of Italian farmers and laborers, many of whom felt drawn to radical socialist and Communist parties in the immediate postwar years; nationwide strikes became common and threatened to cripple the already-damaged economy. The Fascists had their origins in those war veterans who were proud of their service and felt that the radical elements in society were undermining the Italian way of life. Mussolini, after a youthful involvement in socialist politics,

———

[7]   Carried by the bodyguards of Roman magistrates, the fasces represented the republic's authority over its citizens and the notion of strength through unity.

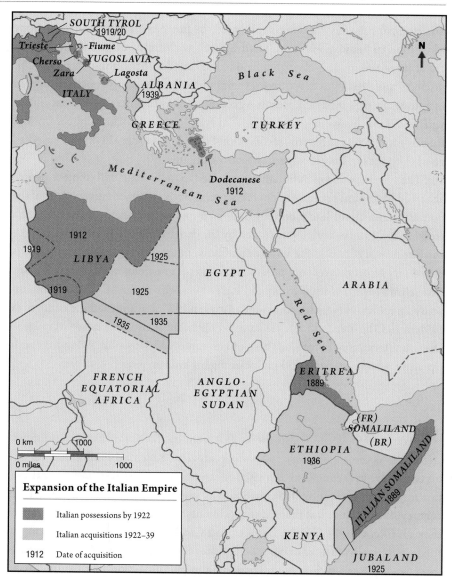

MAP 25.3   Expansion of the Italian Empire, 1922–1939

drew many leaders of his new party from the special-forces units that had fought in the Alps. In 1922, after the threat of yet another general strike, the Fascists marched on Rome by the thousands, determined to take over the government if it was not handed over to them voluntarily. The king chose not to resist and received Mussolini, appointing him the leader of the new government.

Mussolini ran Italy with a combination of terror and traditionalism. Using his special corps of thuggish loyalists, the Blackshirts, he crushed all political dissent, broke the labor unions, suppressed the free press, and brutalized anyone who stood in his way. He ingratiated himself with Italy's economic and aristocratic elites and made it clear that he would gladly leave them in control of their property and privileges in return for their political support. Most of them agreed, including the papacy. The **Lateran Agreement** of 1929 officially recognized the Vatican City as a sovereign nation within Italy—indeed within the confines of Rome—and in return for this recognition Pope Pius XI (r. 1922–1939) urged all good Catholics in Italy to support his government.

The Fascist brand of nationalism appealed to many Italians, but more people accepted Mussolini's regime out of fear of retaliation, or out of a greater fear of the political alternatives like Communism, than out of true enthusiasm. Although workers' rights were severely curtailed by the disbanding of labor unions and the close relations between the government and industrial leadership, the Fascists' enormous expenditures on public works kept unemployment relatively low. Mussolini's determination to expand Italy's authority in the Mediterranean also proved popular. He sent his forces into Libya in 1923 and annexed the country in 1931; in 1935 he invaded Ethiopia, and in 1939 he invaded Albania (see Map 25.3). Despite international protests, these moves improved Mussolini's standing with the army, which was central to maintaining his hold on power.

Military support was also the key element in the rise of Francisco Franco (1892–1975), the leader of Fascist Spain. A career military man, Franco had worked his way through the ranks and in 1920 became Spain's youngest-ever general. Nationalist sentiments ran as strong in Spain as anywhere else in Europe in the 19th century; the problem was that those sentiments were regional and divisive rather than uniting. Groups like the Basques and Catalans regarded themselves as autonomous nations instead of parts of a greater Spain. They sought independence from Madrid, not union with it. Passionate in his conviction that Communism represented the greatest evil of the modern era, Franco believed in monarchy, the Catholic Church, and Spanish (by which he meant Castilian) cultural tradition—and he was determined to eliminate everything that threatened them.

Spain had endured two bloody but inconsequential civil wars (1833–1840 and 1872–1876) that left it with a weak constitutional monarchy and a deeply divided parliament. Industrialization and the loss of Spain's last colonies (Cuba, Guam, the Philippines, and Puerto Rico) to the United States in the Spanish-American War of 1898 had added new strains to the situation, causing Spain to enter the 20th century with even stronger centripetal momentum than in the 19th. Officially neutral in World War I, the government in Madrid had made an ill-fated attempt to conquer Morocco as a salve to wounded pride. In 1923 the army, under the command of a liberal general named Miguel Primo de Rivera, had staged a coup and tried to institute republican reform. This new regime recognized the rights of workers to form unions and admitted moderate socialist parties to the political process. But these concessions had triggered a conservative backlash by Spain's landowning elite and industrial leaders, and in 1930 Primo de Rivera was forced to resign, which opened the door to yet another civil war—and the rise to power of the Fascists.

The **Spanish Civil War** of 1936–1939 began after a six-year experiment with a republican form of government that aggressively pursued a liberal agenda. Franco quickly emerged as the champion of conservative interests. The bulk of the army sided with Franco, while most of the naval and air forces supported the Republicans, which turned the war into a struggle between the inland plains on the one hand and the coastal perimeter on the other. The war drew the attention of anti-Fascist groups across Europe, and tens of thousands of volunteers from Britain, France, the United States, and elsewhere joined the Republicans. So too did a small but highly influential contingent of officers and airmen from the Soviet Union, whose involvement helped to radicalize many of the Republican fighters—a trend that only added urgency to the Fascist cause. The bitterness of the struggle intensified the political divisions: the liberals became increasingly revolutionary, while the conservatives grew increasingly reactionary.

Witness the description of Barcelona in George Orwell's *Homage to Catalonia* (1938):

> Practically every building of any size had been seized by the workers and was draped with red flags or with the red and black flag of the Anarchists; every wall was scrawled with the hammer and sickle and with the initials of the revolutionary parties; almost every church had been gutted and its images burnt. Churches here and there were being systematically demolished by gangs of workmen. Every shop and cafe had an inscription saying that it had been collectivized; even the bootblacks had been collectivized and their boxes painted red and black. Waiters and shop-walkers looked you in the face and treated you as an equal. Servile and even ceremonial forms of speech had temporarily disappeared. Nobody said *Señor* or *Don* or even *Usted*; everyone called everyone else "Comrade" or "Thou," and said *Salud!* instead of *Buenos dias*. Tipping had been forbidden by law since the time of Primo de Rivera; almost my first experience was receiving a lecture from a hotel manager for trying to tip a lift-boy. There were no private motor-cars, they had all been commandeered, and the trams and taxis and much of the other transport were painted red and black. The revolutionary posters were everywhere, flaming from the walls in clean reds and blues that made the few remaining advertisements look like daubs of mud. Down the

The Horror of War   The bombing of a small Basque town in 1937 (by Nazi and Italian Fascist airplanes, acting on behalf of the Nationalist forces led by Francisco Franco) inspired Pablo Picasso to paint his great mural *Guernica*, which he exhibited at the World's Fair in Paris of that year. Using a gloomy black, gray, and white palette, he layered images of horror on top of each other in the center of the scene (note the human skull and the attacking bull located inside the image of the shrieking horse), which he counter-balanced with images of dismemberment along the base and figures of women in pain and despair at either side. Even after a lifetime of seeing reproductions of the painting in books, to stand before the original painting, now housed permanently at the Museo Nacional Centro de Arte Reina Sofia in Madrid, is an unforgettable experience.

Ramblas, the wide central artery of the town where crowds of people streamed constantly to and fro, the loud-speakers were bellowing revolutionary songs all day and far into the night.

The war ended on April 1, 1939, with a decisive Fascist victory. More than half a million people had perished in the fighting, and in the years that followed many tens of thousands more disappeared in retaliatory attacks by the Fascists against their political enemies. The new regime outlawed all competing political parties and imposed strict censorship of the media and school curricula. It mandated the use of Castilian Spanish, promoted conservative Catholicism, and built a network of concentration camps where criminals and political enemies were imprisoned, tortured, and killed.

NAZISM IN GERMANY

The Weimar government was all but powerless in the face of Fascism's rise in Germany. The Nazi Party, formally the National Socialist Party, was in fact only one of many extremist factions that had formed throughout Europe almost immediately after the signing of the Versailles Treaty. Nor was its extremism limited to Fascism. Under Josef Stalin, Communism in Russia became a brutal means of social control.

Adolf Hitler (1889–1945) joined the Nazis in 1919 (he was the fifty-fifth member) and took control of the party in 1921. In November 1923 Hitler and his followers attempted a coup in Munich that they hoped would provide a springboard to seizing power in Berlin—an uprising they thought would mimic Mussolini's March on Rome. The effort collapsed immediately, but a sympathetic judge sentenced Hitler to a mere nine months in prison. He emerged from his cell with a bulky manuscript that he soon published: *Mein Kampf* ("My Struggle"), published in two volumes (1925–1926). The book is odious, rambling, and filled with venom. But whatever personal demons haunted Hitler's mind, his book resonated with the bruised and embittered egos of many Germans.

Mein Kampf devotes most of its pages to a theory of the superiority of the German race, on the basis of which it promotes two strategic goals. The first goal was **Lebensraum**—"living space," literally. By this term Hitler meant not just the return of ethnically German territories carved away from the nation by the Versailles Treaty; he also meant the right of Germany to expand into eastern Europe and the Balkans at the expense of the inferior Slavic peoples who resided there. His second goal was to promote an organic, classless, national community of the Germanic people. It would unite them in spirit and blood and would express its spiritual unity in Nazism and its leader. It insisted that the spiritual purity of the German "folk" (*Volk*) could be achieved only by removing from its midst the polluting presence of Communists, homosexuals, the physically and mentally handicapped, and above all the Jews.

Amid the desperate conditions of postwar Germany, Hitler appealed to ever growing numbers of disaffected and resentful Germans. His skill as a speaker and the brilliance of his propaganda director, Josef Goebbels (1897–1945), made Hitler's political rise seem unstoppable. The impact of the Great Depression provided the last boost needed to bring the Nazis to power. In the national elections of 1928, the Nazis were still a minor, though growing, power; in the next election cycle of 1930 (one year after the onset of the Depression), they became the second largest party in Germany.

My Space   After sending in their troops into Poland in 1939, the Nazis were quick to reorganize the administration of their new territories and to resettle the land with ethnic Germans. The new administrative districts were called "Reichsgaue"—an intentionally archaic-sounding term in German intended to promote the (false) notion of a Germanic historical claim to the land. Here a healthy (and suspiciously tidy-looking) young German tries to look as though she is as connected to the Polish soil as the crops she is pretending to care for.

From this point, the Nazis quickly turned to the use of violence, blackmail, and intimidation in order to strengthen their hand. Hitler purged the party of any possible rivals to his personal rule. The personality cult of "the Leader" (*der Führer*) promoted by Goebbels grew in intensity, and the desire to cleanse Germany of moral guilt for World War I intensified too. Finally, in January 1933, after a new round of elections, the Nazis emerged as victors, and Hitler won appointment as chancellor of the nation. In September he delivered a speech that summarizes the Nazi view of politics and German history:

> In 1919 when the Nazi Party came into existence in order to replace the Marxist-democratic republic with a new nation, the very idea seemed hopeless and foolish—especially to those pseudo-intellectuals who, with their shallow understanding of history, looked upon us with a simpering and pitying smile. Most of them knew that our nation was about to fall upon evil times, because they recognized that the men in charge of the November Republic were both too evil and too inept to lead our great nation. What they did *not* know, however, was that our party would *never* fall victim to the ideas and sentiments that caused *them* to run from the attacks of Marxism for the last fifty years. . . . We were ready from the start for the long and difficult struggle to build up a party that would destroy Marxism. . . . The former leaders, the bourgeois leaders, of society talked endlessly of "quiet progress" . . . while we held hundreds and thousands of demonstrations. . . . They blathered about democracy, but kept away from the people. National Socialism, on the other hand, talked about authority, but engaged with the people, wrestled with the people, as no movement in German history had ever done. . . .
>
> As the sole legitimate possessor of state power, our party understands that it is responsible for the entire course of German history. . . . We may reject the principles of democracy and parliamentary government, but we passionately believe in the peoples' right to govern themselves. Parliaments, we insist, do not express the will of the masses, but actually pervert and violate that will. The will of the people finds its only true and effective expression in its most gifted leaders. . . . Power and its ruthless application can accomplish much.

The appeal of such a message was deep, for it offered a chance to rewrite history as well as to chart a new future. And the people of Germany desperately desired to do both.

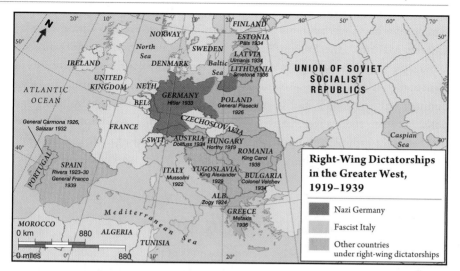

MAP 25.4 Right-Wing Dictatorships in the Greater West, 1919–1939.

Fascism's appeal was wide-reaching (see Map 25.4). Austria had at least two Fascist parties of note—the Fatherland Front and the Home Defense Force; Belgium's Rexist Party grew large enough to hold one-tenth of the seats in the national parliament; Britain had fifty thousand members in its Fascist Union, led by Oswald Mosley. In Croatia the Fascist Insurrection Party was led by the loathsome Ante Pavelic, and in Finland the Lapua Party of Vihtori Kohsola nearly seized power in a coup in 1932, while Ioannis Metaxis presided over Greece's Fascist Party of Free Believers and in Hungary Ferenc Szálasi led the Arrow/Cross Party. The National Union Party, under its leader Vidkun Quisling, came briefly to power in Norway, while Portugal's Fascist group was under the leadership of António Oliveira de Salazar. Poland's Fascist Falanga Party (deriving its name from the ancient Greek phalanx) and its leader Bolesław Piasecki spouted torrents of anti-Semitic bile that rivaled anything uttered by Hitler. Corneliu Codreanu was the charismatic, anti-Semitic head of Romania's leading Fascist party, known primarily as the Iron Guard but occasionally using the names Everything for the Fatherland, the League of Christian Defense, and the Legion of the Archangel Michael.

Even France itself felt the tug towards Fascism, producing as it did an abundance of extremist parties: the Cross of Fire (led by François de la Rocque)

> In all of these countries, Fascism appealed to two very distinct groups: the poor, who wanted retribution against real and perceived enemies, and the industrial and financial elites, who craved social and economic stability.

which may have had as many as a million members, French Action (led by Charles Maurras), the French Popular Party (under Jacques Doriot), French Solidarity (headed by Jean Renaud), and the Young Patriots (led by Pierre Taittinger). It may be the case, in fact, that France avoided becoming a Fascist country only because it had so many Fascist parties, which kept splitting the votes between themselves. In all of these countries, Fascism appealed to two very distinct groups: the poor, who wanted retribution against real and perceived enemies, and the industrial and financial elites, who craved social and economic stability.

OPPRESSION AND TERROR IN RUSSIA

Fascism and Communism stood as opposite ends of the political spectrum in the 1920s and 1930s, and each presented itself as the only defense against the other. Yet they resembled each other closely in methods of social control—so closely that observers as early as 1926 coined the word **totalitarianism** to describe their shared form of political oppression. Like the Fascist groups across Europe, Russia's Communist regime under Josef Stalin (1879–1953) was an intensely centralized society. The Bolshevik Party held all authority and openly used systematic police terror to dominate and manipulate the general population.

Stalin had come to Lenin's attention early in the century and by 1912 was appointed to the Bolshevik Central Committee. An enthusiast from the start for Lenin's insistence on the use of violence against political enemies, Stalin indulged his taste for cruelty, and for the rest of his life he relied on assassinations, purges, enslavement, and intimidation to achieve his ends. After Lenin's death in 1924, Stalin resolved to increase Russia's industrial and agricultural output by any means necessary, and that meant dismantling the economic structures created by Lenin's New Economic Policy. That policy had called for the nationalization of large-scale economic activities while allowing for small-scale private production in local markets. Stalin railed against the independent peasant farmers (*kulaks* in Russian) as enemies of the state and called for their immediate liquidation. State officials massacred hundreds of thousands of farmers and their families, confiscated their lands in order to form new collective farms under the direct control of the government, and forced the rest into exile and starvation. Many millions more perished of famine and exposure.

Stalin relentlessly blamed all food shortages and failures to meet the goals of his vaunted Five-Year Plans on conspiracies led by corrupt officials, lazy workers, inept engineers, political rivals, and, of course, their Jewish financial cronies. Starting in 1936 in the **Great Purge** he orchestrated a series of show trials in

Building Socialism   Women and children were also sent to the gulag during Stalin's murderous reign. Here a group of prisoners work at digging a canal out of the frozen Russian ground.

which phony evidence was used to prove false charges against these "enemies of socialism"—and then to justify their execution. By the next year he did away with even the show trials. He simply ordered mass arrests and confinements in a vast network of brutal concentration camps that stretched across Russia from Moscow to Siberia—the **gulag** (an acronym for the Russian phrase meaning "Central Administration of Corrective Labor Camps").[8] From 1938 to Stalin's death in 1953, roughly one million prisoners died in these camps. Some were starved and worked to death; others were simply beaten to death or shot. And perhaps another million or more died after being sentenced to internal exile.

The Bolshevik regime had improved the social and political status of Russian women by establishing a high-level Women's Department within its ranks, granting women the right to seek divorce, and securing access to abortion ser-

---

[8]   By the time World War II began, Stalin had already murdered 90 percent of his generals and 80 percent of his colonels. That left the army at a decided disadvantage.

Working Mother   This image comes from a children's book called *Mommy's Bridge* (1933). The book aimed to show that women working to create a socialist state could do so without fear of failing as mothers. Stalin emphasized a cult of motherhood in order to encourage women to produce more little socialists.

vices. Stalin rolled back many of these gains, but less out of opposition to women's rights in theory than from a need to stem a demographic hemorrhage. He killed so many millions that the nation had difficulty maintaining a national work-force. He therefore ordered improved health care available to women (although access to birth control was tightly restricted), and education focused on improving literacy rates. The number of female engineers, physicians, and civil officials rose significantly; the lower ranks of the Party itself became in time filled with female members. At the same time, Stalin redefined the family. What Marx had dismissed as an outdated bourgeois institution was officially rehabilitated as a "school for socialism." To encourage large families, Stalin bestowed a new award—that of the "Heroic Mother" (*Mat'eri Geroi*)—on women who produced ten children. Propaganda posters of the 1930s vividly depict all these changes in the significance of women to the socialist dream.

A NEW DEAL?

When Hitler became chancellor on January 3, 1933, his aims could hardly have been clearer. *Mein Kampf* had spelled them out in rambling detail, and the thug-gish tactics used by his uniformed and civilian supporters gave overwhelming evidence of the Nazis' willingness to beat, murder, rob, and swindle to accom-plish those aims. Whatever else might be said about Hitler, he seldom shied away from speaking his mind. Why, then, did the nations of the West give him more or less free rein for six years to do whatever he wanted? Before looking for answers, it is important to emphasize the continuing economic crisis.

The steps needed to confront the Depression seemed clear enough: only spending on public projects like highways, dams and levees, electrical grids, schools, and parks could put enough people to work that it would spark economic recovery. The creation of welfare-state programs could offer nonworking sectors of the population, such as children and the elderly, essential services like housing and health care. This was in fact how Hitler enabled Germany's recovery. Massive investment in rebuilding the military and constructing large-scale projects like the Autobahn system (the highways) all but eradicated Germany's sky-high unemployment rate by 1937. In the United States, Franklin Delano Roosevelt's torrent of new programs known as the **New Deal** followed the same basic path. It put millions of men and women back to work, provided price supports for cash-strapped farmers, offered unemployment insurance and retirement benefits to those no longer working, and made welfare payments to dependent mothers and their children.

Opposition to such schemes was widespread, however, and in many countries the opposition undercut recovery. Some of the opposition was simply personal: those with capital and incomes did not relish paying higher taxes—often dramatically higher—in order to benefit others. Much, however, was a matter of principle, since government intervention on such a scale smacked of socialism. Two brilliant economists squared off in the debate and set the terms for much of the philosophical divide between liberalism and conservatism for the rest of the 20th century—John Maynard Keynes (1883–1946) and Friedrich Hayek (1899–1992).

Keynes was the author of *The Economic Consequences of the Peace* (1919). After his bitter experience at the Paris Peace Conference, he moved between Cambridge, where he was a fellow at King's College, and London, where he advised the Treasury on economic matters. He was also associated with the group of writers, artists, and philosophers (including Virginia Woolf) who became known as the **Bloomsbury Group**. In 1936 he published his greatest work, *The General Theory of Employment, Interest, and Money,* which some have called the most important work of economics of the 20th century. Believing that unemployment was the single most severe problem posed by the Depression, Keynes argues in *The General Theory* that market forces alone cannot solve the problem. As profits decline, wages will fall indefinitely to restore profits, given enough time, and in unacceptably unpredictable ways. The rehiring of displaced workers and the taking on of new laborers will always be the last step taken by businesses on the mend. Moreover, Keynes adds, many failed or failing businesses will simply never return; some might reinvent themselves and produce new manufactures and services that rely less on labor—but this will only extend the problem. The solution to endemic unemployment, he maintains, is direct government action. The wages earned by labor will allow them to spend more, and the return to normal demand levels for products and service will mean a return to normal prices and profits to businesses.

Friedrich Hayek was born in Vienna, then the still-vibrant capital of the Austrian-Hungarian Empire. His family was wealthy and academic, and he fought bravely in an artillery unit on the Italian front. His personal sense of the loss of the comfort, stability, and refinement of the prewar era never left him. After the war he studied law and economics at the University of Vienna, earned a doctorate, and published his first book, on monetary theory, in 1929—the year of the crash. On its strength Hayek was appointed a professor at the London School of Economics, where he taught until 1950. He later taught at the University of Chicago (1950–1962) and the University of Freiburg (1962–1968), and in 1974 he received the Nobel Prize in Economics. Hayek challenged Keynes both theoretically and empirically, book for book, article for article, lecture for lecture, throughout the 1930s and 1940s. Their rivalry was without personal animosity, but the differences between the two men were profound.

Hayek endorsed the pre-1848 vision of classical economic liberalism, one that asserted the prime importance of individual liberty, personal responsibility, and the sacrosanct rights of property. A free market, he insisted, was the best and ultimately the only reliable guarantor of all three. Government intervention is a violent interruption of a natural process and leads only to demands for further interruptions. Think of how erecting a levee or a dam on a river may protect a floodplain: it may protect that particular plain, but it only passes the problem of river flow further downstream—where more calls for action will result in still more levees and dams, built at ever greater expense. Eventually, the river becomes unmanageable and a disaster vastly greater than that posed to the initial floodplain will occur. Better to recognize that rivers sometimes flood, and one should not build homes below the high-water level. Period. Hayek, a somewhat stiff and formal personality, would probably not have used such a homespun analogy, but in a private moment he might have approved.

In his two most famous attacks on Keynesian economics, *The Pure Theory of Capital* (1941) and *The Road to Serfdom* (1944), his conclusion is stark: government intervention in a free economy, no matter how well intentioned, is the first step toward totalitarianism—whether of the liberal (Communist) or conservative (Fascist) variety. "When economic power is centralized as an instrument of political power it creates a degree of dependence scarcely distinguishable from slavery," he famously wrote; "it has been well said that, in a country where the sole employer is the state, opposition means death by slow starvation."

APPEASEMENT AND PACIFISM

How evil does a regime like Fascism have to be before other countries will take preemptive action against it? Who may take such action—only the Fascist state's immediate neighbors? How is it that the churches of Europe, both Catholic and Protestant, failed to make immediate, unqualified, and repeated condemnations of immoral regimes preaching doctrines of hatred and violence? Why did the Western world respond to Fascism by tolerating it? This is the essential, urgent question posed by the 1930s, and it still rankles millions of people.

Why did the Western world respond to Fascism by tolerating it? This is the essential, urgent question posed by the 1930s, and it still rankles millions of people.

There is no single answer. The guiding policy of the West toward Hitler in the 1930s was called **appeasement**—the granting of political and territorial concessions in order to preserve peace—and each Western country appeased Hitler in different ways and for different reasons. And because of the continued economic crisis, the stakes were high. Each nation debated how to confront the Nazi danger without risking a slide of its own into totalitarianism.

France had perhaps the easiest choice to make, since it had really no choice at all. After World War I and the Depression, France could not even feign a direct challenge to Hitler's aggression. It took instead a purely defensive posture by building a barricade along the French-German border—the **Maginot Line**, named after the minister of war, André Maginot. An interlocking chain of artillery casements, machine-gun pillboxes, tank formations, barbed wire, minefields, and concrete bunkers, it was a variation on the trench networks of World War I—and proved in the end to be just as ineffective. The point, though, is that France could do little else.

The causes of American appeasement were rather more complicated. First, a strong popular sentiment in favor of isolationism dominated the 1930s. The Paris Peace Conference had spoiled the hopes of many regarding their country's ability to influence Europe for the better, and the crushing urgency of the Depression—which had left nearly one-half the U.S. population in dire poverty—demanded immediate, unwavering attention. Senate Republicans led the case for nonintervention, by establishing a special commission to examine America's involvement in World War I. Its 1936 report concluded that munitions manufacturers had influenced the U.S. decision to enter the war, out of a simple but coldhearted desire for profits. Outrage at these "war profiteers" fueled noninterventionist passions across America.

But another factor mattered just as much, namely the concern over aggressive Communism. While the full extent of Stalin's humanitarian crimes remained unclear, enough was known to make Washington wary. Hitler clearly sought to force his will over central Europe, but Stalin wanted the entire world under his boot-heel. Given a choice between evils—which many in Washington thought was all they had, in the 1930s—it might make strategic and even moral sense to prefer a strong Nazi Germany as a barricade against a Stalinist Europe.

The causes of British appeasement were perhaps the most complicated of all. Most people in Britain agreed that the Versailles Treaty had been a disaster and that the refusal of the Parliament to ratify it had been correct. But if the West had been wrong in 1919 to strip Germany of its peripheral territories, how could it oppose Germany's desire to have those territories restored? So long as Hitler's demands called only for rolling back an unfair treaty, many British concluded, they were not worth foiling at the cost of another war. For example, Hitler repeatedly demanded the return to Germany of the Ruhr Valley (of 1923–1924 fame). Britain, loath to quarrel yet again with France, at first hesitated and denied the claim, citing the treaty as justification. But when German demands became more shrill and Hitler declared his willingness for war, if necessary, Britain relented. In 1936 it agreed to allow the Nazi regime to take control of and remilitarize the district.

Munich Conference Negotiations between Neville Chamberlain and Adolf Hitler, with attendants, in September 28, 1938, to resolve the issue of Nazi claims to control the Sudetenland region in Czechoslovakia. After returning home from this meeting, Chamberlain spoke to a crowd outside 10 Downing Street: "My good friends, this is the second time in our history that there has come back from Germany to Downing Street peace with honour. I believe it is peace for our time. We thank you from the bottom of our hearts. And now I recommend you to go home and sleep quietly in your beds." World War II broke out almost exactly one year later.

For the moment, tensions calmed, but then Hitler began the gamble again the following year by calling for Germany's right to unite with Austria (the *Anschluss*). Similar demands, similar arguments, similar threats—and once again, British compliance. Then in 1938 Hitler insisted on the return of the Sudetenland—the predominantly ethnically German part of what was then northern Czechoslovakia. Once again the British prime minister Neville Chamberlain (r. 1937–1940) had to explain his position on the floor of the Parliament in March 1938:

> The position that we had to face in July was that a deadlock had arisen in the negotiations which had been going on between the Czechoslovak Government and the Sudeten Germans and that fears were already entertained that if it were not readily broken the German Government might presently intervene in the dispute. For His Majesty's Government there were three alternative courses that we might have adopted. Either (1) we could have threatened to go to war with Germany if she attacked Czechoslovakia, or (2) we could have stood aside and allowed matters to take their course, or, finally, (3) we could attempt to find a peaceful settlement by way of mediation. The first of those courses we rejected. We had no treaty liabilities with Czechoslovakia. We always refused to accept any such obligation. Indeed, this country, which does not readily resort to war, would not have followed us if we had tried to lead it into war to prevent a minority from obtaining autonomy, or even from choosing to pass under some other Government.
>
> The second alternative was also repugnant to us. However remote this territory may be, we knew, of course, that a spark once lighted there might give rise to a general conflagration, and we felt it our duty to do anything in our power to help the contending parties to find agreement.
>
> We addressed ourselves to the third course, the task of mediation. We knew that the task would be difficult, perhaps even perilous, but we felt that the object was good enough to justify the risk.

Chamberlain substitutes the word "mediation" here for "appeasement," which actually had a positive connotation at the time—a sense of reasonableness and diplomatic maturity. Only after World War II did it acquire its current taint.

Another English word entered common use in the West in the 1930s, carried over from French—**pacifism**. It appeared first in 1902 to describe French social reformers who opposed the military buildup that culminated in World

War I. From 1919 on, however, it denoted any principled and total rejection of violence as a means of resolving disputes. In the preface to his play *Heartbreak House* (1919), George Bernard Shaw described prewar Europe as a time and place where "there was only one virtue, pugnacity; only one vice, pacifism. That [combination] is an essential condition of war."[9] In an early treatise dedicated to the subject, the social critic P. S. Mumford wrote in his *Introduction to Pacifism* (1937, that "the Pacifist believes: 1. That war, i.e. mass murder, as a political policy is morally wrong, and consequently will never produce good results. . . . 2. That security for nations, ideals, or personal freedom can be obtained only by nonviolent resistance." Pacifism therefore meant not merely the preference for peace but the belief that any form of violence is intrinsically evil.

The most famous name among British pacifists of the time was the novelist and critic Aldous Huxley (1894–1963), best remembered today for his novel *Brave New World* (1932), in which he warned of the harmful effects of society's growing dependence on technology. Urged on by figures like him, the Student Union of Oxford University in 1935 swore a public oath that it "would not take up arms in defense of King and country . . . under any conditions whatsoever," should conflicts with Nazi Germany, Fascist Italy, or Communist Russia come to war. This "Oxford Oath" circulated through Cambridge University as well before coming to the United States. By the end of 1936 no fewer than sixty thousand American undergraduates had also taken the pledge, starting at Columbia University and Brown University.

Britain found itself in a bind—caught between loathing and distrust of Hitler on the one hand and a grudging willingness to consider his demands on the other. Despite urgent warnings in Parliament from Churchill and others, the ruling Conservative Party hoped to the very last that nations could deal with even a tyrant like Hitler with caution and reasonableness. Many in the country, and in Britain's closest ally, the United States, feared Stalin even more and hoped against hope that Hitler could be used as a foil against him. And leading groups of the generation that would do the actual fighting, if it came to that, had already announced their refusal to fight at all.

In the face of all this, Churchill rose in Parliament on October 5, 1938, with a stirring speech against any further appeasement or pacification. He ended with a quote from the Bible (Daniel 5.27):

> The Prime Minister desires to see cordial relations between this country and Germany. There is no difficulty at all in having cordial

---

9   Winston Churchill wrote in his 1930 memoir *My Early Life* that he had "always been against the Pacifists during [a] quarrel, and against the Jingoes at its close."

relations with the German people. Our hearts go out to them. But they have no power. You must have diplomatic and correct relations, but there can never be friendship between the British democracy and the Nazi Power, that power which spurns Christian ethics, which cheers its onward course by a barbarous paganism, which vaunts the spirit of aggression and conquest, which derives strength and perverted pleasure from persecution, and uses, as we have seen, with pitiless brutality the threat of murderous force. That power cannot ever be the trusted friend of the British democracy.

What I find unendurable is the sense of our country falling into the power, into the orbit and influence of Nazi Germany, and of our existence becoming dependent upon their good will or pleasure. It is to prevent that, that I have tried my best to urge the maintenance of every bulwark of defense—first, the timely creation of an Air Force superior to anything within striking distance of our shores; secondly, the gathering together of the collective strength of many nations; and thirdly, the making of alliances and military conventions. . . . It has all been in vain. Every position has been successively undermined and abandoned on specious and plausible excuses. We do not want to be led upon the high road to becoming a satellite of the German Nazi system of European domination. In a very few years, perhaps in a very few months, we shall be confronted with demands with which we shall no doubt be invited to comply. Those demands may affect the surrender of territory or the surrender of liberty. I foresee and foretell that the policy of submission will carry with it restrictions upon the freedom of speech and debate in Parliament, on public platform, and discussions in the Press. . . .

But [the British public] should know the truth. They should know that there has been gross neglect and deficiency in our defenses; they should know that we have sustained a defeat without a war, the consequences of which will travel far with us along our road; they should know that we have passed an awful milestone in our history, when the whole equilibrium of Europe has been deranged, and that the terrible words have for the time being been pronounced against the Western democracies: "Thou art weighed in the balance and found wanting."

The Nazi regime made an enormous gamble after 1933. It bet its survival on the belief that the nations of the West would acquiesce so long as Nazi demands were couched in terms of the Versailles Treaty. The six years of breathing space accorded Hitler by the policies of appeasement and the popular call for pacifism were all he needed to rebuild Germany's military system and to turn it into the most awesome fighting force in Europe. On September 1, 1939, Hitler took his decisive step by sending his army into Poland—the first territory outside any conceivable German claim to legitimate dominion. At that point it was at last undeniable that Nazi aims were pan-European. Within three days, World War II had begun.

WHO, WHAT, WHERE

appeasement	Lateran Agreement
Balfour Declaration	*Lebensraum*
Bloomsbury Group	League of Nations
Fascism	Maginot Line
Fourteen Points	mandates
gold standard	New Deal
Great Depression	pacifism
Great Purge	Spanish Civil War
gulag	totalitarianism

SUGGESTED READINGS

Primary Sources

Hayek, Friedrich A. *The Road to Serfdom.*
Hitler, Adolf. *Mein Kampf.*
Keynes, John Maynard. *The General Theory of Employment, Interest, and Money.*
Orwell, George. *Homage to Catalonia.*

Spengler, Oswald. *The Decline of the West.*
Toynbee, Arnold J. *A Study of History.*
Valéry, Paul. "A Crisis of the Mind."
Wells, H. G. *The Outline of History.*

Anthologies

Aster, Sidney, ed. *Appeasement and All Souls: A Portrait with Documents, 1937–1939* (2005).

Crew, David F. *Hitler and the Nazis: A History in Documents* (2006).

Studies

Berend, Ivan T. *Decades of Crisis: Central and Eastern Europe before World War II* (2001).
Bosworth, R. J. B. *Mussolini's Italy: Life under the Fascist Dictatorship, 1915–1945* (2007).
Brendon, Piers. *The Dark Valley: A Panorama of the 1930s* (2009).

Caldwell, Bruce J. *Hayek's Challenge: An Intellectual Biography of F. A. Hayek* (2003).
Diepeveen, Leonard. *The Difficulties of Modernism* (2002).
Evans, Richard J. *The Coming of the Third Reich* (2004).

———. *The Third Reich in Power, 1933–1939* (2005).

Fitzpatrick, Sheila. *Everyday Stalinism: Ordinary Life in Extraordinary Times—Soviet Russia in the 1930s* (2000).

Geifman, Anna. *Death Orders: The Vanguard of Modern Terrorism in Revolutionary Russia* (2010).

Gregor, A. James. *Marxism, Fascism, and Totalitarianism: Chapters in the Intellectual History of Radicalism* (2008).

Griffin, Roger. *Modernism and Fascism: The Sense of a Beginning under Mussolini and Hitler* (2011).

Hagedorn, Ann. *Savage Peace: Hope and Fear in America, 1919* (2007).

Hodgson, Keith. *Fighting Fascism: The British Left and the Rise of Fascism, 1919–39* (2010).

Hoffmann, David L. *Stalinist Values: The Cultural Norms of Soviet Modernity, 1917–1941* (2003).

Kennedy, David M. *Over Here: The First World War and America Society* (2004).

Kitchen, Martin. *Europe between the Wars: A Political History* (2006).

Lampe, John R. *Balkans into Southeastern Europe: A Century of War and Transition* (2006).

Lampe, John R., and Mark Mazower, eds. *Ideologies and National Identities: The Case of Twentieth-Century Southeastern Europe* (2004).

North, Michael. *Reading 1922: A Return to the Scene of the Modern* (2001).

Overy, Richard. *The Twilight Years: The Paradox of Britain between the Wars* (2009).

Paxton, Richard O. *The Anatomy of Fascism* (2005).

Pfannestiel, Todd J. *Rethinking the Red Scare: The Lusk Committee and New York's Crusade against Radicalism, 1919–1923* (2003).

Pine, Lisa. *Education in Nazi Germany* (2011).

Romero Salvadó, Francisco J. *The Spanish Civil War: Origins, Course, and Outcomes* (2005).

Steiner, Zara. *The Lights that Failed: European International History, 1919–1933* (2007).

———. *The Triumph of the Dark: European International History, 1933–1939* (2011).

Thomas, Hugh. *The Spanish Civil War* (2001).

Tubach, Frederic C. *German Voices: Life during Hitler's Third Reich* (2011).

Wapshott, Nicholas. *Keynes Hayek: The Clash That Defined Modern Economics* (2011).

Weitz, Eric D. *Weimar Germany: Promise and Tragedy* (2009).

Widdig, Bernd. *Culture and Inflation in Weimar Germany* (2001).

Worley, Matthew. *Oswald Mosley and the New Party* (2010).

For additional resources, including maps, primary sources, visuals, web links, and quizzes, please go to **www.oup.com/us/backman.**

"THIS WORLD CANNOT EXIST HALF SLAVE AND HALF FREE"

SACRIFICE FOR FREEDOM

CHAPTER 26

The World at War (Part II)

1937–1945

Fifty to sixty million deaths. Adolf Hitler's invasion of Poland on September 1, 1939, inaugurated the war in Europe, and Japan's attack on the U.S. naval base at Pearl Harbor, Hawaii, on December 7, 1941, triggered war in the Pacific. World War II ended in 1945 with the unconditional surrenders of Germany in May and Japan in September. It was ruin run wild over three continents. More than 110 million soldiers participated; twenty-seven million of them perished. Six million Jews, almost all of them civilians, were murdered in the Nazi concentration camps; another twenty to twenty-five million civilians from among all the other combatants' nations died of starvation or exposure, in air raids or artillery shelling, or were deported to the death camps. In one way or another the war involved most of the nations on Earth, and the great powers formed into two camps—the Allies (led by Britain, France, the Soviet Union, and the United States) and the Axis (Germany, Italy, and Japan, principally).[1]

The largest, bloodiest, most destructive, and most expensive conflict in human history, World War II nearly wiped out entire races and entire cities. Along with its unparalleled atrocities, however, a recognition of the need for justice after the war led to the attempt to treat the atrocities as war crimes. And along with the atomic bomb, the postwar years also brought the recognition of international

THE WORLD AT WAR, 1937–1945

◉ Major clashes

◀ **Fight for Freedom** A patriotic call to duty in wartime Britain (note the Anglican collar on the clergyman at left—already wholly in shadow). The threatening figure brandishing the whip is artfully drawn: he could be interpreted as either a Nazi German or a Stalinist Russian. Aimed at the British, this poster was produced by the U.S. government.

law in the United Nations. Women had seen the pace of their gains fall with the Great Depression and Fascism, but they also played an active role in wartime. So did territories on the peripheries, in Africa and the Middle East. In the process, they felt evolving definitions of Arab nationalism and Zionism—the drive for a state of Israel.

A PLACE IN MEMORY

Unlike the start of World War I, no jubilant crowds greeted this conflict. Popular sentiments were decidedly grim. After Hitler took the Sudetenland from Czechoslovakia, and the West had acquiesced, few people doubted that a horrible conflict was imminent, and the last six months before the war were filled with desperate strategic maneuvers. Britain and France, fearing the worst, promised to defend Greece, Poland, Romania, and Turkey in case of Nazi aggression. Hitler countered by forging the "Pact of Steel" with Fascist Italy, in May 1939. In Moscow, meanwhile, Stalin was exasperated at the West's delay in protecting eastern Europe and so began his own furtive negotiations with Hitler. In a surprise nonaggression pact signed in August 1939, each side vowed not to attack the other and to remain neutral in the event of war elsewhere. And Stalin counted on that pact. He needed every last month and week of delay, in order to replenish the officer corps that he had decimated with his purges.

The news stunned Europe and the United States, since the ideology of each nation was so opposed to the other. What the West did not know was that a secret clause in the Nazi-Soviet Pact arranged for the two countries to divide the lands of Poland, Estonia, Latvia, and Lithuania. At some future date, their conquest was to be undertaken by either Germany or Russia—and that future arrived more quickly than even Hitler and Stalin may have guessed.

---

[1]   Counting the pre-1939 Sino-Japanese War between China and Japan, estimates of the dead may reach as high as eighty million.

CHAPTER TIMELINE

1937
Japan invades China

August 1939
Nonaggression Pact between Germany and USSR

June 2, 1940
German army captures Paris

1942
Final Solution put into effect

1938
Virginia Woolf, *Three Guineas*

September 1, 1939
Germany invades Poland

December 7, 1941
Japanese attack on Pearl Harbor

World War II holds a special place in memory. To the people of Russia, where by far the greatest number of victims fell, it is called the "Great Patriotic War" to honor their extraordinary suffering. To them, the eastern front marked the center of the conflict, and the battle for Stalingrad was the turning point of the entire war. Western Europe recalls instead the Nazi seizure of Holland, Belgium, and France; the battle of Britain; the Normandy Invasion; the North African and Italian campaigns; and the final march on Berlin. In China, which remained apart from the broader conflict, it is the "War of Resistance" against Japan, while in Japan it is either the "Japan-China Incident" or simply the "China Incident." (After all, neither country ever issued a formal declaration of war.) Japanese historians long described the war against America and her allies as simply one facet of the "Greater East Asian War"—a broad independence movement that aimed to free East Asia of Western meddling. (Japanese officials later drew a parallel with China's own description of its Tiananmen Square massacre of 1989 as an "incident.") Americans speak of World War II, but a widely read history written in the mid-1980s referred to the struggle as the "Good War." That goodness lay, at least in nostalgic memories, in the moral clarity of America's involvement—as a conflict between obvious Good and obvious Evil. By whatever name the war is known, it left scars on the hearts and minds of all who participated in it (see Figure 26–1).

> Americans speak of World War II, but a widely read history written in the mid-1980s referred to the struggle as the "Good War." That goodness lay, at least in nostalgic memories, in the moral clarity of America's involvement—as a conflict between obvious Good and obvious Evil.

THE WAR IN EUROPE

The broad narrative of the war divides easily into three stages—Nazi success after success, decisive battles in Russia and against Italy, and Allied success in France and Germany. From 1939 to 1942 Germany quickly overran, in order,

August 1942-February 1943
Battle of Stalingrad

February-March 1945
Battle of Iwo Jima

August 1945
United States drops atomic bombs on Hiroshima and Nagasaki; Japan surrenders

1948
Universal Declaration of Human Rights

June 6, 1944
D-Day: Allied invasion of Normandy

May 1945
Germany surrenders

1945
Nuremberg and Tokyo War Crimes Trials begin; UN established

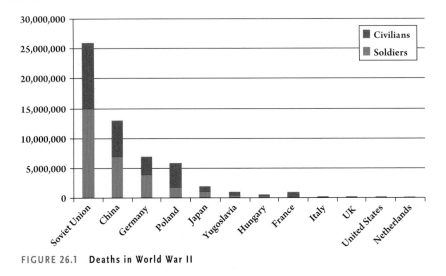

FIGURE 26.1   **Deaths in World War II**

Poland, Denmark, Norway, Holland, Belgium, and France. The Nazis made the fullest possible use of Germany's advantages in technology and numbers to break through defensive barriers at speed. Their **Blitzkrieg** ("lightning war") strategies concentrated heavy but mobile firepower (tanks and aircraft especially) and rapid troop movement in small areas. Having split their opponents' forces, the Germans then rapidly advanced straight ahead rather than contending with the divided flanks, which forced the shattered defense forces to attempt to regroup against a fast-moving enemy.

Time and again, in the first three years of the war, Nazi strategies forced their opponents to capitulate before they ever had a chance to mount a counter campaign. In less than two months in 1940, before the French army could even muster, the Nazis raced through the Low Countries, circumvented the Maginot Line altogether, and occupied Paris. The city surrendered on June 22. An infamous film clip shows a jubilant Hitler, who arrived in Paris shortly thereafter, celebrating the crushing of an era established by the hated Versailles Treaty. Roughly two-thirds of France remained under Nazi occupation for the next four years, while a Nazi-controlled puppet regime under Field Marshal Philippe Pétain (1856–1951) governed southern France from its temporary capital in the city of Vichy. Meanwhile, Poland had been divided with Stalin according to the Nazi-Soviet Pact, which allowed the Nazis to round up Jews for the labor camps rapidly being built in the east. The "ethnic cleansing" of Europe had begun.

In the second half of 1941 Hitler stood at the apogee of his power. True, his attempt to force Britain's capitulation through air raids from August to

October 1940 had failed, ending his dream of conquering Britain. He had also been drawn against his will into fighting in the Balkans and North Africa, thanks to Mussolini's amateurish efforts to establish Fascist control of the central Mediterranean. Yet he was confident enough in late 1941 both to invade Russia in June and to declare war on the United States in December. These events mark the beginning of the second phase of the war in Europe.

The campaign into Russia, called Operation Barbarossa, caught Stalin by surprise and progressed rapidly. Barbarossa was the largest single military action in

Hitler in Paris　After the collapse of French defenses, the Nazi army seized control of France in a matter of a few weeks. Here a triumphant Hitler poses with Albert Speer (1905–1981), his Minister of Armaments and War Production, and Arno Breker (1900–1991), his favorite sculptor, before the Eiffel Tower.

Western history, involving three million German soldiers (75 percent of the entire Nazi army and 66 percent of its total air power), who went east against nearly five million soldiers of the Soviet Red Army. Stalin's forces were already established in the half of Poland ceded to him by Hitler in 1939, and so the initial Blitzkrieg strikes occurred there. After breaking through the Russian ranks, the Germans pressed a three-pronged attack: to the northeast, against Leningrad (Saint Petersburg); due east, toward Moscow; and to the southeast, to Stalingrad (Volgograd). Each of the three campaigns ended in Nazi defeats. The Nazis reached Leningrad in September of 1941 but were unable to storm the city. Instead, a miserably protracted siege lasted over two years, until January 1944, during which more than a million city dwellers died of starvation, cold, and disease. The Nazis themselves incurred extraordinarily high casualties, as they were exposed to brutal winters for which they were unprepared and poorly resupplied.[2] The battle for Moscow, from October 1941 to January

---

[2]　Nazis dropped over one hundred thousand bombs and more than two hundred thousand artillery shells on Leningrad.

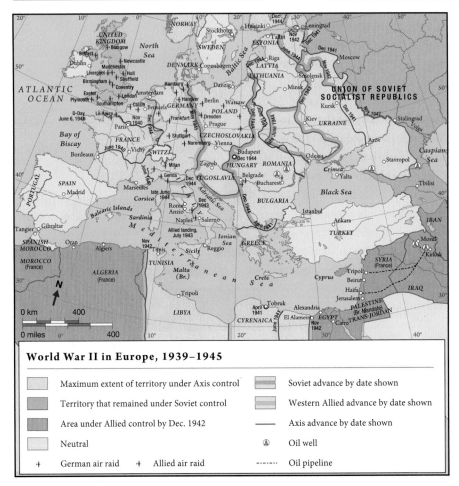

World War II in Europe, 1939–1945

Maximum extent of territory under Axis control	Soviet advance by date shown
Territory that remained under Soviet control	Western Allied advance by date shown
Area under Allied control by Dec. 1942	—— Axis advance by date shown
Neutral	⒜ Oil well
+ German air raid + Allied air raid	------- Oil pipeline

MAP 26.1   World War II in Europe, 1939–1945

1942, ended with a decisive Russian victory, however, as did the battle for Stalingrad, from August 1942 to February 1943 (see Map 26.1).

Matters worsened for the Germans quickly thereafter. The Allies in the west moved steadily through North Africa and turned north, invading Sicily and the Italian mainland in the late summer of 1943. The Fascist government toppled Mussolini and imprisoned him, though he quickly escaped, with German help; he was later captured trying to flee to neutral Switzerland and was lynched by a mob in Milan. Italy then broke with the Axis and joined the Allied side, which set the stage for the third and final stage of the war—which began with the Allied invasion of Normandy on D-Day, June 6, 1944.

The Nazis had long anticipated an invasion but were surprised at the precise location and date when it did finally come. Nevertheless, their defenses were strong. An Allied force of 130,000 men, made up primarily of U.S. and U.K. soldiers, landed on the beaches, while another 20,000 parachuted far behind the Nazi defenses to cut off reinforcements. Though enormously costly in lives, the D-Day landing proved a huge success, and that year Allied forces liberated Holland, Bel-

D-Day   Allied troops landing on the beach at Normandy on D-Day, June 6, 1944.

gium, and France, while their troops in Italy pressed continually northward. Gradually, as 1945 began, Allied armies from the west and the south and Russian forces moving in rapidly from the east closed in on Germany and then on Berlin itself. The war ended in May 1945 after Adolf Hitler committed suicide in his Berlin bomb shelter, and his remaining circle of high officials surrendered unconditionally.

WARS IN THE PACIFIC

The war in the Pacific began on December 7, 1941, when Japan attacked the U.S. naval base at Pearl Harbor in Hawaii, but tensions between the two countries had been rising for at least twenty years before that. Japan had long feared domination from the mainland, from China or Korea, and the coal-powered American maritime rivals added a new threat. Only by rapid industrialization, and the means to deliver its manufactures to world markets, could Japan feel protected. But the islands of Japan have little in the way of mineral ores—which forced them to look for outside sources of raw materials, fuel to process and ship them, and secure markets in which to sell them.

Japan's imperialist adventures had begun in 1904–1905 with the Russo-Japanese War. This war had been fought principally for control of the island of Sakhalin off the coast of Russia, where sizeable deposits of oil were known to exist. In 1910 Japan forcibly annexed Korea too, which had much-needed natural resources and a large population that could serve as a captive market. When World War I broke out, Japan formed an alliance with Britain and laid claim to Germany's east Asian and Pacific Island colonies—which it duly received. Japanese sailors also fought briefly in the Great War in the Mediterranean, against the Ottomans. By this point Japan was fully in the grip of militarism, every bit equal to that of Europe prior to 1914. When the Great Depression hit in 1929, the military took an even more active role in government, touting itself as the only real solution to the economic problem. Its solutions in the 1930s focused on stirring up trouble in China in order to justify direct military action (see Map 26.2).

The Japanese in China, 1931–1941

- Japanese Empire up to Sept 1931
- Japanese protectorate from 1932
- Area occupied by Japan by Dec 1941
- Direction of Japanese advance
- Shaanxi-Gansu-Ningxia border region under Communist control
- Communist offensive against Japanese 1940
- Soviet-Japanese border clashes
- Main supply routes from Allies

MAP 26.2   The Japanese in China, 1931–1941

Two "incidents" provided all the justification Japan needed. In September 1931 the Japanese staged a supposed Chinese terrorist attack on the South Manchurian Railway, which was then under lease to Japan. They placed a small bomb a short distance from a little-used piece of track and detonated it. The explosion caused only minor damage, but it attracted the attention of nearby Chinese soldiers, who hurried to investigate. The sudden "onslaught" of Chinese forces provided a pretext for Japanese action—and the seizure of all of Manchuria within five months of the faked terrorist attack.[3] The United States condemned Japan's action and vowed never to recognize any government established in Manchuria by Tokyo.

The second incident triggered the start of the Second Sino-Japanese War (1937–1945) and was a murkier affair. It occurred in July 1937 at the Marco Polo Bridge (the Lugou Bridge in Chinese, or Roku in Japanese), a long stone bridge over a tributary of the Hai River located a dozen miles southwest of Beijing. The bridge formed part of the rail line that linked Beijing with the rest of the province

---

[3] An exhibit in the Yushukan Military and War Museum in Tokyo still blames the 1931 Manchurian Railway bombing on Chinese militias.

and was thus of great strategic importance. The Chinese government, as a courtesy, had long allowed any nation that had trade legations in Beijing to place armed guards along this rail line. These guards had the right to perform occasional maneuvers—but Japan was the only country actually to do so. Either by plan or by accident, a squad of Japanese soldiers performed night maneuvers without informing local Chinese officials as they were supposed to do. One of the Japanese soldiers disappeared, and when Chinese officials began to search for him and to investigate the matter, Japan claimed that a cover-up conspiracy was under way and used this as a pretext for a full-scale invasion of Beijing and the entire province. When the United States condemned the aggression, announced economic sanctions, and ultimately cut off oil and steel to Japan, the Japanese military began the preparations that led ultimately to the attack on Pearl Harbor.

In broad outline, Japanese imperialism differed little from the European variety. Japan, too, believed in its innate superiority over other cultures, its superior claim to the world's resources, and its destiny to prove that superiority through force. Like the Europeans, the Japanese also showed themselves capable of horrific, wanton violence on occasion. In the First Sino-Japanese War of 1894–1895, a Japanese army division found the mutilated corpses of some of their compatriots who had been wounded and captured by the Chinese in an earlier battle. Infuriated, the division attacked the coastal town of Port Arthur (now Lushunkou) and massacred nearly the entire population, both military and civilian—an estimated population of five to six thousand. A mere three dozen survivors faced the grim task of burying the dead.

Militarism gained pace in Japan as the nation's population grew—forty-five million in 1900, sixty-five million by 1930. The greater numbers of people, combined with the Depression, highlighted the fundamental fact that Japan alone among developed nations could not feed itself.[4] For the generation that fought in World War II, imperial might and the martial spirit that sustained it were the best guarantors of prosperity and proof of the peoples' superior nature.

As with the war in Europe, the war in the Pacific falls neatly into three stages. The years from 1937 to 1941 mark the first stage, when Japan imposed its will throughout eastern and southeastern Asia, snatching up former German colonies and adding new ones through their campaigns in China. The second stage consists of the start of the war with the United States in 1941 to the Battle of

---

[4] Japan today remains the only industrialized nation that survives on imported food.

Midway in 1942. Midway Island lay roughly 1,500 miles (2,400 kilometers) west of Hawaii; though small, it had great strategic value because of its location midway between Hawaii and Japan. When Japan attempted a joint naval and amphibious assault on it, a smaller American force successfully fended off the attackers—and turned the tide of the war (see Map 26.3).

The final stage ran from 1942 to the Japanese surrender in 1945, as the Allies pressed in on the Japanese Empire from all sides. A ferocious battle to take the garrison island of Iwo Jima in February–March 1945 was the most notorious single episode in the campaign. Iwo Jima lay 750 miles due south of Tokyo and was the site of strategic airfields that the Japanese used to resist American air attacks on Japan itself. Of the roughly 18,000 soldiers stationed there, only two hundred survived and were captured; the rest perished in the assault. The United States attacked with a force of 70,000, nearly 7,000 of whom perished; another 20,000 were wounded. Overall, it was a heavier U.S. toll than in the invasion of Normandy on D-Day. The war ended suddenly with the American decision to

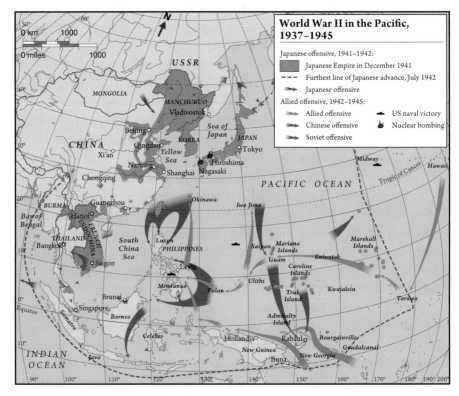

MAP 26.3   World War II in the Pacific, 1937–1945

drop atomic bombs on Hiroshima and Nagasaki in August 1945, and the Japanese government surrendered.

ATROCITIES AND HOLOCAUST

All wars have their atrocities, but technology has made modern warfare particularly grisly. From the introduction of gunpowder weapons and the creation of mass armies, the frequency and scale of massacres in wartime have increased dramatically. The mere pressing of a button or the pulling of a trigger can produce carnage to equal that at Thermopylae or Actium, Hastings or Hattin, Breda or Lepanto. For one generation, World War I seemed the summit of human horror; but airplanes and armored vehicles came into wide use only toward the end of that conflict, and World War II began with even more destructive weapons. Ironically, interwar recovery efforts made those weapons possible, thanks to the heavy investment in industry. The roll call of massacre sites is a long one: Auschwitz, Babi Yar, Dresden, Hiroshima, Katyn, Manila, Nagasaki, Nanking, Novi Sad, Port Arthur, and Treuenbrietzen are simply the best-known episodes. We know as much as we do about the atrocities in part because the Nazis kept meticulous film and documentary archives of their own activities. In part, too, the Allies insisted on international tribunals for investigating and prosecuting war crimes.

> From the introduction of gunpowder weapons and the creation of mass armies, the frequency and scale of massacres in wartime have increased dramatically. The mere pressing of a button or the pulling of a trigger can produce carnage to equal that at Thermopylae or Actium, Hastings or Hattin, Breda or Lepanto.

Four episodes, out of thousands, give a sense of the heartless savagery of the war. First was the Nazis' program to improve the gene pool of the Aryan race by euthanasia. Known as the "T4 Project," this campaign targeted native Germans with any major form of physical or mental handicap. Hundreds of thousands of such ethnic "mercy killings" and forced sterilizations took place.[5] (Exceptions were made for wounded war veterans.) The project took its name from the address of its administrative center in Berlin—4 Tiergartenstrasse—and began in 1939, shortly before the invasion of Poland. Officially closed in 1941, to cover up its

---

[5] Between 1933 and 1939 the Nazis sterilized roughly three hundred thousand undesirables. The T4 Project aimed to be a less costly way of achieving the same "racial hygiene."

Persecuting an Orthodox Jew   Poland was the site of heroic resistance against the Nazis and also a center of intense anti-Semitism. In this photo from 1941 a group of sneering Nazi soldiers cut the beard off an elderly Jew.

actions, the T4 project unofficially operated almost to the end of the war, and another two hundred thousand people were killed. Hitler recruited physicians, engineers, chemists, and administrative personnel with great care, in order to make sure that their ideological zeal matched their technical expertise. His chancellors Philipp Bouhler (1899–1945) and Viktor Brack (1904–1948) served as administrative heads, and Dr. Karl Brandt (1904–1948), oversaw the review, selection, and disposal of the victims. In the end, the Nazis' official T4 records report that some seventy thousand men, women, and children were put to death in a half-dozen sites built especially for the program; in the Nuremberg trials that followed the war, evidence of an additional 150,000 victims emerged. Initially, the victims were killed by lethal injections—but the process took too long and the poisons became too costly once the war began, so Brandt recommended custom-designed gas chambers instead. Bouhler was arrested at the war's end but committed suicide before he could be tried; Brandt and Brack were tried, convicted, and executed for crimes against humanity.

T4 was prologue to a still greater tragedy—the systematic murder of six million Jews, the **Holocaust**, or Shoah (Hebrew for "catastrophe"). Nazi hatred of the Jews was fanatical, but unlike other anti-Semitic episodes in Western history the war on the Jews had primarily a racial rather than a religious basis. The Jews, it was feared, polluted the Aryan race. First, their mere presence in Europe fouled the atmosphere and corrupted the culture; second, by intermarriage they weakened the racial purity of the Germanic people; and third, their supposed championing of both the hated ideologies of Communism and untrammeled capitalism gave them a dangerous degree of control over the material lives of the people. Hitler had made it clear in *Mein Kampf* what he intended to do about the Jewish problem, if he ever had the chance. "We must free ourselves from the forces that now control our public life.... Our first objective must be to wipe out Jewish society as it currently exists."

The Jewish population of prewar Germany had been roughly 500,000; another 200,000 were added when Hitler annexed Austria. Just over half of these had fled the Nazis before the start of the war. When Hitler swept into Poland, however, some two million more Jews came under his control, and the increased numbers added to the frenzy of Nazi hatred. The solution to the Jewish problem, they concluded, was to ship Jews to concentration camps where they could be forced to labor on behalf of the Germans. Although the **Final Solution** of exterminating the Jews was not decided upon until later in 1941, it was clear that the half dozen main camps were set up to kill.

A report written by two escapees from Auschwitz-Birkenau, Alfred Wetzler (1918–1988) and Rudolf Vrba (1924–2006), describes the scene that met them when they arrived at the camp in early 1942:

> By the middle of May a total of four Jewish male transports had reached Birkenau from Slovakia. All received the same treatment as ourselves. From the first and second transports, 120 of us were sent to Auschwitz on orders of the Auschwitz camp command, which had asked for doctors, dentists, university students, and professional administrators and clerks. After one week at Auschwitz 18 doctors and nurses, as well as three clerks, were selected from the 120 professionals. The doctors were assigned to the Auschwitz hospital and the three clerks, including myself, were sent back to Birkenau. Two of my companions, . . . both of whom have since died, went to the Slovak block. I went to the French block, where we were given administrative work. The remaining 99 persons were sent to work in the Auschwitz quarry, where they perished within a short time.
>
> Shortly afterwards a so-called hospital was established in one of the buildings. This was the notorious Block No. 7. I was assigned there as head-nurse at first; later I became the manager. . . . This hospital was nothing other than an assembly point for those awaiting death. All prisoners unable to work were sent here. Naturally, there could be no question of medical treatment or nursing. Every day about 150 people died and their corpses were sent to the Auschwitz crematorium.
>
> At the same time the so-called "selection" was started. The number of prisoners who were to be gassed and their bodies burned was determined twice weekly, on Monday and Thursday, by the camp doctor. Selectees were loaded on a truck and taken to the birchwood. Those who reached there alive were gassed in the big barrack built for the purpose and located next to the hole for burning bodies, and then were cremated in that hole. Approximately 2000 from Block No. 7 died each week, of which about 1200 deaths resulted from "natural causes" and about 800 from "selection." Death reports on those dying from natural causes were made out and sent

to camp HQ at Orianenburg. Selectees were marked up in a book labeled "Special Treatment." I was manager of Block No. 7 until 15 January 1943, during which time I could observe what was going on. About 50,000 prisoners were destroyed during that period, either from "natural causes" or through "selections."

This report, quoted here in its official English translation for the courts, was among the most valuable pieces of evidence presented at the Nuremberg Trials.

The Nazis killed Jews everywhere they found them, but eight camps formed the main sites of industrialized murder: Auschwitz-Birkenau, Belzec, Bergen-Belsen, Chelmno, Lublin/Majdanek, Mauthausen, Sobibor, and Treblinka. Six of the eight (those apart from Bergen-Belsen in Germany and Mauthausen in Austria) are in Poland, where the Nazis shipped their victims from across Europe (see Map 26.4). Those Jews deemed fit for labor received temporary reprieves and were set to work. The rest faced quick annihilation in gas chambers, followed by cremation in special ovens built for the purpose.

For a time, the English language failed before the scale of the evil; a new word was needed for a crime of this magnitude. Fittingly, a Polish Jew, Raphael

MAP 26.4   The Death Camps, 1941–1945

Lemkin, coined the term **genocide** in 1944. Lemkin (1900–1959) had been a public prosecutor in prewar Poland, and in 1939 he joined the army to fight against the Nazis. Wounded in battle, he escaped to Sweden and eventually to America, where he subsequently taught law at Duke, Yale, and Rutgers universities. He served as an adviser to Robert H. Jackson, the U.S. Supreme Court judge who later served as chief counsel at the Nuremberg Trials.

Six million Jews died in the Holocaust—the great majority in a single eighteen-month spasm of psychotic violence from late 1942 to mid-1944. By the time it ended, when advancing Russian and Allied troops closed in on Germany, the Jewish societies of Austria, Germany, Lithuania, Poland, Romania, and the Ukraine had been all but annihilated.

Auschwitz Jewish children in the death-camp at Auschwitz.

Jews were not the only victims of the Nazi's industrialized murder scheme. Somewhere between two and three million Russian prisoners of war died in the camps, as did two million Polish Gentiles who had resisted Nazi power or impeded the Germans' roundup of Jews. Other victims included homosexuals, the physically disabled, the Roma (Gypsies), Freemasons, and Jehovah's Witnesses; this last group was persecuted less for their religious beliefs than for their refusal to serve in the German army.

Six million is also the rough tally of Chinese killed while fighting Japan during the 1941–1945 war alone. If one adds the war of 1932–1937, the tally reaches twenty million. The Chinese-Japanese conflict had many causes

TABLE 26.1 **Non-Jewish Victims of the Concentration Camps**

Soviet POWs	2,000,000–3,000,000
Poles	2,000,000
Roma (Gypsies)	350,000
The Disabled	250,000
Freemasons	120,000
Homosexuals	15,000
Jehovah's Witnesses	4,000

and frequently reached feverish pitches of intensity. The most notorious of atrocities in this conflict was the **Rape of Nanjing.** In the weeks following the Marco Polo Bridge Incident (December 13, 1937), a large force of 150,000 Japanese soldiers advanced on Nanjing, then the capital of China. Accounts of what happened differ—and the Japanese either destroyed or removed their records on the affair, as American forces drew closer to Tokyo in 1945. Enough evidence, however, survives to make it clear that somewhere around 250,000 Chinese civilians were slaughtered by the Japanese army, all in a period of only five to six weeks. Another 20,000–50,000 Chinese women and girls were raped, most of them repeatedly. Civilians were shot, stabbed to death, or be-headed. Others were doused with gasoline and set aflame. Hundreds were plowed, alive, into ditches and covered with tons of dirt. In the end even the Japanese commanding officer, General Iwane Matsui (1878–1948), expressed confusion and regret over how it had all happened; his soldiers, it seemed, had simply gone briefly mad.

The Rape of Nanjing   In just six weeks, after taking the then-capital of Nanjing in December 1937, Japanese soldiers beat, raped, tortured, and killed as many as three hundred thousand Chinese men, women, and children. To many ardent nationalists in Japan, even today, none of this ever happened. Most Japanese today acknowledge that a gruesome battle took place, but they place the number of the dead at only one-tenth of the real casualties and attribute even those deflated numbers to regular battlefield occurrences.

Another crime was the Japanese abduction and sexual enslavement of a quarter million women and girls to serve as prostitutes, or **comfort women**, for their soldiers. These women were taken overwhelmingly from the occupied territories, although there is evidence that some Japanese women—primarily the relatives of critics of the government—were also forced to work throughout the empire. The official purpose of the "comfort stations" was, first, to control the spread of sexually transmitted diseases among the soldiers, by giving them access to a regulated sex trade. Second, it was said to protect against espionage by foreign agents posing as prostitutes. It seems likely that the basic aim was more elemental—to curry favor with the soldiers by giving them what they would have simply taken anyway.

The program began as early as 1932, when the first comfort station was introduced in Shanghai at the start of the Second Sino-Japanese War. The government actively recruited women to work in the brothels, even to the point of placing advertisements in newspapers; but as the empire and the army grew, volunteers no longer sufficed. By 1937, civilian agents hired by the government to manage and provide for the military brothels resorted to fraud and kidnapping. Ultimately, many tens of thousands of Chinese, Indonesian, Korean, Malay, Philippine, Thai, and Vietnamese women were abducted, raped, and humiliated. Although several Japanese prime ministers have apologized for the abuse of women during the war, the government still denies any legal liability for the military brothels. It holds that the total number of comfort women was no larger than twenty thousand—none of whom, it insists, were forced into the work.

MAKING AMENDS

How does a nation make amends for horrors? Can crimes of the magnitude of those committed in World War II be atoned for or forgiven? Who has the right to judge? One result of the war was the creation of a setting where such questions could be debated and decided on the basis of international law. The **Nuremberg Trials** of German leaders and **Tokyo Trials** in Japan did more than set the stage.

The idea of international law dates to the Treaty of Westphalia in 1648 but started to assume its modern character in the 19th century, with the growth of multinational businesses and modern empires. The Allies, however, had planned at least since early 1942 to bring the Nazis to justice for war crimes, and they had worked out

Nazi Germany and Imperial Japan were not the first nations to commit war crimes; nor were they the only ones to commit appalling acts in World War II. Germany and Japan were unique in that their crimes were conceived, implemented, and administered by the state as conscious elements of national policy.

the mechanisms for doing so long before Germany actually surrendered. The Tokyo Trials were another matter. Although the Allies agreed in principle to bring charges against the leaders of Imperial Japan, the joint process was preempted by General Douglas MacArthur (1880–1964), who used his position as supreme commander of the Allied Powers in the Pacific to order the arrests of nearly forty Japanese leaders and to begin their prosecution. The tribunal worked out the details as it conducted its work.

Nazi Germany and Imperial Japan were not the first nations to commit war crimes; nor were they the only ones to commit appalling acts in World War II. Germany and Japan were unique in that their crimes were conceived, implemented, and administered by the state as conscious elements of national policy. At Nuremberg, the Allies placed twenty-four top Nazi officials on trial, twenty-one of whom were convicted; subsequent trials of lower-tier officers convicted 142 of 185 defendants. Still more trials took place in several of the concentration camps, adding hundreds more to the list of criminals brought to justice before the trials closed in 1956. Most of the guilty were either hanged or imprisoned for life, although several of the most prominent defendants, like Herman Göring (1893–1946, the head of the German Air Force, or *Luftwaffe*), committed suicide before their executions could be carried out.

Göring on Trial   Hermann Göring (1893–1946) was the commander-in-chief of the Nazi air force (*Luftwaffe*) and Hitler's designated successor. Convicted of crimes against humanity at the Nuremberg Trials, he committed suicide the night before he was to be hanged. In a late conversation with an interviewer he boasted that " people can always be talked into doing what their rulers want. It's easy—all one has to do is tell them that they are being attacked, and then blame it on unpatriotic pacifists who are exposing everyone to harm. It will work in any country."

These courts marked a crucial point in the establishment of fundamental standards of international justice. As one of the leading judges at the trials, Robert H. Jackson (1892–1954), declared in his opening statement for the prosecution on November 21, 1945:

> Never before in legal history has an effort been made to bring within the scope of a single litigation the developments of a decade, covering a whole continent, and involving a score of nations, countless individuals, and innumerable events. Despite the magnitude of the task, the world has demanded immediate action. This demand has had to be met, though perhaps at the cost of finished craftsmanship. In my country, established courts, following familiar procedures, applying well-thumbed precedents, and dealing with the legal consequences of local and limited events, seldom commence a trial within a year of the event in litigation. Yet less than eight months ago today the courtroom in which you sit was an enemy fortress in the hands of German S.S. troops. Less than eight months ago nearly all our witnesses and documents were in enemy hands....
>
> I should be the last to deny that the case may well suffer from incomplete researches, and quite likely will not be the example of professional work which any of the prosecuting nations would normally wish to sponsor. It is, however, a completely adequate case to the judgment we shall ask you to render, and its full development we shall be obliged to leave to historians.... At the very outset, let us dispose of the contention that to put these men to trial is to do them an injustice, entitling them to some special consideration. These defendants may be hard pressed but they are not ill used.... If these men are the first war leaders of a defeated nation to be prosecuted in the name of the law, they are also the first to be given the chance to plead for their lives in the name of the law.

While few people complain about the trials' outcomes, the manner in which they took place raises questions about the quality of their justice. As pointed out at the time—for instance, by Supreme Court Justice William O. Douglas (1898–1980)—the laws defining war crimes were written after the atrocities had been committed. The trials were therefore ex post facto ("after the fact"), appearing more like revenge rather than fair judgment.[6] Some critics even condemned the processes as sophisticated lynchings. Both Winston Churchill and the American secretary of the Treasury, Henry Morgenthau Jr. (1891–1967) were adamantly

---

[6]   Göring, presented with a copy of the indictment against him, penned the comment, "The victor is always the judge, the defeated is always the accused"—with his signature.

opposed to the trials. Churchill simply advocated summary executions without any kind of trial whatsoever. Morgenthau's position had more nuance. He pointed out that Stalin in his show trials of the 1930s had written the laws under which the defendants were charged, appointed the judges and prosecutors, and determined the place for the proceedings. For the Allied Powers to do so could give the impression of a similar sort of rough justice. It did not help matters that Stalin made a point of repeatedly endorsing the Nuremberg trials in public. In the end, many of the accused, along with the German nation as a whole, recognized that some form of atonement, even an imperfect one, was necessary for the atrocities committed.

The Tokyo Trials were a different matter. At least since the battle at Midway Island in 1942, the Imperial Japanese government had carefully searched out and destroyed documents regarding their crimes, and in the weeks before their surrender in 1945, they undertook a mass purging of their records. Above all, they wanted to protect the emperor Hirohito and his family from any possible legal charge. Second, they wanted political and military leaders to claim plausible deniability about their role in criminal action. The tribunals therefore operated with distinctly inferior standards of evidence: documents could be submitted to the courts, for example, without their authenticity or provenance clearly established. "The tribunal shall not be bound by technical rules of evidence," declared the foundation charter of the Tokyo Trials, "and it shall admit any evidence which it deems to have probative value."

The tribunals forbade the cross-examination of some witnesses for the prosecution. Tribunals disallowed hearsay evidence (third party accounts rather than those of eyewitnesses) that contradicted the hearsay evidence presented by prosecutors, and they adopted a new standard for "negative criminality." Here they condemned Japanese officials for not preventing actions that were legal when they were performed. In the end, the Allies and nearly every nation under Japanese rule after 1932 staged trials of over ten thousand Japanese officials, more than half of whom were convicted, and roughly one thousand were executed.

THE UNITED NATIONS AND HUMAN RIGHTS

The **United Nations (UN)** set in formal order the standards and procedures for maintaining peace and international law. Established in 1945, this organization of member nations established a special tribunal for hearing specific cases as well as the permanently standing International Court of Justice and International Criminal Court. War crimes and crimes against humanity came under the jurisdiction of the International Criminal Court.

To prevent further war crimes and to establish a sounder basis for trials when they should occur, the United Nations on December 10, 1948, approved the **Universal Declaration of Human Rights**, whose drafting and promotion

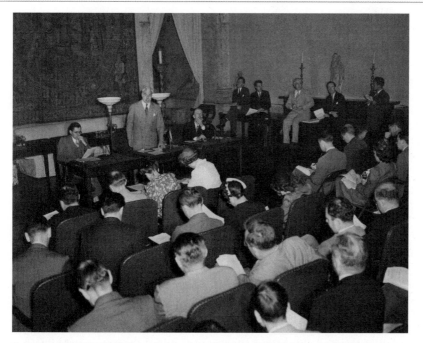

Creating a New World Order   Delegations from the United States, UK, USSR, France, and China meet in Washington, D.C., at the Dumbarton Oakes Conference in August 1944 to draft the charter of a new international institution—what would become the United Nations. The five chartering countries became the permanent members of the Security Council.

were chiefly the work of Eleanor Roosevelt (1884–1962), the wife of President Franklin Delano Roosevelt. It was the first, and is still the most important, statement of global rights in history. Until 1990, when forty-five Muslim nations withdrew from the Universal Declaration and provided a substitute for it, the declaration provided a standard for justice recognized, officially at least, around the globe. (We return to the Cairo Declaration on Human Rights in Islam in chapter 30.)

The key articles of the Universal Declaration assert:

Article 1: All human beings are born free and equal in dignity and rights. They are endowed with reason and conscience and should act towards one another in a spirit of brotherhood.

Article 2: Everyone is entitled to all the rights and freedoms set forth in this Declaration, without distinction of any kind, such as race, color, sex, language, religion, political or other opinion, national or social origin, property, birth or other status. . . .

Article 3: Everyone has the right to life, liberty and security of person.

Article 4: No one shall be held in slavery or servitude; slavery and the slave trade shall be prohibited in all their forms.

Article 5: No one shall be subjected to torture or to cruel, inhuman or degrading treatment or punishment.

Article 6: Everyone has the right to recognition everywhere as a person before the law.

Article 7: All are equal before the law and are entitled without any discrimination to equal protection of the law. . . .

Article 9: No one shall be subjected to arbitrary arrest, detention or exile.

Article 10: Everyone is entitled in full equality to a fair and public hearing by an independent and impartial tribunal, in the determination of his rights and obligations and of any criminal charge against him.

Article 11: (1) Everyone charged with a penal offence has the right to be presumed innocent until proved guilty according to law in a public trial at which he has had all the guarantees necessary for his defense. (2) No one shall be held guilty of any penal offence on account of any act or omission which did not constitute a penal offence, under national or international law, at the time when it was committed. . . .

Article 13: (1) Everyone has the right to freedom of movement and residence within the borders of each state.

Article 14: (1) Everyone has the right to seek and to enjoy in other countries asylum from persecution. . . .

Article 16: (2) Marriage shall be entered into only with the free and full consent of the intending spouses. . . .

Article 18: Everyone has the right to freedom of thought, conscience and religion; this right includes freedom to change his religion or belief, and freedom, either alone or in community with others and in public or private, to manifest his religion or belief in teaching, practice, worship and observance.

Article 19: Everyone has the right to freedom of opinion and expression; this right includes freedom to hold opinions without interference and to seek, receive and impart information and ideas through any media and regardless of frontiers.

Article 20: (1) Everyone has the right to freedom of peaceful assembly and association. . . .

Article 21: (1) Everyone has the right to take part in the government of his country, directly or through freely chosen representatives. (2) Everyone has the right of equal access to public service in his country. (3) The will of the people shall be the basis of the authority of government; this will shall be expressed in periodic and genuine elections which shall be by universal and equal suffrage and shall be held by secret vote or by equivalent free voting procedures.

Article 23: (1) Everyone has the right to work, to free choice of employment, to just and favorable conditions of work and to protection against unemployment. (2) Everyone, without any discrimination, has the right to equal pay for equal work. . . .

Article 26: (1) Everyone has the right to education.

The UN General Assembly adopted the declaration by a nearly unanimous vote: Czechoslovakia, Saudi Arabia, South Africa, the Soviet Union, and Yugoslavia abstained.

Their respective policies of female subjection, apartheid, and rejection of private property and free speech contradicted its central tenets. While sincerely supported by the nations that signed it, the declaration bears the marks of its Western and Enlightenment origins. It could have been written by Rousseau himself—personal safety, political participation, due process, equality before the law, and social egalitarianism. The Enlightenment had championed education but never asserted an individual right to it; Voltaire, for one, would have been horrified at the prospect of teaching the masses to read. That difference sets the declaration ahead of its 18th-century forebears.

> While sincerely supported by the nations that signed it, the declaration bears the marks of its Western and Enlightenment origins. It could have been written by Rousseau himself—personal safety, political participation, due process, equality before the law, and social egalitarianism.

The declaration marked an important step into a better world than the one that had given birth to it. Before long the Cold War between Communist nations and nations to the west raised tensions, which made it impossible for the declaration to be a binding treaty. Eleanor Roosevelt and her colleagues had to settle for its acceptance as universal guidelines or standards of behavior. Subsequent regional treaties such as the European Convention for the Protection of Human Rights and Fundamental Freedoms (1953) and the African Charter of Human and Peoples' Rights (1981), however, based their articles on the declaration and made its principles binding.

ATOMIC FISSURES

Harry S. Truman, U.S. president from 1945 to 1952, gave the orders to drop the atomic bomb on Hiroshima on August 6, 1945, and another on Nagasaki just three days later. The Japanese government capitulated the day after the Nagasaki attack, with surrender taking effect on August 15.

Without unconditional surrender, Truman had warned, Japan would face "the inevitable and complete destruction of [its] armed forces and just as inevitably the utter devastation of the Japanese homeland." It can hardly have been a surprise that the Americans had long been at work on a weapon of unparalleled destructiveness. The **Manhattan Project**, as the secret program to develop an atomic bomb was known, had begun in 1939 under the scientific direction of J. Robert Oppenheimer (1904–1967). It was generally and correctly assumed that Nazi Germany was trying to develop atomic weapons as well. While Hitler would hardly have kept Emperor Hirohito informed of their progress, Japan six years later must have suspected that the United States might be attempting something of dramatic scale. After all, nuclear physicists in Japan had undertaken their graduate studies in the United States with some of the very scientists involved in the Manhattan Project.

Hiroshima and Nagasaki were important but not vital hubs of industry, shipping, and military communications, and neither had been the site of any fighting or bombing prior to that August. The Americans wanted "untouched" targets, the better to assess the effectiveness of their new weapons. According to the *U.S. Strategic Bombing Survey*, a report on the bombs' effectiveness:

> The morning of 6 August 1945 began bright and clear. At about 0700 there was an air-raid alarm and a few planes appeared over the city. Many people within the city went to prepared air-raid shelters, but since alarms were heard almost every day the general population did not seem to have been greatly concerned. . . .

After the all-clear sounded, persons began emerging from air-raid shelters and within the next few minutes the city began to resume its usual mode of life for that time of day. It is related by some survivors that they had watched planes fly over the city. At about 0815 there was a blinding flash. Some described it as brighter than the sun, others likened it to a magnesium flash. Following the flash there was a blast of heat and wind. The large majority of people within 3,000 feet of Ground Zero were killed immediately. Within a radius of about 7,000 feet almost every Japanese house collapsed. Beyond this range and up to 15,000–20,000 feet many of them collapsed and others received serious structural damage. Persons in the open were burned on exposed surfaces, and within 3,000–5,000 feet many were burned to death while other received severe burns through their clothes. In many instances clothing burst into spontaneous flame and had to be beaten out. Thousands of people were pinned beneath collapsed buildings or injured by flying debris.... The people appeared stunned by the catastrophe and rushed about as jungle animals suddenly released from a cage.... Pandemonium reigned as the uninjured and the slightly injured fled the city in fearful panic.

Hiroshima's population then stood at around 350,000, Nagasaki's around 250,000. The bombs killed about 20 percent of each city's population instantly

Atomic Destruction   Nagasaki after the atomic bombing.

and turned their cityscapes instantly into moonscapes.[7] Within five years of the bombings, an equal number people died from the effects of radiation as had died in the explosions themselves—a total of perhaps a quarter million—while many tens of thousands more suffered from radiation wounds and diseases for decades to come.

Why not give Japan an explicit warning, or even a preview by detonating the bomb on a deserted Pacific island? Was it truly necessary to incinerate 70,000 people in Hiroshima and another 40,000 in Nagasaki, most of them civilians? As recalled by Henry Stimson (1867–1950), the American secretary of state:

> We carefully considered such alternatives as a detailed advance warning, or a demonstration, in some uninhabited area. But both of these suggestions were discarded as impractical. They were not regarded as likely to be effective in compelling a surrender of Japan, and both of them would involve risks. Even the New Mexico test did not give final proof that any given bomb was certain to explode when dropped from an airplane. Quite apart from the generally unfamiliar nature of atomic explosives, there was the whole problem of exploding a bomb at a predetermined height in the air by a complicated mechanism which could not be tested in New Mexico. Nothing would have been more damaging to our effort to obtain Japan's surrender than a warning or a demonstration followed by a dud.... Furthermore, we had no bombs to waste. *("The Decision to Use the Atomic Bomb," Harper's Magazine, February, 1947)*

Stimson's matter-of-fact tone masks the complexities of the issue. Japan had expressed a possible willingness to surrender in the spring of that year and passed word to Josef Stalin, who had offered to serve as intermediary with the Americans. But Stalin never forwarded the Japanese offer to Washington, in the hope that by prolonging the struggle in the Pacific, he might strengthen his own hand in East Asia. In fact, he was already racing to send his troops, recently relieved of battle in Europe after the Nazi surrender, across the massive Russian countrywide into Japanese-controlled Manchuria. On August 8, only two days after the bombing of Hiroshima, 1.5 million Soviet troops invaded Manchuria and presumably would have continued into Japan itself. The prospect of Stalin replacing Imperial Japan as the supreme lord of eastern Asia was untenable to the United States, which proceeded to drop their second atomic bomb on Nagasaki the very next day—as much as a warning shot across the Soviet bow as a final blow against Hirohito.

---

[7]   Most of the dead were killed either by the force of the explosions or from "flash burns" caused by the tremendous heat they generated, reaching 7,000°F (3,900°C).

Arguments that the bombings were necessary in order to spare the millions of lives that would have been lost in a conventional attack cannot be wholly dismissed, but neither can they be taken at face value. There is no way of knowing for certain what would have happened had America simply continued its conventional advance. The question therefore changes. America could certainly have defeated Japan without the atomic bombs—but could it have reached Tokyo before Stalin's troops did? By August 1945, it was clear that the Russians had no intention of withdrawing from eastern Europe. Were the Allies ready to confront a Stalin also in control of East Asia?

Except for the iconic images of the mushroom clouds over the two cities, photos and film of the devastation were strictly controlled or suppressed altogether. America may have wished to avoid comparison with images then circulating of the Nazi death camps. Photos of mangled, bloodied, and charred bodies, the government feared, might raise doubts about the legitimacy of American actions precisely when the country faced the possibility of continuing the war against the Communist regime.

Some scientists in Russia, in fact, had been engaged in nuclear research since the early 1930s, but Stalin's government was intensely focused on practical industrial development, so little of this "pure research" was therefore given sufficient funding or encouragement. What changed Stalin's mind was a letter in 1942 from a Russian physicist that pointed out a singular fact: no American, British, or German physicist had published any research on nuclear fission in scientific journals since 1939. Clearly something was up. Why else the sudden and total silence from the most brilliant scientists in the West? Stalin began to give priority to nuclear research in Russia, though progress was slow until after 1945, when Russian troops reached Berlin and started transporting truckloads of German physicists back to Moscow.[8] With the help of these new recruits, the Soviet Union developed its first atomic bomb in 1949. Britain became an atomic power in 1952 and France in 1960. As the postwar tensions between the West and the USSR rose higher and higher, they did so in a frightening new context of potential mass annihilation.

> As the postwar tensions between the West and the USSR rose higher and higher, they did so in a frightening new context of potential mass annihilation.

---

[8] A German-born British physicist named Klaus Fuchs (1911–1988), whose hatred of Nazism inspired him to join the British Communist Party in 1933, began passing sensitive scientific material to Russia as early as August 1941. An early member of the British team investigating the building of an atomic bomb, he eventually was welcomed into the Manhattan Project in 1943. Transferring to Los Alamos itself in 1944, Fuchs kept Stalin's scientists informed of the general developments in atomic research. His espionage continued until 1949. He was tried by the British in 1950 and sentenced to fourteen years in prison. Released in 1959, Fuchs emigrated to Communist East Germany and continued his nuclear research until his death.

WOMEN IN, AND AGAINST, FASCISM

By the 1930s Western women had secured political equality and the right to vote. They found the challenge of *social* equality more stubborn, however; or perhaps they simply settled for what they had newly earned. The Roaring Twenties had seen youthful hedonism and the appearance of major literary and artistic talents. The Depression and the totalitarian threat, in contrast, pressed most women back into the home. Yet when war came, women were in the thick of it.

Nazi ideology, based on a somewhat mythical traditionalism, had made women's place in society clear: it emphasized women's duty to produce more Aryan children in order to offset the growth of Jewish and Slavic peoples. As Hitler put it in a speech to the Nazi Women's League in September 1934:

> The catchphrase "Emancipation for Women!" was coined by Jewish intellectuals, who also shaped the whole of the so-called women's movement. But surely no German woman needs emancipation in an era as full of promise as our own.

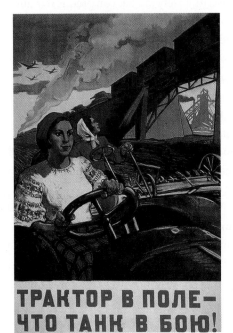

Fighting Fascism on the Farm   This Soviet poster from 1942, with the words "A Tractor in the Field Is Worth a Tank in Battle," proclaims the importance of farm work and of women workers. The poster's calm, reassuring image ignores the wartime devastation that Hitler's armies were then creating in the Soviet Union.

Remilitarization and the revival of heavy industry under the Nazis put men back to work. As in Fascist Spain, however, women were essentially driven from the workplace. (Women did, however, supply much of the clerical and lower administrative staff of the regime.) Italy differed from her totalitarian allies. There, women not only had owned and run businesses and estates, but many worked in factories and served in the civil service. Expectations about their domestic roles did not alter much, but a public life was widely considered acceptable as well. Communist Russia experienced the most dramatic change in women's roles, since the ideology insisted on a radical equality of gender roles. Women worked in factories, toiled on the land, ran offices, and served as bureaucrats, at least on the lower levels. In fact, they served on something like an equal level with men—although also equal to men in their lack of freedom. In order to accelerate industrial production, Stalin outlawed abortion in 1936 and increased state aid to families with young children, so that women could afford to remain in the workplace. When war finally broke out, women in Russia saw active combat.[9]

In western Europe a more complex picture emerged. The poor economic conditions of the 1930s undermined many of the political gains made by women after 1918, since government revenue had declined so precipitously. In Britain, for example, unemployment benefits were withheld from all women who worked as domestic staff—as cooks, maids, and housecleaners—and from women who worked out of their own homes as seamstresses, launderers, or typists. Consider a woman who lost a clerical or manufacturing job and was compelled to take a position in domestic service at dramatically reduced pay. If she accepted, she was ineligible for unemployment insurance, since she was employed; but if she declined, she was ineligible since she was not actively seeking work. As conditions worsened, married women who lost their jobs were denied unemployment payments as well, whether their husbands were working or not. In Austria, government statistics on unemployment regularly consisted only of men who were out of work, since women were regarded as workers but not as employees. And that, too, ate into welfare payments and other social benefits.

Although Mussolini boasted that Fascism had created a utopia, Italian women in the 1930s experienced unending want, oppression, and despair. Most trade unions were broken, and labor strikes were outlawed—which made it difficult for any workers, much less women, to show discontent. Government funding for education, health programs, and unemployment faced regular cuts to make room for military expenditures. The Italian military made up over 30 percent of government costs in the 1930s and approached 40 percent when war finally came. As conditions worsened, birthrates fell. Women either put off marriage or did what they could to avoid pregnancy (contraception was forbidden). The Italian birthrate fell 30 percent between 1911 and 1941, and this came amid a decline in overall population thanks to heavy emigration.

———————   ✦   ———————

Women had featured prominently in the pacifist campaigns of the 1930s too. Taking up where the antiwar groups of World War I had left off, many women's groups that had formed to pursue suffrage turned to the cause of avoiding war. The **Women's International League for Peace and Freedom** (WILPF) convened

---

[9]   By 1940 women made up almost half of the workforce in Russia. Just over one hundred thousand were decorated for valor after service in artillery and tank units or in the signal corps.

for the first time in the Netherlands, in The Hague, in the spring of 1915; it later moved its headquarters to Geneva, Switzerland, where it still resides. Its founders were an American, Jane Addams (1860–1935); two Germans, Anita Augsburg (1857–1943) and Lida Heymann (1868–1943); and a Dutchwoman, Dr. Aletta Jacobs (1854–1929).[10] The WILPF campaigned for equal rights for all citizens, economic justice, and greater understanding and empathy between peoples.

Members were divided, sometimes passionately, on whether socialism had to be a part of the movement for peace and freedom—but the real crisis confronting it was Fascism. To work tirelessly for peace and fairness in the long term is one thing. What should one do, however, when aggressive, violent evil has burst upon the scene? Some activists and writers formed a new group, the Women's Congress against War and Fascism (WCWF). Founded in Paris in 1934, it advocated the use of force as a last resort against international Fascism. Given the general popularity of appeasement, however, anti-Fascist groups like the WCWF came under suspicion of possible connections with Communism.

The decade's most famous statement in favor of pacifism was *Three Guineas* (1938) by Virginia Woolf. Woolf was then at the height of her fame as a novelist and had long been active in, and publicly associated with, women's issues. The bitterness of *Three Guineas* is understandable, even appropriate, although in the end it works against Woolf's aims. The book offers three essays, each written in the form of a letter (to a different person in each case) who has asked the author for a financial contribution to a social cause. The first cause is a drive to enlarge and refurbish a women's college at Cambridge University; the second, to help professional women advance in their careers; and the third, "to prevent war by protecting culture and intellectual liberty." The third essay, which is as long as the first two combined, is not only Woolf's statement of radical pacifism but an attempt to decode the root cause of all war. She sees war as the extreme expression of a uniquely male desire for aggression. To offer direct resistance to Fascism is simply to extend the male need to dominate, to beat down, to control, and to rule.

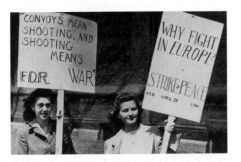

Women and Pacifism   Pacifist protestors at Radcliffe College, April 1941.

In a footnote Woolf equates two newspaper articles that appeared in the same issue of the *Daily Herald* (August 1, 1936). One article quotes a member of Parliament urging "the House of Commons to stand up to

---

[10]   Jane Addams became the first American to win the Nobel Peace Prize in 1931. Another leader of the WILPF, Emily Greene Balch (1867–1961), received the prize in 1946.

dictators (i.e. Hitler)"; the other reports a British woman's suit against her estranged husband for financial support: He "insists that I call him *Sir*," the woman complains. "I also have to clean his boots, fetch his razor when he shaves, and speak up promptly when he asks me questions." Both stories, in Woolf's argument, show the universal brutality of male dominance and chest-thumpery. In fact, the primary target of her scorn, apart from the loutish husband, is the British member of Parliament who advocates action against Hitler.

Woolf contrasts male brutishness with female nurturing and civilizing; she sees the role of guardian of civilized behavior as the special calling of the "daughters of educated men." The lower orders, both male and female, she dismisses as the "ignorantsia." Woolf recognizes the evil of Fascism but sees it as latent in all male aggression—overt or covert, political or social, extreme or mild. She condemns the Nazis for their ugly habit of burning books even while she celebrates her call to women, in the college-fund essay, to

> Woolf recognizes the evil of Fascism but sees it as latent in all male aggression—overt or covert, political or social, extreme or mild.

> burn the college to the ground. Set fire to the old hypocrisies. Let the light of the burning building scare the nightingales and incarnadine the willows. And let the daughters of educated men dance round the fire and heap armful upon armful of dead leaves upon the flames. And let their mothers lean from the upper windows and cry, 'Let it blaze! Let it blaze! For we have done with this "education"!'

Was Woolf's thoroughgoing pacifism heartfelt but naïve? She had visited Germany and Italy with her husband, Leonard Woolf, only a few years earlier and had seen the monstrosity of the regimes at firsthand. The fact that Leonard was Jewish brought the danger of Hitler home. As far as actual resistance to the evil, she vowed only, along with Leonard, to commit joint suicide should Nazi armies set foot in England. The Germans never did land, but Virginia took her life in 1941, when she felt the return of her recurring mental illness and depression. Leonard survived until 1969.[11]

Friedrich II von Hohenzollern, the 18th-century Prussian monarch, once said of warfare that "if it is properly done, it will pass entirely unnoticed by

---

[11] Helena Swanwick (1864–1939) made the case for pacifism more compellingly in *The Roots of Peace*, published the same year as *Three Guineas* and unfortunately now out of print.

civilians, women, and children." For a time the idol of Voltaire, he was probably trying hard to sound like a philosopher himself, rather than the brute he was. His own wars, after all, left scores of thousands of noncombatants dead or despairing. War as it is actually practiced seldom spares the innocent, and at least since medieval times one of the more reliable strategies makes use of just that fact to erode morale among the opposition and to undermine a society's support for conflict by bringing the battlefield directly into their homes.

World War I had been a partial exception. At least along the western front, only a small number of British, French, German, and Italian women witnessed any fighting or were direct casualties of it, though millions of them suffered the loss of loved ones. But World War II was different. The battlefronts were too numerous and too mobile, and air assaults like the London Blitz or the Allies' firebombing of Dresden respected neither gender nor age. No matter which side they were on, and whether they supported the war or not, women were involved from start to finish.

Britain called its women to active service almost immediately once fighting began in 1939, requiring every woman aged eighteen to fifty to register either for military or civil service. By 1941, as soon as the Blitz was over, unmarried British women aged twenty to thirty were drafted directly into one of the noncombat units. In the countryside, women were called into the "Land Army" to maintain food production; in the cities somewhere between 80 and 90 percent of all adult females worked either in industry or directly in the war effort. They served as clerks, radio operators, drivers, warehouse and shipping personnel, instructors, nurses, or searchlight handlers. In Italy, women served as nurses and physicians, teachers, and military staff, although the Fascist regime restricted other types of work to males. Men still dominated industry and farming. France, however, whether Occupied or Vichy, pushed women into traditional household roles as much as possible.

American women probably made the greatest social and economic gains during the war years. Women filled factories, offices, the professions, and schools in record numbers in the 1940s. And one area of particular significance was journalism. Women had long worked in the U.S. news industry, whether print or radio, but usually in behind-the-scenes positions like clerks, production assistants, and general staff; the Women's National Press Club had formed as early as 1919. When female correspondents began losing their jobs during the Great Depression, Eleanor Roosevelt organized weekly press conferences to which only women journalists were invited. The practice sent out a symbolic message and preserved at least a few dozen jobs for women in Washington. When the war came, nearly 150 women journalists became accredited war correspondents and photographers. They reported from foreign battlefields, military bases and ships, hospitals and concentration camps across Europe and East Asia.

We Can Do It!   American women at work constructing B-17 bombers, August 1942, at the Douglas Aircraft Company in Long Beach, California.

Women received only 50–75 percent of the pay men earned for the same work. It did not matter whether they worked in offices, schools, factories, the military, journalism, hospitals, or scientific labs. It did not matter whether they worked alongside men or in place of men who had entered the military. They were also largely expected, and even forced, to give up employment after 1945, as men returned from war. Many of women's gains disappeared after the war ended, setting the stage for the domestic era of the 1950s. Yet women in every country contributed mightily to the war effort—and just as much to the effort to promote peace.

WORLD WAR II AND THE MIDDLE EAST

While not active in the conflict, the peoples of the Near East were profoundly affected by World War II, and their aspirations affected both Allied and Axis strategies. The war also led to growing tensions among European mandates, Arab nationalism, and a Jewish homeland.

The Muslim lands that already existed as autonomous nations—Egypt, Iran, and Turkey most notably—declared neutrality in the conflict but were drawn in nonetheless. The Fertile Crescent regions that existed as European mandates (Lebanon and Syria, under France; Palestine, Jordan, and Iraq, under Britain) were important factors in Allied strategies from the start. Egypt, technically independent since 1922, had endured a British military occupation that aimed above all to keep the Suez Canal open—and popular sentiment against the British presence rose throughout the 1930s. When the war began in 1939, Egyptian hopes of freedom from British influence led the nominal ruler, King Farouk I (r. 1936–1952), to open negotiations secretly with Berlin, offering to join the Axis if Britain should be driven from the region. German forces under Field Marshal Erwin Rommel (1891–1944) advanced almost to Cairo before being turned back at the battle of El Alamein in late 1942, which dashed the prospect of a British withdrawal.

Iran too was a neutral power. Under Reza Shah Pahlavi (r. 1925–1941) it was engaged in an array of ambitious modernization projects. Public schools, modern hospitals, a national system of trains and buses, a comprehensive radio and telephone grid, the University of Tehran—all were paid for with revenues from oil. But oil in wartime becomes a weapon, and neither the Allies nor the Axis wanted Iran's oil to fall to the other side. Roughly a thousand German nationals resided in Iran in the early years of the war; most were engineers and businessmen developing a local steel industry in return for oil. When Reza Shah rejected Allied demands that he deport the Germans, both British and Soviet forces invaded the country and forced him to abdicate in favor of his son, Mohammad Reza Shah Pahlavi (r. 1944–1979), who immediately aligned himself with the Western Allies. Mohammad remained in power until the Iranian Revolution of 1979 toppled him and instituted the Islamic Republic.

Turkey likewise faced pressure from both Allies and Axis governments but remained neutral until the last year of the war, when it seemed clear that Nazi Germany would fall. Like Egypt, the country joined the Allies simply to earn the right to participate in the UN end-of-war negotiations for a permanent settlement. By holding to a neutral position for so long, Turkey was able to advance its internal development as a secular democracy and so to serve as a bridge between the West and the Middle East.

The Fertile Crescent itself was under French and British rule. Nations did not exist here—only an administrative grid of Western mandates and regional governors who tried to manage an interlocking yet fluid array of tribes, clans, and sects. The Ottomans had known better and had not tried to force the Arabs into larger units. France and Britain governed their mandates by allying themselves with self-selected conservative elites—landowners, clerical leaders, leading merchants, tribal chieftains, and military officers. All expressed, and in some cases genuinely felt, a willingness to work with their European masters. In return, Europe tacitly recognized their positions as leaders, ready and fit to take over whenever the Europeans left.

Syria, technically, was enemy territory to the Allies after 1940, since the Nazi seizure of Paris had left control of Syria to the puppet-regime of Vichy, which took its orders from Berlin. Hitler began to use Damascus at a staging and refueling site for planes bringing Iraqi oil to Germany, and this in turn led to the British decision to invade. Aided by "Free France" forces in exile, Britain took control of Syria in July 1941 and held it until the end of the war. When the war ended, however, Syria declared itself an independent republic, wrote a constitution, and elected a prime minister. Newly liberated France responded by bombing Damascus (in May 1945) and reasserting its rights under the UN mandate.

Britain opposed the French claim and wanted to secure an advantageous position with the new Syrian Republic.

New Allies Mohammad Reza Pahlavi, the shah of Iran from 1941 to 1979, established close ties with the US and UK, who supported him in return for his help in bringing Iranian oil to Western markets. Reza Pahlavi wanted to bring Iranian life into line with modern European, secular, and democratic society. Here he confers with U.S. President Franklin D. Roosevelt at the Tehran Conference in late 1943.

First, it pressured France to withdraw its troops (done by April 1946). Second, it recognized the republic's claim to a "Greater Syria" that extended its borders to the Mediterranean. Finally, Britain promised to do all it could to prevent further Jewish immigration into Palestine; at the same time, Britain was formally committed to a Jewish homeland there.

ARAB NATIONALISM AND GROWING ZIONISM

Arab nationalism differed from its European models, in that it emphasized shared language and culture over shared territory. Autonomy from the West meant more than an independent form of government. Secularism was a means to an end, rather than an ideal. Most Arabs, whether Sunni or Shi'i, were devout Muslims and desired to recreate an Islamic caliphate—though only in the sense of a symbolic spiritual realm. But most declared allegiance to secularism in order to placate Western concerns for the many Jews and Arab Christians that lived in the region. As one writer expressed it:

> The nationalism we are talking about is nothing more than Love—the feeling that binds a man to his family. For our country is simply a large household, our nation a large family. Nationalism thus makes the heart glad and the soul joyful, just as any form of love does, and whoever feels

this joy shares it with everyone who feels the same. It raises one beyond oneself and brings one closer to spiritual perfection. *(The Battle for Our Destiny, 1958)*

The writer was Michel Aflaq (1910–1989), an Arab Christian from Damascus who founded the **Ba'ath Party**—which he envisioned as the representation of secular **Pan-Arabism**, combined with socialist ideals of state-sponsored care for the masses. To Ba'ath supporters, and many other "nationalist" groups of the 1930s and 1940s, the "nation" of the Arabs implied something larger than any political arrangement and should not be thought of in Western political terms; the Arab nation, to them, was a spiritual state, an elevated sense of communal and cultural identity, a renewal of the original, founding community of the united Arab *peoples*.[12]

Britain had established a pro-Western monarchy in Iraq with the elevation of King Faisal I (r. 1921–1933), who maintained good relations with Britain. After a brief coup that was caused in part by the effects of the Depression, Faisal's grandson took over and ruled as Faisal II (r. 1939–1958). They hoped to foster a sense of political unity among the peoples living in Iraq. Ethnic, sectarian, and even geological divisions, unfortunately, stood in the way. As it had been determined by the UN mandate, Iraq consisted of two oil-rich zones, one in the north and one in the south, with an arid desert zone in between and centered on the ancient capital of Baghdad. The Kurds live in the north, the Iranian-allied Shi'a in the south, and the Ba'athist, pan-Arab, Sunnis in the arid middle. Without the resources of the north or south, the Sunni middle could hold Iraq together and impose its will only by force.

Palestine was both the most and least significant of the mandate territories. In earlier centuries its religious importance had matched its commercial significance: it bridged the Mediterranean-based economy of the West and the caravan-route-based economy of Asia. Trade routes, however, had long since moved, with the development of modern shipping, rail, and air-cargo traffic. The Suez Canal, opened in 1869, and the Trans-Siberian Railroad, completed in 1916, opened still more routes for goods. When Mark Twain visited Palestine in the latter half of the 19th century he described it as a barren expanse of dust, rocks, and weeds that was almost devoid of habitation. As he famously put it in *The Innocents Abroad* (1869):

> The further we went the hotter the sun got, and the more rocky and bare, repulsive and dreary the landscape became. There could not have been more fragments of stone strewn broadcast over this part of the world, if every ten square feet of the land had been occupied by a

---

12 The Arabic word ba'ath means "renaissance."

separate and distinct stonecutter's establishment for an age. There was hardly a tree or a shrub anywhere. Even the olive and the cactus, those fast friends of a worthless soil, had almost deserted the country. No landscape exists that is more tiresome to the eye than that which bounds the approaches to Jerusalem. The only difference between the roads and the surrounding country, perhaps, is that there are rather more rocks in the roads than in the surrounding country.

Conditions had changed by the mid-20th century, of course, and the most dramatic change was the growing Jewish presence. Between 1869 and 1923 roughly fifty thousand Russian and European Jews had immigrated to the Holy Land, where they purchased farmlands, pastures, homes, and businesses from departing Turks and emigrating Arabs. Another sixty thousand arrived by 1932; and during the early years of Hitler's rule, while the West pursued appeasement, perhaps 150,000 more Jews came. The British did all they could to restrict immigration during the war, to avoid upsetting their Arab subjects. The British also saw it as a first step toward resolving the tensions between Arab claims and the founding of a Jewish state.

The Jews were still a minority in the Holy Land in 1945, although they constituted a majority in Jerusalem and several other cities. The Jews who moved into Palestine included poor farmers and laborers, but also large numbers of professionals—physicians, lawyers, business managers, engineers, teachers, labor organizers, and scholars—and their skills transformed the landscape. New industries, schools, and trades appeared on the scene, health care improved, malarial swamps were drained, and transportation and communication networks were established. New political and legal institutions were introduced as well. Unlike their Arab neighbors, the Jews formed modern political parties based

Exodus to Nowhere   The SS *Exodus 1947* was a packet steamer that carried 4,500 German Jews, most of them Holocaust survivors, to the Holy Land. Britain was then still in possession of the Palestinian Mandate and had a determined policy not to worsen their relations with the Arabs by allowing increased Jewish immigration, and hence when the *Exodus 1947* reached port in Haifa, British authorities refused to let them disembark. Taking control of the ship, British officials sought other sites to unload the passengers but no place seemed suitable—and so they made the decision to return them to Germany. The predictable uproar occurred, and the fate of the Jews became international news for months on end. With the formal creation of the nation of Israel in 1948, all bars to the group's repatriation were removed, but by then half of the original 4,500 had either died or fled.

on ideology—pro-labor, pro-business, pro-socialist, secular, or religious. These organizations unified the populace across the region. Palestinian Arabs remained wedded to a more traditional tribal and clan-based social organization. The Jews, in other words, developed a Western variety of political nationalism that proved more effective than the cultural and spiritual variety of nationalism familiar to the Arab world. This powerful sense of nationhood, and the legal and institutional practices that operated within it, combined with the immense emotions produced by the Holocaust, which demanded a safe homeland for the Jews. Together, they created the unstoppable drive toward a State of Israel in 1948.

WHO, WHAT, WHERE

Ba'ath Party
Blitzkrieg
comfort women
Final Solution
genocide
Holocaust
Manhattan Project
Nuremberg Trials
Pan-Arabism

Rape of Nanjing
Tokyo Trials
United Nations (UN)
Universal Declaration
 of Human Rights
Women's International
 League for Peace
 and Freedom

SUGGESTED READINGS

Primary Sources

Gilbert, G. M. *Nuremberg Diary.*

Levi, Primo. *Survival in Auschwitz.*

Stimson, Henry L., and McGeorge Bundy. *On Active Service in Peace and War.*

Swanwick, Helena. *The Roots of Peace* (1938).

Woolf, Virginia. *Three Guineas* (1938).

Zweig, Stefan. *The World of Yesterday.*

Anthologies

Coetzee, Frans, and Marilyn Shevin-Coetzee, eds. *The World in Flames: A World War II Sourcebook* (2010).

Goldensohn, Leon. *The Nuremberg Interviews* (2005).

Laqueur, Walter, and Barry Rubin, eds. *The Israel-Arab Reader: A Documentary History of the Middle East Conflict* (2008).

Madison, James H. *World War II: A History in Documents* (2009).

Marrus, Michael R., comp. *The Nuremberg War Crimes Trial, 1945–46: A Documentary History* (1997).

Martel, Gordon, ed. *The World War Two Reader* (2004).

Simmons, Cynthia, and Nina Perlina. *Writing the Siege of Leningrad: Women's Diaries, Memories, and Documentary Prose* (2005).

Studies

Bass, Gary Jonathan. *Stay the Hand of Vengeance: The Politics of War Crimes Tribunals* (2001).

Bellamy, Chris. *Absolute War: Soviet Russia in the Second World War; A Modern History* (2008).

Bix, Herbert. *Hirohito and the Making of Modern Japan* (2000).

Carpenter, Stephanie. *On the Farm Front: The Women's Land Army in World War II* (2003).

Evans, Richard J. *The Coming of the Third Reich* (2003).

———. *The Third Reich at War, 1939–1945* (2008).

———. *The Third Reich in Power, 1933–1939* (2005).

Friedländer, Saul. *Nazi Germany and the Jews.* Vol. 1, *The Years of Persecution, 1933–1939* (1998).

———. *Nazi Germany and the Jews.* Vol. 2, *The Years of Extermination, 1939–1945* (2008).

Gelvin, James L. *The Modern Middle East: A History* (2011).

Glendon, Mary Ann. *A World Made New: Eleanor Roosevelt and the Universal Declaration of Human Rights* (2002).

Gregor, Neil. *Haunted City: Nuremberg and the Nazi Past* (2008).

Hasegawa, Tsuyoshi. *Racing the Enemy: Stalin, Truman, and the Surrender of Japan* (2006).

Hitchcock, William I. *The Struggle for Europe: The Turbulent History of a Divided Continent, 1945 to the Present* (2004).

Knox, Macgregor. *Common Destiny: Dictatorship, Foreign Policy, and War in Fascist Italy and Nazi Germany* (2009).

Laucht, Christoph. *Elemental Germans: Klaus Fuchs, Rudolf Peierls and the Making of British Nuclear Culture, 1939–59* (2012).

Mawdsley, Evan. *Thunder in the East: The Nazi-Soviet War, 1941–1945* (2007).

Megargee, Geoffrey P. *War of Annihilation: Combat and Genocide on the Eastern Front, 1941* (2007).

Merridale, Catherine. *Ivan's War: Life and Death in the Red Army, 1939–1945* (2007).

O'Shea, Paul. *A Cross Too Heavy: Pope Pius XII and the Jews of Europe* (2011).

Pike, Francis. *Empires at War: A Short History of Modern Asia since World War II* (2011).

Rees, Laurence. *World War II behind Closed Doors: Stalin, the Nazis, and the West* (2008).

Steiner, Zara. *The Lights That Failed: European International History, 1919–1933* (2007).

———. *The Triumph of the Dark: European International History, 1933–1939* (2011).

Thorpe, Julie. *Pan-Germanism and the Austrofascist State, 1933–38* (2012).

Totani, Yuma. *The Tokyo War Crimes Trial: The Pursuit of Justice in the Wake of World War II* (2009).

Vaizey, Hester. *Surviving Hitler's War: Family Life in Germany, 1939–48* (2010).

Weikart, Richard. *Hitler's Ethic: The Nazi Pursuit of Evolutionary Progress* (2011).

Wendehorst, Stephan E. C. *British Jewry, Zionism, and the Jewish State, 1936–1956* (2011).

Wette, Wolfram. *The Wehrmacht: History, Myth, Reality* (2007).

Wintle, Michael, and Menno Spiering, eds. *European Identity and the Second World War* (2011).

For additional resources, including maps, primary sources, visuals, web links, and quizzes, please go to **www.oup.com/us/backman.**

CHAPTER 27

The Theater of the Absurd

1945–1968

THE GREATER WEST, ca. 1950

— "Iron Curtain"

I t was no easy thing to survive the first half of the 20th century and still believe in the goodness of mankind, the inevitability of progress, or a loving God. And in fact millions of people ceased to believe in all three. An immense task of rebuilding once again confronted the West. Hundreds of thousands of corpses needed burial, and millions of wounded and displaced people needed care. Billions of tons of rubble had to be cleared. Rivers and fields had to be reopened. Whole cities had to be fixed up or entirely reconstructed. Homes, schools, hospitals, factories, offices, sewage systems, communications networks, roads, subways, theaters, waterways, airports, harbors, train stations, rail lines, power grids, warehouses, and places of worship all demanded attention. The agricultural sector, too, needed to be reestablished. The destruction was immense, even awe-inspiring.

The Italian novelist Elsa Morante (1912–1985), who was half Jewish, spent part of the war hiding in the Apennine Mountains from the Nazis. She described the physical and emotional desolation of the time in a wrenching novel called *History* (*La storia*, 1974). It depicts the brutality of everyday

◀ **Postwar** On November 27, 1944, more than three hundred RAF bombers all but obliterated the city center of Freiburg im Breisgau, in far southwestern Germany. The home of one of Europe's great universities, Freiburg was the hometown of such notables as the philosopher-theologians Hannah Arendt, Walter Benjamin, Martin Heidegger, Edmund Husserl, Karl Rahner, and Edith Stein. In this stark photo, a lonely resident—still dressed in proper clothes for polite society—searches for food after the bombing.

life in war-torn Rome—searching for food and cast-off clothing, trying to find a safe place to sleep amid ruins, running from looters and rapists. Morante evokes the horror of the war not by narrating large-scale scenes of battle but by describing small, even intimate, betrayals of trust and decency. The main character, a shy southern Italian woman named Ida, is raped by a passing Nazi soldier; while Ida's travails form the bulk of the narrative, Morante goes out of her way to present the death of the soldier who raped her in a sympathetic light. (An Allied bomb lands directly on his transport, and he is obliterated.) When Ida encounters a train filled with Jews on their way to the death camps, she singles out of the noise within the closed car the sound of several children singing a song—and rushes to the door in order to join in with the doomed children.

The effect is all the more powerful because of the smallness of its scale. Ida's quest is both material and ethereal: to survive, keep her children safe, and restore some kind of normal life, but also to make sense of horrors. Suffering that does not *mean something* is unbearable. "Man in his fundamental nature needs to explain the world into which he was born," Morante writes. "This is what separates him from other animals. Every last person, even the least intelligent and the lowest of the world's castaways, explains the world to himself from childhood on, and this is what enables him to keep living. Without it, all would be madness."

Many in Europe never found safety or meaning, and an aura of persistent gloom lasted long after the war. It influenced literature with the idea of "the absurd." Millions of others, however, rolled up their sleeves and set to work. They rebuilt nations and economies. They faced down the tensions and violence of the Cold War—a world divided between the West and Communism—by moving away from imperialism as well as into a "second wave" of feminism. Some of the same tensions stirred conflict and change in Islamic states as well. They also created new systems of literature and philosophy that, it just so happened, described thought and language as systems.

CHAPTER TIMELINE

1942
Camus, *The Stranger*

1945
End of World War II

1947
Marshall Plan begins; start of the Cold War

1948
State of Israel founded

1948–49
Berlin Airlift

1949
NATO founded

1953
Kirk, *The Conservative Mind*; Barthes, *Mythologies*

1955
West Germany admitted into NATO

SETTING TO WORK

The refugee crisis called for attention first. Roughly fifty million refugees and several million prisoners of war had to be repatriated—that is, sent home. The difficult process was made even more confusing by new national boundaries and by Stalin's unwillingness to withdraw his troops from eastern Europe. Germany was divided into zones of Allied control. Brutal forms of ethnic cleansing became commonplace in the east, as ethnic minorities were shuffled from one location to another. In Poland, for example, the non-Polish population constituted one-third of the nation before the war; it was reduced to a mere five percent (see Map 27.1). Wartime criminals, collaborators, and postwar looters were sought out for punishment. Judicial punishments and mob justice reached many who had collaborated with the Nazis. In Belgium alone over six hundred thousand people (roughly 8 percent of the population) were prosecuted.

Europe could not feed itself. Agricultural production in 1945 was less than half its prewar level, and strict rationing was put in place everywhere. Lacking markets in which to sell, and having no fuel with which to operate their machinery, farmers refrained from growing crops and turned instead to raising livestock. Shipments of food from the United States helped to keep people alive, but rationing continued in many countries well into the 1950s. The **Marshall Plan**, named after U.S. secretary of state George Marshall (1880–1959), began in 1947. It provided cash, credit, raw materials, and technical assistance to jump-start industrial production.[1]

Marshall described the agricultural crisis in a public lecture he delivered at Harvard University in June of 1947:

> The farmer has always produced the foodstuffs to exchange with the city dweller for the other necessities of life. This division of labor is the basis of modern civilization. At the present time it is threatened with breakdown.

---

[1] Within five years the Marshall plan provided over $13 billion dollars in aid—worth more than $100 billion dollars today.

1956
USSR invades
Hungary

1964
Martin Luther King, Jr.
awarded Nobel Peace Prize

1966
National Organization
of Women founded in
the United States

1967
Six-Day War

1968
Prague Spring and
subsequent Soviet
invasion of Czechoslovakia

1969
Organization of the Islamic
Conference founded

1975
Decolonization
nearly complete

Displaced Peoples in East and Central Europe, 1942–1955

● Baltic peoples ● Czechs ● Finns ○ Germans ● Greeks ○ Hungarians ● Italians ○ Poles ● Romanians
● Russians ◌ Russians forcibily repatriated ● Turks ✡ Jewish emigration to Israel 1945–50 in thousands

(300) Number of refugees in thousands (with color of peoples)   ——— "Iron Curtain" 1948

MAP 27.1   Displaced Peoples in East and Central Europe, 1945–1952

The town and city industries are not producing adequate goods to exchange
with the food-producing farmer. Raw materials and fuel are in short supply.
Machinery is lacking or worn out. The farmer or the peasant cannot find the
goods for sale which he desires to purchase. So the sale of his farm-
produce for money which he cannot use seems to him an unprofitable trans-
action. He, therefore, has withdrawn many fields from crop cultivation and
is using them for grazing. He feeds more grain to stock and finds for himself
and his family an ample supply of food, however short he may be on clothing
and the other ordinary gadgets of civilization. Meanwhile people in the
cities are short of food and fuel. So the governments are forced to use their
foreign money and credits to procure these necessities abroad. This process
exhausts funds which are urgently needed for reconstruction. Thus a very
serious situation is rapidly developing which bodes no good for the world.
The modern system of the division of labor upon which the exchange of

products is based is in danger of breaking down. The truth of the matter is that Europe's requirements for the next three or four years of foreign food and other essential products—principally from America—are so much greater than her present ability to pay that she must have substantial additional help or face economic, social, and political deterioration of a very grave character.

Under Stalin's orders the nations of eastern Europe, now under Communist control, declined U.S. assistance and denounced it as a disguised effort to reestablish economic imperialism. In the West, the aid provided by the Marshall Plan jump-started the economy as hoped, and industrial capacity returned quickly to prewar levels. By the mid-1950s western Europe was again exporting manufactured goods around the globe. Currencies had stabilized, and Europe began a long period of steady growth that allowed it to perform a great social experiment—the modern welfare state.

Full Speed Ahead "The Open Road of the Marshall Plan," a German poster promoting the rebuilding effort.

ALIENATION AND THE ABSURD

The determination and hard work of so many people did not translate, however, into optimism. Gloom predominated, even among the war's victors. In fact, much of European culture and at least some in America hardly believed what it saw—a vast ruin of shattered hopes and beliefs. The notion of **absurdity** summed up, for many, the meaningless of existence and the inscrutability of fate. The French-Algerian writer Albert Camus (1913–1960), the first great writer of postwar Europe, made the quest for meaning in an absurd world an emblem of his generation.

> To Camus that is the drama of life, and its tragedy. A world that can continue to exist after sixty million deaths is a world in which no individual life has real meaning.

As he sees it, we can bear the unhappiness of today because we have some hope for tomorrow. That uncertainty, or ambiguity, is endurable. But it still leaves a tension, however, that can be resolved only by a lie: we believe that our lives matter, but if we are honest we must acknowledge that they do not. To Camus that is the drama of life, and its tragedy. A world that can continue to exist after sixty million deaths is a world in which no individual life has real meaning. We do not choose to come into this world, but we are powerless to leave it, short of suicide. Life is thus reduced to mere existence—and the absurdity of it all.

Camus enjoyed enormous success with his first novel, *The Stranger* (1942), and he followed it with more novels, plays, critical essays, and philosophical works. He won the Nobel Prize in Literature in 1957, before dying in an automobile accident. His brilliant career, his reputation as a man of action,[2] and his remarkable good looks made him a cultural icon. He was the alienated modern man as smoldering romantic hero—a brooding James Dean with advanced degrees in philosophy and a war record to boast of.

In *The Stranger* the protagonist, Meursault, argues with a priest who is trying to redeem his soul after he commits a murder:

> Something inside me snapped. I do not know why. I began to scream at him, as loudly as I could, berating him, telling him his prayers were wasted on me. I seized him by the collar of his cassock and let fly with all the anger and passion in my heart: *You're so confident about everything, aren't you? But there's not a belief in your head that is weightier than a hair, a single hair on a woman's head!* The poor fellow couldn't even be sure he was alive, since he was living like one already dead. And he thought *I* was the one with an empty existence! But I knew the truth—about me, about everything—better than he ever did; I knew my life and the death that was coming for me. Yes, that was all, is all. But I had as strong a grip on it as it had on me. . . . I had done this, but not that; a third thing, but not a fourth—and so what? It was like I had been waiting just for this moment, this crack of light at dawn, to win my vindication. Nothing mattered, nothing, and I knew why. . . . What did it matter that some people died, or that a mother loved her child? What could his God, or the lives that people choose for themselves, or the fates they think they control, possibly mean to me?

Camus summarizes the problem of absurdity in *The Myth of Sisyphus* (1942):

> I do not know if the world has any transcendent meaning, but I do know that if such meaning exists I cannot know it; it is impossible for me to know it. What can a meaning outside of my own existence possibly

---

2   Camus had been a member of the Resistance during World War II.

mean to me? I can understand things only in human ways—the things that I touch, the things that press back against me. These things I understand. But I also know that I cannot reconcile my desire for absolute truth and unity with the impossibility of reducing the world to a rational, understandable principle. What truth about these things can I state without lying? Without invoking a sense of hope that I do not possess—a hope that means nothing outside my own existence?

The Philosopher as Rock Star   Albert Camus dedicated his life to attacking the nihilism and despair that Nietzsche had warned of. "Do not wait for the Last Judgment; it takes place every day."

Camus ultimately pulled back from nihilism, that denial of all meaning to life, in the 1950s, when he devoted himself to political action. He campaigned energetically for human rights on behalf of the United Nations. His dedication to action, however, resulted in (or was a result of) a severe case of writer's block, which cut short his literary and philosophical career. Deciding that "courage is the only moral virtue," he championed the rights of the poor and oppressed around the world, campaigned against admitting Fascist Spain into the United Nations, protested the brutality of the Soviet regime, and advocated an end to capital punishment. He never renounced his ideas about the absurdity of life. He simply decided that he could still try to create a better existence for himself and others.

Much of Western literature and philosophy took up the themes of absurdity and alienation. The view of life that they portrayed was grim—from the philosophy of Camus's contemporary Jean-Paul Sartre to the plays and novels of the Irish writer Samuel Beckett (1906–1989) and or the French-Romanian playwright Eugène Ionesco (1909–1994). Many of the plays and novels were comic, but the laughter they produced was nervous and never far from despair.

THE COLD WAR AND DECOLONIZATION

To some politicians and military commanders, the fall of Berlin in 1945 should not have been the end of the war. Worries about Stalin's Russia and the role it would play had emerged as early as 1943 and were an important factor in the closing military strategies of the Allies. Communism under Lenin and then Stalin had always been feared, but Communist Russia had looked inward during the run-up to the war. Now that the war had left Stalin in possession of half of Europe locked behind an **Iron Curtain**, his long-stated goal of exporting revolution to other nations now was put into effect. An American general, George Patton, proclaimed his readiness in 1945 to keep his tank divisions rolling eastward until they brought Moscow to its knees, and he had his share of supporters.

Winston Churchill, too, wanted to continue on to Russia after Hitler's defeat—which explains why the British voted him out of office in the first postwar election. They were grateful for his role in saving the country from the Nazis, but they wanted no part in a new war with their former ally in the east. To many observers, President Truman's decision to drop the atomic bombs on Hiroshima and Nagasaki was motivated at least in part by Russia. It was, they felt, a warning to Russia not to expand its role in the east as it had done in Europe.

The **Cold War** between the Soviet bloc and western European nations allied with the United States received its name from Bernard Baruch (1870–1965), a wealthy American financier and presidential adviser who was appointed in 1946 to the UN Atomic Energy Commission. He advocated a World Atomic Authority that would have complete control over atomic weapons. By this point, however, Stalin's scientists had begun work on their own atomic program. Baruch borrowed the term from George Orwell; the British writer had used it to describe the "peace that is no peace" that would exist if two atomically armed countries opposed one another. Neither nation would dare to use its weapons, and yet neither would dare to disarm. Orwell coined the term in 1945, before Stalin had begun the Soviet nuclear program. Baruch applied it to the high-tech rivalry that became real when Russia tested its first atomic bomb in 1949.

The Cold War unfolded in three main stages. The years from 1947 to 1962 marked the first and most hostile stage. The United States and Western Europe were determined to prevent any revival of Fascism by promoting democracy and capitalism. They naturally viewed Soviet expansion with suspicion. Most Russians, however, had no doubts that the West was the real aggressor. How many times had a European power invaded Russia? Hitler had been only the most recent would-be conqueror, in a line that stretched back through Kaiser Wilhelm, Napoleon, Selim III, Charles XII of Sweden, and the Polish-Lithuanian Confederation of the 17th century. In fact, it ran all the way back to the Crusades and the age of the Vikings. Yet when had Russia ever invaded Europe? After 1945, Russia at last possessed a buffer zone of European states that allowed it to export its Communist ideals while remaining somewhat safe from attack.

The second stage of the Cold War stretched from 1962 to 1979. This was the era of **détente**, when the USSR and the West tried to ease tensions between them by diplomacy, cultural exchange, and treaties to limit arms. West Germany played an important role here by pursuing closer relations with Communist East Germany. A younger generation increasingly warned of the dangers of the weapons buildup.

We pick up the final phase of the Cold War in chapter 29. It began with the Soviet invasion of Afghanistan in 1979, the effort to suppress the Solidarity reform movement in Poland, and the rise to power in Moscow of Mikhail Gorbachev in 1985. Gorbachev's willingness to tear down the Berlin Wall in 1989 began the end of the Cold War—a process that both sides declared complete in 1991.

The Berlin Airlift In June 1948 the Soviet Union imposed a land-blockade on Berlin in the hope of bringing the Allied-controlled western half of the city under Soviet control. This was the first major crisis of the Cold War. The Allies responded by delivering food, water, clothing, and other supplies by air. By the time the blockade ended in May 1949, over 200,000 flights had delivered roughly 5,000 tons of supplies a day.

Throughout the initial phase of the Cold War, each side aggravated tensions. The United States and Russia supported separate sides in the Greek Civil War of 1946–1948. Stalin blockaded West Berlin (1948–1949) in an effort to starve the city until it accepted Soviet rule; the Allies responded by dropping over two hundred thousand planeloads of food.[3] The United States created the **North Atlantic Treaty Organization (NATO)**, a defensive alliance to protect Western Europe. The Soviet Union saw it instead as a marshalling of forces to attack Russia, and with every country added to the alliance, the battlefront moved closer and closer to the Soviet border (see Map 27.2). Even such peaceable institutions as the International Monetary Fund (IMF) and the World Bank (both started in 1946) struck Moscow as aggressive, for they aimed to promote capitalism.

The Korean War (1950–1953) pitted the U.S.-backed South Koreans against the Communist-led North Koreans. Stalin's death in 1953 led to a temporary calming of hostilities, but these roared back to life with the **Cuban**

---

[3] During the Berlin Airlift, an average of one plane every three minutes delivered food to the German capital.

MAP 27.2   Military Blocs in Europe, 1948–1955

Missile Crisis of 1962, when the USSR's new leader, Nikita Khrushchev (1894–1971), built military bases in Cuba equipped to launch nuclear missiles. After two weeks of intense negotiations, threats, and a U.S. blockade of Cuba, Khrushchev withdrew the missiles. The world had come within minutes of a full-scale nuclear war. After this close escape, both sides agreed to ease hostilities and, if possible, to limit the spread of nuclear weapons.

DECOLONIZATION

This was also the era of **decolonization**, when Europe gave up, willingly or unwillingly, the bulk of its overseas territories. Independence movements had already picked up their pace when the Depression made it harder for the imperial nations to afford their overseas involvements. First, the former colonies of the Ottomans gained freedom (though often only a partial freedom, under a government named by the Europeans), followed by those of the Japanese Empire.[4] The European-held colonies followed. First came those in south Asia.

---

4   Japan had held Burma, Cambodia, parts of China, Laos, and Vietnam for only a decade, after seizing them from the Europeans who had held them much longer.

Burma, India-Pakistan, Indonesia, and Sri Lanka all gained freedom in the late 1940s. In the 1950s the decolonizing wave passed to Southeast Asia, and in the 1960s it came at last to Africa. By 1975 the process was virtually complete (see Map 27.3).

A host of problems confronted each of the newly independent countries, often before the ink had dried on their new charters. One problem was particularly prevalent in Africa: the political borders of the new nations did not correspond to ethnic, religious, or cultural boundaries. The borders of Somalia, for example, consisted only of the extent of Italian military conquest. The new "country" after the Italian withdrawal did not exist in any meaningful way for the native peoples, who found themselves lumped together in a state not of their own choosing. Nigeria was formed from no fewer than 420 distinct ethnic and tribal groups. While Kenya, for instance, had a more traditional structure to it, the problem of borders accounted for much of the political instability in African nations.

Independence from Europe also did not translate directly into economic self-sufficiency. Too many natural resources had been stripped away, in cases such as Cambodia, the Congo, and India. Elsewhere resources remained monopolized by foreign corporations or the descendants of the colonizers, who often remained

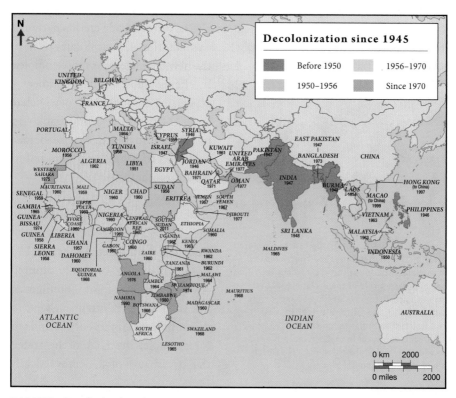

MAP 27.3 Decolonization since 1945

in what was for them their homeland. Even as the 20th century drew to a close, Africans and Asians of European descent and their associates held much of the productive land, mineral resources, and commercial properties in the former European colonies. They also dominated political life. In Zimbabwe, for instance, white citizens made up a mere 1.5 percent of the total population but as late as 1987 were guaranteed 20 percent of the seats in parliament. The Dutch East Indies, colonized in 1602, had been seized by Japan in World War II, and after the war the independent nation of Indonesia began to draft a constitution. The Dutch, however, waged a four-year war (1946–1950) to reestablish control; they were willing to compromise on sovereignty but fought bitterly to retain possession of the profitable trades in coal, coffee, oil, rubber, and spices. In the end, as many as eighty thousand Indonesians were killed and several million were displaced from their homes, especially on the islands of Java and Sumatra.

Decolonization also added to the rivalry between the West and the Soviet Union. In nearly every former colony hundreds, if not thousands, of diplomatic, economic, and military agents worked to encourage the new country to join their paths of development. Communism appealed strongly among the poorest and most powerless of the freed peoples and to many left-leaning intellectuals. Its message of economic equality resonated with desires to settle old scores with the West. Khrushchev supported independence movements across Africa and Asia but lacked capital for direct investment. Hence he offered trade credits in return for the raw materials that could supply Russia's factories. America's sales pitch to the new countries was more complex. It offered substantial investment—especially through the newly-chartered IMF and the World Bank—in return for guarantees to keep markets open to American goods and to resist Communism.

To keep an eye on Soviet attempts to spread their influence, the United States developed the **Central Intelligence Agency (CIA).** Its mission was officially limited to the gathering of intelligence but in practice it often engaged in direct political intervention. In Iran, for example, the CIA orchestrated the overthrow of a democratically

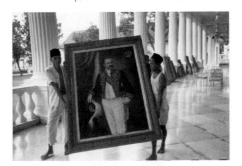

Cleaning House   The United East India Company, chartered by the government of The Netherlands, had controlled Indonesia from the late-16th century to 1800, when the government took over direct rule of the archipelago. Seized by imperial Japan in 1941, Indonesia demanded independence after the war but the Dutch fought to re-establish their colony. After two years of fighting, Indonesia won independence in December 1949. In this photo, Indonesian workers remove the portraits of the three hundred Dutch governors who had ruled the country since 1595.

elected new prime minister, Muhammad Mosaddegh, in 1953, when he nationalized the oil industry and its petroleum reserves. For good measure, they also had Mussadegh arrested by the new government of Muhammad Reza Pahlavi, who ruled as shah until his own overthrow in the Iranian Revolution of 1979. Such actions did not endear the United States to many, but were considered necessary to stop Soviet expansion. In Korea (1950–1953) and Vietnam (1955–1975) the confrontation of Communist and Western interests reached the point of military action. Neither war ended satisfactorily for either side.

THE WELFARE SOCIETY AND THE ECONOMIC BOOM

While trying to contain Communist expansion, Europe also devised programs to put economic development back on track and to prevent a reemergence of Fascism. These programs aimed at the creation of **welfare states**—societies in which the central government, funded by heavy taxation, provided all essential social services. They did this out of two central convictions: that education, health care, and a secure retirement are human rights and that people who have their basic needs met will not be tempted by radicalism.

The welfare state differed in each country. In France, for example, the government focused on protecting children through education, family allowances, and childcare assistance. The British placed special emphasis on security for adults through health care, unemployment insurance, and pensions. The fundamental goal of maintaining stable life for all citizens remained the same, though. The United States did not travel as far down this road as western Europe did, but it went farther than many people today remember. By the 1960s it offered a broad range of social benefits—Social Security for retirees, unemployment insurance, health care for the elderly and the indigent (Medicare and Medicaid), assistance with securing mortgages through the Federal Housing Administration (FHA), and access to college education (the GI Bill, Pell Grants, and loan guarantees)—even while undertaking massive infrastructure projects like the interstate freeway system and while subsidizing the oil and automobile industries.

Sir William Beveridge (1879–1963), a prominent economist, stated the British case for social welfare in 1942, in a report to Parliament called *Social Insurance and Allied Services* but known commonly as the Beveridge Report. He called on three essential principles:

> The first principle is that any proposals for the future, while they should use to the full the experience gathered in the past, should not be restricted by consideration of sectional interests established in the

Subsidized Housing   Architects and urban planners review plans for creating more high-rise housing in a poor district in postwar Glasgow (1953). Post-colonial immigration increased demand for housing in western Europe's bigger cities, and the development of the welfare state gave high priority to providing housing.

obtaining of that experience. Now, when the war is abolishing land-marks of every kind, is the opportunity for using experience in a clear field. A revolutionary moment in the world's history is a time for revolutions, not for patching. . . .

The second principle is that organisation of social insurance should be treated as one part only of a comprehensive policy of social progress. Social insurance fully developed may provide income security; it is an attack upon Want. But Want is one only of five giants on the road of reconstruction and in some ways the easiest to attack. The others are Disease, Ignorance, Squalor and Idleness. . . .

The third principle is that social security must be achieved by co-operation between the State and the individual. The State should offer security for service and contribution. The State in organising security should not stifle incentive, opportunity, responsibility; in establishing a national minimum, it should leave room and encouragement for voluntary action by each individual to provide more than that minimum for himself and his family.

Beveridge was arguing that the purpose of the state is to remove want, disease, ignorance, squalor, and idleness—as opposed simply to guaranteeing an individual's freedom to do so on his or her own.

This marks a significant change in 19th-century liberalism. Yet as early as 1848 liberalism had insisted on the state's responsibility to intervene. Free-market capitalism, for all its positive elements, gives profound advantages to some parts of society and not others. Intervention should thus be seen as re-establishing the freedom of the majority rather than curtailing the freedom of the minority. In protecting workers, for example, the state is simply correcting the imbalance that the marketplace gives to company owners. Workers must have the right to form unions and negotiate collectively for wages and work conditions, because company owners otherwise control labor. Another example is progressive taxation—requiring those with higher incomes to pay higher percentages of that income in tax. In this way, the state breaks up self-perpetuating concentrations of wealth, so that a larger number of people gain the freedom to achieve success themselves.

The postwar welfare state extended such thinking. No one is free who is born into want, disease, ignorance, and squalor—and no such person can achieve freedom. Even idleness, Beveridge thought, is not simply a vice. It is imposed by unemployment, lack of education, and lack of opportunity. Removing these bars to freedom, liberalism argued, is the responsibility of the state. The purpose of government is to care for its citizens rather than to preserve owners' rights to control their property. Higher taxes on the wealthy are needed to pay for basic services.

> Even idleness, Beveridge thought, is not simply a vice. It is imposed by unemployment, lack of education, and lack of opportunity. Removing these bars to freedom, liberalism argued, is the responsibility of the state.

Not everyone was pleased. F. E. Hayek in the 1930s and 1940s warned of the "road to serfdom" (see chapter 25). Economic freedom was to Hayek the engine of all other freedoms, and any interference in capital, goods, services, and labor invited totalitarianism. (After reading a subsequent report by Beveridge in 1944 called *Full Employment in a Free Society*, Hayek declared that Beveridge knows "no economics whatever.") A leading American theorist who dissented from welfare-state orthodoxy was Russell Kirk (1918–1994), the author of *The Conservative Mind: From Burke to Santayana* (1953).[5] Kirk's brand of conservatism emphasizes morality, tradition, and right living: "All culture arises out of

---

[5]   "When religious faith decays, culture must decline, though often seeming to flourish for a space after the religion which has nourished it has sunk into disbelief."—Russell Kirk

religion." No amount of wealth or poverty can stand in the way of living by, and for, shared values. Nevertheless, Kirk insisted that the rights of private property were essential to freedom, since without the means to support oneself one cannot be truly free; attacks on property, as represented by the taxation required for the welfare state, undermined freedom.

British voters reelected the Conservative Party, then still under the leadership of Churchill, in 1951 largely out of fear of the welfare state. While welcome in the abstract, the welfare society was proving expensive to sustain. As the party's manifesto put it:

> The attempt to impose a doctrinaire Socialism upon an Island which has grown great and famous by free enterprise has inflicted serious injury upon our strength and prosperity. Nationalisation has proved itself a failure which has resulted in heavy losses to the taxpayer or the consumer, or both. . . . Our finances have been brought into grave disorder. No British Government in peace time has ever had the power or spent the money in the vast extent and reckless manner of our present rulers. Apart from the two thousand millions they have borrowed or obtained from the United States and the Dominions, they have spent more than 10 million pounds a day, or 22 thousand millions in their six years. No community living in a world of competing nations can possibly afford such frantic extravagances. . . . A Conservative Government will cut out all unnecessary Government expenditure, simplify the administrative machine, and prune waste and extravagance in every department. . . . British taxation is higher than in any country outside the Communist world. It is higher by eight hundred millions a year than it was in the height of the war. We have a population of fifty millions depending on imports of food and raw materials which we have to win by our exertions, ingenuity, and craftsmanship. . . . We are a hardworking people. We are second to none in ability or enterprise so far as we are allowed to use these gifts. We now have the only Socialist Government in the Empire and Commonwealth. Of all the countries in the world Britain is the one least capable of bearing the Socialist system. . . . We must free ourselves from our impediments. Of all impediments the class war is the worst. At the time when a growing measure of national unity is more than ever necessary, the Socialist Party hope to gain another lease of power by fomenting class hatred and appealing to moods of greed and envy. . . . There is no means by which this Island can support its present population except by allowing its native genius to flourish and fructify. We cannot possibly keep ourselves alive without the individual effort, invention, contrivance, thrift, and good housekeeping of our people.

While successful in the short run, this line of thinking was too colorless. There had to be more to the conservative program than an argument that the nation could not afford the liberal program. After four brief years, the British returned the more liberal Labour Party to power in 1955 and gave the welfare state a renewed endorsement. It was not until Margaret Thatcher took the leadership in 1979 that conservatism reemerged as a powerful force in British life.

SOCIAL CONSERVATISM, ECONOMIC LIBERALISM, AND THE POSTWAR BOOM

Germany lay divided into the democratic Federal Republic of Germany (FDR), or West Germany, and the Soviet-dominated Democratic Republic of Germany (GDR), or East Germany. West Germany, aided by the Marshall Plan and various UN programs, achieved a stunning economic and political recovery under Konrad Adenauer (1887–1967), its chancel-

lor from 1949 to 1963. Adenauer led the Christian Democratic Union (CDU), the party that has dominated German politics for the last sixty years. He was polite but reserved, and he could be coldly autocratic, especially in his later years, yet his vision for Germany was generous, welcoming, and humble regarding the sins of the Nazi past.

Adenauer was determined to create a prosperous and decent society that would integrate with the rest of western Europe. He set German-French relations on a better course by agreeing to the transfer of the Saarland to France, and he started the effort to reconcile Germany with the new State of Israel. He acknowledged the horror of the Holocaust, offered unconditional and repeated apologies, and extended reparations and aid to the fledgling Jewish state. By 1955 he had restored West Germany's

Konrad Adenauer   The tag-line on this photo reads: "Together with the Chancellor, all Germans eye with worry their capital city." Adenauer was one of the founders of the Christian Democratic party in postwar West Germany and served as Chancellor of the Federal Republic from 1949 to 1963. He oversaw the reconstruction of the nation and its economy, restored diplomatic relations with Britain, France, and the US, advocated restitution to all Jews, and was a resolute champion of the new state of Israel. Participants in a television poll in 2003 named him "the greatest German of all time."

reputation so much that NATO welcomed it into the alliance. At home Adenauer set in motion the welfare state. Education, health care, pensions, and unemployment insurance all became hallmarks of the Christian Democrats. Austria, Belgium, Italy, the Netherlands, and Norway for many years were (and in some instances, still are) dominated by Christian Democratic parties. Other nations with prominent Christian Democrat parties include Czechoslovakia, Denmark, France, Hungary, Ireland, Luxembourg, Portugal, Poland, Romania, and Sweden.

Christian Democrats have figured large in most western European nations—and in fact in most developed non-Communist countries worldwide since World War II. As an ideology, **Christian Democracy** is a hybrid of social conservatism and economic liberalism. It blends forward-looking economic growth with a regard for traditionally Christian moral values. The movement started in the 19th century with a Catholic twist. Pope Leo XIII's encyclical *On New Things (De Rerum Novarum)* had discussed the impact of industrial capitalism on society (see chapter 20). Yet the thrust of most Christian Democrat parties has been moral, not theological—the importance of family, help to the poor and oppressed, communal identity, and social justice. After World War I many Protestant groups joined forces with the early Christian Democrat parties, out of concern for the rise of secularism across European society. They affirmed the Christian heritage of their societies, not in order to exclude other religious communities but to challenge secular ethics and Communism.

On the economic front, Christian democracy staked out a position midway between free-market capitalism and socialism. Commercial competition is generally good, it holds, but needs to be used for the benefit of society as a whole, and that requires regulation. Unchecked capitalism creates wealth, but the problems of the 20th century resulted not from lack of wealth but from its unequal distribution. Hence the welfare state. Substantial and indexed taxation, with tax rates increasing with income levels, exists both in order to fund essential services and to engineer a society that has less income disparity. To a significant degree, however, western Europe could afford its welfare structure because the United States provided the cost of military defense through direct aid and subsidization of NATO.

─────────── ✦ ───────────

With the state providing for their basic needs, western Europeans could spend more of their incomes on the new consumer goods that rolled off factory lines: televisions, automobiles, refrigerators, laundry machines, record players, mass-produced cigarettes and alcohol, motorcycles, electric coffee makers, vacuum cleaners, hair dryers, power tools, gas and electric ovens. High taxes naturally reduced "disposable income," the money left over to buy such items, but a new tool kept the purchases coming—consumer credit. Credit has been the fuel for capitalism since the 13th century, but it had always been limited to governments, banks, investment houses, companies, merchants, and entrepreneurs. Now that consumers too could purchase items on credit, consumption could keep pace, and more so, with production, assuring manufacturers of steady demand for their products. Demand spurred continuous production and continual innovation, which in turn generated profits that could be taxed to fund the welfare state.[6]

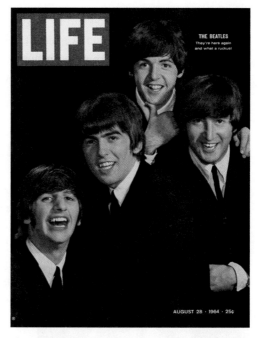

"Can't Buy Me Love"—But You Can Buy the Album   On August 28, 1964 *Life* magazine ran this photo of the Beatles on its cover. "They're here again—and what a ruckus!"

It worked well, until the late 1960s. As long as the economies kept growing, so did tax revenues, and governments remained solvent. But economic growth depended on the growing postwar population, the **baby boom**. It demanded more goods—more food and toys, more athletic equipment, more clothing, more schools and school supplies, more stereo systems, and more ways to care for all of them. But when the population increase leveled off, so too did demand for goods. Prices tumbled and profits along with them. To continue funding the welfare state, taxes rose and credit became tighter. The miracle of the West suddenly appeared vulnerable.

A GENERATION OF REBELLION

Ballooning public costs also contributed to that vulnerability. Welfare spending grew steadily through the 1960s until, as early as 1964, it strained budgets across western Europe and the United States. In Britain, annual costs for social services

---

[6]   The first true credit card, the Diners Club Card, appeared in 1950, and American Express brought out its card in 1958. Sweden introduced the Eurocard in 1960. France's Carte Bleue appeared in 1967.

rose 50 percent between 1964 and 1970. With the U.S. military shield protecting Europe from the Soviet Union, western states were still able to sustain their generous welfare programs with ease. In the United States, however, the combination of social spending and military costs threatened ruin. For millions of baby boomers coming of age in the 1960s, the economy and society appeared to be unraveling, along with the political system that oversaw it. As America entered the war in Vietnam, it seemed to many to have lost its moral authority as well. A generation of rebellion began to question received values and to protest against unjust norms and failed policies.

A Generation in Rebellion   University students in Paris, in 1968, seized the buildings of the Sorbonne in protest against the Cold War and the failures of the welfare state. The photos visible here are portraits of Karl Marx, Friedrich Engels, Josef Stalin, and Mao Zedong. Workers across the nation joined in a general strike, which nearly brought down the government of Charles de Gaulle. De Gaulle agreed to hold new elections to the National Assembly, but as he did so he marshaled the French army outside Paris. The rebellion broke up soon thereafter. The motives of the rebels are still debated. Clearly many were Communists or Socialists, but many also seem to have joined in a spirit of unfocused anarchy. One of the many graffiti left behind by the students on the walls of the Sorbonne read: "We do not want a world in which the price for a guarantee of not starving to death is to die of boredom."

In western Europe, however, the rebellious 1960s had a different focus. Heavy public investment in higher education continued. Britain created dozens of public universities in the 1950s and 1960s, which British students attended for free. Discontent arose not from denied access to education but from social prejudices that preserved old privileges. One could be brilliantly educated at a new "red brick" university—yet one could get the best jobs or most promising careers, many believed, only if one had attended the private universities of Oxford and Cambridge.

France too expanded access to its universities, but at a much slower rate—and with preferred treatment for the middle class. As late as 1968 only 4 percent of university students nationwide came from the working class. Italy invested in fewer new universities but admitted students in large numbers and also helped pay for their tuition; the average student-to-faculty ratio rose higher than 200:1. The quality of their education, or at least the perception of its quality, declined proportionally. By 1968 only half of university graduates were able to find work in the fields of their study. The liberalization of higher education across western Europe, in other words, had failed to alter ingrained social privilege and class stratification.

Similar complaints arose about economic strata. In 1967 in West Germany, despite twenty years of reform, the top 2 percent of the population still owned more than one-third of the nation's wealth—a pattern that echoed the inequity of the era before World War I. France and Britain had comparable concentrations of wealth. Western society, overall, was better off than ever before, but the ideal of social justice, many complained, had been sold out. People had ceased to be thinking and feeling actors on the world stage and had become mere consumers.

> Western society, overall, was better off than ever before, but the ideal of social justice, many complained, had been sold out. People had ceased to be thinking and feeling actors on the world stage and had become mere consumers.

The 1960s were also the age of **civil rights** struggles in the United States—the struggles for equal access for African Americans to transportation, lunch counters, jobs, schools, and every other part of society. Dr. Martin Luther King Jr. (1929–1968) was a powerful moral force who advocated the use of civil disobedience to obtain these goals. He won the Nobel Peace Prize in 1964. His shocking assassination in 1968 did not deter other groups, including Hispanic Americans, American Indians, and gays and lesbians, from also advocating for their own rights in the face of sometimes enormous hostility. Major civil rights laws were passed by the U.S. Congress starting in 1964. But the decade also saw immigration conflicts in western Europe. Millions of Africans, South Asians, and Muslim Arabs migrated into Europe during decolonization. They came for many different reasons. Some feared the instability of the postcolonial societies and their underdeveloped economies. Others felt a keen sense of cultural identity with the withdrawing Europeans. Still others were openly recruited by Western powers that, after eighty million war deaths, faced the hard work of rebuilding. Jobs were plentiful in western Europe, and economic futures in Africa, Asia, and the Middle East seemed uncertain, so why not migrate?

Germany had the greatest need for workers, given the scale of reconstruction and given that half its population was captive behind the Iron Curtain. Konrad Adenauer invited "guest workers" (*Gastarbeiters*) from Turkey to work in construction and in factories. In 1964 the FDR's labor minister, Theodor Blank (1905–1972), commemorated the arrival of the one-millionth Turkish guest worker:

> These million workers contribute vitally to the steady growth of German industry, the maintaining of stable prices, and upholding

> Germany's reputation on the world marketplace.... To judge from available statistics, our native labor pool will continue to shrink for the foreseeable future.... We are in fact wholly dependent on the guest workers to keep our economy moving forward.... In fact we can no longer even imagine economic life without them, a situation that entitles them to share in the benefits of our [welfare] society.

Tensions between the guest workers and their German hosts were growing, he acknowledged, but "the coming together of people from different backgrounds and cultures has worked—and for that we owe our guest workers our gratitude."

But popular resistance to immigration kept growing. In 1982 a group of professors at the University of Heidelberg went so far as to publish an open letter that warned of

> the infiltration of our German people by millions of foreign immigrants and their families—the infiltration of our language, our culture, our national traditions.... In many workplaces and neighborhoods, in fact, our German people are made to feel like strangers in their own land.

In Britain, immigrants included Indians, Pakistanis, Arabs, Africans, Chinese, and Southeast Asians. Throughout the 1960s a Conservative British politician, Enoch Powell (1912–1998), warned of the growing expense of the welfare state. He is best remembered, however, for a speech in the spring of 1968 on the threat of immigration:

> In 15 or 20 years, on present trends, there will be in this country three and a half million Commonwealth immigrants and their descendants. That is not my figure. That is the official figure given to parliament by the spokesman of the Registrar General's Office.
>
> There is no comparable official figure for the year 2000, but it must be in the region of five to seven million, approximately one-tenth of the whole population, and approaching that of Greater London. Of course, it will not be evenly distributed from Margate to Aberystwyth and from Penzance to Aberdeen. Whole areas, towns and parts of towns across England will be occupied by sections of the immigrant and immigrant-descended population.
>
> As time goes on, the proportion of this total who are immigrant descendants, those born in England, who arrived here by exactly the same route as the rest of us, will rapidly increase. Already by 1985 the native-born would constitute the majority. It is this fact which creates the extreme urgency of action now, of just that kind of action which is hardest for

politicians to take, action where the difficulties lie in the present but the evils to be prevented or minimised lie several parliaments ahead. . . .

For reasons which they could not comprehend, and in pursuance of a decision by default, on which they were never consulted, they found themselves made strangers in their own country. They found their wives unable to obtain hospital beds in childbirth, their children unable to obtain school places, their homes and neighbourhoods changed beyond recognition, their plans and prospects for the future defeated; at work they found that employers hesitated to apply to the immigrant worker the standards of discipline and competence required of the native-born worker; they began to hear, as time went by, more and more voices which told them that they were now the unwanted. On top of this, they now learn that a one-way privilege is to be established by Act of Parliament; a law which cannot, and is not intended to, operate to protect them or redress their grievances, is to be enacted to give the stranger, the disgruntled and the agent provocateur the power to pillory them for their private actions. . . .

As I look ahead, I am filled with foreboding. Like the Roman, I seem to see "the River Tiber foaming with much blood". That tragic and intractable phenomenon which we watch with horror on the other side of the Atlantic but which there is interwoven with the history and existence of the States itself, is coming upon us here by our own volition and our own neglect. Indeed, it has all but come. In numerical terms, it will be of American proportions long before the end of the century. Only resolute and urgent action will avert it even now. Whether there will be the public will to demand and obtain that action, I do not know. All I know is that to see, and not to speak, would be the great betrayal.

Powell's "Rivers of Blood" speech set off a stormy debate. While many Britons denounced his comments as racist, most rallied to his cause. The argument against immigration was the same one used by societies dating back to Roman efforts to block Germanic tribesmen from overwhelming the empire in the 3rd century CE: too many, too fast. Mass assimilations can be difficult for the host society, as they are for the immigrants themselves. Popular support for Powell's comments swelled, because immigration was seen as a threat to the welfare state.[7] Powell argued that welfare programs could continue at steady levels even while reducing Britain's basic tax rate (just over 40 percent in 1968)—but only if the country avoid military entanglements abroad and reduce the immigrant population. Those were two big ifs.

---

[7]   In polls between 1969 and 1974, Enoch Powell was repeatedly identified as the single most admired politician in Britain.

Migrant Labor   An immigrant from Portugal arrives in Britain, in search of a better life. He was lucky to get out. A repressive quasi-Fascist regime, led by António de Oliveira Salazar, ran Portugal from 1932 to 1974.

TURNING POINT: 1967–1968

Cold War tensions had eased somewhat after the near-catastrophe of the Cuban Missile Crisis, but they roared back to life in 1967 and 1968. They were fueled by three events—the Six-Day War in the Middle East, the Soviet invasion of Czechoslovakia, and the Tet Offensive against American forces in Vietnam.

Relations between Israel and her Arab neighbors had remained difficult, since the Arab states refused to recognize Israel and continued to call for its destruction. Border clashes occurred regularly, and members of the **Palestinian Liberation Organization (PLO)** regularly carried out terrorist attacks on Israeli citizens and property. Rivalries and disagreements between the Arab states, however, impeded any sort of collective action against Israel until 1967, when alliances between Egypt, Jordan, and Syria left Israel surrounded by declared enemies. Fearing invasion from all sides, Israel launched the **Six-Day War**. Air strikes and rapid troop movements paralyzed the Arabs' military capabilities, and in only six days Israel seized the Gaza Strip, the Golan Heights along the Israeli border with Syria, the Sinai Peninsula, and the entire West Bank. It also took possession of the eastern part of the then-divided city of Jerusalem (see Map 27.4).

The speed and completeness of the Israeli victory deeply embarrassed the Arab nations, including the eight countries that had provided armed assistance: Algeria, Iraq, Kuwait, Libya, Morocco, Saudi Arabia, Sudan, and Tunisia. Apart

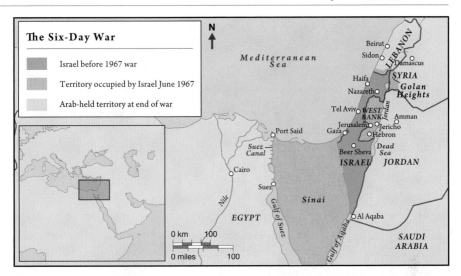

The Six-Day War

- Israel before 1967 war
- Territory occupied by Israel June 1967
- Arab-held territory at end of war

N

Mediterranean Sea

Beirut
Sidon
Damascus
LEBANON
Haifa
SYRIA
Nazareth
Golan Heights
Tel Aviv
WEST BANK
Amman
Jerusalem
Jericho
Gaza
Hebron
Port Said
Suez Canal
Beer Sheva
Dead Sea
Cairo
ISRAEL
JORDAN
Suez
Sinai
Nile
Gulf of Suez
EGYPT
Al Aqaba
SAUDI ARABIA
Gulf of Aqaba

0 km   100
0 miles   100

MAP 27.4   The Six-Day War

from what it meant to the combatants and local populations, the war had important implications for the Cold War. Arab popular opinion quickly decided that the stunning defeat was possible only through secret U.S. intervention on Israel's behalf. Although America staunchly supported the state of Israel prior to the war, most Arabs had regarded the British and French as the biggest meddling outsiders. After the war, much of Arab popular resentment turned toward the United States.

The following year, on the night of August 20, 1968, Soviet tanks rolled into Czechoslovakia and put an end to the liberalizing reforms of its Communist government. Czechoslovakia had been Communist since 1948, but a new leader, Alexander Dubcek (1921–1992), hoped to create a less repressive form of government, a "socialism with a human face." Reforms instituted early in 1968 (known as the **Prague Spring**) permitted independent political parties; this appalled the Soviet ruler, Leonid Brezhnev (1906–1982), who ordered the military intervention. The action was more threatening than violent, but it sent a chill throughout Europe; the USSR, after all, had killed over twenty thousand civilians in its 1956 invasion of Hungary. Even the most liberal of western Europeans could not easily deny the brutality of Communist government or try to dismiss that brutality as something unique to Josef Stalin's rule. Under Stalin's successor, Khrushchev, and then again under Khrushchev's successor, Brezhnev,

> The attack on Czechoslovakia was the first direct experience of Soviet brutality for the generation that came of age in the late 1960s, and it made clearer than ever the perilous state of the world.

The Prague Spring   "Ivan, go home!" shouted this young Czech woman to the Soviet soldiers who rode their tanks through the streets of Prague in 1968. The invasion of Czechoslovakia was a turning point in the Cold War, since it challenged Communist sympathizers across Europe and America to reconsider their idealistic view of the Soviet Union.

the leadership in Moscow had shown its willingness to secure and expand its dictatorial authority. The attack on Czechoslovakia was the first direct experience of Soviet brutality for the generation that came of age in the late 1960s, and it made clearer than ever the perilous state of the world.

Also in 1968, a surprise wave of attacks by the troops of North Vietnam against the U.S.-supported government in South Vietnam nearly toppled the American-backed regime in Saigon. Called the Tet Offensive, these attacks targeted roughly 120 separate towns and cities in the south and left 10,000 South Vietnamese and American soldiers dead and another 35,000 wounded. America had become directly involved in Vietnam in 1955, when President Eisenhower deployed several hundred military advisers to the regime in Saigon. By 1963 U.S. troops were still as few as 16,000, but under President Lyndon Johnson the military presence escalated dramatically, passing the half million mark by 1968. The sharp impact of the Tet Offensive made it abundantly clear that, even with increased numbers and superior technology, the United States could look forward to no quick and easy victory in Vietnam. Chinese and Soviet support for the Communist North Vietnamese further assured a long and drawn-out war (see Map 27.5).

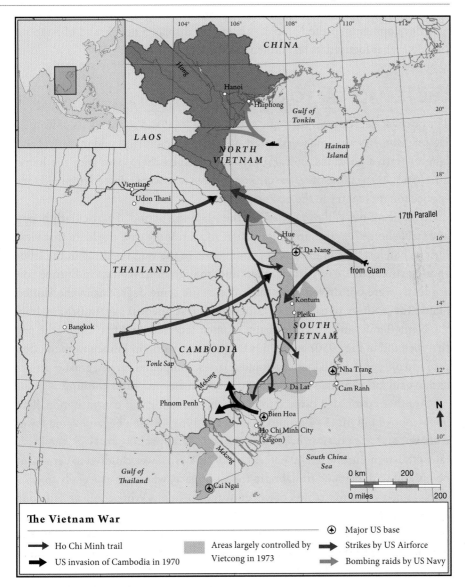

MAP 27.5   **The Vietnam War**

The 1967–1968 turning point drove home some harsh realities. The economic bonanza of the postwar years was coming to a halt, and that threatened to unravel the safety net provided by the welfare state. The Cold War turned out not to be merely a strategic game between bureaucrats and armchair generals; the threat was real and deadly. In the United States the struggle for civil rights showed that prejudices and racial hatreds still roiled, while conflicts in Europeans over immigrants threatened hard-won social stability everywhere.

And developments in the Middle East put on display a new brand of Arab nationalism that focused its resentment on the United States.

THE FEMALE FACTOR

The postwar decades saw dramatic shifts in the legal and social rights of women. Despite women's wartime work in farming, in manufacturing, and in clerical and administrative positions, cultural pressures pushed them back into the home after 1945. At the same time, the millions of men who were released from military service sought reentry in the postwar economy.

Americans often like to remember the 1950s as a period of particularly happy and stable home life. In Europe, privation and rationing gave the lie to that view. Europe had lost tens of millions of young men in the war, resulting in the labor shortage that had led to guest workers and immigration. Women in Europe consequently were not driven from their jobs to the same degree as in the United States; the primary injustice they experienced was unequal pay. In Britain, Italy, the Netherlands, and West Germany, women received only two-thirds the pay that men did in the 1950s and 1960s for the same work; in France women often received only half. With low wages and salaries, companies earned greater profits and so paid more in taxes—which in turn kept social programs running.

Another factor also came into play—the availability of contraception. The birth-control pill hit the European market in 1961, women began having fewer children, and the postwar baby boom ended. After peaking in 1955, the birthrate in western Europe fell 40 percent by 1975. With fewer children to care for at home, and with demand for labor in the workplace, women—especially middle-class women—began to think of work outside the home. Work could be a lifelong career, rather than a way to support oneself until marriage.

By 1970 fully one-half of European mothers had stopped having children by the age of twenty-seven or twenty-eight, which meant that forty years of productive work still lay ahead of them, if they were interested. And they *were* interested. They wanted careers, not merely jobs, and they demanded equal pay for equal work. The rise of feminism thus aimed specifically at economic justice. Men still predominated in heavy industry and manufacturing, but new careers opened up in schools and universities, in health care, in management, in journalism, and in law. Women were drawn to these "white collar" careers in large numbers.

The movement for equality for women in the 1960s and 1970s came to be known as **second wave feminism**. Feminism's first wave, starting in the 19th century, had a single goal—the right of women to vote. Crusaders for contraception were then relatively few, and they were seen as radicals. The second wave focused on personal life, sexual health, access to abortion and contraception, equal rights in the workplace, the availability of child care services, gender roles in society, and the portrayals of women in popular culture. Since then, a third wave of feminism, from the 1990s to the present, has had two main streams. One was a broadening of the movement to include the poor and ethnic minorities. The other was an examination of the very concepts of gender, race, and sexuality.

The second wave scored signal achievements. In the United States, new institutions dedicated to improving women's lives were established—from the Presidential Commission on the Status of Women (1961) to the National Organization for Women (1966), the National Abortion Rights Action League (1968), and the Coalition of Labor Union Women (1974). The Supreme Court in 1965 struck down states' bans on the sale of contraception, and in 1973 it upheld women's right to abortion. The first shelters for battered women opened their doors. Universities across the nation created programs in women's studies. Laws and procedures regarding rape were revised with a new emphasis on the protection of rape victims. Military academies admitted women applicants, while female undergraduates in colleges outnumbered males by 1978.

Feminism in western Europe did not have the vibrancy of America's reform movement, largely because the extensive welfare-state structures had already achieved—at least on paper—many of its goals. The new French constitution of 1946, for example, had mandated equal legal rights for men and women, and

Second Wave Feminists   Italian women march in front of the Coliseum in Rome to protest the country's divorce laws, in 1974. The banner reads: "Movement for the Liberation of Women."

women were already vital to the workforce. While discrimination persisted, especially in pay, political instability seemed the more immediate problem. Between 1946 and 1958 the French government went through no fewer than twenty-seven cabinet reshufflings, which made it difficult to mount any extended campaigns for reform. Only in 1968 was the first national organization for women's rights formed—the Mouvement de Libération des Femmes (MLF). Even then, the MLF saw itself as a network of psychologists, psychoanalysts, philosophers, and legal scholars rather than a group of activists. Practical, hands-on reform had to wait until the 1971 formation of Choisir ("Choice"), a group that advocated for contraception and abortion rights.

In West Germany too, the welfare state had addressed many women's issues. That assumption helps explain why no government between 1945 and 1961 had a single woman in a cabinet-level post. As Franz Josef Würmeling, the West German minister for the family and social affairs, put it in 1961:

> The [German] family has responded to the economic constraints of our time in two main ways: with housewives and mothers taking jobs outside the home, and then limiting the number of children they have. . . . But for housewives and mothers to work outside the home is not a solution; it is in fact a compulsive evil.

In Britain feminist concerns were the program of the Labour Party, along with social welfare and reform. Labour was in power from 1945 to 1951 under Clement Atlee (1883–1967), then again from 1964 to 1970 and 1974 to 1976 under Harold Wilson (1916–1995). The laws regarding abortion, contraception, divorce, education, and sexual preference were all liberalized, but a vital feminist movement failed to appear.

WOMEN, ISLAM, AND THE STATE

The status of women in postcolonial Islamic society played out between the opposing forces of modernization and traditionalism. The ideologies of the Cold War did not affect Muslim states directly, since atheistic Communism held no appeal, but the political conflict mattered to them very much. Three broad issues had a particular impact on women: national identity, the role of Islamic law in civic life, and the nature of state government.

First, national identity. The states created out of European decolonization sometimes crossed, and sometimes divided, traditional ethnic borders. Creating a sense of national identity thus represented a challenge to traditional social structures and values. Some factions believed that Western-style pluralism could be harnessed to produce a modern democratic society based on individual rights and capitalism even while retaining the core values of Islam. This reformed tradition, they believed, would allow Islamic states to remain open to the West and rid Muslim life of centuries-old norms regarding women, while still retaining an authentic religious identity.

One example of this reform-minded strain emerged in Turkey. There the secular constitution ensured equal treatment of women before the law, moderated customs regarding marriage and divorce, and allowed women economic freedom, access to education, and freedom of dress. In Algeria after liberation in 1962, men and women came to possess full and equal civil rights. Lebanon also experimented with democracy, civil rights, religious pluralism, and greater participation and freedom for women in public life. Conflicts with Israel and Syria kept Lebanon a fragile society, but the capital city of Beirut became known in the 1960s and 1970s as the "Paris of the eastern Mediterranean." In Iran, too, under the autocratic regime of Shah Muhammad Reza Pahlavi, westernizing policies opened the state to economic development, the growth of a vivid cosmopolitan culture, and an easing of restrictions on female participation in society. No political freedom existed, of course, and the rewards of economic development were hoarded by the Shah and his cadre. But Iranian society seemed set on a liberalizing trajectory, prior to the Islamic revolution of 1979.

Learning New Ways   An Iranian teacher assists one of her students during class, late 1960s.

Other factions in response raised the second issue of importance to women—the role of Islamic law, or **shariah**. They argued that Islam cannot be harmonized with Western ways, and the only correct path was complete rejection of Western values and the embrace of ancient Islamic practices. In the words of one conservative reformer, Mona Fayyad Kawtharani, ancient practices like the veiling of women represent resistance to the West.[8] Ethnic and tribal traditions also contributed, but civic rights and social freedoms for women became ideological statements. After the overthrow of the shah and the declaration of Iran as an Islamic Republic, in 1979, the fundamentalist new regime ordered women to relinquish Western styles of dress, forbade them from venturing out in public without an accompanying male family member, and pressed them back into domestic life.

The role of religion in national life thus became crucial to determining women's fates. The Organization of the Islamic Conference (OIC) formed in 1969 to present a united Islamic face to the world. With fifty-seven member states, it is the largest international organization in the world after the United Nations itself, and it came to reject the UN Declaration on Human Rights (1948) because of its basis in secular values. The OIC's **Cairo Declaration on Human Rights**, adopted in 1990, states in its preamble that the only valid foundation for human rights is in faith:

> Convinced that mankind which has reached an advanced stage in materialistic science is still, and shall remain, in dire need of faith to support its civilization as well as a self-motivating force to guard its rights;
>
> [and] believing that fundamental rights and freedoms according to Islam are an integral part of the Islamic religion and that no one shall have the right as a matter of principle to abolish them either in whole or in part or to violate or ignore them inasmuch as they are binding divine commands, which are contained in the Revealed Books of Allah and which were sent through the last of His Prophets to complete the preceding divine messages;
>
> and [believing] that safeguarding those fundamental rights and freedoms is an act of worship whereas the neglect or violation thereof is an abominable sin, and that the safeguarding of those fundamental rights and freedom is an individual responsibility of every person and a collective responsibility of the entire *Ummah*;
>
> [We do] hereby and on the basis of the above-mentioned principles declare as follows.

---

8   As a sign of its rejection of Western ways, a society could accept a simple head scarf, the head-to-toe burka, or something in between.

Among the Declaration's highlights:

Article 1: (a) All human beings form one family whose members are united by submission to God and descent from Adam. All men are equal in terms of basic human dignity and basic obligations and responsibilities, without any discrimination on the grounds of race, colour, language, sex, religious belief, political affiliation, social status or other considerations. . . .

Article 2: Life is a God-given gift and the right to life is guaranteed to every human being. It is the duty of individuals, societies and states to protect this right from any violation, and it is prohibited to take away life except for a Shari'ah-prescribed reason. . . .

Article 5: The family is the foundation of society, and marriage is the basis of its formation. Men and women have the right to marriage, and no restrictions stemming from race, colour or nationality shall prevent them from enjoying this right. . . .

Article 6: (a) Woman is equal to man in human dignity, and has rights to enjoy as well as duties to perform; she has her own civil entity and financial independence, and the right to retain her name and lineage. (b) The husband is responsible for the support and welfare of the family. . . .

Article 9: (a) The quest for knowledge is an obligation, and the provision of education is a duty for society and the State . . . . (b) Every human being has the right to receive both religious and worldly education from the various institutions of education and guidance, including the family, the school, the university, the media, etc. . . .

Article 10: Islam is the religion of unspoiled nature. It is prohibited to exercise any form of compulsion on man or to exploit his poverty or ignorance in order to convert him to another religion or to atheism.

Article 11: (a) Human beings are born free, and no one has the right to enslave, humiliate, oppress or exploit them, and there can be no subjugation but to God the Most-High. (b) Colonialism of all types being one of the most evil forms of enslavement is totally prohibited. . . .

Article 12: Every man shall have the right, within the framework of Shari'ah, to free movement and to select his place of residence whether inside or outside his country and, if persecuted, is entitled to seek asylum in another country. . . .

Article 19: (a) All individuals are equal before the law, without distinction between the ruler and the ruled. (b) The right to resort to justice is guaranteed to everyone. . . .

Article 22: (a) Everyone shall have the right to express his opinion freely in such manner as would not be contrary to the principles of the Shari'ah. (b) Everyone shall have the right to advocate what is right, and propagate what is good, and warn against what is wrong and evil according to the norms of Islamic Shari'ah. (c) Information is a vital necessity to society. It may not be exploited or misused in such a way as may violate sanctities and the dignity of Prophets, undermine moral and ethical values or disintegrate, corrupt or harm society or weaken its faith. (d) It is not permitted to arouse nationalistic or doctrinal hatred or to do anything that may be an incitement to any form of racial discrimination.

Article 25: The Islamic Shari'ah is the only source of reference for the explanation or clarification to any of the articles of this Declaration.

The Cairo Declaration recognizes the innate dignity of all people. It asserts their rights to live in peace, to own property, and to receive health care and an education. It also protects people from enslavement and war; and it prohibits anyone from taking another's life "except for a Shari'ah-prescribed reason." But since "the Islamic Shari'ah is the only source of reference for the explanation or clarification to any of the articles of this Declaration" (article 25), exceptions exist to almost every one of its guarantees. As far as women are concerned, the OIC's declaration recognizes that "woman is equal to man to human dignity, and has rights to enjoy as well as duties to perform," but that is not the same thing as saying that a woman has equal rights—as the UN declaration explicitly declares.

The third issue affecting women's status was the debate regarding the role of the state itself. In order to hold together their ethnically plural nations, with diverging interpretations of the role of religion in national life, postcolonial governments have relied on centralized authority. Propping up their militaries and police structures has proved expensive, however, and many Muslim governments have pushed hard for economic development. "Strongmen" with authoritarian regimes have included the shah in Iran, Hafez al-Assad in Syria (r. 1971–2000), General Muhammad Zia ul-Haq in Pakistan (r. 1978–1988), or Muammar al-Qaddafi in Libya (r. 1969–2011). In each case, wealth has been hoarded by elites rather than distributed throughout society, and countries without oil have been mired in poverty. In the poorer states—Afghanistan, Bangladesh, Jordan, Libya, Pakistan, Syria—lack of economic opportunity drove women into isolation within the home, so that they could not compete with men for available jobs.[9]

---

[9]   Even in oil-rich Saudi Arabia, wealth is so centralized that millions of women and men live in poverty.

THE STRUCTURES OF THOUGHT

Catastrophes can have their beneficial aspects. They can sweep history's slate clean; they can trigger a willingness to rethink basic assumptions. Something like this happened in the late Middle Ages, when the Black Death carried off one-third of Europe's population. People questioned why God would permit so much suffering, how society had responded, and what truly matters in life. All these questions contributed to the great Renaissance of the 15th and 16th centuries. In the ancient world, the destruction of the Temple in Jerusalem and the Jews' being hauled away to Babylon in slavery, in 586 BCE, inspired the creation of rabbinical Judaism, the Oral Torah, and the revival of Jewish thought. In the 20th century, the blow of two World Wars, the Depression, the Holocaust, and the threat of global nuclear annihilation again stimulated thought about fundamental questions in life.

The intellectual and artistic life of the second half of the 20th century in the West has been rich. The experimental spirit of modernism has combined with new developments in science, linguistics, technology, and psychology. If much of this work has been bleak and despairing, it also contains intense feeling and ironic, if unsettling, humor. **Structuralism**, most notably in the 1950s through 1970s, had a particular focus on language. The **post-structuralism** that followed is more skeptical of systems of thought. Both, however, are difficult to define once and for all. The writing style of their leading thinkers is often difficult, too, and highly technical.

Such a style of prose is not accidental. The massive expansion of higher-education systems in the postwar era resulted in the professionalization of philosophy. Philosophers, in short, became academics. Their investigations were not conducted with popular audiences in mind, and they could write in a way that few others could understand. Consider just a sampling. For Jürgen Habermas (b. 1929) in Germany, critical theory can still speak directly to the role of the individual in politics, but most individuals would be lost reading it:

> Under the functional aspect of reaching understanding, communicative action serves the transmission and renewal of cultural knowledge; under the aspect of coordinating action, it serves social integration and the establishment of group solidarity; under the aspect of socialization, it serves the formation of personal identities. *(Habermas, The Theory of Communicative Action, 1981)*

For Hilary Putnam (b. 1926), an American philosopher, the very idea of explanation is in question. He works in a tradition that scrutinizes every term, in a specialized and technically precise language:

On the internalist view, we recall, explanation depends on factors internal to the body of knowledge (on structuring the body of knowledge so that the parts stand in appropriate logical and epistemic relations) *except*, of course, for the truth of the statements comprising the explanans.
(*Putnam, The Threefold Cord: Mind, Body, and World, 1999*)

Despite its difficulty, post-structuralism has allowed feminists, ethnic minorities, and others to look for the hidden assumptions in the critical thinkers of the past. Perhaps the most famous stream within post-structuralism, however, began with Jacques Derrida (1930–2004). His theory of "deconstruction" involves close readings of past thinkers. Even to quote it is daunting, so we must first get a better handle on structuralism.

Structuralism emerged in response to the collapse of belief in values portrayed by the absurdists, such as Camus and Beckett. It emphasizes the structured ways in which we see, participate in, and comprehend the world. The world itself may be incomprehensible, said the structuralists, but our perceptions of it are not. They arise from structured systems of language, thought, and social interaction.

> The world itself may be incomprehensible, said the structuralists, but our perceptions of it are not. They arise from structured systems of language, thought, and social interaction.

Structuralism has its roots in the work of a Swiss linguist, Ferdinand de Saussure (1857–1913). Saussure argued that all languages are arbitrary systems. They are *systems* because they are held together by self-dependent rules of grammar, syntax, and etymology; they are *arbitrary* because they bear no necessary relation to the world they describe. Consider a book. English speakers centuries ago, when books were invented, could have selected *any* combination of letters or sounds to denote the new object. But *B, O, O,* and *K* are what they settled on. And that choice had all sorts of side-effects: a person who sells books became a BOOK-SELLER, and his or her place of business became a BOOKSTORE. Someone who learned a great deal from reading books became BOOK-SMART. Saussure's point is that the relationships that matter are not those that connect the words to the things they describe, like B-O-O-K to a book. They are the relationships that connect words together. All our statements—all of our "speech acts," as some linguists call them—say as much about our language itself as about the world.

Claude Levi-Strauss (1908–2009) emerged in the 1950s and 1960s as the most brilliant of structuralist anthropologists. Levi-Strauss maintained that the differences between cultures are local variations of shared human traits. Human actions, desires, emotions, and ideas emerge from a single, though complex, structure of instinctive needs. Every human society, for example, abhors the idea of incest. This is no coincidence. But cultural norms about incest can still vary enormously. In the West, biologists might talk about the danger to the species from marrying too closely within a family. (Incest, they would say, "narrows the gene pool." If the environment changes and wipes out people with just some genes, then everybody is gone.) Other societies would have very different words and practices. To Levi-Strauss, human beings all perceive the world in certain ways; I see this pen, that piece of paper, this desk, that lamp. Yet we interpret it in different ways, thanks to the connections we make. Just as Saussure said about words, we define things in relation to one another. Levi-Strauss made his life's work showing the hidden parallels that exist across cultures.

As we saw in earlier chapters, Sigmund Freud and Karl Marx describe, in their different ways, patterns in human life. Freud wrote about the lures of Eros and Thanatos, Marx about class conflict and modes of production. Not surprisingly, then, structuralists of the 1960s and 1970s revived their ideas. The French literary theorist Roland Barthes (1915–1980) showed in *Mythologies* (1953) the cultural values in ordinary middle-class life. Everything from fashion magazines to televised wrestling matches, from advertisements for household cleaning prod-

ucts to striptease shows, has hidden meanings that can be decoded. A poem, a novel, or an essay has hidden meanings too. The point is not what the author tried to say, but what he could not avoid not saying. A text, as Barthes put it, represents the "death of the author."

The belief in hidden systems or codes in all human activity carries a risk. If humans can only operate within limits, even without awareness of them, then is it possible to be a free moral agent? Or are human beings instead just a part of the vast system of the world? And if so, can we be held morally responsible for our actions? The question is not just theoretical. A number of early structuralists, especially in France, had unsavory pasts. Louis Althusser (1918–1990), a Marxist philosopher, resisted efforts to reform the Communist Party after

Consuming Hidden Meanings   A modishly dressed young Swede shows off her Levi's shopping bag in 1973, in Stockholm. The image of a woman's bottom that adorns the bag—also displayed on a poster in the store window—is a play on the phrase "skin-tight jeans". The advertisement is intended as playful rather than demeaning, as it reflected the spirit of sexual liberation among the young generation of the late 1960s and early 1970s. Cheeky chic.

Stalin's death; he also strangled his wife. (In court, he explained that he was massaging her neck absentmindedly, and when he stopped he realized she was dead. He was sentenced to a mental institution.) He also added his name to a petition in 1977 that called for the repeal of "age of consent" laws, so that adults could legally have sex with children under the age of fifteen. Other figures had even more sordid pasts. An earlier German philosopher whose ideas influenced structuralism, Martin Heidegger (1889–1976), had affairs with two of his Jewish graduate students shortly before joining the Nazi Party, which he served for twelve years. Paul de Man (1919–1983), a Belgian literary critic schooled in structuralism, wrote over two hundred pro-Nazi articles.

But ideas should be judged for themselves, not for the individuals who derive them. Structuralist thinking at its best helped to assuage the bleakness felt by the postwar generations. It reoriented the mental map of Western intellectual life. It was, in its way, an antidote to modernism. And, with Jacques Derrida, it provided the antidote by creative but sympathetic readings of many of the great modernists. The horrors of the century shattered faith in progress, goodness, meaning, and purpose in life for millions of people. Structuralism rebuilt some essential scaffolding in a ruined landscape. People still wanted something to believe in.

WHO, WHAT, WHERE

absurdity

baby boom

Cairo Declaration on Human Rights

Central Intelligence Agency (CIA)

Christian democracy

civil rights

Cold War

Cuban Missile Crisis

decolonization

détente

Iron Curtain

Marshall Plan

North Atlantic Treaty Organization (NATO)

Palestinian Liberation Organization (PLO)

post-structuralism

Prague Spring

second wave feminism

shariah

Six-Day War

structuralism

welfare states

SUGGESTED READINGS

Primary Sources

Barthes, Roland. *Mythologies.*

Camus, Albert. *The Myth of Sisyphus.*

——. *The Stranger.*

Kirk, Russell. *The Conservative Mind.*

Lévi-Strauss, Claude. *The Savage Mind.*

Powell, Enoch. *Freedom and Reality.*

Anthologies

Hanhimäki, Jussi, and Odd Arne Westad, eds. *The Cold War: A History in Documents and Eyewitness Accounts* (2003).

Pierson, Christopher, and Francis G. Castles, eds. *The Welfare State Reader* (2007).

Prince, Althea, and Susan Silva-Wayne, eds. *Feminisms and Womanisms: A Women's Studies Reader* (2004).

Winkler, Allan M. *The Cold War: A History in Documents* (2011).

Studies

Azoulay, Ariella. *From Palestine to Israel: A Photographic Record of Destruction and State Formation, 1947–1950* (2011).

Barrett, Roby C. *The Greater Middle East and the Cold War: US Foreign Policy under Eisenhower and Kennedy* (2010).

Fraser, Derek. *The Evolution of the British Welfare State: A History of Social Policy since the Industrial Revolution* (2009).

Gaddis, John Lewis. *The Cold War: A New History* (2005).

Geller, Jay Howard. *Jews in Post-Holocaust Germany, 1945–1953* (2005).

Grossmann, Atina. *Jews, Germans, and Allies: Close Encounters in Occupied Germany* (2009).

Harrison, Brian. *Seeking a Role: The United Kingdom, 1951–1970* (2011).

Hilton, Matthew. *Consumerism in Twentieth-Century Britain: The Search for a Historical Movement* (2003).

Judt, Tony. *Postwar: A History of Europe since 1945* (2005).

Lüthi, Lorenz. *The Sino-Soviet Split: Cold War in the Communist World* (2008).

Palier, Bruno, ed. *A Long Goodbye to Bismarck?: The Politics of Welfare Reforms in Continental Europe* (2010).

Patten, Howard A. *Israel and the Cold War: Diplomacy, Strategy, and the Policy of the Periphery at the UN* (2012).

Pugh, Martin. *Women and the Women's Movement in Britain, 1914–1959* (2000).

Roth, Benita. *Separate Roads to Feminism: Black, Chicana, and White Feminist Movements in America's Second Wave* (2004).

Sturrock, John. *Structuralism* (2003).

Wendehorst, Stephan E. C. *British Jewry, Zionism, and the Jewish State, 1936–1956* (2011).

Westad, Odd Arne. *The Global Cold War: Third World Interventions and the Making of Our Times* (2007).

Zubok, Vladislav M. *A Failed Empire: The Soviet Union in the Cold War from Stalin to Gorbachev* (2008).

For additional resources, including maps, primary sources, visuals, web links, and quizzes, please go to **www.oup.com/us/backman.**

CHAPTER 28

Something to Believe In

1945–1988

PREDOMINANT RELIGIONS OF THE GREATER WEST, ca. 1988

Predominant/state-supported religion:
- Roman Catholicism
- Orthodox and other Eastern Churches
- Protestantism
- Sunni Islam
- Shiite Islam
- Judaism

Europe's movement away from Christian religious observance accelerated in the second half of the 20th century. The revolt was intuitive rather than intellectual. Many who had survived World War II simply concluded that no god would allow such suffering, and any god who would allow it did not deserve worship. Others retained their belief but not their former practice; with entire cities in ruins, there were not enough churches left standing. Still others felt that Europe could not afford the time for churchgoing. The task of rebuilding was too important—and once the economies did begin to hum along, there were too many opportunities to "get ahead." Millions of Europeans felt trapped by the tension between the United States and the Soviet Union. Regardless of what happened with missiles, few doubted that Europe itself would once again become a battlefield and responded to the knowledge with despair.

Yet amid secularism and spiritual anxiety, there was also revival. As attendance in churches declined, both Catholic and Protestant thinking became more diverse. Pope John XXIII began the most sweeping Catholic reform in centuries, with concern for the plight of Jews after the Holocaust and for Catholics behind the Iron Curtain. Protestantism saw a "new orthodoxy" in Europe, but also new modes of worship and new spiritual energy in the United States and the Third World. Postwar realities also brought on important changes in Jewish and Islamic observance across the Greater West. Jews fractured into new denominations

◀ **Believing in Prosperity**
The 60s generation, Italian-style. Postwar youths, full of energy and brio, secure in their comfort and care, but already showing signs of rebellion against conformity.

and contested histories of Israel, and the tensions between traditional Islamic cultures and modernity sparked another revolution.

RELIGIOUS OBSERVANCE AND "SPIRITUAL ANXIETY"

One factor in the decline of religious observance was the welfare state. The governments of western Europe assumed much of the social role formerly filled by churches. Meanwhile eastern Europe under Communism suppressed churches altogether. Soviet regimes confiscated church lands, buildings, and bank accounts. They forbade religious education and practice and imprisoned anyone who offered resistance. Technology played a role too. Modern transportation and communication meant that people did not have to make friends with their neighbors in order to have a social life. Parishes as a social institution went into decline, and people who still wanted a religious life could go "church shopping."

Many people ceased active religious life out of sheer frustration and anger. While countless Christians were brave and generous during the 1930s and 1940s, the sad fact is that most church leaders failed to respond to the threat of Fascism. Most of them, in fact, had made compromises of one sort or another with Franco, Hitler, and Mussolini. How could the moral leadership of Christian Europe have failed so wretchedly? Whatever the reasons, the generation that survived the war in Europe turned away from traditional Christian practice. Much of the baby-boom generation that came of age in the 1960s therefore grew up without ever knowing it.

In 1950 western Europeans overwhelmingly identified themselves as Christians and claimed to attend church regularly. By the end of the century, all that had changed. While most people still identified as Christians, they tended to mean it in a cultural sense only, without regular practice—often defined as attending ordinary religious services (not counting weddings, baptisms, and funerals) at least once a month for a whole year. By 2010, for example, in Austria only 18 percent of the population attended church; in Belgium, only 7 percent;

CHAPTER TIMELINE

1945
"Stuttgart Confession of Guilt"

1954
European Organization for Nuclear Research established

1968
Papal encyclical, *Humanae vitae*

1952
International Humanist and Ethical Union founded

1962–65
Second Vatican Council

in France, Germany, and Hungary, only 12 percent. Only 30 percent of Italians attended Mass, as did only 20 percent of Spaniards. Only 10 percent of the British were practicing Christians. For Protestants and Catholics alike, the trends pointed downward (see Figure 28.1).

These are only national averages. Christian practice in most countries still thrives in rural areas, villages, and small towns—but not in large cities. In Paris, as little as 2 percent of the population attends services; in Milan, by the turn of the millennium, the figure had sunk to 5 percent. Barcelona's three hundred churches, if crammed to capacity, could hold 450,000 faithful; but the city's

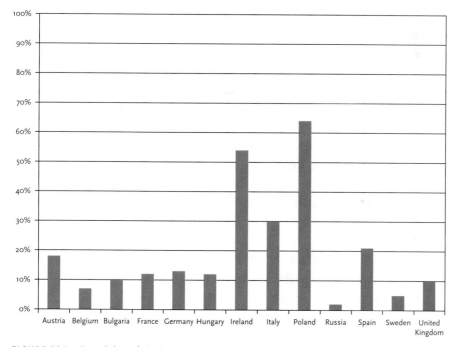

FIGURE 28.1   Practicing Christians in Europe: 2010

1975
European Space Agency founded; UN
Resolution 3379 condemns Israel

1987
Benny Morris, *The Birth of the Palestinian
Refugee Problem, 1947–1949*; Hamas founded

1973
Yom Kippur
War

1979
Peace treaty between Egypt and
Israel; Iranian revolution

population is 1.8 million, and the churches are virtually empty, apart from tourists. Moreover, the figures do not describe an important demographic shift. Many practicing Christians in Europe—perhaps one-tenth of the total—are recent immigrants from Africa.

Was the decline in religious culture a positive or a negative development? Was it an awakening to reason after two millennia of superstition, or was it a loss of cultural identity? However one interprets the trend, its historical significance is undeniable. Christianity, for good or ill, has been a foundation stone of Western culture and identity. While its decline does not foretell the end of Western life, it does indicate a momentous change.

> Christianity, for good or ill, has been a foundation stone of Western culture and identity. While its decline does not foretell the end of Western life, it does indicate a momentous change.

The change was noticed from the start. Paul Tillich (1886–1965), a German Protestant theologian, identified the "spiritual anxiety" of the postwar era. Every era, he argued in 1952, has its own unique form of anxiety. The ancient world's spiritual crisis was the fear of death, for which Christianity was the cure. The Christian era's crisis was guilt for not living up to God's expectations. But now, to Tillich, the spiritual crisis was different—a crisis of meaninglessness. To live without purpose, as Tillich asserts in *The Courage to Be* (1952), is not to live at all:

> The anxiety of meaninglessness is anxiety about the loss of an ultimate concern, of a meaning which gives meaning to all meanings. This anxiety is aroused by the loss of a spiritual center, of an answer, however symbolic and indirect, to the question of the meaning of existence. . . . The breakdown of absolutism, the development of liberalism and democracy, the rise of a technical civilization with its victory over all enemies and its own beginning disintegration—these are the sociological presupposition for the third main period of anxiety. In this [era] the anxiety of emptiness and meaninglessness is dominant. We are under the threat of spiritual non-being.

A secular world, in Tillich's eyes, is a soulless one. The West after the loss of faith knows that this is true, yet feels powerless to do anything about it.

SCIENCE AND SECULARISM

Advances in science, generally speaking, did not cause the loss of faith. Although it took some time to understand ideas like evolutionary theory and Einstein's relativity, most mainstream Christian denominations absorbed them. Smaller groups resisted any compromise with Biblical literalism, but mostly in the United States. European Christians, both Protestant and Catholic, were, if anything, invigorated by the intellectual challenge.

The sheer volume of new discoveries is not surprising, since government and industry invested so much money in the sciences. The Cold War was the era of "big science," involving everything from the space race to subatomic particle colliders, from cancer research to genetic engineering, and from biochemical processes to digital microprocessing.[1] Spending on scientific research in Europe

TABLE 28.1 **Breakthroughs in Science, 1950–1998**

1952	Polio vaccine developed by Jonas Salk.
1953	Francis Crick and James Watson model DNA molecule.
1962	Thomas Kuhn publishes *The Structure of Scientific Revolutions*.
1963	Tectonic plate theory confirmed.
1964	Louis Leaky identifies *Homo habilis*.
1965	Cosmic microwave background radiation (echo of Big Bang) detected; Noam Chomsky posits theory of generative grammar.
1968	ARPANET (precursor of Internet) established.
1969	First microprocessor; Neil Armstrong lands on the Moon.
1970	Stephen Hawking and Robert Penrose prove the universe must have had a beginning in time.
1971	Biologists identify the gene that controls an organism's sense of time
1972	Astronomers identify the first-ever confirmed black hole; Stephen J. Gould presents theory of evolution by punctuated equilibria.
1973	First successful experiment of recombinant DNA; Development of TCP/IP, allowing diverse computer networks to communicate with each other.
1796	Confirmation of theory of a genetic component in development of cancer.
1977	First transmission of television signals on optical fibers.
1978	Mary Leaky discovers fossilized human footprints 3.5 million years old.
1981	Programmers at Microsoft Corporation develop MS-DOS operating system.
1982	Experimental proof of Einstein's predicted "spooky action at a distance" theorem.
1984	Discovery of Homo erectus skeleton, 1.6 million years old.
1987	Genealogical model shows how all human mitochondrial DNA can be traced back to a common African maternal ancestor.
1988	Etienne Baulieu develops the RU-486 abortion pill.
1990	Tim Berners-Lee invents the World Wide Web.
1993	First evidence published of a possible genetic role in homosexuality in humans.
1995	Discovery of first extra-solar planet; first complete sequencing of a genome of a living organism (hemophilus influenzae); first preventative treatment for sickle cell anemia
1996	First lander/rover on Mars; Java programming language released.
1997	First cloning of an adult mammal: Dolly, the sheep; Fermilab reports discovery of the Top Quark.
1998	The expansion of the universe is discovered to be accelerating; construction begins, in orbit, on the International Space Station; vaccines discovered for Lyme disease and for rotavirus.

---

[1] Few may have noticed the invention of the microprocessor the same year that Neil Armstrong became the first man to walk on the moon.

and the United States quintupled between 1945 and 1980 (even after adjusting for inflation); so did the number of scientists and engineers engaged in research. Spending on so vast a scale produced results, of course. But the gains in knowledge are remarkable all the same.

Given the high costs of scientific research, these achievements could not have occurred without the support of governments and other institutions. In nuclear physics, for example, leadership belonged to the European Organization for Nuclear Research (known as CERN, an acronym of its original French name—Conseil Européen pour la Recherche Nucléaire), established in Geneva in 1954. Funded by twelve governments, CERN had an operating budget in 2010 of approximately 650 billion dollars. The European Molecular Biology Laboratory, established in 1974, conducts research at five principal sites, with a 2010 operating budget of $170 million. The European Space Agency (created in 1975), with a 2010 budget of five billion dollars, is headquartered in Paris. The Institute for Reference Materials and Measurements, based in Belgium, maintains the standardization of units of measure; it was created in 1957 as the Central Bureau for Nuclear Measurements. Supervising a dozen other groups is the Joint Research Council of the European Union, with expenditures in 2010 of roughly five hundred million dollars.[2]

Scientific Breakthrough   ENIAC, the first digital computer (1946).

---

[2]   Publicly funded research and development in 2005 was approximately $275 billion.

But few believers abandoned their faith after learning about quasars, DNA, stem cells, or the fossils of human ancestors. Besides, secularization is not the same thing as irreligion. It does not mean atheism or hostility to faith. Rather, most secular Europeans since the 1960s have been indifferent to organized religion, making it difficult to keep tradition going.

Groups dedicated to a secularized society proliferated after World War II. The International Humanist and Ethical Union, formed in Amsterdam in 1952, brought together over a hundred smaller groups across Europe. The union, which claims a membership of five million people around the world, promotes a secular basis for society but recognizes the right to freedom of belief:

> Humanism is a democratic and ethical life stance, which affirms that human beings have the right and responsibility to give meaning and shape to their own lives. It stands for the building of a more humane society through an ethic based on human and other natural values in the spirit of reason and free inquiry through human capabilities. It is not theistic, and it does not accept supernatural views of reality.

In 1956 several thousand secularists came together in Oslo and formed the Norwegian Humanist Association to campaign against the established Lutheran Church. The British Humanist Association came together in 1967 (although its origins lay in the 19th century); among its chief aims is to maintain the strict separation of church and state. Activists in Stockholm created the Swedish Humanist Association in 1979. The European Humanist Federation brought together several smaller institutions when it formally organized in Berlin in 1993. Now based in Brussels, it participates actively in the work of the European Union. Membership in such groups has grown steadily, and their chief goals have been to remove religion from civic life and to encourage reasoned interpretations of science, government, ethics, and society.

The great bulk of Europe's secularization, however, has resulted from waning participation in organized faith. It was not an intellectual rebellion or a conscious rejection, but a fading away. Even in staunchly secular France (with church attendance only 12 percent), the majority self-identifies as Christian.

Three factors head the list of probable causes: the nature of capitalist society, religious pluralism, and antagonism toward institutional churches. First, life in the West offered unending opportunities for work, leisure, and entertainment—cinemas, television, sports events, restaurants, cafes, radio, museums, theaters, concerts, parks. These took over part of the social function of churchgoing, just as the welfare state assumed the caring role of churches. Second, the many religious choices eroded a strong sense of religious identity, especially among Protestants. So did intermarriage. Since at least the 1960s, fewer and fewer people say that they can

No Time for Church   Scottish flags wave atop one end of Wembley Stadium in London for a football match between England and Scotland, in 1955. The popularity of professional sports—aided by the construction (often at public expense) of vast stadiums and by the advent of television coverage—is one of many factors that has contributed to the secularization of Europe.

differentiate between the teachings of various denominations. The third factor was consciousness of the churches' real and perceived failings. For many who came of age in the late 1960s, the institutional churches had much to answer for.

THE CATHOLIC REFORMATION

A series of crises rocked the Roman Catholic Church throughout the 20th century and contributed to the loss of lay members. Especially painful for many Catholics was the Church's response to Fascism and the Holocaust—or rather its lack of one. Pope Pius XII (r. 1939–1958), though personally opposed to Fascism, charted a moderate course in opposing Mussolini and Hitler; officially, the Vatican remained neutral throughout the war. Pius feared a military assault on Catholic communities across Europe or even on the Vatican itself if it took public positions on political matters. Many Jews looked to Rome to take a strong moral position, and Pius secretly protected thousands, in churches and monasteries as well as in the Vatican. In the end, roughly 80 percent of Rome's Jewish population received direct aid from the Church in avoiding capture by the Nazis via their Fascist allies.

Still, Pius never unmistakably condemned the ongoing Holocaust. The closest he came was in a radio speech on Christmas Day in 1942. Near the end of his talk, he called for the restored promise of honesty, fairness, generosity, and mercy toward all of God's people:

> Humanity owes such a vow to the innumerable dead who lie buried on battlefields: the sacrifice of their lives in their fulfillment ought to be a holocaust for a new and better social order. Humanity owes such a vow to the unending cries of mothers, widows, and orphans who have had the light, comfort, and sustenance of their lives torn from them. Humanity owes such a vow to the innumerable exiles whom the hurricane of war has blown from their homes and left stranded in foreign lands: they can lament with the Prophet [Jeremiah], "Our inheritance has been handed over to strangers, our homes to foreigners" [Lamentations 5.2]. Humanity owes such a vow to the hundreds of thousands of people who, without any just cause and only on account of their nationality or race, have been sent either to their deaths or to a gradual decline. Humanity owes such a vow to the many millions of noncombatants—women, children, the sick, the elderly—to whom the aerial bombardments (whose horrors we have repeatedly condemned from the start) have destroyed lives, goods, possessions, houses, hospitals, and places of worship without discernment or sufficient care. Humanity owes such a vow to the rivers of tears and bitterness, to the clouds of sorrow and torment, which have proceeded from the deadly ruin of the present conflict, darkening the heavens and calling out for the descent of the Holy Spirit—that It might free the world from the spread of violence and terror.

Even this moving invocation does not specify the suffering of the Jews. His description of persecution and his quotation from Jeremiah might be veiled references to the Jews, but many Catholics wanted something more from their leader. Pius was no anti-Semite, but to his critics he is the pope who failed to speak out. To them the church—or at least the papacy—lost moral authority.

After the war, Pius encouraged the rebuilding of Europe and the creation of the European Union of 1957 (see chapter 29). He also focused on the plight of Catholics behind the Iron Curtain. His positions on the State of Israel mixed altruism and stubbornness.[3] The crux of the conflict was Jerusalem, which the Vatican maintained should be an internationally controlled city. Pius's legacy

---

[3]   Pius showed concern for everyone suffering from persecution and war, but he refused to recognize Israel. The Vatican finally recognized Israel late in 1993.

regarding Judaism is complex, and it will become clear only when the archives of his pontificate are fully available to researchers.

Pius XII's successor was Pope John XXIII (r. 1958–1963), who dedicated his pontificate to **aggiornamento**, or bringing the church up to date. John believed that the church needed to confront head-on the rift between the practices of the church and the lived realities of everyday Catholics. He convened the **Second Vatican Council** (known as Vatican II), which met from 1962 to 1965. John did not live to see the conclusion of the council, but his spirit dominated its proceedings. The council's work was wide ranging. It refined the relations between the papacy and bishops. It reformed the liturgy, to allow greater lay participation. It expressed regret for the centuries-long hostilities between the Catholic and Orthodox Churches. It renewed a spirit of missionary work around the globe. And it rededicated the church to seeking union, whenever possible, with the Protestant and other churches.

Most controversially, the council rejected the tradition of blaming the Jews for the killing of Christ:

> True, the Jewish authorities and those who followed their lead pressed for the death of Christ; still, what happened in His passion cannot be charged against all the Jews, without distinction, then alive, nor against the Jews of today. Although the Church is the new people of God, the Jews should not be presented as rejected or accursed by God, as if this followed from the Holy Scriptures. All should see to it, then, that in catechetical work or in the preaching of the word of God they do not teach anything that does not conform to the truth of the Gospel and the spirit of Christ. Furthermore, in her rejection of every persecution against any man, the Church, mindful of the patrimony she shares with the Jews and moved not by political reasons but by the Gospel's spiritual love, decries hatred, persecutions, displays of anti-Semitism, directed against Jews at any time and by anyone. (*Nostra Aetate, "In Our Time"*)

Many bishops had opposed the change. Except for a few individuals, they were motivated not by anti-Semitism but by a desire to uphold another tradition—the church's "infallibility," or freedom from error. How could the central ritual of the church, the Mass, have been wrong when for centuries it had blamed the "perfidious Jews" for the Crucifixion? The reformers won the day, however.

The end of Vatican II did not stop further reforms. Pope Paul VI (r. 1963–1978), John XXIII's successor, instituted the Mass in languages other than Latin, by simple decree. For liberal-minded Catholics, the work of the council and then the reforms of Paul offered hope for a faith adapted to the needs of contemporary society. In

Adapting to the Needs of Contemporary Society   Roman Catholicism, though still the single largest branch of Christianity, has struggled to keep abreast with the social and cultural changes since World War II—and has in fact debated whether or not it should do so. The reforms of the Second Vatican Council (1962–1965) displeased many Catholics, many of whom thought the council had compromised too much with modernity, and many others who felt that it had not reformed nearly enough. Shown here is a Mass on behalf of the then gravely ill Pope John Paul II (r. 1978–2005), at Our Lady of Angels Cathedral in Los Angeles.

sheer numbers, however, they were proved wrong. Attendance at Mass continued its steep decline, and pursuit of the priesthood fell off at a startling rate. Conservative Catholics attributed the decline to the reforms themselves. They argued that, in the attempt to make the church relevant to the modern world, it had cut itself off from its roots. Liberal Catholics pointed to two other issues—the church's ban on contraception and its refusal to allow women to be priests.

The debate over artificial contraception had been around for a long time, at least since the 12th century, but it became urgent with the availability of the birth-control pill in 1961. Paul VI spent several years investigating the science behind the new method. He also reviewed church doctrine on the nature of sexuality and the purpose of marriage. He set up advisory committees that included laymen and laywomen, both married and unmarried. He reviewed the documents of Vatican II and consulted with both physicians and theologians. Finally, in 1968, he issued *Humanae Vitae* ("Of Human Life"), perhaps the most famous papal encyclical in history.

The encyclical recognizes (in an innovation) that sex has a twofold purpose. Besides producing offspring, it expresses love. All the more reason, then, that marriage is the only licit venue for sex, for without a lifelong commitment, sex is reduced to coupling. Marriage does more than unite a man and woman into "one flesh." It unites the married couple with the loving God who brought them together:

> Marriage, then, is far from being the effect of chance or the result of the blind evolution of natural forces. It is in reality the wise and provident institution of God the Creator, whose purpose was to effect in man His loving design. As a consequence, husband and wife, through that mutual gift of themselves, which is specific and exclusive to them alone, develop that union of two persons in which they perfect one another, cooperating with God in the generation and rearing of new lives.
>
> The marriage of those who have been baptized is, in addition, invested with the dignity of a sacramental sign of grace, for it represents the union of Christ and His Church.

Married love, then, is a human analogue to the Holy Trinity itself. *Humanae Vitae* consequently rejects all forms of artificial contraception and insists that "each and every" act of sexual union must be left open to the possibility of new life.

The crowds stayed away in droves. Studies of European Catholics from 1970 on showed that a major factor in their falling away from church attendance was the church's stance on contraception. A clash was perhaps inevitable—even more so with the rise of second wave feminism. To many women, *Humanae Vitae* resentenced them to lives of endless reproduction just when they were winning their freedom to pursue other goals.

Of secondary significance was the issue of women's ordination as priests—secondary because fewer women were interested in pursuing the priesthood than in avoiding pregnancy. The church's traditional position was that Jesus, in selecting his twelve apostles, had chosen only men, and so only men were called to priesthood. The church therefore did not have the authority to ordain women, even if it wanted to do so. At Vatican II many bishops and their theological advisers argued against this strict interpretation of the Gospel. The apostles, they pointed out, were also all married men and all Jewish. Did it not then follow that the church does not have the authority to ordain anyone other than Jewish husbands to the Catholic priesthood? Moreover, the New Testament clearly distinguishes between the apostles and bishops. The church would have none of this, however. Paul VI and his successor, John Paul II (r. 1978–2005), insisted that the priesthood is a uniquely male calling, and the question is closed.

Vatican II was the most thoroughgoing reform of the church since the Renaissance. But the legacy of the Council is still debated. To conservatives, the council is to blame for the church's European decline; it substituted modern fashions for a two-thousand-year tradition. To liberals, the council failed to enact enough reform; it left the same old patriarchy, perhaps with a friendlier face. In either case, the results are still to be seen Sunday after Sunday, in row after row of empty seats in the pews.

POSTWAR PROTESTANTISM

The story of postwar Protestantism is also one of loss, and yet Protestant Christianity grew as fast in the postcolonial Third World as it faded in Europe. Moreover, when it came to spiritual energy, the United States became a leader in the Protestant world.

Attendance at and active membership in church life declined at roughly the same pace and to the same extent as with Catholic Europeans. Protestantism in Europe, however, experienced a fragmentation that the Catholic Church did not. The decline began in the 19th century, gained pace with the disillusionment of World War I, and turned severe after World War II. By 1989, when the Soviet Union began to disintegrate, it became apparent that Protestant Christianity had survived four decades of Communist persecution in eastern Europe better than it had survived in the postwar west. This tenacity of faith in the east perhaps resulted from the persecution itself, as Protestants resisted the official state atheism. In the west, Protestantism faced many of the same factors that affected Catholic Christians—modern capitalism, religious pluralism, and frustration with the institutional churches.

The Protestant churches, as institutions, had been organized along national lines since the 16th century. Many, in fact, had been established as the official churches of their countries, led by national councils and ruled (at least symbolically) by the monarchies. The blow that the World Wars dealt to nations, and to nationalism, thus affected the churches as well. In Nazi Germany, a National Socialist brand of Lutheranism, the "German Christian" movement, had received official support. The German Evangelical Church (EKD, for Evangelische Kirche in Deutschland), formed in 1933, had roots in the World War I era. Some six hundred thousand members strong, the EDK had supported Hitler and defrocked all Lutheran ministers of Jewish descent. It also established a "research institute" charged with preparing a new translation of the

Nazi Resister   Lutheran pastor and theologian Dietrich Bonhoeffer.

New Testament—one that would eliminate all references to the Jewishness of Jesus and his apostles and turn them all into Aryans.

Although the EKD survived until the end of the war, there was heroic resistance to it. A group of Lutheran, Calvinist, and Moravian theologians and pastors met in Barmen (the birthplace of Friedrich Engels, ironically enough) and formed the Confessing Church. As a religious group, they did not denounce Nazism itself but only the Nazification of their faith in the EKD. Nevertheless, several leading figures in the Confessing Church became prominent activists against the Nazi regime, most notably the Lutheran pastors Hermann Maas (1877–1970) and Dietrich Bonhoeffer (1906–1945). Maas, an ardent Zionist from his youth, risked his life many times to shield Jews from arrest and helped many to flee Germany.[4] Bonhoeffer campaigned actively against the Nazi regime and in 1943 even joined the conspiracy of some German intelligence officers to assassinate Hitler. Bonhoeffer was arrested and died in the Flossenbürg concentration camp on April 9, 1945, only three weeks before the end of the war.

Uneasy over their churches' collusion with the Nazis during the war, and left without a clear leadership after it, German Protestantism lost momentum. The faithful had enough to do clearing rubble, finding food and shelter, reviving the economy, reorganizing the state, and (until the Berlin Wall was erected in 1961) maintaining a connection with their countrymen and family members living under Soviet control. Churchgoing, to many of them, was hardly a priority. In October 1945 ecumenical figures from outside Germany persuaded the Protestant leaders to issue a somewhat tepid and vague acknowledgement of their failures during the Nazi years; known as the "Stuttgart Confession of Guilt," it acknowledged that "enormous wrong befell many peoples and countries on account of us," but insisted, "We fought for many years, in the name of Jesus Christ, against the mindset that exemplified the Nazi's violent regime." The leaders' shortcomings, the "Confession" said, consisted of "not standing up for our beliefs more courageously, not praying more faithfully, not believing more joyfully, and not loving more ardently." The murders, pogroms, book burnings, arrests, deportations, and concentration camps of the previous twenty-five years are never mentioned.

---

4   Israel placed Hermann Maas on the list of "Righteous among the Nations" at the official Yad Vashem Holocaust Memorial in Jerusalem.

This is no time, the leaders seemed to say, for looking back. Besides, the main Protestant denominations were undergoing some painful rifts. Theologians and church leaders across the Continent began reinterpreting their traditions. They sought to expunge ideas that, in their eyes, had contributed to the two World Wars—national pride, belief in progress, support for liberal capitalism, confidence in "justification by faith" and the guidance of the elect. Among the most important of these new schools of thought was Protestant **neoorthodoxy** (sometimes known as dialectical theology). Its founder was the Swiss Calvinist theologian Karl Barth (1886–1968); Dietrich Bonhoeffer was also active before his arrest. So later

> Neoorthodoxy tried to restore the transcendent mystery of God, but it prepared the way for its own end. Europe's struggling Protestants craved a more immediate, approachable, and comforting deity.

were the Swiss writer Emil Brunner (1889–1962), the Frenchman Jacques Ellul (1912–1994), and the Americans Reinhold Niebuhr (1892–1971) and William Stringfellow (1928–1985).

Neoorthodox thought is difficult, and intentionally so. Protestant theology up to that point, it assumed, had made God too easy to understand. It had made him a Protestant minister "writ large," as Bonhoeffer put it. Neoorthodoxy emphasized instead the absolute strangeness and "complete Otherness" of God. Unlike the confident liberal Protestant writers of the 19th century, Barth and his followers stressed that God's nature could not be known. The human intellect will never be up to the task—and thus we are helpless in the face of God's will. He will save whom he chooses to save. Try as we might, we will never be able to understand or predict whom he will choose. Neoorthodoxy tried to restore the transcendent mystery of God, but it prepared the way for its own end. Europe's struggling Protestants craved a more immediate, approachable, and comforting deity.

In Britain, the decline of religious life also became apparent after the war. Economic straits meant less money for the support and maintenance of church buildings, and the sunny tone of much Anglican preaching seemed out of place. The loss of empire also meant the decay of prestige for the Church of England and its head, the archbishop of Canterbury. Just as Britain ceased to be a political superpower, so too did mainstream Anglicanism and Episcopalianism lose ground.

THE FUNDAMENTALS OF PROTESTANTISM

In Africa, Asia, and South America, Protestant communities ceased to look to Europe for leadership. Missionary work in the Third World increased steadily starting in the 1950s, bringing many new faithful into the fold. It also affected the substance of the faiths themselves. As described by an Anglican missionary to India, William Robertson (1894–1955):

> Christianity is not a product of the West. Its divine Founder lived in an Eastern land. The great churches of its glorious youth with that roll of doctors and martyrs belonged chiefly not to Europe but to Africa and the East. We must therefore desire to go to a land like India as little as possible as Westerners. We must give every encouragement to the clothing of the catholic faith and the worship that enshrines it in Indian garments. Our vision must be that of a real Indian Church.
>
> Our ideal is to live in simplicity as far as possible in the Indian way. Our hope is that if we are faithful God will enable us to make some contribution to the Church in India by helping forward the naturalizing of her theology and worship . . . .
>
> Our hope is that our Ashram will be so Indian in character that many Hindus will feel at home in it, and will readily stay with us. Hospitality will always be part of our programme, and we hope to have accommodation for a number of guests. We hope also to undertake works of social service, and some of us may teach in schools. It has been suggested that we should visit the prison, the leper asylum, and the hospitals. In this way rather than in preaching we believe that we can show forth the spirit of Jesus, our Lord. *(From Love's Redeeming Work: The Anglican Quest for Holiness, by Geoffrey Rowell, Kenneth Stevenson, and Rowan Williams, 2004)*

By the end of the Cold War, the number of practicing Christians outside of Europe vastly exceeded the number within Europe. And they stamped the faith with elements of their native cultures.

Despite upheaval in the 1960s and 1970s, the United States never experienced the severe popular decline in Christian practice seen in Europe.[5] America was also the site of three important developments—Pentecostalism, fundamentalism, and evangelicalism. All three are styles of worship rather than separate denominations, and all three took root in the mainstream Protestant churches.

Pentecostalism takes its name from the descent of the Holy Spirit upon the original twelve apostles, as told in the New Testament. Taking the appearance of tongues of flame, the Spirit filled the twelve with heavenly grace; and the sign of this gift was that they could suddenly speak in foreign tongues. Pentecostalism first appeared in the last years of the 19th century, a revival movement among poor

---

5   The nation with the highest proportion of active Christians today is Nigeria, where 85 percent of the Christian population attends church regularly.

rural groups in the American South. It is at root a mystical union with God. The believer is seized by a spiritual ecstasy, speaks aloud in unrecognizable speech, and often receives or performs miraculous healings. It preaches of a second baptism "in the Holy Spirit," and it celebrates a surrender of the believer's heart to the Resurrected Christ. As such, Pentecostalism is openly, even proudly, anti-intellectual in its approach—based on a conviction that traditional Protestantism has tied itself into knots by a dependence on rational inquiry. By the 1960s and 1970s it entered mainstream Protestantism as a charismatic reform that has proved highly popular. Moreover, Pentecostal missionaries in the 1980s and 1990s found many welcoming audiences in South America and parts of Asia, especially China, where it now forms the fastest-growing Christian movement. But it has failed to take root in Europe.

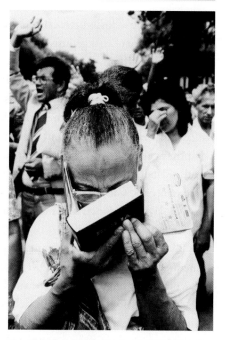

Mystical Union with God   Worshippers at a Pentecostal revival in Brazil. The explosive growth of Pentecostalism has been in a statistical sense, one of the major success stories in recent Christian history. Its appeal has been particularly strong in South America. Estimates of the worldwide Pentecostal population are difficult to make, since Pentecostalism is more a style of worship than a discrete denomination; figures range from two hundred to five hundred million.

The key element of **fundamentalism** is "Scriptural inerrancy." It too is a mode of worship rather than a distinct denomination, and scholars trace its origins to 19th-century debates in the United States over Darwinian theory and the Biblical record.[6] It can mean the strictest and simplest type of literalism when reading the Bible, but more commonly it insists merely on the presence of a fundamental Truth in every Scriptural passage. For example, when the Bible states that Abraham lived 175 years (Genesis 25.7), it is not talking about calendar years; it is simply proclaiming that obedience to God guarantees a heavenly blessing—in this case, long life. Fundamentalism rose to the forefront of several Protestant denominations in the 1980s and was embraced by large sectors of the Republican Party. Morally earnest, fundamentalism has an element that urges personal and societal reform before the approach

---

6   The publication in 1910–1915 of a twelve-volume anthology of pamphlets called *The Fundamentals: A Testimony to the Truth* is often taken as the symbolic start of the movement.

of Armageddon—Jesus's return and the final battle between good and evil, which certain fundamentalist groups describe as the "Rapture."

Evangelicalism, too, emphasizes the work of the Holy Spirit in the world and the centrality of Biblical truth. However, it retains more of the traditional elements of Protestant denominations than Pentecostalism does—and less millennial urgency than fundamentalism. Evangelicals also focus more on *ecumenicalism*, or bringing Protestant churches together. They seek simply to enliven what they regard as staid forms of Protestant worship. Evangelicalism is the only trend of the three that has gained any footing within Europe, where it tries to bring energetic Christian worship back into Anglican, Calvinist, and Lutheran life. The World Council of Churches formed in Amsterdam in 1948, to staunch the spiritual loss in Europe.

In sum, European Protestantism in the later 20th century struggled to disassociate itself from the elements that, for many people, had made it complicit in two world wars. It attempted to do so both in a highly intellectualized way, with dialectical theology, but also with a stripped-down version of evangelicalism that emphasized feeling over intellect and a return to Biblical basics. Neither attempt succeeded in Europe, and the vital centers of Protestant Christianity thus passed beyond Europe's borders. In the United States, Latin America, Africa, and Asia, the faith has adapted itself to local worship traditions, giving it new life in new forms.

JEWISH REVIVAL—AND CONFLICT

World Jewry experienced both elation and sorrow in the years after Israel's success in the Six-Day War. Although still surrounded by hostile neighbors, Israel had proven its might and extended its borders to more easily defensible positions. Jews from throughout the Diaspora migrated in a large new wave, especially from Muslim countries, now that the fledgling state seemed likely to survive (see Map 28.1). More than 90 percent of the quarter-million Jews living in Morocco, for example, returned to the Holy Land within a decade of the 1967 war, while virtually the entire Jewish population in Libya (roughly 35,000) did the same.

Not all Arab Jews showed such confidence in Israel. The quarter-million or so Jews in Algeria, for example, migrated instead to France, with some continuing on to the United States. Their Sephardic traditions and greater degree of religious observance changed the tone of French Jewish life. Yet tens of thousands poured into Israel from Iraq and Iran, and the small number of Jews remaining in Egypt were essentially forced out by the government of Gamal Abdul Nasser

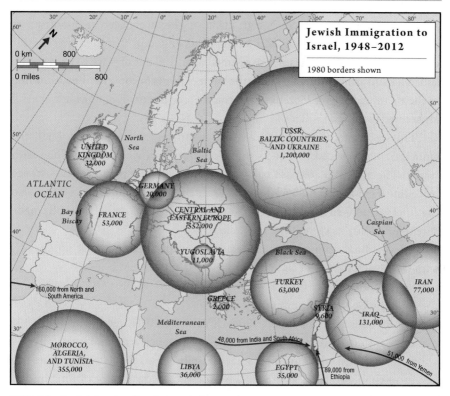

MAP 28.1   Jewish Immigration to Israel since 1948.

(r. 1956–1970). For the first time, many Jews arrived from the United States and western Europe as well.

The new wave of immigrants profoundly altered Israeli society. The nation had been founded earlier in the 20th century largely by refugees and immigrants from the Ashkenazim of central and eastern Europe. Many were secular, and they brought with them a passionate Zionism and a commitment to socialism. The new arrivals of the 1950s, 1960s, and 1970s were different. The North African Jews were Sephardic, spoke Ladino and Arabic rather than Yiddish and Hebrew, were highly observant, and were generally blue-collar laborers eager for an opportunity to prosper. Meanwhile the Oriental Jews (immigrants from the Arabian Peninsula, Iraq, and Iran) and the Jews returning from the United States and western Europe were educated professionals and entrepreneurs. A new money-driven consumer culture developed in challenge to the older, idealistic communal identity.

Israel's compulsory military service was still an engine of social integration. Yet strong prejudices between many of these groups polarized society. Survivors of the Holocaust and their descendants often regarded the Sephardim and the

Jews from the prosperous West with disdain. They were seen as opportunists who wanted to connect with their Jewish roots only now that the suffering was over. Sephardic religious traditions seemed alien and out of place to many established Israelis, and so did the Sephardic habit of living in communities according to their national origin. Moreover, the commercial orientation of the newer arrivals seemed crass and shallow.

This reorientation of Israeli life had significant consequences. First, the United States replaced France as the Western nation most closely allied with Israel.[7] The United States also became the chief supplier of military assistance, by selling its most technologically sophisticated weaponry to Israel. (It was also the chief weapons supplier to several Arab states in the 1970s, but it usually made sure to offer only its second-tier technology.)

International opinion turned decidedly against Israel—most notoriously with UN Resolution 3379, in 1975:

> The General Assembly,
>
> Recalling its resolution 1904 (XVIII) of 20 November 1963 . . . . that "any doctrine of racial differentiation or superiority is scientifically false, morally condemnable, socially unjust and dangerous" and its expression of alarm at "the manifestations of racial discrimination still in evidence in some areas in the world, some of which are imposed by certain Governments by means of legislative, administrative or other measures",
>
> Recalling also that, in its resolution 3151 G (XXVIII) of 14 December 1973, the General Assembly condemned, inter alia, the unholy alliance between South African racism and Zionism,
>
> Taking note of . . . the principle that "international co-operation and peace require the achievement of national liberation and independence, the elimination of colonialism and neo-colonialism, foreign occupation, Zionism, apartheid and racial discrimination in all its forms, as well as the recognition of the dignity of peoples and their right to self-determination",
>
> Taking note also of Resolution 77 (XII) adopted by the Assembly of Heads of State and Government of the Organization of African, . . . which considered "that the racist regime in occupied Palestine and the racist regimes in Zimbabwe and South Africa have a common imperialist origin,

---

7   America was home to six million Jews, more than lived in the Holy Land itself, and American public and private economic aid to Israel grew rapidly.

forming a whole and having the same racist structure and being organi-
cally linked in their policy aimed at repression of the dignity and integrity
of the human being",

Taking note also of the Political Declaration and Strategy to
Strengthen International Peace and Security and to Intensify Solidarity
and Mutual Assistance among Non-Aligned Countries, ... which most
severely condemned Zionism as a threat to world peace and security and
called upon all countries to oppose this racism and imperialist ideology,

Determines that Zionism is a form of racism and racial discrimination. *(http://www.un.org/documents/ga/res/30/ares30.htm)*

This diplomatic shift had many causes, including anti-Americanism as a consequence of the Cold War and the war in Vietnam. Moreover, yet another war had
been fought in the Middle East on October 6, 1973. On Yom Kippur, the holiest
day in the Jewish calendar, united Egyptian and Syrian forces had launched a
surprise assault on Israel. Caught unawares, the Israeli forces nearly fell, but after
two weeks they managed to drive off
their attackers and advanced far toward
Cairo and Damascus before agreeing
to a cease-fire. The war did not change
territorial borders very much, but it destroyed Israel's aura of invincibility, as-
suaged hurt Arab pride, and emboldened
anti-Israel forces to push for the UN resolution. Under pressure from the United
States, the UN ultimately revoked Resolution 3379 in 1991. It is the only revoked
declaration in UN history.

Within Israel, by the mid-1970s the
majority of the population consisted
of the non-European immigrants of
the previous decades or their offspring.
That change placed the earlier settlers
in the minority for the first time. One
consequence was a sharp shift to the
political right, since Arab and Oriental
Jews generally took a more hard-line
stance toward the Arabs. The conservative Likud Party, led by Menachem

U.S. and Israeli Assault This Egyptian political
cartoon, published in the run-up to the Yom Kippur
War in September 1973, shows a joint U.S.-Israeli
bomb falling on the home of an Egyptian boy. In
reality, the war began when Egypt and Syria launched
a surprise two-front assault on Israel.

Begin (r. 1977–1983), now rivaled the Labor Party for dominance, and Israel's governments for the next twenty-five years were coalitions. Neither Likud nor Labor could win an outright majority. In an effort for peace, Egypt's President Anwar Sadat (r. 1970–1981) boldly traveled to Jerusalem to deal directly with the government. Begin and Sadat had a surprisingly good rapport and, aided by U.S. president Jimmy Carter (r. 1977–1981), signed a peace treaty in 1979.

The political shift reflected a second major development in Israel, religious conflict. Israel had had a diverse population from the start. In 1948, at the nation's founding, about 10 percent of Israel's citizenry was Arab; by 2010 Arabs comprised nearly 20 percent of the population, not counting Palestinians residing in the occupied West Bank and Gaza Strip. The Jews themselves were divided between wholly secular Jews (roughly 20 percent), those who identified as nonobservant but believing Jews (50–55 percent), observant Orthodox Jews (15–20 percent), and *Haredim* (or Ultra-Orthodox) Jews (5–10 percent). Between 5 and 7 percent of Israel's citizens are Christian; another 1–2 percent of the citizens are Druze. But Israel's constitutional system of proportional representation has meant that small and even fringe parties have figured in every governing coalition.

Together with the virtual deadlock between Labor and Likud since the 1970s, the divisions make it difficult to unify the government behind any plan to resolve the conflict with the Palestinians. Moreover, the Ultra-Orthodox have demanded, as the price of their joining any coalition, control of the ministry that determines and enforces religious law regarding marriage. (Israel has no civil marriage.) That has largely meant strict Orthodoxy on marriage law. Many Reform immigrants, converts, and children of a Jewish father and non-Jewish mother have found, to their surprise, that the government does not legally recognize them as Jews at all—even though it grants them citizenship.

INTERNATIONAL JUDAISM AND THE MYTH OF ISRAEL

International Judaism has undergone a wide range of changes and evolutions. Nearly one-third of all Jewish marriages in the United States and in western Europe since the 1970s have been mixed, and the majority of families resulting from those mixed marriages have become culturally or religiously Christian by the third, and sometimes by the second, generation.[8] Reform Jews, whether observant or not, have proved the most willing to enter mixed marriages, Orthodox and Conservative Jews the least. Reform Jews in the west have also been quickest

---

8   In the United Kingdom, fully half of all Jewish marriages were mixed by the year 2000.

to accept homosexuality as a normal aspect of human life, regardless of Biblical and halakhic (rabbinical legal) condemnations of it. They have been the first to allow women to enter the rabbinate as well.[9]

Conservative Judaism, in contrast, permits men and women to sit together during worship but accepted female rabbis only starting in the late 1980s. Conservative Judaism also initiated the formal ritual of a bat mitzvah for girls, to correspond to the centuries-old bar mitzvah for boys. Both rituals take place at the traditional coming of age at thirteen years. The bat mitzvah, begun only in 1922 in the United States, proved popular and was gradually accepted by all major Jewish traditions, although the Orthodox held out against it the longest. Orthodox Judaism rejects women rabbis as contrary to halakha and tradition, but several rabbinical schools since 2000 allow women to

Rabbi Naamah Kelman   Born in New York City in 1955, Kelman moved to Israel in 1976 to pursue graduate studies. She received ordination as a Conservative rabbi in 1992, making her the first woman rabbi in Israel. Since 2009 she has served as dean of Hebrew University in Jerusalem.

participate in rabbinical study and to qualify as educators. In recent decades several new versions of Judaism have emerged in the West: Humanistic, Liberal, Reconstructionist, Renewal, and Tradition Jews have all emerged since the 1970s.

Jews of every denomination have also endured continued persecution, and Jews trapped behind the Iron Curtain faced some of the worst of it. Under Stalin and Khrushchev, thousands of synagogues, schools, Jewish newspapers, theaters, and youth clubs were all closed. By the middle of the 1960s there were fewer than a hundred synagogues in the entire USSR. More than a million Jews left eastern Europe and Russia in the 1990s, heading chiefly to Israel and the United States. As late as 2002, in Russia proper, Jews made up less than one-fifth of 1 percent of the total population. Lower birth rates combined with emigration to reduce what had once been the center of Jewish population to the tiniest fraction of what it had been.

Hundreds of thousands asked to emigrate to Israel but were denied exit visas on the excuse that they had access to information vital to state security. And in fact Jews were prominent in many professions. In the 1960s a mere four thousand were allowed to repatriate to the Holy Land. In Poland and Czechoslovakia, where Soviet officials often appointed Jewish members of the Communist Party to administrative positions, anti-Communist rebellions took on an ugly anti-Semitism. The Soviets could always blame, and did blame, government failures on Jews in positions of power. Romania's dictator Nicolae Ceaușescu (1918–1989), in power

---

[9]   The first woman rabbi, Regina Jonas (1902–1944), was killed at Auschwitz after two years caring for fellow concentration-camp prisoners and delivering lectures on Jewish history and law.

from 1965 until his death, held his Jewish subjects for ransom; he granted them exit visas only in return for large cash payments to support his lavish lifestyle.

An unexpected challenge to Jews everywhere came from within Israel itself, starting in the 1980s, with the young scholars and journalists known as the **New Historians**. Mostly born in Israel, they came of age just when the thirty-year hold (a common practice internationally) expired on government records pertaining to the establishment of the state of Israel. With access to these declassified documents, historians like Benny Morris (b. 1948), Tom Segev (b. 1945), and Avi Shlaim (b. 1945) offered fresh—and to many older Israelis, treacherous—views of Zionism.

The standard history up until then had described the early Zionists as peaceful idealists. These stout pioneers longed to settle in the Holy Land side by side with their Arab neighbors. When Hitler came to power, they spared no effort to save their doomed European compatriots, but could do nothing in the face of such evil. And when the nation of Israel was formally proclaimed in 1948, these Zionist heroes watched in surprise as their good Palestinian neighbors suddenly abandoned the land. Surrounding Arab states had ordered it, promising a glorious return once Arab armies trounced the inexperienced Jewish forces. But when that plan failed, the Zionist victors had no alternative but to claim the abandoned land as Jewish territory. "We did not have real history in this country," argued Segev; "we had mythology."

The debate began in earnest in 1987, with the publication of Benny Morris's study *The Birth of the Palestinian Refugee Problem, 1947–1949*. Here Morris argues that the seven hundred thousand Palestinians who fled the Holy Land at the time of Israel's war of independence did so for a variety of reasons—but the chief cause was the Israeli army, which forced village after village to flee. Morris sees no evidence of a central policy of ethnic cleansing. Rather, he insists that Palestinians were expelled in location after location, on orders of commanders on the ground, depending on their strategic needs in the war.

Another New Historian, Ilan Pappé (b. 1954), entered the fray in 1988. His *Britain and the Arab-Israeli Conflict, 1948–1951* maintains that the British colonial government had favored the establishment of a Palestinian Arab, not a Jewish, state. Most disturbing of all was Tom Segev's *The Seventh Million: The Israelis and the Holocaust* (1993), which criticizes the Zionist leaders of the 1930s for caring more about the establishment of Israel than about helping the Jews facing mass murder under the Nazis. To older Israelis, this was inexcusable slander.

The debate was intense, and it remains so today. Morris and his peers insist that they want only to discover the truth about their nation. A permanent peace settlement, they say, can come about only if both sides confront honestly the strengths and weaknesses of their claims to the land. But to their critics, the New Historians

Palestinian Refugees　　Palestinian refugee camp in Gaza, 1967.

are mounting an assault on Zionist belief itself—the belief in a unique Jewish identity and a unique Jewish fate, both tied to the Holy Land. The impact of the New Historians probably would not have been so great had not Jewish identity already been so endangered by secularization, assimilation, mixed marriages, and divisions among denominations. To attack the "myth of Israel" was, to many, to attack Judaism itself. Without that, what does it mean to be a Jew? As more records become declassified, the historical picture changes and takes on more detail. But this remains only half the story. Modern Arab archives remain largely closed to researchers—and absolutely closed to Jews. Until full access is available to all, the truth of what happened to those seven hundred thousand Palestinians, how, and why will be unknown. A just and permanent settlement of the Israeli-Palestinian dispute will be impossible.

> To attack the "myth of Israel" was, to many, to attack Judaism itself. Without that, what does it mean to be a Jew?

Jews around the world, but especially in Israel and France, faced yet another threat starting in the 1970s: terrorism. It started with the surprise attack on the Israeli athletic team at the 1972 Olympic Games held in Munich. Small acts of violence were then commonplace, but organized and well-funded campaigns of guerrilla violence became the preferred strategy of those opposed to Israel.

ISLAMIC REVOLUTIONS

The idea of revolution holds an uneasy place in classical Islamic teaching. Unlike the English word *revolution*, which is morally neutral ("digital revolution," anyone?), the most frequent Arabic terms are decidedly negative. *Al-fitnah* ("rebellion"), *al-ma'siyah* ("disobedience"), and *al-riddah* ("apostasy")—all imply efforts to overturn a divinely established order. Misrule is no justification for revolution; only impiety is. A ruler may be autocratic, corrupt, and venal, but unless he has violated religious law and damaged the spiritual well-being of the community, he must be obeyed. To oppose a ruler who is guilty of impiety is not "revolution" but jihad. But even a righteous jihad poses dangers, since the anarchy it produces if it fails might lead believers astray. It is best to accept any government that does not flout the basic tenets of the faith, no matter how inept or despotic it may be. Thus Ibn Taymiyyah (d. 1328), the inspiration for the modern Wahhabi movement, justified rebellion against the Mongols (who had described Genghis Khan as the Son of Allah) but insisted on acceptance of the despised Mamluks.

In the 18th century, in response both to the Enlightenment and to European incursions into the Islamic world, a new word entered the popular vocabulary. *Al-thawrah* ("uprising") implied secular insurrection against a foreign regime and thus had an element of nationalist sentiment. Wahhabi groups across North Africa and throughout the Middle East used this term when calling for Arab rebellion against the Ottoman Turks and their European enablers. Both the Arab struggle under Muhammad ibn Saud (d. 1765) against the Turks and the Egyptian insurrection against the British in 1919 were described by contemporaries as *al-thawrah*.

The Islamic world of the late 20th century was filled with political upheavals and refusal to settle for an unacceptable status quo. The 1950s saw military coups d'état in Egypt, Iran, Iraq, and Pakistan. Uprisings in the 1960s occurred in Libya, Syria (four times), and Yemen. Still more revolts came in the 1970s in Iran, Iraq, Lebanon, Pakistan, Syria, and Yemen. The 1980s were relatively quiet, with civil insurrection only in Lebanon and Yemen, but the 1990s saw rebellion in Lebanon, Pakistan, and Yemen. And these were only the successful uprisings; scores more failed revolts took place in every country. It is an impressive record of determined opposition.

Still, what was the status quo against which they rebelled? And why was it unacceptable? There are two obvious explanations and another two that are less obvious. All four are colored by profound religious concerns.

First was the issue of nationalism and the emotional residue of European imperialism and the Cold War. Many Muslim states were the creation of Europe. The imperialist countries left not only international borders but as often as not new nativist regimes and new constitutions to prop them up. European motives were seldom altruistic. If a government was willing to oppose the spread of Communism, open its country's markets to Western commerce, and keep oil production going, then the West cared little how corrupt and oppressive it might be. The result was a series of pro-Western autocracies that were widely viewed by their Arab subjects as puppets. They were also constant targets for ambitious new leaders who wanted to show their eagerness to confound the West and to stoke Arab pride.

Time magazine in 1973 described Muammar al-Qaddafi, who had seized power in Libya in 1969, this way:

> The leadership of the 100 million Arabs is, in the famous words of Egypt's Gamal Abdel Nasser, "a role wandering aimlessly about in search of an actor to play it." Now that Nasser is dead, now that his successors are gray and conventional, it is the implausible figure of Muammar Gaddafi that has acquired the role of an Arab Parsifal. He is a mere 31 years old, handsome, devout, ardent, even fanatical. "The Arabs need to be told the facts," he is fond of saying. "The Arabs need someone to make them weep, not someone to make them laugh." Nasser once told the young Gaddafi: "You remind me of myself when I was your age." Gaddafi was profoundly moved. To be the new Nasser is his obsession—to succeed where Nasser failed.

The new Arab leaders, while anti-Western in their public stances, were often eager to retain good relations with Europe and the United States privately, in order to preserve the flow of Western dollars. By Islamic standards, their false piety was cause for legitimate revolt.

Second was the issue of Israel. With the possible exception of Jordan, few of the Arab countries cared about the plight of the Palestinians, whom popular prejudice among the broader Arab populace regarded as poor, backward rustics. But other countries cared very much about using them as a cudgel with which to beat the Israelis. Repeated defeats at the hands of the Israeli Defense Force wounded Arab pride. It also threatened to undermine the legitimacy of the national governments. As Islamist groups repeatedly pointed out, the Qur'an itself (3.110–112) had proclaimed of the Arabs:

> You are the best nation formed out of mankind, commanding what is good, forbidding what is evil, and believing in Allah. If only the People of the Book [Jews and Christians] had had faith, it would have been well for them. Some of them do have faith, but most of them are perverted transgressors. They will never be able to do you any serious harm, only minor annoyance. When they come out to fight you, they will turn their backs [to flee], and will

not be succored. Shame is their lot, pitched over them [like a tent] wherever they might go.... They have incurred Allah's wrath, and humiliation covers them [like a blanket]—all because they rejected Allah's signs, impiously killed His prophets, and have continually rebelled and transgressed.

That was a hard pill to swallow after seven straight military defeats. The need to take the lead in opposing Israel, and to be seen to take the lead, became a central plank of Middle Eastern politics. Any regime that faltered or failed in this regard paid a price in popular discontent.

A third explanation is less obvious: decolonization let loose long-simmering ethnic and tribal rivalries. These contests frequently played themselves out as power struggles within nations, but from the 1970s on they took the form of angling for leadership of the broader Islamic world. Ethnic Arabs had not been in such a role since the late 8th century, when power passed to the Persians. In the 14th and 15th centuries, leadership in the Muslim world passed to the Ottoman Turks, who held it until World War I. Wahhabism originated in the 18th century as an intellectual movement to restore Arab primacy, but the Arab states began to adopt it after World War II. The rebel

Demonstrating for Pan-Arabism   Gamal Abdel Nasser was the president of Egypt from 1956 to 1970 and one of the leading statesmen for the pan-Arab movement. Among his achievements was a brief formal union of Egypt and Syria into a single United Arab Republic. Formed in 1958, the union ended when Syria withdrew in 1961. Here, an Egyptian crowd, carrying Nasser's portrait, protest the Syrian secession.

leaders who managed to hold onto power through the 20th century consistently presented themselves as leaders of a pan-Arab movement to guide Islam into the new age. The state-run media in ethnically Arab countries referred to the 1979 uprising in Iran as *al-shawrah al-Iraniyyah* ("Iranian secular rebellion"). They wished to deny both the ethnic Persians and the dominant Shi'a of that country the honor of leading an "Islamic revolution."

Which brings up, at last, the fourth issue—Islam's relationship with modern culture. Islamic modernism had emerged in the 19th century, when progressive religious scholars were eager to adapt Islamic life to technological and secular society. These modernizers included the Young Turks at the Ottoman court, the Islamic Enlightenment in Egypt, and writers as broadly based as Beirut, Damascus, and Baghdad. The ideas associated with Islamic modernism fell into disrepute, however, in the 20th century. Religious and nationalist conservatives rejected modernism out of hand because of its pro-Western taint. The enduring problems in the Islamic world, to the conservatives, did not need a Western solution but rather a traditional Islamic one, rooted in ancient values and customs.

> The enduring problems in the Islamic world, to the conservatives, did not need a Western solution but rather a traditional Islamic one, rooted in ancient values and customs.

The theocratic government established in Iran after the overthrow of the shah in 1979 offered one variation on this theme. As the Ayatollah Khomeini put it in his best-known book, *Islamic Government:*[10]

> Islamic government is a government of law. In this form of government, sovereignty belongs to God alone and law is His decree and command. The law of Islam, divine command, has absolute authority over all individuals and the Islamic government. Everyone, including the Most Noble Messenger(s) and his successors, is subject to law and will remain so for all eternity—the law that has been revealed by God, Almighty and Exalted, and expounded by the tongue of the Qur'an and the Most Noble Messenger(s). If the Prophet(s) assumed the task of divine vice-regency upon earth, it was in accordance with divine command.

Free-market capitalism, with its emphasis on individual freedom and the rights of property, did not fit well with a conservative Islamic view that championed community and egalitarianism. Better suited to Muslim values, and specifically to Arab ones, was the political ideology known as Ba'athism.

---

[10] "In Islam," wrote Khomeini, "government has the sense of adherence to law; it is law alone that rules over society."

BA'ATHISM AND BROTHERHOOD

Ba'athism is at root a form of Islamic socialism. It calls for a state-run capitalism in which the government, or the Ba'athist Party, provides essential services to all citizens. Ba'athism originated in Syria in the 1940s and gained popularity in the postwar decades. Although a secular political ideology, it complemented the conservative religious movement of the Wahhabis. Like them, it emphasized the unique role of the Arabs in securing a new future for international Islam. Its mission was to turn back the course of history to the social and cultural ideal of the first Arab caliphate.[11] This vision may or may not have been a genuine political goal; what mattered was Arab unity as an expression of religious culture.

The desire to restore an Islamic culture of the past meant first the rejection of Western ideas, values, and civic norms. Democracy, equal rights for women, freedom of speech, and the separation of religion and government appear not as universal ideals but as Western customs incompatible with Islamic culture. Hence the decision to replace the UN Declaration of Human Rights with the Cairo Declaration (see chapter 27), which, as we saw in the last chapter, subordinates all claims of human rights to shariah. Hence too the 1988 charter of **Hamas**, a conservative religious-political Palestinian group that devoted itself equally to charitable campaigns and social work among the Palestinians and to a terrorist war upon Israel.

Hamas, which originated as an offshoot of the Egyptian **Muslim Brotherhood**, took as its slogan the declaration that "Allah is our goal, the Prophet [Muhammad] our model, the Qur'an our constitution, jihad our method, and death for Allah's sake our most sublime conviction." Its well-known view on the Palestinian issue is expressed clearly in its founding charter.

> In the name of Allah the Merciful and Compassionate . . .
> "You are the best nation" [Qur'an 3.110].
> [Hamas] is a free-standing Palestinian movement; ever loyal to Allah, it embraces Islam as its way of life and aims to raise Allah's flag over the entirety of Palestine. Those who follow other religions [of the Book] may continue to live in the secure enjoyment of their lives, property, and personal rights, even though without Islam disagreements arise, injustice spreads, and corruption thrives, leading to never-ending strife and war . . . .
> Ours is a global movement, worthy to fulfill our role because of the clarity of our ideals, the loftiness of our purpose, the exalted nature of our goals . . . .

---

[11]   The Ba'athist Party's constitution proclaimed "a single Arab nation from the Persian Gulf to the Atlantic Ocean, a nation with an eternal mission."

Marching to Annihilate the Zionist Enemy Hamas members and sympathizers rally in Gaza City on the first anniversary of the death of Abdel Aziz al-Rantissi (1947–2004), the group's co-founder. Rantissi helped to popularize the false notion that the Holocaust was the result of a secret Jewish conspiracy with the Nazi leaders; the conspiracy, he claimed, aimed to drive more Jews to emigrate to Palestine while making the rest of the world feel sorry for them and thereby allow the creation of Israel. Many Palestinian leaders, including Mahmoud Abbas, the current president of the Palestinian Authority, have endorsed the idea. (In fact, Abbas used an elaborated version of the theory for his Ph.D. dissertation.)

We are one element in the jihad-struggle to confront the Zionist invasion.... The Prophet (may Allah's prayer and peace be ever upon him!) himself said: "The hour of judgment will not come until the Muslims fight the Jews and kill them all—such that every tree and stone will say "Oh Muslim, servant of Allah! There is a Jew hiding behind me. Come kill him!"' ... There is no solution to the Palestinian problem except by *jihad*.

Less well known is its position regarding modernism:

Our movement began at a time when true Islam had all but disappeared from Arab life: its laws had been broken, its teachings ignored, its values altered. Wicked people had seized power, and under them there was nothing but oppression and darkness .... Homelands were usurped, people sent into exile and made to wander aimlessly through the world; justice disappeared and lies took its place. Nothing was as it should have been—which is the case whenever true Islam is driven out ....

In order to bring up the generations in an authentic Islamic way, it is necessary to teach the duties of religion, to study the Qur'an and the Prophet's traditions in their completeness, and to learn Islam's history and ways from authentic sources . . . .

We respect [nationalist] movements, understanding the conditions and circumstances that gave birth to them, and so long as they reject both the Communist East and the Crusading West we encourage them in their work . . . . We detest opportunism and seek only the good of all people. We reject material wealth and celebrity, seeking no return from any human being.

Such groups commanded significant popular support, but less for their anti-modern stance than for their anti-Zionism. A unified pan-Arab movement, they confidently believed, emboldened by a pure and disciplined application of traditional Islamic morality, could not fail to achieve the annihilation of the Zionist enemy. And success would be the crowning achievement of the Arab campaign to regain its rightful place at the head of international Islam. This is why Israel's repeated military victories in the 1960s and 1970s stung: while the Zionist state continued to thrive at the physical center of the Arab lands, Arab dreams to regain their status remained frustrated.

Groups like the Muslim Brotherhood and Hamas shared that frustration with political parties like the Ba'athists. They wished to revitalize a past vision of Islamic-Arab greatness rather than pursue a new one. They sought not a revolution but a restoration.

WHO, WHAT, WHERE

aggiornamento	neoorthodoxy
evangelicalism	New Historians
fundamentalism	Pentecostalism
Hamas	Second Vatican Council
Muslim Brotherhood	

SUGGESTED READINGS

Primary Sources

John XXIII. *Pacem in terris.*

Paul VI. *Humanae vitae.*

Tillich, Paul. *The Courage to Be.*

———. *Theology of Culture.*

Anthologies

Bonhoeffer, Dietrich. *Conspiracy and Imprisonment, 1940–1945* (2006).

Hahnenberg, Edward P. *A Concise Guide to the Documents of Vatican II* (2007).

Studies

An-Na'im, Abdullahi Ahmed. *Islam and the Secular State: Negotiating the Future of Shari'a* (2010).

Asad, Talal. *Formations of the Secular: Christianity, Islam, Modernity* (2003).

Bauman, Zygmunt. *Modernity and the Holocaust* (2001).

Bethge, Eberhard. *Dietrich Bonhoeffer: A Biography* (2000).

Calvert, John. *Sayyid Qutb and the Origins of Radical Islamism* (2010).

Campos, Michelle U. *Ottoman Brothers: Muslims, Christians, and Jews in Early Twentieth-Century Palestine* (2011).

Gerlach, Wolfgang. *And the Witnesses Were Silent: The Confessing Church and the Persecution of the Jews* (2000).

Heschel, Susannah. *The Aryan Jesus: Christian Theologians and the Bible in Nazi Germany* (2010).

Hockenos, Matthew D. *A Church Divided: German Protestants Confront the Nazi Past* (2004).

Jenkins, Philip. *God's Continent: Christianity, Islam, and Europe's Religious Crisis* (2009).

Karsh, Efraim. *Fabricating Israeli History: The "New Historians"* (2000).

Lamb, Matthew L., and Matthew Levering, eds. *Vatican II: Renewal within Tradition* (2008).

Morris, Benny. *Righteous Victims: A History of the Zionist-Arab Conflict, 1881–2001* (2001).

———. *The Birth of the Palestinian Refugee Problem Revisited* (2004).

O'Malley, John W. *What Happened at Vatican II* (2010).

Roy, Olivier. *Holy Ignorance: When Religion and Culture Part Ways* (2009).

Sánchez, José. *Pius XII and the Holocaust: Understanding the Controversy* (2002).

Segev, Tom. *One Palestine, Complete: Jews and Arabs under the British Mandate* (2001).

———. *1967: Israel, the War, and the Year That Transformed the Middle East* (2008).

———. *The Seventh Million: The Israelis and the Holocaust* (2000).

Taylor, Charles. *A Secular Age* (2007).

Warner, Michael, Jonathan VanAntwerpen, and Craig Calhoun, eds. *Varieties of Secularism in a Secular Age* (2010).

Young, Julian. *The Death of God and the Meaning of Life* (2003).

For additional resources, including maps, primary sources, visuals, web links, and quizzes, please go to **www.oup.com/us/backman.**

CHAPTER 29

Global Warmings

1989–2001

In late 1989 Mikhail Gorbachev, the general secretary of the Soviet Union from 1985 to 1991, opened the Berlin Wall. The collapse of the Soviet Union followed quickly thereafter. As winter came and 1990 began, another Soviet-bloc country emerged into freedom almost every month: East Germany, Bulgaria, Czechoslovakia, Romania, Lithuania, Latvia, Estonia, Poland, Hungary. Soon even nations within the Russian Confederation declared their independence, most notably Ukraine and Georgia. Every emergent state, and eventually Russia itself, announced its intent to write a new constitution, to dismantle its state-run economy, and to adopt democracy and free-market capitalism. The transitions were rocky, but people everywhere spoke optimistically of a "postideological era." The ideological battle between East and West belonged, it seemed, to the past. Western values and ideas had become the norm (see Map 29.1).

WORLD POPULATION, 1950–2000

Country where population increased by:
0–50% | 100–150% | 200–250% | over 300%
50–100% | 150–200% | 250–300%

A surprise international bestseller, *The End of History and the Last Man* (1992) by Francis Fukuyama, argued that with Communism's failure the battle for human hearts and minds was ended. Conflicts still lay ahead, but they would be mere economic or territorial disputes, not philosophical ones:

> What we may be witnessing is not just the end of the Cold War, or the

◀ **The End of History?** And the walls came tumbling down. . . . German youths celebrate the opening of the Berlin Wall on November 9, 1989. Ironically, that date is also the anniversary of other crucial events in German history: the end of the Revolution of 1848, the declaration of the Weimar Republic (1918), Adolf Hitler's failed "Beer Hall Putsch"—his first attempt to seize power in the country (1923), and the Kristallnacht attacks by the Nazis upon Germany's Jews (1938).

passing of a particular period of postwar history, but the end of history as such: that is, the end point of mankind's ideological evolution and the universalization of Western liberal democracy as the final form of human government.

The debate between differing visions was settled—or so it seemed.

However, triumph soon gave way to profound tensions. Open markets and democratic government, it turned out, are difficult to institute overnight. Outgoing government figures in many ex-Soviet nations made private deals to share power, sell off national industries and public resources, and arrange guarantees of immunity from prosecution for crimes committed while in power. With price controls lifted on consumer goods, inflation skyrocketed. The opening of secret-service archives triggered disputes over the settling of old scores with informants. The need to secure nuclear weapons and fissile-material laboratories raised concerns for safety. Many earnest, and many overearnest, emissaries from Western churches rushed in to win godless former-Communist souls for Christ, numb to local desires to revive their Orthodox traditions.

The end of the Cold War and the independent demands of peoples and nations thus introduced a host of new challenges. Globalized capitalism and the enormous influence of the United States as the only remaining superpower raised both hopes and fears that the norms of the West would become universalized. Among the most immediate concerns were the debates over how to promote economic development while protecting the environment and how to protect the rights of women and the poor without imposing, or appearing to impose, Western cultural values that were at odds with those of non-Western states. These concerns dramatically and suddenly complicated relations within the Greater West as the Muslim states struggled to determine their own relations with modernity. Trouble emerged right from the start in 1989.

CHAPTER TIMELINE

1984
Luce Irigaray, *An Ethics of Sexual Difference*

1992
Francis Fukuyama, *The End of History and the Last Man*

1989
Publication of *Satanic Verses* leads to uproar in the Muslim world; *Exxon Valdez* environomental disaster; Ayatollah Khomeini dies; Berlin Wall breached

1993
Treaty of Maastricht creates European Union

ONE YEAR, FOUR CRISES

A popular video game called World in Conflict, released in 2007 by software developers in Sweden, is set in 1989 and presents the fictional scenario of the Soviet Union, in a last desperate gamble to stay in power before collapse, invading western Europe. That done, the Soviets promptly attack the U.S. city of Seattle in order to immobilize the Americans' missile-defense mechanisms; the United States responds by unleashing a tactical nuclear strike on the Soviet forces, annihilating the city in the process. Meanwhile, China enters the fray as a Soviet ally, and the war quickly becomes global in scale.

The scenario is unlikely, if not preposterous, but not because of its attribution to the USSR of a military strength that it simply did not possess at that time. A more realistic scenario for the game would have been for the threat to world peace to come from China and parts of the Islamic world, for that is where signs of discontent with world developments were most visible, most determined, and most violent.

In the wake of Communism's fall what remained to do, it seemed at first, was to set to work bringing the world into the golden dawn of prosperity, freedom, and progress. Freed of the need for Cold War nuclear deterrence, people spoke of a "peace dividend." Now governments could balance their books, lower taxes, promote economic growth, and even expand social services. It was heady optimism unlike anything the West had seen since before the two World Wars. Hundreds of thousands rushed into western Europe, fleeing poverty and oppression, and were received as heroic survivors of despotism. Manufacturing

> Freed of the need for Cold War nuclear deterrence, people spoke of a "peace dividend." Now governments could balance their books, lower taxes, promote economic growth, and even expand social services. It was heady optimism unlike anything the West had seen since before the two World Wars.

1995
UN Women's Conference in Beijing; WTO founded

2000
World population 6.1 billion

1999
Euro currency introduced; Good Friday accord signed; "Battle of Seattle" against WTO

2001
Terrorist attacks on the United States

The Fall of Communism in Eastern Europe and the Soviet Union

Former republics of the Soviet Union gaining independence in 1991	Independence from Soviet Union declared 1991; at war with Russia, 1994–2000	▬▬	Boundary of the former Soviet Union to 1991
Boundary of Russian Federation after December 1991	Former Warsaw Pact country holding free elections, 1990–1992	⚑	Violent ethnic conflicts

MAP 29.1   The Fall of Communism in Eastern Europe and the Soviet Union

companies from the West saw huge potential markets in the East. Churches looked to the millions who had been denied religious life for forty years.

Three other events in that remarkable year of 1989 presaged a less rosy future. First, the leader of the Islamic Republic of Iran, the Ayatollah Ruhollah Khomeini (1902–1989), ghoulishly declared a death sentence on a British novelist, Salman Rushdie (b. 1947), and offered $3 million to any Muslim who murdered him. Earlier that year Rushdie had published a novel, *The Satanic Verses*, that Khomeini—without having read it—declared blasphemous:

> I would like to inform all courageous Muslims throughout the world that the author of the novel *The Satanic Verses* . . . as well as those

publishers who were aware of its contents, are hereby sentenced to death. I call upon all pious Muslims to execute them all, quickly, wherever they might find them, so that afterwards no one will dare to insult the holiness of Islam. Anyone who is killed in carrying out this sentence will be regarded as a martyr and will go directly to heaven.

The novel takes its title from a dream sequence in which the fever-stricken main character imagines that the Prophet Muhammad has made a deal with three ancient pagan deities to insert some of their pseudo-revelations into the text of the Qur'an. Even more repugnant to some Muslims was an episode set in India, in which the prostitutes in a certain brothel have all taken the names of the Prophet's wives as pseudonyms.

Khomeini died four months after pronouncing the death sentence, but his call spurred fanatics into action. The novel's Japanese translator, a recent convert to Islam, was stabbed to death; its Italian translator, knifed in Milan, survived; its Norwegian publisher was shot in the back four times, but also survived. A mob set fire to a hotel where the novel's Turkish translator was participating in a literary conference; thirty-five people burned to death. The Turkish translator himself escaped the fire, but several of the firefighters beat him senseless. Rushdie stayed in protective custody with the British government for nine years, and the death sentence remains, although Iran has agreed not to pursue it. Iranian officials announced in 1998 that they have "no intention, nor is it going to take any action whatsoever, to threaten the life of the author of *The Satanic Verses* or anybody associated with his work, nor will it encourage or assist anybody to do so."

A handful of would-be assassins do not represent an entire religion or culture, but the reaction of the Muslim world alarmed the West. The Union of Muslim Organisations, Britain's largest Islamic group, petitioned Parliament to ban the distribution of the novel.[1] Thousands of Muslims poured into the streets in protest, and a crowd in the town of Bolton staged a public burning of the book. Bookshops were vandalized and firebombed, and hundreds more received bomb threats. The Organisation of the Islamic Cooperation, a group for coordinating policy between Muslim states at the United Nations, requested all its member states to ban the book. In May 1989 a crowd of twenty thousand burned an effigy of Rushdie in Parliament Square in London. The Islamic Union of Students' Associations in Europe also endorsed the demand for Rushdie's murder. Numerous other Islamic groups opposed the killing, but on legal rather than moral grounds.

---

[1] Within a year of publication, *The Satanic Verses* was banned in nineteen countries, including Egypt, Saudi Arabia, and South Africa.

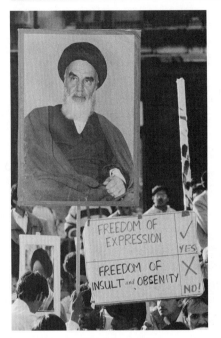

Demonstrating Against *The Satanic Verses* Ayatollah Khomeini's call for the assassination of novelist Salman Rushdie prompted dozens of demonstrations worldwide, both for and against the *fatwa*. In this photo, Khomeini supporters in Tehran declare their support for the *fatwa* with the assertion that freedom of speech does not extend to religious insult.

They argued that Khomeini's fatwa, or Islamic legal pronouncement, had not followed the proper guidelines, and anyway a fatwa could not be enforced in a non-Islamic country such as Britain.

The Rushdie affair brought home the anger of many Muslims worldwide at Western values. The Khomeini regime had instituted public whippings, stonings, beheadings, and firing squads for its enemies. "Those who attempt to undermine or ruin our Republic in the name of democracy," Khomeini warned, "will be suppressed; they are worse than the Jews of Banu Qurayza, and must be hanged." (The reference is to a group of 7th-century Jews from Medina, some eight hundred of them, who had opposed Muhammad's rise and were consequently captured and beheaded.) The Iranian Revolution pursued not only a separate path of development for Islamic nations but active opposition to the West's "oppressive, un-Islamic" ways of life.

Arab states feared the Iranian Revolution as both Shi'a and Persian, and therefore a threat to Arab and Sunni dominance. Iran and its neighbor Iraq fought a bitter eight-year war (1980–1988) that left hundreds of thousands dead. But rejection of the West's politics, economy, popular culture, and moral values proved popular, and militant organizations had at least the tacit support of the broader population—and even several governments. Soon news and debates in the West regularly referred to such names as Islamic Jihad, Party of God, Party of Islam, and Party of Liberation. Like the nations in which they were founded, most of these institutions are of recent origin; many of their founders are still active. All promote a restoration of conservative Islamic values, but not all promote anti-Western violence. Many of these groups are quite small, with only a few hundred members. But some claim membership in the hundreds of thousands.

Until the Rushdie affair, the West had generally regarded developments in the Islamic world as regional concerns, of interest only as they affected Israel or the price of oil. Muslim immigration into Europe and the United States still worried relatively few. But the tens of thousands of angry European Muslims on the streets of Berlin, Copenhagen, The Hague, London, Paris, Rome, and dozens of smaller cities provided a wake-up call. This might not be the "end of history" after all.

The second alarming incident of 1989 was the grounding of the *Exxon Valdez*, an oil tanker, in Prince William Sound, Alaska. The tanker was plump with 55 million gallons (over 200,000 cubic meters) of heavy, thick crude oil from Alaska's far-northern Prudhoe Bay when its hull was crushed against a reef.[2] It created an environmental disaster greater than anything the United States had experienced. The responsibility lay with the Exxon Corporation; an Alaskan court ordered it to pay over a quarter billion dollars in compensation and another five billion dollars in punitive damages. To finance its payments, Exxon received a multibillion-dollar line of credit from the J.P. Morgan investment bank, which invented a new kind of financial instrument in order to provide the capital. They

Environmental Disaster   The work to clean up the oil spilled by the *Exxon Valdez* took years. Here workers use high-power sprays on coastal rocks and the beach. Technologies for cleaning up after oil spills are today essentially the same as they were in 1989.

---

2   The *Valdez* released somewhere between 11 and 32 million gallons (42,000 to 120,000 cubic meters) of oil into the sound.

called it a **credit default swap**, and it was to play a role in a still larger disaster—the economic collapse of 2008.

The spill showed that the oil industry's recovery and cleanup techniques were ineffective, and so was the government's oversight. Immediate efforts included a controlled burn of the oil and the application of a chemical dispersant; both had only modest success owing to bad weather conditions. In fact, the dispersant created underwater plumes of oil that could no longer be reached. Mechanical skimmers arrived after a delay and began to collect oil from the water's surface. The rocky shorelines suffered heavy contamination, which crews addressed with high-pressure sprays of scalding water. Workers and volunteers spent thousands of hours cleaning by hand the sea birds, seals, and otters that were coated with thick sheens of oil. The loss of wildlife was immense; the hot water sprays also killed the plankton that form the first link in the marine food chain. Even twenty years later, marine and coastal wildlife were dramatically reduced in numbers. While the sound itself now appears surprisingly clean, as much as 20,000 gallons of oil still lie beneath the surface. Many local plant species and the animal populations that feed on them have declined over 90 percent and show little likelihood of recovering.

The spill awakened millions in the West to the threat that industrial development can pose to the environment (see Map 29.2). Concerns about pollution were hardly new, but they took on new urgency after a 1973 boycott by the **Organization of Petroleum Exporting Countries** (OPEC) drove gasoline prices to record levels. The first Green Parties appeared on the political scene in Belgium and West Germany, where they won parliamentary seats. Debates about Western dependency on oil, its effects on the environment, and the dangers of what seemed the only real alternative—nuclear energy—continued. After a drought in 1988, government officials spoke for the first time of global warming, a sweeping change in the earth's climate. Britain's prime minister Margaret Thatcher in 1988 called for political action to combat climate change, but promoted nuclear energy as the solution. The *Valdez* oil spill accelerated calls for international action.

The first significant step was the UN Conference on Environment and Development, or Earth Summit, held in Rio de Janeiro in 1992. Its Rio Declaration called environmental protection an "integral part of the development process," one that "cannot be considered in isolation from it." It also committed nations to "the essential task of eradicating poverty as an indispensable requirement for sustainable development." Critics complained that the two goals were contradictory, at least in the short term, since only economic development could overcome Third World poverty. The demand to reduce carbon emissions from fossil fuels while also resisting the spread of nuclear energy, critics said, was simply unrealistic. Transportation of goods and people alone accounted for 40 percent of carbon emissions. For all its ecological drawbacks, oil is effective, relatively inexpensive,

Water Pollution

Carbon Monoxide

Water Pollution and Carbon Monoxide Emissions Worldwide

▼ Offshore dumpsite for waste

  Great Pacific Garbage Patch

  Severe pollution

  Moderate pollution

  Area of frequent oil pollution

Emissions of CO_2 in tonnes per person per year (2008):

  over 10   1–5

  5–10   under 1

MAP 29.2   Water Pollution and Carbon Monoxide Emissions Worldwide

and easy to move. One can have economic health or environmental health, critics insisted, but not both.

The conflict between economic development and environmental preservation came to a head with the document known as the **Kyoto Protocol**, an international response to global warming in 1997. Thomas Malthus (1766–1834) had raised a related issue as long ago as 1826, in his *Essay on the Principle of Population*. To Malthus, human history has always been the contest of a growing population for the finite material goods of the earth. "The power of population is indefinitely greater than the power in the earth to produce subsistence for man." When the tension between the two powers becomes too great, nature alleviates it by famine and disease. Knowingly or not, those who argued most for environmental protections were Malthusians. They believed that human and economic catastrophe could be averted only by protecting the environment.

Others took the opposite view, insisting that economic growth was the answer to the ecological problem. In two books, *The Ultimate Resource* (1981) and *The Resourceful Earth* (1984), the American economist Julian Simon (1932–1998) laid the intellectual foundation for many conservative leaders at the end of the century. For Simon, the competition for scarce resources in a free market promotes innovations, as he wrote in *The Ultimate Resource*:

> The basic idea is that growth in population creates a demand that provokes an increase in prices. The increase in prices creates opportunities that attract businesses and scientists to be able to satisfy the demand and thus increase their income. Most of them fail and they personally absorb the costs. But after a while, some are successful and find solutions. At the end you have a situation better than if there had not been a problem of scarcity.

If environmental doomsayers were too negative, the "free-market environmentalists" may have been naïve idealists. But once again the "end of history"—either as the birth of a capitalist utopia or the death of planet Earth—had not yet arrived.

———————— ✦ ————————

A third crucial event of 1989 occurred in China. In April, students at Beijing University used the funeral of a popular dissenting politician as an occasion to demonstrate for reform in Tiananmen Square. Over one hundred thousand people joined the demonstration, which soon became a direct challenge to the government. The demonstrators in the square were peaceful and stopped short of calling for the Communists to leave office; rather, they demanded democracy, freedom of speech, freedom of association, an end to political cronyism, and increased funding for education. As the crowd swelled, demonstrators issued a call for university students and faculty throughout China to boycott classes. Urban

Tank Man   The identity of this lone figure, staring down a column of tanks en route to Tiananmen Square, is still unknown—and he may well be grateful for that fact, given the continuing crackdown on dissidents by China's ruling elite.

workers, who generally supported the government's economic liberalization but had begun to experience inflation, voiced support for the students.

Violent rioting broke out in several cities, though not in Beijing itself. The government portrayed the demonstrators as plotting to overthrow the state, which only strengthened student resolve. On June 4, the army took action, both within Beijing and across the nation. Estimates of the number of protestors, onlookers, and soldiers killed nationwide ranges from 241 (the official government reckoning) to as many as five thousand, as estimated by the local branch of the Red Cross. Thousands, and possibly tens of thousands, were wounded.

The government tried to control how these events appeared to the world, but too late. Satellite phones and radio and television broadcasts had leaked too many reports and videos. The benign image that the regime had presented was stripped away, to reveal a brutal autocracy with the power of tanks and fact-twisting propaganda:

> This turmoil was not a chance occurrence. It was a political turmoil incited by a very small number of political careerists after a few years of plotting and scheming. It was aimed at subverting the socialist People's Republic. By making use of some failings in the work of the Chinese

government and the temporary economic difficulties, they spread far and wide many views against the Constitution, the leadership of the Chinese Communist Party and the People's Government, preparing the ground for the turmoil ideologically, organizationally and in public opinion. . . .

Even under this circumstance, the Party and the government exercised great restraint towards the students' extremist slogans and actions and had all along given due recognition to the students' patriotic enthusiasm and reasonable demands. At the same time, the Party and the government warned the students not to be made use of by a handful of people and expressed the hope for solving the problems through dialogues and by normal, democratic and legal procedures. . . .

A group of ruffians banded together about 1,000 people to push down the wall of a construction site near Xidan and seized large quantities of tools, reinforcing bars and bricks, ready for street fighting. They planned to incite people to take to the streets the next day, a Sunday, to stage a violent rebellion in an attempt to overthrow the government and seize power at one stroke.

At this critical juncture, the martial law troops were ordered to move in by force to quell the anti-government rebellion. . . . Over 1,280 vehicles were burned or damaged in the rebellion, including over 1,000 military trucks, more than 60 armoured cars, over 30 police cars, over 120 public buses and trolley buses and over 70 motor vehicles of other kinds. More than 6,000 martial law officers and soldiers were injured and scores of them killed.

Such heavy losses are eloquent testimony to the restraint and tolerance shown by the martial law enforcement troops. For fear of injuring civilians by accident, they would rather endure humiliation and meet their death unflinchingly, although they had weapons in their hands. It can be said that there is no other army in the world that can exercise restraint to such an extent. *(Official Report of the Editorial Board of the Truth about the Beijing Turmoil, Beijing Publishing House, 1990)*

In response to the crackdown, the European Union and the United States embargoed the sale of weaponry to China, and the World Bank suspended all developmental loans to Beijing. Billions of dollars in foreign investments were canceled, and international tourism to China fell by 25 percent.

Communist and Maoist ideology no longer convinced most Chinese, but the Party could still command obedience by appeals to nationalism. The Party presented itself as the only sure guarantor of stable economic reform and the protector of national pride. The Communists in effect played a double game. It showed a friendly face to the outside world and courted international investment. Yet internally it portrayed the Chinese people as the victims of misunderstanding and imperialist aggression. The Party now stood as the paragon of patriotism. When the 2000 Olympic Games were awarded to Sydney, Australia, instead of Beijing, China's press condemned the decision as another example of entrenched pro-Western bias.[3]

The rise of radical Islamism, the debate between environmentalism and economic development, and the flourishing of Arab and Chinese nationalism have shaped Western life ever since. The Cold War may have ended in 1989, but a profoundly unsettled world took its place.

> The rise of radical Islamism, the debate between environmentalism and economic development, and the flourishing of Arab and Chinese nationalism have shaped Western life ever since. The Cold War may have ended in 1989, but a profoundly unsettled world took its place.

The post-1989 changes in fact echoed many of the experiences of the post-1815 era, when an economic and social time lock opened, and an accelerating wave of aggressive capitalism rushed in. Scores of huge fortunes were amassed almost instantly, as people with access to capital snatched up privatized state monopolies while the bulk of the populations, unaccustomed to and suspicious of Western-defined "market forces," found themselves with no means to support themselves. Unemployment in Poland, for example, hit 20 percent, and an investigative report from members of the European Union classified fourteen percent of the nation as "severely materially deprived." The gross national product (GNP) of Ukraine collapsed 50 percent within ten years of the Soviet breakup, while hyperinflation threatened to make the national currency useless; even after another decade (that is, by 2009) more than one-third of the adult population was unemployed. Hungary lost three-fourths of its export markets when protectionist measures closed access to its former trading partners; the national trade deficit soon grew to nearly triple the amount of total exports.

Soon enough, the predictable backlash occurred, and currents of political ultraconservatism emerged across eastern Europe that advocated a return to centralized control. Intense nationalistic sentiments rose, which prompted many nonmajority populations—especially large numbers of Jews—to emigrate. Right-wing coups were attempted in Georgia, as people denounced the

---

[3] "Give China a chance!" had been the slogan for Beijing's 1993 bid to host the 2000 Olympic Games.

corruption and cronyism of democratically chosen administrations. Assassinations and attempted assassinations poisoned the political atmospheres.

The West responded by injecting capital through the IMF, increasing private investment, bringing at least some of the nations (Bulgaria, Estonia, Hungary, Latvia, Lithuania, Poland, Romania) into the European Union and most of the same into NATO. The economic malaise improved through the 1990s as a result, but improvement came at the cost of leaving the not-included nations feeling exposed and vulnerable, especially in the face of renewed political swagger from Russia's leader, Vladimir Putin.

THE UNITED STATES OF EUROPE

The idea of uniting Europe in a single superstate can be traced back at least to Charlemagne in the early 9th century. Several medieval popes had imagined it. Habsburgs had probably fantasized about it. Napoleon almost achieved it. Hitler almost destroyed the place in his sick attempt make it happen. But the idea existed outside the minds of would-be dictators too.

Unification's appeal lay into the hope that it might be the one force powerful enough to contain nationalist passions, and it expressed the idea that European civilization stood for more than material progress. At the Continent's center, German thinkers have traditionally been at the forefront of the call to unification. The Romantic writer Novalis (the pen name of Georg Freiherr von Hardenberg; 1772–1801) had prophesied that "blood will stream over Europe until the nations fully understand this terrifying madness that drives them in circles." Novalis believed in the power of culture and art to save Europe. His contemporary Justus Friedrich von Schmidt-Phiseldek (1769–1851), a German politician and writer, had warned that unless Europe united into a large confederation it would soon lose its place on the international stage. The young but robust United States would rise not only as an economic power but also as the symbolic leader of Western life. Another German, Julius Fröbel (1805–1893), had raised an even sharper alarm. If Europe did not unite, he had warned, it would become a battleground in a war between the United States and Russia.

Nietzsche had devoted a long section of *Beyond Good and Evil* (1886) to the question of national and civilizational identity:

> No matter what you wish to call the thing by which Europe is made distinctive—its "civilization," "humanization," or "progress"—or if you

simply call it (without praise or blame) Europe's political "democratization," there is an overarching physiological process occurring, indeed accelerating, behind all the moral and political theorizing around it: namely, Europeans are becoming more and more alike, more and more detached from those elements of climate and class that lead to the creation of separate races.... An essentially super-national, free-wandering European man is emerging, one who physiologically possesses as his defining trait a superfluity of the ability to adapt. *(Chapter 242)*

Because of the pathological soul-estrangement created by the utter insanity of nationalism ... and because of the short-sighted sleight-of-hand performed by today's politicians (who got to where they are precisely by playing off this madness), ... people are overlooking or perhaps (willfully?) misunderstanding the most obvious thing in the world: namely, that *Europe wants to unite.*   *(Chapter 256)*

The aspiration to unite was cultural, moral, esthetic, and even spiritual. At stake were shared values and beliefs, a commitment to human rights, civic-mindedness, reason, and personal freedom. Politics and the economy played their roles, but what mattered most was the idea of Europe as a civilization, not just a commercial entity.

How much the horrors of the 20th century changed things. The leaders of western Europe, after years of wrangling, agreed in March 1957 to the first step toward union—the **Treaty of Rome**, which established the European Economic Community (EEC). The treaty's preamble proclaimed its purpose:

Determined to lay the foundations of an ever-closer union among the peoples of Europe,

Resolved to ensure the economic and social progress of their countries by common action to eliminate the barriers which divide Europe,

Affirming as the essential objective of their efforts the constant improvement of the living and working conditions of their peoples,

Recognising that the removal of existing obstacles calls for concerted action in order to guarantee steady expansion, balanced trade and fair competition,

Anxious to strengthen the unity of their economies and to ensure their harmonious development by reducing the differences existing between the various regions and the backwardness of the less favoured regions,

Desiring to contribute, by means of a common commercial policy, to the progressive abolition of restrictions on international trade,

Intending to confirm the solidarity which binds Europe and the overseas countries and desiring to ensure the development of their prosperity, in accordance with the principles of the Charter of the United Nations,

Resolved by thus pooling their resources to preserve and strengthen peace and liberty, and calling upon the other peoples of Europe who share their ideal to join in their efforts, they announced the creation of the EEC.

More of a corporate merger than a cultural confluence, the EEC created a competitive commercial bloc that could hold its own on the world market.

The EEC's goals were to help postwar recovery and to counterbalance American economic power. Two other groups, the European Coal and Steel Community and the European Atomic Energy Community, were merged with the EEC in 1967, creating the European Community. Already it sounded less like a chamber of commerce and more like an association of cultures.

The next step to full integration came late in 1993, when a treaty signed a year earlier at Maastricht, in the Netherlands, took effect. This treaty established the **European Union** (EU), as not a single institution but as a united group of independent European nations. This flexible web of institutions would provide a process for coordinating policies formed at the level of member states:

The European Union (EU) is not a federation like the United States. Nor is it simply an organisation for co-operation between governments, like the United Nations. It is, in fact, unique. The countries that make up the EU (its "member states") remain independent sovereign nations but they pool their sovereignty in order to gain a strength and world influence none of them could have on their own. Pooling sovereignty means, in practice, that the member states delegate some of their decision-making powers to shared institutions they have created, so that decisions on specific matters of joint interest can be made democratically at the European level.

From the six members of the original European Economic Community of 1957 (Belgium, France, West Germany, Italy, Luxembourg, and the Netherlands), the EU grew steadily (see Map 29.3). It now numbers twenty-seven member

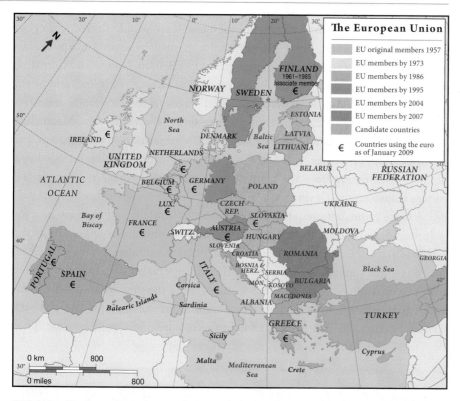

The European Union

- EU original members 1957
- EU members by 1973
- EU members by 1986
- EU members by 1995
- EU members by 2004
- EU members by 2007
- Candidate countries
- € Countries using the euro as of January 2009

MAP 29.3   The European Union

states, with another five official candidates for membership. Each nation must meet three criteria before joining:

- It must have a democratic government that recognizes human rights and the rule of law.
- It must have a free-market economy.
- It must meet administrative standards to participate seamlessly with other member states.

Of those standards, the most crucial is the ability to limit governmental debt to an acceptable percentage of GNP. Once a member, each country may choose to join in a common currency—the euro—which was introduced in 1999. By eliminating or reducing bureaucratic barriers, the EU promoted the free movement of workers, goods, services, and capital. All these, combined with the low price of oil caused by Middle East overproduction, made the 1990s an economic boom time. Still-developing economies in countries like Greece, Ireland, and Portugal benefitted from substantial investment in new manufacturing and financial ventures.

Unified Europe was not without problems. More people flowed from poor nations into wealthy ones than euros flowed from wealthy nations into poor ones. This meant rising unemployment in countries like Britain, France, and Germany; it also meant uncertain growth in countries like Greece, Portugal, and Spain. Labor surpluses put downward pressure on wages in the developed countries, since by far the most migration took place among the working class. Meanwhile the developing nations took on excessive debt in proportion to their growth. For the time being, however, the availability of cheap capital, which included substantial investments from the United States and China, made the decade feel more prosperous than it was.

A more immediate problem was the social assimilation of so many new foreign workers. Concern about immigration had become an issue as early as the late 1960s, but the creation of the union put increased numbers on the move. And this was the movement of Europeans within Europe rather than the migration of Africans or Asians into Europe. It was also chiefly the migration of individuals rather than entire families. Since many such workers sent parts of their pay back to their families, they often could afford only crowded and squalid housing. They

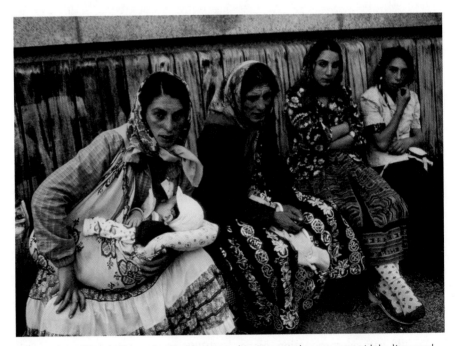

Roma   The Roma people, or Gypsies, originated in Romania but are now widely dispersed across Europe, and they remain largely unwelcome immigrants. Here a group of Gypsy women sit on a street corner in Berlin. The Roma were another group singled out for elimination by the Nazis. Estimates of the number of Gypsies killed in the death camps range from 300,000 to 1.5 million.

remained socially isolated in their host countries and struggled for acceptance. They were also the first workers to be laid off during bad times. The need for their wages back home, however, often kept them in their host countries where they looked for new work. The emotional strain on these workers, not to mention on their distant families, was great.

When a recession hit, the unemployed in Britain alone grew from 1.6 million workers to 3.0 million between 1990 and 1993. The downturn contributed to the rise of reactionary popular movements in Europe. Neo-Nazi skinheads led race riots and railed against "foreigners," both European and non-European. "France for the French!" became the cry of the far-right National Front Party, which by the middle of the decade was earning 15 percent of the vote. The French government, eager to capitalize on anti-immigrant passions, in 1996 chartered aircraft to fly undocumented workers back to their native countries. In Austria and the Netherlands as well, immigration was the crucial issue in determining the outcome of elections.

FEMINISM'S THIRD WAVE

The 1990s were a crucial period in the history of Western women, too. The collapse of Communism introduced eastern European women to the ideas of modern feminism. And the expansion of the EU to include countries like the Czech Republic, Hungary, and Poland provided opportunities for women to migrate westward in search of work and a new life. However, that only heightened awareness of the differences between national cultures when it comes to women's rights and roles.

For every move toward liberalization in the 1990s, there was an equal trend toward conservatism. In both Ireland and Italy, efforts to liberalize laws pertaining to divorce met powerful resistance from traditional-minded women's groups. While homosexuality to most people was no longer a pathology or a crime, the "gender wars" brought thuggish attacks on homosexuals. Other disadvantaged groups in society—from ethnic minorities to the physically disabled, from underrepresented religious groups to the urban poor—demanded more attention to their own agendas.

This was the decade of feminism's third wave, and while its active center was firmly fixed in the United States, much of its intellectual leadership came from Europe. The two leading figures were French-speaking. Luce Irigaray (b. 1932), a Belgian psychoanalyst, became especially influential as her books appeared in

English translation. Both *An Ethics of Sexual Difference* (1984, in English in 1993) and *Speculum of the Other Woman* (1974, in English in 1985) display her eclectic ideas and methods. (She holds two doctorates—one in philosophy, another in linguistics—and is also a certified psychoanalyst.) Her central theme is the struggle to create an authentic understanding of femaleness. For her, ideas of gender are socially constructed around a system of binary relations. Every aspect of Western culture, Irigaray writes, right down to the use of gendered nouns and adjectives in Western languages, presents the male as the norm. Everything that is "She," meaning "not He," fails to comprehend fully the Otherness of the female. Business practice, too, tends to use male experience as the default. Would men ever have thought of maternity leaves had women not fought for them?

> Every aspect of Western culture, Irigaray writes, right down to the use of gendered nouns and adjectives in Western languages, presents the male as the norm.

Is Irigaray too cavalier in seeing a "gendered nature" in everything?[4] In one essay she criticizes the sexual tyranny of men, in often technical language:

> It is important to rediscover the uniqueness of female sexual delight.... Are not these women being de-personalized, abandoned without vitality, sensations, perceptions, gestures or images of their own, things expressive of their own true identity? For women, at least two types of orgasms exist—one that is attuned to the male sexual economy...; but there is another more in harmony with women's true identity, their true sexual nature. There are many women who feel nothing but guilt and unhappiness, who are paralyzed and dismissed as frigid, simply because they cannot enjoy their true sensations, their true sexuality..., within the norms established by the phallocratic sexual economy. Such women could embrace sexuality if they were allowed to pursue a norm of sexual delight more attuned to their bodies and their sex.

To Irigaray's critics, the relentless focus on language defeats any practical social change. In the last decade, however, she has been involved in several studies for the EU investigating the conditions of women's lives. She has also played a role in developing possible legislation for the European Parliament.

---

4   "Is E = mc^2 a gendered equation?" Irigaray once asked. "It may be." She explained her reasoning: "The equation is sexist because, like male-ness, it is hierarchical. In privileging the speed of light over all other speeds, it enacts a form of domination that is expressive of gendered relations."

If Irigaray made her name by drawing attention to language, Julia Kristeva (b. 1941) made hers by rejecting "essentialism." To this Bulgarian-French sociologist and literary critic, there is no such thing as femaleness in the first place. Rather than a fixed essence, Kristeva writes, femaleness is an ongoing process. All that one can do is to take a snapshot of it at any particular moment in time. She herself attempted such a snapshot in an unfortunate early book called *About Chinese Women* (1975), in which she praised Chairman Mao's Cultural Revolution. But process, to Kristeva, is also crisis. She posits an instinct called the *semiotic* that underlies self-consciousness. Resembling Freud's concept of the id, the semiotic consists of the unspoken—the thing that we are trying to say when we use language but can never get quite right. Our lived experiences, she argues, can never be completely described in language, since language is fixed in time. Think of a photograph of a speeding car. The photograph can present a perspective of the car's shape and color, but it can never tell us what it is like to drive the car, what makes it move, or how to operate it. Reality is always more complex, yet also more immediate and simple, than language can convey. It is more dynamic, yet also more static and reassuring, more richly mysterious and compelling, yet also more familiar and calming.

Kristeva calls the gap between language and reality the *space of abjection*. For her, this space is the domain of women, ethnic minorities, gays, lesbians, and the poor, since the language and value systems that create our "snapshot" of experience are inevitably male, white, heterosexual, and prosperous. To be outside the dominant structure is therefore to live in continuous crisis.

To her critics, Kristeva also distances herself from the everyday problems of women in the world—discrimination, violence, unequal pay, and control over sexual reproduction. Unless it is dedicated to programs for social change, they argue, feminism risks becoming only an interesting academic specialty. To discuss the space of abjection does little to improve the lives of Portuguese girls trapped in French textile sweatshops. It cannot help Turkish daughters who fear "honor killing" at the hands of their own fathers or brothers in Germany. Admirers of the third wave, however, have a reply: this is exactly what we are talking about. Why should women *have* to justify feminism through its results? No one, after all, discounts intellectual fields like literary criticism, art history, mathematics, or astronomy for not addressing social problems. Criticism of the irrelevance of third wave writers, they say, is simply another form of sexism.

WOMEN AND THE GLOBAL WORLD

Feminism as practical action did not cease in the 1990s. In fact, it went global. Under the leadership of institutions like the **UN Women's Conference**, the call to recognize women's rights as human rights grew louder. Meetings in

Third Wave Feminism in India   India's centuries-old caste system has proven resilient to change, which has led many oppressed groups to join forces. In this photo members of the National Federation of Dalit ("untouchable") community unite with reformers on behalf of women's rights.

Mexico City (1975), Copenhagen (1980), and Nairobi (1985) recognized the different priorities of Western and non-Western women. Western speakers, in general, had addressed economic, legal, and political rights, while representatives from the non-Western countries emphasized disease, hunger, poverty, and violence. The difference did not show a lack of caring or understanding. It showed instead how much Western women had achieved—on fundamental issues still faced every day by women in Africa, Asia, and Latin America.

A rousing call to action came in the 1995 conference held in Beijing. Hillary Rodham Clinton (b. 1947), then the First Lady of the United States, enumerated the plain horrors confronting women around the globe:

> It is a violation of human rights when babies are denied food, or drowned, or suffocated, or their spines broken, simply because they are born girls.
>
> It is a violation of human rights when women and girls are sold into the slavery of prostitution for human greed—and the kinds of reasons that are used to justify this practice should no longer be tolerated.
>
> It is a violation of human rights when women are doused with gasoline, set on fire, and burned to death because their marriage dowries are deemed too small.

It is a violation of human rights when individual women are raped in their own communities and when thousands of women are subjected to rape as a tactic or prize of war.

It is a violation of human rights when a leading cause of death worldwide among women ages 14 to 44 is the violence they are subjected to in their own homes by their own relatives.

It is a violation of human rights when young girls are brutalized by the painful and degrading practice of genital mutilation.

It is a violation of human rights when women are denied the right to plan their own families, and that includes being forced to have abortions or being sterilized against their will.

If there is one message that echoes forth from this conference, let it be that human rights are women's rights and women's rights are human rights once and for all. Let us not forget that among those rights are the right to speak freely—and the right to be heard.

The rising ethnic pluralism in Europe probably did more than the Internet to increase awareness of women's global plight. Poverty and violence are harder to ignore when they happen here rather than thousands of miles away.

The "United States of Europe" began to resemble the United States itself, not only as an institution but also in its cultural pluralism. And not everyone was pleased.

ISLAM AND ITS DISCONTENTS

Militant Islamism continued to spread throughout the 1990s and caused sharp political ruptures in North Africa and the Middle East. With the exception of Iran, most of the foment came from nongovernmental groups. Indeed, most militants opposed their own governments as much as they resented what they regarded as Western neocolonialism. These groups turned to terrorist tactics as their main form of political action, fearing that no other tactic could bring reform. The danger lay not only in the attacks themselves but also in the response of Arab governments. These states hoped to co-opt popular support for Islamic groups by manipulating the passions stirred up by the Israeli-Palestinian conflict.

The funeral of Ruhollah Khomeini in 1989 was a riot of religious enthusiasm. Tens of thousands lined the streets of Tehran, weeping and beating their breasts. Hundreds of thousands more repeated the scene in city after city. When the open coffin was brought out of the mosque in Tehran, people surged forward in a frenzy. Hoping to touch the body or to grab a piece of its shroud, they nearly tore the corpse to pieces. The scene played endlessly on European and American media, driving home viscerally the new religious energy in parts of the Islamic world. Uproar followed in Algeria and Tunisia, where the governments cracked down on Islamist parties that had gained majority support among the poor masses.

In Algeria, for example, the Islamic Salvation Front (FIS) won local and national elections with its calls for government by Islamic law, or shariah. The Algerian government voided the elections and declared martial law, triggering a civil war (1991–1992) that killed one hundred thousand. Fearing comparable scenes in their own countries, the governments of Egypt and Tunisia also suppressed Islamist groups. In Egypt President Hosni Mubarak placed every mosque under direct government control, in an effort to root out radical clerics. In Turkey, the Rifah (or Welfare) Party rose quickly, scoring local electoral victories in 1994 and two years later electing Necmettin Erbakan as prime minister.

Erbakan had the demeanor of an academic, which he was (he was a professor of mechanical engineering), but his political convictions were those of an Islamist radical. A personal manifesto that he had published, called *Millî Görüş* ("A National Vision"), warned of a decline in Islamic moral standards as a result of Muslims' too-close relations with the corrupt West. He rejected the idea of Turkey joining the European Common Market, which he disparaged as a joint Catholic and Zionist conspiracy to engulf and assimilate the Islamic world. His policies antagonized the overwhelmingly secular Turkish army, however, which pressed him to resign after only twelve months in office. Also appearing on the scene in 1994 was the Taliban (literally "students"), a group of young radicals in Afghanistan. Some had fought against the Soviet invasion; by 1996 they were in control of the country with their own ultraconservative interpretations of shariah.

Finding the legal paths to power blocked, many of these extremist groups turned to violence and made the 1990s a golden age of terrorism. The most frequently used techniques were car bombings and shootings, although by the end of the decade suicide bombings became increasingly common as well. And the victims were global. Colombia suffered the greatest number of terrorist attacks, all connected to the trade in illegal drugs. Other hot spots included India, Indonesia, Pakistan, and Sri Lanka.

The greatest number of attacks came from domestic rather than foreign enemies. Algerians fought against their own government, separatists in Northern Ireland against the United Kingdom, Kurdish rebels against the Turkish state, and Basque separatists in the Spanish capital of Madrid. In only a handful of cases was terrorism directed outward against foreign nations. Those cases, however, included Libya's brutality in France and Britain, Israel's struggle with the Palestinians, and the horrific attack on the United States on September 11, 2001 (see Map 29.4).

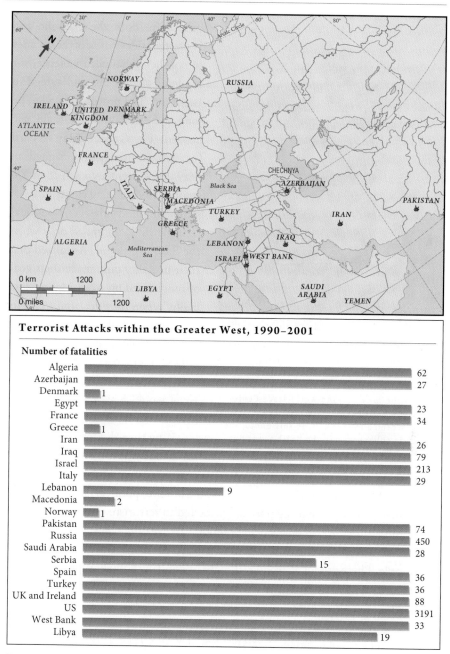

MAP 29.4   **Terrorist Attacks within the Greater West, 1990–2001**

BUT WHY TERRORISM?

Fringe-group terrorism seldom works. In the short term it terrifies, even paralyzes, whole populations; but it also steels their resolve not to give in to the terrorists' aims. The conflict in Northern Ireland, for example, was resolved only after terrorist

Day of Infamy   September 11, 2001. Terrorists from Osama bin Laden's group known as al-Qaeda hijacked four U.S. airliners and intentionally flew them into chosen targets. One plane crashed into the Pentagon in Washington, D.C. Two others took down the towers of the World Trade Center in lower Manhattan. The fourth crashed in rural Pennsylvania when the passengers stormed the cockpit. In this photo, the south tower has already collapsed, and the north tower has just been hit by the airplane targeting it. More than 2,700 people died, and 2,200 more were injured.

groups on both the Catholic and Protestant sides, tiring of the decades of conflict, renounced violence, surrendered their arms, and agreed to negotiate. The process proved to be long and difficult, but it finally succeeded. The **Good Friday Accord** (or Belfast Agreement), signed in May 1998, went into effect in December 1999, ending eighty years of strife. Similarly, the constitutional struggle in Spain ended only when the Basque group ETA realized that their brutality only made their goal of more freedom from Madrid less likely. When they declared a halt to terrorism in 2006, negotiations for greater autonomy began at once; by 2011 a permanent settlement had been made. If terrorism worked, Israel would have been brought to her knees decades ago.[5]

Why then did terrorism spread so viciously at the end of the 20th century? Two schools of thought predominate, one pointing to economic and the other to political factors. The economic theorists argue that the poor are attracted to terrorism out of desperation. They are recruited to become suicide bombers by wealthy elites, who use terrorism against a declared enemy as a tool to gain power and influence among their own people. These groups also build strength by courting popular support through social work and by appealing for aid outside of their country. Sustained terrorist campaigns, after all, require money—lots of money.

For example, Hamas, the Palestinian group founded in Gaza in 1987 by a poor religious scholar named Shaikh Ahmed Yassin (1937–2004), acquired financial backing from the Muslim Brotherhood. Yassin quickly brought physicians into the leadership and set to work providing free health services to the Gazan poor, which helped establish a popular base. Tens of millions of dollars annually (an estimated 50 percent of its money) comes from Saudi Arabia; perhaps

---

[5]   State-run terrorism, of course, is another matter. Testimonials could be given by any number of people—the ancient Assyrians, Attila the Hun, Genghis Khan, Tamerlane, and Stalin come to mind.

another 10 percent comes from the government in Iran. Ironically, Hamas in its first years also received financial backing from the Israeli government, which had sought to draw support away from the PLO under Yasser Arafat. As it gained financial heft, however, Hamas supplemented its charitable work with armed terrorism. Most recent Western estimates of Hamas's funding place it in the range of $400 to $500 million dollars a year.

The case of **al-Qaeda**—the group behind the September 11, 2001, assault on the World Trade Center and the Pentagon in the United States—is similar. Its founder, Osama bin Laden (1957–2011), was born to wealth, a member of the Saudi royal family. He expanded his fortune through owning and managing several large construction companies. A longtime religious conservative, bin Laden fought against the Soviet Union in Afghanistan with the mujahideen, and his politics became radicalized during the first Gulf War (1989), when he objected to "infidel armies" in the land of the Prophet. From this point on, he called the United States the greatest of the four "enemies of Islam" against which he dedicated his life. The other three were Jews, Shi'i Muslims, and unspecified "heretics."

IRA Funeral   Masked members of an IRA (Irish Republican Army) honor guard carry the coffin of one of their colleagues, Bobby Sands, who died on hunger strike in a British prison in 1981. Sands had been a low-ranking member in the Provisional IRA and was arrested on a charge of illegal possession of weapons. When he and nine other IRA cellmates began their hunger strike they attracted considerable media attention—as a result of which Sands was elected a member of the British parliament to represent a district at the western edge of Northern Ireland, even though he was in prison. Sands died after sixty-six days without food.

The second leading theory sees political and social conditions as terrorism's richest source. Repressive governments and discriminatory societies, this line of thinking goes, create their own terrorists as individuals come to feel the need for dramatic action. The **Irish Republican Army** (IRA) in Northern Ireland is the best example. Originating in the 1910s, the IRA had as its goal a single objective—to overthrow what it regarded as 750 years of English tyranny over the Irish people. IRA fighters saw themselves as champions of Irish freedom and of Catholic vengeance on Protestant persecutors. Consider, too, the Kurdish PKK (Partiya Karkerên Kurdistan, or Kurdistan Workers' Party), which Abdullah Öcalan (b. 1948) founded in 1978. Nursing an intense resentment of the Republic of Turkey, the PKK fought to gain independence for the Turkish Kurds. It also had the long-term aim of a united Kurdistan, made up of the Kurds in northern Iran and Iraq too. Financial support poured in from Syria, which hoped to profit from Turkey's trouble. Later the bulk of its funding came from extortion, racketeering, and the drug trade.

> If a strong-armed regime can persuade its subjects that the real cause of their misery is foreign meddling, then the repressed people will lash out against that enemy. In this scenario the tyrannical authority casts itself as the true champion of the people, its only alternative to corruption and humiliation from abroad.

However, a political explanation of terrorism must be more subtle than a simple formula like "terrorism as revenge." If a strong-armed regime can persuade its subjects that the real cause of their misery is foreign meddling, then the repressed people will lash out against that enemy. In this scenario the tyrannical authority casts itself as the true champion of the people, its only alternative to corruption and humiliation from abroad.

In the case of Syria, for example, which is perhaps the most repressive Arab regime of the last forty years, the Assad family has held control, even though it represents the small, and largely detested, Alawite minority. In fact, it has turned its minority status into its strength, by building up a national myth, thanks to a steady diet of anti-Semitic and anti-American propaganda. Only the Assads, they repeat, can hold at bay the strife between Arab tribes and sects within Syria. Only they can stand up to Zionists and Western imperialists.

In an editorial published in *Tishreen* (September 16, 2003), Syria's largest and state-run newspaper, Ghazi Hussein declared that the Holocaust was an invention of the Jews—a plan they had hatched with the Nazis. Why arrange to have six million fellow Jews killed? So that the world will feel sorry for the survivors and allow them to create the Zionist state:

> Zionism lurks in the darkest chapter of [Israel's] history, and invents fictions about Jewish suffering in the "Nazi Holocaust" which it then inflates astronomically.... The fundamental problem is not the fact that

the Zionists attempt to re-write history but that Zionist groups use this false history to deceive international opinion, win the world's sympathy, and then engage in blackmail. . . . Two goals are paramount to Israel and the Zionist organizations that support it: to get more money out of Germany and the other European entities, and to use the myth of the Holocaust as a sword held over the necks of anyone who opposes Zionism and to accuse them of anti-Semitism. . . . The truth though is that Israel herself—the supposed heir of Holocaust victims everywhere—has committed in the past and still commits today crimes much worse than anything supposedly done to them by the Nazis.

Hussein was not a random commentator. At the time he wrote the article he was both a legal advisor to the Syrian government and the head of the political section of the Palestinian Liberation Organization's office in Damascus.

Similar stories run in other newspapers, like *Balsam*, published in the West Bank by the Palestinian Red Crescent, and appear regularly on Syria's state-operated radio. The thuggish rule of Saddam Hussein in Iraq used the same technique, blaming the country's woes on American imperialists and Muslim-hating Zionists.

Both the economic and political interpretations of terrorism have had their followers. Europeans have often favored the first, the United States the second. Some, however, have raised a third possibility—that Islam itself promotes violence as a way to attain martyrdom. This sentiment is found more frequently in the United States than in Europe—or at least it is given freer expression in America. Predictably, it also feeds the belief of many Muslims that the West is biased against Islam. Whatever the causes, bitter discontent and terrorism show no signs of abating.

ECONOMIC GLOBALIZATION

Protesters gathered in Seattle in 1999, in advance of the scheduled ministerial conference of the **World Trade Organization** (WTO), an intergovernmental organization seeking to liberalize trade between nations. They blocked intersections and organized large street demonstrations. Speeches and worker protest songs rang out from street corners. Some protestors set fire to dumpsters. Others broke shop windows and halted almost the entire city's commerce. Police reacted with pepper spray, tear gas, and rubber bullets in order to clear the streets. In the end, police arrested over six hundred people. The disruption of business and the task of cleaning up cost the city over $20 million.

Protesting Globalization   A protestor against the World Trade Organization, one of the institutions most closely identified with economic globalization.

The "Battle of Seattle" drew attention to the intense emotions surrounding economic globalization—the development of a single, interconnected global market. A global market is much like the digital Internet, a network of networks, crossing all borders of nationality, language, culture, and class. Globalization itself was nothing new. One can think of it as an extension of long-standing regional or continental trade. The arc dates back at least to the wave of European imperialism in the 1880s and 1890s. Some historians of antiquity, fancifully enough, date the movement all the way back to the Sumerian era, when the grain-rich Mesopotamian south was linked with northernmost reaches of the Fertile Crescent, rich in iron ore. What is new today are of course modern systems of communication and transportation. Strawberries harvested one day in California can appear the next day in markets in Tokyo.

> What is new today are of course modern systems of communication and transportation. Strawberries harvested one day in California can appear the next day in markets in Tokyo.

The WTO, formed in 1995, promotes international trade by resolving disputes between nations (see Map 29.5). It also implements trade agreements between nations and, most controversially, oversees the national trade policies of individual countries. The protestors in Seattle represented labor unions, environmental groups, women's organizations, immigration activists, and others. Their

The World Trade Organization

Countries that joined WTO 1995-2000 — Countries that joined WTO 2001-2012 — Observer governments

MAP 29.5 **The World Trade Organization**

opposition to the WTO—indeed to globalization itself—sprang from many issues, but all ones related to the differing standards and legal protections between countries. Workers in countries like China and India do not have the same rights as American workers in regard to wages, work conditions, and employment benefits. It is therefore to any manufacturer's advantage to shift its production overseas. The savings in labor costs vastly outweigh the expense of transporting their finished goods. Some countries offer tax benefits to companies that other countries cannot afford. Still others do not require industry to observe the same environmental protection. The uneven international playing field represented a danger to the standards of living that Westerners had come to expect. Hence the trouble in Seattle.

Globalization had been opposed before, but never in such a dramatic way. More demonstrations followed, all across the United States, in opposition to the World Bank and the International Monetary Fund, two institutions viewed as the financiers of globalization. Opposition to globalization occurred in Europe too, though generally in quieter forms.

World population is rising sharply and will continue to do so until 2050 (see Figure 29.1). And that means a steady rise in the demand for everything from food and textiles to pharmaceuticals and computer components. Yet the

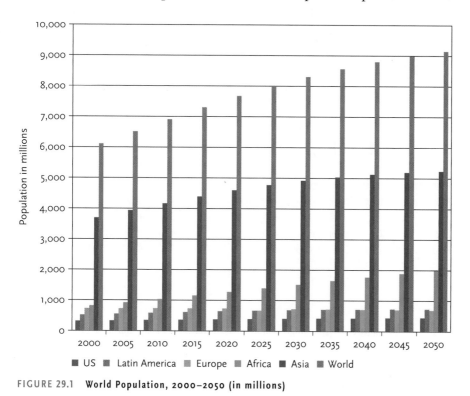

FIGURE 29.1 **World Population, 2000–2050 (in millions)**

populations of Europe and the United States are stagnating. Between 2010 and 2050 the U.S. population is projected to grow from 300 million to 400 million (a 33 percent growth, compared to the global increase of 100 percent), and the population of Europe will actually decline from 700 million to 690 million.[6] For Western corporations that want to expand their businesses, the choices are clear—either import workers (which means immigration, whether legal or illegal) or export jobs. Or both. And in their varying ways, institutions like the WTO, the IMF, and the World Bank help them do just that.

Both responses to the demographic gap between the West and the world—exporting jobs and immigrating workers—present political and social challenges. Our last chapter looks to the future.

WHO, WHAT, WHERE

al-Qaeda

credit default swap

European Union

Good Friday Accord

Irish Republican Army

Kyoto Protocol

Organization of Petroleum Exporting Countries

Treaty of Rome

UN Women's Conference

World Trade Organization

SUGGESTED READINGS

Primary Sources

Fukuyama, Francis. *The End of History and the Last Man.*

Irigaray, Luce. *The Ethics of Sexual Difference.*

Khomeini, Ruhollah. *Islamic Government.*

National Commission on Terrorist Attacks upon the United States. *The 9/11 Commission Report* (2004).

Rushdie, Salman. *The Satanic Verses.*

---

6   In 2010, the United States and Europe held 15 percent of the world's population; by 2050, they may hold as little as 8.5 percent.

Anthologies

Freedman, Estelle B., ed. *The Essential Feminist Reader* (2007).

Kamrava, Mehran, ed. *The New Voices of Islam: Rethinking Politics and Modernity—A Reader* (2007).

Oliver, Kelly, ed. *The Portable Kristeva* (2002).

Roded, Ruth, ed. *Women in Islam and the Middle East: A Reader* (2008).

Volpi, Frédéric, ed. *Political Islam: A Critical Reader* (2010).

Studies

Berman, Eli. *Radical, Religious, and Violent: The New Economics of Terrorism* (2009).

Budgeon, Shelley. *Third Wave Feminism and the Politics of Gender in Late Modernity* (2011).

Castells, Manuel. *The Information Age: Economy, Society, and Culture* (2009–2011).

Garcelon, Marc. *Revolutionary Passage: From Soviet to Post-Soviet Russia, 1985–2000* (2005).

Frieden, Jeffry A. *Global Capitalism: Its Fall and Rise in the Twentieth Century* (2007).

Gillis, Stacy, Gillian Howie, and Rebecca Munford, ed. *Third Wave Feminism: A Critical Exploration* (2007).

Hoffman, Bruce. *Inside Terrorism* (2006).

Hoogvelt, Ankie. *Globalization and the Postcolonial World: The New Political Economy of Development* (2001).

Judt, Tony. *Postwar: A History of Europe since 1945* (2005).

Keddie, Nikki R. *Modern Iran: Roots and Results of Revolution* (2006).

Kenney, Padraic. *The Burdens of Freedom: Eastern Europe since 1989* (2006).

Krueger, Alan B. *What Makes a Terrorist: Economics and the Roots of Terrorism* (2008).

Laqueur, Walter. *The Last Days of Europe: Epitaph for an Old Continent* (2009).

Malik, Kenan. *From Fatwa to Jihad: The Rushdie Affair and Its Aftermath* (2010).

Mittelman, James H. *The Globalization Syndrome: Transformation and Resistance* (2000).

Mockaitis, Thomas R. *The "New" Terrorism: Myths and Reality* (2008).

Mottahedeh, Roy. *The Mantle of the Prophet: Religion and Politics in Iran* (2008).

Post, Jerrold M. *The Mind of the Terrorist: The Psychology of Terrorism from the IRA to al-Qaeda* (2008).

Rashid, Ahmed. *Jihad: The Rise of Militant Islam in Central Asia* (2002).

Reid, T. R. *The United States of Europe: The New Superpower and the End of American Supremacy* (2005).

Roy, Sara. *Failing Peace: Gaza and the Palestinian-Israeli Conflict* (2006).

———. *Hamas and Civil Society in Gaza: Engaging the Islamist Social Sector* (2011).

Sinno, Abdulkader, ed. *Muslims in Western Politics* (2008).

Suri, Jeremi. *Power and Protest: Global Revolution and the Rise of Détente* (2005).

Westad, Odd Arne. *The Global Cold War: Third World Interventions and the Making of Our Times* (2007).

Zürcher, Christoph. *The Post-Soviet Wars: Rebellion, Ethnic Conflict, and Nationhood in the Caucasus* (2009).

For additional resources, including maps, primary sources, visuals, web links, and quizzes, please go to **www.oup.com/us/backman**.

CHAPTER 30

Hearts and Minds Going Forward

2001–Present

On September 11, 2001, long-simmering tensions between the West and the Muslim Middle East came to a full boil. And well after the "9/11" terrorist attacks on New York and Washington, DC, the violence kept coming. Hardly a week passed in 2002 without a suicide bomber maiming innocents in Israel; in 2003 the pace slowed to perhaps one massacre every other week. In March 2004 a coordinated sequence of bombs on train lines in Madrid killed 191 and wounded more than two thousand innocents. On July 7, 2005, or "7/7" in British common parlance, a team of bombers struck London's public transport system, killing fifty-two and injuring over seven hundred. Only a few months later, in September 2005, a Danish newspaper published a dozen cartoons that depicted the Prophet Muhammad in ways that Muslims around the world found offensive and blasphemous. One Danish cartoon depicted the Prophet with a black turban that was actually a lit bomb. Scores of angry demonstrations took place, and arsonists set the Danish embassies in Beirut, Damascus, and Tehran aflame. A wealthy regional politician in India offered a $10 million reward to any Muslim who beheaded the cartoonist who had drawn the most offensive of the cartoons.

DISTRIBUTION OF WEALTH IN THE GREATER WEST

A country's GDP per capita as percentage of world average ($10,500):
over 400%   100–200%   25–50%   under 10%
200–400%   50–100%   10–25%

◀ **The Cultures of the West, 2011.** This street scene from Marseilles captures some of the problems and promise of Greater Western society today. In the background stands the Église des Réformés, looking almost tangled in the utility lines that cross the sky. In the foreground a diverse group of women stroll by, chiefly involved in their cellphone conversations. Cars move past. Though a bustling scene, it evinces an odd atmosphere of isolation and disconnectedness.

"Americans are asking," said U.S. President George W. Bush, "'Why do they hate us?'" Terrorism, though, was not by any means the whole story—perhaps not even the most important one when it comes to understanding Islam or the future of the West. The challenges include independence movements and recovery from a war in eastern Europe, hopes for strengthening of the European Union, a second Iraq war, and the status of Muslim women. The turmoil includes the glory and optimism of an "Arab Spring," a deep economic downturn, and conflict over taxation and liberty—especially between conservatives and liberals in the United States. Ultimately, adaption is underway in Europe and the Greater West.

"WHY DO THEY HATE US?"

The political resolution of the problems in Northern Ireland and in Spain largely ended the problem of domestic terrorism within Europe after 2001, except for a few fringe groups. The tensions with Europe's immigrant Muslim population became largely a matter of passionate but nonviolent demonstrations and occasional street crime. This relative quiet, though, was not so much a calming of grievances. Well-funded terrorist groups like al-Qaeda and Islamic Jihad simply had their hands full, thanks to U.S.-led wars in Afghanistan and Iraq and the spread of military activities into Pakistan. Meanwhile in Israel and the West Bank arsonists, assassins, and bombers drove the casualty counts on both sides ever higher. An Egyptian terrorist group with connections to al-Qaeda launched a bomb attack in 2005 on the popular resort city of Sharm el-Sheikh on the Red Sea, killing eighty-eight and wounding more than two hundred.

As the killings continued, non-Muslim majorities in Europe and the United States reacted in horror. That was sensible enough, but many of them also reacted less sensibly, by seeing all Muslims as terrorists, potential terrorists, or supporters of terrorism. Racism lies behind such attitudes, but so does a willing

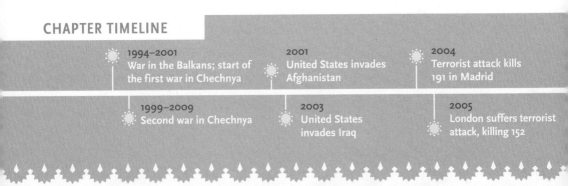

CHAPTER TIMELINE

1994–2001
War in the Balkans; start of the first war in Chechnya

2001
United States invades Afghanistan

2004
Terrorist attack kills 191 in Madrid

1999–2009
Second war in Chechnya

2003
United States invades Iraq

2005
London suffers terrorist attack, killing 152

ignorance—and, in Europe, a greater indifference to religion. Few non-Muslim Westerners knew much about Islam prior to 9/11 and 7/7, and surprisingly few are better informed even ten years later.

Both the best and worst instincts of Western society were on display only ten days after the 9/11 attacks. In his speech to Congress, President George W. Bush was somber, dignified, and powerful. Yet his address also reflected widely held ambivalence about the Muslim world.

> The terrorists practice a fringe form of Islamic extremism that has been rejected by Muslim scholars and the vast majority of Muslim clerics. A fringe movement that perverts the peaceful teaching of Islam. The terrorists' directive commands them to kill Christians and Jews, to kill all Americans and make no distinctions among military and civilians, including women and children. This group and its leader, a person named Osama bin Laden, are linked to many other organizations in different countries, including the Egyptian Islamic Jihad and the Islamic Movement of Uzbekistan.
>
> There are thousands of these terrorists in more than sixty countries. They are recruited from their own nations and neighborhoods and brought to camps in places like Afghanistan, where they are trained in the tactics of terror. They are sent back to their homes or sent to hide in countries around the world to plot evil and destruction. The leadership of al-Qaeda has great influence in Afghanistan and supports the Taliban regime in controlling most of that country.
>
> In Afghanistan we see al-Qaeda's vision for the world. Afghanistan's people have been brutalized. Many are starving and many have fled. Women are not allowed to attend school. You can be jailed for owning a television. Religion can be practiced only as their leaders dictate. A man can be jailed in Afghanistan if his beard is not long enough.

2007
Hamas assumes control of Gaza

2008–2009
Economic downturn and financial crisis in the Greater West

2011
U.S. special forces kill Bin-Laden; Libya falls to rebel forces, Qaddafi killed

2008
Israel invades Gaza

2010
Completion of withdrawl of Western armed forces from Iraq; beginning of Arab Spring

2012
Deepening debt crisis in Euro Zone

After stating his demand that the Taliban then in control of Afghanistan hand over the al-Qaeda terrorists or else face retribution, he then addressed a few words to peaceful Muslims everywhere:

> I also want to speak tonight directly to Muslims throughout the world. We respect your faith. It's practiced freely by many millions of Americans and by millions more in countries that America counts as friends. Its teachings are good and peaceful. And those who commit evil in the name of Allah blaspheme the name of Allah. The terrorists are traitors to their own faith, trying in effect to hijack Islam itself.
>
> The enemy of America is not our many Muslim friends. It is not our many Arab friends. Our enemy is a radical network of terrorists and every government that supports them.
>
> Our war on terror begins with al-Qaeda, but it does not end there. It will not end until every terrorist group of global reach has been found, stopped, and defeated.
>
> Americans are asking, "Why do they hate us?"
>
> They hate what they see right here in this chamber, a democratically elected government. Their leaders are self-appointed. They hate our freedoms, our freedom of religion, our freedom of speech, our freedom to vote and assemble and disagree with each other. They want to overthrow existing governments in many Muslim countries, such as Egypt, Saudi Arabia, and Jordan. They want to drive Israel out of the Middle East. They want to drive Christians and Jews out of vast regions of Asia and Africa.
>
> These terrorists kill not merely to end lives but to disrupt and end a way of life. With every atrocity they hope that America grows fearful, retreating from the world and forsaking our friends. They stand against us because we stand in their way. We're not deceived by their pretenses to piety. We have seen their kind before. They are the heirs of all the murderous ideologies of the 20th century. By sacrificing human life to serve their radical visions, by abandoning every value except the will to power, they follow in the path of fascism, Nazism and totalitarianism. And they will follow that path all the way to where it ends: in history's unmarked grave of discarded lies.

The 21st century begins with the Greater West on a new learning curve. It opens on societies that have had too little contact between them and increasingly find themselves as neighbors and colleagues.

In fact, the Muslim world in general does not hate democracy, human rights, or free speech; it hates only what it perceives as Western hypocrisy about them.

Demonstrating for Religious Freedom   Muslim women and girls demonstrate, in 2004, for the right to wear Islamic headscarves in publicly funded schools. French law requires that public schools be entirely secular, which means, among other things, a ban on religious clothing and religious symbols (Jewish skullcaps and Christian crucifixes are likewise forbidden). The protestors carry a banner that calls for "Equality" and "Fraternity"—echoes of the call-to-arms of the French Revolution of 1789. Critics of the Muslim protests point out that demonstrators have left out the first word in the call-to-arms, "Liberty."

How committed is the United States to democracy, Muslims have asked, when it overthrew the democratically elected prime minister of Iran (Mohammad Mossadegh, r. 1951–1953) and installed an autocrat like the shah, Mohammed Reza Pahlavi? How committed is it when it lavished military aid on a dictatorial regime like Hosni Mubarak's in Egypt? How dedicated to religious freedom is a country like France when it forbids Muslim schoolgirls to wear the traditional covering, the hijab? How committed to freedom of speech is Germany when it forbids, on penalty of imprisonment, the expression of doubt about the extent of the Holocaust? In the minds of many Muslims, we have been weighed in our own balance and found wanting.

The 21st century begins with the Greater West on a new learning curve. It opens on societies that have had too little contact between them and increasingly find themselves as neighbors and colleagues. The need to deal with Islamist terrorism is urgent, but a more difficult challenge awaits us all—to move from ignorance and indifference to understanding and acceptance.

WAR AND PEACE, FROM THE BALKANS TO PALESTINE

"The next great European war will begin over some damned foolish incident in the Balkans." That bit of wisdom, sometimes attributed to Otto von Bismarck, predicted the start of World War I. It also presaged opinions in much of the West about the end of the 20th century. Unfortunately, those opinions failed to understand or foresee 21st-century nationalist passion and Muslim rage beyond that region (see Map 30.1).

Nationalist passions in the Balkans had been kept in check by the heavy hand of totalitarian rulers. After the collapse of Communism, they sprang back to poisonous life. Serbs, Croats, Bosnians, and Slovenians after 1991 all wanted to secede from the political union that the Communists had forced on them, but a demographic mixing had taken place during Yugoslavia's forty years of existence. It was impossible to draw satisfying political borders when every configuration left remnants of some group as a minority among others.

Of all the peoples involved, the Serbs proved the most willing, even eager, to resort to war. Under their leader Slobodan Milosevic (1941–2006), who commanded what was left of the old Yugoslav army (the fourth largest military machine on the Continent), the Serbs began a series of wars against their neighbors. They hoped to establish a Greater Serbia that would unite all ethnic Serbs, to reclaim Balkan land claimed as their patrimony, and to purge those lands of non-Serbs. In 1994, after Serbian soldiers had massacred tens of thousands of Bosnians and driven hundreds of thousands more into exile, NATO forces finally took action with bombing raids against Serb artillery. Eventually the United Nations brought in peacekeeping forces. These wars lasted until 1995 and witnessed many scenes of horror and near-genocide. A peace deal was finally negotiated with the help of the United States, but the Serbs soon opened a new front in Kosovo and Albania, extending the violence until 2001. Milosevic himself was arrested in that year and brought to The Hague to face trial for crimes against humanity. He died in prison before the trial had run its course.

Apart from bookending the 20th century with Balkan violence, the wars here added fuel to Muslim rage against the West. The Bosnians, who were the chief victims of Serb massacre, are a predominantly Muslim people.[1] Would the European and American powers have waited two years to come to the rescue if the Bosnians had been Christians and the Serbs were Muslims? To countless Muslims around the world, the wholesale slaughter of the Bosnians took place with the silent complicity of the West. The mass murder of eight thousand Bosnian men and boys at Srebrenica in July 1995 would never have occurred, they insisted, had the religions of attackers and victims been reversed.

---

[1]   Bosnians are the largest Islamic population in Europe after the Turks.

MAP 30.1   Wars and Conflicts in the Greater West, 1990–2012

Mourning the Dead   In July 1995, soldiers of the Serbian army massacred eight thousand Muslim men and boys in the Bosnian city of Srebrenica. The massacre was preceded by several days of horrendous torture of civilians, including the systematic rape of Bosnian women, even as a Dutch-staffed UN peacekeeping force looked on. Here a Srebrenica survivor, Hajra Èatiae, who lost her husband and son in the attack, helps to maintain a photo archive of the victims.

Many critics perceived a similar anti-Muslim bias in the West's reaction to the warfare between Russia and Chechnya. Chechnya is a Muslim territory in the North Caucasus, with a native population of roughly 1.5 million. As the USSR eroded in the 1980s, a Chechen independence movement arose. The Chechen National Congress achieved independence in 1991, but only three years later Russia sent in a large army to end it. The war lasted from 1994 to 1996, when a truce was declared. War broke out again shortly thereafter, lasting from 1999 to 2009. The conflicts were marked by atrocities on both sides. Russia proved unable to bring the province to heel despite enormously superior numbers and weaponry and its reckless artillery bombardment. The Chechens could not drive the Russians from the region, but they proved ruthless and adept at terrorist bombings in Moscow and elsewhere. Muslims felt a lack of interest in the West in their suffering. Europe barely responded to Russia's heavy-handedness, but it condemned the terrorism that many Chechens felt was their only option. As if to prove their point, the Chechen War drew little media attention in the West.

Two wars in the Persian Gulf, however, claimed the attention of the entire world. The first war (1990–1991) was a tense but brief affair. Iraq's ruler, Saddam Hussein, deeply in debt after his disastrous war with neighboring Iran (1980–1988), needed new oil revenues and invaded the tiny but wealthy Gulf nation of Kuwait. Kuwait was in fact one of Iraq's two principal creditors, the other being Saudi Arabia. International condemnation of Iraq came swiftly, and in seven months a U.S.-led coalition drove the Iraqis from Kuwait and established a "no-fly zone" over southern Iraq. Its goal was to protect Kuwait from fresh attack and to protect Shi'i Iraqis from retribution by Saddam Hussein's Sunni army. The coalition's forces were mostly American soldiers, with the next largest contingents from the United Kingdom and the Arab League.[2] Saudi Arabia was the staging post of the coalition's armies, and it paid the bulk of the war's cost. Both facts had dramatic consequences, since they drew the ire of Osama bin Laden, the head of al-Qaeda. They became his justification for launching the 9/11 and 7/7 terrorist attacks on the United States and United Kingdom.

The United States launched air assaults against the Taliban regime in Afghanistan in October 2001, since the Taliban had granted refuge to al-Qaeda for years. Within a matter a weeks the Taliban were crushed, although Osama bin Laden escaped into Pakistan. Rather than focusing on building up the shaky new government in Afghanistan, however, the United States under President George W. Bush turned its attention to Saddam Hussein in Iraq. He had been behind the 9/11 attacks, Bush argued, and was stockpiling advanced chemical, biological, and perhaps even nuclear weapons. In March 2003, after months of diplomatic pressure and posturing, the United States invaded Iraq—but no link between Iraq and al-Qaeda was ever found. Indeed, Hussein had long been an active hunter of groups like al-Qaeda, since their religious ideology undermined his secular Ba'athism. Nor were any of the advanced weapons systems ever found, which left the United States and its British allies open to charges of willful war making. Most Iraqis cheered the capture, trial, and execution of Hussein, but few felt that his downfall was worth the price of the invasion.

Charges of imperialism were levied against the West throughout the Arab world, charges supported by critics within the West. Accusations of oil theft, war crimes, corruption, and high-handedness swirled around the Western forces, and scandals only added to the West's public-relations difficulties with the Muslim world. American forces mistreated Iraqi prisoners at the Abu Ghraib prison

---

[2]   The Arab League consists of Egypt, Morocco, Oman, Qatar, Saudi Arabia, Syria, and the United Arab Emirates.

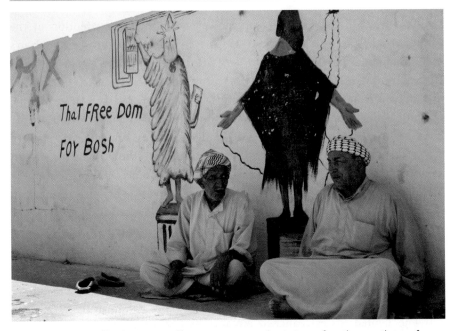

Public Relations Difficulties US efforts to restore order in Iraq after the overthrow of Saddam Hussein confronted one challenge after another. One of the most infamous episodes was the public release of photos showing the torture of Iraqis held in the US-controlled prison at Abu Ghraib in 2004. This photos shows two Iraqi men resting in the shade provided by a wall—a wall bearing graffiti criticizing the US behavior. "That freedom for Bosh" castigates the president's policies.

complex, at a military facility in Guantanamo Bay in Cuba, and at secret prisons operated by the CIA. Such episodes undercut the positive image the West tried to create for its involvements in the region, which it sees as efforts to bring democracy to nations that have known only tribalism and corrupt dictatorship.

In 2007 Great Britain got a new prime minister, Gordon Brown (2007–2010), and one year later President Barack Obama was elected in the United States. Under these two leaders the West began to withdraw its troops from Iraq, bringing to a gradual end (in October 2010) a struggle that had lasted for seven years. A democratic government under a new constitution now runs Iraq, but it remains to be seen if it can withstand the separatist leanings of parts of the country and the continued attacks of Islamist splinter groups. The United States temporarily boosted its involvement in Afghanistan, in a last-ditch effort to bring down the Taliban—before effecting a transition to civilian Afghan rule under its president, Hamid Karzai.

Meanwhile, al-Qaeda's relocation to Pakistan opened a new front in the war against terrorism. Pakistan's diplomatic position had always been delicate, since its chief diplomatic and military concern has always been its troubled relations with India, to the east. The issue of Afghanistan was important to the Pakistani government chiefly as a way to coax military and economic aid out of the United States. That led the government in Islamabad to play a double game of claiming to oppose al-Qaeda and the Taliban, even while privately giving them aid and refuge. American support for Pervez Musharraf, the head of the Pakistani military and president of the country from 2001 to 2008, fueled claims about Western hypocrisy—since Musharraf had come to power in 1999 by staging a military takeover of a democratically elected government. On May 2, 2011, U.S. special forces launched a secret raid on a secure compound in Abbottabad in Pakistan, where it found and killed Osama bin Laden, who was still directing the activities of al-Qaeda after ten years on the run. His discovery at a safe house only a short distance from a Pakistani military academy prompted questions about Pakistan's role in harboring him.

ISRAEL, PALESTINE, AND THE ARAB SPRING

Meanwhile, the conflict between Israel and the Palestinians showed no sign of nearing resolution. In 2007 Palestinian leadership split between two rival factions—the Fatah party under Mahmoud Abbas, which administers the West Bank, and Hamas, which took control of the Gaza Strip. This split introduced an unexpected difficulty into the peace process, for Hamas, despite its genuine social and charitable work, is a terrorist organization, on account of which Israel steadfastly refuses to negotiate with it. Yet Hamas rose to power through open election by the Gazan Palestinians. To Israel, the way in which Hamas won power is irrelevant. Above all, what matters most is what the group has done in the past with the power it had: it has murdered and maimed thousands of innocent Israelis.

But there is more. Since 2007 Hamas has actively encouraged the radicalization of the populace. It instituted an official "Virtue Committee" whose members patrol the streets in search of anyone not observing strict rules of sexual segregation, dress, and comportment. Verbal harassment and physical coercion are common tactics. Critics have likened their actions to the excesses of the Taliban in Afghanistan.

For three weeks at the end of 2008 and the start of 2009, Israel conducted a surprise bombing campaign against Hamas called Operation Cast Lead. Inevitably, interpretations of it vary widely. Hamas and Fatah claim that the Israeli action was a callous act of aggression that killed well over a thousand Palestinian civilians and virtually destroyed Gaza's infrastructure. Israel maintains that it launched a precisely limited series of strikes against known sites of Hamas's terrorist activity and provided warnings in advance to local residents to clear each target area. A flawed UN investigation into the campaign was widely criticized, leaving the dispute alive.

Finally, a chain of spontaneous popular rebellions against corruption, oppression, and ineptitude spread through the Arab world starting in December 2010. The first eruption occurred in Tunisia, where a local street vendor, Muhammad Bouazizi, who was in despair after years of mistreatment by local officials, set himself ablaze in a busy intersection and killed himself. Crowds took to the street by the hundreds of thousands to protest the actions of the government. They saw Bouazizi as a martyr to civic freedom, and they chanted over and over their demand for vengeance. After attempting to calm the protests, the Tunisian president, who had held dictatorial authority for twenty-three years, fled to France, and a new government came to power. Only a week later the government in neighboring Algeria surrendered the emergency powers it had held for nearly twenty years.

Lebanon and Jordan came next, with crowds demanding, and receiving, new parliamentary regimes. Demonstrations in Sudan prompted its controversial president, Omar al-Bashir, to announce that he would step down from office at the end of his current term. Apart from his oppression of the people in Darfur, he is believed to have embezzled as much as $8 billion of the nation's funds.[3] Bashir is charged with crimes against humanity, including genocide, by the International Criminal Court. In Oman and Saudi Arabia, protestors won economic concessions and the right to hold elections to fill local government offices and to initiate legislation at that level.

The most spectacular revolt yet occurred in Egypt, where massive demonstrations in Cairo's Tahrir Square in 2011 brought down the forty-year dictatorship of Hosni Mubarak (in June 2012 he was sentenced to life in prison). The military took temporary control of the government, dissolved the parliament, and suspended the constitution. Subsequent mass movements arose in Morocco, Yemen, Iraq, Bahrain, and Kuwait and won at least a partial lifting of heavy-handed governments, the shifting of cabinets, release of political prisoners, and certain economic concessions. The reforms are ongoing though the prospect for the future is unclear.

The only Arab regimes to have mounted prolonged resistance to uprisings have been Libya and Syria, both nations where the government's military forces remained reliably on the regime's side. In each case, civilians withstood months of repressive measures—beatings and arrests, artillery bombardments, systematic rape, and the cutting off of food, water, and electricity. Rebels against Libya's Muammar Qaddafi finally defeated the regime after NATO airstrikes paralyzed the dictator's defenses, which allowed the rebels to stage a decisive land campaign into the capital of Tripoli. Qaddafi himself was captured and killed by a rebel mob when he fled to his home town of Sirte in October 2011.

---

[3]   The atrocities in Darfur have killed as many as four hundred thousand people and left 2.5 million homeless.

The Arab Spring   Tawakkol Karman, the leader of the organization "Women Journalists without Chains," protests against the government of Yemen in 2011. Yemen's president, Ali Abdullah Saleh, had been in power since 1978; he was forced to resign his office in early 2012.

Government intransigence has been even stronger in Syria, where the Assad regime, as of summer 2012, has not only held out but has violated UN-brokered cease-fires and intensified its resistance. The political and military situation in Syria, however, is considerably more complicated than it was in Libya. Syria's historical role as the original center of the Islamic empire and its proximity to Israel (with which it has had officially hostile yet surprisingly stable relations since the 1990s), together with international concerns to have an Arab counterweight to the regional ambitions of Iran, have disinclined groups like the UN, NATO, or the Arab League to provide direct support to the rebels.

These rebellions are known collectively as the **Arab Spring**. They are taking place in the ethnically Arab lands and represent part of the broad awakening of Arab national identity and pride (see Map 30.2). A revitalized and democratic belt of Arab nations across North Africa and throughout the Middle East could do much to help the people of the region prosper. As things have stood, the immense oil wealth of the area has been monopolized by either royal or dictatorial families and their cronies. Freer societies could mean not only a broader sharing of that wealth but more varied and diverse economies that

Islamist groups have inevitably been involved at the margins, but the Arab Spring has been overwhelmingly a civic movement, a demand of the masses for control over their own lives.

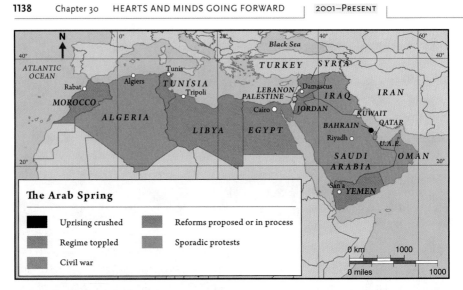

MAP 30.2   The Arab Spring

would help strong democratic traditions to take root. At the same time, the re-bellions have been secular. Islamist groups have inevitably been involved at the margins, but the Arab Spring has been overwhelmingly a civic movement, a demand of the masses for control over their own lives. If they can succeed, and in their success remove one of the chief factors behind the desperate appeal of radical Islamism, the possibility of a real, lasting, and just peace in the region could be within reach.

VEILED THREATS

The future of its women may yet determine the fate of Greater Western society in the 21st century. Despite discouraging trends in places like India and China, where gender-selective abortion thrives despite its official illegality, women still outnumber men and comprise the bulk of global society. Within the Greater West, however, a sharp divide exists in how women are treated in society.

The **World Economic Forum** (WEF) publishes an annual "Report on the Global Gender Gap," using statistics provided by the member countries them-selves, that examines the status of women worldwide. The reports examine five criteria in each country: the level of economic opportunity available to women; educational opportunity and attainment; the availability of health care, whether publicly or privately funded; levels of gender-specific crimes like rape; and the degree of political empowerment, which includes female participation in gov-ernment, the right to vote, and equal treatment under the law. The 2010 report highlights and quantifies the divide within the Greater West. Fourteen of the highest-scoring twenty nations—that is, those countries that provide the greatest equality and respect to women—are members of the European West. Fifteen of the lowest-scoring twenty nations are Muslim nations.

The WEF's criteria can be, and often are, argued to have a pro-Western bias. They represent the values of the UN Declaration of Human Rights rather than those of the Cairo Declaration. They assume that individually based gender values matter as much as family cohesion, for example, and that personal independence is superior to communal stability and cultural tradition.

The Muslim West treats women and girls profoundly differently than men and boys. In the most conservative lands women may not vote, drive a car, give testimony in court, or hold a job. Education for girls, when available at all, is often limited to the elementary level and is focused on religious schooling. In many Islamic countries the law allows women greater choice in deciding whom to marry, and it has liberalized the criteria that allow women to seek divorce. Yet domestic violence remains commonplace. It may be technically illegal, as in the case of **honor killings**—the deaths of women who are thought to have tarnished the family's reputation. Even then, however, the violence is seldom prosecuted and frequently

TABLE 30.1 **The Global Gender Gap**

20 BEST NATIONS FOR WOMEN	20 WORST NATIONS FOR WOMEN
Iceland	Nepal
Norway	Lebanon
Finland	Qatar
Sweden	Nigeria
New Zealand	Algeria
Ireland	Jordan
Denmark	Ethiopia
Lesotho	Oman
The Philippines	Iran
Switzerland	Syria
Spain	Egypt
South Africa	Turkey
Germany	Morocco
Belgium	Benin
United Kingdom	Saudi Arabia
Sri Lanka	Ivory Coast
The Netherlands	Mali
Latvia	Pakistan
United States	Chad
Canada	Yemen

goes unpunished.[4] In 2003 the government of Pakistan alone documented over twelve hundred such killings. Thanks to the Internet, the practice is far harder to overlook. Gruesome videos of women being beaten, whipped, and stoned to death are readily available to anyone with the stomach to watch them.

The phenomenon has spread to the West with the rise in Muslim immigration to Europe (see Map 30.3). Recent reports estimate that two hundred Muslim girls and women have been killed by their families in Spain in the last twenty years. Roughly a dozen honor killings occur each year in the United Kingdom. In a recent BBC poll, in fact, 10 percent of Muslim British men—which would calculate to some fifty thousand of them, nationwide—said that they would unhesitatingly kill a daughter or sister who had dishonored the family.

But 90 percent of them said they would not. Worldwide, Muslims who reject the idea of honor killing are clearly in the majority, but proponents of the practice remain a sufficiently large minority that concern for the persecution of women cannot abate. The Western media predictably but understandably focus on the most horrifying cases. They told of the 2002 gang rape of a young Pakistani woman that was ordered by a tribal court as punishment for her brother's sexual immodesty. They told of the 2004 fire at a girls' school in Saudi Arabia, where firefighters allowed only those girls who had stopped to cover themselves head-to-foot to flee the burning building. Or of the sixteen-year-old girl in Hamburg whose brother stabbed her twenty-three times in a parking lot for dishonoring the family by her refusal to wear a hijab and to marry the man (a cousin) selected for her by her father. Or of the Afghan-Canadian husband and wife who drowned all three of their teenage daughters in 2011 because they had boyfriends without their permission.

Recent studies have shown that the predominant motive behind honor killings, when they occur in Islamic countries, is some sort of real or perceived sexual impropriety. But when they occur among Muslims within Europe, the main cause—by more than a two-to-one margin—is that the women or girls were considered to have "become too Western." Even more disturbing, the honor killings committed for the supposed crime of becoming Westernized usually involve some sort of torture before the victims are actually killed. Given the virulence of such crimes, it is no wonder that Europe's Muslims have not assimilated into their surrounding cultures at a rate fast enough to please their non-Muslim neighbors. Yet the media pay little attention to the slow but steady advances made by Muslim women both

---

[4]   According to the UN Population Fund, roughly five thousand honor killings take place yearly around the world, the majority in Muslim societies.

MAP 30.3   European Muslim Population, 2012

in Europe and in the Middle East.[5] Girls' schools in Egypt and Jordan are growing, albeit slowly, in number and in sophistication. Prominent women teach at some of the premier universities in Egypt, Iraq, and Turkey.

Violence against women, equal access to education and civil rights, and the right to work—all these issues are being discussed. That fact alone might have seemed impossible a generation ago. The Internet's influence here is unmistakable. Videos of the stoning of women cannot be easily ignored or dismissed; nor can the jubilant celebrations among the men who hurled the rocks. Blogs by dissidents evade censors and bring to the world news of government crackdowns on protestors. When Bill Gates (b. 1955), cofounder of Microsoft, spoke to a crowd of business leaders in Riyadh, he was asked if he thought Saudi Arabia would ever become a global leader in technology: "Not if you aren't fully utilizing half of the talent in your country," he replied. For the time being, that "half of the talent" is underappreciated.

Aside from traditional cultural conservatism, economic factors also play a role in shaping Arab attitudes toward women. Since 85 to 90 percent of Arab wealth comes from a single industry, petroleum, their nations do not have the varied

---

[5]   Women in Iran hold 10 percent of the nation's political offices, including three of its twelve vice presidencies.

Leaders of the Revolution   A group of Iranian schoolgirls listen to their president, Mahmoud Ahmadinejad, addressing the parliament in February 2011. Women have the right to vote in Iran, and currently about eight percent of parliamentary seats are held by women.

economies that would allow women to advance as they have done in Europe and in the non-Arab Muslim countries. Proven oil reserves in the Middle East, at current rates of production and consumption, will run dry by the year 2050, leaving the region economically crippled unless other sources of revenue can be found. As of 2010 plastics and petrochemicals are the two largest non-oil industries—but together they produce only enough money to cover the cost of food imports into the region.

> Proven oil reserves in the Middle East, at current rates of production and consumption, will run dry by the year 2050, leaving the region economically crippled unless other sources of revenue can be found.

Muslim women's growing involvement in the post-oil economy should lighten some of the social strictures under which they lived throughout the 20th century. But given the experience of women in Europe, this may take some time.

DEBT, TAXES, AND LIBERTY

The economic crash of 2008 highlighted painfully the problem of Western debt. Since capitalism runs on credit, debt and even long-term indebtedness are inescapable—and are not in itself harmful. People commonly purchase homes that leave them in debt to their banks or mortgage servers for thirty years. They may even refinance their loans at any point, lowering their payments but extending the indebtedness farther into the future. They also pay for college with loans that may extend into their middle age or even beyond. Cities and states issue bonds in order to provide revenues to improve infrastructure or to pay for school construction. National governments borrow domestically and internationally to fund special projects or to spur economic growth. Small companies rely on loans to expand their business, invest in new products, and modernize their equipment. Large corporations take on debt in order to acquire smaller companies—and sometimes even larger debt in order to purchase companies larger than themselves.

Problems arise, however, when too much red ink appears on the ledger. How much is too much? It depends on one's assets and their current and projected values, but also on other factors. These include the viability of the project for which the debt is assumed, the interest rate charged, and the security of the revenue stream that will repay the loan. This is all elementary finance—but the West still got itself into a mess only a few years ago. Public and private debt threatens to collapse the Euro Zone and has brought the United States close to default. Looking at public debt as a percentage of gross domestic product (GDP)—the value of all goods and services produced in a year and the best way to judge the problem—is a sobering exercise.

The problem with Greece, for example, is obvious. The nation's debt is almost one hundred times its annual GDP, and its 2010 budget added another GDP's worth of debt to the pile. At the same time, its national revenues are declining by more than 12 percent a year. Caught in so severe a bind, the nation has no way to ever pay its creditors and return to fiscal health without help. Portugal, in comparison, owes sixty-four times its GDP and slashed its 2010 budget by almost 3 percent of GDP. Its growth rate is only enough to hold steady, and it can avoid drowning only by forcing its creditors underwater. The euro, the single currency of the EU, was supposed to lessen problems like this. The easy availability of credit, though, enticed too many people, in all countries, to take on more debt. For a time it seemed that economic growth and the increase in value of what they owned would compensate.

Something similar happened in the United States. Government debt had been on the rise since the 1960s but had remained manageable, as a percentage of GDP, until the 1990s under President Clinton. At that point, a series of tax increases and cuts in social programs, combined with a decade-long rise in the stock market, created a significant budget surplus. The federal budget entered the 21st century well under control, but three events reversed the trend. First, a surge of interest in high-tech companies had driven the stock market upward in the nineties, but now the collapse of this "dot-com bubble" put many Americans

TABLE 30.2 **GDP and Government Debt Compared, 2011**

COUNTRY	GDP (by millions US)	GOVERNMENT DEBT (% of GDP)	NET VALUE OF ECONOMIC GROWTH (minus cost of debt)
Austria	379,047	40.9	0.2
Belgium	469,347	83.3	0.4
Canada	1,577,040	30.3	3.2
Czech Republic	197,674	4.8	0.6
Denmark	309,866	0.5	1.2
Finland	238,731	–57	2.4
France	2,559,850	57.2	0.3
Germany	3,280,334	52.7	0.5
Greece	301,065	97.8	–12.2
Hungary	128,629	60.1	–2.2
Ireland	206,600	39.9	–4.8
Italy	2,051,290	104.1	–1.3
Netherlands	779,310	34.4	0.4
Norway	413,056	–153.4	3
Poland	469,393	27.9	1.1
Portugal	228,859	64.3	–3
Sweden	458,725	–19.6	2.6
Switzerland	527,920	6.2	1.4
UK	2,253,552	53.5	–0.2
United States	14,447,100	66.6	2.2

out of work. Second, President George W. Bush pressed for substantial tax cuts that radically reduced federal revenues just as demand for social services began to rise dramatically. Third, the country went to war in Afghanistan and Iraq without raising taxes in order to pay for either conflict—essentially funding two wars on a credit card.

These factors combined to produce the largest budget deficits in the country's history. Soon millions of Americans took on enormous personal debt, in part because of artificially high housing values. Unscrupulous and even fraudulent loan agencies and mortgage brokers walked right in, earning specious profits by extending loans to people who could not afford them and then selling the mortgages. The sale went to the financial markets, repackaged as the hazily understood "collateralized debt obligations," that together with the credit default swaps made popular twenty years earlier by the *Exxon Valdez* settlement, helped trigger the financial crisis of 2008.

The combination of widespread debt and economic recession presents a problem—how to spur economic growth and get unemployed people back to work. To do both, governments have traditionally invested heavily in infrastructure and other projects, and they have done so by taking on debt. As more people become wage earners, their taxes pay off the public loan. But opposition to tax increases remained fervid in 2010 in the United States, especially among conservatives who prefer to balance budgets by cutting expenditures. In Europe, calls for debt financing to help out countries in critical condition (Greece, Ireland, Italy, Portugal, Spain) and to fuel job growth have been resisted by those nations (Germany especially) that would have to provide the credit.

> The Greater West has entered the 21st century engaged in full-throttle disputes over the purpose and limits of government and the responsibilities of individuals in society.

More is involved in these debates than reconciling figures in a ledger. The Greater West has entered the 21st century engaged in full-throttle disputes over the purpose and limits of government and the responsibilities of individuals in society. The disputes are not new, but they are being addressed with a fervor not seen since the middle of the 19th century.

Two related issues are at stake. The first is taxation as economic stimulus: do higher taxes help the economy or not? Remember that the story of capitalism is capital—wealth that can be used to produce more wealth. No one disputes that injecting new capital into an economy spurs investment, production, and consumption. But should that capital come from the public (that is, the government) or from private sources?

The conservative argument holds that the best way to trigger growth is to reduce taxes and spending on social programs in order to "free" capital. We should allow business owners to keep more of their wealth in order to invest in production, and we should let consumers retain more of their own wealth in order to spur the purchase of goods. That way, activity will be stimulated throughout the economy. This is the free-market view described in the mid-20th century by economists like F. A. Hayek. It was also the view of Milton Friedman, an American economist later in the 20th century (see chapter 25). An unregulated market, these economists wrote, will produce the greatest efficiency. A small but thriving portion of the economy will always produce more than a larger, intrusive portion of a halting, staggering economy. Moreover, it respects individuals' rights to control their own property.

The second issue is taxation as wealth redistribution: Taxes take from those with money and give it to those without it, in the form of social services—but should that be the goal of society? The **libertarian** argument holds that any taxation at all is evil because it is theft. By claiming a right to a portion of my income, a government is claiming a right to a portion of my labor—the labor that produces the income. But to claim someone else's capital as one's own is theft. Even worse, the ownership of someone else's labor is slavery. Once, before the American Revolution, colonists protested British taxes. No taxation, they

Campaigning against Austerity Members of the right-wing Independent Greeks party stage a rally in Thessaloniki in May 2012 against the austerity budgets put forth by the government in Athens at the behest of the European Union. The Independent Greeks currently hold twenty seats (out of three hundred) in the Greek parliament. Their most notable political plank is to call for Germany to pay reparations to Greece for the damage done to the country in World War II.

cried, without representation. Now, the argument goes, any form of taxation at all is an attack on individual liberty. Obviously, certain services are essential ones that people need not provide for themselves. National defense, most obviously, cannot be provided for without public funding. And it is unreasonable, for another example, to expect each of us to build our own roads when we wish to travel somewhere. So some compromise on principle is necessary. But libertarians hold that government ought to be as small and inexpensive as possible: it should provide only those services that citizens cannot be expected to provide for themselves.

What might those services be? Infrastructure, certainly (meaning roads, electrical grids, sewer systems, and so on), and national defense. But anything beyond that is debatable. Retirement pensions? Health care? Many conservatives would respond by asking why people shouldn't be expected to save for their own retirement. A publicly funded pension, after all, might be a disincentive to save. And if someone *has* saved but finds, on retirement, that his or her savings still fall short of what is needed, why shouldn't the individual's family help first? Why is it *everyone*'s responsibility to care for individuals who chose to spend all of their money as they were making it? For government to step in is not only contrary to an efficient economy; it actually weakens society by lessening the role of the family.

As for health care, shouldn't people be responsible for themselves? If you choose to smoke forty cigarettes a day, avoid exercise, and drink to excess, that is absolutely your right. But why is it then society's responsibility to pay for your cancer treatment, liver transplants, and physical therapy? Or consider school lunches, a fine idea for those who wish to purchase them. Why should they be publicly subsidized? Is it wrong to expect parents to feed their own children? Why is it right to subsidize a lunch provided by the school, but not the lunch a parent prepares for a child to carry to school?

The conservative argument against taxation rests on the simple principle that people are responsible for themselves and for their own families. Taxation to provide services that ought not to be the government's business in the first place is therefore unjustifiable. In the end, it does more harm than good. For the state to intrude on such matters is unprincipled, inefficient, costly, harmful to the economy, and damaging to the moral well-being of society.

FREE MARKET? WHAT FREE MARKET?

All this is willful blindness and moral idiocy, counter liberals. The blindness consists of a refusal to see that no such thing as a "free market" exists. People are not autonomous, self-owned, rational actors in a marketplace of open and equal competition. Capitalism is at root a numbers game, especially as the libertarians claim to practice it. Real human actions are not governed by and cannot be understood by numbers and formulas alone. A skilled electrician who cannot get hired because he is a member of a racial or religious minority is not subject merely to market forces. No matter how good his work or how low his rates, his struggle against prejudices—even if successful—is not played out on the same economic playing field as his white competitor. Or take a midlevel manager working for a software firm who earns only 80 percent of what her male colleagues in the same position receive. She confronts daily something more than "rational choice" in the corporate marketplace. Equal pay for equal work is a matter of fundamental justice, not of artificial manipulation of a free market. The problem with the call for small government and unregulated economies, liberals argue, is that free-market economists don't believe in sin. Or at least they talk as though they don't, whenever the subject is the economy.

> The problem with the call for small government and unregulated economies, liberals argue, is that free-market economists don't believe in sin. Or at least they talk as though they don't, whenever the subject is the economy.

Not only are injustices like racism, sexism, cronyism, and class discrimination built into the system, but so are inequalities of opportunity. Large, well-stocked supermarkets provide full selections of fresh produce, artisanal breads, and shelves packed with dietary supplements. They are almost always located in suburbs, with ample parking, not in inner cities and in poorer neighborhoods. Why then is it solely the responsibility of the urban poor to maintain their own healthy diets? Even when suburban supermarkets are located near bus lines, it may take a city dweller an hour and a half to get there. A simple grocery trip can turn into an all-day affair that may get in the way of work and other responsibilities.

Moreover, even in a perfect world, capitalism has a built-in bias toward the concentration of capital. For one thing, property is inheritable but labor is not: the owner of a manufacturing plant can hand over that ownership to a son or daughter, but the factory workers cannot pass on their jobs to their heirs. Even allowing for business failures, real assets generally grow in value over time, while the long-term value of labor diminishes as workers age or as technology replaces them. Thus thriving capitalist societies do experience a degree of enrichment overall, but within that general trend lives another pattern entirely—the consolidation of wealth at the top.[6] So much for total assets, but what about annual income? In the United States more than twenty cents out of every dollar in new income is paid to the top one percent of wage and salary earners. In the United Kingdom from 1997 to 2007, the overwhelming bulk of the new jobs created were added at the very top and the very bottom of the pay scale: the executives, in other words, and their minimum-wage workers.

Economists measure wealth and income distributions using a standard called the **Gini coefficient**, named after the Italian statistician (and one-time Fascist bureaucrat) Corrado Gini (1884–1965).[7] The Gini scale ranges from a score of 0, meaning that a country has perfect equality of wealth among all citizens, to a score of 100, meaning that 100% of the wealth is owned by a single individual. According to the Gini scale, the West maintained the lowest concentrations of wealth during the decades of the welfare state. Since free-market economic policies came into effect beginning with President Reagan and Prime Minister Thatcher in 1980, however, the trend has been toward ever-greater concentrations of wealth in their two countries. From 1980 to the present, these pro-market economies have improved overall wealth, but the concentration of that wealth

---

[6]   In the United States in 2010, the four hundred richest individuals (0.000125 percent of the population) owned as much wealth (capital and assets) as the least wealthy 150 million Americans combined.

[7]   When he wasn't busy calculating his coefficients and indexing the birth rates of inferior peoples, Gini wrote a pamphlet called *The Scientific Basis of Fascism* (1927).

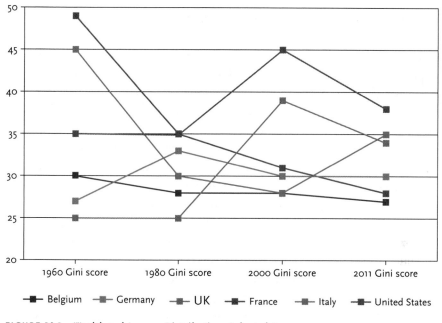

FIGURE 30.1   **Wealth and Income Distribution: Selected Scores**

among the richest citizens (a 50 percent increase in Britain between 1980 and 2000, a 33 percent increase in the United States) is clear (see Figure 30.1).

These trends lead to another idea: redistributive taxation—taxes intended not only to pay for essential services but to force a broader distribution of wealth as well. Liberal economists argue that these taxes *must* exist, as a matter of justice. Besides, taxes also assure continued economic growth, as a matter of practical policy. Take redistribution as justice, first. A just society gives priority to treating its people, not its material wealth, with fairness and respect, goes the argument. If there are human rights, then all people possess them, and society should see that every citizen has his or her rights recognized and protected. Does that mean that all wealth should be handed out in equal parcel to everyone? Socialists might say yes, but most liberals say no. Rather, society serves justice by seeing to it that everyone has an equal opportunity to prosper. The children of a billionaire investor and the children of a coal miner do not begin life with the same opportunities and the same chances to succeed, and hence the state has a responsibility and a right to extract, in taxes, more of the billionaire's wealth so that it can be directed to the coal miner.

Liberal thinking often follows a line of thought articulated by John Rawls, in *A Theory of Justice* (1971). Rawls imagined each of us cloaked in a "veil of ignorance." Sure, inequalities of wealth, intelligence, social class, and talents exist.

Yet none of us know where we or anyone else stands. In that case, we must all choose a future regardless of our good or bad fortune in history's lottery. An economy that lets some people begin with vastly greater means than others is unfair from the start. Fairness to all is more important than any individual's right to inherit parental wealth. In Rawls's words, "Justice is fairness," and fairness includes redistributive taxation.

> Rawls imagined each of us cloaked in a "veil of ignorance." Sure, inequalities of wealth, intelligence, social class, and talents exist. Yet none of us know where we or anyone else stands.

No one lives independently, in this view, and all our fates are connected. You can wear a seatbelt while driving a car, for example, or not—but you had better wear one. The choice is not simply a matter of personal freedom versus a paternalist state, and it is gross selfishness to think that it is.

If you are without a seatbelt in an accident, your medical costs will be vastly greater than if you had worn one. Even if private insurance pays that bill, the rest of society remains affected because the demand on medical services raises the prices of medical care and insurance for all. The accident also increases the need for police officers and ambulances, as well as interrupting traffic.

Justice Is Fairness   The distribution of wealth has become increasingly a focus of political attention. Here a well-dressed figure in London's financial district walks past a homeless beggar outside the Royal Exchange (formerly a financial center, now a luxury shopping mall).

Two other major issues stand out, among many, as pressing challenges to economic growth. First is the aging of the West. The population of Europe, especially the western half of it, is getting older, since birth rates are in decline and the advantages of skilled medicine allow people to live longer lives. This problem also exists to some extent, though a lesser one, in the United States, where immigration, both legal and illegal, makes up for some of the stagnation in net population. As Britain discovered at the end of the 19th century, its aging population factored heavily in its economic and political competition with Germany, whose larger and younger population was a catalyst for its imperial growth. In parts of eastern Europe, and especially throughout the Islamic part of the Greater West, populations are growing rapidly and average ages are declining (see Map 30.4). In Iran alone, nearly two-thirds of the entire population is under the age of thirty-five; moreover, overall growth, in absolute numbers, has been dramatic: the population has nearly doubled in size since the Islamic Revolution in 1979.

An aging population means increased health costs—which forms the other major challenge to the West. The European countries provide cradle-to-grave medical care to their people, but this generosity depends on two factors to keep it going: continuing military subsidies from the United States, which frees up capital for the EU nations to dedicate to social programs, and a sizable labor force whose taxes can support the cost of medical care. Both factors are currently in doubt for the foreseeable future. In the United States, the cost of entitlement programs (Medicare for the elderly, Medicaid for the poor, and Social Security pensions for the retired) have been straining or breaking budgets for decades. The need both to address these ballooning costs and to balance that effort against the need to stimulate a sluggish recessionary economy will dominate national politics for at least another generation.

WHAT IS THE GREATER WEST NOW?

The names of historical periods and movements matter. It matters that the educated of the 18th century called themselves *the Enlightened*—even if only to expose their self-regard. In the 3rd century CE, when Germanic tribes swept into the western Roman Empire, the Romans called it an *invasion*, but the Germans later described it as a *migration* (*Völkerwanderung*). And they were both right, each from their own point of view.

The Greater West may be experiencing a similar two-faced moment now. Migration within and immigration from without is changing the entire European

MAP 30.4   **Population Growth in the Greater West, 2012**

continent. New faiths are filling the spaces left by a declining Christianity. The languages heard on the streets are unfamiliar; so are the smells and tastes emanating from shops and restaurants. Nationalist passions contend with a vision of European unity that, like new clothing, seems to fit but still feels uncomfortable. Political and economic rivalries come and go, but most Europeans are cheered that no wars have broken out between any members of the EU, the EC before it, or the EEC before that. This most warlike of continents may finally have stumbled on the path to peace.

Other parts of the Greater West are undergoing almost precisely the opposite pressures and trends. The ethnic makeup of the Arab countries is becoming more, not less, homogenous. Christian populations are small and declining; the Jewish populations even more so. Israel is the most pluralistic of the Middle East nations and the most democratic, although optimists see in the Arab Spring the start of a pronounced democratic swing. Iraq may yet prove to be the first viable Arab democracy. Religious conviction runs deep, but the rifts between Sunni and Shi'i Muslims and the rivalries between clans are a continuous challenge. The likely major struggle to come within the Islamic world will be the rivalry between Arabs, Persians, and Turks; and in the working out of that contest the fate of Islam's women will be both cause and consequence. Iran's nuclear ambitions are perhaps the most pressing issue at present, but the contest will continue to heat up, especially as Arab oil wealth declines. For now, the two halves of the Greater West are confronting the challenge of understanding their own identity—as nations? Religions? Economic actors?

> Political and economic rivalries come and go, but most Europeans are cheered that no wars have broken out between any members of the EU, the EC before it, or the EEC before that. This most warlike of continents may finally have stumbled on the path to peace.

The question has already run into roadblocks. Speaking to the Council of Europe in 2005, Pope Benedict XVI (r. 2005–present) urged the European Union not to deny its own history. Christianity, for good or ill, has been a central element in the development of European culture. He insisted that the faith still has a crucial role to play in the future:

> Only a Europe with peaceful social coexistence and the exchange of cultural riches, both material and non-material, will be able to be featured as the common house of all Europeans, in which each and every one is accepted and feels at home, no one is subject to discrimination but all are required to live as responsible members of one great family of peoples.... Christianity has been an essential factor of unity among peoples and cultures. For two millennia, it has never ceased to promote an integral vision of the human being and human rights, and the history of the nations of the Continent as a whole attests to its extraordinary cultural fruitfulness.
>
> Eager to honour the modern requirement of a proper secularism of States, and hence of Europe with all its religious and secular elements running counter to a reductive secularism that inspires certain policies, the Holy See reaffirms its willingness and the ability of religions to help build the common European home, contributing in particular to remedy

the challenge of social disintegration and to give meaning to life and to history.

Did not European modernism, which gave the world the ideal of democracy, the meaning of the dignity of every human person and his or her inalienable rights, find in the crucible of Christianity the loftiest values in its 1,000-year-old culture, the heir to Greek thought, in the Roman institutions and in many other cultural contributions, particularly the Celtic, Anglo-Saxon, German and Slav?

In the period subsequent to the Second World War, the Fathers of Europe courageously pointed out the challenge of "justice without freedom." Today, an equally ruinous "utopia" threatens our societies with disintegration: the indifference that relativizes everything, advances nothing and, masked by its appearance of tolerance, endangers the humanity of men and women.

To confront this new challenge together at the dawn of the third millennium, to build Europe as a human community, means giving the European Cultural Convention a new impetus, to which, for its part, the Holy See fully intends to contribute.

There is an obvious difficulty here. To deny the significance of the Christian faith in shaping the Western tradition is historical nonsense, but the Western world is increasingly Muslim. To center Western identity on Christianity is just bad politics; hence the EU's refusal to acknowledge a Christian core to Western culture. But the Islamic world, too, will have to adapt to non-Muslim society. It has done so in the past, with notable success. The challenge to Islam today is the small but violent minority of Muslims who oppose any adaptation. They demand an immediate and uncompromising return to the strictest shariah. The only reform they desire is a return to a mythical pure past—a common trope of Greater Western culture, but not necessarily the most admirable or helpful one.

Efforts are underway to speed adaptation along, to improve understanding across religious lines. A controversial figure, the Swiss academic Tariq Ramadan (b. 1962), has emerged with a distinctive European version of Islam. Born and raised in Geneva, Ramadan is the grandson of the founder of the Muslim Brotherhood in Egypt, a family connection that makes many of his critics suspicious of his claims that he is not a fundamentalist. After studying philosophy and French literature at the University of Geneva, he completed a PhD in Islamic studies. He has taught at several prestigious universities and is currently on the faculty at Oxford. Ramadan argues that the Qur'an is the essential authority in Islamic life, but it must be interpreted in light of the time and place in which one lives. Muslims within Europe, he insists, have an obligation to observe the laws of the

The Face of the Greater West   A group of Berlin youths gather at the annual Holocaust Remembrance Day for an activity known as "Cleaning the Cobblestones [*Stolpersteine*]." Christian, Muslim, Jewish, and Bahai youths walk through the streets to clean and care for the roughly 3,500 commemoration-stones planted along sidewalks. Each stone bears the name of local Jewish citizens of Berlin who became victims of the Holocaust. The idea has grown in popularity, and hundreds of cities all across Europe now have *Stolpersteine*. By the end of 2011 more than thirty thousand stones had been created.

secular state. They should devise a code of Islamic life that harmonizes Qur'anic teaching and social expectation. As he expressed it in his book entitled *To Be a European Muslim* (1999):

> The European environment is a space of responsibility for Muslims. This is exactly the meaning of the notion of "space of testimony" (*dar al-shahada*) that we propose here, a notion that totally reverses perspectives: whereas Muslims have, for years, been wondering whether and how they would be accepted, the in-depth study and evaluation of the Western environment entrusts them, in light of their Islamic frame of reference, with a most important mission .... Muslims now attain, in the space of testimony, the meaning of an essential duty and of an exacting responsibility: to contribute, wherever they are, to promoting good and equity within and through human brotherhood. Muslims' outlook must now change from the reality of "protection" alone to that of an authentic "contribution."

Ramadan's outlook is not altogether new. We have often forgotten that Islam has been a Western religion from the start. The events of the Arab Spring are still recent, but the slow integration of the post-Christian European and Muslim worlds now underway in the Greater West has a chance to succeed. As it happens, one of its first test cases will occur where Western civilization began—in Iraq.

WHO, WHAT, WHERE

Arab Spring
Gini coefficient
honor killings

libertarian
World Economic Forum

SUGGESTED READINGS

Primary Sources

Ramadan, Tariq. *Islam, the West, and the Challenges of Modernity.*

———. *The Quest for Meaning: Developing a Philosophy of Pluralism.*

———. *Western Muslims and the Future of Islam.*

Anthologies

Laqueur, Walter, and Barry Rubin, eds. *The Israel-Arab Reader: A Documentary History of the Middle East Conflict* (2008).

Sandel, Michael J., ed. *Justice: A Reader* (2007).

Vallentyne, Peter, and Hillel Steiner, eds. *The Origins of Left-Libertarianism: An Anthology of Historical Writings* (2007).

Studies

Browers, Michaelle. *Political Ideology in the Arab World: Accommodation and Transformation* (2009).

Calhoun, Craig, and Georgi Derluguian, eds. *Business as Usual: The Roots of the Global Financial Meltdown* (2011).

Council on Foreign Relations. *The New Arab Revolt: What Happened, What It Means, and What Comes Next* (2011).

Holton, Robert J. *Globalization and the Nation State* (2011).

Huntington, Samuel P. *The Clash of Civilizations and the Remaking of World Order* (2011).

İnce, Başak. *Citizenship and Identity in Turkey: From Atatürk's Republic to the Present Day* (2012).

Marquand, David. *The End of the West: The Once and Future Europe* (2011).

Mearsheimer, John J. *The Tragedy of Great Power Politics* (2003).

Nussbaum, Martha C. *The New Religious Intolerance: Overcoming the Politics of Fear in an Anxious Age* (2012).

Ohana, David. *Israel and Its Mediterranean Identity* (2011).

Pope, Nicole. *Honor Killings in the Twenty-First Century* (2011).

Ruiz, Teofilo F. *The Terror of History: On the Uncertainties of Life in Western Civilization* (2011).

Sandel, Michael J. *What Money Can't Buy: The Moral Limits of Markets* (2012).

Sarotte, Mary Elise: *1989: The Struggle to Create Post-Cold War Europe* (2009).

Sen, Amartya. *The Idea of Justice* (2011).

———. *Identity and Violence: The Illusion of Destiny* (2008).

Shapiro, Daniel. *Is the Welfare State Justified?* (2007).

Stiglitz, Joseph E. *Globalization and Its Discontents* (2003).

Tavassoli, Sasan. *Christian Encounters with Iran: Engaging Muslim Thinkers after the Revolution* (2011).

Van Dam, Nikolaos. *The Struggle for Power in Syria: Politics and Society under Asad and the Ba'th Party* (2011).

Wikan, Unni. *Generous Betrayal: Politics of Culture in the New Europe* (2002).

Wilkinson, Richard, and Kate Pickett. *The Spirit Level: Why More Equal Societies Almost Always Do Better* (2009).

Young, Elise G. *Gender and Nation Building in the Middle East: The Political Economy of Health from Mandate Palestine to Refugee Camps in Jordan* (2012).

For additional resources, including maps, primary sources, visuals, web links, and quizzes, please go to **www.oup.com/us/backman.**

Reference Maps

The Greater West: Physical Features

The Greater West, 2012

N

PORTUGAL
Lisbon
Rabat
MOROCCO
SPAIN
Madrid
ANDORA
Balearic Is.
Algiers
ALGERIA
IRELAND
Dublin
UNITED KINGDOM
London
FRANCE
Paris
MONACO
Corsica
Sardinia
Tunis
TUNISIA
Tripoli
NETHERLANDS
Amsterdam
BELGIUM
Brussels
LUX.
LIECH.
SWITZ.
Bern
Rome
ITALY
Sicily
Malta
NORWAY
Oslo
DENMARK
Copenhagen
GERMANY
Berlin
AUSTRIA
Vienna
SLOVENIA
Ljubljana
CROATIA
Zagreb
BOSNIA
HERZ.
Sarajevo
MONT.
Podgorica
ALB.
Tirana
LIBYA
SWEDEN
Stockholm
FINLAND
Helsinki
ESTONIA
Tallinn
LATVIA
Riga
LITHUANIA
Vilnius
POLAND
Warsaw
CZECH REP.
Prague
SLOVAKIA
Bratislava
HUNGARY
Budapest
SERBIA
Belgrade
KOSOVO
MAC.
Skopje
GREECE
Athens
Crete
RUSSIA
Moscow
BELARUS
Minsk
UKRAINE
Kiev
MOLDOVA
Chişinău
ROMANIA
Bucharest
BULGARIA
Sofia
TURKEY
Ankara
Cyprus
Cairo
EGYPT
KAZAKHSTAN
UZBEKISTAN
Tashkent
Dushanbe
TURKMENISTAN
Ashgabat
GEORGIA
Tbilisi
ARMENIA
Yerevan
AZERBAIJAN
Baku
Tehran
IRAN
AFGHANISTAN
Kabul
PAKISTAN
Muscat
OMAN
QATAR
UAE
Abu Dhabi
BAHRAIN
Riyadh
SAUDI ARABIA
KUWAIT
Kuwait
IRAQ
Baghdad
SYRIA
Damascus
LEBANON
Beirut
ISRAEL
Jerusalem
Amman
JORDAN

0 km   540
0 miles   540

A-2

Glossary

A

Abbasids Dynasty of Islamic caliphs who came to power in 750 and remained titular heads of the Islamic empire until 1258, when they were unseated by the Mongols. Moved Islamic capital from Damascus to Baghdad.

absolutism Political theory granting limitless authority to a sovereign ruler, holding that a sovereign entrusted with absolute power will best protect the sovereign's subjects from disorder and chaos.

absurdity Postwar cultural concept, associated with the French-Algerian writer Albert Camus (1913–1960), that sees life as essentially meaningless.

Academy The school founded by the philosopher Plato in Athens in 385 BCE.

Act of Union Parliamentary acts (1800) that united Great Britain and Ireland.

Acts of Toleration Throughout the 17th and 18th centuries, laws promulgated to offer full or partial constitutional rights to Jews.

Afrikaners The descendants of the first Dutch settlers of South Africa; formerly known as the Boers; the language they speak is called Afrikaans.

Aggiornamento Among the issues addressed by the Second Vatican Council's meetings (1962–1965) were a reformation of the liturgy to allow for the participation of the congregation, a call for missionary work, an expression of regret for hostilities between the Catholic and Orthodox churches, and a rejection of the tradition of blaming the Jews for the killing of Christ. The word used by Pope John XXIII to describe his goal in summoning the Vatican II council—to bring the Church "up to date," literally.

Ahura Mazda The One Lord or eternal God, worshiped by Zoroastrians who believe he is the creator of all living things.

Almohads Reformist Islamic sect, made up chiefly of ethnic Berbers from North Africa, who invaded Muslim Spain in the 1170s.

amir al-umara' "Commander of commanders," a title held by those who seized civil authority from the Abbasid caliphs after 936.

Anabaptists Apocalyptic sect of Swiss exiles who rejected infant baptism, called for a second baptism in adulthood, and embraced a literal reading of Scripture and the imminent approach of Christ's Second Coming.

analytical geometry Developed by René Descartes, the application of algebra to the study of geometry.

analytic philosophy Branch of philosophy that emphasizes close and careful reasoning (as distinct from rationalist philosophy, which studies the movement of the human mind itself).

Ancien Régime The French aristocracy from 1648 to 1789, seen as a golden age (for those privileged enough to enjoy it) before the French Revolution.

anno Domini System of dating that reckons the years since the birth of Christ.

Annunaki Collective name for the gods and goddesses of the Sumerians.

Anschluss "Union," literally; the term has come to refer specifically to the political unification of Austria and Germany under the Nazi regime.

anti-Semitism Term coined in 1881 to describe the vicious hatred toward and persecution of Jews, both officially and unofficially, that emerged across Europe in the 19th century.

apartheid Official policy of racial segregation instituted in South Africa by the Afrikaner-dominated National Party in 1948.

appanage A land or estate held by a nobleman from the king of France without the requirement of performing feudal service in return.

Appeasement In the 1930s, the granting of political and territorial concessions to Hitler's Germany by many Western countries in order to preserve peace.

Arab Revolt Uprising (1916) of Middle Eastern Arab tribes against Turkish rule, which aimed to replace Ottoman imperial rule with autonomous Arab countries but instead furthered the European imperialist project by dividing the Middle East between England and France (see **Sykes-Picot Agreement**).

Arab Spring Wave of rebellions in ethnically Arab countries, beginning in Tunisia in December 2010 and rippling across Morocco, Yemen, Iraq, Bahrain, Egypt, and Kuwait. The rebellions turned violent in Libya, resulting in the eventual overthrow and death of dictator Muammar Qaddafi, and in Syria, which at the time of publication was on the brink of an all-out civil war.

Archaic period From 750 to 500 BCE, a time marked by the extension of networks of Greek colonies—primarily for peaceful, entrepreneurial purposes—around the Aegean rim, the Black Sea, and the entire perimeter of Asia Minor, across southern Italy and Sicily, and along the southern coast of France and the eastern coast of Spain, and along the northern coast of Africa.

Ark of the Covenant A chest containing the stone tables on which the Ten Commandments were inscribed, which Moses received from God on Mount Sinai. Captured by the Philistines around 1050 BCE, the ark was recovered by King David (r. 1005–965 BCE), whose son Solomon (r. 965–928 BCE) built a temple in Jerusalem to house it. The ark vanished after the Babylonians conquered Jerusalem in 586 BCE.

art nouveau   Popular style in art and design in the late 19th century, featuring flowing lines, flower-tracery, and gently erotic female forms.

Ashkenazim   Northern European Jewish cultural tradition uniquely focused on the preservation of Talmudic tradition.

askesis   Stoic term for the peace of mind acquired by the philosophical life. Later used to refer to the Christian "ascetics" who cut themselves off from society.

Assyrians   A strongly militaristic and powerful society (ca. 12th century BCE—612 BCE) of upper Mesopotamia, whose use of iron and steel for weaponry contributed to their formidable conquests.

Atheism   The rejection, or absence, of religious belief.

Augustus   Original title of the Roman emperors; given first to Octavius.

auto-da-fé   A Portuguese term meaning "act of faith." This was a public ritual of confession of sin and consequent humiliation for those deemed heretics by the Inquisition.

avant-garde   "Vanguard," literally. Term popularized by the Dada movement to describe bold artistic experimentation that questions the very idea of art.

Avesta   The holy book of the Zoroastrians.

ayatollah   Arabic, "sign from God"; the supreme clerical authority in Iran.

B

Ba'ath Party   Founded in 1947 by Arab Christian writer Michel Aflaq as the political representation of secular **Pan-Arabism**, applying socialist ideals of state-sponsored care for the masses (from the Arab word for "renaissance").

baby boom   Demographic bubble in the United States (1946–1964) when postwar prosperity and the return of soldiers from combat resulted in an elevated birthrate.

Babylonian Captivity   After the Chaldaeans destroyed Jerusalem and the Temple in 587, they took many of the surviving Jews back east as slaves, where they remained until they were released in 538 BCE by the Persian emperor Cyrus the Great (r. 576–530 BCE).

Balfour Declaration   Agreement (1917) that announced Britain's support for a national Jewish homeland in Palestine.

baptizein   Greek verb meaning "to baptize." Ritual of purification popularized by John the Baptist in 1st-century BCE Palestine. "To plunge or to dunk," literally.

barbaroi   General and pejorative term among ancient Greeks for any non-Greek peoples. English word "barbarian" derives from it.

Baroque Age   Concurrent with the **Ancien Régime**, an era in Europe of extraordinary artistic accomplishment in the service of the tremendously wealthy and privileged aristocratic class.

basileus   Title of the emperors of Byzantium.

Black Death   Successive outbreaks of bubonic plague, beginning in 1347, that killed up to a third of European and Muslim populations over the course of the 14th century.

Blitzkrieg   Nazi strategy of "lightning war" that used rapid motorized firepower to overwhelm an enemy before it could mount a defense.

Bloomsbury Group   Affiliation of writers, artists, and philosophers (including Virginia Woolf and John Maynard Keynes) who met socially in the Bloomsbury district of London in the first decades of the 20th century.

Bolsheviks   Political party led by Vladimir Lenin in the Russian Revolution that overthrew the Russian government in 1917, establishing a form of Communism that maintained power in the Soviet Union until 1991. A variation on classical Marxism, requiring the systematic use of violence, the establishment of a supposedly temporary dictatorship by Party members to effect the overthrow of prerevolutionary practices, and the violent exportation of revolution to other countries.

Book of the Dead   An anthology of prayers, poems, and similar texts collected during the Egyptian Middle Kingdom (2035 BCE–1640 BCE). Placed in the coffin, the Book of the Dead was believed to allow the deceased to enter paradise.

bourgeoisie   The prosperous and primarily urban middle class of Enlightenment Europe.

Boxer Rebellion   Violent attempt (1898–1901) by Chinese peasants, motivated by millennial Buddhist beliefs, to purge Westerners and Western influence from China.

Boyle's law   Discovered by Robert Boyle, states that the volume and pressure of a gas at constant temperature vary inversely.

Bronze Age   The period between 4000 and 1500 BCE characterized by the ability of early Near East inhabitants to smelt copper (and its alloy, bronze, which combines copper with tin) for weapons, farm implements, and tools.

Byzantine Empire   Eastern half of the Roman Empire, with its capital in Constantinople; at its height in the 4th and 5th centuries it included all of today's countries of Libya, Egypt, Israel, Jordan, Lebanon, Syria, Turkey, and most of the Balkan states.

C

caesar Title of the vice emperors under the constitutional reforms created by Diocletian. Later evolved into German and Russian terms for emperor (*kaiser* and *tsar*, respectively).

cahiers de doléances "Grievance notebooks," literally. Records of commoners' complaints compiled for the use of representatives to the Estates General in 1789.

Cairo Declaration on Human Rights Adopted in 1990 by the Organization of the Islamic Conference to replace the earlier (and secular) **Universal Declaration of Human Rights** with a specifically Islamic conceptualization.

caliph Successor to the Prophet Muhammad as political and religious leader of the Islamic world. Meaning "deputy" in the literal sense, in common usage it was roughly comparable to the English word "emperor."

capitulations Trade agreements between the Ottoman Empire and European nations that by the 19th century overwhelmingly favored European interests.

Carolingians Ambitious Frankish dynasty that overthrew the Merovingians, defended western Christendom against Muslim invaders, and united France.

Cathars Christian heresy that posited the existence of two equally strong but diametrically opposed gods—one absolutely good, who created human souls, and one absolutely evil, who created the physical world. Humans are trapped in a cycle of reincarnation until they overcome materialism.

censor A powerful office in the Roman Republic, whose duties were to maintain the census, to administer the state's finances for public works, and to preserve public morals.

census The official list of all citizens of Rome, their property, and legal class.

Central Intelligence Agency (CIA) American governmental agency originally created in 1947 to monitor and deter global Soviet influence. Its mission was officially limited to the gathering of intelligence but in practice the CIA has often engaged in direct political intervention.

chansons de geste Vernacular epic poems of the 11th to 13th century about the heroic deeds of knights. "Songs of deeds."

Chartist movement Labor movement begun by the London Working Men's Association in 1838.

chivalry In 12th-century Europe, an ethic that embraced ideal knightly behavior: comportment, noble demeanor, learning, and piety.

Chosen People The Hebrew Bible describes the Hebrews as God's "Chosen People," by which is meant not just the favor and protection God gives them but their obligation to obey God in all things and to live up to the high moral standards God expects of them.

Christian Democracy Western European ideological hybrid of social conservatism and economic liberalism.

Christian humanism Anticlerical movement of the northern Renaissance that emphasized the simple reading of Scripture (especially the New Testament), the singing of hymns, and communal prayer.

christianities The dozens of versions of early Christianity, each with its own beliefs, liturgical traditions, and customs, that emerged in the earliest years following the death of Jesus.

Church of England Protestant church founded by King Henry VIII of England when he broke with the Catholic Church in 1533. Also known as the Anglican Church; the monarchy is its supreme head.

Ciompi Rebellion Popular uprising in Italy in 1378.

citizenship As articulated by the 19th-century Egyptian reformer Rifa'a al-Tahtawi, a form of group identity that is not determined by race, creed, or ethnicity.

civil rights The guarantee of equal access to all parts of government and society for all members of a society. In the United States, the civil rights movement refers primarily to the struggle of African Americans in the 1960s for equal access.

Classical Age The era beginning with the defense of Greece against Persia lasting until the conquest of Persia by the Greeks under Alexander the Great (479–323 BCE), marked by vitality in civic life, economic prosperity, artistic expression, and literary achievement.

Classicism Artistic movement that replaced the flourishes of the Baroque with a more controlled and formal sensibility.

Cold War Term coined by American financier and presidential adviser Bernard Baruch to describe the relationship (1947–1991) between the Soviet bloc and western nations allied with the United States; each side possessed nuclear weapons, yet neither side dared to either use those weapons or disarm.

College of Cardinals Created by Pope Nicholas II (r. 1059–1061) and given sole power to elect the next pope.

comfort women Term used in imperial Japan for the quarter-million Chinese, Filipino, and other women captured and forced into sexual slavery in World War II.

comitatus An assembly or council of tribal elders among the early Germanic peoples. Term coined by Roman writer Tacitus.

comites Title of the regional governors ("counts") established under the Carolingian emperors in Europe. The term designated officeholders, not a hereditary class.

command economies Economies that aim to provide the highest possible yield for whoever held the raw materials and captive markets

Communism Socialist movement that advocates the destruction of capitalism and the development of a new, classless society of freedom.

The Communist Manifesto Book by Karl Marx and Friedrich Engels (1848) that presents a Marxist view of history as class struggle.

Concordat of Worms Established the independence of the papacy in 1122.

Conference of Berlin International conference (1884–1885) of European nations that established the standards by which any European country could claim an African territory over another European rival, touching off the "Scramble for Africa."

Congress of Vienna Conference of European diplomats convened from 1814 to 1815 to redraw boundaries and work toward peace after decades of conflict.

conquistadores The 16th-century Spanish forces that subdued South and Central America.

conservatism Political approach that values tradition and stability above the individual.

consul In the Roman Republic, the executive office in charge of the government.

Continental System Economic system, implemented by Napoleon, with two key aims: to create an integrated Continental economy and to bring about the collapse of Britain through the imposition of a strict trade embargo.

cottage industry The transfer of textile production from urban industry, where it was controlled by guilds, to rural producers, particularly women. Also known as the "putting-out system."

Council of Trent Ecumenical council convened from 1546 to 1563 to address the challenges of Protestantism by clarifying the teachings and practices of the Catholic church.

Counter-Reformation General reform of Catholic life initiated by the Council of Trent.

covenant The special promise God made to the Jews, symbolized by Moses's leading of the Hebrews out of bondage in Egypt and into the Promised Land; in return, the Jews agreed to live by the Torah.

credit default swap A new kind of financial instrument invented by the J.P. Morgan investment bank in 1994; misuse of the instrument contributed to the 2008 global economic collapse.

Crimean War Rooted in the long-standing desire of Russia to increase its influence over the Ottoman Empire, the immediate cause of the war had to do with Russian claims to protective oversight over Orthodox Christians in the Ottoman Empire, but more strategic goals were at stake. The war (1853–1856) pitted France and Britain, who were allied with the Ottomans, against Russia. While Russia accepted unfavorable terms at a conference in Paris in 1856 that ended the conflict, both sides performed ineptly, a fact that became widely known because the war was the first conflict to be covered by journalists and photographers.

crossbow Brutally efficient weapon, whose metal darts could pierce armor; it was the first weapon to be banned by the Catholic Church.

Cuban Missile Crisis Standoff between the Soviet Union and the United States in 1962, when Soviet leader Nikita Khrushchev built military bases in Cuba equipped with nuclear missiles. After two weeks of intense negotiations, Khrushchev withdrew the missiles.

cuius regio Full phrase is *Cuius regio, eius religio,* meaning "the religion of the ruler decides the religion of the realm." Compromise determined to settle the Wars of Religion in the 16th and 17th centuries. The policy guaranteed certain basic rights to the nonestablished religions.

cult of domesticity Sentimental cultural view in the 19th century that idealized women's role in the home, discouraging them from seeking work or other opportunities outside of their domestic duties.

cuneiform Technique of writing developed in Mesopotamia whereby wedge-shaped marks were impressed in clay tablets.

curiales The class of urban elites in ancient Rome who, though unsalaried, were responsible for municipal government and tax collection; obliged to make up any shortfalls in civic finance from their own personal wealth, they were entitled to retain a portion of the tax revenues they collected for personal use.

D

Dark Ages The period in Western Europe from the 4th to the 8th centuries, so named because of the chaos that reigned after the fall of the western Roman Empire and the endless depredations of various barbarian invasions.

decolonization European withdrawal during the 20th century from its former colonies.

Deism   Enlightenment-era belief in a single and possibly benevolent God who created the cosmos—but who plays no active role in it. As a result, a dual policy of religious freedom and of freedom from religious intolerance is essential to human progress.

Delian League   A military alliance formed in 478 BCE (Athens assumed control a year later) among all the Greek poleis, dedicated to maintaining a strong defense—particularly against Persia.

détente   A "loosening" of tensions between two nations. Used especially to describe efforts to improve diplomatic ties between the United States and the Soviet Union in the 1970s and 1980s. Ironically, *détente* is also a colloquial French term for the trigger of a gun.

dhimmi   Legal status of Jewish and Christian populations living under Muslim rule; officially granted freedom of religion, Jews and Christians had to accept certain restrictions on their communal practice and pay a poll tax (jizya) in return for Islamic protection. Restrictions include bans on any public expression of faith and curtailment of the ability to build or repair synagogues and churches.

dialectical materialism   In Marxist theory, the idea that history is driven forward by materialist concerns; to Lenin, this led inevitably to confrontation between the proletariat and the bourgeoisie.

Diaspora   The "exile" or "scattering" of the Hebrews after the Assyrians brutally conquered the Kingdom of Israel in 721 BCE and the Chaldaeans (or Neo-Babylonians) conquered Judah in 587 BCE.

Diet   The medieval German parliament.

Directory   In Prussia, companies of royal commissioners and civil servants who controlled financial and judicial affairs in the provinces on behalf of the king.

Documentary Hypothesis   The belief of many modern Biblical scholars that the Torah was compiled from four original sources: "J," by the Yahwist (ca. 950 BCE); "E," by the Elohist (ca. 750 BCE); "D," by the Deuteronomist (ca. 650 BCE); and "P," by the Priestly Author (ca. 550 BCE).

Dominicans   Mendicant order focused on education that established schools across Europe.

E

Edict of Milan   Issued by Constantine in 313 CE, legalizing Christianity and guaranteeing religious freedom for all faiths within the empire.

Edict of Nantes   Decree by Henri IV in 1598 that guaranteed religious freedom, with certain restrictions, throughout France.

Edict of Toleration   See **Edict of Milan**.

Elect   To Calvinists, those predestined for salvation.

emir   A military or naval commander, petty prince, or provincial governor.

enclosure movement   Trend of aristocratic landowners toward evicting small farmers (by enclosing formerly open fields with stone walls or hedges) and instead using those fields for the more profitable grazing of livestock, especially sheep.

Enlightenment   Term coined in the second half of the 18th century to describe an array of intellectual and cultural activities of the 1700s distinguished by a worldview informed by rational values and scientific inquiry.

Entente Cordiale   Diplomatic agreement between England and France in 1904, whereby each country recognized the other's spheres of influence in northern Africa.

Epic of Gilgamesh   One of the earliest known works of literature, originating in Sumer but first recorded by Babylonian scribes; relates the adventures of the semimythical Sumerian king Gilgamesh as he battles gods and monsters in pursuit of enlightenment.

Epicureanism   Philosophy based on the work of the Greek philosopher Epicurus (341 BCE—270 BCE) that promoted a life free of pain and fear as the way to happiness.

epistemology   The philosophical inquiry into the nature of knowledge (and, by extension, learning).

Essenes   An ascetic and eschatological sect within Second Temple Judaism.

Estates General   French parliament, established by the Capetian kings. Reestablished in 1789 (after having last met in 1614) at the behest of the French aristocracy. The three estates were the nobles, the clergy, and the common people.

Etruscans   A literate and prosperous people who associated with the Latins and profoundly influenced the emerging religious and moral culture of Rome.

European Union   United group of independent European nations established in 1993 to provide a process for coordinating policies formed at the level of member states.

evangelicalism   Protestant style of worship developed in Protestant church that emphasizes the work of the Holy Spirit in the world and the centrality of Biblical truth while retaining more of the traditional elements of Protestant denominations.

existentialism   Rationalist philosophy associated with Jean-Paul Sartre whose key tenet, "existence precedes essence," demands that we take action and make something of the world, or at least of our lives in it.

F

familia The essential social unit of the Roman Republic, comprising an entire household.

fasces Name of the symbol of Roman power over its citizenry—a battle-ax lashed to a bundle of birch rods. The root of the modern term **Fascism**.

Fascism The belief that force, directly applied to achieve a specific end, is the best form of government, exemplified by the dictatorships of Adolf Hitler (r. 1934–1945)and Benito Mussolini (r. 1922–1945).

Fatimids Dynasty of Shi'a rulers in 10th-century Egypt in parts of the Holy Land and Syria; they derived their name from Fatimah, the daughter of the Prophet Muhammad.

fatwa An Islamic legal pronouncement.

feminist movement A series of movements from the 19th century through the present day that aim to reform policies and practices that oppress the rights and well-being of women.

Fertile Crescent The region of the Middle East roughly framed by the Mediterranean to the west, the Arabian Peninsula to the south, and the Tarsus and Zagros Mountains to the north and east. The Tigris and Euphrates rivers flow through the center of this region, whose rich soils and abundant water gave rise to early agriculture. The Fertile Crescent connected central Asian and eastern Mediterranean economies.

feudal bonds The relationship between lord and vassal, whereby the lord granted dominion over property to the vassal in exchange for the vassal's pledge of service to the lord.

Final Solution Nazi program of systematic deportation and murder of Jews throughout Germany and all German-occupied territories during World War II.

al-fitnah "Rebellion." Used to describe an uprising against an impious ruler (not merely an unjust one).

Fourteen Points Woodrow Wilson's proposal, presented to the Paris Peace Conference (1919), for rebuilding Europe in the aftermath of World War I; ultimately rejected because of French and British concerns.

Franciscans Mendicant order established by Saint Francis of Assisi (1181–1226) dedicated to preaching and service to the urban poor.

Freemasonry Secret society that claimed its origins lay in medieval trade guilds; its members, wealthy bourgeoisie and noblemen alike, met in private clubs (or "lodges") to conduct business.

Freidenkerbund "Freethinkers' League." An early secularist group in Germany, formed in the 19th century.

Fronde Rebellion of French aristocrats against the tax policies of Cardinal Mazarin, during the regency for the underage King Louis XIV. Began in 1648.

fundamentalism American Protestant style of worship that insists on the presence of a fundamental Truth in every Scriptural passage and urges personal and societal reform before the approach of Armageddon; from the 1980s, fundamentalism has had considerable influence on American politics, particularly the Republican Party.

G

Gastarbeiter The "guestworkers," chiefly from Turkey, welcomed into Germany in the postwar era to rebuild the nation. German labor shortage necessitated the importing of workers.

General Theory of Relativity Einstein's theory (1915) describing gravity's relationship to space-time.

genocide Term coined in 1944 by Raphael Lemkin , a lawyer and Polish Jew, to describe the extermination of a particular racial or ethnic group, such as Germany's **Final Solution**.

Ghettos Segregated communities of Jews in European cities.

Gini coefficient Standard for measuring wealth and income distributions, named for Italian statistician Corrado Gini (1884–1965).

Girondins One of several factions during the French Revolution; a relatively moderate group, they championed a constitutional monarchy until they were driven from power by the more radical Jacobins.

glasnost "Openness," literally, in Russian. Specifically, the policy in the Soviet Union under Premier Mikhail Gorbachev to relax the traditional censorship of Soviet television, radio, and print media and to permit greater freedom of speech.

Glorious Revolution Coup in 1688 that deposed the Catholic king James II of England and replaced him with the popular Protestant ruler of Holland, William of Orange (who was married to James II's daughter Mary).

gold standard Monetary system, initially introduced in the West by Britain in 1821 and abandoned by most countries in the aftermath of the Great Depression, that pegs a currency to the price of gold.

Good Friday Accord Treaty signed in 1998 that ended eighty years of terrorist conflict in Northern Ireland.

Great Depression (1929–1936) Global economic depression that began with the crash of the New York Stock Exchange on October 29, 1929, resulting in massive unemployment and economic crises worldwide.

Greater West   The matrix of European and Near Eastern cultures originating in the Fertile Crescent and still resonant today through bonds of trade, intellectual cross-fertilization, cultural overlap, and religious rivalry.

Great Purge   Brutal efforts, beginning with show trials in 1936, by Josef Stalin (r. 1931–1953) to eliminate anyone he considered an enemy of the Soviet Union.

guild   Artisanal and commercial trade associations that set prices, quality standards, methods and volume of production, and wages paid to workers. Guilds also assigned market shares to individual artisans or merchants.

gulag   Network of Soviet Russian prison camps used to incarcerate political dissidents and enemies. Begun under Lenin and greatly expanded under Stalin, the gulag accounted for the deaths of roughly a million prisoners annually from the 1930s to the 1980s.

gynaeceum   Area of a private home in ancient Greece restricted to women, their children, and their servants. Greek women were strictly segregated from public life and did not enter public areas of their own homes without the permission of their husbands.

H

hadith   The written record of the actions and non-Qur'anic teachings of the Prophet Muhammad. The two most significant collections are those by al-Bukhari (d. 870) and al-Muslim (d. 875).

haeresis   Term for the "philosophical sects" among the Jews of ancient Palestine (Pharisees, Sadducees, Essenes). Later used to refer to the "heresies" of post-Nicean Christianity.

hajj   The pilgrimage of Muslims to Mecca, held annually. All able-bodied Muslims are expected to undertake the hajj at least once in their lives.

Hamas   Conservative religious-political Palestinian group (and offshoot of the **Muslim Brotherhood**) equally devoted to charitable campaigns and social work among the Palestinians and to a terrorist war upon Israel.

Haredim   The so-called Ultra-Orthodox Jews of Israel; they make up somewhere between 5 and 10 percent of the population.

Hasidim   Adherents to a revivalist movement in Judaism, started in the mid-18th century in the Polish-Lithuanian Commonwealth by the Ba'al Shem Tov (d. 1760). Using highly emotive language and physical expression, Hasidic Judaism challenged the rather staid formalism of synagogue worship.

Haskalah   Hebrew term for "enlightenment."

Hellenistic Age   The era beginning with the death of Alexander the Great (323 BCE) and concluding with the conquest of the East by the Romans (327 BCE) and marked by a broader degree of cultural cohesion than previous eras, including the development of a common dialect of Greek (**Koine**) used across the territories. Although art and literature did not flourish as they did in the Classical Age, tremendous advances were made in the sciences.

heliocentrism   First articulated by Copernicus, the observation that Earth is one of several planets that orbit around a stationary sun.

helot   Slave owned by the city-state of ancient Sparta. Comprising roughly 75 percent of the Spartan population, they performed virtually all the labor, leaving the Spartans themselves free to perform military and civic service.

hetaera   Ancient Greek courtesan, skilled in music and witty conversation in addition to her erotic services.

hieroglyphs   System of writing used in ancient Egypt, especially in official records.

higher criticism   Scholarly study of the Bible that seeks to determine the origins of the Biblical texts in time and place, in the process challenging long-held beliefs about the authority of Scripture. Synonymous with **historical criticism**.

hijab   The "covering" of women required in Islamic society. Varies widely from country to country, depending on ethnicity, denomination, and to some extent to class. Least extensive covering is a simple headscarf; most extensive is the full-length burqa.

Hijrah   The migration, or exodus, of Prophet Muhammad and his company of the faithful from Mecca to Madina in 622 CE. Marks Year 1 in the Islamic calendar (1 AH).

historical criticism   See **higher criticism**.

historical materialism   In Marxist theory, the process by which economic concerns propel historical change.

Hittites   Indo-European group that settled in north-central Anatolia and by 1700 BCE had united into a single kingdom whose military repeatedly challenged Mesopotamia and Egypt.

Holocaust   The systematic murder of six million Jews by the Nazis.

honestiores   The senatorial and equestrian classes, municipal officials, and army veterans and their status entitling them to immunity from torture, lesser criminal fines, and, in capital crimes, exemption from crucifixion.

honor killings   In some Muslim countries, and among some Arab immigrant communities in the

West, the murder of Arab women thought to have tarnished the honor of their families. The murder of these women by family members is believed to restore the family's honor.

hoplites   Ancient Greek infantrymen serving in a phalanx; name derives from Greek word (*hoplos*) for the smallish, circular shields they carried.

household gods   Family deities who watched over the family's farmland, household, and possessions. The daily worship of the household gods was the responsibility of the paterfamilias.

hubris   Arrogant self-pride, the deadliest of moral sins to the ancient Greeks; specifically, the delusional belief that one was in control of one's own fate. Frequently used as the plot device to trigger the dire events in Greek tragedy.

Huguenots   The Calvinists in 16th-century France, led by Henri de Navarre.

humiliores   Everyone in the Roman Empire apart from the honestiores and the slaves (the latter, in terms of the law, were counted as property rather than people). The humiliores were expected to obey the law, pay their taxes, participate in public religious rites, and hold to the ethical duties of family care and public service.

Hundred Years' War   From 1337 to 1453 CE; fought between England and France, beginning when England's king Edward III (r. 1327–1377) laid claim to the French throne; France (led, at one point, by the young girl Joan of Arc) eventually won.

Hyksos ascendancy   The Second Intermediate Period (1640–1570 BCE) of the Middle Kingdom, so named because of the revolt of foreign laborers against the Egyptian government.

I

Ideal Forms   In Plato's philosophy, the concept of a perfect and ultimate reality, of which our own perceived reality is but a flawed and flimsy reflection. Because we have a dualistic nature composed of an eternal soul temporarily housed in a flawed and mortal body, we can apprehend and aspire to that perfection.

ijma'   Arabic, "consensus"; in the Sunni tradition, a principle that embraced the use of reason to resolve a religious question among a community of scholars. Once the community's answer on any given questioned had been authoritatively expressed, the question was considered closed for all time.

The Iliad   Epic composed by Homer (ca. 750 BCE) recounting the events of the Trojan War in the Mycenaean age many centuries earlier. The epic evokes a lost, heroic, semimythological, and highly romanticized version of Greek history.

illuminationism   Twelfth-century Persian philosophical program that attempts to harmonize Sufism, Shi'ism, and rational philosophy.

imam   In Sunni Islam, a community leader who recites Qur'anic verses during prayer services. In Shi'ite Islam, a charismatic spiritual leader, a successor and descendant of Prophet Muhammad through the line of Fatima and Ali.

imperator   Title assumed by Augustus and all subsequent rulers of Rome; often translated as "emperor" but in the Republic referred to a triumphant military general.

imperialism   European (and, later, American as well) dominance of non-Western cultures for the exploitation of natural resources as well as political gain.

Index of Forbidden Books   A list of books proscribed by the Catholic Church, first published in 1599 and continually revised until its final suppression in 1966.

Indo-European   A horde of nomadic and herding nations, loosely related by their dialects of the language family, who began to migrate from their homeland near the Black Sea toward western Europe, the Aegean, and Asia Minor from about 2000 BCE. Other groups migrated eastward.

indulgences   Donations to the Catholic Church as a means of satisfying the requirements for the forgiveness of sin.

industrial revolution   The burgeoning 19th-century economy driven by mechanization, factories, an investment in infrastructure, and a growing workforce

Inquisition   Campaign by the Catholic Church to identify and correct heresy; heretics who would not admit their errors were punished, in some instances brutally.

intendants   Officials appointed by the royal court in Versailles to oversee the administrative work of the aristocracy during the Age of Absolutism.

intifada   "Uprising." Organized mass protests of Palestinians against Israeli occupation of the West Bank and Gaza (1987–1993). The Second Intifada lasted from 2000 to 2005.

Ionian League   An alliance (ca. 750 BCE) of several Greek coastal cities in Asia Minor organized by the vibrant and prosperous city of Miletus.

'ird   Arabic, "honor" or "purity"; in Islam, a quality that women either possessed or did not possess. If a woman lost that quality, the moral shame spread to her family; the only way to redeem the family's honor was to kill the woman who had transgressed.

Irish Republican Army   Terrorist group founded in the 1910s to fight what it saw as

English tyranny and Protestant oppression of Catholics in Northern Ireland

Iron Curtain   Military and ideological barrier dividing the Soviet bloc from western Europe between 1945 and 1990.

Islam   Religion founded by the Prophet Muhammad (570–632). In Arabic, the word "islam" means "surrender" and implies the fundamental duty of mankind to submit to the absolute authority of Allah.

isonomia   Equality before the law. The term originates with the ancient Greek reformer Cleisthenes, but the notion of a single standard of behavior for all members of a community dates back to the ancient Hebrews.

Israel   One of two Hebrew kingdoms (937–721 BCE), this one in the north of Palestine with Shechem as its capital.

J

Jacobins   Radical party that seized power from the Girondists during the French Revolution. Resolutely antimonarchist, the Jacobins executed King Louis XVI and his family in 1793, outlawed Christianity, and sought to create a classless society based on radical principles.

Jacquerie   Popular uprising in France (1358).

al-Jahiliyya   Term (literally "Age of Ignorance" or "Age of Barbarism") used by Arab historians to describe the era between the death of Jesus and the birth of Muhammad.

Janissaries   Elite military caste in the Ottoman Empire, 14th–19th centuries. The ranks of Janissaries were filled with Christian children, either orphaned or kidnapped from their parents, who were then converted and given a special, highly disciplined, military upbringing.

Jesuits   Ecclesiastical order, founded by Saint Ignacio de Loyola in 1540, particularly devoted to education and missionary work.

jihad   "Struggle," literally. Refers to any conscious, intentional, and persistent effort to advance the cause of Islam in the world. The term has a broad range of meanings, from something as innocuous as a personal vow to live a more committed Islamic life to a determination to wage religious war against the perceived enemies of God.

jizya   Poll tax levied on all non-Muslims in an Islamic state.

Judah   One of two Hebrew kingdoms (937—721 BCE), this one in the south of Palestine and centered on Jerusalem. (See **Israel**.)

judges   As described in the Bible, the leaders of each of the twelve tribes of Hebrews who moved into Palestine around 1200 BCE, after being delivered from Egypt.

Junkers   Landed aristocracy in Brandenburg-Prussia in the 17th–18th centuries. In popular usage the term came in the 19th century to designate all types of conservative, wealthy elites.

justification by faith alone   Luther's understanding that one attains salvation not through the purchasing of **indulgences** or other outward acts but simply by having faith in Christ.

K

Ka'ba   The holiest shrine of Islam. Temple in Mecca housing the stone believed to mark the site of Abraham's altar to Allah. Originally a pagan shrine dedicated to all the deities of the pre-Islamic Arab tribes. Site of the **hajj**.

Kabbala   A mystical interpretation of scripture developed by rabbis that became newly popular in the 17th century in part via the influence of Sabbatai Zvi (1626–1676).

kalam   "Theology." Unsystematic effort to provide rational explanation of basic religious mysteries in early Islam on the nature of the Qur'an and the attributes of Allah.

khalifah al-rasul Allah   "Deputy of the Prophet of God," literally. Title of the ruler (caliph) of the Islamic empire.

khan   The hereditary leader of a given tribe of Mongols.

King James Bible   English translation of the Scriptures commissioned in 1604 by King James I of England.

Koine   The demotic form of Greek used throughout the Middle East during the Hellenistic Age and the early Christian era.

Kristallnacht   "Crystal Night," literally; the "Night of Broken Glass," poetically. The organized Nazi attacks on Jewish businesses, synagogues, and homes throughout Germany on November 9, 1938. Widely regarded as the turning point from Nazi anti-Semitic discrimination to blatant pursuit of genocide.

kulak   "Fist," literally. Term popularized by Lenin and Stalin to designate relatively wealthy peasant freeholders who opposed the Communist regime in early 20th-century Russia.

Kulturkampf   Otto von Bismarck's "cultural war" against Catholicism in Germany.

Kyoto Protocol   International agreement, adopted in 1997, to combat global warming by reducing greenhouse gas emissions. The United States is not among the almost two hundred nations who have since signed and ratified the protocol.

L

laissez-faire "Leave it alone," literally. Term used to identify the economic doctrine of allowing markets to self-regulate, without government interference. First articulated by Adam Smith in *The Wealth of Nations* (1776).

Lares The ancestral household gods that protected homes in the Roman world; also the statuettes that represented them in family shrines.

Late Antiquity Term ancient historians use for the Dark Ages.

Lateran Agreement Agreement (1929) between Mussolini and Pope Pius XI that recognized the Vatican as a sovereign state in exchange for the Catholic Church's support of Mussolini's Fascist regime.

latifundia Slave-worked plantations in ancient Rome, especially during the republic.

Latins Name of the original settlers of the region of Latium.

League of Augsburg Alliance forged by Holy Roman emperor Leopold I in 1686 for defense against French expansionism; members included England, the Low Countries, Sweden, and several German principalities as well as the Holy Roman Empire.

League of Nations Woodrow Wilson's proposed international body that would arbitrate disputes, oversee demilitarization, and provide for collective security.

Lebensraum "Living space," literally. The conviction that the territorial losses forced upon Germany by the Treaty of Versailles (1919) had denied the German people sufficient space in which to live and thrive. Under the Nazis, it evolved into the policy of demanding the unification of all German-inhabited lands.

legatus Commander of a legion selected by the Roman emperor from members of the Senate. In smaller provinces, the legate also served as the provincial governor.

liberalism Political view calling for civil liberties, equality under the law, the right to vote, and a free market economy.

Libertas ecclesie "Freedom for the Church!" Popular rallying cry of the Peace of God reform movement in the 10th and 11th centuries.

libertarian Political stance that supports very small and highly limited government and opposes almost all forms of taxation.

Linear A Script used by Minoan culture on ancient Crete. Underlying language has not been identified, and hence the script has not been deciphered.

Linear B Syllabic script used by ancient Mycenaeans in Crete. Underlying Language is an early dialect of Greek, and the script was deciphered by 1953.

logos "Word," literally. Neoplatonic term for the spirit of wisdom that lies at the center of creation, from which emanate the **Ideal Forms** and all the elements of the cosmos. Term adopted by early Christians (see Gospel of John) to refer to Christ as the "Word of God" made flesh.

Lollards Anticlerical heretical group that condemned Catholic corruption and worldliness, believed in the right of nonpriests to preach, and taught that to live according to the spirit of Christ was more important than to follow the many letters of the church's laws.

longbow Fourteenth-century innovation in weapons technology that, by moving bow-and-arrow weapons from cavalry to infantry, allowed for the length of the bow to be greatly increased and therefore the range of its arrows considerably expanded.

lord In the feudal system, the figure who could grant vassals dominion over manors.

lugal Old Sumerian title of city-state kings in Mesopotamia.

Lyceum School founded by the philosopher Aristotle in Athens in 335 BCE.

M

ma'at Concept of cosmic order in ancient Egypt, everything being in perfect balance; includes the notions of meaning, justice, and truth, although in a passive sense, asking people not to upset divine harmony by attempting to alter the political and religious order.

madrasa Islamic religious school attached, administratively and often physically, to a mosque. Study focused on memorization of the Qur'an, with subsequent forays into Islamic law and literature.

magi Zoroastrian priests.

Maginot Line Barricade of artillery casements, machine-gun pillboxes, tank formations, barbed wire, minefields, and concrete bunkers built by France along its border with Germany.

Magna Carta Agreement in 1215 between the king of England and English lords, establishing certain constraints on royal power.

Magna Mater The "Great Mother," Cybele. There was a passionate religious cult dedicated to this life-giving goddess. A rival for popularity with Christianity.

Mahdi Messianic figure expected by Shi'ite Muslims; believed to be the return of the "Hidden Imam" who has gone into seclusion until the end of time.

mamluk A slave-soldier in the medieval Islamic world.

mandates Semi-independent states created in the Middle East by the League of Nations after World War I, dividing territories of the former Ottoman Empire between Britain and France.

Manhattan Project Secret American program to develop an atomic bomb, begun in 1939 under the scientific direction of J. Robert Oppenheimer.

manors In a feudal system, collective farms under the authority of lords.

Mare Nostrum To Romans, the Mediterranean ("Our Sea" in Latin).

market Term coined by economist Adam Smith (1776) to describe commerce as a rational pattern of human behavior.

Marshall Plan American plan to rebuild western Europe after World War II by providing cash, credit, raw materials, and technical assistance to jump-start industrial production.

al-ma'siyah "Disobedience." Justified resistance to a ruler or government who violates religious law.

maskilim "Enlightened Ones," literally. Jewish religious scholars in the 18th century who worked to harmonize Jewish tradition with the principles of the Enlightenment.

mawali Non-Arab Muslim converts in the Islamic empire.

medieval In western Europe, the period between the end of the Dark Ages and the beginning of the Renaissance.

Mehmet Ali Pasha Pro-Western dynastic leader of Egypt (r. 1805–1848) who built a powerful Egyptian military force, professionalized the government along Western lines, and developed both industry and education.

mendicant orders Groups (such as the Dominicans and the Franciscans) dedicated to assisting the clergy in the performance of their evangelical mission.

Mensheviks Faction of the Russian Revolution that was generally more moderate than Lenin's **Bolshevik** faction and was ultimately defeated by the Bolsheviks in 1917.

mercantilism The economic policy of absolutism, defining economic wealth as tangible assets and promoting protectionism with the aim of concentrating wealth among as few individuals as possible.

Merovingians Warrior dynasty who ruled as kings of the Franks from ca. 500 to the ascent of the Carolingians (ca. 754).

messiah In the Jewish tradition, an earthly savior who would bring justice and create a safe, unified state for the Jews.

Midrash Rabbinic literature that explicates Biblical texts.

miles/milites Term for the warlord(s) of the 10th and 11th centuries who emerged from the breakup of the Carolingian Empire. By 12th century the term is translated as "knight(s)."

Minoan An ancient and wealthy commercial culture that flourished from 2000 to 1500 BCE, centered on the island of Crete and named for its legendary founder, King Minos. Later Greek culture and mythology were profoundly influenced by the Minoans, and one of the two written scripts (called Linear B) used by Minoans records an early form of Greek.

missi dominici Itinerant representatives of the Carolingian emperor, sent out to check on the job performance of the comites in the provinces.

modernism 1. To the Catholic Church in the early 20th century, a deplorable trend toward intellectual novelty that trivialized Scriptural truth and claimed "that there is nothing divine in sacred tradition [of the Church]." 2. Highly diverse cultural movement (roughly 1860–1950) that simultaneously rejects previous attitudes about how artists should work and resists the contemporary impersonality of mass-produced culture.

monasticism In the rapidly Christianizing world, the movement to reject normal family and social life, along with the concern for wealth, status, and power, in favor of a harsh life of solitude and spiritual discipline in communities of other monks.

Mongols Diverse group of nomadic Asian tribes that, through a series of brutal conquests in China, Russia, and the Muslim world, covered at its height in 1279 nearly one quarter of the Earth's land surface.

monotheism The belief in a single, supreme deity.

Morgengab The morning gift owed by a husband to his bride after the wedding night, in compensation for her lost virginity, among early Germanic peoples.

mullah A Persian word used primarily in non-Arabic speaking Shi'i Muslim countries (e.g., Iran, Afghanistan, Pakistan) to designate a low-level cleric. It is a term of respect rather than a designation of office. With a literal meaning of "guardian" or "caretaker," it carries a colloquial sense analogous to the English word *reverend*, stripped of any ecclesial meaning. Used primarily by Shi'i Muslims and throughout Pakistan and India by both Sunnis and Shi'a.

Mulla Sadra The greatest Muslim philosopher of the modern era; his most important book is *The Four Journeys of the Intellect* (1638).

Muslim Brotherhood Religious-political group founded in Egypt in 1928 that, after years of repression by Egypt's military and secular regime, assumed power following elections in 2011.

mut'a A form of concubinage or "temporary marriage" permitted among Shi'i Muslims. Such marriages could be as short as twenty-four hours, as a means of legitimizing sexual activity.

Mu'tazilites Dissident Muslim scholars who, counter to the tradition of **ijma'**, believed that whenever tradition and reason were in conflict, the scale tipped in reason's favor.

Mycenaean Greece Society (1600 to 1200 BCE) marked by the dominance of mainland Hellenes in the Aegean region; named for the city of Mycenae, which according to tradition was the city ruled by the legendary King Agamemnon.

N

al-Nahda Arabic, "awakening" or "renaissance"; nineteenth-century Islamic intellectual and cultural movement centered in Egypt that advocated the integration of Islamic and European culture.

Napoleonic Code Systematic law code established by Napoleon that (among other principals) emphasized individuals' rights to property and standardized the legal structures for contracts, leases, and establishing stock corporations.

nationalism A collective consciousness or awareness that the members of an individual nation-group share a depth of feelings, values, and attitudes toward the world.

naturalism European literary movement (1850–1914) that aimed to depict the whole array of pressures, demands, irritations, and longings that shape human lives in as much specific and realistic detail as possible. Sometimes used (though inaccurately) as a synonym for Realism.

Neo-Lutheranism German religious movement of the mid-19th century that sought to reaffirm the distinctive Lutheran heritage. However, adherents were divided among conservatives who argued for scriptural inerrancy, moderates who privileged the institutional tradition of Lutheranism, and more liberally inclined believers who believed that traditional faith and the new sciences could be harmonized.

neoorthodoxy Protestant theology founded by Swiss Calvinist theologian Karl Barth (1886–1968) that emphasizes the absolute strangeness and "complete Otherness" of God.

Neoplatonism Spiritual philosophy derived from Plato that influenced both late Roman paganism and early Christian theologians.

New Deal American economic initiatives launched by Franklin Delano Roosevelt to help the nation recover from the Great Depression by increasing government spending to employ men and women, provide price supports for farmers, offer unemployment insurance and retirement benefits, and create welfare programs.

New Historians Young Jewish scholars and journalists, mostly born in Israel, whose archival research and writing has led to a more complex and less idealistic understanding of Zionism and the founding of Israel.

New Testament Canon of twenty-seven works written after the death of Christ by or about various apostles.

new woman The subject of innumerable journalistic and literary works in Europe, America, and parts of the Islamic world; a woman who, thanks to tremendous economic, cultural, and political shifts, was free to travel, get an education, and have a career.

Nicene Creed Statement of fundamental Christian beliefs issued by an ecumenical council convened by Constantine in 323–325.

nihilism Philosophical position of extreme skepticism that holds existence to be random, even meaningless.

Ninety-Five Theses A list, published by Martin Luther in 1517, of assertions condemning the theology of indulgences.

noble savage The idea, popularized by Jean Jacques Rousseau (1712–1778), that non-Europeans are untainted by civilization's corrupting influences.

nome An economic and administrative district in ancient Egypt, composed of towns and villages along defined segments of the Nile River. The chief administrator of each nome was called a *nomarch*.

North Atlantic Treaty Organization (NATO) Defensive alliance created by the United States in 1949 to protect Western Europe.

Nuremberg Trials Trials of Nazi leaders for war crimes before an international tribunal of judges and prosecutors from the Allied countries, held in 1945–1946 in Nuremberg, Germany.

O

Oath of Supremacy In Britain, an oath to recognize the monarch as the supreme head of the church within the realm. The oath effectively excluded Irish Catholics from holding public office or playing any part in public life.

Olympian deities   The numerous gods, worshipped by the ancient Greeks, whose passions and exploits are recounted in Greek mythology.

On the Origin of Species by Means of Natural Selection   Book by Charles Darwin (1859) that set forth his theory of natural selection as the means by which evolution occurs.

Organization of Petroleum Exporting Countries   Group of twelve oil-exporting countries that strongly influences both the production and the pricing of oil. A 1973 boycott by OPEC drove gas prices to record levels, disrupting the American economy.

Ottoman Turks   Dynasty founded by Osman (r. 1281–1324) that established a powerful state from the Balkans to Mesopotamia to North Africa.

Oxford Movement   Mid-19th-century English movement to reinforce the traditions of Anglican Christianity.

P

pacifism   In the aftermath of World War I, a term used to describe any principled and total rejection of violence as a means of resolving disputes.

Pale of Settlement   Region of Russian Empire where Jews were allowed to live (they were generally not allowed to live anywhere else in Russia), and the site of devastating pogroms in the late 19th century.

Palestinian Liberation Organization (PLO)   Political organization of Palestinian Arabs created in 1964 in opposition to the existence of the Jewish state of Israel.

Pan-Arabism   Ideology promoting the unification of all Arabs, particularly in opposition to Western imperialism. See **Ba'ath Party**.

Pan-Slavism   Populist approach of Tsar Aleksandr III (r. 1881–1894) that resulted in vicious persecution of Russian Jews, who were portrayed as exploiters of the common Russian people.

Pantheon   A temple built by the emperor Hadrian (r. 117–138 CE) in Rome and dedicated to the whole roster of major deities within the empire.

parlements   Ancient French aristocratic-led system of legal courts reestablished during the regency of Louis XV as a way to extend aristocratic privileges; Louis XV tried to overturn the parlements when he came of age.

paterfamilias   In the Roman Republic, the head (always male) of a household. The paterfamilias had complete authority over the familia and was the sole possessor of its property.

patria potestas   "Paternal power," the authority given by Roman law and custom to the male head of a household. Patria potestas gave the man possession of everything owned by the members of his household and gave him the power of life and death over every member except his wife.

patrilinear   Describes a social system in Mesopotamia and elsewhere, a society in which only men can inherit property.

Pax Romana   The "Roman Peace," a period of general peace and prosperity in the Roman Empire from Augustus (d. 14 CE) to Marcus Aurelius (d. 180 CE).

Peace of Augsburg   Compromise settlement (1555) between Charles V and Lutheran princes that granted Lutheranism legal recognition. With this policy, the religion of the local ruler determined the state religion of the principality, with certain guarantees offered of the rights of the religious minority.

Peace of God   Tenth-century rallies, initiated by peasants, for reform of the control warlords had over the church.

Peace of Westphalia   A collection of treaties (1648) negotiated by the first general diplomatic congress in Western history. Involving over one hundred delegations, it brought a century of European conflict to a close.

Peasants' Revolt   Popular uprising in England in 1381.

Peloponnesian War   (431–404 BCE) Prolonged war between Athens, which sought to dominate all of Greece, and Sparta, one of the last holdouts against Athenian supremacy. An epidemic of typhus in 429 BCE weakened Athens, while the Spartans' alliance with Persia allowed them to challenge and defeat the Athenian navy.

Pentecostalism   American Protestant style of worship that is charismatic, even antiintellectual, in its emphasis on a mystical union with God manifested by the ability to speak in tongues and perform miraculous healings.

perestroika   Collective term for the economic policies of Mikhail Gorbachev in the Soviet Union that allowed for the limited introduction of free-market mechanisms. "Restructuring," literally.

phalanx   A fighting unit of Greek foot soldiers: eight horizontal lines of ten to twenty men each, who stood shoulder to shoulder and moved as a single unit.

Pharisees   One of three "philosophical sects" into which Judean society was divided. Unlike other Jews, they held a belief in the immortality of the soul and the resurrection of the dead; they also anticipated the arrival of a messiah.

phenomenology Philosophy associated with Edmund Husserl (1859–1938) and based on the belief that whereas the world may or may not be rationally ordered, our reactions to it are.

Philistines An urban, commercial people with origins in Mycenaean Greece who settled just south of Phoenicia and engaged in hostilities against the Hebrews.

philosophes Self-chosen term for the thinkers and writers of the Enlightenment, applied to all regardless of their ethnicity.

Phoenicians A seafaring culture that established a trade network across the islands of the Mediterranean and the northern coast of Africa; the Phoenician alphabet formed the basis of the later Greek alphabet, and their great city of Carthage (established in the 9th century BCE) later challenged Rome for domination of the entire Mediterranean.

picaresque Like *Gargantua and Pantagruel*, a literary work that is a series of loosely connected and frequently funny or scatological episodes.

plebeians The class of free landowning Roman citizens, represented in the government of the Roman Republic by the plebeian council.

plenitudo potestatis The Roman Catholic Church's "fullness of power." Describes the church's obligation to speak out on any aspect of life with a significant moral component and its right to be heard. The policy was fully enunciated in the 13th century.

pogroms Beginning in 1881, vicious attacks from 1648 on against entire Jewish communities in the **Pale of Settlement**.

polis The ancient Greek city-state (plural form *poleis*).

pontifex maximus In ancient Rome, a title ("chief priest") held by the pagan emperor; the Christian emperor Constantine used this precedent to declare himself the head of the Christian church as well.

populism As Lenin understood it, moral compromise dressed up as common sense; more generally, a political approach that pits (often cynically) the common people against an (often imaginary or exaggerated) elite. See **Pan-Slavism**.

post-structuralism Intellectual movement associated with French philosopher Jacques Derrida (1930–2004) that, by challenging the authority of language, allows feminists, ethnic minorities, and others to look for the hidden assumptions in the work of critical thinkers of the past.

Prague Spring Reforms initiated in 1968 Communist Czechoslovakia by moderate leader Alexander Dubček, who described it as "socialism with a human face"; the reforms were squashed by a Soviet military intervention in August 1968.

Princeps Epithet taken by the emperor Octavian, meaning "first in honor" (because his name appeared first on the censor's list of Roman citizens).

proletariat A term popularized by Marx to describe the working classes. A revolution of the proletariat, Marx believed, would bring about the end of capitalism and the birth of a classless society.

protectionism The blocking of imports by tariff barriers or other legal means in order to promote the interests of a domestic mercantilist economy.

Protestant Reformation Movement initiated by Martin Luther that sought to recreate what he believed to be Christian belief and practice as they had existed in the apostolic church.

psychoanalysis Technique associated with Sigmund Freud (1856–1939) that seeks to understand the unconscious mind.

Punic Wars Three wars Rome fought with Carthage between 264 and 146 BCE, resulting in Roman dominance of the entire western Mediterranean basin.

putting-out system See **cottage industry**.

Pythagoreans Group of philosophers named after Pythagoras (570–495 BCE), who had developed the famous theorem about right triangles. They sought to identify rational order and laws governing the natural world; hence their focus on mathematics.

Q

qadi Islamic religious judge.

al-Qaeda "The Base," literally. Islamic terrorist organization created in the late 1980s by former rebels against the Soviet Army in Afghanistan. Led by Usamah bin Laden until his death in 2011.

Qajar Dynasty that ruled Iran from 1796 to 1925.

Qizilbash Network of militant units who fought to defend and uphold the Safavid dynasty of Iran.

quantum theory New theory of physics proposed by Max Planck (1858–1947) suggesting that both light and matter exist as waves and as particles.

Qur'an The holy book of Islam, revealed to the Prophet Muhammad.

R

rabbi An honorific Hebrew word meaning "my master." Rabbis were originally teachers of Jewish law. During the Babylonian Captivity, far from their ruined temple, many Jews turned to their rabbis for religious guidance. Rabbis became leaders of the exiled Jews and during this time refined the laws governing Jewish life.

Rape of Nanjing Atrocities perpetrated by invading Japanese soldiers in the Chinese capital of Nanjing in December 1937–January 1938. Hundreds of thousands of Chinese civilians were brutally murdered.

rationalism The essential characteristic of Greek thought, from Mycenaean times to the earliest known philosophers of Miletus (Thales, Anaximander, and Anaximenes); attempts to explain the natural world through observation rather than through mythology.

rationalist philosophy Branch of philosophy that studies the movement of the human mind itself (as distinct from analytic philosophy, which emphasizes close and careful reasoning).

realist See **naturalist**.

Realpolitik Politics based on strategic and tactical realities instead of idealism.

Reconquista "Reconquest," in Spanish. Refers to the long struggle (985–1492) between Christian and Muslim warlord-princes for control of the Iberian Peninsula.

Reichstag Name of the lower parliamentary chamber in the German imperial government, 1871–1945.

Reign of Terror Brutal period of French Revolution (1792) during which, at the direction of Robespierre, tens of thousands of French citizens believed to be opposed in any way to the Revolution were executed.

relativity In physics, the concept that every vantage point in the universe, whether moving or stationary, is as valid as every other vantage point; as a cultural metaphor, the new and possibly frightening idea that there are no fixed points, no absolute time, and no absolute space.

religiones licitae The legally approved religions of ancient Rome. Christianity became one in 375.

Renaissance Literally "rebirth" (French); an era of tremendous cultural achievement as artists, scholars, and philosophers rediscovered the works of classical Greece and Rome and applied those ideas and aesthetics to contemporary arts, humanism, and modern statecraft.

Renaissance humanism Movement of philosophers such as Pico della Mirandola to develop human potential, to value the particular, and to assert the inherent dignity of each person.

Rerum Novarum (Latin, "of new things.") Encyclical issued by Pope Leo XIII (1891) that recognized the intrinsic rights of private property but insisted on the equal right of workers to form labor unions.

res publica Latin term for "republic" or "commonwealth"; a form of government based on a system of checks and balances that emerged in Rome in 509 BCE.

al-riddah "Insubordination" or "apostasy," depending on circumstance.

Risorgimento "Resurgence," literally. This was the name given to the 19th-century movement for Italian national reunification.

Romanticism Cultural and artistic movement in opposition to industrialization, preferring emotion and instinct over structural order and rational thought.

Rub' al-Khali The "Empty Quarter" of the Arabian peninsula. Area of vast and almost impenetrable desert.

Rule of Saint Benedict A communal handbook written by Saint Benedict of Nursia (480–547) to guide the monastery he had established; its focus on the physical and intellectual as well as spiritual well-being of monks led to its being widely adopted by monastic communities across medieval Europe.

Rumi Sufi poet (1207–1273) whose work championed Islam without disparaging other faiths.

S

Sadducees One of three "philosophical sects" into which Judean society was divided; an aristocratic party who were reputedly strict upholders of Temple ritual, dedicated to the literal reading of Scripture and the rejection of the Oral Torah.

Saint Bartholomew's Day Massacre Riot (August 23–29, 1572) between Catholics and Protestant Huguenots that began in Paris and spread across France, resulting in the deaths of thousands.

salons In urban, Enlightenment-era France, regular gatherings, often hosted by wealthy or aristocratic women in their own homes, to which philosophers, artists, and other cultural figures were invited to discuss ideas.

samizdat Secret literature of political dissidents in Soviet Russia and Communist Eastern Europe, who passed officially condemned information, literature, and uncensored documents; important especially in the 1960s and 1970s.

sans-culottes "Those without breeches," literally. Colloquial reference to political revolutionary militants in Paris drawn from the lower orders.

satire Literary genre, originally popular among the Romans, that flourished during the

Renaissance. Satirical writers use humor or figurative language to mock and criticize powerful people and institution.

Schlieffen Plan Military strategy created by German chief of general staff Alfred Graf von Schlieffen in 1905 that called for German forces to circumvent French defenses by striking swiftly through Belgium and Luxembourg; this was exactly how Germany proceeded at the start of World War I nine years later.

scholasticism Method of research and teaching in medieval universities, characterized by the application of Aristotelian logic and the attempt to harmonize all knowledge.

scientific management Management theory that increases the productivity of labor by breaking down manufacturing into small, distinct steps.

Scientific Revolution From 1500 to 1700, a cultural, philosophical, and intellectual shift from a view of the universe as divinely created to a concept of the natural world as a system that could be understood through study and observation.

Sea Peoples Indo-European invaders (ca. 1200 BCE) who conquered the Hittites, ended the Egyptian dominance of Palestine, and wrought enormous destruction across southern and southeastern Europe before vanishing, possibly through assimilation into local groups.

Second Industrial Revolution Continuation of the earlier industrial revolution but with a focus instead on producing capital goods (goods, such as steel and chemicals, used to produce other goods).

Second Vatican Council Convened by Pope John XXIII (r. 1958–1963) as part of the effort to modernize the Church's teachings and governance.

second wave feminism Women's movement in the 1960s and 1970s that focused on sexual health, access to abortion and contraception, equal rights in the workplace, childcare services, gender roles in society, and portrayals of women in popular culture. (The "first wave" of feminism had focused almost exclusively on women's suffrage.)

secularism The declining power of religious beliefs and institutions and the subsequent decline in religious practice.

Sephardim Jewish people centered around the Mediterranean, where they remained in constant contact with Arab, Greek, and Latin cultural developments.

Septuagint A Greek translation of the Hebrew Bible created by a group of seventy-two scholars who convened in Alexandria around 260 BCE (the name is derived from the Greek word for

"seventy". It includes several books later excluded from the Jewish canon.

serfs Dependent farmers who performed labor on manors in exchange for the security and primitive justice provided by the landlord.

shah Persian term for "emperor."

shari'ah Islamic religious law.

She'ol The underworld of the Hebrew Bible, to which all the dead are sent; not analogous to later Christian concepts of hell as a place of punishment.

Shi'a Muslims who believe that political and religious legitimacy could pass only to members of the Prophet Muhammad's hereditary line.

Shoah See **Holocaust**

simony Paying money or presenting gifts in return for ecclesiastical office, a widespread abuse in the Roman Catholic Church in post-Carolingian era and inspiring the Gregorian Reform.

Six-Day War Military action (June 5–June 10, 1967) initiated by Israel against Egypt, Jordan, and Syria; Israel seized the Gaza Strip, the Golan Heights along the Israeli border with Syria, the Sinai Peninsula, and the entire West Bank, including the eastern part of the then-divided city of Jerusalem. After the stunning defeat of Arab allies, much of Arab popular resentment turned toward the United States.

Social Catholicism Nineteenth-century European Catholic movement founded on the idea that the challenge to Christian society under industrialism was structural rather than personal.

social contract Articulated in Thomas Hobbes's *Leviathan* (1651), the theory that when people decide to live in community they enter a covenant with each other, compromising their individual free wills in return for the benefits of society. Government, which bears responsibility for preserving social stability, may therefore legitimately assert its will on the community whenever it deems it necessary to do so.

social Darwinism Misuse of Darwin's theory of evolution by natural selection to morally justify imperialism as a healthy competition among societies.

sodalitia Special "fellowships" within the Roman Catholic Church—that is, groups of less formal rank than religious orders, organized usually around a special theme or mission. In the debates over religious modernism, numerous sodalitia loyal to the pope were granted oversight authority of parish clergy.

sola fide "By faith alone." Central concept in Martin Luther's theology—the notion that faith in Christ alone is sufficient to gain salvation.

sola Scriptura "By Scripture alone." Protestant belief, also originating with Luther, that the Bible is the sole source and sufficient authority (as opposed to tradition or the church) for divine teaching.

Sol Invictus The Unconquered Sun. Pagan cult devoted to the sun god in the Roman Empire. Identified with the emperor Constantine, who encouraged it despite his personal Christianity.

Song of Songs Biblical book, also known as the Song of Solomon, consisting of a poetic dialogue between a bride and bridegroom. Centuries of scholars have interpreted the Song of Songs as an allegory of the covenant between God and his people.

Sophists In Greece in the 5th century BCE, a group of thinkers who traveled from city to city teaching rhetoric and philosophy.

South Sea Bubble Economic crash (1720) sparked when the South Sea Company, an English company formed to trade with Spanish colonies in the New World, encouraged investors to speculate wildly on its supposed ventures but then could not make good on its unrealistic promises.

space-time Einstein's concept of time and space as elastic and therefore understood as different facets of a single dimension.

Spanish Civil War Internal conflict (1936–1939) between conservative and liberal forces in Spain that drew anti-Fascist support from around the world. The conservatives, under the Fascist dictator Francisco Franco (r. 1936–1975), won.

special theory of relativity Einstein's theory (1905) that maintains that all measurements of space and time are relative; the basis of the idea that nothing can go faster than the speed of light.

stadtholder Dutch term for "Head of State" in the 17th century, usually drawn from the noble house of Orange.

Stoicism Philosophy most famously described and taught by Seneca (4 BCE–65 CE) and Epictetus (55–135 CE) that conformed to Roman morals through an emphasis on duty, forbearance, self-discipline, and concern for others.

streltsi Semifeudalized noble cavalrymen who made up the Russian army until it was disbanded and reorganized by Tsar Piotr I in 1698.

structuralism Philosophy rooted in the work of Swiss linguist Ferdinand de Saussure (1857–1913) that emphasizes the structured ways in which we see, participate in, and comprehend the world.

subsidiarity Introduced by Pope Leo XIII, the principle that sought to preserve the dignity of persons and to help them recognize their own moral responsibilities and sought to safeguard against an overreaching centralized government.

suffrage The right to vote.

suffragettes European activists for women's rights who, in contrast with **suffragists**, favored confrontation, aggressive action, and, whenever they thought it necessary, even violence in order to change society.

suffragists Activists for women's rights who, in contrast with **suffragettes**, worked peaceably and within the legal system for women's rights.

Sufism A mystical, esoteric approach to Islam that flourished in the Ottoman Empire.

sultan "Commander," literally. Term for chief military officer in the Turkish empire. Under the Ottomans, the word came to represent the head of state.

Sultanate of Women Period (1640s and 1650s) of the Ottoman Empire when leading members of the imperial harem effectively controlled the state, directed foreign policy, and oversaw the fiscal system.

summa A "summary," or an encyclopedic effort to organize all thought on a given topic; a popular genre among the scholastic writers of the 13th and 14th centuries, representing the conviction that a rational order underlay all of human life.

sumptuary codes Dress codes in the cosmopolitan, diverse mercantile cultures of the Mediterranean that regulated styles of dress in order to establish the rules of engagement among different peoples.

sunnah The collected sayings and actions of Prophet Muhammad, used to establish Islamic legal precedents.

Sunni Muslims who regard selection by the community as the sole legitimate means to leadership of the Islamic world.

supermen Term used by Friedrich Nietzsche (1844–1900) to describe cultural, political, and intellectual figures with a will to power.

Sykes-Picot Agreement Pact between England and France (1916) that took advantage of the **Arab Revolt** to divide the dominions of the Middle East between the two nations.

Syllabus of Errors Sixty-five teachings Pope Pius X decreed irredeemably anti-Catholic in two 1907 encyclicals.

symposia All-male drinking parties in ancient Greece where philosophical ideas were discussed.

syncretism The union of religious doctrines.

T

taifas Petty princedoms in Muslim Spain, after the collapse of the caliphate in Cordoba in 1031.

takiyya "Concealment," literally. Practice of religious disguise permitted to Shi'i Muslims as a means to avoid persecution.

Talmud Codification of rabbinical law and commentary that became central to Jewish life starting in the Middle Ages. Two dominant forms exist: the Babylonian Talmud, compiled around 500 CE, and the Palestinian Talmud (also known as the Jerusalem Talmud), compiled around 400 CE. Reference to the "Talmud" usually means the Babylonian Talmud.

Tanakh A common name for the canonical Hebrew Bible—an acronym based on the letters T (for Torah, meaning "Instructions"), N (for Nevi'im, or "Prophets"), and K (for Ketuvim, or "Writings"). Traditionally believed to have been assembled by the "Men of the Great Assembly" around 450 BCE, modern scholars believe the compilation occurred later, between 200 BCE and 200 CE.

Tanzimat (Turkish, "reorganization"); a 19th-century movement by the Ottoman government to promote economic development and the integration of the empire's non-Muslims and non-Turks into civil society.

telos According to Aristotle, the intrinsic purpose or necessary role in the cosmic drama of every existing thing.

Tetrarchy Under Diocletian, a new system whereby the empire was formally divided into two halves with a separate emperor (**augustus**, in Latin) for each. Each half was further divided in half again, and each *augustus* therefore had a subordinate vice-emperor or *caesar*.

al-thawrah "Uprising," literally. Describes opposition to a government or ruler on account of the injustice of its rule. No directly religious overtone.

themes New system of organizing army under Byzantine emperor Heraclius in the 7th century that redistributed land to military officers and soldiers.

theory of evolution by natural selection As explained by Charles Darwin in his 1859 book *On the Origin of Species by Means of Natural Selection*, the process by which the superabundance of offspring produced by all living beings results in their competition for resources; over time, that competition favors traits in offspring that provide an advantage over their rivals.

Third Estate The branch of the French legislative body made up of elected representatives of the common people, including the bourgeoisie and wage earners. See **Estates General**.

Thirty Tyrants Committee of thirty Athenians appointed by the Spartan conquerors of Athens to rule the city.

Thirty Years' War Conflict that began in 1618 between Protestants and Catholics in Germany and gradually enveloped most of Europe, ending in 1648 after massive losses of life and property.

Tokyo Trials Trials (1946–1948) of Japanese officials for war crimes before an international tribunal of judges and prosecutors from the Allied countries.

Torah The first five books of the **Tanakh**, attributed to Moses.

totalitarianism A system of government that controls all aspects of society, using fear and intimidation to maintain power.

Treaty of Rome Treaty agreed to by Western European leaders in 1957 that established the European Economic Community to help post-war recovery and counterbalance American economic power.

Treaty of Versailles Controversial agreements that formally ended World War I on June 28, 1919, but ruinous concessions demanded from a defeated Germany were a contributing factor in the run-up to World War II.

Trinity For Christians, the doctrine in the existence of a single God in a union of three separate and divine "Persons."

trireme Ancient Greek warship with three tiers of oarsmen and a bronze-tipped battering ram on the prow.

troubadours Vernacular love poets popular in the aristocratic courts of southern France and northern Italy in the 12th and 13th centuries.

Truce of God An 11th-century decree by the reformed church banning warfare on holy days as well as the assault of religious pilgrims.

Twelve Tables The first written law code of the Roman Republic, ca. 450 BCE.

tyrant A person in a Greek polis who took power temporarily in order to bring about dramatic reform in a politically deadlocked state. In terms of social class, the tyrants were aristocrats but were allied with the masses.

U

'ulama Arab for "brotherhood" or "community," a central focus of Sunni life.

Umayyads Name of the ruling dynasty in the Islamic empire, 661–750. Governing the empire from their new capital at Damascus, the Umayyads were overthrown in 750 by the Abbasids, who transferred the capital to newly built Baghdad.

ummah   The community of Muslim believers.

uniformitarianism   Geologist James Hutton's theory that geological change consists of the slow accumulation of smaller changes—and these changes continue to happen in the present.

United Nations (UN)   Organization of member nations established in 1945, including a permanently standing International Court of Justice and International Criminal Court.

Universal Declaration of Human Rights   The first statement of global rights in history, drafted and promoted by American First Lady Eleanor Roosevelt and approved on December 10, 1948, by most members of the United Nations (Saudi Arabia, South Africa, and the Soviet Union abstained).

UN Women's Conference   International conferences sponsored by the United Nations to promote women's rights as *human* rights.

ushabti   Figures made of clay or wood, buried with well-to-do Egyptians, that represented servants who would work for one in the afterlife.

Utilitarianism   Philosopher John Stuart Mill's ethical principal that "holds that actions are right in proportion as they tend to promote happiness, wrong as they tend to produce the reverse of happiness"; based on this principle he argued that women should have the right to vote and determine their own destiny.

V

vassal   In a feudal system, a free man who pledged to serve a lord in exchange for dominion over a manor or manors bestowed by the lord.

vizier   Regional administrator under the Abbasid dynasty and later under the Ottomans. From the word meaning "burden sharer."

Volk   The German people. Related etymologically to the English word *folk* but with a different meaning. Used in a combined colloquial and mystical sense.

W

wadi   Seasonal river in Middle East.

Wahhabism   Conservative reform movement within Sunni Islam, taking its name from the 18th-century figure Muhammad ibn Abd al-Wahhab. The movement stresses returning to strict reliance on Qur'an and hadith, purging Islam of non-Arabic traditions, and restoring ethnic Arabs to leadership in international Islam.

The official sect in Saudi Arabia in the 20th and 21st centuries.

War of the Roses   English civil war for the throne (1455–1485) fought between the noble houses of York and Lancaster.

welfare states   In post–World War II Western Europe, societies in which the central government, funded by heavy taxation, provided all essential social services.

wergild   Old Germanic term—"man money," literally—for the compensation owed by an offender to his victim, according to custom.

will to power   Term used by Friedrich Nietzsche (1844–1900) to describe the passionate striving to make meaning and leave a mark on the world.

Women's International League for Peace and Freedom   Pacifist group founded in 1915 that campaigned for equal rights for all citizens, economic justice, and greater understanding and empathy between peoples.

World Economic Forum   Nonprofit foundation that encourages global political and business leaders to work together to address and resolve global business, industrial, and environmental issues.

World Trade Organization   Intergovernmental organization seeking to liberalize trade between nations.

Y

YHWH   The term for "God" used by the Yahwist author of the Torah (see **Documentary Hypothesis**), represented in English-language Bibles by the all-capitals word LORD.

Young Turks   Modernizing faction in Turkey that promoted pan-ethnic Islamic nationalism, overthrowing the sultan Abdul Hamid II in 1909 and replacing him with his half brother Mehmed V (r. 1909–1918).

Z

zakat   The giving of alms to the poor, required of Muslims.

ziggurat   Step-pyramid temples of ancient Mesopotamia, believed to be the dwelling places of the gods.

Zionism   From Hebrew *Tsiyon*, the name for the central portion of Jerusalem, but by extension referring to all of Israel/Palestine. Movement by Jews (especially from Eastern Europe) to establish a Jewish state in the Holy Land as a refuge from European persecution beginning in the 19th century.

Zollverein "Customs union." The free-trade zone established by Prussia in the early 19th century; an important early step in German unification.

Zoroastrianism Monotheistic religion founded by Zoroaster in Persia ca. 1300 BCE. In its emphasis on moral behavior, personal salvation, and the eventual victory of Good in a cosmic battle with Evil, Zoroastrianism is considered by many a precursor of Judaism (and, by extension, Christianity).

zunnar Identifying belt worn by non-Muslims in the early Islamic empire.

Credits

Bristol Record Office BRO 04720 (folio 152); pg. 343 Gianni Dagli Orti / The Art Archive at Art Resource, NY; pg. 345 © DeA Picture Library / Art Resource, NY; pg. 348 Réunion des Musées Nationaux / Art Resource, NY; pg. 351 Snark / Art Resource, NY; pg. 354 Scala / White Images / Art Resource, NY; pg. 358 National Palace Museum, Beijing; pg. 359 Image copyright © The Metropolitan Museum of Art. Image source: Art Resource, NY; pg. 363 Image copyright © The Metropolitan Museum of Art. Image source: Art Resource, NY; pg. 368 Erich Lessing / Art Resource, NY; pg. 370 Eileen Tweedy / The Art Archive at Art Resource, NY.

CHAPTER 11: pg. 372 Erich Lessing / Art Resource, NY; pg. 376 The Bodleian Libraries, The University of Oxford; pg. 379 © National Gallery, London / Art Resource, NY; pg. 382 Scala / Art Resource, NY; pg. 385 Courtesy of the Library of Congress; pg. 386 Erich Lessing / Art Resource, NY; pg. 389 public domain; pg. 391 Scala / Art Resource, NY; pg. 393 bpk, Berlin / Kunstmuseum / Art Resource, NY; pg. 395 © DHM; pg. 399 Photo: Albertina, Vienna, from Geisberg, Der deutsche Holzschnitt in der ersten Halfte des 16. Jahrhundert, Munchen 1923–1930; 30. Lieferung, Nr. 1243; pg. 402 The Pierpont Morgan Library / Art Resource, NY; pg. 406 Snark / Art Resource, NY; pg. 409 Courtesy of the Library of Congress.

CHAPTER 12: pg. 414 The Pierpont Morgan Library / Art Resource, NY; pg. 422 Snark / Art Resource, NY; pg. 424 Library of Congress, Rare Book and Special Collections Division; pg. 425 Peter Newark American Pictures; pg. 430 National Portrait Gallery, London; pg. 433 Rijksmuseum, Amsterdam, Langdurig bruikleen van de Gemeente Amsterdam, SK-C-232; pg. 436 Kharbine-Tapabor / The Art Archive at Art Resource, NY; pg. 439 public domain; pg. 445 Scala / White Images / Art Resource, NY; pg. 448 © The Trustees of the British Museum; pg. 450 Index / The Bridgeman Art Library; pg. 452 Snark / Art Resource, NY; pg. 455 Gianni Dagli Orti / The Art Archive at Art Resource, NY; pg. 457 Erich Lessing / Art Resource, NY.

CHAPTER 13: pg. 464 Plate XX from Volume I of *The Mathematical Principles of Natural Philosophy* by Sir Isaac Newton (1642–1727) engraved by John Lodge (fl. 1782) 1777 (engraving), English School, (18th century) / Private Collection / The Bridgeman Art Library; pg. 468 public domain;

pg. 471 (left) Erich Lessing / Art Resource, NY; pg. 471 (right) Courtesy of the Library of Congress; pg. 472 Courtesy of the Library of Congress; pg. 475 (left) Scala / Ministero per i Beni e le Attività culturali / Art Resource, NY; pg. 475 (right) Réunion des Musées Nationaux / Art Resource, NY; pg. 477 Courtesy José Luís Fernández-Castañeda, S.J., parish priest of the Church of San Pedro, Lima, and Administrator of the Jesuit Order in Peru; pg. 479 (left) Erich Lessing / Art Resource, NY; pg. 479 (right) Erich Lessing / Art Resource, NY; pg. 481 to Index ; pg. 483 Museo Galileo. Florence—Photo Franca Principe; pg. 487 Erich Lessing / Art Resource, NY; pg. 489 (left) Scala / Art Resource, NY; pg. 489 (right) Bridgeman-Giraudon / Art Resource, NY; pg. 490 Royal Asiatic Society, MSS 35; pg. 492 bpk, Berlin / National Portrait Gallery / Jochen Remmer / Art Resource, NY; pg. 495 Réunion des Musées Nationaux / Art Resource, NY.

CHAPTER 14: pg. 502 National Trust Photo Library / Art Resource, NY; pg. 507 public domain; pg. 509 Réunion des Musées Nationaux / Art Resource, NY; pg. 512 HIP / Art Resource, NY; pg. 514 Gianni Dagli Orti / The Art Archive at Art Resource, NY; pg. 518 akg-images; pg. 519 Giraudon; pg. 522 © Bristol City Museum and Art Gallery, UK / The Bridgeman Art Library; pg. 525 © The Trustees of the British Museum; pg. 527 Nimatallah / Art Resource, NY; pg. 518 © Photo: Bayerisches Nationalmuseum München, Bastian Krack. Fork: Inv. No. 36/37; Knife: Inv. No. 36/38; pg. 530 © Danita Delimont / Alamy; pg. 532 public domain; pg. 535 The Pierpont Morgan Library / Art Resource, NY; pg. 542 © Roger Wood / CORBIS; pg. 548 Eileen Tweedy / The Art Archive at Art Resource, NY.

CHAPTER 15: pg. 552 Alfredo Dagli Orti / The Art Archive at Art Resource, NY; pg. 558 Gianni Dagli Orti / The Art Archive at Art Resource, NY; pg. 564 Erich Lessing / Art Resource, NY; pg. 566 (left) SSPL/Science Museum / Art Resource, NY; pg. 566 (right) Alfredo Dagli Orti / The Art Archive at Art Resource, NY; pg. 567 Erich Lessing / Art Resource, NY; pg. 569 Gianni Dagli Orti / The Art Archive at Art Resource, NY; pg. 570 Erich Lessing / Art Resource, NY; pg. 571 Eileen Tweedy / The Art Archive at Art Resource, NY; pg. 575 public domain; pg. 579 Kimbell Art Museum, Fort Worth, Texas / Art Resource, NY; pg. 584 bpk, Berlin / Art Resource, NY; pg. 585 Erich Lessing / Art Resource, NY.

Index

Page numbers followed by *t* indicate a table. Page numbers followed by *m* indicate a map. Italicized page numbers indicate a figure or photo.